THE POLITICAL ECONOMY
OF DEVELOPMENT
AND UNDERDEVELOPMENT

THE POLITICAL ECONOMY OF DEVELOPMENT AND UNDERDEVELOPMENT

EDITED BY

Charles K. Wilber

University of Notre Dame

Random House Business Division New York

I have a dream that one day every valley shall be exalted,
every hill and mountain shall be made low, the rough
places will be made plain, and the crooked places will
be made straight, and the glory of the Lord shall be
revealed, and all flesh shall see it together.

Martin Luther King, Jr.
The March on Washington
August 1963

For my granddaughters, Heather Jean, Ashley Marie, and Erin Michelle,
that they may live in a world that cherishes and pursues this dream.

Fourth Edition
987654321
Copyright © 1973, 1979, 1984, 1988 by Random House, Inc.

Library of Congress Cataloging-in-Publication Data

The Political economy of development and underdevelopment.

 Bibliography: p.
 Includes indexes.
 1. Economic development. 2. Developing countries—
Economic conditions. I. Wilber, Charles K.
HD82.P546 1987   330.9172'4   87–9668
ISBN 0–394–37499–1

Manufactured in the United States of America

PREFACE TO THE FOURTH EDITION

The decade of the 1960s was marked by an optimism that world poverty could be conquered by economic growth. The 1970s saw that hope dashed by growing unemployment and inequality and the intractability of absolute poverty in the Third World. The first edition of this book charted that disillusionment.

The 1970s witnessed the birth of a new optimism to replace the old. The pursuit of "growth with equity" or a strategy of targeting "basic human needs" would succeed where economic growth failed. The second edition of this book captured the beginnings of this movement.

The 1980s have ushered in a period of greater caution. World poverty will not be eliminated with simple economic panaceas. Resource shortages (particularly of energy), rising protectionism in the industrial world, militarism in the Third World, the international arms race, the structure of the world economy all make the design of development strategies a complex problem in political economy. The third edition charted the progress of debate among the contending schools of thought with emphasis on issues of political economy rather than on narrowly economic problems.

This fourth edition updates the continuing debate among the contending schools of thought, highlights the international debt crisis along with the attendent stabilization and readjustment programs, and charts the resurgence of free market economics with its attack upon "development" economics.

Once again, I am indebted to many people for the valuable help they have given me in preparing this fourth edition. They provided critiques of the third edition, suggested new readings, and encouraged me to go ahead. I particularly want to thank James H. Weaver of The American University and Kenneth P. Jameson at the University of Notre Dame. Their ideas have become so entangled with mine that it is no longer possible to sort out ownership. This fourth edition would not have been possible without the work of my graduate research assistant, Jim Harder. Finally, I want to thank Paul Shensa for his continued support.

Charles K. Wilber
UNIVERSITY OF NOTRE DAME
JULY 1987

PREFACE TO THE FIRST EDITION

Economists assume that the problem of a more human society is solved by expertise, by know-how. Since they assume that the question of the nature of a good society is already answered, the issue becomes one of solving certain practical problems. The good society is simply assumed to be an idealized version of the United States economy, that is, a consumer society. The key to a consumer society is growth of per capita income. Thus the vast bulk of the development literature has focused on growth rates as the *deus ex machina* to solve all problems. Even much of the socialist writing on development argues that the superiority of socialism over capitalism lies in faster growth rates.

There is much to be said for this approach because some minimum level of food, clothing, shelter, recreation, etc., is necessary before a person can be free to be human. However, the emphasis on consumption and growth of per capita income has not led to a decrease of poverty in the underdeveloped world. If anything it has increased. A thin layer has prospered while the vast majority of the population sinks ever deeper into the backwater of under-development. Therefore, during the past several years a new look has been taken at the meaning of development. Dudley Seers, Mahbub ul Haq, Ivan Illich, and others have questioned the emphasis on chasing the consumption standards of the developed countries via economic growth. Instead they argue for a direct attack on poverty through employment and income redistribution policies. Denis Goulet and Paulo Freire argue that development must include "liberation" from oppression, cultural as well as political and economic.

Both of these positions have merit, and they are not necessarily mutually exclusive. That is, the study of political economy should lead one to ask whether stressing the importance of rapid economic growth has to mean that the growth will consist of movies, bikinis, deodorants, key clubs, and pollution. An analysis of political economic systems should lead one to see why growth has meant luxuries being produced for some while others go hungry.

This book is about economic development and underdevelopment, and is designed to be used with a standard textbook in advanced undergraduate and beginning graduate courses. The readings emphasize the *political economy* rather than the narrowly *economic* approach and issues.

Many of the readings are excellent examples of radical political economy. Political economy recognizes that man is a social being whose arrangements for the production and distribution of economic goods must be, if society is to be livable, consistent with congruent institutions of family, political, and cultural life. As a result, a political economy analysis must incorporate such noneconomic influences as social structures, political systems, and cultural values as well as such factors as technological change and the distribution of income and wealth. The readings are radical in the sense that they are willing to question and evaluate the most basic institutions and values of society.

While I hope that the work presented here is objective, there is no artificial stance of neutrality. I am committed to certain values that undoubtedly influence the choice of questions asked and the range of variables considered for selection. In general, my system of values posits material progress (at least up to some minimum level), equality, cooperation, democratic control of economic as well as political institutions, and individual freedom as positive goods. It should be noted that there may be contradictions among these criteria, and thus society is faced with choices. With these values in mind the reader can judge the degree of objectivity attained.

It is a pleasure to acknowledge my indebtedness to those who have helped me shape my ideas on economic development and underdevelopment. First of all I want to thank Professors W. Michael Bailey, James H. Weaver, Celso Furtado, Branko Horvat, E. J. Mishan, Ronald Müller, Brady Tyson, Albert Waterston, and Irving Louis Horowitz—critics, colleagues, and friends. Some of my greatest debts are to those whom I know only through their writings—Karl Polyanyi and R. H. Tawney. Their example of scholarship and social commitment has been a guide and inspiration. I want to thank Sandy Kelly for her invaluable help in editing and typing, and Bob Devlin for his assistance in research and editing. Barbara Conover and Nancy Perry, editors at Random House, have been invaluable in seeing the book through to publication.

My greatest debt, however, in this as in all my endeavors, is to my wife, Mary Ellen, and our children: Kenneth, Teresa, Matthew, Alice, Mary, Angela, and Louie. I owe all to their love and encouragement.

Charles K. Wilber
WASHINGTON, D.C.
SEPTEMBER 1973

CONTENTS

PART ONE

THEORY AND METHOD IN ECONOMIC DEVELOPMENT

Development economics is an art. Like the cultural arts, the understanding of the object studied varies among schools of thought. We all see a painting, but we each experience it differently, conditioned by the way we perceive the world in general and by our proficiency with the tools of art appreciation.

There are competing stories or explanations of development and underdevelopment. Our diagnosis of the problems and the specification of economic change depend upon underlying theories. These theories, in turn, are grounded in our world view—the "facts" as we see them through value-biased eyes. Therefore, to construct a robust story of the dynamics of development, we must clearly articulate the building blocks of values, facts, and theories.

The concept of *paradigms,* offered by Thomas Kuhn, helps us to organize these competing schools of thought. A paradigm is a world view shared by a group working or thinking about a particular topic. In the first essay Wilber and Jameson highlight two dominant paradigms in economic development, the orthodox and the political-economy approach. The orthodox paradigm is a theoretical umbrella spanning free market models, planning approaches, and the distributional issues raised by the growth-with-equity critique. Its unifying thread is the underlying value assumption that economic growth and consequent high mass consumption are desirable ends that rational and efficient utility-maximizing agents will pursue.

The political economy paradigm challenges economic growth as a static end-goal, contending instead that the *nature of the process* of economic development is crucial. What is important is the *means* by which economic development is pursued and how these means affect the everyday lives of people. This approach is historical and appreciates the dialectic relationship between the society, the polity, and the economy.

Within a given paradigm or world view several competing theories may exist. These internal arguments are part of any school of thought's historical legacy—varying interpretations of what happened and why. In "The Misconceptions of 'Development Economics,'" Deepak Lal claims that the attempt to create an economics of development is fundamentally misguided. This is so because it involves a denial of the applicability of traditional economic theory to the problems of developing countries. In particular it denies the universal existence of economizing behavior, exaggerates the importance of market failures, and believes that political authorities can allocate resources better than the market. Amartya Sen defends the record of "development economics," claiming both that the criticisms are inaccurate and that there has been substantial development.

Howard J. Wiarda claims in "Toward a Nonethnocentric Theory of Development: Alternative Conceptions from the Third World," that rejection of the Western model of development, in its several varieties, is now widespread in the Third World. There are many new and exciting efforts to construct indigenous models of development that are more compatible with local values and traditions. In this sense they are more in line with the political economy paradigm.

1

Paradigms of Economic Development and Beyond

Charles K. Wilber and Kenneth P. Jameson

I. INTRODUCTION

During the more than thirty years since the end of World War II and the founding of the United Nations, "development" has captured the attention of economists and statesmen alike. Of course international inequalities are not new, but three factors account for this recent emphasis: (1) the realization that the worldwide spread of markets has not automatically brought the benefits promised by nineteenth-century economic theory; (2) the emergence of socialism as a viable development alternative; and (3) the pressure for economic development exerted by the newly independent countries of Latin America, Asia, and Africa with the resulting challenge to existing economic relations. In all of these cases, the meaning of "development" is a crucial element.

Theorists and practitioners of development have written and labored in universities, government agencies, and international institutions. International conferences have been held, billions have been spent on foreign aid, and thousands of experts now earn their living from development. However, this prolonged preoccupation has not resulted in a generally accepted explanation of the process of development. Indeed, an initial survey of the field would seem to suggest an analogy with the Tower of Babel. Closer examination, however, shows that there are two main categories of treatments of development, one we will term "orthodox" and the other "political economy."

One of the purposes of this chapter is to suggest how the diverse writings on development can be understood as belonging to these two competing

From Charles K. Wilber and Kenneth P. Jameson, "Paradigms of Economic Development and Beyond," in *Directions in Economic Development* (Notre Dame, Ind.: University of Notre Dame Press, 1975) pp. 1–41. Reprinted by permission.

3

categories. But a second goal is to show that the intellectual strictures which accompany work within either of these two traditions may actually hamper our understanding of development; we must move beyond them to an approach based on what we term "convoluted history. . . ."

The initial problem is to establish the context in which the interplay of the two main approaches is played out. Thus the question of intellectual competition in economics must be considered.

II. INTELLECTUAL COMPETITION IN ECONOMICS

The status of economics as a science has provoked active debate in recent years. Some claim that economics has indeed gained the coherence and explanatory power to qualify as a science, while others claim that it is presently in a prescientific state and is likely to remain there forever. Of course the entire debate traces back to the work of Thomas Kuhn,[1] who in his history of science used the construct of the "paradigm" to show that science and its development are much more complex than the simple march of value-free knowledge which progresses by its own persuasiveness.

There is no need to enter into the debate on the nature of economics nor into the hot philosophical debate sparked by Kuhn. As a device for ordering thinking about economic development, the concept of a paradigm will be useful.

For our purposes a paradigm is a world view shared by a group working on or thinking about a particular topic, e.g., economic development. Such a world view affects their activity across the board: the questions which are asked, the information which is collected, the method of interpretation of that information, and even the group with which there will be communication about the questions. Because of the functioning of this world view and this scientific community, advances in knowledge about the particular concerns of this community are facilitated; but it is very difficult to move from one world view or one community to another. As long as the paradigm relates successfully to the questions addressed, there is substantial "progress" in understanding and knowledge. On the other hand, even when the questions are not addressed with a high degree of success, i.e., when there is a crisis in the community, members of the community continue to follow the paradigm's guidelines rather than breaking with that world view and adopting another.

This paradigm or general theory—whether it be neoclassical economics, Marxism, or some other—is usually so much a part of the very thought process that empirical disconfirmation of some particular hypothesis is almost automatically rejected. There are a variety of specific problems that make it easy in economics to reject a disconfirmation as invalid and thus to protect the scientist's theory or paradigm.

First is the *ceteris paribus* problem. Hypotheses in economics must always be stated in the form of "if . . . then" propositions. Since the "ifs" do change, an econometric test that disconfirms the theory can always be rejected as "mis-specified." In addition, since hypotheses are stated in probabilistic terms, a nonoccurrence of the predicted event cannot be used as a refutation of the general law from which the particular hypothesis was deduced.

Second is the difficulty of constructing a clear-cut test of a hypothesis in economics. Most of the traditional statistical tests (for example, null hypotheses) are very weak and a large number of different theories are capable of passing them. The choice among alternative theories, therefore, cannot be settled on empirical grounds. Instead, the desirable qualities of a logical model—simplicity, generality, specificity, and aesthetic quality—are used, and the relative evaluation of these qualities is probably determined by one's own paradigm.

In the area of development—which is multidisciplinary by nature—these problems of verification are multiplied many times over. When a general theory or paradigm has achieved a high level of insulation from falsification it might best be termed an ideology or, less pejoratively, a parable. As parables, both the orthodox and political-economy paradigms of economic development serve two essential and related functions. Each acts to restrict the scope of what is considered "scientific" inquiry and each serves as a policy stance for molding society in its image.

Before turning to specific consideration of the two paradigms, let us indicate in a general manner what the main components of paradigms or parables of development are. It will be seen that a major consideration is the view of history implicit in the paradigm, a theme to which we will return in later sections.

An Outline of Development Paradigms

Both the orthodox and the political-economy paradigms grow out of Western modes of thought, and thus they have similarities in their patterns of analysis and thinking. This fundamental similarity can be seen by going back to the definition of development given in *Webster's Third New International Dictionary.* Development is defined as "the act, process, or result of developing: the state of being developed: a gradual unfolding by which something . . . is developed: gradual advance or growth through progressive changes." This obviously requires examination of the word "develop," which is defined as "to cause to unfold gradually: conduct through a succession of states or changes each of which is preparatory for the next."

From this we see that development has the implication of a gradual unfolding or of a passing through stages, each of which prepares for the next. When applied to the context of countries existing in time, it shows that development must be dealt with in a historical context. The historical experience will condition the stage in which a country finds itself and the degree to which its development has unfolded.

From the definition, there is another sense in which history is important. To talk of an "unfolding" implies the stripping off of overlays which are hiding the true nature of the subject; it suggests the gradual emergence of the nature of the entity which for some reason has been hidden but which reveals itself with the passage of time. There is in this view a type of teleology, an end to which history is tending or should tend. So development is more than simply change or the passage of time; it is change in some particular direction. Such a stance fits quite nicely with the other definition of development, the passage from stage to stage. As long as each succeeding stage is a "higher" stage, then the process of history and development is again teleological. This can be seen most clearly in the writings of W. W. Rostow on the stages of economic growth,[2] but it also appears in a close reading of virtually any text on development. Thus, Bauer and Yamey talk of "the widening of the range of alternatives open to people as consumers and producers";[3] Higgins sees development as "a discernible rise in total and in per capita income, widely diffused throughout occupational and income groups, continuing for at least two generations and becoming cumulative":[4] Seers says that it must be treated in relation to a "universally acceptable aim—the realization of the potential of human personality";[5] while, finally, Denis Goulet in talking of the French school describes their view as "development itself is simply a means to the human ascent."[6]

Joining together the historical element of development with the teleological, it is rather easy to arrive at a view of history as a parable of "progress" toward that final goal. It is this aspect of development thinking whose philosophical roots are examined by Celso Furtado.[7] . . .

In his *Economic Development,* Culbertson[8] points out that "belief in progress" characterized the classical writers and Marx as well as the neoclassical school of development thinking, i.e., that progress is a component of both of the competing paradigms of development. The fundamental role of "history = progress" will be emphasized in the final section of this chapter.

Two other components complete the skeleton of the analytical framework of the two paradigms. The first is their attempt to deal with the continued existence of "underdevelopment." Obviously few if any countries have developed fully, and an explanation for this must be a part of the paradigm. More particularly, why is it that the range of performance is so vast, from that of the United States or Sweden on one end, to a Chad or Guinea-Bissau on the other? Thus, a complete view of development must contain a "theory of underdevelopment" which can provide a plausible explanation for the existing state of events. The second component, naturally, is a "theory of development." In other words, there must be offered some explanation of the mechanism or motive force which moves countries through history in their process of development. It is in the theories of development and underdevelopment that the two paradigms differ most radically.

With this as background, we are now ready for a rapid tour through the two main paradigms of development before turning to an alternative view of history and to the essays in this volume and their contribution to an understanding of the process of development.

III. THE ORTHODOX PARADIGM

Development thinking in the United States has long been dominated by what we term the "orthodox" paradigm. Although it has certainly undergone an evolution and has several variants, its basic outlines adequately encompass a majority of the writers on economic development in this country. Following the schema outlined above in terms of its major components, we can sketch out the general outlines of this paradigm.

The basic goal of development has been seen traditionally as the attainment of a "high mass consumption" society, to use Rostow's term. It is understandable, therefore, that orthodox development economists have usually measured the level of economic development by the level of per capita income or product. The implicit goal of development appears to be the creation of societies that replicate the political-economic system of the United States: a private enterprise economy combined with a representative, democratic political structure.

The view of the historical process contained in the orthodox paradigm is clear from this characterization: it is one in which developing societies move toward ever greater availability of goods and services for their citizens. This is the nature of progress, and, as a result, growth in the per capita output of goods and services is often used synonomously with development. Since the general unit of analysis is the nation-state, it is the average per capita income of the whole population of the nation-state that moves to higher and higher levels as the historical process of development continues.

As might be expected, the treatment of this historical process is closely intertwined with the theory of development incorporated in the paradigm. It is often held that development and progress are almost natural and lawlike and that history is simply a continuum from the poorest to the richest countries. The main difference between them, aside from natural resource base, is the time which separates them from underdevelopment.

Rostow's stages-of-growth model is the best known and most explicit presentation of this view of historical development. The use of this model as a framework for analysis of the process of development assumes that present-day countries correspond to the "traditional society" stage or, at best, the "preconditions" stage in the Western developed countries. That is, the present-day developed countries were once underdeveloped and all countries move through all these stages.

How can this development best be brought about, that is, what mechanisms will most surely lead to growth and development? Of course there are a variety of approaches to this problem, but the one which has greatest claim to the orthodox position is the view that development will be facilitated by doing nothing, by letting things alone: "laissez faire."

This view grows out of the model of competitive market capitalism. Since an uncoerced person can be depended upon to act rationally to maximize his/her individual self-interest, it is thought that an automatic, self-regulated mechanism to manage economic affairs naturally emerges in the course of history. These free choices are expected to overcome scarcity and to result in progress through the automatic adjustments of free exchange in markets. The forces of competition ensure that the economy produces those goods which people desire and that maximum output is produced in the most efficient manner.

Since the process is virtually automatic and technically determined, this suggests the theory of underdevelopment. If development has not occurred, then the reason must be that something interferes with this automatic process. The analysis of obstacles to development is, in effect, the theory of underdevelopment contained in the orthodox paradigm. Two examples can illustrate the concept of obstacles. One obstacle to growth may be nonrational behavior, that is, nonmaximizing behavior. Because of cultural dualism,[9] lack of n-achievement,[10] or other social/cultural/psychological constraints, people tend to behave in ways that perpetuate traditional forms of economy, and thus retard development. Another is the obstacle to the free working of markets created by government regulation and participation in the economy[11] and by the imperfections of markets caused by the low level of development.[12] These two categories of obstacles hamper the automatic progress of development which otherwise would take place.

The possible existence of such obstacles represents a challenge to policy-making, and two main responses to this challenge have developed since World War II. In addition a third response, growth with equity, has developed in recent years as a reaction to what is perceived as the failure of development programs.

Laissez Faire and Planning Responses

Suggested policies to overcome these obstacles to the automatic process of development have been quite varied. However, they fall into two major groupings: a continued defense of the laissez faire strategy[13] or a belief that substantial government planning will be required to overcome these obstacles.[14]

The laissez faire response is twofold. On the one hand, it questions the observations of nonrational behavior. There is a large literature in the economic anthropology area which finds rational maximizing behavior in widely varying situations that would seem on the surface to preclude such rationality. While this may only indicate the protean nature of the concept of "economic rationality," it is a viable response. Similarly the apparent market failures can be dismissed either as nonexistent or as causing minimal economic loss. Harberger's earlier work[15] examines the question for the problem of monopoly power, and his chapter in this book presents a similar view critical of claims of inappropriate factor proportions in production. If such problems do not exist, then it is apparent that the policy of laissez faire continues to be viable and indeed desirable from a development standpoint. Once again the problem of development will be solved with the passage of time as the underdeveloped countries pass through the same stages as did the now developed countries.

On the other hand, it is admitted that there may indeed be deviations from laissez faire. The best example of this is the role which government has come to play in Third World countries. Government interferes in all areas, setting prices by nonmarket considerations, distorting the operation of labor markets through minimum-wage legislation and through providing employment in the government sector. In addition, the government artificially stimulates demand through deficit spending, thereby generating inflation in the domestic economy. In this case, the detrimental aspects cannot be overlooked; action must be taken. Government interference must be curtailed and the size of government deficits must be cut drastically. The best example of such an attempt is the effort to implement a "social market economy" in Chile after the military coup in 1973. This was seen as necessary because of the distortions caused to the economy by the previous socialist regime. Following the dictates of economic policymakers, generally trained at the University of Chicago, the government is attempting to implement the above policies, in essence moving the economy back to a market-based operation.

The planning response is quite different. Those with this perspective conclude that government must intervene in the economy to offset the antidevelopment impact of the two types of obstacles to development. On the side of nonrational behavior, the government can attempt to convince its citizens of the need for "modernization" while at the same time substituting its own entrepreneurial ability and knowledge to fill that vacuum. On the side of markets, the government can again offset the difficulties through economic planning. By developing a coherent overview of the economy and by forcing this on the actors in the economy through the various means at its disposal, the orthodox result of growth in income can be attained.

It should be pointed out here that the willingness of government to begin to supplement or supplant the market has another important result. It also opens the door to a deviation from consumer sovereignty in deciding the availability of goods to the economy and brings to the fore questions about the distribution of income which are generally submerged in the laissez faire approach. These questions can no longer be ignored because it is obvious in a planned economy that income distribution is highly conditioned by the political process, not given by some endowment of ability and drive. This suggests that the problem of the "social-welfare function" must be taken into consideration, and the definition of development must be consciously decided rather than simply taken as growth in output.

The preponderance of work in the orthodox mold can fit into either of the two responses noted above. We must now take note of the recent work of the "growth-with-equity" group which is a response to the historical record of development programs in the postwar period.

The Growth-with-Equity Response

While there are important differences between the laissez faire theorists and the planners, they both agree in their assessment of the success of postwar development. They both point to the resounding success of the effort to raise growth rates of GNP. As Morawetz[16] points out, "GNP per capita of the developing countries grew at an average rate of 3.4% per annum during 1950–75, or 3.0% if the People's Republic of China is excluded. This was faster than either the developed or the developing nations had grown in any comparable period prior to 1950, and exceeded both official goals and private expectations." While there is diversity in GNP performance across countries, there is an almost universal increase in other indicators of welfare such as life expectancy, which has increased as much in the past two decades in developing countries as it did in a century in the industrialized nations.[17] The same can be said about the tremendous increase in the availability of education and about performance on measures of literacy.[18] Of course, these data take into account both the socialist and the capitalist countries, and thus the success cannot be ascribed solely to the advance of capitalism. But the capitalist countries have succeeded in these terms, which seems to indicate the success of the orthodox strategy.

Despite its success in raising growth rates of GNP, the orthodox strategy of economic development has seemingly failed in some crucial areas: there is continued unemployment, increased income inequality within and among nations, and the stagnation of real income levels among the poorest. The common theme that animates all of these criticisms is that the benefits of the orthodox strategy of development have failed to "trickle down" to the poor of the world, and thus there must be a new strategy, growth with equity. Let us look at these failures more closely.

In employment, the general experience has been that unemployment has risen despite the high growth rates; it exists in the world today on an enormous scale, much more severe than in the 1930s. Some economists argue that open unemployment in the world is going up at the rate of 8 percent a year, though Morawetz is much less alarmed. Of note is that this widespread unemployment emerged during the 1960s, a decade of worldwide expansion of trade and rapid growth in the economies of developed countries, and that it often appeared in the countries that were growing the most rapidly.

The second change that is apparent in the data is an increase in the inequality of income distribution in underdeveloped countries. While there is an active debate on the meaning of the data, since 1965 the share of Brazil's national income going to the top 5 percent of the people has risen from 29 percent to 38 percent, and by some estimates to 46 percent. In Kenya, the top 20 percent appears to receive 68 percent of the income; in Ecuador, 74 percent of the income; and in Turkey, 61 percent of the income.

The third problem area is absolute poverty: the inability of persons to provide for their basic needs. Adelman and Morris studied income shares in 43 noncommunist, underdeveloped countries during the post-World War II period.[19] They found that as economic growth proceeded, the share of the bottom 60 percent of the people fell relatively. But they also found that in poorer countries the income of the bottom 40 percent had fallen absolutely as well, i.e., these people had less income in absolute terms at the end of these two decades of development than they had had in the beginning. Adelman and Morris's statistical results correspond well with evidence gathered in certain areas: India, Pakistan, northern Mexico.

In response to these depressing results many orthodox development economists began to search for ways to modify their vision of "development = growth in per capita GNP" to include a concern for channeling the benefits of growth to the poorest. Thus there is emerging a third major response within the orthodox paradigm, one that has been termed "growth with equity."[20]

The growth-oriented theory of economic development stresses that inequality of income is necessary to provide incentives for investment. If self-interested, maximizing individuals are allowed to seek differential rewards for their efforts and risk-taking, total income will be maximized in the process. Then (if you are a conservative) the benefits will eventually "trickle down" to the less successful in the form of higher wages; or (if you are a liberal) the state could redistribute the benefits when society is rich enough so that incentives will not be drastically impaired. Unfortunately, as seen above, the results of these two strategies in underdeveloped countries are not very encouraging. Forty percent of the people live and die all too early in the meantime.

The growth-with-equity adherents argue that the "grow now, trickle later" approach not only has problems of execution but is badly flawed in its conception of strategy. Three problems are cited most commonly.

First, a country cannot grow now and redistribute income later because of the structures which develop with unequal growth. For example, as growth proceeds, those receiving the income obtain increased political power to op-pose any attempt to redistribute later. In addition, income becomes embodied in goods—Mercedeses, luxury apartments, college educations—which cannot be redistributed. There is no way to turn a Mercedes into bicycles or a luxury apartment into public housing. Thus income becomes a stock which cannot be redistributed.

A second problem with the growth strategy is that the poor moved into the cities in far greater numbers than theory assumed. Todaro[21] argues that for every job opening up in the cities, three people migrate from rural areas looking for jobs. Thus, for every job created, two people are attracted who end up unemployed. In addition, the demonstration effect of urban life has been a major magnet in drawing people from the rural sectors to the urban areas.

Finally the argument is made that certain key aspects of the development process simply have been ignored. Agriculture is one of these. It was given the role of fueling the industrialization process by providing various sur-pluses. But it turns out that this was often at the expense of the vitality of the sector, and in many cases agriculture has become unable to provide the basic food needs of the population. Similar benign neglect was accorded broader social and political aspects of development, with little concern given to social and political mobilization and participation.

Growth-with-equity economists are relatively united in their critique of the economic growth strategy and there are other areas of basic agreement as well. They generally accept the idea that social revolution is unlikely and probably undesirable for most poor countries in the near future. Thus these theorists are struggling to come up with an approach that will achieve some degree of equity short of social revolution. They are convinced that the poor can improve their standard of living without revolution, and they cite Tai-wan, Hong Kong, Israel, Japan, Singapore, and Sri Lanka as examples of countries where this has happened. This places them to some degree in the "history = progress" school, but they are much less sure of this than of other orthodox responses.

Another common factor is their implicit assumption concerning the peasants in less developed countries. They regard most people in the poor countries as responsive to economic opportunities; thus the bottleneck in the poor countries is not the peasant, but is more likely the capital city's powerful elite who have failed to design projects that provide meaningful opportunities to peasants. Common explanations of this failure are: first, the people at the top do not understand the people at the local level and their needs; second, they have been following a development-from-above syndrome, keeping all the incentives, all the management, all the cash in the hands of the central planners; or, finally, they have been following misguided policies favoring urban consumers. Any effort at growth with equity must correct these inade-quate economic policies.

Finally, growth-with-equity theorists all give considerable emphasis to the social and political variables in achieving growth and equity. They argue that one of the crucial limitations of past approaches was their narrow focus on simple economic factors—land, labor, and capital—to the exclusion of political, social, and cultural factors.

Despite these common starting points, growth-with-equity theorists espouse a wide variety of development strategies; in fact, some seven growth-with-equity strategies are discernible: employment generation, the redirecting of investment, the meeting of basic needs, human resource development, agriculture-first development, integrated rural development, and the New International Economic Order.[22] They are not all mutually exclusive, of course, and some are quite complementary. They simply approach the problem of eliminating poverty from different angles. Their unifying thread is the intention to deliver greater benefits to the bottom half of the population.

The two most fundamental strategies are "meeting basic needs"[23] and the "New International Economic Order."[24] . . . Streeten argues that the goal or target of development should be to meet the basic needs of all people everywhere—food, water, clothing, shelter, medical care, education, and participation in decisionmaking. In addition to meeting these needs directly, employment generation,[25] the redirection of investment,[26] human resource development,[27] agriculture-first development,[28] and integrated rural development[29] can all be seen as indirect ways of meeting basic needs.

All but one of these strategies focus on efforts within the underdeveloped countries. However, those who call for a New International Economic Order argue that while internal changes are necessary they cannot succeed without a major restructuring of those international institutions—the international monetary system, tariffs, multinational corporations, etc.—that at present result in discrimination against the poor countries.

It should be noted that growth with equity has not brought unanimity to the orthodox camp. The traditionalists within the orthodox paradigm retort that the growth-with-equity case is built on sand. They claim that the data are insufficient to prove a worsening of living standards and, in addition, that traditional strategies are being judged too soon. Western development exhibited increasing unemployment and income inequality as a stage before growth finally spread its benefits to the poorest part of the population. More time is needed before the growth approach can be declared a failure.

While the growth-with-equity approach developed within the orthodox paradigm and still has one foot firmly planted there, its tendency to endorse policies that supplant markets and deliver goods and services directly begins to move it closer to the political-economy paradigm. Certainly many of those who call for a New International Economic Order are adherents of dependency theory, one of the two main variants of the political economy paradigm. Celso Furtado is one of the best examples.

At this point the boundaries between the two paradigms become blurred, and the view of history as progress is not so clear. The growth of unemployment, inequality, and absolute poverty certainly have tarnished that belief. We will return to these questions after consideration of the political-economy paradigm.

IV. THE POLITICAL-ECONOMY PARADIGM

The other main approach to development is what we term the political-economy paradigm. It takes a very different stance from the orthodox approach, and the contrast highlights the arena of paradigm competition.

Within the orthodox paradigm the more traditional laissez faire and planning economists focus on economic growth as the key to development, while the growth-with-equity economists concentrate on the distribution of the benefits of growth to the poor. Political economists are more concerned with the *nature of the process* by which economic growth is achieved.[30] In addition, traditional economists look on people's values as means. Since the goal is growth, if people's values have to change in order to get growth, then society must effect that change. But for political economists, one goal is to enhance people's core values. Development becomes the means, not the end, for the end is to enhance what people value. Development or growth is desirable only if it is consistent with people's deepest values. Thus, political economists such as Denis Goulet define development as "liberation."[31]

This means liberation from oppressive and exploitative relationships both internally, among people within the country, and externally, among nations. The key question is: Who is controlling the development process? To apply Paulo Freire's terminology of the educational process[32] to the development process implies the question: Are people (or classes) and nations *objects* of development under someone else's control or are they *subjects* of development, in control of their own destiny?

Development is thus seen as the unfolding, in human history, of the progressive emancipation of peoples and nations from the control of nature and from the control of other peoples and nations. A major task then becomes that of explaining why this process has progressed much more with some peoples and nations than others. At this point there emerge within the political-economy paradigm two major schools of thought—the Marxists and the dependency theorists. The key difference between them resides in where they identify the locus of power and control. The control and use of the economic surplus of society is seen as the key to power and control of development. The Marxists focus on the internal class structure as the key to understanding control of the economic surplus. Dependency theorists focus on relationships between nations. This is primarily a matter of emphasis. Marxists have always been concerned with imperialism, and dependency theorists are concerned with the connection between the internal class structure and external dependency. But the different emphasis is important in understanding the political-economy paradigm.

The economic or social surplus is viewed as a residual factor—that which remains after necessary consumption has been subtracted from total output. Political economists argue that control of this economic surplus determines the nature of the development process. If a landed aristocracy controls the surplus you will get one style of development, if the middle class controls it then you will get a different style. The degree of foreign control of the surplus also will shape the strategy of development.

The economic-surplus concept is used by both Marxists and dependency theorists to analyze historical development and explain the existence of underdevelopment. We now turn to that analysis.

Development and Underdevelopment

At least at a superficial level, the stance of the political economist vis-à-vis history is quite similar to that of the orthodox writer. As Marx said, "the developed countries simply show the less developed countries their future." Thus the forces of nature will of necessity push economies from a precapitalist stage through the capitalist stage into either a socialist stage, which is the prelude to a communist society for the Marxist, or into self-reliance within a New International Economic Order for the dependency theorist. The process is inexorable, ensuring that history will bring progress. Nonetheless, there is a substantial difference between the two paradigms on specifics of the process. Whereas an automatic process was simply assumed by the orthodox approach, no such automatic transit is assumed by the political economists. The progress of history will come about only through the efforts of men: "Man makes himself." It will be through a long and costly struggle that history will advance, with each phase containing within it contradictions which must be exploited and which in their resolution will move the system the next step on the path. But those who control the economic surplus at a given time will not give in easily and thus progress will always be difficult. But it will come about as history and development move synchronously.

In this paradigm, the theory of underdevelopment has received the bulk of the interest, for it is only by understanding the forces of underdevelopment that the contradictions can be located and the struggle launched to resolve them. Let us take as our starting point the treatment of Western capitalist development, common to both variants of the political-economy paradigm, which, in turn, is the springboard for their separate theories of underdevelopment.

Capitalist Development in Europe and the United States

The development of capitalism in the West faced the need for change in the social structure so that the change-oriented middle class could become the leaders of society. This often involved a more or less violent struggle for supremacy between the old social order and the emerging new one. The English Revolution of 1640, ending with the supremacy of Parliament in 1688, replaced the feudal lords with the landed gentry and urban middle class as the dominant classes in England, thus preparing the way for later economic progress. The French Revolution of 1789 replaced the old aristocracy with the new middle class. The lack of such social change was a major factor in the economic stagnation of Spain after the seventeenth century.

This change in social structure enabled the economic surplus to be productively used. As Professor Dudley Dillard has pointed out: "Productive use of the 'social surplus' was the special virtue that enabled capitalism to outstrip all prior economic systems. Instead of building pyramids and cathedrals, those in command of the social surplus chose to invest in ships, warehouses, raw materials, finished goods and other material forms of wealth. The social surplus was thus converted into enlarged productive capacity."[33]

Before this productive investment could take place, the economic surplus had to be channeled into the hands of the new progressive class of society. In England, the profit inflation (the rise of money prices faster than rents and/or money wages) of 1540–1640 and 1795–1815 redistributed income in the first instance from landlords with fixed money rents to the rising gentry and merchants, and in the second from wage earners to profits on capitalist enterprise. Also the lag of real wages behind increases of productivity in the eighteenth and nineteenth centuries further increased profits from which new investment was made. This accumulation of capital enabled new technology to be utilized, which, by reducing costs, enabled more capital to be accumulated.

Such a period of development is always characterized by discontent and unrest because of the great changes taking place. In the case of the development of the capitalist countries, this required action on the part of a powerful national state to facilitate the social changes and accumulation of capital and to suppress any attempted interference with the process.

The appearance of a new "spirit" not only facilitated social change in the capitalist countries but also promoted capital accumulation and economic development. The Protestant ethic encouraged thrift and reinvestment of savings by the middle classes, and hard work and obedience by the working classes.

The sum of these historical events was a social revolution that destroyed the old feudal social order and brought to the fore a new class that was change oriented, and into whose hands the economic surplus was channeled for productive use. This, coupled with the rationalization of agriculture that took place, enabled capital to accumulate and economic development to proceed.

Since this process revolutionized the economies of Western Europe and North America, why did it fail to do so in Asia, Africa, and Latin America? That is, what are the causes of underdevelopment suggested by the two political economy variants?

Two Theories of Underdevelopment

Let us start with the Marxist view. Capitalism entered most underdeveloped countries the "Prussian way"—not through the growth of small, competitive enterprise but through the transfer abroad of advanced large-scale business. Thus, capitalist development in these countries has not been accompanied by the rise of a strong property-owning middle class and by the overthrow of landlord domination of society. Rather, an accommodation has taken place between the newly arrived business class and the socially and politically entrenched agrarian aristocracy.[34]

Therefore, there is neither vigorous competition between enterprises striving for increased output and rationalized production, nor accumulation of the economic surplus in the hands of entrepreneurs forced by the competitive system and the spirit of a middle class society to reinvest as much as possible in the continuous expansion and modernization of their businesses. The result is that production is well below the potential level, with agriculture still being operated on a semifeudal basis, and with waste and irrationality in industry protected by monopoly, high tariffs, and other devices.

For these and other reasons the actual economic surplus is much lower than the potential social surplus, which is the difference between the output that could be produced in a given natural and technological environment and what might be regarded as necessary consumption. A large share of the potential social surplus is used by aristocratic landlords in excess consumption and the maintenance of unproductive laborers. In addition, a large share of the actual social surplus is taken by businessmen for commercial operations promising large and quick profits, or for the accumulation of investments or bank accounts abroad as a hedge against domestic social and political hazards. Furthermore, in order to obtain social status and the benefits and privileges necessary for the operation of a business, they must emulate the dominant aristocracy in its mode of living. The potential social surplus is further reduced by the substantial quantity of resources used to maintain elaborate and inefficient bureaucratic and military establishments.

Although other factors undoubtedly have much to do with the inadequacy of the amount and composition of investment, the waste of a large portion of the social surplus due to the prevailing social structure is probably one of the major causes of economic stagnation.

In addition, the prevailing social and economic structure breeds a system of social relations, habits, customs, and culture that retards social and economic development. The preindustrial attitudes of peasants and workers operate against change, but even more important is the attitude of the ruling classes and the state which they usually dominate. These ruling classes know that if social and economic development comes, their power, status, and way of life will be threatened. Therefore, they continuously and actively oppose all kinds of social change.

The governments of these countries are poor agencies for enforcing the necessary changes, even though they claim the desire to do so, because often they are controlled or at least heavily influenced by these same wealthy classes. Governments which have attempted basic alterations in the social and economic structure have usually fallen, victims of a coup d'etat.

Many of these governments fear the prospects of development; their ruling classes realize better than we do the revolutionary potential which is contained in social change. They realize that even an attempt at peaceful, evolutionary development could quickly gain momentum and proceed to a situation where whole social classes are destroyed and basic institutions remolded.

John Gurley has elsewhere encapsulated this view quite succinctly:

Social scientists these days usually suppose that all governments really want economic development, and if they do not achieve it, then it must be because the problems are unusually difficult to solve, or that solutions take a rather long time to work themselves out. Persistence and technical knowledge are what is required for success. This supposition, however, does not adequately take account of the class structure of societies, the often conflicting aims that exist among the various classes, and the class nature of "success" and "failure." When poverty is looked at from the standpoint of the ruling classes, it may not be a failure of the system at all but rather a prerequisite for the continuation of their accumulation of wealth, their privileges, and their social, political, and economic domination of the society. . . .

A thorough-going programme of economic development, which is spread widely and reaches deeply into the structure of the society, is a dangerous thing to ruling classes, for it tends to undermine the very attributes of the masses of people that nourish the wealthy and powerful. Such a programme awakens people, and it is often best that they doze; it mobilizes people for gigantic economic efforts and such organization can be turned into political subversion; it sweeps away illusions, but may open their eyes to the causes of their own oppression.

Furthermore, any serious economic development programme that involves industrialization threatens existing class structures by creating new economic bases from which arise new social classes, and weakens the economic foundations which support the present dominant classes.[35]

Thus there is little likelihood that underdeveloped countries will simply progress along the path which has been traversed before. Capitalism has failed in its historic mission to develop the Third World. Rather, they are doomed to underdevelopment unless they undertake a process of struggle to take advantage of the contradictions of the capitalist order.

Dependency theorists would not necessarily disagree with this view of Third World underdevelopment; but they would argue that it does not give enough emphasis to the underdeveloped countries' own history and to their interaction with the developed countries.

Starting with the historical studies of underdevelopment pioneered by Celso Furtado, André Gunder Frank, Keith Griffin, Osvaldo Sunkel, and others, a dependency perspective on this process of development and underdevelopment has been in the making, particularly in regard to Latin America. This structural approach builds on the history of capitalist development presented above. The development of capitalism and the world market is seen as a twofold process. A highly dualistic *process of underdevelopment* of Africa, Asia, and Latin America is the consequence of the *process of development* of Europe and North America. This twofold process created a situation of dependence in which the underdeveloped countries became appendages of the developed countries.

This approach emphasizes the role of dependence in shaping the internal economic, social, and political structures (and thus control of the economic surplus) and in shaping the external relations of underdeveloped countries. Dependency means that many of the most important decisions about development strategies—decisions about prices, investment patterns, government macroeconomic policies, etc.—are made by individuals, firms, and institutions external to the country.

The simplest way to understand the meaning of underdevelopment in dependency theory is to see it as a process whereby an underdeveloped country, characterized by subsistence agriculture and domestic production, progressively becomes integrated as a dependency into the world market through trade or investment. Its production becomes geared to the demands of the world market and particularly of the developed countries, with a consequent lack of integration between the parts of the domestic economy. Thus both agriculture and industry become export oriented.

Two Views of Development

The final component of the models is their theory of development. Here the lack of elaboration is as notable as the wealth of analysis in the theory of underdevelopment. The Marxist theory of development suggests that the capitalist structures which exist and inhibit the development of Third World countries must be overthrown and replaced by a socialist society. This will in turn become a communist society over time, but the basic step must be the overthrow, violent or otherwise, of the capitalist structures.

What is to be done after the revolution? Political economists, Marxists, and dependency theorists alike have not developed any *theories* of development. Rather Marxists and many dependency theorists have drawn empirical generalizations from the historical development experience of the Soviet Union and China. Until recently the Soviet model of development was looked to for guidance in development strategies. Thus it is worthwhile to take a closer look at it.

The Soviet model,[36] as historically derived, can be subdivided into three aspects: the preconditions of the model, the institutions characteristic of the model, and the strategy of development in the model.

The preconditions of the model include severance of any existing colonial bond with capitalist countries, elimination of economic domination by foreign capitalists, and redistribution of political and economic power. In sum, this will usually mean a social revolution which, at least nominally, redistributes political and economic power to the workers and peasants.

The institutions characteristic of the model include collectivized agriculture, publicly owned enterprises, comprehensive central planning, centralized distribution of essential materials and capital goods, and a system of administrative controls and pressures on enterprises, in addition to incentives, to ensure compliance with the plan.

The strategy of development in the model encompasses high rates of capital formation; priority of basic capital goods industries; bias in favor of modern, capital-intensive technologies in key processes combined with labor-intensive techniques in auxiliary operations; an import-substitution policy in international trade; utilization of underemployed agricultural labor for capital formation; and heavy investment in human capital.

Parallel, in time and intent, to the revolt of the growth-with-equity theorists within the orthodox paradigm, many Marxists and dependency theorists turned to Chinese experience as an alternative to the Soviet model of development. Many factors played a role in this shift in allegiance: the Soviet obsession with growth that relegated people's values to a secondary position, the concentration of power in the hands of the Communist party at the expense of the mass of people, the focus on industrialization to the neglect of agriculture, and so on.

To many political economists China seems a more appropriate model of development.[37] A great deal of work has been done on the accomplishments in China. A review of this literature finds extensive and numerous treatments of China's gains in health care, sanitation, worker organization in industry, rural development, and rural mobilization. It is apparent that if China had not existed, political economists would have had to invent it, for the validation that it gives to the political-economy approach is substantial and crucial.

The general model drawn from Chinese experience is one in which self-reliant development is pursued with an emphasis on fulfilling people's basic human needs (food, shelter, health, education) and on providing institutional structures (brigades, communes, etc.) that enable people to exert control over the conditions in which they lead their lives.

. . . . . .

Most dependency theorists are more circumspect about citing China as their model of development. They concentrate instead on the elimination of dependency relations through the call for a New International Economic Order. This is frequently coupled with a rather vague endorsement of a self-reliant socialism that is without the dictatorial political control of China. Thus, their major concern is returning control of the development process to the individual nation-states. Some dependency theorists realize that eliminating external dependency does not necessarily empower the mass of poor people in the underdeveloped countries. A class analysis demonstrates that the leading elites in many underdeveloped countries—particularly those countries most integrated into the international economy—are less than eager to pass control to the poor.[38]

In general, then, political economists see the historical process of development sidetracked into the blind alley of underdevelopment. Traditional Marxists see this as due to the failure of the middle class to perform its historical mission of creating a dynamic capitalist society. Dependency theorists argue that specific conditions led to a dependent relationship between center and periphery countries that distorted the development of the latter. Marxists call for social revolution to replace the middle class with control by workers and peasants, and dependency theorists call for an end to dependency so nation-states can take control of their own development.

In closing this discussion of the political-economy paradigm it should be noted that this reading of historical development is not universally agreed upon by political economists. . . . [W]riters such as Bill Warren, although speaking from a Marxist perspective, claim that there have been tremendous increases in the forces of production in the postwar period, that development is indeed occurring in exactly the way that Marx would have predicted. Countries such as Brazil, Mexico, and Nigeria are going though a capitalist revolution. This process and its success will bring forth the contradictions which will eventually lead to a socialist overthrow of the capitalist system. Thus, these political economists agree with the traditional economists of the orthodox paradigm that development is occurring. They differ in believing that, after development occurs, conflict that will eventually lead to socialist revolutions will develop among all the advanced capitalist countries. Here again, the boundaries between the two paradigms become blurred, but these two sections should have made clear the basic utility of the paradigm division.

Nonetheless, it is the contention of the remainder of this chapter that it is necessary to pass beyond these paradigms and, in particular, to break free of their implicit belief in the natural progress of history. We suggest that seeing history as "convoluted" avoids many of the reductionist failings of our postwar paradigms, and in general that the remaining chapters of the volume should be taken as examples of analyses which do move beyond these confines.

. . . . . .

V. CONVOLUTED HISTORY

A look at the postwar record indicates that countries prospered and stagnated regardless of social system or development strategy. Brazil and Mexico grew while their poor suffered. Costa Rica grew and Cuba failed to grow while their poor prospered. Both China and Taiwan are cited as "models" of development. Both Tanzania and Peru are floundering. Capitalism has not brought freedom to Chile or South Korea and socialism has not brought liberation to Cambodia or North Korea. There have been increases in both per capita GNP and malnutrition, decreases in both infant mortality and political freedoms, and decreases in both external dependency and control by the poor of their own lives. This concrete record of "progress" challenges us to rethink our approach to "development."

As noted above, the starting point for thinking about development is some conception of history. An initial response to our idea of convoluted reality which might aid in understanding the later chapters would be to become wary of the accepted conception of history and to attempt to avoid assuming the view of historical progress which is common to both of the paradigms. History as we live it simply does not seem to be moving in that direction. The parable of historical progress common to both the orthodox and political-economy paradigms is a metaphor that may be useful in studying an abstraction—civilization or socialism—but it is misplaced in studying the actual development of Peru or Uganda.

Nisbet summarizes the difficulty succinctly and elegantly:

> The relevance and utility of the metaphor of growth are in direct proportion to the cognitive distance of the subject to which the metaphor is applied. The larger, more distant or more abstract the subject, the greater the utility of metaphor-derived attributes. . . .
>
> We may now state the proposition in reverse. The less the cognitive distance, the less the relevance and utility of the metaphor. In other words, the more concrete, empirical and behavioral our subject matter, the less the applicability to it of the theory of development and its several conceptual elements.
>
> It is tempting enough to apply these elements to the constructed entities which abound in Western social thought: to civilization as a whole, to mankind, to total society; to such entities as capitalism, democracy, and culture; to social systems as functionalists and others conceive them; and to so-called evolutionary universals. Having endowed one or

other of these with life through the familiar process of reification, it is but a short step to further endowment with growth—with internal mechanisms of growth and development around which laws of progress and evolution are constructed. Such has in very large measure been the history of social thought in the West since the time of Aristotle.

It is something else entirely, however, when we try, as much social theory at present is trying, to impose these concepts of developmentalism upon, *not* constructed entities, but the kind of subject matter that has become basic in the social sciences today: *the social behavior of human beings in specific areas and within finite limits of time.* Efforts to extract this further from the metaphor of growth are . . . wholly unsuccessful.[39]

Convoluted History, Convoluted Development

It might be well to examine an alternative view of history, one which comes out of the writings of the Latin American novelist, Gabriel García Márquez. In his major work, *One Hundred Years of Solitude,* [40] García Márquez provides us with a parable of Latin American history since independence which is quite at variance with our progress notion. History moves forward, progresses, but it is always doubling back upon itself. In some cases the march of history gets mixed up and only later resumes its "natural" course. This view we can call "convoluted history."

Let us briefly review the story of the book to aid our understanding. It is the history of a village, Macondo, from its founding to its demise, as seen through the eyes and lives of one family, the Buendías. Ostensibly there is the progress which we call development. From an obscure, virtually deserted swamp Macondo grows and its people prosper. Macondo experiences technical or scientific progress as new inventions become known: ice, the astrolabe, the pianola. It experiences economic progress as the diversity of activities increases, the capstone being the arrival of a banana company which raises per capita GNP substantially. It also experiences political modernization as the national political structure develops and incorporates Macondo into its bosom.

Throughout these experiences of progress, there are doubts. The inventions of science, known for years elsewhere, are used by the gypsies to dominate the people of Macondo. The banana company effects substantial changes in the town and the people; but when the company cannot have its own way, it leaves town and calls down a tremendous rain which "purifies" the town of its past. In addition, the political structure is often quite repressive and unresponsive.

But the real questioning of historical progress comes from viewing the lives of the Buendías. Every generation has two recurring tendencies. One is the "Aurelio" tendency, calm and reflective, given to studying the historical manuscript of the family, yet when challenged, able to react with fury. In one case the fury was so great as to drive Colonel Aurelio to lead thirty-two unsuccessful rebellions.

The other recurring tendency is the "José Arcadio" tendency. This describes modernizers, the entrepreneurs, who participate and enjoy the new changes which history is bringing them, and usually die a violent death. But history is more complex than simply continuity and repetition. For at one point the twins, Aureliano Segundo and José Arcadio Segundo, are mixed up; and they live part of their lives acting as the other. Finally history triumphs and brings them back to their own nature.

But underlying the currents of history is one consistent concern: the attempt to understand and to decipher the parchments left by Melquiades the gypsy. There is a gradually growing understanding, which reaches its fruition when the last Aureliano, Babilonia, learns to read the parchments which are the entire history of his family condensed into one moment. As he reads, that history ends and is blown away by the wind "because races condemned to one hundred years of solitude did not have a second opportunity on earth."

This is certainly a different version of history.

Yet it is a version which may fit the process of development better than the idea of "progress," and it is one which can place the chapters of this book in a useful perspective. In some sense the writers of the later chapters are attempting to decipher the parchments of development, to read and understand the history of development in Third World countries. In addition, they are doing so in an effort to wipe out that history, to call forth the wind to banish underdevelopment and to facilitate policy which can bring about meaningful development.

The import of Garcia Márquez's parable of convoluted history is that there is no simple historical march of progress. There are no general paths to development just as there is no general definition of development. Each people must write its own history. As Denis Goulet says regarding the strategy of development pursued by Guinea-Bissau: "Paradoxically, the lesson of greatest importance is that *the best model of development is the one that any society forges for itself on the anvil of its own specific conditions.*"[41]

What does this mean for the development economist? There is an interesting parallel in modern medicine in a tension between the "scientific" explanation of a disease and the diagnosis a clinician makes for a particular patient.[42] This is well described by Tolstoy in *War and Peace:*

> Doctors came to see Natasha, both separately and in consultation. They said a great deal in French, German and in Latin. They criticised one another, and prescribed the most diverse remedies for all the diseases they were familiar with. But it never occurred to one of them to make the simple reflection that they could not understand the disease from which Natasha was suffering, as no single disease can be fully understood in a living person; for every living person has his complaints unknown to

medicine—not a disease of the lungs, of the kidneys, of the skin, of the heart, and so on, as described in medical books, but a disease that consists of one out of the innumerable combinations of ailments of these organs.

While Tolstoy's depiction of every illness as a unique event may no longer be justified, economic development is even more of an art than medical diagnosis. Economic theorists can scientifically explain the results of under-pricing capital regardless of country or time. Development economists, on the other hand, are diagnosticians of the particular illnesses of particular countries at specific points in time. They are forced to transcend a specific scientific paradigm to become artisans of the particular.

. . . . . .

This throwing off of the conceptual blinders of the paradigms holds out hope that development will become a means to serve people and that there will be fewer tragedies like Chile and Cambodia, where people are seen as a means to promote development. "If there is to be a possibility of choosing a human path so that all human beings may become the active subjects of their own history, it must begin at the level of new analysis. . . . Development should be a *struggle* to create criteria, goals, and means for self-liberation from misery, inequity, and dependency in all forms. Crucially, it should be the process a people choose, which heals them from historical trauma, and enables them to achieve a newness on their own terms."[43]

NOTES

1. Thomas Kuhn, *The Structure of Scientific Revolution,* 2nd ed. (Chicago: University of Chicago Press, 1970).
2. W. W. Rostow, *The Stages of Economic Growth: A Non-Communist Manifesto* (New York: Cambridge University Press, 1960).
3. P. Bauer and B. Yamey, *The Economics of Underdeveloped Countries* (New York: Cambridge University Press, 1967), p. 151.
4. B. Higgins, *Economic Development: Problems, Principles and Policies* (New York: W. W. Norton, 1968), p. 147.
5. D. Seers, "The Meaning of Development," in Charles K. Wilber, *The Political Economy of Development and Underdevelopment* (New York: Random House, 1973), p. 6.
6. Denis Goulet, " 'Development' . . . or Liberation," in Wilber, *Political Economy,* p. 355.
7. Furtado also points out how development and progress have come to be focused on the nation-state as the major operational entity. In our treatment we will take as an unexamined premise that the basic unit of analysis is the nation-state. Gurley's essay indicates the empirical validity of this approach even with reference to the socialist states which place "internationalism" on a very high plane.
8. J. Culbertson, *Economic Development: An Ecological Approach* (New York: Alfred A. Knopf, 1971).

9. See J. H. Boeke, *Economics and Economic Policy in Dual Societies* (New York: Institute of Pacific Relations, 1953) and Higgins, *Economic Development,* chap. 12, "Cultural Determinism."

10. See David C. McClelland, *The Achieving Society* (Princeton, N.J.: D. Van Nostrand, 1961).

11. See David E. Novack and Robert Lekachman, eds., *Development and Society: The Dynamics of Economic Change* (New York: St. Martins, 1964), "Part Two: The Social Order"; Bert F. Hoselitz, *Sociological Aspects of Economic Growth* (New York: Free Press, 1960); Everett E. Hagen, *The Economics of Development,* rev. ed. (Homewood, Ill.: Richard D. Irwin, 1975), chap. 11, "Entrepreneurship."

12. See Ragnar Nurkse, *Problems of Capital Formation in Underdeveloped Countries* (Oxford: Basil Blackwell, 1958). See also the relevant chapters in Higgins, *Economic Development,* and Hagen, *Economics of Development.*

13. See particularly Bauer and Yamey, *Economics of Underdeveloped Countries.*

14. See Hagen, *Economics of Development;* Higgins, *Economic Development;* Culbertson, *Economic Development;* and a host of other works.

15. A. Harberger, "Using the Resources at Hand More Effectively," *American Economic Review,* May 1959.

16. D. Morawetz, "Twenty-Five Years of Economic Development," *Finance and Development,* September 1977, p. 10.

17. Ibid., p. 12.

18. Ibid., p. 13.

19. I. Adelman and C. Morris, *Economic Growth and Social Equity in Developing Countries* (Stanford: Stanford University Press, 1973).

20. See James H. Weaver, Kenneth P. Jameson, and Richard N. Blue, "Growth and Equity: Can They Be Happy Together?" *International Development Review,* 1978/1, pp. 20–27, reprinted in Charles K. Wilber, ed., *The Political Economy of Development and Underdevelopment,* 2nd ed. (New York: Random House, 1978). Also see Mary Evelyn Jegen and Charles K. Wilber, eds., *Growth with Equity: Essays in Economic Development* (New York: Paulist Press, 1979).

21. Michael P. Todaro, "A Model of Labor Migration and Urban Unemployment in Less Developed Countries," *American Economic Review,* March, 1969, pp. 138–148.

22. This is based on Weaver, Jameson, and Blue, "Growth and Equity . . ."

23. In addition to the essay by Paul Streeten in this volume, see Overseas Development Council, *The United States and World Development: Agenda 1977* (New York: Praeger, 1977).

24. See the following: Mahbub ul Haq, *The Third World and the International Economic Order,* Overseas Development Council, Development Paper 22, (September 1976); Guy F. Erb and Valeriana Kallab, eds., *Beyond Dependency: The Developing World Speaks Out* (Washington, D. C.: Overseas Development Council, 1975); Antony J. Dolman and Jan van Ettinger, eds., *Partners in Tomorrow: Strategies for a New International Order* (New York: E. P. Dutton, 1978).

25. See International Labour Office, *Employment, Growth and Basic Needs: A One-World Problem* (New York: Praeger, 1977); Kenneth P. Jameson and Charles K. Wilber, "Employment, Basic Human Needs, and Economic Development," in Jegen and Wilber, *Growth with Equity.*

26. See Hollis Chenery, et al., *Redistribution with Growth* (Oxford: Oxford University Press, 1974).

27. See Irma Adelman, "Growth, Income Distribution, and Equity Oriented Development Strategies," *World Development,* February–March, 1975; reprinted in Wilber, *Political Economy,* 2nd ed.

28. See John Mellor, *The New Economics of Growth* (Ithaca: Cornell University Press, 1976).

29. See Albert Waterson, "A Viable Model for Rural Development," *Finance and Development,* December 1974 and March 1975; reprinted in Wilber, *Political Economy,* 2nd ed.

30. For a full discussion of alternative definitions of development see Peter J. Henriot, "Development Alternatives: Problems, Strategies, Values," in Wilber, *Political Economy,* 2nd ed.

31. See Goulet, " 'Development' . . . or Liberation," in Wilber, *Political Economy,* 2nd ed.

32. See Paulo Freire, *Pedagogy of the Oppressed* (New York: Herder and Herder, 1970). Chapter 1 is reprinted in Wilber, *Political Economy,* 2nd ed.

33. Dudley Dillard, s.v. "Capitalism" *Encyclopedia Britannica* (1963); reprinted in Wilber, *Political Economy,* 2nd ed.

34. See Paul A. Baran, "On the Political Economy of Backwardness," in Wilber, *Political Economy,* 2nd ed. Celso Furtado, a dependency theorist, has a similar analysis. See Celso Furtado, *Diagnosis of the Brazilian Crisis* (Berkeley: University of California Press, 1965), pp. 20–21, 115–118.

35. John Gurley, "Rural Development in China 1949–72, and the Lessons to Be Learned from It," *World Development,* July–August 1975, p. 456.

36. For a full treatment see Charles K. Wilber, *The Soviet Model and Underdeveloped Countries* (Chapel Hill: University of North Carolina Press, 1969).

37. For the classic statement of the Chinese model see John Gurley, "Maoist Economic Development: The New Man in the New China," in Wilber, *Political Economy,* 2nd ed.

38. Fernando Henrique Cardoso and Enzo Faletto, *Dependencia y Desarrollo en América Latina* (Santiago: ILPES, 1967).

39. Robert A. Nisbet, *Social Change and History: Aspects of the Western Theory of Development* (New York: Oxford University Press, 1969), pp. 267–268.

40. Gabriel Garcia Márquez, *One Hundred Years of Solitude* (New York: Harper and Row, 1970).

41. Denis Goulet, *Looking at Guinea-Bissau: A New Nation's Development Strategy,* Occasional Paper no. 9: Overseas Development Council, March 1978, p. 52.

42. The following is based on the discussion of a related issue taken from Stanley Hauerwas, David Burrell, and Richard Bondi, *Truthfulness and Tragedy: A Further Investigation in Christian Ethics,* "An Alternative Pattern for Rationality in Ethics" (Notre Dame, In.: Notre Dame Press, 1977).

43. James J. Lamb, "The Third World and the Development Debate," *IDOC-North America,* January–February 1973, p. 20.

2

The Misconceptions of "Development Economics"

Deepak Lal

Ideas have consequences. The body of thought that has evolved since World War II and is called "development economics" (to be distinguished from the orthodox "economics of developing countries") has, for good or ill, shaped policies for, as well as beliefs about, economic development in the Third World. Viewing the interwar experience of the world economy as evidence of the intellectual deficiencies of conventional economics (embodied, for instance, in the tradition of Marshall, Pigou, and Robertson) and seeking to emulate Keynes' iconoclasm (and hopefully renown), numerous economists set to work in the 1950s to devise a new unorthodox economics particularly suited to developing countries (most prominently, Nurkse, Myrdal, Rosen-stein-Rodan, Balogh, Prebisch, and Singer). In the subsequent decades numerous specific theories and panaceas for solving the economic problems of the Third World have come to form the corpus of a "development econom-ics." These include: the dual economy, labor surplus, low level equilibrium trap, unbalanced growth, vicious circles of poverty, big push industrializa-tion, foreign exchange bottlenecks, unequal exchange, "dependencia," redis-tribution with growth, and a basic needs strategy—to name just the most influential in various times and climes.

Those who sought a new economics claimed that orthodox economics was (1) unrealistic because of its behavioral, technological, and institutional assumptions and (2) irrelevant because it was concerned primarily with the efficient allocation of given resources, and hence could deal neither with the so-called dynamic aspects of growth nor with various ethical aspects of the alleviation of poverty or the distribution of income. The twists and turns that the unorthodox theories have subsequently taken may be traced in four major areas: (1) the role of foreign trade and official or private capital flows in

From *Finance and Development,* 22 (June 1985), pp. 10–13.

promoting economic development, (2) the role and appropriate form of industrialization in developing countries, (3) the relationship between the reduction of inequality, the alleviation of poverty, and the so-called different "strategies of development," and (4) the role of the price mechanism in promoting development.

The last is, in fact, the major debate that in a sense subsumes most of the rest, and it is the main concern of this article; for the major thrust of much of "development economics" has been to justify massive government intervention through forms of direct control usually intended to supplant rather than to improve the functioning of, or supplement, the price mechanism. This is what I label the *dirigiste dogma,* which supports forms and areas of *dirigisme* well beyond those justifiable on orthodox economic grounds.

The empirical assumptions on which this unwarranted *dirigisme* was based have been repudiated by the experience of numerous countries in the postwar period. This article briefly reviews these central misconceptions of "development economics." References to the evidence as well as an elucidation of the arguments underlying the analysis (together with various qualifications) can be found in A. O. Hirschman's *Essays in Trespassing* (Cambridge, 1981).

DENIAL OF "ECONOMIC PRINCIPLE"

The most basic misconception underlying much of development economics has been a rejection (to varying extents) of the behavioral assumption that, either as producers or consumers, people, as Hicks said, "would act *economically;* when the opportunity of an advantage was presented to them, they would take it." Against these supposedly myopic and ignorant private agents (that is, individuals or groups of people), development economists have set some official entity (such as government, planners, or policymakers) which is both knowledgeable and compassionate. It can overcome the defects of private agents and compel them to raise their living standards through various *dirigiste* means.

Numerous empirical studies from different cultures and climates, however, show that uneducated private agents—be they peasants, rural-urban migrants, urban workers, private entrepreneurs, or housewives—act economically as producers and consumers. They respond to changes in relative prices much as neoclassical theory would predict. The "economic principle" is not unrealistic in the Third World; poor people may, in fact, be pushed even harder to seek their advantage than rich people.

Nor are the preferences of Third World workers peculiar in that for them too (no matter how poor), the cost of "sweat" rises the harder and longer they work. They do not have such peculiar preferences that when they become richer they will not also seek to increase their "leisure"—an assumption that underlies the view that there are large pools of surplus labor in developing countries that can be employed at a low or zero social opportunity cost. They are unlikely to be in "surplus" in any meaningful sense any more than their Western counterparts.

Nor are the institutional features of the Third World, such as their strange social and agrarian structures or their seemingly usurious informal credit systems, necessarily a handicap to growth. Recent applications of neoclassical theory show how, instead of inhibiting efficiency, these institutions—being second-best adaptations to the risks and uncertainties inherent in the relevant economic environment—are likely to enhance efficiency.

Finally, the neoclassical assumption about the possibilities of substituting different inputs in production has not been found unrealistic. The degree to which inputs of different factors and commodities can be substituted in the national product is not much different in developed or developing countries. Changes in relative factor prices do influence the choice of technology at the micro level and the overall labor intensity of production in Third World economies.

MARKET *VS.* BUREAUCRATIC FAILURE

A second and major strand of the unwarranted *dirigisme* of much of development economics has been based on the intellectually valid arguments against *laissez-faire.* As is well known, *laissez-faire* will only provide optimal outcomes if perfect competition prevails; if there are universal markets for trading all commodities (including future "contingent" commodities, that is, commodities defined by future conditions, such as the impact of weather on energy prices); and if the distribution of income generated by the *laissez-faire* economy is considered equitable or, if not, could be made so through lump-sum taxes and subsidies. As elementary economics shows, the existence of externalities in production and consumption and increasing returns to scale in production, or either of them, will rule out the existence of a perfectly competitive utopia. While, clearly, universal markets for *all* (including contingent) commodities do not exist in the real world, to that extent market failure must be ubiquitous in the real world. This, even ignoring distributional considerations, provides a *prima facie* case for government intervention. But this in itself does not imply that any or most forms of government intervention will improve the outcomes of a necessarily imperfect market economy.

For the basic cause of market failure is the difficulty in establishing markets in commodities because of the costs of making transactions. These transaction costs are present in any market, or indeed any mode of resource allocation, and include the costs of excluding nonbuyers as well as those of acquiring and transmitting the relevant information about the demand and supply of a particular commodity to market participants. They drive a wedge, in effect, between the buyer's and the seller's price. The market for a particular good will cease to exist if the wedge is so large as to push the lowest price at which anyone is willing to sell above the highest price anyone is willing to pay. These transaction costs, however, are also involved in acquiring, processing, and transmitting the relevant information to design public policies, as well as in enforcing compliance. There may, consequently, be as many instances of bureaucratic as of market failure, making it impossible to attain a full welfare optimum. Hence, the best that can be expected in the real world of imperfect markets and imperfect bureaucrats is a second best. But judging between alternative second best outcomes involves a subtle application of second-best welfare economics, which provides no general rule to permit the deduction that, in a necessarily imperfect market economy, particular *dirigiste* policies will increase economic welfare. They may not; and they may even be worse than *laissez-faire.*

FORETELLING THE FUTURE

Behind most arguments for *dirigisme,* particularly those based on directly controlling quantities of goods demanded and supplied, is the implicit premise of an omniscient central authority. The authority must also be omnipotent (to prevent people from taking actions that controvert its diktat) and benevolent (to ensure it serves the common weal rather than its own), if it is to necessarily improve on the working of an imperfect market economy. While most people are willing to question the omnipotence or benevolence of governments, there is a considerable temptation to believe the latter have an omniscience that private agents know they themselves lack. This temptation is particularly large when it comes to foretelling the future.

Productive investment is the mainspring of growth. Nearly all investment involves giving hostages to fortune. Most investments yield their fruits over time and the expectations of investors at the time of investment may not be fulfilled. Planners attempting to direct investments and outputs have to take a view about future changes in prices, tastes, resources, and technology, much like private individuals. Even if the planners can acquire the necessary information about current tastes, technology, and resources in designing an investment program, they must also take a view about likely changes in the future demand and supply of myriad goods. Because in an uncertain world there can be no agreed or objective way of deciding whether a particular investment gamble is sounder than another, the planned outcomes will be better than those of a market system (in the sense of lower excess demand for or supply of different goods and services) only if the planners' forecasts are more accurate than the decentralized forecasts made by individual decision makers in a market economy. There is no reason to believe that planners, lacking perfect foresight, will be more successful at foretelling the future than individual investors.

Outcomes based on centralized forecasts may, indeed, turn out to be worse than those based on the decentralized forecasts of a large number of participants in a market economy, because imposing a single centralized forecast on the economy in an uncertain world is like putting all eggs in one basket. By contrast, the multitude of small bets, based on different forecasts, placed by a large number of decision makers in a market economy *may be* a sounder strategy. Also, bureaucrats, as opposed to private agents, are likely to take less care in placing their bets, as they do not stand to lose financially when they are wrong. This assumes, of course, that the government does not have better information about the future than private agents. If it does, it should obviously disseminate it, together with any of its own forecasts. On the whole, however, it may be best to leave private decision makers to take risks according to their own judgments.

This conclusion is strengthened by the fact, emphasized by Hayek, that most relevant information is likely to be held at the level of the individual firm and the household. A major role of the price mechanism in a market economy is to transmit this information to all interested parties. The "planning without prices" favored in practice by some planners attempts to supersede and suppress the price mechanism. It thereby throws sand into one of the most useful and relatively low-cost social mechanisms for transmitting information, as well as for coordinating the actions of large numbers of interdependent market participants. The strongest argument against centralized planning, therefore, is that, even though omniscient planners might forecast the future more accurately than myopic private agents, there is no reason to believe that ordinary government officials can do any better—and some reason to believe they may do much worse.

It has nevertheless been maintained that planners in the Third World can and should directly control the pattern of industrialization. Some have put their faith in mathematical programming models based on the use of input-output tables developed by Leontief. But, partly for the reasons just discussed, little reliance can be placed upon either the realism or the usefulness of these models for deciding which industries will be losers and which will be winners in the future. There are many important and essential tasks for governments to perform (see below), and this irrational *dirigisme* detracts from their main effort.

REDRESSING INEQUALITY AND POVERTY

Finally, egalitarianism is never far from the surface in most arguments supporting the *dirigiste dogma*. This is not surprising since there may be good theoretical reasons for government intervention, even in a perfectly functioning market economy, in order to promote a distribution of income desired on ethical grounds. Since the distribution resulting from market processes will depend upon the initial distribution of assets (land, capital, skills, and labor) of individuals and households, the desired distribution could, in principle, be attained either by redistributing the assets or by introducing lump-sum taxes and subsidies to achieve the desired result. If, however, lump-sum taxes and subsidies cannot be used in practice, the costs of distortion from using other fiscal devices (such as the income tax, which distorts the individual's choice between income and leisure) will have to be set against the benefits from any gain in equity. This is as much as theory can tell us, and it is fairly uncontroversial.

Problems arise because we lack a consensus about the ethical system for judging the desirability of a particular distribution of income. Even within Western ethical beliefs, the shallow utilitarianism that underlies many economists' views about the "just" distribution of income and assets is not universally accepted. The possibility that all the variegated peoples of the world are utilitarians is fairly remote. Yet the moral fervor underlying many economic prescriptions assumes there is already a world society with a common set of ethical beliefs that technical economists can take for granted and use to make judgments encompassing both the efficiency and equity components of economic welfare. But casual empiricism is enough to show that there is no such world society; nor is there a common view, shared by mankind, about the content of social justice.

There is, therefore, likely to be little agreement about either the content of distributive justice or whether we should seek to achieve it through some form of coercive redistribution of incomes and assets when this would infringe other moral ends, which are equally valued. By contrast, most moral codes accept the view that, to the extent feasible, it is desirable to alleviate abject, absolute poverty or destitution. That alleviating poverty is not synonymous with reducing the inequality of income, as some seem still to believe, can be seen by considering a country with the following two options. The first option leads to a rise in the incomes of all groups, including the poor, but to larger relative increases for the rich, and hence a worsening of the distribution of income. The second leads to no income growth for the poor but to a reduction in the income of the rich; thus the distribution of income improves but the extent of poverty remains unchanged. Those concerned with inequality would favor the second option; those with poverty the first. Thus, while the pursuit of efficient growth may worsen some inequality index, there is no evidence that it will increase poverty.

SURPLUS LABOR AND "TRICKLE DOWN"

As the major asset of the poor in most developing (as well as developed) countries is their labor time, increasing the demand for unskilled labor relative to its supply could be expected to be the major means of reducing poverty in the Third World. However, the shadows of Malthus and Marx have haunted development economics, particularly in its discussion of equity and the alleviation of poverty. One of the major assertions of development economics, preoccupied with "vicious circles" of poverty, was that the fruits of capitalist growth, with its reliance on the price mechanism, would not trickle down or spread to the poor. Various *dirigiste* arguments were then advocated to bring the poor into a growth process that would otherwise bypass them. The most influential, as well as the most famous, of the models of development advanced in the 1950s to chart the likely course of outputs and incomes in an overpopulated country or region was that of Sir Arthur Lewis. It made an assumption of surplus labor that, in a capitalist growth process, entailed no increase in the income of laborers until the surplus had been absorbed.

It has been shown that the assumptions required for even under-employed rural laborers to be "surplus," in Lewis' sense of their being available to industry at a constant wage, are very stringent, and implausible. It was necessary to assume that, with the departure to the towns of their relatives, those rural workers who remained would work harder for an unchanged wage. This implied that the preferences of rural workers between leisure and income are perverse, for workers will not usually work harder without being offered a higher wage. Recent empirical research into the shape of the supply curve of rural labor at different wages has found that—at least for India, the country supposedly containing vast pools of surplus labor—the curve is upward-sloping (and not flat, as the surplus labor theory presupposes). Thus, for a given labor supply, increases in the demand for labor time, in both the industrial and the rural sectors, can be satisfied only by paying higher wages.

The fruits of growth, even in India, will therefore trickle down, in the sense either of raising labor incomes, whenever the demand for labor time increases by more than its supply, or of preventing the fall in real wages and thus labor incomes, which would otherwise occur if the supply of labor time outstripped the increase in demand for it. More direct evidence about movements in the rural and industrial real wages of unskilled labor in developing countries for which data are available has shown that the standard economic presumption that real wages will rise as the demand for labor grows, relative to its supply, is as valid for the Third World as for the First.

ADMINISTRATIVE CAPACITIES

It is in the political and administrative aspects of *dirigisme* that powerful practical arguments can be advanced against the *dirigiste dogma*. The political and administrative assumptions underlying the feasibility of various forms of *dirigisme* derive from those of modern welfare states in the West. These, in turn, reflect the values of the eighteenth-century Enlightenment. It has taken nearly two centuries of political evolution for those values to be internalized and reflected (however imperfectly) in the political and administrative institutions of Western societies. In the Third World, an acceptance of the same values is at best confined to a small class of Westernized intellectuals. Despite their trappings of modernity, many developing countries are closer in their official workings to the inefficient nation states of seventeenth- or eighteenth-century Europe. It is instructive to recall that Keynes, whom so many *dirigistes* invoke as a founding father of their faith, noted in *The End of Laissez-Faire:*

> But above all, the ineptitude of public administrators strongly prejudiced the practical man in favor of *laissez-faire*—a sentiment which has by no means disappeared. Almost everything which the State did in the 18th century in excess of its minimum functions was, or seemed, injurious or unsuccessful.

It is in this context that anyone familiar with the actual administration and implementation of policies in many Third World countries, and not blinkered by the *dirigiste dogma,* should find that oft-neglected work, *The Wealth of Nations,* both so relevant and so modern.

For in most of our modern-day equivalents of the inefficient eighteenth-century state, not even the minimum governmental functions required for economic progress are always fulfilled. These include above all providing public goods of which law and order and a sound money remain paramount, and an economic environment where individual thrift, productivity, and enterprise is cherished and not thwarted. There are numerous essential tasks for *all* governments to perform. One of the most important is to establish and maintain the country's infrastructure, much of which requires large, indivisible lumps of capital before any output can be produced. Since the services provided also frequently have the characteristics of public goods, natural monopolies would emerge if they were privately produced. Some form of government regulation would be required to ensure that services were provided in adequate quantities at prices that reflected their real resource costs. Government intervention is therefore necessary. And, given the costs of regulation in terms of acquiring the relevant information, it may be second best to supply the infrastructure services publicly.

These factors justify one of the most important roles for government in the development process. It can be argued that the very large increase in infrastructure investment, coupled with higher savings rates, provides the major explanation of the marked expansion in the economic growth rates of most Third World countries during the postwar period, compared with both their own previous performance and that of today's developed countries during their emergence from underdevelopment.

Yet the *dirigistes* have been urging many additional tasks on Third World governments that go well beyond what Keynes, in the work quoted above, considered to be a sensible agenda for *mid-twentieth-century* Western polities:

> the most important *Agenda* of the State relate not to those activities which private individuals are already fulfilling, but to those functions which fall outside the sphere of the individual, to those decisions which are made

by no one if the State does not make them. The important thing for governments is not to do things which individuals are doing already, and to do them a little better or a little worse; but to do those things which at present are not done at all.

From the experience of a large number of developing countries in the postwar period, it would be a fair professional judgment that most of the more serious distortions are due not to the inherent imperfections of the market mechanism but to irrational government interventions, of which foreign trade controls, industrial licensing, various forms of price controls, and means of inflationary financing of fiscal deficits are the most important. In seeking to improve upon the outcomes of an imperfect market economy, the *dirigisme* to which numerous development economists have lent intellectual support has led to policy-induced distortions that are more serious than, and indeed compound, the supposed distortions of the market economy they were designed to cure. It is these lessons from accumulated experience over the last three decades that have undermined development economics, so that its demise may now be conducive to the health of both the economics and economies of developing countries.

Development: Which Way Now?

Amartya Sen

I. THE PROMISE AND THE DEFAULT

'Development economics is a comparatively young area of inquiry. It was born just about a generation ago, as a subdiscipline of economics, with a number of other social sciences looking on both skeptically and jealously from a distance.'[1] So writes Albert Hirschman, but the essay that begins so cheerfully turns out to be really an obituary of development economics—no longer the envy of the other social sciences. In this illuminating essay, aptly called 'The Rise and Decline of Development Economics', Hirschman puts his main thesis thus:

> our subdiscipline had achieved its considerable lustre and excitement through the implicit idea that it could slay the dragon of backwardness virtually by itself or, at least, that its contribution to this task was central. We now know that this is not so.[2]

The would-be dragon-slayer seems to have stumbled on his sword.

There is some plausibility in this diagnosis, but is it really true that development economics has no central role to play in the conquest of under-development and economic backwardness? More specifically, were the original themes in terms of which the subject was launched really so far from being true or useful? I shall argue that the obituary may be premature, the original themes—while severely incomplete in coverage—did not point en-

Presidential Address of the Development Studies Association given in Dublin on 23 September 1982. In preparing the final version of the paper, I have benefited from the comments of Carl Riskin, Louis Emmerij, Albert Hirschman, Seth Masters, Hans Singer, and the editorial referees of this Journal, and from the discussions following my DSA address, and also that following a talk I gave on a related theme at the Institute of Social Studies in the Hague on 11 October 1982. Published in *Economic Journal*, 93 (December 1983), pp. 745–762. Copyright © 1983 by The Royal Economic Society. Reprinted by permission of Cambridge University Press.

tirely in the wrong direction, and the discipline of development economics does have a central role to play in the field of economic growth in developing countries. But I shall also argue that the problematique underlying the approach of traditional development economics is, in some important ways, quite limited, and has not—and could not have—brought us to an adequate understanding of economic development. Later on, I shall take up the question as to the direction in which we may try to go instead.

There is a methodological problem in identifying a subject—or a subdiscipline as Hirschman calls it—with a given body of beliefs and themes rather than with a collection of subject matters and problems to be tackled. But Hirschman is certainly right in pointing towards the thematic similarities of the overwhelming majority of contributions in development economics. While some development economists such as Peter Bauer and Theodore Schultz have not been party to this thematic congruence, they have also stood outside the mainstream of what may be called standard development economics, as indeed the title of Peter Bauer's justly famous book, *Dissent on Development,* [3] indicates. The subdiscipline began with a set of favourite themes and the main approaches to the subject have been much moulded by these motifs. Clearly, the subject cannot live or die depending just on the success or failure of these themes, but the main approaches would need radical reformulation if these themes were shown to be fundamentally erroneous or misguided.

Hirschman identifies two major ideas with which development economics came into being, namely 'rural underemployment' (including so-called 'disguised unemployment') and 'late industrialisation'. The former idea led naturally to a focus on utilisation of underemployed manpower and to acceleration of capital accumulation. The latter called for an activist state and for planning to overcome the disadvantages of lateness through what Hirschman calls 'a deliberate, intensive, guided effort'. The subject expended a lot of time in developing 'new rationales . . . for protection, planning, and industrialisation itself'. [4]

While there have been differences in assertion and emphasis *within* the mainstream of the subdiscipline, it is fair to say that in terms of policy the following have been among the major strategic themes pursued ever since the beginning of the subject: (1) industrialisation, (2) rapid capital accumulation, (3) mobilisation of underemployed manpower, and (4) planning and an economically active state. [5] There are, of course, many other common themes, e.g. emphasis on skill formation, but they have not typically been as much subjected to criticism as these other themes, and there is thus much to be said for concentrating on these four.

These themes (especially the need for planning, but also the deliberate fostering of industrialisation and capital accumulation and the acceptance of the possibility of surplus labour) are closely linked to criticisms of the traditional neoclassical models as applied to developing countries. Hirschman calls this eschewal of 'universal' use of neoclassical economics the rejection of 'monoeconomics'. Monoeconomics sounds perhaps a little like a disease that one could catch if not careful. I shall avoid the term, though some would no doubt have thought it quite appropriate to characterise universal neoclassical economics as a contagious affliction.

It was argued by development economists that neoclassical economics did not apply terribly well to underdeveloped countries. This need not have caused great astonishment, since neoclassical economics did not apply terribly well anywhere else. However, the role of the state and the need for planning and deliberate public action seemed stronger in underdeveloped countries, and the departure from traditional neoclassical models was, in many ways, more radical.

The discrediting of traditional development economics that has lately taken place, and to which Hirschman made reference, is undoubtedly partly due to the resurgence of neoclassical economics in recent years. As Hirschman (1981) rightly notes, 'the claim of development economics to stand as a separate body of economic analysis and policy derived intellectual legitimacy and nurture from the prior success and parallel features of the Keynesian Revolution' (p. 7). The neoclassical resurgence against Keynesian economics was to some extent paralleled by the neoclassical recovery in the field of economic development. The market, it was argued, has the many virtues that standard neoclassical analysis has done so much to analyse, and state intervention could be harmful in just the way suggested by that perspective.

The neoclassical resurgence has drawn much sustenance from the success of some countries and the failure of others. The high performance of economies like South Korea, Taiwan, Hong Kong and Singapore—based on markets and profits and trade—has been seen as bringing Adam Smith back to life. On the other hand, the low performance of a great many countries in Asia, Africa and Latin America has been cited as proof that it does not pay the government to mess about much with the market mechanism. Recently, doubts raised about the record of China, and the vocal desire of the Chinese leadership to make greater use of material incentives, have been interpreted as proof that even a powerful socialist regime cannot break the basic principles on which the market mechanism is founded.

The attack on state activism and planning has been combined with criticism of some of the other features of traditional development economics. It has been argued that enterprise is the real bottleneck, not capital, so that to emphasise capital accumulation and the creation of surplus—as was done for example by Maurice Dobb (1951; 1960) and Paul Baran (1957)—was to climb the wrong tree. The charge of misallocation of resources has been levelled also against industrialisation, especially for the domestic market. Hirschman (1981) notes: 'By itself this critique was highly predictable and might not have carried more weight than warnings against industrialisation emanating from essentially the same camp ten, or twenty, or fifty years earlier.' But—as he goes on to say—the effectiveness of this critique was now greater for various reasons, including the fact that 'some of the early advocates of industrialisation had now themselves become its sharpest critics' (p. 18). Hirschman refers in this context to some 'neo-Marxist' writings and the views of some members of the so-called 'dependency' school. Certainly, the particular pattern of industrial expansion in Latin America provides many examples of exploitative relations with the metropolitan countries, particularly the United States of America, and the internal effects were often quite terrible in terms of fostering economic inequality and social distortion. But to move from there to a rejection of industrialisation as such is indeed a long jump.

I should explain that Hirschman, from whom I have been quoting extensively, does not in many cases endorse these attacks on the policy strategies of traditional development economics. But he provides excellent analyses of the arguments figuring in the attacks. I believe Hirschman is more hesitant in his defence of traditional development economics than he need have been, but his own reasons for rejecting that tradition—to which he himself has of course contributed much[6]—rests primarily on the argument that development economics has tended to be contemptuous of underdeveloped countries, albeit this contempt has taken a 'sophisticated form'. These countries have been 'expected to perform like wind-up toys and "lumber through" the various stages of development single-mindedly'. As Hirschman (1981) puts it, 'these countries were perceived to have only *interests* and *no passions*' (p. 24).[7]

I believe this diagnosis has much truth in it. But I also believe that, contemptuous and simplistic though development economics might have been in this respect, the main themes that were associated with the origin of development economics, and have given it its distinctive character, are not rejectable for that reason. I shall argue that they address common problems, which survive despite the particular passions.

II. TRADITIONAL THEMES IN THE LIGHT OF RECENT EXPERIENCES

Growth is not the same thing as development and the difference between the two has been brought out by a number of recent contributions to development economics.[8] I shall take up the complex question of the content of economic development presently (in Sections III–V below). But it can scarcely be denied that economic growth is one aspect of the process of economic development. And it happens to be the aspect on which traditional development economics—rightly or wrongly—has concentrated. In this section I do not assess the merits of that concentration (on which more later), but examine the appropriateness of the traditional themes, given that concentration. Dealing specifically with economic growth as it is commonly defined, the strategic relevance of these themes is examined in the light of recent experiences. How do these theories—formulated and presented mainly in the 'forties and 'fifties—fare in the light of the experiences of the 'sixties and the 'seventies?

The World Development Report 1982 (henceforth WDR) presents comparative growth data for the period 1960–80 for 'low-income economies' and 'middle-income economies', with a dividing line at US $410 in 1980. Leaving out small countries (using a cut-off line of 10 million people) and excluding the OPEC countries which have had rather special economic circumstances during the 'seventies, we have 14 countries in the low-income category for which data on economic growth (GNP or GDP) are given in WDR. Correspondingly, there are 18 such countries in the middle-income category. Table 1 presents these data. For three of the low-income countries, namely China, Bangladesh and Afghanistan, the GNP growth figures are not given in WDR and they have been approximately identified with GDP growth. In interpreting the results, this has to be borne in mind, and only those conclusions can be safely drawn which would be unaffected by variations of these estimates within a wide range.

The fourteen low-income economies vary in terms of growth rate of GNP *per capita* during 1960–80 from *minus* 0.7% in Uganda to 3.7% in China. The top three countries in terms of economic growth are China (3.7%), Pakistan (2.8%) and Sri Lanka (2.4%). (Note that China's pre-eminent position would be unaffected even if the approximated growth figure is substantially cut.) In the middle-income group, the growth performance again varies a great deal, ranging from *minus* 1.0% for Ghana to 8.6% for Romania. The top three countries in terms of economic growth are Romania (8.6%), South Korea (7.0%) and Yugoslavia (5.4%).

How do these high-performance countries compare with others in the respective groups in terms of the parameters associated with the main theses of traditional development economics? Take capital accumulation first. Of the three top growth-performers, two also have the highest share of gross domestic investment in GDP, namely Sri Lanka with 36% and China with 31%. Pakistan comes lower, though it does fall in the top half of the class of fourteen countries.

Turning now to the middle-income countries, the top three countries in terms of growth are also the top three countries in terms of capital accumulation, namely Yugoslavia with 35%, Romania with 34%, and South Korea with 31%. Thus, if there is anything to be learned from the experience of these successful growers regarding the importance of capital accumulation, it is certainly not a lesson that runs counter to the traditional wisdom of development economics.

It might, however, be argued that to get a more convincing picture one should look also at failures and not merely at successes. I don't think the cases are quite symmetrical, since a failure can be due to some special 'bottleneck' even when all other factors are favourable. Nevertheless, it is not useless to

TABLE 1

COUNTRY	GNP Per Head		1980 GROSS DOMESTIC INVESTMENT (% OF GDP)	1980 SHARE OF INDUSTRY IN GDP (%)
	1980 VALUE ($)	1960–80 GROWTH (%)		
Low-income				
Bangladesh	130	1.3*	17	13
Ethiopia	140	1.4	10	16
Nepal	140	0.2	14	13
Burma	170	1.2	24	13
Afghanistan	—	0.9*	14	—
Zaire	220	0.2	11	23
Mozambique	230	−0.1	10	16
India	240	1.4	23	26
Sri Lanka	270	2.4	36	30
Tanzania	280	1.9	22	13
China	290	3.7*	31	47
Pakistan	300	2.8	18	25
Uganda	300	−0.7	3	6
Sudan	410	−0.2	12	14
Middle-income				
Ghana	420	−1.0	5	21
Kenya	420	2.7	22	21
Egypt	580	3.4	31	35
Thailand	670	4.7	27	29
Philippines	690	2.8	30	37
Morocco	900	2.5	21	32
Peru	930	1.1	16	45
Colombia	1,180	3.0	25	30
Turkey	1,470	3.6	27	30
S. Korea	1,520	7.0	31	41
Malaysia	1,620	4.3	29	37
Brazil	2,050	5.1	22	37
Mexico	2,090	2.6	28	38
Chile	2,150	1.6	18	37
South Africa	2,300	2.3	29	53
Romania	2,340	8.6	34	64
Argentina	2,390	2.2	—	—
Yugoslavia	2,620	5.4	35	43

SOURCE: *World Development Report 1982,* tables 1–5. The countries included are all the ones within the 'Low-income' and 'Middle-income' categories, other than those with less than 10 million population, members of OPEC, and countries without GNP or GDP growth figures. Asterisked growth rates are based on GDP growth figures per head (tables 2 and 17).

examine the cases of failure as well, especially with respect to capital accumulation, since it has been seen in traditional development economics to be such a *general* force towards economic growth.

The three worst performers in the low-income category in terms of growth rate are, respectively, Uganda with *minus* 0.7%, Sudan with *minus* 0.2%, and Mozambique with *minus* 0.1%. In terms of capital accumulation, Uganda's rank is also the worst there, with only 3% of GDP invested. Mozambique is the second lowest investor, and Sudan the fifth lowest.

What about growth failures in the middle-income countries? The worst performers in terms of growth rate are Ghana with *minus* 1%, Peru with 1.1%, and Chile with 1.6%. As it happens these countries are also respectively the lowest, the second lowest and the third lowest accumulators of capital in the category of the middle-income countries.

So both in terms of cases of success and those of failure, the traditional wisdom of development economics is scarcely contradicted by these international comparisons. Quite the contrary.

Hans Singer (1952) in his paper entitled 'The Mechanics of Economic Development', published thirty years ago, seems to be almost talking about today's worst case of growth failure in the combined category of low-income and middle-income countries, namely Ghana. Using the Harrod-Domar model with an assumed capital-output ratio, Singer argues that a country with 6% savings and a population growth rate of 1.25% will be a 'stationary economy'. While Ghana has managed an investment and savings ratio of just below 6% (5% to be exact) it has had a population growth between 2.4 and 3.0% during these decades as opposed to Singer's assumption of 1.25%. Rather than being stationary, Ghana has accordingly slipped back, going down at about 1% a year. The Harrod-Domar model is an over-simplification, of course, but the insight obtained from such reasoning is not altogether without merit.

I turn now to the theme of industrialisation. In the category of low-income countries, the top performers—China, Pakistan and Sri Lanka—happen to be among the four countries with the highest share of industries in GDP. In the middle-income group, the top growers—Romania, South Korea and Yugoslavia—are among the top five countries in terms of the share of industries in GDP.[9]

The picture at the other end, i.e. for countries with growth failures, is certainly less neat than at the top end in this case, or at either end in the case of capital accumulation. It is, however, certainly true that Uganda, which occupies the bottom position in the low-income category in terms of growth rate, also has the bottom position in terms of the share of industries, and similarly Ghana, with the lowest record of growth in the middle-income group, also has the lowest share of industries in that group. But the positions of second and third lowest are not quite so telling. In the low-income category, low-performing Sudan and Mozambique have middling industrial ratios. In the middle-income group, the second-lowest growth performer, Peru, has the third *highest* ratio of industries in that group, though the third-lowest growth performer, Chile, has a middling industrial ratio. The picture is, thus, a bit more muddled at the lower end of growth performance.[10]

Altogether, so far as growth is concerned, it is not easy to deny the importance of capital accumulation or of industrialisation in a poor pre-industrial country. Turning to the thesis of underemployment and the role of labour mobilisation, there have been several powerful attempts at disestablishing the thesis of 'disguised unemployment', e.g. by Theodore Schultz (1964), but they have not been altogether successful.[11] Furthermore, what is really at issue is the crucial role of labour mobilisation and use, and not whether the opportunity cost of labour is exactly zero.[12] It is worth noting, in this context, that the high growth performers in both groups have distinguished records of labour-using economic growth, and some (e.g. China and South Korea) have quite outstanding achievements in this area. While they have very different political systems, their respective successes in labour mobilisation have been specially studied and praised.[13]

The question of planning and state activism is a field in which comparative quantitative data is particularly difficult to find. But some qualitative information is of relevance. Of the three top growing economies in the low-income group, one—China—is obviously not without an active state. While Pakistan is in no way a paradigmatic example of determined state planning, it has been frequently cited as a good example of what harm government meddling can do.[14] The third—Sri Lanka—has been recently studied a great deal precisely because of its active government intervention in a number of different fields, including health, education and food consumption.

In the middle-income group, of the three top performers, Romania and Yugoslavia clearly do have a good deal of planning. The third—South Korea—has had an economic system in which the market mechanism has been driven hard by an active government in a planned way. Trying to interpret the South Korean economic experience as a triumph of unguided market mechanism, as is sometimes done, is not easy to sustain. I have discussed this question elsewhere,[15] and I shall not spend any time on it here. I should only add that, aside from having a powerful influence over the direction of investment through control of financial institutions (including nationalised banks), the government of South Korea fostered an export-oriented growth on the secure foundations of more than a decade of intensive import substitution, based on trade restrictions, to build up an industrial base. Imports of a great many items are still prohibited or restricted. The pattern of South Korean economic expansion has been carefully planned by a powerful government. If this is a free market, then Walras's auctioneer can surely be seen as going around with a government white paper in one hand and a whip in the other.

The point is not so much that the government is powerful in the high-growth developing countries. It is powerful in nearly *every* developing country. The issue concerns the systematic involvement of the state in the *economic* sphere, and the pursuit of *planned* economic development. The carefully planned government action in, say, China or Sri Lanka or South Korea or Romania, contrasts—on the whole strongly—with the economic role of the government in such countries as Uganda or Sudan or Chile or Argentina or Ghana.

This examination of the main theses of traditional development economics has been too brief and tentative, and certainly there is no question of claiming anything like definitiveness in the findings. But, in so far as anything has emerged, it has not gone in the direction of debunking traditional development economics; just the contrary.

Before I move on to develop some criticisms of my own, I should make one last defensive remark about traditional development economics. The general policy prescriptions and strategies in this tradition have to be judged in terms of the climate of opinion and the over-all factual situation prevailing at the time these theories were formulated. Development economics was born at a time when government involvement in deliberately fostering economic growth in general, and industrialisation in particular, was very rare, and when the typical rates of capital accumulation were quite low. That situation has changed in many respects, and, while that may suggest the need to emphasise different issues, it does not in any way invalidate the wisdom of the strategies then suggested.

The point can be brought out with an example. In the 1952 paper of Hans Singer from which I have already quoted, one of the conclusions that Singer emphasised is the need to raise the then existing rate of saving. He argued, with some assumptions about production conditions, that to achieve even a 2% rate of *per capita* growth, with a population growing at 1.25% per year, 'a rate of net savings of 16.25% is necessary', and that 'this rate of saving is about three times the rate actually observed in underdeveloped countries' (Singer, 1952, pp. 397–8). The current average rate of saving is no longer a third of that figure, but substantially *higher* than the figure. The weighted average ratio of gross domestic saving for low-income developing countries is estimated to be about 22%, and that for middle-income developing countries about 25%; and, even after deducting for depreciation, Singer's target has certainly been exceeded. And, even with a faster growth of population than Singer anticipated, the weighted average of GDP growth rates *per capita* has been about 2.5% per year for low-income countries and more than 3% per year for middle-income countries over the 'seventies.[16]

The point of policy interest now is that, despite these *average* achievements, the performances of different countries are highly divergent. There is still much relevance in the broad policy themes which traditional development economics has emphasised. The strategies have to be adapted to the particular conditions and to national and international circumstances, but the time to bury traditional development economics has not yet arrived.

III. FAST GROWTH AND SLOW SOCIAL CHANGE

I believe the real limitations of traditional development economics arose not from the choice of means to the end of economic growth, but in the insufficient recognition that economic growth was no more than a means to some other objectives. The point is not the same as saying that growth does not matter. It may matter a great deal, but, if it does, this is because of some associated benefits that are realised in the process of economic growth.

It is important to note in this context that the same level of achievement in life expectancy, literacy, health, higher education, etc., can be seen in countries with widely varying income per capita. To take just one example, consider Brazil, Mexico, South Korea, China and Sri Lanka.[17]

China and Sri Lanka, with less than a seventh of GNP per head in Brazil or Mexico, have similar life expectancy figures to the two richer countries. South Korea, with its magnificent and much-eulogised growth record, has not yet overtaken China or Sri Lanka in the field of longevity, despite being now more than five times richer in terms of *per capita* GNP. If the government of a poor developing country is keen to raise the level of health and the expectation of life, then it would be pretty daft to try to achieve this through raising its income per head, rather than going directly for these objectives through public policy and social change, as China and Sri Lanka have both done.

Not merely is it the case that economic growth is a means rather than an end, it is also the case that for some important ends it is not a very efficient means either. In an earlier paper (Sen, 1981*b*) it was shown that had Sri Lanka been a typical developing country, trying to achieve its high level of life expectancy not through direct public action, but primarily through growth (in the same way as typical developing countries do), then it would have taken Sri Lanka—depending on assumptions—somewhere between 58 years and 152 years to get where it already now happens to be.[18] It might well be the case that 'money answereth all things', but the answer certainly comes slowly.

TABLE 2

COUNTRY	LIFE EXPECTANCY AT BIRTH 1980 (YEARS)	GNP PER HEAD, 1980 (U.S. DOLLARS)
Brazil	63	2,050
China	64	290
Mexico	65	2,090
South Korea	65	1,520
Sri Lanka	66	270

IV. ENTITLEMENTS AND CAPABILITIES

Perhaps the most important thematic deficiency of traditional development economics is its concentration on national product, aggregate income and total supply of particular goods rather than on 'entitlements' of people and the 'capabilities' these entitlements generate. Ultimately, the process of economic development has to be concerned with what people can or cannot do, e.g. whether they can live long, escape avoidable morbidity, be well nourished, be able to read and write and communicate, take part in literary and scientific pursuits, and so forth. It has to do, in Marx's words, with 'replacing the domination of circumstances and chance over individuals by the domination of individuals over chance and circumstances'.[19]

Entitlement refers to the set of alternative commodity bundles that a person can command in a society using the totality of rights and opportunities that he or she faces. Entitlements are relatively simple to characterise in a purely market economy. If a person can, say, earn $200 by selling his labour power and other saleable objects he has or can produce, then his entitlements refer to the set of all commodity bundles costing no more than $200. He can buy any such bundle, but no more than that, and the limit is set by his ownership ('endowment') and his exchange possibilities ('exchange entitlement'), the two together determining his over-all entitlement.[20] On the basis of this entitlement, a person can acquire some capabilities, i.e. the ability to do this or that (e.g. be well nourished), and fail to acquire some other capabilities. The process of economic development can be seen as a process of expanding the capabilities of people. Given the functional relation between entitlements of persons over goods and their capabilities, a useful—though derivative—characterisation of economic development is in terms of expansion of entitlements.[21]

For most of humanity, about the only commodity a person has to sell is labour power, so that the person's entitlements depend crucially on his or her ability to find a job, the wage rate for that job, and the prices of commodities that he or she wishes to buy. The problems of starvation, hunger and famines in the world could be better analysed through the concept of entitlement than through the use of the traditional variables of food supply and population size. The intention here is not, of course, to argue that the supply of goods— food in this case—is irrelevant to hunger and starvation, which would be absurd, but that the supply is just one influence among many; and, in so far as supply is important, it is so precisely because it affects the entitlements of the people involved, typically through prices. Ultimately, we are concerned with what people can or cannot do, and this links directly with their 'entitlements' rather than with over-all supplies and outputs in the economy.[22]

The failure to see the importance of entitlements has been responsible for millions of people dying in famines. Famines may not be at all anticipated in situations of good or moderate over-all levels of supply, but, notwithstanding that supply situation, acute starvation can hit suddenly and widely because of failures of the entitlement systems, operating through ownership and exchange. For example, in the Bangladesh famine of 1974, a very large number died in a year when food availability per head was at a peak—higher than in any other year between 1971 and 1975. The floods that affected agriculture did ultimately—much later than the famine—reduce the food output, but its first and immediate impact was on the rural labourers who lost jobs in planting and transplanting rice, and started starving long before the main crop that was affected was to be harvested. The problem was made worse by forces of inflation in the economy, reducing the purchasing power especially of rural labourers, who did not have the economic muscle to raise their money wages correspondingly.[23]

Entitlements may not operate only through market processes. In a socialist economy entitlements will depend on what the families can get from the state through the established system of command. Even in a non-socialist economy, the existence of social security—when present—makes the entitlements go substantially beyond the operation of market forces.

A major failing of traditional development economics has been its tendency to concentrate on supply of goods rather than on ownership and entitlement. The focus on growth is only one reflection of this. Extreme concentration on the ratio of food supply to population is another example of the same defective vision.[24] Recently the focus has shifted somewhat from growth of *total incomes* to the *distribution of incomes.* This may look like a move in the right direction, and indeed it is. But I would argue that 'income' itself provides an inadequate basis for analysing a person's entitlements. Income gives the means of buying things. It expresses buying power in terms of some scalar magnitude—given by one real number. Even if there are no schools in the village and no hospitals nearby, the income of the villager can still be increased by adding to his purchasing power over the goods that are available in the market. But this rise in income may not be able to deal at all adequately with his entitlement to education or medical treatment, since the rise in income as such guarantees no such thing.

In general, one real number reflecting some aggregate measure of market power can scarcely represent so complex a notion as entitlement. The power of the market force depends on relative prices and, as the price of some good rises, the hold of income on the corresponding entitlement weakens. With nonmarketability, it slips altogether. In the extreme case, the entitlement to live, say, in a malaria-free environment is not a matter of purchase with income in any significant way.

In dealing with starvation and hunger, the focus on incomes—though defective—is not entirely disastrous. And of course it is a good deal better than the focus on total food output and population size. The weighting system of real income and cost-of-living pays sufficient attention to food in a poor community to make real income a moderately good 'proxy' for entitlement to food in most cases.[25] But when it comes to health, or education, or social equality, or self-respect, or freedom from social harassment, income is miles off the target.

V. POLITICAL COMPLEXITIES

To move from concentrating on growth to supplementing that with an account of income distribution is basically an inadequate response to what is at issue. It is also, in effect, an attempt to refuse to come to terms with the complexity of entitlement relations. The metric of income, as already discussed, is much too crude. Indeed, entitlements related even to purely economic matters, e.g. that to food, may actually require us to go beyond the narrow limits of economics altogether.

Take the case of famine relief. A hungry, destitute person will be *entitled* to some free food *if* there is a relief system offering that. Whether, in fact, a starving person will have such an entitlement will depend on whether such a public relief operation will actually be launched. The provision of public relief is partly a matter of political and social pressure. Food is, as it were, 'purchased' in this context not with income but with political pressure. The Irish in the 1840s did not have the necessary political power. Nor did the Bengalis in the Great Bengal Famine of 1943. Nor the Ethiopians in Wollo in the famine of 1973. On the other hand, there are plenty of examples in the world in which timely public policy has averted an oncoming famine completely.

The operation of political forces affecting entitlements is far from simple. For example, with the present political system in India, it is almost impossible for a famine to take place. The pressure of newspapers and diverse political parties make it imperative for the government in power to organise swift relief. It has to act to retain credibility. No matter how and where famine threatens—whether with a flood or a drought, whether in Bihar in 1967–8, in Maharashtra in 1971–3, or in West Bengal in 1978—an obligatory policy response prevents the famine actually occurring.

On the other hand, there is no such relief for the third of the Indian rural population who go to bed hungry every night and who lead a life ravaged by regular deprivation. The quiet presence of non-acute, endemic hunger leads to no newspaper turmoil, no political agitation, no riots in the Indian parliament. The system takes it in its stride.[26]

The position in China is almost exactly the opposite of this. On the one hand, the political commitment of the system ensures a general concern with eradicating regular malnutrition and hunger through more equal access to means of livelihood, and through entitlements *vis-à-vis* the state; and China's achievements in this respect have been quite remarkable. In a normal year, the Chinese poor are much better fed than the Indian poor. The expectation of life in China is between 66 and 69 years in comparison with India's miserable 52 years. On the other hand, if there is a political and economic crisis that confuses the regime and makes it pursue disastrous policies with confident dogmatism, then it cannot be forced to change its policies by crusading newspapers or by effective pressure from opposing political groups.

It is, in fact, now quite clear that in China during 1959–61 there were deaths on a very large scale due to famine conditions. The extent of the disaster has only recently become evident, even though there are still many uncertainties regarding the exact estimation of extra mortality.[27] Important mortality data were released in 1980 by Professor Zhu Zhengzhi of Beijing University,[28] indicating that the death rate rose from about 10.8 per thousand in 1957 to an average of 16.58 per thousand per year during 1958–61. This yields a figure of extra mortality of 14–16 million in China in the famine-affected years—a very large figure indeed. It is, in fact, very much larger than the extra mortality (calculated in the same way) even in the Great Bengal Famine of 1943 (namely about 3 million[29]), the largest famine in India in this century.

In 1981 the noted economist Sun Yefang released some further mortality data,[30] referring to 'the high price in blood' of the economic policy pursued at that time. He reported that the death rate per thousand had risen to as high as 25.4 in 1960, indicating an extra mortality of 9 million in that year alone. His figures for the four years also yields a total of around 15 million extra deaths during the Chinese famine of 1959–61.[31] Others have suggested even higher mortality.[32]

These are truly staggering figures. Even if we take a level quite a bit below the lower limit of the estimates, the sudden extra mortality caused by the famine[33] would still be on a scale that is difficult to match even in pre-independent India (and there has of course been no famine in India since independence).

Is it purely accidental that a famine—indeed one on an enormous scale—could take place in China while none has occurred in post-independent India? The contrast is particularly odd when viewed in the context of the undoubted fact that China has been very much more successful than India in eliminating regular malnutrition. There may well be an accidental element in the comparative records on famines, but as already noted, on a number of occasions potentially large famines have been prevented in India through quick, extensive and decisive government intervention. Reports on deaths from hunger reach the government and the public quickly and dramatically through active newspapers, and are taken up vigorously by parties not in power. Faced with a threatening famine, any government wishing to stay in office in India is forced to abandon or modify its on-going economic policy, and meet the situation with swift public action, e.g. redistribution of food within the country, imports from abroad, and widespread relief arrangements (including food for work programmes).

Policy failures in China during the famine years (and the Great Leap Forward period), which have been much discussed in China only recently, relate not merely to factors that dramatically reduced output, but also to distributional issues, e.g. inter-regional balances, and the draconian procurement policy that was apparently pursued relentlessly despite lower agricultural output.[34] Whatever the particular policy errors, the government in power was not forced to re-examine them, nor required to face harrowing newspaper reports and troublesome opposition parties. The contrast may not, therefore, be purely accidental.

In an interesting and important speech given in 1962—just after the famine—Chairman Mao made the following remarks to a conference of 7,000 cadres from different levels: 'If there is no democracy, if ideas are not coming from the masses, it is impossible to establish a good line, good general and specific policies and methods. . . . Without democracy, you have no understanding of what is happening down below; the situation will be unclear; you will be unable to collect sufficient opinions from all sides; there can be no communication between top and bottom; top-level organs of leadership will depend on one-sided and incorrect material to decide issues, thus you will find it difficult to avoid being subjectivist; it will be impossible to achieve unity of understanding and unity of action, and impossible to achieve true centralism.'[35] Ralph Miliband (1977), who has provided an illuminating and far-reaching analysis of the issue of democracy in capitalist and socialist societies from a Marxist perspective, points out that Mao's 'argument for "democracy" is primarily a "functional" one' (pp. 149–50), and argues that this is an inadequate basis for understanding the need for 'socialist democracy'.[36] That more general question certainly does remain, but it is worth emphasising that even the purely 'functional' role of democracy can be very crucial to matters of life and death, as the Chinese experiences of the famine of 1959–61 bring out.[37]

Finally, it is important to note that the protection that the Indian poor get from the active news distribution system and powerful opposition parties has very severe limits. The deprivation has to be dramatic to be 'newsworthy' and politically exploitable (see Sen, 1982c). The Indian political system may prevent famines but, unlike the Chinese system, it seems unable to deal effectively with endemic malnutrition. In a normal year when things are running smoothly both in India and China, the Indian poor is in a much more deprived general state than his or her Chinese counterpart.[38]

VI. CONCLUDING REMARKS

I shall not try to summarise the main points of the paper, but I will make a few concluding remarks to put the discussion in perspective.

First, traditional development economics has not been particularly unsuccessful in identifying the factors that lead to economic growth in developing countries. In the field of causation of growth, there is much life left in traditional analyses (Section II).

Secondly, traditional development economics has been less successful in characterising economic development, which involves expansion of people's capabilities. For this, economic growth is only a means and often not a very efficient means either (Section III).

Thirdly, because of close links between entitlements and capabilities, focusing on entitlements—what commodity bundles a person can command—provides a helpful format for characterising economic development. Supplementing data on GNP *per capita* by income distributional information is quite inadequate to meet the challenge of development analysis (Section IV).

Fourthly, famines and starvation can be more sensibly analysed in terms of entitlement failures than in terms of the usual approach focusing on food output per unit of population. A famine can easily occur even in a good food supply situation, through the collapse of entitlements of particular classes or occupation groups (Section IV).

Fifthly, a study of entitlements has to go beyond purely economic factors and take into account political arrangements (including pressure groups and news distribution systems) that affect people's actual ability to command commodities, including food. These influences may be very complex and may also involve apparently perplexing contrasts, e.g. between (1) India's better record than China's in avoiding famines, and (2) India's total failure to deal with endemic malnutrition and morbidity in the way China has been able to do (Section V). Whether the disparate advantages of the contrasting systems can be effectively combined is a challenging issue of political economy that requires attention. Much is at stake.

REFERENCES

Aird, J. (1980). 'Reconstruction of an official data model of the population of China.' U.S. Department of Commerce, Bureau of Census, 15 May.

―――― (1982). 'Population studies and population policy in China.' *Population and Development Review,* vol. 8, pp. 267–97.

Alailima, P. J. (1982). 'National policies and programmes of social development in Sri Lanka.' Mimeographed, Colombo.

Alamgir, M. (1978). *Bangladesh: A Case of Below Poverty Level Equilibrium Trap.* Dhaka: Bangladesh Institute of Development Studies.

―――― (1980). *Famine in South Asia—Political Economy of Mass Starvation in Bangladesh.* Cambridge, Mass.: Oelgeschlager, Gunn and Hain.

Arrow, K. J. (1982). 'Why people go hungry.' *New York Review of Books,* vol. 29, July 15, pp. 24–6.

Aziz, S. (1975) (ed.). *Hunger, Politics and Markets: The Real Issues in the Food Crisis.* New York: NYU Press.

—— (1982) (ed.). 'The fight against world hunger.' Special number of *Development,* 1982:4.

Baran, P. A. (1957). *Political Economy of Growth.* New York: Monthly Review Press.

Bardhan, P. (1974). 'On life and death questions.' *Economic and Political Weekly,* vol. 9, pp. 1293–304.

Bauer, P. (1971). *Dissent on Development.* London: Weidenfeld and Nicolson.

—— (1981). *Equality, the Third World, and Economic Delusion.* Cambridge, Mass.: Harvard University Press.

Bernstein, T. P. (1983*a*). 'Starving to death in China.' *New York Review of Books,* vol. 30, 6 June, pp. 36–8.

—— (1983*b*). 'Hunger and the state: grain procurements during the Great Leap Forward; with a Soviet perspective.' Mimeographed, East Asia Center, Columbia University.

Chattopadhyay, B. (1981). 'Notes towards an understanding of the Bengal famine of 1943.' *Cressida,* vol. 1.

Coale, A. J. (1981). 'Population trends, population policy, and population studies in China.' *Population and Development Review,* vol. 7, pp. 85–97.

Datta, B. (1952). *Economics of Industrialization.* Calcutta: World Press.

Datta-Chaudhuri, M. K. (1979). 'Industrialization and foreign trade: an analysis based on the development experience of the Republic of Korea and the Philippines.' ILO Working Paper WP II-4, ARTEP, ILO, Bangkok.

Desai, M. J. (1983). 'A general theory of poverty.' Mimeographed, London School of Economics, To be published in *Indian Economic Review.*

Dobb, M. H. (1951). *Some Aspects of Economic Development.* Delhi: Delhi School of Economics.

—— (1960). *An Essay on Economic Growth and Planning.* London: Routledge.

Fei, J. C. H., and Ranis, G. (1964). *Development of the Labour Surplus Economy: Theory and Practice.* Homewood, Ill.: Irwin.

George, S. and Paige, N. (1982). *Food for Beginners.* London: Writers and Readers Publishing Cooperative.

Ghose, A. (1979). 'Short term changes in income distribution in poor agrarian economies.' ILO Working Paper WEP 10-6/WP 28, Geneva.

Grant, J. (1978). *Disparity Reduction Rates in Social Indicators.* Washington, D.C.: Overseas Development Council.

Griffin, K. (1978). *International Inequality and National Poverty.* London: Macmillan.

Gwatkin, D. R. (1979). 'Food policy, nutrition planning and survival: the cases of Kerala and Sri Lanka.' *Food Policy,* November.

Hirschman, A. O. (1958). *The Strategy of Economic Development.* New Haven, Conn.: Yale University Press.

—— (1970). *Exit, Voice, and Loyalty.* Cambridge, Mass.: Harvard University Press.

—— (1977). *The Passions and the Interests.* Princeton: P.U. Press.

—— (1981). *Essays in Trespassing: Economics to Politics and Beyond.* Cambridge University Press.

Isenman, P. (1978). 'The relationship of basic needs to growth, income distribution and employment—the case of Sri Lanka.' Mimeographed, World Bank.

Ishikawa, T. (1981). *Essays on Technology, Employment and Institutions in Economic Development.* Tokyo: Kinokuniya.

Jayawardena, L. (1974). 'Sri Lanka.' In *Redistribution with Growth* (ed. H. Chenery *et al.*). London: Oxford University Press.

Kynch, J. and Sen, A. K. (1983). 'Indian women: survival and well-being.' Mimeographed; to be published in *Cambridge Journal of Economics.*

Lappé, F. M. and Collins, J. (1979). *Food First: Beyond the Myth of Scarcity.* New York: Ballantine Books.

Lewis, W. A. (1954). 'Economic development with unlimited supplies of labour.' *Manchester School* vol. 22, pp. 139–91.

——— (1955). *The Theory of Economic Growth.* Homewood, Ill.: Irwin.

Little, I. M. D. (1982). *Economic Development: Theory, Policy and International Relations.* New York: Basic Books.

——— Scitovsky, T. and Scott, M. (1971). *Industry and Trade in Some Developing Countries.* London: Oxford University Press.

McLellan, D. (1977) (ed.). *Karl Marx: Selected Writings.* Oxford: Oxford University Press.

Mandelbaum (Martin), K. (1945). *The Industrialization of Backward Areas.* Oxford: Blackwell.

Mao Tse-tung (Zedong) (1974). *Mao Tse-tung Unrehearsed, Talks and Letters: 1956–71* (ed. Schram). London: Penguin Books.

Marga Institute (1974). *Welfare and Growth in Sri Lanka.* Colombo: Marga Institute.

Marglin, S. A. (1976). *Value and Price in the Labour Surplus Economy.* Oxford: Clarendon Press.

Marx, K. and Engels, F. (1846). *The German Ideology.*

Miliband, R. (1977). *Marxism and Politics.* London: Oxford University Press.

Morris, M. D. (1979). *Measuring the Condition of the World's Poor: The Physical Quality of Life Index.* Oxford: Pergamon Press.

Nurkse, R. (1953). *Problems of Capital Formation in Underdeveloped Countries.* Oxford: Blackwell.

Oughton, E. (1982). 'The Maharashtra drought of 1970–73: an analysis of scarcity.' *Oxford Bulletin of Economics and Statistics,* vol. 44, pp. 169–97.

Parikh, K. and Rabar, F. (1981) (eds.). *Food for All in a Sustainable World.* Laxenburg: IIASA.

People's Republic of China (1981). *Foreign Broadcast Information Service,* no. 58, 26 March.

Rao, V. K. R. V. (1982). *Food, Nutrition and Poverty in India.* Brighton: Wheatsheaf Books.

Ravallion, M. (1983). *The Performance of Rice Markets in Bangladesh during the 1974 famine.* Mimeographed, University of Oxford.

Research Group of the Feng Yang County Communist Party Committee (1982). 'An investigation into the household production contract system in Liyuan Commune.' *New York Review of Books,* vol. 30, 16 June, pp. 36–8; translated from *Nongye Jingji Congkan* (Collected Material on Agricultural Economics), 25 November 1980.

Rosenstein-Rodan, P. (1943). 'Problems of industrialization in Eastern and South-eastern Europe.' ECONOMIC JOURNAL, vol. 53, pp. 202–11.

Schultz, T. W. (1964). *Transforming Traditional Agriculture.* New Haven, Conn.: York University Press.

Sen, A. K. (1967). 'Surplus labour in India: a critique of Schultz's statistical test.' ECONOMIC JOURNAL, vol. 77, pp. 154–61.

——— (1975). *Employment, Technology and Development.* Oxford: Clarendon Press.

——— (1976). 'Famines as failures of exchange entitlement.' *Economic and Political Weekly,* vol. 11, pp. 1273–80.

—— (1977). 'Starvation and exchange entitlement: a general approach and its application to the Great Bengal Famine.' *Cambridge Journal of Economics,* vol. 1, pp. 33–59.

—— (1981*a*). *Poverty and Famines: An Essay on Entitlement and Deprivation.* Oxford: Clarendon Press.

—— (1981*b*). 'Public action and the quality of life in developing countries.' *Oxford Bulletin of Economics and Statistics,* vol. 43, pp. 287–319.

—— (1981*c*). 'Family and food: sex bias in poverty.' Mimeographed, Oxford Institute of Economics and Statistics. To be published in *Rural Poverty in South Asia* (ed. P. Bardhan and T. N. Srinivasan).

—— (1982*a*). *Choice, Welfare and Measurement.* Oxford: Blackwell, and Cambridge, Mass.: MIT Press.

—— (1982*b*). 'Food battles: conflict in the access to food.' Coromandel Lecture, 13 December 1982. Reprinted in *Mainstream,* 8 January 1983.

—— (1982*c*). 'How is India doing?' *New York Review of Books,* vol. 29, Christmas Number, pp. 41–5.

—— (1982*d*). *Commodities and Capabilities.* Hennipman Lecture, April 1982. To be published by North-Holland, Amsterdam.

—— (1983). 'Poor, relatively speaking.' *Oxford Economic Papers,* vol. 35,

—— and S. Sengupta (1983). 'Malnutrition of rural children and the sex-bias.' *Economic and Political Weekly,* vol. 18.

Singer, H. W. (1952). 'The mechanics of economic development.' *Indian Economic Review;* reprinted in *The Economics of Underdevelopment* (ed. A. N. Agarwala and A. P. Singh). London: Oxford University Press, 1958.

Sinha, R. and Drabek, A. G. (1978) (eds.). *The World Food Problem: Consensus and Conflict.* Oxford: Pergamon Press.

Spitz, P. (1978). 'Silent violence: famine and inequality.' *International Social Science Journal,* vol. 30.

Srinivasan, T. N. (1982). 'Hunger: defining it, estimating its global incidence and alleviating it.' Mimeographed. To be published in *The Role of Markets in the World Food Economy* (ed. D. Gale Johnson and E. Schuh).

Streeten, P. (1981). *Development Perspectives.* London: Macmillan.

—— with S. J. Burki, Mahbub ul Haq, N. Hicks and F. Stewart (1981). *First Things First: Meeting Basic Needs in Developing Countries.* New York: Oxford University Press.

Sun Yefang (1981). Article in *Jingji Guanli* (Economic Management), no. 2, 15 February; English translation in People's Republic of China (1981).

Taylor, L. (1975). 'The misconstrued crisis: Lester Brown and world food.' *World Development,* vol. 3, pp. 827–37.

Zhu Zhengzhi (1980). Article in *Jingji Kexue,* no. 3.

NOTES

1. Essay 1 in Hirschman (1981).
2. Hirschman (1981), p. 23.
3. Bauer (1971). See also Schultz (1964) and Bauer (1981). For a forceful critical account without breaking from traditional development economics, see Little (1982).
4. Hirschman (1981), pp. 10–11.

5. See Rosenstein-Rodan (1943), Mandelbaum (1945), Dobb (1951), Datta (1952), Singer (1952), Nurkse (1953) and Lewis (1954, 1955).
6. See particularly Hirschman (1958, 1970).
7. For the conceptual framework underlying the distinction, see Hirschman (1977).
8. See, for example, Streeten (1981). See also Grant (1978), Morris (1979) and Streeten *et al.* (1981).
9. An additional one in this case is South Africa, and its industrial share is high mainly because mining is included in that figure. In fact, if we look only at manufacturing, South Africa falls below the others.
10. The rank correlation coefficient between *per capita* growth and the share of gross domestic investment in GDP is 0.72 for middle-income countries, 0.75 for low-income countries and 0.82 for the two groups put together. On the other hand, the rank correlation coefficient between *per capita* growth and the share of industries is only 0.22 for middle-income countries, even though it is 0.59 for the low-income countries and 0.68 for the two groups put together.
11. My own views on this are presented in Sen (1975). See also Sen (1967), and the exchange with Schultz following that in the same number of this JOURNAL.
12. See Marglin (1976), chapter 2. Also Sen (1975), chapters 4 and 6. See also Fei and Ranis (1964).
13. See Little (1982). See also the important study of Ishikawa (1981), which discusses the empirical role of labour absorption in different Asian economies.
14. For example, Little *et al.* (1971).
15. Sen (1981*b*), and the literature cited there, especially Datta-Chaudhuri (1979).
16. See tables 2, 5, and 17 of the *World Development Report 1982.*
17. Taken from *World Development Report 1982,* table 1. The 1982 Chinese census indicates a higher expectation of life—around 69 years. The Sri Lankan figure of 66 years relates to 1971, and the current life expectancy is probably significantly higher.
18. See Sen (1981*b*), pp. 303–6. See also Jayawardena (1974), Marga Institute (1974), Isenman (1978), Alailima (1982), Gwatkin (1979).
19. Marx and Engels (1846); English translation taken from McLellan (1977), p. 190.
20. The notion of 'entitlements' is explored in Sen (1981*a*). It is worth emphasizing here, to avoid misunderstandings that seem to have occurred in some discussions of the concept, that (1) 'exchange entitlement' is only a *part* of the entitlement picture and is incomplete without an account of ownership or endowment, and (2) 'exchange entitlement' includes not merely trade and market exchange but also the use of production possibilities (i.e. 'exchange with nature').
21. Capabilities, entitlements and utilities differ from each other. I have tried to argue elsewhere that 'capabilities' provide the right basis for judging the advantages of a person in many problems of evaluation—a role that cannot be taken over either by utility or by an index of commodities (Sen, 1982*a,* pp. 29–38, 353–69). When we are concerned with such notions as the well-being of a person, or standard of living, or freedom in the positive sense, we need the concept of capabilities. We have to be concerned with what a person can do, and this is not the same thing as how much pleasure or desire fulfilment he gets from these activities ('utility'), nor what commodity bundles he can command ('entitlements'). Ultimately, there-fore, we have to go not merely beyond the calculus of national product and aggregate real income, but also that of entitlements over commodity bundles

viewed on their own. The focus on capabilities differs also from concentration on the mental metric of utilities, and this contrast is similar to the general one between pleasure, on the one hand, and positive freedom, on the other. The particular role of entitlements is *through* its effects on capabilities. It is a role that has substantial and far-reaching importance, but it remains derivative on capabilities. On these general issues, see Sen (1982*a, d,* 1983) and Kynch and Sen (1983).

22. See Sen (1981*a, b*), Arrow (1982), Desai (1983).

23. See Sen (1981*a*), chapter 9. Other examples of famines due to entitlement failure without a significant—indeed any—reduction of overall food availability can be found in chapter 6 (the Great Bengal Famine of 1943) and chapter 7 (the Ethiopian famine of 1973–4); see also chapter 7 (the Sahelian famines of the 1970s). On related matters, see also Sen (1976, 1977), Ghose (1979), Alamgir (1978, 1980), Chattopadhyay (1981), Oughton (1982), Ravallion (1983). See also Parikh and Rabar (1981) and Srinivasan (1982). Also the special number of *Development,* Aziz (1982).

24. On this and related issues, see Aziz (1975), Taylor (1975), Griffin (1978), Sinha and Drabek (1978), Spitz (1978), Lappé and Collins (1979), George and Paige (1982), Rao (1982).

25. However, the index of real income will continue to differ from the index of food entitlement since the price deflators will not be the same, though the two will often move together. A problem of a different sort arises from *intra-*family differences in food consumption (e.g. through 'sex bias'), as a result of which both the real income and the food entitlement of the family may be rather deceptive indicators of nutritional situations of particular members of the family. On this issue, see Bardhan (1974), Sen (1981*c*), Kynch and Sen (1983) and Sen and Sengupta (1983).

26. See Sen (1982*b, c*).

27. See Aird (1982), pp. 277–8.

28. Zhu Zhengzhi (1980), pp. 54–5. These data have been analysed by Coale (1981). See also Bernstein (1983*b*).

29. See Sen (1981*a*), Appendix D. In both cases the death rate immediately preceding the famine-affected year is taken as the bench mark in comparison with which the 'extra' mortality in famine-affected years are calculated.

30. Sun Yefang (1981) and People's Republic of China (1981).

31. See Bernstein (1983*a, b*).

32. See Bernstein's (1983*b*) account of the literature. See also Aird (1980). For a description of the intensity of the famine in a particular commune (the Liyuan Commune in Anhui province), see Research Group of the Fen Yang County Communist Party Committee (1983). 'The commune's population of 5,730 people in 1957 had dropped to 2,870 people in 1961. More than half died of starvation [*e si*] or fled the area. . . . In 1955, the Houwang production team was a model elementary cooperative. The village had twenty-eight families, a total of 154 people. . . . fifty-nine people starved to death [*e si*], and the survivors fled the area' (p. 36).

33. The number of deaths due to a famine must not be confused with the number actually dying of starvation, since most people who die in a famine tend to die from other causes (particularly from diseases endemic in the region) to which they become more susceptible due to undernutrition, and also due to breakdown of

sanitary arrangements, exposure due to wandering, eating non-eatables, and other developments associated with famines. See Sen (1981*a*), pp. 203–16.

34. See Bernstein (1983*b*), who also argues that the harsh procurement policies in China did not have the ideologically 'anti-peasant' character that similar policies in the USSR did during 1932–3, but reflected 'erroneous' reading of the level of output and of the economic situation.

35. Mao Zedong (1974), p. 164.

36. Miliband goes on to argue: 'Much may be claimed for the Chinese experience. But what cannot be claimed for it, on the evidence, is that it has really begun to create the institutional basis for the kind of socialist democracy that would effectively reduce the distance between those who determine policy and those on whose behalf it is determined' (p. 151).

37. The Soviet famines of the 1930s and the Kampuchean famine of more recent years provide further evidence of penalties of this lacuna.

38. The crude death rate in China in 1980 was reported to be 8 per thousand in contrast with India's 14 (*World Development Report 1982,* table 18, p. 144). Only in famine situations did the reported death rate in China (e.g. 25.4 reported in 1960) exceed that in India.

4

Toward a Nonethnocentric Theory of Development: Alternative Conceptions from the Third World

Howard J. Wiarda

*[The Ayatullah] Khomeini has blown apart the comfortable
myth that as the Third World industrializes, it will also adopt
Western values.*

Time *(7 January 1980)*

A revolution of far-reaching breadth and meaning is presently sweeping the Third World, and we in the West are only partially and incompletely aware of it. This revolution carries immense implications not only for the Third World and our relations with it but also, more generally, for the social sciences and the way we comprehend and come to grips with Third World change.

We are all aware of the new social and economic forces of modernization sweeping the Third World and perhaps to a somewhat lesser extent of the political and value changes also occurring, including anti-Americanism and anticolonialism. What has received less attention is the way these changes are now finding parallel expression in a rejection of the basic developmental models and paradigms originating in the West, both Marxian and non-Marxian varieties, and a corresponding assertion of non-Western, nonethnocentric, and indigenous ones.[1]

The ongoing Iranian Revolution may not be typical, but it is illustrative. At the popular level, awareness of the profound changes occurring in Iran has

From *Journal of Developing Areas*, Vol. 17 (July 1983), pp. 433–452. © 1984 by Western Illinois University.

been warped and obscured by events surrounding the revolution and the 1979 seizure of the American hostages, by the discomfort those in the more plural-ist societies of the West feel toward the Islamic fundamentalists' assertion that there is a single right way and a wrong way to do everything, and by the general "ugliness" (at least as portrayed on our TV screens) of some of the revolution's leaders. Even scholars and others more sympathetic to such radical transformations, in Iran and elsewhere, have tended to focus on the changes occurring in their one area or country of specialization and have not analyzed the more general phenomenon or placed it in a broader, global perspective.[2] Alternatively, they have preferred to see the Iranian Revolution and the coming to power of its ayatullah as an isolated event, readily subject to ridicule and agreed-upon moral outrage and therefore not representing a serious challenge to established Western values and social science under-standings.

The proposition argued here, however, is that the rejection of the West-ern (that is, North-West European and United States) model of development, in its several varieties, is now widespread throughout the Third World, and that there are many new and exciting efforts on the part of intellectuals and political elites throughout these areas to assert new and indigenous models of development. Furthermore, these efforts represent serious and fundamen-tal challenges to many cherished social science assumptions and understand-ings and even to the presumption of a universal social science of develop-ment. Thus, we underestimate or continue to disregard such changes at the risk of both perpetuating our malcomprehension of the Third World areas and retaining a social science of development that is parochial and ethnocen-tric rather than accurate and comprehensive.[3]

The Iranian Revolution, with its assertion of Islamic fundamentalism and of a distinctively Islamic social science (or model) of development, is in fact but one illustration of a far more general Third World phenomenon. There are common themes in the reexaminations presently under way by many Third World leaders: of Indian caste associations and their role in moderniza-tion; of African tribalism not as a traditional institution that is necessarily dysfunctional and therefore to be discarded into the ashcans of history but as a base upon which to build new kinds of societies; of Latin American organicism, corporatism, populism, and new forms of bureaucratic-authoritarianism; of family and interpersonal solidarities in Japan; of the overlaps of Confucian and Maoist conceptions in China. These themes relate to the hostility toward and often the inappropriateness of the Western devel-opmental models in non-Western or only partially Western areas, the nation-alistic and often quite realistic assertion of local and indigenous ones, and the questioning of some basic notions regarding the universality of the social sciences. They relate also to the realization that there are not just one or two (First and Second World) paths to development but many and diverse ones, and that the dichotomies between traditional and modern represent not real but false choices for societies where the blending and fusion of these is both likely and more widespread than the necessary or automatic replacement of the former by the latter.[4]

These themes are controversial and provocative, and not all the dimensions and issues can be dealt with here. Rather, my purposes are to present the critique Third World areas are now directing at the Western and, we often presume, universal developmental model; to examine the alternatives they themselves are now in the process of formulating; to assess the problems and difficulties in these alternative formulations; and to offer some conclusions regarding the issue of particularism versus universalism in the social sciences.

THE THIRD WORLD CRITIQUE OF THE WESTERN DEVELOPMENTAL MODEL

> *In all frankness, much of our self-inflicted disaster has its intellectual roots in our social sciences faculties.*
>
> West Indian economist Courtney N. Blackman,
> in "Science, Development, and Being Ourselves,"
> Caribbean Studies Newsletter (Winter 1980)

The Third World critique of the Western model and pattern of development as inappropriate and irrelevant, or partially so, to their circumstances and conditions is widespread and growing. There has long been a powerful strain of anti-Westernism (as well as anticolonialism) on the part of Third World intellectuals, but now that sentiment is stronger and well nigh universal. The recent trends differ from the earlier critiques of Western modernization theory in that the attacks have become far more pervasive, they are shared more generally by the society as a whole, they have taken on global rather than simply area- or country-specific connotations, and the criticisms are no longer solely negative but are now accompanied by an assertion of other, alternative, often indigenous approaches. Moreover the debate is no longer just a scholarly one between competing social science development models; rather, it has powerful policy implications as well.

One should not overstate the case. As yet, the critiques one reads are frequently as inchoate and uncertain as the concept of the Third World itself. They tend sometimes to be partial and incomplete, fragmented and unsystematic, long on rhetoric but short on reality, often as nationalistic and parochial as the very Western theories they seek to replace. Yet one cannot but be impressed by the growing strength of these critiques, the increasing acceptance and receptivity of them by Third World leaders, and the dawning realization of common themes, criticisms, and problems encountered with the Western model across diverse continents, nations, and cultural traditions.

The criticism centers, to begin with, on the bias and ethnocentrism perceived in the Western model and on its inapplicability to societies with quite different traditions, histories, societies, and cultural patterns.[5] For societies cast in quite different traditions from the Judeo-Christian one, lacking the sociopolitical precepts of Greece, Rome, and the Bible, without the same experiences of feudalism and capitalism, the argument is that the Western model has only limited relevance.[6] Western political theory is faulted for its almost entirely European focus and its complete lack of attention to other intellectual traditions; political sociology in Durkheim, Comte, Weber, or Parsons is shown to be based almost exclusively on the European transition from "agraria" to "industria" and its accompanying sociopolitical effects, which have proved somewhat less than universal;[7] and political economy, in both its Marxian and non-Marxian variants, is criticized for the exclusively European and hence less-than-universal origins of its major precepts: philosophical constructs derived (especially in Marx) from Germany, a conception of sociopolitical change derived chiefly from the French tradition, and an understanding of industrialization and its effects stemming chiefly from the English experience. Even our celebrated "liberal arts education" (basically Western European) has come in for criticism as constituting not an experience of universal relevance but merely the first area studies program.[8] These criticisms of the narrowness and parochialism of our major social science traditions and concepts, as grounded essentially on the singular experience of Western Europe and without appreciation of or applicability to the rest of the world, are both sweeping and, with proper qualification, persuasive.

Third World intellectuals have begun to argue secondly that the timing, sequence, and stages of development in the West may not necessarily be replicable in their own areas. Again, this argument is not new, but its sophisticated expression by so many Third World leaders is. For example, Western political sociology generally asserts, based on the European experience, that bureaucratization and urbanization accompanied and were products of industrialization; in Latin America and elsewhere, however, many Third World scholars are arguing that the phenomena of preindustrial urbanization and bureaucratization would seem to require different kinds of analyses.[9] With regard to timing, it seems obvious that countries developing and modernizing in the late twentieth century should face different kinds of problems than those that developed in the nineteenth; because their developmental response must necessarily be different, there seems to be no necessary reason why the former should merely palely and retardedly repeat the experience of the latter.[10] In terms of stages, the European experience would lead us to believe that capitalism must necessarily replace feudalism; in much of the Third World, however, feudalism in accord with the classic French case seems never to have existed,[11] capitalism exists in forms (populist, patrimonialist, etatist) that hardly existed in the West, and rather than capitalism definitely *replacing* feudalism, it seems more likely that the two will continue to exist side by side.

The timing, sequences, and stages of development in most Third World nations are sufficiently different, indeed, that virtually all our Western precepts require fundamental reinterpretation when applied there: the so-called demographic transition, the role of the emerging middle classes, military behavior and professionalization, the role of peasants and workers, the presumption of greater pluralism as societies develop, notions of differentiation and rationalization, and so on.[12]

Not only are the timing, sequences, and stages of Third World development likely to be quite different, but the international context is entirely altered as well. In the nineteenth century, countries like Britain, Japan, and the United States were able to develop relatively autonomously; for today's Third World nations, that is no longer possible. To cite only a handful of many possible illustrations, these nations are often caught up in Cold War struggles over which they have no control and in which they are cast as mere pawns; they are absolutely dependent on outside capital, technology, and markets for their products;[13] they are part of an international community and of a web of international military, diplomatic, political, commercial, cultural, communications, and other ties from which they cannot divorce themselves; moreover, many of them are entirely dependent for their continued development on external energy sources and thus are the victims of skyrocketing prices that they can ill afford to pay and that have wreaked havoc with their national economies. In these and other ways it seems clear the international context of development is entirely different than that of a century to a century and a half ago.

A fourth area of difference perceived by leaders from the Third World relates to the role of traditional institutions. Western political sociology largely assumes that such traditional institutions as tribes, castes, clans, patrimonialist authority, and historic corporate units must either yield and give way (the liberal tradition) under the impact of modernization or be overwhelmed (the revolutionary tradition) by it. Nevertheless, we have learned that in much of the Third World so-called traditional institutions have, first of all, proved remarkably resilient, persistent, and long-lasting; rather than fading or being crushed under the impact of change, they have instead proved flexible, accommodative, and adaptive, bending to the currents of modernization but not being replaced by them.[14] Second, these traditional institutions have often served as filters of the modernization process, accepting what was useful and what they themselves could absorb in modernity while rejecting the rest. Third, we have learned that such traditional institutions as India's caste associations, African tribalism, and Latin American corporatism can often be transformed into agents of modernization, bridging some wrenching transitions and even serving as the base for new and more revered forms of indigenous development.[15] Indeed one of the more interesting illustrations of this process is the way a new generation of African leaders, rather than rejecting tribalism as traditional and to be discarded, as the *geist* of Western political sociology would have them do, are now reexamining tribalism's persistent presence as an indigenous, realistic, and perhaps viable base on which to construct a new kind of authentic African society.[16]

Fifth, Third World intellectuals are beginning to argue that the Eurocentrism of the major development models has skewed, biased, and distorted their own and the outside world's understanding of Third World societies and has made them into something of a laughingstock, the butt of cruel, ethnic, and sometimes racial gibes. For example, the Western bias had led scholars, those from the West and sometimes those from the Third World, to study and overemphasize such presumably modernizing institutions as trade unions and political parties; yet in many Third World countries these institutions may not count for very much, and their absence or weakness often leads these societies to be labeled underdeveloped or dysfunctional. At the same time, institutions that Western political sociology has proclaimed traditional and hence inevitably fated to die or disappear, such as patronage networks, clan groups, religious institutions and movements, extended families and the like, have been woefully understudied and represent some immense gaps in our knowledge concerning these societies; consequently, there exist some fundamental misinterpretations of them.[17]

Meanwhile, these nations actually do modernize and develop, in their terms if not always in ours—that is, through coups and barracks revolts that contribute to an expanding circulation of elites, through larger patronage and spoils systems now transferred to the national level, through assistance from abroad that is often employed not entirely inappropriately in ways other than those intended, and through elaborated corporate group, family, clan and/or tribal networks. Yet the actual dynamics of change and modernization in these nations have often been made the stuff of opéra bouffe in *New York Times* headlines or *New Yorker* cartoons or have led to appalled and holier-than-thou attitudes on the part of Westerners who would still like to remake the Third World in accord with Judeo-Christian morality and Anglo-American legal and political precepts. The excessive attention to some institutions that our ofttimes wishful sociology would elevate to a higher plane than they deserve, the neglect of others, and our ethnocentrism and general ignorance as to how Third World societies do in fact develop has perpetuated our woeful misunderstanding and inadequate comprehension of them.[18] Indeed it is one of the greater ironies, and a result of what we might call our cultural or social-scientific imperialism, that for a long time Third World intellectuals bought, or were sold, the same essentially Western categories as the Westernizers themselves had internalized, and that their understanding of their own societies therefore was often no greater than our own. That condition is now changing very rapidly.[19]

The Western development perspective, furthermore, has recently been subjected to an additional criticism: that it is part of the Western ideological and intellectual offensive to keep the Third World within the Western orbit.[20]

This is perhaps the most widespread of the criticisms of the Western development model current in the Third World. Western modernization and development theory is thus seen as still another imperialist Cold War strategy aimed at tying Third World nations into a Western and liberal (that is, United States) development pattern, of keeping them within our sphere of influence, and of denying them the possibilities of alternative developmental patterns. Of course it should be said that not all of those who fashioned the early and influential development literature had such manifest Cold War or New Mandarin goals in mind. Some clearly did,[21] but among others the development literature was popular chiefly because it corresponded to cherished notions about ourselves (that we are a liberal, democratic, pluralist, socially just, and modern nation) and to the belief that the developing nations could emulate us if they worked hard and recast themselves in accord with the American or Western way. This strategy, one would have to admit, was remarkably successful from the late 1950s, when the first development literature began to appear, until the early 1970s. Since that time, however, development has been increasingly tarred with the imperialist brush and discredited throughout the Third World, and hence a whole new generation of young Third World leaders and intellectuals no longer accepts the Western developmentalist concepts and perspectives and is searching for possible alternatives.[22]

Finally, and perhaps most harmful in terms of the long-term development of the Third World, is the damage that has been inflicted on their own institutions because of the Western biases. "Development" is no mere intellectual construct nor is it benignly neutral. There are consequences, often negative, in following a Western-oriented development strategy. I will not discuss here the damage inflicted on countries such as the Congo, Angola, Guatemala, or the Dominican Republic by Cold War rivalries or by such agencies as the International Monetary Fund, whose financial advice to Third World nations has often been ruinous. Instead what concerns us here is the role development has had in undermining such viable institutions as extended family networks, patronage ties, clan and tribal loyalties, corporate group linkages, churches and religious movements, historic authority relations, and the like. By undermining and often eliminating these traditional institutions before any more modern ones were created, development helped destroy some of the only agencies in many Third World nations that might have enabled them to make a genuine transition to real modernity. The destruction, in the name of modernization, of such traditional institutions throughout the Third World may well be one of the most important legacies that development left behind, and it will powerfully affect our future relations with them. For by our actions and our patronizing, condescending, and ethnocentric efforts to promote development among the LDCs, we may have denied them the possibility of real development while at the same time destroying the very indigenous and at one time viable institutions they are now attempting, perhaps futilely and too late, to resurrect.[23]

The Third World critique of the Western development model as biased, ethnocentric, and often damaging is thus strong, sweeping, and, in its essentials, difficult to refute. Although many of the arguments are not new and though not all Third World critiques are as coherent, global, and organized as presented here, the criticisms are spreading and becoming global, the common elements are being analyzed, and they are increasingly informed by solid facts and argument. It remains for us to examine what the Third World offers in place of the Western schema.

THE ASSERTION OF INDIGENOUS THIRD WORLD DEVELOPMENT MODELS

> The problem with us Africans is that we've not been educated to appreciate our art and culture. So many of us have been influenced by the British system of education. I went through this system here not knowing enough about my own country. It was almost as if what we natives did wasn't important enough to be studied. I knew all about British history and British art, but about Ghana and Africa nothing.
>
> Ghanaian art historian and intellectual Nana Apt,
> quoted in New York Times, 13 September 1980, p. 16

The purpose of this section is to provide a sense of the kinds and varieties of new development models emerging from the Third World. Space constraints rule out any detailed treatment here; our survey and tour provide only a hint and surface gloss of the new ideas, concepts, and theories.[24] Nevertheless, even in a brief passage it is possible to convey some of the main themes from each of the major areas, to show their common currents, and to begin to analyze the larger patterns. More detailed treatment is reserved for a planned book-length study.[25]

In his influential work Beyond Marxism: Towards an Alternative Perspective, Indian political theorist Vrajenda Raj Mehta argues that neither liberal democracy nor communism are appropriate frameworks for Indian development. He attributes their inadequacy to their unidimensional views of man and society. The liberal-democratic view that man is a consumer of utilities and producer of goods serves to legitimize a selfish, atomistic, egoistic society. Communism, he says, reduces all human dimensions to one, the economic, and transforms all human activity into one, state activity, which erodes all choice and destroys life's diversities.[26]

Mehta further argues for a multidimensional conception of man and society incorporating (1) the objective, external, rational; (2) the subjective, internal, intuitive; (3) the ethical, normative, harmonious; and (4) the spiritual and fiduciary. For the development of man's multidimensional personality, society must be structured as an "oceanic circle," an integral-pluralist system of wholes within wholes. The four social wholes of Mehta's well-organized society consist of "those devoted to the pursuit of knowledge, those who run the administration and protect the community from external aggression, those who manage the exchange of services of goods, and those who attend to manual and elementary tasks" (p. 54). Mehta claims that such an integral-ist-pluralist order will overcome the atomistic limitations of liberal democracy and the economic and bureaucratic collectivism of communism. The logic of "developing wholes" means that each sector of society must have autonomy or *swaraj* within an overall system of harmony and oceanic circles. Emphasizing both the autonomy of the several societal sectors and their integration within a larger whole, Mehta calls this essentially Indian-organic-corporatist system "integral pluralism":

> Integral pluralism insists that the development of society has to be the development of the whole society. The whole is not one, but itself consists of various wholes, of economics and politics, ethics, and religion, as also of different types of individuals. The relationship of each of them to each other is in the nature of oceanic circles (p. 60).

Particularly interesting for our purposes are Mehta's attempts to ground his theory in the reality of Indian culture, history, and civilization. "Each national community," he says, "has its own law of development, its own way to fulfill itself." "The broken mosaic of Indian society," he goes on, "cannot be recreated in the image of the West—India must find its own strategy of development and nation-building suited to its own peculiar conditions" (p. 92). Instead of being dazzled by the national progress of the West and futilely trying to emulate its development model, India should define its goals and choose its means "separately in terms of its own resources and the role it wants to play on the world scene." Rejecting the thesis of a single and universal pattern of development, Mehta advocates an indigenous process of change attuned to the needs of individual societies: "A welcome process of social change in all societies is a process towards increasing self-awareness in terms of certain normatively-defined goals in each case, and that the direction of the process and the definition of ends is largely defined by the society's own distinct history and way of life" (p. 104).

Mehta's theory of integral pluralism is a bold and erudite exposition of a model of indigenous development for India. Although he draws some of his ideas eclectically from the West, the specific sources of inspiration for his model are Indian: the Vedic seers, the *Mahabharata,* Tagore, and Gandhi. In contemporary India the model derives particular support from nationalists and from those who advocate the Gandhian model of development, which emphasizes a decentralized economy based on small industries, a reorientation of production in terms of criteria besides prosperity only, a possible decentralized defense industry, and hence a particularly Indian route to development.

Mehta believes that the form of liberal democracy derived from England, the colonial power, is inappropriate and unworkable in the Indian context. Political events in India in recent years would seem to provide abundant though still incomplete evidence for that argument. But neither is communism in accord with India's traditions, he argues. Mehta states that the crisis in Indian politics is due to the fact the constitution and political system are not based on what he calls the "hidden springs" or the underlying institutional and cultural heritage of Indian society. That is why, he writes, there are presently disillusionment, institutional atrophy, spreading chaos, and a concomitant widespread desire to adopt the Gandhian model. Accordingly, the successful ruler and developer in the Indian context

> will be the one who will not only have an idea of the system of international stratification and the position of the dominant powers in it, but also the one who will weave into a holistic view the fact that his society once had a glorious civilization which, due to certain structural defects and rigidities, gave way to conquerors from the outside; he will be conscious of the continuity amidst all the shifts in the historical scene, of the underlying unity amongst a panorama of immense and baffling diversities (p. 115).

No claim is made here that Mehta's book captures the essence of contemporary Indian thinking or that it is necessarily representative of the newer currents emanating from Indian intellectuals or public opinion.[27] It is, nevertheless, illustrative of the kind of thinking and writing now beginning to emerge, and there is no doubt that its clarion call for a nationalistic and indigenous model of development has struck in his country an immensely responsive chord. Moreover, it corresponds closely to other observed phenomena in contemporary India: the increased repudiation of English and Western influences, the rising tide of Indian nationalism, the revival of various religious movements and the corresponding criticisms of Western secularism and pluralism, the justifications for authoritarian rule and of integral and harmonious development, and the reinterpretation of caste associations no longer as traditional institutions that must be destroyed but as indigenous agencies capable themselves of modernization and of serving as transitional bridges of development. These deep-rooted trends help make Mehta's book, and the voluminous writings of numerous other scholars and popularizers, worthy of serious attention.[28]

The new and often parallel currents stirring the Islamic world have received far more popular attention than have those in India. There can be no doubt that a major religious revival is sweeping the world of Islam,[29] but our understanding of the forces at work has been obscured, biased, and retarded by events in Iran and by general Western hostility to them. It is relatively easy in the Iranian case to express our appalled indignation at the summary trials and executions, the brutal treatment of the hostages, and the sometimes wild fulminations of an aging ayatullah; but by doing so we may miss some of the deeper permanent, and more important aspects of the changes under way.[30]

Two major features of the Islamic revival command special attention here. Both are also present in the Indian case. One is the criticism of the Western models, either liberal or communist, as inappropriate and undesirable in the Islamic context. The widespread sentiment in favor of rejecting Western values and the Western developmental model has again been obscured in the popular media by their focusing only on the sometimes ludicrous comments of Iran's religious leaders that the Western model is sinful and satanic. That focus makes it easy to satirize, parody, and dismiss what is, in fact, a widespread criticism and which, coming from other Islamic mouths and pens—in, for instance, Saudi Arabia and Pakistan—is quite realistic and telling. The argument is that the excessive individualism of the liberal model and the excessive statism of the communist one are both inappropriate in the Islamic context: they violate its customs and traditions by importing a system without strong indigenous roots, and they are positively damaging in terms of the Islamic world's own preferred values and institutions.[31]

The second aspect commanding attention, complementary to the first, is the effort on the part of the Iranians and others, once the Western influences were excised or repudiated, to reconstruct society and polity on the bases of indigenous and Islamic concepts and institutions. Once more, what is in fact a serious process has frequently been made ludicrous in the media where only the comic-opera and the most brutal aspects have received attention. But surely the efforts to reforge the links between the state and society that had been largely destroyed by the shah, to lay stress on the family, the local community, a corporate group life and solidarity, and the leader who provides both direction and moral values—in contrast to the alienation and mass society that are among the more visible results of the Western pattern of development—are serious and therefore must command our attention. Important too are the efforts at religious revival and the attempts to reconstruct law, society, and behavior in accord with religious and moral principles, to rejoin politics and ethics in ways that in the West have been nearly irrevocably broken since Machiavelli. Rather than reject such developments out of hand, which further postpones our understanding of them, Westerners must begin to take Islamic society on its own terms, not from the point of view of automatic rejection or a haughty sense of superiority, but with empathy and understanding. Indeed one of the more fascinating aspects that has emerged from this Islamic revival is not only a set of new, innovative, and indigenous institutions but a whole, distinctive Islamic social science of development to go with it.[32]

In Africa the institution around which the discussion revolves is tribalism. Tribalism is one of those traditional institutions, like India's caste associations or Islamic fundamentalism, that was supposed to decline or disappear as modernization went forward. The sentiment that tribalism was to be consigned to the dustbins of history was so deeply ingrained that African leaders themselves were often made to feel ashamed of their own background and origins. Tribalism had to be repressed and denied and the nation-state or the single-party mass-mobilizing system elevated to an artificial importance, which in fact it did not have.[33] When tribalism refused to die, it was rebaptized under the rubric of ethnicity and ethnic conflict, which somehow made it seem more modern.

There are still Westerners and Africans alike who would deny the existence of tribalism and would seek to stamp it out, but among other Africans there is a new and refreshing realism about tribalism, even some interesting albeit not as yet overly successful efforts to reconstruct African society using tribalism as a base. These attempts include new variations on the federal principle, new forms of consociationalism, a corporately based communalism as in Tanzania, or the African authenticity of Zaire. Whatever the precise name and form, these newer approaches to tribalism would seem to be both more realistic and more interesting than the past denial of or wishful thinking about it.

At a minimum, the tribe often gives people what little they have in rural Africa: a patch of land for their huts and maize, leadership, order, and coherence. The tribe often has its own police force, which offers a measure of security. In countries sometimes without effective national welfare or social security, tribal authority and tradition help provide for the old and sick. Tribal ties and solidarities in the cities also help provide jobs, patronage, and positions within the army or bureaucracy. Parties and interest associations are often organized along tribal lines. In the absence of strong states and national political structures, the tribe may be an effective intermediary association providing services and brokering relations between the individual, family, or clan and the national government. Hence while tribalism may weaken over time, it surely will not disappear, and there is a growing and realistic recognition on the part of African leaders that tribalism is part of Africa. Many will find this new realism refreshing and the effort to refashion African polities and social structures in accord with its own indigenous traditions exciting and innovative.[34]

The case of Latin America is somewhat different since it is an area that we think of as already Western.[35] Properly qualified (taking into account Latin America's large indigenous populations, the periodic efforts to resurrect and glorify its Indian past, or the efforts of nations such as Mexico to ground their nationalism in part upon their mestizoness—the new "cosmic race"), this assertion is valid; one must also remember, however, that Latin America is an offshoot or historical fragment of a special time and of a special part of the West, Iberia circa 1500,[36] whose own conformity to the Western model has been and in many ways still is somewhat less than 100 percent.[37] With this in mind, Latin America may be looked on as something of a mixed case, Western and Third World at the same time.

In various writings I have sought to wrestle with this issue of where and in what ways Latin America conforms to the Western pattern and where it is distinctive.[38] In the context of this paper, however, what is striking are the remarkable parallels between the newer currents in Latin America and in other Third World areas. First, there is a growing nationalistic rejection of the United States-favored route to development, a rejection that has even stronger historical roots than in other Third World areas and that found expression as early as the nineteenth century in fears and hostility toward the "colossus of the north" and in the widespread acceptance of the arguments of Jose E. Rodo, who contrasted the spiritualism, Catholicism, personalism, and humanism of Latin America (Ariel) with the crassness, materialism, secularism, pragmatism, and utilitarianism of the United States (Caliban).[39]

Second, and the reverse side of this coin, is the effort to identify what is distinctive in Latin America's own past and present and to determine whether these characteristics can be used to erect a separate Latin American political sociology of development. Such a formulation would emphasize Latin America's persistent corporatism and organic statism, its neomercantilist and state-capitalist economic structures, its personalism and kinship patterns, its Catholicism and the institutions and behavioral patterns of Catholic political culture, its patrimonialism and unabashed patriarchalism, its patron-client networks now extended to the national political level, its distinctive patterns and arenas of state-society relations, and its historic relations of dependency (particularly in recent times) vis-a-vis the United States.[40] There are, as we shall see in the next section, problems with these formulations, not the least of which is that not all Latin Americans accept them or wish to accept them, still preferring to see themselves in terms of and to cast their lot with the Western model. Nevertheless the parallels with other Third World areas are striking, and the attempts by Latin Americans to fashion their own indigenous model and social science of development must command our attention.

Analogous developments in other areas also merit serious study, though here only passing mention can be made of them. In China, for example, the combination of Marxist and Confucian elements in Mao's thought provided not only a new and fascinating synthesis but also some of the key ingredients in the distinctively Chinese model of development.[41] Japan has achieved phenomenal economic growth rates by borrowing, copying, or synthesizing the technology and organizational models of the West and adapting these to historic and preferred Japanese forms, structures, and ways of doing things.[42]

In Poland and elsewhere in Eastern Europe, Marxism is being adapted to local and home-grown institutions such as Catholicism and nationalism. In the Soviet Union there is of course a Marxist socialist state, but no one would disagree it is also a *Russian* Marxist state (however ambiguous and open to disagreement may be its precise meaning).[43] Finally, in Western Europe itself, in whose development patterns the Western model obviously originated, there is both a new questioning of what the Western model consists of and whether even the nations of Western Europe conform to it, as well as a rethinking of whether that Western model is in fact applicable to the rest of the world.[44]

These various national and regional traditions need to be examined in detail and the arguments more fully amplified. What seems clear even from this brief survey, however, is that there is a growing rejection of the Western model as irrelevant and inappropriate in areas and nations where the traditions and institutions are quite different and that there exists a growing search for indigenous national institutions and models, based on local traditions instead of those imported from or imposed by the West. These trends seem now to cut across and transcend national and cultural boundaries.

PROBLEM AREAS AND DILEMMAS

> *The notion of a bright new world made up of young emerging nations is a fairy tale.*
>
> V. S. Naipaul, Among the Believers

There can be no doubt that the idea of a native, indigenous model and social science of development, reflecting and deeply rooted in local practices and institutions rather than imported and surface ones, is enormously attractive. Social scientists need to analyze this rather than merely celebrate it, however, and when that is done numerous problems arise.

First, the search for indigenous models of development may prove to be more romantic and nostalgic than realistic.[45] In some areas and nations (several of the Central American countries, for example), indigenous institutions may well prove weak or nonexistent, incapable of serving as the base for national development. They may, as with the Western model, reflect the preferences of intellectuals rather than those of the general population—or they may reflect the nostalgic longing for a past that no longer exists and cannot be recreated. Such indigenous institutions may have been destroyed in whole or in part by the colonial powers or discredited by the earlier generation of Western-oriented local elites. There may not be an institutional foundation based on indigenous institutions and practices on which to build and hence, for many Third World nations, no light of whatever sort at the end of the development tunnel. The Western model seems not to have worked well, but an indigenous one may not work out either if it reflects the politics of romance and nostalgia rather than the politics of reality.[46]

Second, there are class, partisan, and other biases often implicit in a political strategy that seeks to fashion a model of development based upon indigenous institutions. Such a strategy may serve (though it need not necessarily do so) as a means to defend an existing status quo or to restore a status quo ante, both nationally and internationally. It may serve to justify an existing class, caste, leadership group, or clan remaining in power. It may be manipulated for partisan or personal advantage. For example, in Francisco Franco's efforts to restore and maintain traditional historic Spanish institutions and practices, it was clear that only his rather narrow and particular interpretation of what that special tradition was would be allowed and that other currents and possibilities within that tradition would be suppressed.[47]

Third, the actual practice of regimes that have followed an indigenous development strategy has not produced very many successes. Even on its own terms, it is hard to call the Iranian Revolution, so far, a success. The Mexican Revolution that was once trumpeted as providing an indigenous third way is acknowledged to have sold out, run its course, or died.[48] There has been a lot of talk about African authenticity in recent years, but in countries such as Togo or Zaire the application of the concept has served mainly to shore up corrupt and despotic regimes. Even in Tanzania, which has been widely cited as an example of a serious attempt to build an original African development model, there are immense difficulties accompanying this experiment and a notable lack of enthusiasm on the part of both the peasants who are presumably its prime beneficiaries and the government officials charged with implementing it.[49]

Fourth, it may be that in the present circumstances such indigenous developmental models are no longer possible. The time when a nation could maintain itself in isolation and could develop autonomously and on its own terms may well have passed. All of the Third World is now affected by what Lucian Pye once called the "world culture"—not only styles in dress and music (largely Western) but in social and political systems as well.[50] They are also caught up in what Immanuel Wallerstein called the "world system"— factors such as trade patterns, economic dependency relationships, world market prices, oil requirements, and so on, which have major effects on them but over which they have no control.[51] Additionally, whether one speaks of Afghanistan, El Salvador, or numerous other Third World nations, they are often involved in Cold War and other international political conflicts that cast them as pawns in the global arena and often affect in major ways their internal development as well. All these conditions make it virtually impossible that the outside world would not impinge on any effort at indigenous development, if not destroying it then certainly requiring compromise in numerous areas.[52]

Not only does the outside world impose itself but, fifth, indigenous elites and intellectuals are not all convinced that they wish to follow such a native path. For them, traditional and indigenous institutions are not necessarily symbols of pride and nationalism but of backwardness and underdevelopment. Or they may have mixed feelings that breed confusion, irresolution, and lack of direction. Not all African leaders by any means are convinced that tribalism can serve as a new basis of political organization; hence in Kenya and elsewhere concerted efforts are under way not to build it up but to snuff it out. Indian intellectuals, especially from the lower castes, do not as yet seem ready to accept the arguments concerning the modernizing role the castes may play. Not all Iranian intellectuals accept the virtues of a theocratic state led by the Ayatullah or, even if they are believers in Islamic fundamentalism, are agreed on what precise institutional form that should take.

Latin America is an especially interesting area in this regard, for while most of its intellectuals share varying degrees of antipathy to the United States model and the U.S.-favored development route and want to have a hand in fashioning a nationalistic and Latin American one, they are also terribly uncomfortable with the implications of that position. That new route would imply acceptance of a political system built in some degree upon the principles of corporatism, hierarchy, authoritarianism, and organic-statism— none of which are popular or fashionable in the more democratic nations and salons of the modern world, into which Latin America and its intellectuals, historically plagued by a sense of inferiority and backwardness, also wish to be accepted. Hence they have ambivalent feelings regarding indigenous models and prefer theories of dependency or international stratification that conveniently and more comfortably place the blame on external instead of internal forces.[53]

Sixth and finally, emphasis must be placed on the sheer diversity of these nations and areas and hence the immense difficulties of achieving a consensus on any development strategy, whether indigenous or otherwise. At some levels of analysis, Latin America (and Iberia) may be thought of as part of a single culture area, but it must also be kept in mind that Paraguay is quite different from Argentina, Brazil and Peru from Chile, Nicaragua from Mexico—and that all are at different levels of development. Hence different strategies and models of modernization, even if they could be conceptualized within certain common parameters, would have to be designed for each country of the area.[54] In the Islamic world the same qualifications would have to be introduced; it obviously also makes a major difference if we are talking of the Sunni, the Shiite, or other traditions and combinations of them.[55] A similar case exists in Africa: some observers feel that Islam is the only organized cultural and ideological force capable of offering a coherent and continent-wide alternative to the heretofore dominant Western model. This point of view, however, ignores the still-strong Christian and Western influences, the fact that only a small minority of African states are essentially Muslim (that is, at least 75 percent Islamic), the continuing influence of traditional beliefs, and the fact that parts of Africa have no strong cultural identity of any sort. All of these and many other diversities and differentiations would have to be taken into account in creating for each of these areas an indigenous model, or models, of development. Nor should one underestimate the sheer confusion, uncertainty, and chaos surrounding these issues in many Third World nations. For the Third World as a whole and for its component geographic regions and distinct cultural areas, there is too much diversity to be subsumed under any one single theory or set of concepts.

CONCLUSION: TOWARD A NONETHNOCENTRIC THEORY OF DEVELOPMENT

> *The aspiration for something different, better, more truly indigenous than Western systems of development and yet as socially and materially effective is palpable everywhere. "Our own way" is the persistent theme; but it is far more often advanced as a creed than as a plan.*
>
> *Flora Lewis,* New York Times, *31 December 1979*

In numerous areas, the West and the Western model of development intimately associated with its earlier progress seem to be in decline. Western Europe suffers from various malaises of uncertain and often obscure origins, the United States and many of its institutions seem to be in decline, NATO and the Western Alliance are in disarray, and the global system of American hegemony and dominance is being undermined. With this Spenglerian "Decline of the West"[56] has also come a new questioning of and challenge to the development model that was a part of the nearly 500-year-long Western era of domination. It is not just the model itself that is now being challenged, however, but the larger, preeminently Western, and for that reason parochial and ethnocentric, philosophical and intellectual tradition that went with it. What we in the West, because our entire lifespans and those of our intellectual forebears were entirely encompassed within this time frame, assumed to be a universal set of norms and processes by which societies developed and modernized, and of which the West was presumably the leader and model, has now been demonstrated to be somewhat less than that.

With the decline of Western hegemony and the pretension to universalism of the intellectual constructs that are part and parcel of it, and concomitantly with the rise and new assertiveness of various non-Western and Third World areas, has also come the demand for local, indigenous models of development. The critique of the Western model as particularistic, parochial, Eurocentric, considerably less than universal, and hopelessly biased, as not only perpetuating our lack of understanding regarding these areas but also of wreaking downright harm upon them, seems devastating, persuasive, and perhaps unchallengeable. The question is no longer whether the Western model applies or whether it is salvageable but what is the precise nature of the models that have risen to take its place and whether these new models are functional and viable in terms of the Third World areas from which they are emerging.

These issues would seem to represent the next great frontier in the social sciences.[57] Shorn of its romantic and nostalgic aspects, unfettered by the class or partisan biases that sometimes surround it, incorporating both national currents and international ones, taking account of practical realities and not just intellectual constructs, cognizant of both the mixed sentiments of the local elites and the diversities of the societies studied—or at least recognizing these when they do occur—the notion of a nonethnocentric theory of development is now on the front burner. The study of such local, indigenous, native cultural traditions and models, Samuel P. Huntington has said, may well be the wave of the future for the social sciences.[58]

We need now for the first time to begin to take non-Western areas and their ofttimes peculiar institutions seriously, in their own context and traditions rather than from the slanted perspective of the Western social sciences. We need, hence, to reexamine virtually all of our Western social science notions of development. A serious mistake made by Western scholars, for example, is to assume that as people become modernized and educated, they also become Westernized. In fact in much of the Middle East, urbanization and the growth of a literate middle class are prime causes in the growth of interest in Islam. The examples could easily be multiplied. Hence, we need to see local indigenous institutions not necessarily as dysfunctional or doomed to history's ashcans but frequently as viable and necessary in the society we are studying, as filters and winnowers of the modernization process, as agencies of transition between traditional and modern, and as means for reconciling and blending the global with the indigenous, the nationalist with the international. Such an undertaking implies both greater empathy on our part and greater modesty in terms of the claims made for the universalism of the Western examples.

The implications of such a coming to grips with indigenous institutions and of nonethnocentric theories and concepts of development are enormous.[59] Three major areas of impact may be noted here. The first has to do with the Third World and non-Western nations themselves: their efforts to overcome historical inferiority complexes, their reconceived possibilities for development, the new-found importance of their traditional institutions, the rediscovery of many and complex routes to development, their new sense of pride and accomplishment, and so on. It will take some time before the Third World is able to articulate and mold these diverse concepts into viable and realistic development models; the translation of concepts like authenticity into concrete political institutions, educational policies, health programs and the like is liable to take even longer. Nevertheless, we cannot doubt the reality or growth of such new interpretations, outlooks, perspectives, and syn-theses—as between Marxism and an indigenous development tradition, for example, or in the form of a homegrown type of democracy, or as an updated and modernized Islam.

Second, the arguments presented here have immense implications for the social sciences. Not only must we reexamine a host of essentially Western social science assumptions but we must also be prepared to accept an Islamic social science of development, an African social science of development, a Latin American social science of development, and so on—and to strike some new balances between what is particular in the development process and what does in fact conform to more universal patterns. In exploring such indigenous models, we will need to fashion a dynamic theory of change as well as to examine a variety of normative orientations;[60] we will need also to distinguish between a theory of development that comes from many sources and different theories of development for different regions. In the process the rather tired, even moribund, study of development itself, in all its dimensions, is likely to be revived.

Third, there are major implications for policy. In the past three decades not only have virtually all our intellectual concepts and models with regard to developing nations been based upon the Western experience, but virtually all our assistance programs, developmental recommendations, and foreign policy presumptions have been grounded on these same conceptual tools.[61] Hence the approach here suggested is likely to upset many cherished social science notions and, if considered seriously, will necessitate a fundamental set of foreign policy reconsiderations as well.

NOTES

1. P. T. Bauer, *Dissent on Development* (Cambridge: Harvard University Press, 1976); David E. Schmitt, ed., *Dynamics of the Third World* (Cambridge, MA: Winthrop, 1974); Frank Tachau, ed., *The Developing Nations: What Path to Modernization?* (New York: Dodd, Mead, 1972); W. A. Beling and G. O. Totten, eds., *The Developing Nations: Quest for a Model* (New York: Van Nostrand, 1970); Robert E. Gamer, *The Developing Nations* (Boston: Allyn and Bacon, 1976); Lyman Tower Sargent, *Contemporary Political Ideologies* (Homewood, IL: Dorsey, 1981); Paul E. Sigmund, ed., *The Ideologies of the Developing Nations* (New York: Praeger, 1972); John Kenneth Galbraith, *The Voice of the Poor* (Cambridge: Harvard University Press, 1982); and Howard J. Wiarda, ed., *New Directions in Comparative Politics* (forthcoming).

2. For example, Edward Said, *Orientalism* (New York: Pantheon, 1978); Howard J. Wiarda, ed., *Politics and Social Change in Latin America: The Distinct Tradition,* 2nd ed. rev. (Amherst: University of Massachusetts Press, 1982).

3. These arguments are expanded in Howard J. Wiarda, "The Ethnocentrism of the Social Sciences: Implications for Research and Policy," *The Review of Politics* 42 (April 1981): 163–97. It might be noted that an editor's mistake resulted in the mistitling of this paper in the published version.

4. For some parallel arguments see Reinhard Bendix, "Tradition and Modernity Reconsidered," *Comparative Studies in Society and History* 9 (April 1967): 292–346, reprinted in his *Embattled Reason* (New York: Oxford University Press, 1970); also Joseph R. Gusfield, "Tradition and Modernity: Misplaced Polarities in the Study of Social Change," *American Journal of Sociology* 72 (January 1967): 351–62.

5. This and other criticisms will not be new to many students of political development. What is new is the widespread articulation of such views within the Third World. Moreover, this critique of the Western model needs to be presented as a prelude to the discussion of indigenous models that follows. For some earlier critiques of the Western development model see Wiarda, "Ethnocentrism"; Bendix, "Tradition and Modernity;" Dean C. Tipps, "Modernization Theory and the Comparative Studies of Society: A Critical Perspective," *Comparative Studies of Society and History* 15 (March 1973): 199–226; C. D. Hah and J. Schneider, "A Critique of Current Theories of Political Development and Modernization," *Social Research* 35 (Spring 1968): 130–58. See also the statements on the different meanings of democracy by Costa Rican President Luis Alberto Monge and Nigerian President Alhaji Shehu Shagari at the Conference on Free Elections, Department of State, Washington, DC, 4–6 November 1982; also R. William Liddle, "Comparative Political Science and the Third World," mimeographed (Columbus: Ohio State University, Department of Political Science).

6. An excellent treatment of these themes is Claudio Veliz, *The Centralist Tradition in Latin America* (Princeton, NJ: Princeton University Press, 1980); also Clifford Geertz, *Negara: The Theatre State in Nineteenth Century Bali* (Princeton, NJ: Princeton University Press, 1980), in which he shows that the culture and the theater are the substance, not just superstructure.

7. Especially relevant is the general critique of the Western sociological bias in T. O. Wilkinson, "Family Structure and Industrialization in Japan," *American Sociological Review* 27 (October 1962): 678–82; also Alberto Guerreiro Ramos, "Modernization: Toward a Possibility Model," in *Developing Nations*, ed. Beling and Totten, pp. 21–59; and Gusfield, "Tradition and Modernity."

8. William P. Glade, "Problems of Research in Latin American Studies," in *New Directions in Language and Area Studies* (Milwaukee: University of Wisconsin at Milwaukee for the Consortium of Latin American Studies Programs, 1979), pp. 81–101.

9. Veliz, *The Centralist Tradition.*

10. For a general statement, Leonard S. Binder et al., eds., *Crises and Sequences in Political Development* (Princeton, NJ: Princeton University Press, 1971).

11. See the classic statement by Marc Bloch, *Feudal Society* (Chicago: University of Chicago Press, 1961).

12. Daniel Bell, *The Coming of Post-Industrial Society* (New York: Basic Books, 1973). On 26 May, 1981, in a personal conversation, Professor Bell asserted that by a quite different route he had also "come to similar conclusions regarding the inadequacies of many social science concepts since they derive almost exclusively from a particular Western tradition." Much of the new social science literature emanating from Latin America since the 1960s makes many of the same arguments.

13. The dependency literature is extensive; among the best statements is Fernando Henrique Cardoso and Enzo Faletto, *Dependency and Development in Latin America* (Berkeley: University of California Press, 1978).

14. For a general discussion, S. N. Eisenstadt, "Post-Traditional Societies and the Continuity and Reconstruction of Tradition," *Daedalus* 102 (Winter 1973): 1–27; and idem, *Modernization: Protest and Change* (Englewood Cliffs, NJ: Prentice-Hall, 1966).

15. Lloyd I. Rudolph and Susanne Hoeber Rudolph, *The Modernity of Tradition* (Chicago: University of Chicago Press, 1967).

16. The case of Tanzania is especially interesting in this regard.

17. The arguments are detailed in Wiarda, "Ethnocentrism."

18. A more complete discussion with regard to one region is in Howard J. Wiarda, ed., *The Continuing Struggle for Democracy in Latin America* (Boulder, CO: Westview Press, 1980).

19. G. A. D. Soares, "Latin American Studies in the United States," *Latin American Research Review* 11 (1976); and Howard J. Wiarda, "Latin American Intellectuals and the 'Myth' of Underdevelopment" (Presentation made at the Seventh National Meeting of the Latin American Studies Association, Houston, 2–5 November 1977 and published in Wiarda, *Corporatism and National Development in Latin America* [Boulder, CO: Westview, 1981], pp. 236–38.)

20. Susanne J. Bodenheimer, *The Ideology of Developmentalism: The American Paradigm-Surrogate for Latin American Studies* (Beverly Hills, CA: Sage, 1971); Teresa Hayter, *Aid as Imperialism* (Baltimore, MD: Penguin, 1971); Ronald H. Chilcote, *Theories of Comparative Politics: The Search for a Paradigm* (Boulder, CO: Westview Press, 1981); Hah and Schneider, "Critique."

21. In a faculty seminar I chaired in 1980–81 on "New Directions in Comparative Politics" at the Center for International Affairs, Harvard University, several of whose members were part of the original and highly influential SSRC Committee on Comparative Politics, it was striking to note in the occasional seminar remarks by these members how strongly the anticommunist ideology of that time pervaded the SSRC Committee's assumptions. One of our seminar members, himself part of the original SSRC Committee, flatly stated that the purpose of this group was to formulate a noncommunist theory of change and thus to provide a non-Marxian alternative for the developing nations. Gabriel A. Almond's now virtually forgotten *The Appeals of Communism* (Princeton, NJ: Princeton University Press, 1954) was especially important in helping shape this sentiment. In a volume that grows out of this seminar (*New Directions in Comparative Politics,* forthcoming), I have sought to explain the context and biases undergirding the early development literature.

22. Selig S. Harrison, *The Widening Gulf: Asian Nationalism and American Policy* (New York: Free Press, 1978). My critique of the development paradigm is contained in "Is Latin America Democratic and Does It Want to Be? The Crisis and Quest of Democracy in the Hemisphere," in *The Continuing Struggle,* ed. Wiarda, 3–24.

23. Samuel P. Huntington, *Political Order in Changing Societies* (New Haven: Yale University Press, 1968); and Wiarda, "Ethnocentrism."

24. See also Sigmund, *Ideologies.* Especially striking are the differences between the old and new editions of this study, and the differences in Sigmund's own thinking as contained in his introductions.

25. Tentatively entitled *Third World Conceptions of Development* and also growing out of the Harvard seminar on "New Directions in Comparative Politics."

26. Vrajenda Raj Mehta, *Beyond Marxism: Towards an Alternative Perspective* (New Delhi: Manohar Publications, 1978), p. 12. I am grateful to my colleague Thomas

Pantham for bringing this work and the debate that swirls about it to my attention. Subsequent page references to Mehta will be in parentheses in the text. A parallel volume from Latin America is Jose Arico, *Marx e a America Latina* (Rio de Janeiro: Paz e Terra, 1982).

27. For a critique see Thomas Pantham, "Integral Pluralism: A Political Theory for India?" *India Quarterly* (July–December 1980): 396–405.

28. For another outstanding Indian contribution to the theory of development see Rajni Kothari, *Footsteps into the Future* (New York: Free Press, 1975).

29. G. H. Jansen, *Militant Islam* (New York: Harper and Row, 1980), as well as the special series by Sir Willie Morris in the *Christian Science Monitor*, August–September 1980, and that by Flora Lewis in *New York Times*, December 1979.

30. An especially good statement is by Harvard anthropologist Mary Catherine Bateson, "Iran's Misunderstood Revolution," *New York Times*, 20 February 1979, p. 14.

31. Jansen, *Militant Islam*; Said, *Orientalism*; Barry Rubin, *Paved with Good Intentions* (New York: Oxford University Press, 1980); Shahrough Akhavi, *Religion and Politics in Contemporary Iran* (Albany: State University of New York Press, 1980); Ali Masalehdan, "Values and Political Development in Iran" (Ph.D. diss., University of Massachusetts at Amherst, 1981); and Michael Fischer, *Iran: From Religious Dispute to Revolution* (Cambridge, MA: Harvard University Press, 1980). See also the discussion led by Fischer on "Iran: Is It an Example of Populist Neo-Traditionalism?" Joint Seminar on Political Development (JOSPOD), Cambridge, MA, Minutes of the Meeting of 15 October 1980.

32. Anwar Syed, *Islam and the Dialectics of National Solidarity in Pakistan* (University of Alabama Press, forthcoming). The implications of Syed's discussion are considerably broader than the case he discusses.

33. David Apter, *Ghana in Transition* (New York: Atheneum, 1967); and Ruth Schachter Morgenthau, "Single Party Systems in West Africa," *American Political Science Review* 55 (June 1961) have both helped to popularize (and, to a degree, romanticize) the notion of the viability of African single party systems. Henry L. Bretton, *Power and Politics in Africa* (Chicago: Aldine, 1973) helped to explode those myths.

34. My understanding of these currents in Africa has been enriched by various exchanges with and the seminar presentations of Africanist Naomi Chazan, a colleague in both Jerusalem and Cambridge; and by the writings of Swiss sociologist Pierre Pradervand, *Family Planning Programmes in Africa* (Paris: Organization for Economic Cooperation and Development, 1970); and idem, "Africa—The Fragile Giant," a series of articles in the *Christian Science Monitor*, December 1980. See also Crawford Young, *The Politics of Cultural Pluralism* (Madison: University of Wisconsin Press, 1976).

35. For a partial and inconclusive exchange on this theme see the comments of Susan Bourque, Samuel P. Huntington, Merilee Grindle, Brian Smith, and me in a JOSPOD seminar on "Neo-Traditionalism in Latin America," in Minutes of the Meeting of 19 November 1980.

36. Louis Hartz et al., *The Founding of New Societies* (New York: Harcourt, Brace, 1964).

37. Howard J. Wiarda, "Spain and Portugal," in *Western European Party Systems*, ed. Peter Merkl (New York: Free Press, 1980), pp. 298–328; and idem, "Does Europe Still Stop at the Pyrenees, or Does Latin America Begin There? Iberia, Latin America, and the Second Enlargement of the European Community," in *The Impact of an Enlarged European Community on Latin America*, ed. Georges D. Landau and G. Harvey

Summ (forthcoming); also published under the same title as Occasional Paper no. 2 (Washington: American Enterprise Institute for Public Policy Research, January 1982).

38. Wiarda, *Politics and Social Change, Corporatism and Development; The Continuing Struggle,* and (earlier) "Toward a Framework for the Study of Political Change in the Iberic-Latin Tradition: The Corporative Model," *World Politics* 25 (January 1973): 206–35.

39. Jose E. Rodo, *Ariel* (Montevideo: Dornaleche y Reyes, 1900); an English translation by F. J. Stimson was published under the same title (Boston: Houghton-Mifflin, 1922).

40. Among others, Veliz, *The Centralist Tradition;* Glen Dealy, *The Public Man: An Interpretation of Latin America and Other Catholic Countries* (Amherst: University of Massachusetts Press, 1977); Leopoldo Zea, *The Latin American Mind* (Norman: University of Oklahoma Press, 1963); Octavio Paz, *The Labyrinth of Solitude* (New York: Grove Press, 1961); Richard M. Morse, "The Heritage of Latin America," in *The Founding,* ed. Hartz.

41. H. G. Creel, *Chinese Thought: From Confucius to Mao Tse-tung* (Chicago: University of Chicago Press, 1963); Stuart H. Schram, *The Political Thought of Mao Tse-tung* (New York: Praeger, 1976).

42. T. O. Wilkinson, *The Urbanization of Japanese Labor* (Amherst: University of Massachusetts Press, 1965); Ezra F. Vogel, *Japan as No. 1* (Cambridge: Harvard University Press, 1979); and Peter Berger, "Secularity—West and East" (Paper presented at the American Enterprise Institute Public Policy Week, Washington, DC, 6–9 December 1982).

43. For example, Stanley Rothman and George W. Breslauer, *Soviet Politics and Society* (St. Paul, MN: West, 1978); Archie Brown and Jack Gray, eds., *Political Culture and Political Change in Communist States* (New York: Holmes and Meier, 1978); Jerry F. Hough and Merle Fainsod. *How the Soviet Union Is Governed* (Cambridge: Harvard University Press, 1979).

44. See, for instance, Raymond Grew, ed., *Crises of Political Development in Europe and the United States* (Princeton, NJ: Princeton University Press, 1978); and Charles Tilly, ed., *The Formation of Nation States in Western Europe* (Princeton, NJ: Princeton University Press, 1975).

45. This is one of the criticisms leveled in Pantham, "Integral Pluralism?" against Mehta's *Beyond Marxism.*

46. Pradervand, "Africa."

47. Pantham, "Integral Pluralism"; and idem, "Political Culture, Political Structure, and Underdevelopment in India," *Indian Journal of Political Science* 41 (September 1980): 432–56; also Wiarda. *Corporatism and National Development.*

48. Susan Eckstein, *The Poverty of Revolution: The State and the Urban Poor in Mexico* (Princeton, NJ: Princeton University Press, 1977); Kenneth F. Johnson, *Mexican Democracy: A Critical View* (Boston: Allyn and Bacon, 1971); Octavio Paz, *The Other Mexico* (New York: Grove Press, 1972).

49. Pradervand, "Africa."

50. Lycian Pye, *Aspects of Political Development* (Boston: Little, Brown, 1966).

51. Immanuel Wallerstein, *The Modern World-System* (New York: Academic Press, 1976).

52. Unless of course a nation is willing to withdraw entirely and consciously into isolation, but as Cambodia illustrates that strategy may not work very well either.

53. These issues are addressed in the Introduction to the Portuguese language version of Wiarda, *Corporatism and National Development,* published as *O Modelo Corporativo na America Latina e a Latinoamericanizacao dos Estados Unidos* (Rio de Janeiro: Ed. Vozes, 1983). For an example of such ambivalence see Norbert Lechner, ed., *Estado y Politica en America Latina* (Mexico City: Siglo Veintiuno Editores, 1981); also Carlos Franco, *Del Marxismo Eurocentrico al Marxismo Latinoamericano* (Lima: Centro de Estudios para el Desarrollo y la Participacion, 1981).

54. For a country-by-country analysis combined with a common set of theoretical concepts see Howard J. Wiarda and Harvey F. Kline, *Latin American Politics and Development* (Boston: Houghton-Mifflin, 1979).

55. Masalehdan, *Values and Political Development in Iran.*

56. Oswald Spengler, *The Decline of the West* (New York: Knopf, 1932); and much recent literature.

57. See my research agenda as set forth in the edited volumes *New Directions in Comparative Politics* and *Third World Conceptions of Development,* forthcoming.

58. In a personal conversation with the author, December 1979.

59. The research perspectives suggested here and the implications of these as set forth in the concluding paragraphs are explored in greater detail in Wiarda, "Ethnocentrism"; *Politics and Social Change, The Continuing Struggle for Democracy;* and *Corporatism and National Development.*

60. I have attempted to formulate such a theory in "Toward a Framework for the Study of Political Change in the Iberic-Latin Tradition," and in *Corporatism and National Development.*

61. For example, our community development, family planning, agrarian reform, military assistance, labor, economic development, and numerous other foreign aid programs have all been based on the "Western" (i.e., United States and North-West Europe) model, which is one key reason, I would argue, that few of them have worked or produced their anticipated consequences. On this see Robert A. Packenham, *Liberal America and the Third World: Political Development Ideas in Foreign Aid and Social Science* (Princeton, NJ: Princeton University Press, 1973).

PART TWO

ECONOMIC DEVELOPMENT AND UNDERDEVELOPMENT IN HISTORICAL PERSPECTIVE

Because the essence of economic development is rapid and discontinuous change in institutions and the value of economic parameters, it is impossible to construct a rigorous and determinate model of that process. An economist must be willing to settle for less. Elegance and rigor are important attributes of economic theory, but they take second place to relevance and applicability. The more rigorous the model, the higher its degree of technical success may be, but the greater its inability to explain economic development. Such a model necessarily omits too many of the most significant variables in economic development. An inquiry into the origin of economic development and underdevelopment ought not to commence with a highly generalized and abstract model. If a rigorous and determinate model cannot be utilized to study the process of economic development, a less rigorous but more richly textured model that accounts for the most important socioeconomic variables must be constructed. For this we must turn to history.

Probably the greatest weakness of mainstream economic theorists is their lack of understanding of the process of development in the West between the seventeenth and twentieth centuries. The development of capitalism in the West was faced with the need for change in the social structure so that the progress-oriented middle class could become the leaders of society. This change often involved a violent struggle for supremacy between the old social order and the emerging new one. The English Revolution of 1640, ending with the Supremacy of Parliament Act in 1688, replaced the feudal lords with the landed gentry and urban middle class as the dominant classes in England, thus preparing the way for later economic progress. The French

Revolution of 1789 replaced the old aristocracy with the new middle class. The lack of such social change was a major factor in the economic stagnation of Spain after the seventeenth century.

This change in social structure enabled the social surplus to be productively used. The social surplus may be viewed as a residual, that part of society's total product remaining after basic consumption needs are met. How a society chooses to use this net product of its labor—squandering it in luxury consumption or adding to the country's capital stock—conditions the pattern of development. Of critical importance is who controls the surplus. Are decisions made to favor elites or is the social surplus used to develop society for the good of all?

Because the Western capitalist model forms the core of many Third World development strategies, it is important to have a clear sense of the dynamics of early capitalism and how they are like and different from development demands today. Dudley Dillard's article outlines some of the crucial elements in the historical development of capitalism in the West. As Dillard points out in the first reading in this part, "Productive use of the 'social surplus' was the special virtue that enabled capitalism to outstrip all prior economic systems."

In "On the Political Economy of Backwardness," Paul Baran argues the virtual impossibility of capitalist development in the Third World. Focusing on the class relations between the masses, internal elites, and foreign investors, he highlights the contradiction between imperialism, the process of industrialization, and the general economic development of poor nations. For Baran continuous capitalist development is implausible for the Third World because of the power configuration between foreign and domestic decisionmakers and the people. Capitalism entered most underdeveloped countries the "Prussian Way"—not through the growth of small, competitive enterprise, but through the transfer from abroad of advanced, monopolistic business. Thus capitalist development in these countries was not accompanied by the rise of a strong, property-owning middle class and by the overthrow of landlord domination of society. Instead, an accommodation was reached between the newly arrived monopolistic business and the socially and politically entrenched agrarian aristocracy.

Therefore, there was neither vigorous competition between enterprises striving for increased output nor accumulation of the social surplus in the hands of entrepreneurs, who would be forced by the competitive system to reinvest in the expansion and modernization of their businesses. The result was that production was well below the potential level, with agriculture still being operated on a semifeudal basis and with waste and irrationality in industry protected by monopoly, high tariffs, and other devices.

For these and other reasons the actual social surplus was much lower than the potential social surplus. A large share of the potential social surplus was used by aristocratic landlords on excess consumption and the maintenance of unproductive laborers. In addition, a large share of the actual social surplus was taken by businessmen for commercial operations promising large and quick profits or for the accumulation of investments or bank accounts abroad as a hedge against domestic social and political hazards. Furthermore, in order to obtain social status and the benefits and privileges necessary for the operation of a business, they emulated the dominant aristocracy in its mode of living. The actual social surplus was further reduced by the substantial quantity of resources used to maintain elaborate and inefficient bureaucratic and military establishments.

Andre Gunder Frank, in "The Development of Underdevelopment," tells us that this stagnation in the periphery is generated by the same historical process as successful capitalist development. Instead of focusing on relations between classes, Frank concentrates on the nation-state and the incorporation of Latin America and other periphery economies into the world capitalist order. Hierarchical relations between the First and Third World prevent the effective possibility of sustained, dynamic capitalist development for the periphery. Integration into the global economy is achieved through an intermediate metropolis-satellite chain, in which the surplus generated at each stage is successively drawn to the center. The most underdeveloped regions are therefore those with the strongest ties in the past; the strongest developing economies are those which, usually through some crisis, had looser colonial ties.

David Ruccio and Lawrence H. Simon highlight the schism in the political-economy paradigm between Marxists and *dependendistas*. The problem stems from an argument both about the historical facts of development and about how we ought to interpret these facts to articulate a coherent story. Dependency theorists assert that the major decisions affecting socioeconomic development are made by individuals and institutions outside of the underdeveloped countries. Because these countries must rely on the developed world for infusion of capital and technology and are subsequently drained of the benefits of accumulation by the dominant center, dependent relations create in undeveloped countries a self-perpetuating situation of blocked capitalist development. Marxists take issue with the external orientation in describing underdevelopment. They concentrate, instead, on the internal development of the means of production and the social relations that characterize them. They argue that periods of stagnation and imbalance are inherent in the processes of capitalist development strategies and that the Third World is indeed successfully pursuing the capitalist growth path.

The concluding article of this section provides a fascinating historical case study of modernization without development. E. Bradford Burns's study of El Salvador provides a striking example of how the rapid and profound modernization of a once-neglected outpost of the Spanish empire was accompanied by increasing impoverishment of the majority of the inhabitants.

5

Capitalism

Dudley Dillard

Capitalism [is] a term used to denote the economic system that has been dominant in the western world since the breakup of feudalism. Fundamental to any system called capitalist are the relations between private owners of nonpersonal means of production (land, mines, industrial plants, etc., collectively known as capital) and free but capital-less workers, who sell their labour services to employers. Under capitalism, decisions concerning production are made by private businessmen operating for private profit. Labourers are free in the sense that they cannot legally be compelled to work for the owners of the means of production. However, since labourers do not possess the means of production required for self-employment, they must, of economic necessity, offer their services on some terms to employers who do control the means of production. The resulting wage bargains determine the proportion in which the total product of society will be shared between the class of labourers and the class of capitalist entrepreneurs.

. . . . . .

HISTORICAL DEVELOPMENT

1. Origins of Capitalism

Although the continuous development of capitalism as a system dates only from the 16th century, antecedents of capitalist institutions existed in the ancient world, and flourishing pockets of capitalism were present during the later middle ages. One strategic external force contributing to the breakup of medieval economic institutions was the growing volume of long-distance trade between capitalist centres, carried on with capitalist techniques in a capitalist spirit. Specialized industries grew up to serve long-distance trade, and the resulting commercial and industrial towns gradually exerted pres-

Reprinted from *Encyclopaedia Britannica,* pp. 839–842, by permission of the publisher and the author. © *Encyclopaedia Britannica,* 1972.

sures which weakened the internal structure of agriculture based on serfdom, the hallmark of the feudal regime. Changes in trade, industry and agriculture were taking place simultaneously and interacting with one another in highly complex actual relations, but it was chiefly long-distance trade which set in motion changes that spread throughout the medieval economy and finally transformed it into a new type of economic society.

Flanders in the 13th century and Florence in the 14th century were two capitalist pockets of special interest. Their histories shed light on the conditions that were essential to the development of capitalism in England. The great enterprise of late medieval and early modern Europe was the woolen industry, and most of the business arrangements that later characterized capitalism developed in connection with long-distance trade in wool and cloth.

In Flanders revolutionary conflict raged between plebeian craftsmen and patrician merchant-manufacturers. The workers succeeded in destroying the concentration of economic and political power in the hands of cloth magnates, only to be crushed in turn by a violent counterrevolution that destroyed the woolen industry and brought ruin to both groups. A similar performance was repeated in Florence, which became one of the great industrial cities of Europe during the 14th century. Restless, revolutionary urban workers overthrew the ruling hierarchy of merchants, manufacturers and bankers, and were in turn crushed in a bloody counterrevolution. Thus both Flanders and Florence failed to perpetuate their great industries because they failed to solve the social problem arising from conflicting claims of small numbers of rich capitalists and large numbers of poor workers.

2. Early Capitalism (1500–1750)

By the end of the middle ages the English cloth industry had become the greatest in Europe. Because of the domestic availability of raw wool and the innovation of simple mechanical fulling mills, the English cloth industry had established itself in certain rural areas where it avoided the violent social strife that had destroyed the urban industries of Flanders and Florence. Although it was subject to many problems and difficulties, the English rural cloth industry continued to grow at a rapid rate during the 16th, 17th and 18th centuries. Hence, it was the woolen industry that spearheaded capitalism as a social and economic system and rooted it for the first time in English soil.

Productive use of the "social surplus" was the special virtue that enabled capitalism to outstrip all prior economic systems. Instead of building pyramids and cathedrals, those in command of the social surplus chose to invest in ships, warehouses, raw materials, finished goods and other material forms of wealth. The social surplus was thus converted into enlarged productive capacity. Among the historical events and circumstances that significantly influenced capital formation in western Europe in the early stage of capitalist development, three merit special attention: (1) religious sanction for hard work and frugality; (2) the impact of precious metals from the new world on the relative shares of income going to wages, profits and rents; and (3) the role of national states in fostering and directly providing capital formation in the form of general-purpose capital goods.

Capitalist spirit. The economic ethics taught by medieval Catholicism presented obstacles to capitalist ideology and development. Hostility to material wealth carried forward the teachings of the Christian fathers against mammonism. Saint Jerome said, "A rich man is either a thief or the son of a thief." Saint Augustine felt that trade was bad because it turned men away from the search for God. Down through the middle ages commerce and banking were viewed, at best, as necessary evils. Moneylending was for a time confined to non-Christians because it was considered unworthy of Christians. Interest on loans was unlawful under the anti-usury laws of both church and secular authorities. Speculation and profiteering violated the central medieval economic doctrine of just price.

Expansion of commerce in the later middle ages stirred controversies and led to attempts to reconcile theological doctrines with economic realities. In Venice, Florence, Augsburg and Antwerp—all Catholic cities—capitalists violated the spirit and circumvented the letter of the prohibitions against interest. On the eve of the Protestant Reformation capitalists, who still laboured under the shadow of the sin of avarice, had by their deeds become indispensable to lay rulers and to large numbers of people who were dependent upon them for employment.

The Protestant Reformation of the 16th and 17th centuries developed alongside economic changes which resulted in the spread of capitalism in northern Europe, especially in the Netherlands and England. This chronological and geographical correlation between the new religion and economic development has led to the suggestion that Protestantism had causal significance for the rise of modern capitalism. Without in any sense being the "cause" of capitalism, which already existed on a wide and expanding horizon, the Protestant ethic proved a bracing stimulant to the new economic order. Doctrinal revision or interpretation seemed not only to exonerate capitalists from the sin of avarice but even to give divine sanction to their way of life. In the ordinary conduct of life, a new type of wordly asceticism emerged, one that meant hard work, frugality, sobriety and efficiency in one's calling in the market place similar to that of the monastery. Applied in the environment of expanding trade and industry, the Protestant creed taught that accumulated wealth should be used to produce more wealth.

Acceptance of the Protestant ethic also eased the way to systematic organization of free labour. By definition, free labourers could not be compelled by force to work in the service of others. Moreover, the use of force would have violated the freedom of one's calling. Psychological compulsion arising from religious belief was the answer to the paradox. Every occupation was said to be noble in God's eyes. For those with limited talents, Christian conscience demanded unstinting labour even at low wages in the service of God—and, incidentally, of employers. It was an easy step to justify economic inequality because it would hasten the accumulation of wealth by placing it under the guardianship of the most virtuous (who were, incidentally, the wealthiest) and remove temptation from weaker persons who could not withstand the allurements associated with wealth. After all, it did not much matter who held legal title to wealth, for it was not for enjoyment. The rich like the poor were to live frugally all the days of their lives. Thus the capitalist system found a justification that was intended to make inequality tolerable to the working classes.

The price revolution. Meanwhile treasure from the new world had a profound impact on European capitalism, on economic classes and on the distribution of income in Europe. Gold and silver from the mines of Mexico, Peru and Bolivia increased Europe's supply of precious metals sevenfold and raised prices two- or threefold between 1540 and 1640. The significance of the increased supply of money lay not so much in the rise in prices as in its effect on the social and economic classes of Europe. Landlords, the older ruling class, suffered because money rents failed to rise as rapidly as the cost of living. The more aggressive landlords raised rents and introduced capitalistic practices into agriculture. In England the enclosure movement, which developed with ever increasing momentum and vigour during the 17th and 18th centuries, encouraged sheep raising to supply wool to the expanding woolen industry. Among labourers, money wages failed to keep pace with the cost of living, causing real wages to fall during the price revolution. The chief beneficiaries of this century-long inflation were capitalists, including merchants, manufacturers and other employers. High prices and low wages resulted in profit inflation, which in turn contributed to larger savings and capital accumulation. Profit inflation and wage deflation created a more unequal distribution of income. Wage earners got less and capitalists got more of the total product than they would have received in the absence of inflation. Had the new increments of wealth gone to wage earners instead of to capitalists, most of it would have been consumed rather than invested, and hence the working classes of the 16th century would have eaten better, but the future would have inherited less accumulated wealth.

Mercantilism. Early capitalism (1500–1750) also witnessed in western Europe the rise of strong national states pursuing mercantilist policies. Critics have tended to identify mercantilism with amassing silver and gold by having a so-called favourable balance of exports over imports in trading relations with other nations and communities, but the positive contribution and historic significance of mercantilism lay in the creation of conditions necessary for rapid and cumulative economic change in the countries of western Europe. At the end of the middle ages western Europe stood about where many underdeveloped countries stand in the 20th century. In underdeveloped economies the difficult task of statesmanship is to get under way a cumulative process of economic development, for once a certain momentum is attained, further advances appear to follow more or less automatically. Achieving such sustained growth requires virtually a social revolution.

Power must be transferred from reactionary to progressive classes; new energies must be released, often by uprooting the old order; the prevailing religious outlook may constitute a barrier to material advancement. A new social and political framework must be created within which cumulative economic change can take place.

Among the tasks which private capitalists were either unable or unwilling to perform were the creation of a domestic market free of tolls and other barriers to trade within the nation's borders; a uniform monetary system; a legal code appropriate to capitalistic progress; a skilled and disciplined labour force; safeguards against internal violence; national defense against attack; sufficient literacy and education among business classes to use credit instruments, contracts and other documents required of a commercial civilization; basic facilities for communication and transportation and harbour installations. A strong government and an adequate supply of economic resources were required to create most of these conditions, which constitute the "social overhead capital" needed in a productive economy. Because the returns from them, however great, cannot be narrowly channeled for private gain, such investments must normally be made by the government and must be paid for out of public revenues.

Preoccupation with productive use of the social surplus led mercantilist commentators to advocate low wages and long hours for labour. Consumption in excess of bare subsistence was viewed as a tax on progress and therefore contrary to the national interest. Mercantilist society was not a welfare state; it could not afford to be. Luxury consumption was condemned as a dissipation of the social surplus. Restrictions on imports were directed especially at luxury consumption.

Opportunities for profitable private investment multiplied rapidly as mercantilist policy succeeded in providing the basic social overhead capital. Rather paradoxically, it was because the state had made such an important contribution to economic development that the ideology of *laissez-faire* could later crystallise. When that occurred, dedication to capital accumulation remained a basic principle of capitalism, but the shift from public to private initiative marked the passage from the early state of capitalism and the beginning of the next stage, the classical period.

3. Classical Capitalism (1750–1914)

In England, beginning in the 18th century, the focus of capitalist development shifted from commerce to industry. The Industrial Revolution may be defined as the period of transition from a dominance of commercial over industrial capital to a dominance of industrial over commercial capital. Preparation for this shift began long before the invention of the flying shuttle, the water frame and the steam engine, but the technological changes of the 18th century made the transition dramatically evident.

The rural and household character of the English textile industry continued only as long as the amount of fixed capital required for efficient production remained relatively small. Changes in technology and organization shifted industry again to urban centres in the course of the Industrial Revolution, although not to the old commercial urban centres. Two or three centuries of steady capital accumulation began to pay off handsomely in the 18th century. Now it became feasible to make practical use of technical knowledge which had been accumulating over the centuries. Capitalism became a powerful promoter of technological change because the accumulation of capital made possible the use of inventions which poorer societies could not have afforded. Inventors and innovators like James Watt found business partners who were able to finance their inventions through lean years of experimentation and discouragement to ultimate commercial success. Aggressive entrepreneurs like Richard Arkwright found capital to finance the factory type of organization required for the utilization of new machines. Wealthy societies had existed before capitalism, but none had managed their wealth in a manner that enabled them to take advantage of the more efficient methods of production which an increasing mastery over nature made physically possible.

Adam Smith's great *Inquiry Into the Nature and Causes of the Wealth of Nations* (1776) expressed the ideology of classical capitalism. Smith recommended dismantling the state bureaucracy and leaving economic decisions to the free play of self-regulating market forces. While Smith recognized the faults of businessmen, he contended they could do little harm in a world of freely competitive enterprise. In Smith's opinion, private profit and public welfare would become reconciled through impersonal forces of market competition. After the French Revolution and the Napoleonic wars had swept the remnants of feudalism into oblivion and rapidly undermined mercantilist fetters, Smith's policies were put into practice. *Laissez-faire* policies of 19th-century political liberalism included free trade, sound money (the gold standard), balanced budgets, minimum poor relief—in brief, the principle of leaving individuals to themselves and of trusting that their unregulated interactions would produce socially desirable results. No new conceptions of society arose immediately to challenge seriously what had become, in fact, a capitalist civilization.

This system, though well-defined and logically coherent, must be understood as a system of tendencies only. The heritage of the past and other obstructions prevented any full realization of the principles except in a few cases of which the English free trade movement, crystallised by the repeal of the Corn Laws in 1846, is the most important. Such as they were, however, both tendencies and realizations bear the unmistakable stamp of the businessman's interests and still more the businessman's type of mind. Moreover, it was not only policy but the philosophy of national and individual life, the scheme of cultural values, that bore that stamp. Its materialistic utilitarianism, its naive confidence in progress of a certain type, its actual achievements in the field of pure and applied science, the temper of its artistic creations, may all be traced to the spirit of rationalism that emanates from the businessman's office. For much of the time and in many countries the businessman did not rule politically. But even noncapitalist rulers espoused his interests and adopted his views. They were what they had not been before, his agents.

More definitely than in any other historical epoch these developments can be explained by purely economic causes. It was the success of capitalist enterprise that raised the bourgeoisie to its position of temporary ascendancy. Economic success produced political power, which in turn produced policies congenial to the capitalist process. Thus the English industrialists obtained free trade, and free trade in turn was a major factor in a period of unprecedented economic expansion.

The partition of Africa and the carving out of spheres of influence in Asia by European powers in the decades preceding World War I led critics of capitalism to develop, on a Marxist basis, a theory of economic imperialism. According to this doctrine, competition among capitalist firms tends to eliminate all but a small number of giant concerns. Because of the inadequate purchasing power of the masses, these concerns find themselves unable to use the productive capacity they have built. They are, therefore, driven to invade foreign markets and to exclude foreign products from their own markets through protective tariffs. This situation produces aggressive colonial and foreign policies and "imperialist" wars, which the proletariat, if organized, turn into civil wars for socialist revolution. Like other doctrines of such sweeping character, this theory of imperialism is probably not capable of either exact proof or disproof. Three points, however, may be recorded in its favour; first, it does attempt what no other theory has attempted, namely, to subject the whole of the economic, political and cultural patterns of the epoch that began during the long depression (1873–96) to comprehensive analysis by means of a clear-cut plan; second, on the surface at least, it seems to be confirmed by some of the outstanding manifestations of this pattern and some of the greatest events of this epoch; third, whatever may be wrong with its interpretations, it certainly starts from a fact that is beyond challenge—the capitalist tendency toward industrial combination and the emergence of giant firms. Though cartels and trusts antedate the epoch, at least so far as the

United States is concerned, the role of what is popularly called "big business" has increased so much as to constitute one of the outstanding characteristics of recent capitalism.

4. The Later Phase (Since 1914)

World War I marked a turning point in the development of capitalism in general and of European capitalism in particular. The period since 1914 has witnessed a reversal of the public attitude toward capitalism and of almost all the tendencies of the liberal epoch which preceded the war. In the prewar decades, European capitalism exercised vigorous leadership in the international economic community. World markets expanded, the gold standard became almost universal, Europe served as the world's banker, Africa became a European colony, Asia was divided into spheres of influence under the domination of European powers and Europe remained the centre of a growing volume of international trade.

After World War I, however, these trends were reversed. International markets shrank, the gold standard was abandoned in favour of managed national currencies, banking hegemony passed from Europe to the United States, African and Asian peoples began successful revolts against European colonialism and trade barriers multiplied. Western Europe as an entity declined, and in eastern Europe capitalism began to disintegrate. The Russian Revolution, a result of the war, uprooted over a vast area not only the basic capitalist institution of private property in the means of production, but the class structure, the traditional forms of government and the established religion. Moreover, the juggernaut unleashed by the Russian Revolution was destined to challenge the historic superiority of capitalist organization as a system of production within less than half a century. Meanwhile, the inner structure of West European economies was tending away from the traditional forms of capitalism. Above all, *laissez-faire,* the accepted policy of the 19th century, was discredited by the war and postwar experience.

Statesmen and businessmen in capitalist nations were slow to appreciate the turn of events precipitated by World War I and consequently they misdirected their efforts during the 1920s by seeking a "return to prewar normalcy." Among major capitalist countries, the United Kingdom failed conspicuously to achieve prosperity at any time during the interwar period. Other capitalist nations enjoyed a brief prosperity in the 1920s only to be confronted in the 1930s with the great depression, which rocked the capitalist system to its foundations. *Laissez-faire* received a crushing blow from Pres. Franklin D. Roosevelt's New Deal in the United States. The gold standard collapsed completely. Free trade was abandoned in its classic home, Great Britain. Even the classical principle of sound finance, the annually balanced governmental budget, gave way in both practice and theory to planned deficits during periods of depressed economic activity. Retreat from the free market philosophy was nearly complete in Mussolini's Italy and Hitler's Germany. When World War II opened in 1939, the future of capitalism looked bleak indeed. This trend seemed confirmed at the end of the war when the British Labour party won a decisive victory at the polls and proceeded to nationalize basic industries, including coal, transportation, communication, public utilities and the Bank of England. Yet a judgment that capitalism had at last run its course would have been premature. Capitalist enterprise managed to survive in Great Britain, the United States, western Germany, Japan and other nations [with a] remarkable show of vitality in the postwar world.

6

On the Political Economy of Backwardness

Paul A. Baran

I

The capitalist mode of production and the social and political order concomitant with it provided, during the latter part of the eighteenth century, and still more during the entire nineteenth century, a framework for a continuous and, in spite of cyclical disturbances and setbacks, momentous expansion of productivity and material welfare. The relevant facts are well known and call for no elaboration. Yet this material (and cultural) progress was not only spotty in time but most unevenly distributed in space. It was confined to the Western world; and did not affect even all of this territorially and demographically relatively small sector of the inhabited globe.

. . . . . .

Tardy and skimpy as the benefits of capitalism may have been with respect to the lower classes even in most of the leading industrial countries, they were all but negligible in the less privileged parts of the world. There productivity remained low, and rapid increases in population pushed living standards from bad to worse. The dreams of the prophets of capitalist harmony remained on paper. Capital either did not move from countries where its marginal productivity was low to countries where it could be expected to be high, or if it did, it moved there mainly in order to extract profits from backward countries that frequently accounted for a lion's share of the increments in total output caused by the original investments. Where an increase in the aggregate national product of an underdeveloped country took place, the existing distribution of income prevented this increment from raising the living standards of the broad masses of the population. Like all general statements, this one is obviously open to criticism based on particular cases.

Reprinted from *The Manchester School* (January 1952), pp. 66–84, by permission of the publisher.

There were, no doubt, colonies and dependencies where the populations profited from inflow of foreign capital. These benefits, however, were few and far between, while exploitation and stagnation were the prevailing rule.

But if Western capitalism failed to improve materially the lot of the peoples inhabiting most backward areas, it accomplished something that profoundly affected the social and political conditions in underdeveloped countries. It introduced there, with amazing rapidity, all the economic and social tensions inherent in the capitalist order. It effectively disrupted whatever was left of the "feudal" coherence of the backward societies. It substituted market contracts for such paternalistic relationships as still survived from century to century. It reoriented the partly or wholly self-sufficient economies of agricultural countries toward the production of marketable commodities. It linked their economic fate with the vagaries of the world market and connected it with the fever curve of international price movements.

A *complete* substitution of capitalist market rationality for the rigidities of feudal or semi-feudal servitude would have represented, in spite of all the pains of transition, an important step in the direction of progress. Yet all that happened was that the age-old exploitation of the population of underdeveloped countries by their domestic overlords, was freed of the mitigating constraints inherited from the feudal transition. This superimposition of business *mores* over ancient oppression by landed gentries resulted in compounded exploitation, more outrageous corruption, and more glaring injustice.

Nor is this by any means the end of the story. Such export of capital and capitalism as has taken place had not only far-reaching implications of a social nature. It was accompanied by important physical and technical processes. Modern machines and products of advanced industries reached the poverty stricken backyards of the world. To be sure most, if not all, of these machines worked for their foreign owners—or at least were believed by the population to be working for no one else—and the new refined appurtenances of the good life belonged to foreign businessmen and their domestic counterparts. The bonanza that was capitalism, the fullness of things that was modern industrial civilization, were crowding the display windows—they were protected by barbed wire from the anxious grip of the starving and desperate man in the street.

But they have drastically changed his outlook. Broadening and deepening his economic horizon, they aroused aspirations, envies, and hopes. Young intellectuals filled with zeal and patriotic devotion travelled from the underdeveloped lands to Berlin and London, to Paris and New York, and returned home with the "message of the possible."

Fascinated by the advances and accomplishments observed in the centers of modern industry, they developed and propagandized the image of what could be attained in their home countries under a more rational economic and social order. The dissatisfaction with the stagnation (or at best, barely perceptible growth) that ripened gradually under the still-calm political and social surface was given an articulate expression. This dissatisfaction was not nurtured by a comparison of reality with a vision of a socialist society. It found sufficient fuel in the confrontation of what was actually happening with what could be accomplished under capitalist institutions of the Western type.

II

The establishment of such institutions was, however, beyond the reach of the tiny middle-classes of most backward areas. The inherited backwardness and poverty of their countries never gave them an opportunity to gather the economic strength, the insight, and the self-confidence needed for the assumption of a leading role in society. For centuries under feudal rule they themselves assimilated the political, moral, and cultural values of the dominating class.

While in advanced countries, such as France or Great Britain, the economically ascending middle-classes developed at an early stage a new rational world outlook, which they proudly opposed to the medieval obscurantism of the feudal age, the poor, fledgling bourgeoisie of the underdeveloped countries sought nothing but accommodation to the prevailing order. Living in societies based on privilege, they strove for a share in the existing sinecures. They made political and economic deals with their domestic feudal overlords or with powerful foreign investors, and what industry and commerce developed in backward areas in the course of the last hundred years was rapidly moulded in the straitjacket of monopoly—the plutocratic partner of the aristocratic rulers. What resulted was an economic and political amalgam combining the worst features of both worlds—feudalism and capitalism—and blocking effectively all possibilities of economic growth.

It is quite conceivable that a "conservative" exit from this impasse might have been found in the course of time. A younger generation of enterprising and enlightened businessmen and intellectuals allied with moderate leaders of workers and peasants—a "Young Turk" movement of some sort—might have succeeded in breaking the deadlock, in loosening the hide-bound social and political structure of their countries and in creating the institutional arrangements indispensable for a measure of social and economic progress.

Yet in our rapid age history accorded no time for such a gradual transition. Popular pressures for an amelioration of economic and social conditions, or at least for some perceptible movement in that direction, steadily gained in intensity. To be sure, the growing restiveness of the underprivileged was not directed against the ephemeral principles of a hardly yet existing capitalist order. Its objects were parasitic feudal overlords appropriating large slices of the national product and wasting them on extravagant living; a government machinery protecting and abetting the dominant interests; wealthy businessmen reaping immense profits and not utilizing them for productive purposes; last but not least, foreign colonizers extracting or believed to be extracting vast gains from their "developmental" operations.

This popular movement had thus essentially bourgeois, democratic, anti-feudal, anti-imperialist tenets. It found outlets in agrarian egalitarianism; it incorporated "muckraker" elements denouncing monopoly; it strove for national independence and freedom from foreign exploitation.

For the native capitalist middle-classes to assume the leadership of these popular forces and to direct them into the channels of bourgeois democracy—as has happened in Western Europe—they had to identify themselves with the common man. They had to break away from the political, economic, and ideological leadership of the feudal crust and the monopolists allied with it; and they had to demonstrate to the nation as a whole that they had the knowledge, the courage, and the determination to undertake and to carry to victorious conclusion the struggle for economic and social improvement.

In hardly any underdeveloped country were the middle-classes capable of living up to this historical challenge. Some of the reasons for this portentous failure, reasons connected with the internal make-up of the business class itself, were briefly mentioned above. Of equal importance was, however, an "outside" factor. It was the spectacular growth of the international labor movement in Europe that offered the popular forces in backward areas ideological and political leadership that was denied to them by the native bourgeoisie. It pushed the goals and targets of the popular movements far beyond their original limited objectives.

This liaison of labor radicalism and populist revolt painted on the wall the imminent danger of a social revolution. Whether this danger was real or imaginary matters very little. What was essential is that the awareness of this threat effectively determined political and social action. It destroyed whatever chances there were of the capitalist classes joining and leading the popular anti-feudal, anti-monopolist movement. By instilling a mortal fear of expropriation and extinction in the minds of *all* property-owning groups the rise of socialist radicalism, and in particular the Bolshevik Revolution in Russia, tended to drive all more or less privileged, more or less well-to-do elements in the society into one "counterrevolutionary" coalition. Whatever differences and antagonisms existed between large and small landowners, between monopolistic and competitive business, between liberal bourgeois and reactionary feudal overlords, between domestic and foreign interests, were largely submerged on all important occasions by the over-riding *common* interest in staving off socialism.

The possibility of solving the economic and political deadlock prevailing in the underdeveloped countries on lines of a progressive capitalism all but disappeared. Entering the alliance with all other segments of the ruling class, the capitalist middle-classes yielded one strategic position after another. Afraid that a quarrel with the landed gentry might be exploited by the radical populist movement, the middle-classes abandoned all progressive attitudes in agrarian matters. Afraid that a conflict with the church and the military might weaken the political authority of the government, the middle-classes moved away from all liberal and pacifist currents. Afraid that hostility toward foreign interests might deprive them of foreign support in a case of a revolutionary emergency, the native capitalists deserted their previous anti-imperialist, nationalist platforms.

The peculiar mechanisms of political interaction characteristic of all underdeveloped (and perhaps not only underdeveloped) countries thus operated at full speed. The aboriginal failure of the middle-classes to provide inspiration and leadership to the popular masses pushed those masses into the camp of socialist radicalism. The growth of radicalism pushed the middle-classes into an alliance with the aristocratic and monopolistic reaction. This alliance, cemented by common interest and common fear, pushed the populist forces still further along the road of radicalism and revolt. The outcome was a polarization of society with very little left between the poles. By permitting this polarization to develop, by abandoning the common man and resigning the task of reorganizing society on new, progressive lines, the capitalist middle-classes threw away their historical chance of assuming effective control over the destinies of their nations, and of directing the gathering popular storm against the fortresses of feudalism and reaction. Its blazing fire turned thus against the entirety of existing economic and social institutions.

III

The economic and political order maintained by the ruling coalition of owning classes finds itself invariably at odds with all the urgent needs of the underdeveloped countries. Neither the social fabric that it embodies nor the institutions that rest upon it are conducive to progressive economic development. The only way to provide for economic growth and to prevent a continuous deterioration of living standards (apart from mass emigration unacceptable to other countries) is to assure a steady increase of total output—at least large enough to offset the rapid growth of population.

An obvious source of such an increase is the utilization of available unutilized or underutilized resources. A large part of this reservoir of dormant productive potentialities is the vast multitude of entirely unemployed or ineffectively employed manpower. There is no way of employing it usefully in agriculture, where the marginal productivity of labor tends to zero. They could be provided with opportunities for productive work only by transfer to industrial pursuits. For this to be feasible large investments in industrial plant and facilities have to be undertaken. Under prevailing conditions such investments are not forthcoming for a number of important and interrelated reasons.

With a very uneven distribution of a very small aggregate income (and wealth), large individual incomes exceeding what could be regarded as "reasonable" requirements for current consumption accrue as a rule to a relatively small group of high-income receivers. Many of them are large landowners maintaining a feudal style of life with large outlays on housing, servants, travel, and other luxuries. Their "requirements for consumption" are so high that there is only little room for savings. Only relatively insignificant amounts are left to be spent on improvements of agricultural estates.

Other members of the "upper crust" receiving incomes markedly surpassing "reasonable" levels of consumption are wealthy businessmen. For social reasons briefly mentioned above, their consumption too is very much larger than it would have been were they brought up in the puritan tradition of a bourgeois civilization. Their drive to accumulate and to expand their enterprises is continuously counteracted by the urgent desire to imitate in their living habits the socially dominant "old families," to prove by their conspicuous outlays on the amenities of rich life that they are socially (and therefore also politically) not inferior to their aristocratic partners in the ruling coalition.

But if this tendency curtails the volume of savings that could have been amassed by the urban high-income receivers, their will to re-invest their funds in productive enterprises is effectively curbed by a strong reluctance to damage their carefully erected monopolistic market positions through creation of additional productive capacity, and by absence of suitable investment opportunities—paradoxical as this may sound with reference to underdeveloped countries.

The deficiency of investment opportunities stems to a large extent from the structure and the limitations of the existing effective demand. With very low living standards the bulk of the aggregate money income of the population is spent on food and relatively primitive items of clothing and household necessities. These are available at low prices, and investment of large funds in plant and facilities that could produce this type of commodities more cheaply rarely promises attractive returns. Nor does it appear profitable to develop major enterprises the output of which would cater to the requirements of the rich. Large as their individual purchases of various luxuries may be, their aggregate spending on each of them is not sufficient to support the development of an elaborate luxury industry—in particular since the "snob" character of prevailing tastes renders only imported luxury articles true marks of social distinction.

Finally, the limited demand for investment goods precludes the building up of a machinery or equipment industry. Such mass consumption goods as are lacking, and such quantities of luxury goods as are purchased by the well-to-do, as well as the comparatively small quantities of investment goods needed by industry, are thus imported from abroad in exchange for domestic agricultural products and raw materials.

This leaves the expansion of exportable raw materials output as a major outlet for investment activities. There the possibilities are greatly influenced, however, by the technology of the production of most raw materials as well as by the nature of the markets to be served. Many raw materials, in particular oil, metals, certain industrial crops, have to be produced on a large scale if costs are to be kept low and satisfactory returns assured. Large-scale production, however, calls for large investments, so large indeed as to exceed the potentialities of the native capitalists in backward countries. Production of raw materials for a distant market entails, moreover, much larger risks than those encountered in domestic business. The difficulty of foreseeing accurately such things as receptiveness of the world markets, prices obtainable in competition with other countries, volume of output in other parts of the world, etc., sharply reduces the interest of native capitalists in these lines of business. They become to a predominant extent the domain of foreigners who, financially stronger, have at the same time much closer contacts with foreign outlets of their products.

The shortage of investible funds and the lack of investment opportunities represent two aspects of the same problem. A great number of investment projects, unprofitable under prevailing conditions, could be most promising in a general environment of economic expansion.

In backward areas a new industrial venture must frequently, if not always, break virgin ground. It has no functioning economic system to draw upon. It has to organize with its own efforts not only the productive process *within* its own confines, it must provide in addition for all the necessary *outside* arrangements essential to its operations. It does not enjoy the benefits of "external economies."

There can be no doubt that the absence of external economies, the inadequacy of the economic milieu in underdeveloped countries, constituted everywhere an important deterrent to investment in industrial projects. There is no way of rapidly bridging the gap. Large-scale investment is predicated upon large-scale investment. Roads, electric power stations, railroads, and houses have to be built *before* businessmen find it profitable to erect factories, to invest their funds in new industrial enterprises.

Yet investing in road building, financing construction of canals and power stations, organizing large housing projects, etc., transcend by far the financial and mental horizon of capitalists in underdeveloped countries. Not only are their financial resources too small for such ambitious projects, but their background and habits militate against entering commitments of this type. Brought up in the tradition of merchandizing and manufacturing consumers' goods—as is characteristic of an early phase of capitalist development—businessmen in underdeveloped countries are accustomed to rapid turnover, large but short-term risks, and correspondingly high rates of profit. Sinking funds in enterprises where profitability could manifest itself only in the course of many years is a largely unknown and unattractive departure.

The difference between social and private rationality that exists in any market and profit-determined economy is thus particularly striking in under-developed countries.

. . . . . .

But could not the required increase in total output be attained by better utilization of land—another unutilized or inadequately utilized productive factor?

There is usually no land that is both fit for agricultural purposes and at the same time readily accessible. Such terrain as could be cultivated but is actually not being tilled would usually require considerable investment before becoming suitable for settlement. In underdeveloped countries such outlays for agricultural purposes are just as unattractive to private interests as they are for industrial purposes.

On the other hand, more adequate employment of land that is already used in agriculture runs into considerable difficulties. Very few improvements that would be necessary in order to increase productivity can be carried out within the narrow confines of small-peasant holdings. Not only are the peasants in underdeveloped countries utterly unable to pay for such innovations, but the size of their lots offers no justification for their introduction.

Owners of large estates are in a sense in no better position. With limited savings at their disposal they do not have the funds to finance expensive improvements in their enterprises, nor do such projects appear profitable in view of the high prices of imported equipment in relation to prices of agricultural produce and wages of agricultural labor.

Approached thus *via* agriculture, an expansion of total output would also seem to be attainable only through the development of industry. Only through increase of industrial productivity could agricultural machinery, fertilizers, electric power, etc., be brought within the reach of the agricultural producer. Only through an increased demand for labor could agricultural wages be raised and a stimulus provided for a modernization of the agricultural economy. Only through the growth of industrial production could agricultural labor displaced by the machine be absorbed in productive employment.

Monopolistic market structures, shortage of savings, lack of external economies, the divergence of social and private rationalities do not exhaust, however, the list of obstacles blocking the way of privately organized industrial expansion in underdeveloped countries. Those obstacles have to be considered against the background of the general feeling of uncertainty prevailing in all backward areas. The coalition of the owning classes formed under pressure of fear, and held together by the real or imagined danger of social upheavals, provokes continuously more or less threatening rumblings under the outwardly calm political surface. The social and political tensions to which that coalition is a political response are not liquidated by the prevailing system; they are only repressed. Normal and quiet as the daily routine frequently appears, the more enlightened and understanding members of the ruling groups in underdeveloped countries sense the inherent instability of the political and social order. Occasional outbursts of popular dissatisfaction assuming the form of peasant uprisings, violent strikes or local guerrilla warfare, serve from time to time as grim reminders of the latent crisis.

In such a climate there is no will to invest on the part of monied people; in such a climate there is no enthusiasm for long-term projects; in such a climate the motto of all participants in the privileges offered by society is *carpe diem.*

IV

Could not, however, an appropriate policy on the part of the governments involved change the political climate and facilitate economic growth? In our time, when faith in the manipulative omnipotence of the State has all but displaced analysis of its social structure and understanding of its political and economic functions, the tendency is obviously to answer these questions in the affirmative.

Looking at the matter purely mechanically, it would appear indeed that much could be done by a well-advised regime in an underdeveloped country to provide for a relatively rapid increase of total output, accompanied by an improvement of the living standards of the population. There are a number of measures that the government could take in an effort to overcome backwardness. A fiscal policy could be adopted that by means of capital levies and a highly progressive tax system would syphon off all surplus purchasing power, and in this way eliminate non-essential consumption. The savings thus enforced could be channelled by the government into productive investment. Power stations, railroads, highways, irrigation systems, and soil improvements could be organized by the State with a view to creating an economic environment conducive to the growth of productivity. Technical schools on various levels could be set up by the public authority to furnish industrial training to young people as well as to adult workers and the unemployed. A system of scholarships could be introduced rendering acquisition of skills accessible to low-income strata.

Wherever private capital refrains from undertaking certain industrial projects, or wherever monopolistic controls block the necessary expansion of plant and facilities in particular industries, the government could step in and make the requisite investments. Where developmental possibilities that are rewarding in the long-run appear unprofitable during the initial period of gestation and learning, and are therefore beyond the horizon of private businessmen, the government could undertake to shoulder the short-run losses.

In addition an entire arsenal of "preventive" devices is at the disposal of the authorities. Inflationary pressures resulting from developmental activities

(private and public) could be reduced or even eliminated, if outlays on investment projects could be offset by a corresponding and simultaneous contraction of spending elsewhere in the economic system. What this would call for
is a taxation policy that would effectively remove from the income stream
amounts sufficient to neutralize the investment-caused expansion of aggregate money income.

In the interim, and as a supplement, speculation in scarce goods and
excessive profiteering in essential commodities could be suppressed by rigorous price controls. An equitable distribution of mass consumption goods in
short supply could be assured by rationing. Diversion of resources in high
demand to luxury purposes could be prevented by allocation and priority
schemes. Strict supervision of transactions involving foreign exchanges could
render capital flight, expenditure of limited foreign funds on luxury imports,
pleasure trips abroad, and the like, impossible.

What the combination of these measures would accomplish is a radical
change in the structure of effective demand in the underdeveloped country,
and a reallocation of productive resources to satisfy society's need for economic development. By curtailing consumption of the higher-income groups,
the amounts of savings available for investment purposes could be markedly
increased. The squandering of limited supplies of foreign exchange on capital
flight, or on importation of redundant foreign goods and services, could be
prevented, and the foreign funds thus saved could be used for the acquisition
of foreign-made machinery needed for economic development. The reluctance of private interests to engage in enterprises that are socially necessary,
but may not promise rich returns in the short-run, would be prevented from
determining the economic life of the backward country.

The mere listing of the steps that would have to be undertaken, in order
to assure an expansion of output and income in an underdeveloped country,
reveals the utter implausibility of the view that they could be carried out by
the governments existing in most underdeveloped countries. The reason for
this inability is only to a negligible extent the nonexistence of the competent
and honest civil service needed for the administration of the program. A
symptom itself of the political and social marasmus prevailing in underdeveloped countries, this lack cannot be remedied without attacking the
underlying causes. Nor does it touch anything near the roots of the matter
to lament the lack of satisfactory tax policies in backward countries, or to
deplore the absence of tax "morale" and "discipline" among the civic virtues
of their populations.

The crucial fact rendering the realization of a developmental program
illusory is the political and social structure of the governments in power. The
alliance of property-owning classes controlling the destinies of most underdeveloped countries cannot be expected to design and to execute a set of
measures running counter to each and all of their immediate vested interests.
If to appease the restive public, blueprints of progressive measures such as

agrarian reform, equitable tax legislation, etc., are officially announced, their enforcement is wilfully sabotaged. The government, representing a political compromise between landed and business interests, cannot suppress the wasteful management of landed estates and the conspicuous consumption on the part of the aristocracy; cannot suppress monopolistic abuses, profiteering, capital flights, and extravagant living on the part of businessmen. It cannot curtail or abandon its lavish appropriations for a military and police establishment, providing attractive careers to the scions of wealthy families and a profitable outlet for armaments produced by their parents—quite apart from the fact that this establishment serves as the main protection against possible popular revolt. Set up to guard and to abet the existing property rights and privileges, it cannot become the architect of a policy calculated to destroy the privileges standing in the way of economic progress and to place the property and the incomes derived from it at the service of society as a whole.

Nor is there much to be said for the "intermediate" position which, granting the essential incompatibility of a well-conceived and vigorously executed developmental program with the political and social institutions prevailing in most underdeveloped countries, insists that at least *some* of the requisite measures could be carried out by the existing political authorities. This school of thought overlooks entirely the weakness, if not the complete absence, of social and political forces that could induce the necessary concessions on the part of the ruling coalition. By background and political upbringing, too myopic and self-interested to permit the slightest encroachments upon their inherited positions and cherished privileges, the upper-classes in underdeveloped countries resist doggedly all pressures in that direction. Every time such pressures grow in strength they succeed in cementing anew the alliance of all conservative elements, by decrying all attempts at reform as assaults on the very foundations of society.

Even if measures like progressive taxation, capital levies, and foreign exchange controls could be enforced by the corrupt officials operating in the demoralized business communities of underdeveloped countries, such enforcement would to a large extent defeat its original purpose. Where businessmen do not invest, unless in expectation of lavish profits, a taxation system succeeding in confiscating large parts of these profits is bound to kill private investment. Where doing business or operating landed estates is attractive mainly because it permits luxurious living, foreign exchange controls preventing the importation of luxury goods are bound to blight enterprise. Where the only stimulus to hard work on the part of intellectuals, technicians, and civil servants is the chance of partaking in the privileges of the ruling class, a policy aiming at the reduction of inequality of social status and income is bound to smother effort.

The injection of planning into a society living in the twilight between feudalism and capitalism cannot but result in additional corruption, larger and more artful evasions of the law, and more brazen abuses of authority.

V

There would seem to be no exit from the impasse. The ruling coalition of interests does not abdicate of its own volition, nor does it change its character in response to incantation. Although its individual members occasionally leave the sinking ship physically or financially (or in both ways), the property-owning classes as a whole are as a rule grimly determined to hold fast to their political and economic entrenchments.

If the threat of social upheaval assumes dangerous proportions, they tighten their grip on political life and move rapidly in the direction of unbridled reaction and military dictatorship. Making use of favourable international opportunities and of ideological and social affinities to ruling groups in other countries, they solicit foreign economic and sometimes military aid in their efforts to stave off the impending disaster.

Such aid is likely to be given to them by foreign governments regarding them as an evil less to be feared than the social revolution that would sweep them out of power. This attitude of their friends and protectors abroad is no less short-sighted than their own.

The adjustment of the social and political conditions in underdeveloped countries to the urgent needs of economic development can be postponed; it cannot be indefinitely avoided. In the past, it could have been delayed by decades or even centuries. In our age it is a matter of years. Bolstering the political system of power existing in backward countries by providing it with military support may temporarily block the eruption of the volcano; it cannot stop the subterranean gathering of explosive forces.

Economic help in the form of loans and grants given to the governments of backward countries, to enable them to promote a measure of economic progress, is no substitute for the domestic changes that are mandatory if economic development is to be attained.

Such help, in fact, may actually do more harm than good. Possibly permitting the importation of some foreign-made machinery and equipment for government or business sponsored investment projects, but not accompanied by any of the steps that are needed to assure healthy economic growth, foreign assistance thus supplied may set off an inflationary spiral increasing and aggravating the existing social and economic tensions in underdeveloped countries.

If, as is frequently the case, these loans or grants from abroad are tied to the fulfillment of certain conditions on the part of the receiving country regarding their use, the resulting investment may be directed in such channels as to conform more to the interests of the lending than to those of the borrowing country. Where economic advice as a form of "technical assistance" is supplied to the underdeveloped country, and its acceptance is made a prerequisite to eligibility for financial aid, this advice often pushes the governments of underdeveloped countries toward policies, ideologically or otherwise attractive to the foreign experts dispensing economic counsel, but not necessarily conducive to economic development of the "benefitted" countries. Nationalism and xenophobia are thus strengthened in backward areas—additional fuel for political restiveness.

For backward countries to enter the road of economic growth and social progress, the political framework of their existence has to be drastically revamped. The alliance between feudal landlords, industrial royalists, and the capitalist middle-classes has to be broken. The keepers of the past cannot be the builders of the future. Such progressive and enterprising elements as exist in backward societies have to obtain the possibility of leading their countries in the direction of economic and social growth.

What France, Britain, and America have accomplished through their own revolutions has to be attained in backward countries by a combined effort of popular forces, enlightened government, and unselfish foreign help. This combined effort must sweep away the holdover institutions of a defunct age, must change the political and social climate in the underdeveloped countries, and must imbue their nations with a new spirit of enterprise and freedom.

Should it prove too late in the historical process for the bourgeoisie to rise to its responsibilities in backward areas, should the long experience of servitude and accommodation to the feudal past have reduced the forces of progressive capitalism to impotence, the backward countries of the world will inevitably turn to economic planning and social collectivism. If the capitalist world outlook of economic and social progress, propelled by enlightened self-interest, should prove unable to triumph over the conservatism of inherited positions and traditional privileges, if the capitalist promise of advance and reward to the efficient, the industrious, the able, should not displace the feudal assurance of security and power to the well-bred, the well-connected and the conformist—a new social ethos will become the spirit and guide of a new age. It will be the ethos of the collective effort, the creed of the predominance of the interests of society over the interests of selected few.

The transition may be abrupt and painful. The land not given to the peasants legally may be taken by them forcibly. High incomes not confiscated through taxation may be eliminated by outright expropriation. Corrupt officials not retired in orderly fashion may be removed by violent action.

Which way the historical wheel will turn and in which way the crisis in the backward countries will find its final solution will depend in the main on whether the capitalist middle-classes in the backward areas, and the rulers of the advanced industrial nations of the world, overcome their fear and myopia. Or are they too spell-bound by their narrowly conceived selfish interests, too blinded by their hatred of progress, grown so senile in these latter days of the capitalist age, as to commit suicide out of fear of death?

7

The Development of Underdevelopment

Andre Gunder Frank

I

We cannot hope to formulate adequate development theory and policy for the majority of the world's population who suffer from underdevelopment without first learning how their past economic and social history gave rise to their present underdevelopment. Yet most historians study only the developed metropolitan countries and pay scant attention to the colonial and underdeveloped lands. For this reason most of our theoretical categories and guides to development policy have been distilled exclusively from the historical experience of the European and North American advanced capitalist nations.

Since the historical experience of the colonial and underdeveloped countries has demonstrably been quite different, available theory therefore fails to reflect the past of the underdeveloped part of the world entirely, and reflects the past of the world as a whole only in part. More important, our ignorance of the underdeveloped countries' history leads us to assume that their past and indeed their present resembles earlier stages of the history of the now developed countries. This ignorance and this assumption lead us into serious misconceptions about contemporary underdevelopment and development. Further, most studies of development and underdevelopment fail to take account of the economic and other relations between the metropolis and its economic colonies throughout the history of the world-wide expansion and development of the mercantilist and capitalist system. Consequently, most of our theory fails to explain the structure and development of the capitalist system as a whole and to account for its simultaneous generation

Reprinted from *Monthly Review,* Vol. 18, No. 4 (September 1966), pp. 17–31, by permission of Monthly Review Press.

of underdevelopment in some of its parts and of economic development in others.

It is generally held that economic development occurs in a succession of capitalist stages and that today's underdeveloped countries are still in a stage, sometimes depicted as an original stage of history, through which the now developed countries passed long ago. Yet even a modest acquaintance with history shows that underdevelopment is not original or traditional and that neither the past nor the present of the underdeveloped countries resembles in any important respect the past of the now developed countries. The now developed countries were never *under*developed, though they may have been *un*developed. It is also widely believed that the contemporary underdevelopment of a country can be understood as the product or reflection solely of its own economic, political, social, and cultural characteristics or structure. Yet historical research demonstrates that contemporary underdevelopment is in large part the historical product of past and continuing economic and other relations between the satellite underdeveloped and the now developed metropolitan countries. Furthermore, these relations are an essential part of the structure and development of the capitalist system on a world scale as a whole. A related and also largely erroneous view is that the development of these underdeveloped countries and, within them of their most underdeveloped domestic areas, must and will be generated or stimulated by diffusing capital, institutions, values, etc., to them from the international and national capitalist metropoles. Historical perspective based on the underdeveloped countries' past experience suggests that on the contrary in the underdeveloped countries economic development can now occur only independently of most of these relations of diffusion.

Evident inequalities of income and differences in culture have led many observers to see "dual" societies and economies in the underdeveloped countries. Each of the two parts is supposed to have a history of its own, a structure, and a contemporary dynamic largely independent of the other. Supposedly, only one part of the economy and society has been importantly affected by intimate economic relations with the "outside" capitalist world; and that part, it is held, became modern, capitalist, and relatively developed precisely because of this contact. The other part is widely regarded as variously isolated, subsistence-based, feudal, or precapitalist, and therefore more underdeveloped.

I believe on the contrary that the entire "dual society" thesis is false and that the policy recommendations to which it leads will, if acted upon, serve only to intensify and perpetuate the very conditions of underdevelopment they are supposedly designed to remedy.

A mounting body of evidence suggests, and I am confident that future historical research will confirm, that the expansion of the capitalist system over the past centuries effectively and entirely penetrated even the apparently most isolated sectors of the underdeveloped world. Therefore, the economic, political, social, and cultural institutions and relations we now observe there are the products of the historical development of the capitalist system no less than are the seemingly more modern or capitalist features of the national metropoles of these underdeveloped countries. Analogously to the relations between development and underdevelopment on the international level, the contemporary underdeveloped institutions of the so-called backward or feudal domestic areas of an underdeveloped country are no less the product of the single historical process of capitalist development than are the so-called capitalist institutions of the supposedly more progressive areas. In this paper I should like to sketch the kinds of evidence which support this thesis and at the same time indicate lines along which further study and research could fruitfully proceed.

II

The Secretary General of the Latin American Center of Research in the Social Sciences writes in that Center's journal: "The privileged position of the city has its origin in the colonial period. It was founded by the Conqueror to serve the same ends that it still serves today; to incorporate the indigenous population into the economy brought and developed by that Conqueror and his descendants. The regional city was an instrument of conquest and is still today an instrument of domination."[1] The Instituto Nacional Indigenista (National Indian Institute) of Mexico confirms this observation when it notes that "the mestizo population, in fact, always lives in a city, a center of an intercultural region, which acts as the metropolis of a zone of indigenous population and which maintains with the underdeveloped communities an intimate relation which links the center with the satellite communities."[2] The Institute goes on to point out that "between the mestizos who live in the nuclear city of the region and the Indians who live in the peasant hinterland there is in reality a closer economic and social interdependence than might at first glance appear" and that the provincial metropoles "by being centers of intercourse are also centers of exploitation."[3]

Thus these metropolis-satellite relations are not limited to the imperial or international level but penetrate and structure the very economic, political, and social life of the Latin American colonies and countries. Just as the colonial and national capital and its export sector become the satellite of the Iberian (and later of other) metropoles of the world economic system, this satellite immediately becomes a colonial and then a national metropolis with respect to the productive sectors and population of the interior. Furthermore, the provincial capitals, which thus are themselves satellites of the national metropolis—and through the latter of the world metropolis—are in turn provincial centers around which their own local satellites orbit. Thus, a whole chain of constellations of metropoles and satellites relates all parts of the whole system from its metropolitan center in Europe or the United States to the farthest outpost in the Latin American countryside.

When we examine this metropolis-satellite structure, we find that each of the satellites, including now-underdeveloped Spain and Portugal, serves as an instrument to suck capital or economic surplus out of its own satellites and to channel part of this surplus to the world metropolis of which all are satellites. Moreover, each national and local metropolis serves to impose and maintain the monopolistic structure and exploitative relationship of this system (as the Instituto Nacional Indigenista of Mexico calls it) as long as it serves the interest of the metropoles which take advantage of this global, national, and local structure to promote their own development and the enrichment of their ruling classes.

These are the principal and still surviving structural characteristics which were implanted in Latin America by the Conquest. Beyond examining the establishment of this colonial structure in its historical context, the proposed approach calls for study of the development—and underdevelopment—of these metropoles and satellites of Latin America throughout the following and still continuing historical process. In this way we can understand why there were and still are tendencies in the Latin American and world capitalist structure which seem to lead to the development of the metropolis and the underdevelopment of the satellite and why, particularly, the satellized national, regional, and local metropoles in Latin America find that their economic development is at best a limited or underdeveloped development.

III

That present underdevelopment of Latin America is the result of its centuries-long participation in the process of world capitalist development, I believe I have shown in my case studies of the economic and social histories of Chile and Brazil.[4] My study of Chilean history suggests that the Conquest not only incorporated this country fully into the expansion and development of the world mercantile and later industrial capitalist system but that it also introduced the monopolistic metropolis-satellite structure and development of capitalism into the Chilean domestic economy and society itself. This structure then penetrated and permeated all of Chile very quickly. Since that time and in the course of world and Chilean history during the epochs of colonialism, free trade, imperialism, and the present, Chile has become increasingly marked by the economic, social, and political structure of satellite underdevelopment. This development of underdevelopment continues today, both in Chile's still increasing satellization by the world metropolis and through the ever more acute polarization of Chile's domestic economy.

The history of Brazil is perhaps the clearest case of both national and regional development of underdevelopment. The expansion of the world economy since the beginning of the sixteenth century successively converted the Northeast, the Minas Gerais interior, the North, and the Center-South (Rio de Janeiro, São Paulo, and Paraná) into export economies and incorporated them into the structure and development of the world capitalist system. Each of these regions experienced what may have appeared as economic development during the period of its respective golden age. But it was a satellite development which was neither self-generating nor self-perpetuating. As the market or the productivity of the first three regions declined, foreign and domestic economic interest in them waned; and they were left to develop the underdevelopment they live today. In the fourth region, the coffee economy experienced a similar though not yet quite as serious fate (though the development of a synthetic coffee substitute promises to deal it a mortal blow in the not too distant future). All of this historical evidence contradicts the generally accepted theses that Latin America suffers from a dual society or from the survival of feudal institutions and that these are important obstacles to its economic development.

IV

During the First World War, however, and even more during the Great Depression and the Second World War, São Paulo began to build up an industrial establishment which is the largest in Latin America today. The question arises whether this industrial development did or can break Brazil out of the cycle of satellite development and underdevelopment which has characterized its other regions and national history within the capitalist system so far. I believe that the answer is no. Domestically the evidence so far is fairly clear. The development of industry in São Paulo has not brought greater riches to the other regions of Brazil. Instead, it converted them into internal colonial satellites, decapitalized them further, and consolidated or even deepened their underdevelopment. There is little evidence to suggest that this process is likely to be reversed in the foreseeable future except insofar as the provincial poor migrate and become the poor of the metropolitan cities. Externally, the evidence is that although the initial development of São Paulo's industry was relatively autonomous it is being increasingly satellized by the world capitalist metropolis and its future development possibilities are increasingly restricted.[5] This development, my studies lead me to believe, also appears destined to limited or underdeveloped development as long as it takes place in the present economic, political, and social framework.

We must conclude, in short, that underdevelopment is not due to the survival of archaic institutions and the existence of capital shortage in regions that have remained isolated from the stream of world history. On the contrary, underdevelopment was and still is generated by the very same historical process which also generated economic development: the development of capitalism itself. This view, I am glad to say, is gaining adherents among students of Latin America and is proving its worth in shedding new light on the problems of the area and in affording a better perspective for the formulation of theory and policy.[6]

V

The same historical and structural approach can also lead to better development theory and policy by generating a series of hypotheses about development and underdevelopment such as those I am testing in my current research. The hypotheses are derived from the empirical observation and theoretical assumption that within this world-embracing metropolis-satellite structure the metropoles tend to develop and the satellites to underdevelop. The first hypothesis has already been mentioned above: that in contrast to the development of the world metropolis which is no one's satellite, the development of the national and other subordinate metropoles is limited by their satellite status. It is perhaps more difficult to test this hypothesis than the following ones because part of its confirmation depends on the test of the other hypotheses. Nonetheless, this hypothesis appears to be generally confirmed by the non-autonomous and unsatisfactory economic and especially industrial development of Latin America's national metropoles, as documented in the studies already cited. The most important and at the same time most confirmatory examples are the metropolitan regions of Buenos Aires and São Paulo whose growth only began in the nineteenth century, was therefore largely untrammelled by any colonial heritage, but was and remains a satellite development largely dependent on the outside metropolis, first of Britain and then of the United States.

A second hypothesis is that the satellites experience their greatest economic development and especially their most classically capitalist industrial development if and when their ties to their metropolis are weakest. This hypothesis is almost diametrically opposed to the generally accepted thesis that development in the underdeveloped countries follows from the greatest degree of contact with and diffusion from the metropolitan developed countries. This hypothesis seems to be confirmed by two kinds of relative isolation that Latin America has experienced in the course of its history. One is the temporary isolation caused by the crises of war or depression in the world metropolis. Apart from minor ones, five periods of such major crises stand out and seem to confirm the hypothesis. These are: the European (and especially Spanish) Depression of the seventeenth century, the Napoleonic Wars, the First World War, the Depression of the 1930's, and the Second World War. It is clearly established and generally recognized that the most important recent industrial development—especially of Argentina, Brazil, and Mexico, but also of other countries such as Chile—has taken place precisely during the periods of the two World Wars and the intervening Depression. Thanks to the consequent loosening of trade and investment ties during these periods, the satellites initiated marked autonomous industrialization and growth. Historical research demonstrates that the same thing happened in Latin America during Europe's seventeenth-century depression. Manufacturing grew in the Latin American countries, and several of them such as Chile became exporters of manufactured goods. The Napoleonic Wars gave rise to independence movements in Latin America, and these should perhaps also be interpreted as confirming the development hypothesis in part.

The other kind of isolation which tends to confirm the second hypothesis is the geographic and economic isolation of regions which at one time were relatively weakly tied to and poorly integrated into the mercantilist and capitalist system. My preliminary research suggests that in Latin America it was these regions which initiated and experienced the most promising self-generating economic development of the classical industrial capitalist type. The most important regional cases probably are Tucumán and Asunción, as well as other cities such as Mendoza and Rosario, in the interior of Argentina and Paraguay during the end of the eighteenth and the beginning of the nineteenth centuries. Seventeenth- and eighteenth-century São Paulo, long before coffee was grown there, is another example. Perhaps Antioquia in Colombia and Puebla and Querétaro in Mexico are other examples. In its own way, Chile was also an example since, before the sea route around the Horn was opened, this country was relatively isolated at the end of the long voyage from Europe via Panama. All of these regions became manufacturing centers and even exporters, usually of textiles, during the periods preceding their effective incorporation as satellites into the colonial, national, and world capitalist system.

Internationally, of course, the classic case of industrialization through nonparticipation as a satellite in the capitalist world system is obviously that of Japan after the Meiji Restoration. Why, one may ask, was resource-poor but unsatellized Japan able to industrialize so quickly at the end of the century while resource-rich Latin American countries and Russia were not able to do so and the latter was easily beaten by Japan in the War of 1904 after the same forty years of development efforts? The second hypothesis suggests that the fundamental reason is that Japan was not satellized either during the Tokugawa or Meiji period and therefore did not have its development structurally limited as did the countries which were so satellized.

VI

A corollary of the second hypothesis is that when the metropolis recovers from its crisis and re-establishes the trade and investment ties which fully re-incorporate the satellites into the system, or when the metropolis expands to incorporate previously isolated regions into the world-wide system, the previous development and industrialization of these regions is choked off or channelled into directions which are not self-perpetuating and promising. This happened after each of the five crises cited above. The renewed expansion of trade and the spread of economic liberalism in the eighteenth and nineteenth centuries choked off and reversed the manufacturing development which Latin America had experienced during the seventeenth century, and in some places at the beginning of the nineteenth. After the First World War, the new national industry of Brazil suffered serious consequences from American economic invasion. The increase in the growth rate of Gross National Product and particularly of industrialization throughout Latin America was again reversed and industry became increasingly satellized after the Second World War and especially after the post-Korean War recovery and expansion of the metropolis. Far from having become more developed since then, industrial sectors of Brazil and most conspicuously of Argentina have become structurally more and more underdeveloped and less and less able to generate continued industrialization and/or sustain development of the economy. This process, from which India also suffers, is reflected in a whole gamut of balance-of-payments, inflationary, and other economic and political difficulties, and promises to yield to no solution short of far-reaching structural change.

Our hypothesis suggests that fundamentally the same process occurred even more dramatically with the incorporation into the system of previously unsatellized regions. The expansion of Buenos Aires as a satellite of Great Britain and the introduction of free trade in the interest of the ruling groups of both metropoles destroyed the manufacturing and much of the remainder of the economic base of the previously relatively prosperous interior almost entirely. Manufacturing was destroyed by foreign competition, lands were taken and concentrated into latifundia by the rapaciously growing export economy, intraregional distribution of income became much more unequal, and the previously developing regions became simple satellites of Buenos Aires and through it of London. The provincial centers did not yield to satellization without a struggle. This metropolis-satellite conflict was much of the cause of the long political and armed struggle between the Unitarists in Buenos Aires and the Federalists in the provinces, and it may be said to have been the sole important cause of the War of the Triple Alliance in which Buenos Aires, Montevideo, and Rio de Janeiro, encouraged and helped by London, destroyed not only the autonomously developing economy of Paraguay but killed off nearly all of its population which was unwilling to give in. Though this is no doubt the most spectacular example which tends to confirm the hypothesis, I believe that historical research on the satellization of previously relatively independent yeoman-farming and incipient manufacturing regions such as the Caribbean islands will confirm it further.[7] These regions did not have a chance against the forces of expanding and developing capitalism, and their own development had to be sacrificed to that of others. The economy and industry of Argentina, Brazil, and other countries which have experienced the effects of metropolitan recovery since the Second World War are today suffering much the same fate, if fortunately still in lesser degree.

VII

A third major hypothesis derived from the metropolis-satellite structure is that the regions which are the most underdeveloped and feudal-seeming today are the ones which had the closest ties to the metropolis in the past. They are the regions which were the greatest exporters of primary products to and the biggest sources of capital for the world metropolis and which were abandoned by the metropolis when for one reason or another business fell off. This hypothesis also contradicts the generally held thesis that the source of a region's underdevelopment is its isolation and its precapitalist institutions.

This hypothesis seems to be amply confirmed by the former super-satellite development and present ultra-underdevelopment of the once sugar-exporting West Indies, Northeastern Brazil, the ex-mining districts of Minas Gerais in Brazil, highland Peru, and Bolivia, and the central Mexican states of Guanajuato, Zacatecas, and others whose names were made world famous centuries ago by their silver. There surely are no major regions in Latin America which are today more cursed by underdevelopment and poverty; yet all of these regions, like Bengal in India, once provided the life blood of mercantile and industrial capitalist development—in the metropolis. These regions' participation in the development of the world capitalist system gave them, already in their golden age, the typical structure of underdevelopment of a capitalist export economy. When the market for their sugar or the wealth of their mines disappeared and the metropolis abandoned them to their own devices, the already existing economic, political, and social structure of these regions prohibited autonomous generation of economic development and left them no alternative but to turn in upon themselves and to degenerate into the ultra-underdevelopment we find there today.

VIII

These considerations suggest two further and related hypotheses. One is that the latifundium, irrespective of whether it appears as a plantation or a hacienda today, was typically born as a commercial enterprise which created for itself the institutions which permitted it to respond to increased demand in the world or national market by expanding the amount of its land, capital, and labor and to increase the supply of its products. The fifth hypothesis is that the latifundia which appear isolated, subsistence-based, and semi-feudal today saw the demand for their products or their productive capacity decline and that they are to be found principally in the above-named former agricultural and mining export regions whose economic activity declined in general. These two hypotheses run counter to the notions of most people, and even to the opinions of some historians and other students of the subject, according to whom the historical roots and socio-economic causes of Latin American latifundia and agrarian institutions are to be found in the transfer of feudal institutions from Europe and/or in economic depression.

The evidence to test these hypotheses is not open to easy general inspection and requires detailed analyses of many cases. Nonetheless, some important confirmatory evidence is available. The growth of the latifundium in nineteenth-century Argentina and Cuba is a clear case in support of the fourth hypothesis and can in no way be attributed to the transfer of feudal institutions during colonial times. The same is evidently the case of the postrevolutionary and contemporary resurgence of latifundia particularly in the North of Mexico, which produce for the American market, and of similar ones on the coast of Peru and the new coffee regions of Brazil. The conversion of previously yeoman-farming Caribbean islands, such as Barbados, into sugar-exporting economies at various times between the seventeenth and twentieth centuries and the resulting rise of the latifundia in these islands would seem to confirm the fourth hypothesis as well. In Chile, the rise of the latifundium and the creation of the institutions of servitude which later came to be called feudal occurred in the eighteenth century and have been conclusively shown to be the result of and response to the opening of a market for Chilean wheat in Lima.[8] Even the growth and consolidation of the latifundium in seventeenth-century Mexico—which most expert students have attributed to a depression of the economy caused by the decline of mining and a shortage of Indian labor and to a consequent turning in upon itself and ruralization of the economy—occurred at a time when urban population and demand were growing, food shortages became acute, food prices skyrocketed, and the profitability of other economic activities such as mining and foreign trade declined.[9] All of these and other factors rendered hacienda agriculture more profitable. Thus, even this case would seem to confirm the hypothesis that the growth of the latifundium and its feudal-seeming conditions of servitude in Latin America has always been and still is the commercial response to increased demand and that it does not represent the transfer or survival of alien institutions that have remained beyond the reach of capitalist development. The emergence of latifundia, which today really are more or less (though not entirely) isolated, might then be attributed to the causes advanced in the fifth hypothesis—i.e., the decline of previously profitable agricultural enterprises whose capital was, and whose currently produced economic surplus still is, transferred elsewhere by owners and merchants who frequently are the same persons or families. Testing this hypothesis requires still more detailed analysis, some of which I have undertaken in a study on Brazilian agriculture.[10]

IX

All of these hypotheses and studies suggest that the global extension and unity of the capitalist system, its monopoly structure and uneven development throughout its history, and the resulting persistence of commercial rather than industrial capitalism in the underdeveloped world (including its most industrially advanced countries) deserve much more attention in the study of economic development and cultural change than they have hitherto received. Though science and truth know no national boundaries, it is probably new generations of scientists from the underdeveloped countries themselves who most need to, and best can, devote the necessary attention to these problems and clarify the process of underdevelopment and development. It is their people who in the last analysis face the task of changing this no longer acceptable process and eliminating this miserable reality.

They will not be able to accomplish these goals by importing sterile stereotypes from the metropolis which do not correspond to their satellite economic reality and do not respond to their liberating political needs. To change their reality they must understand it. For this reason, I hope that better confirmation of these hypotheses and further pursuit of the proposed historical, holistic, and structural approach may help the peoples of the underdeveloped countries to understand the causes and eliminate the reality of their development of underdevelopment and their underdevelopment of development.

NOTES

1. *América Latina,* Año 6, No. 4, October-December 1963, p. 8.
2. Instituto Nacional Indigenista, *Los centros coordinadores indigenistas,* Mexico, 1962, p. 34.
3. Ibid., pp. 33–34, 88.
4. "Capitalist Development and Underdevelopment in Chile" and "Capitalist Development and Underdevelopment in Brazil" in *Capitalism and Underdevelopment in Latin America,* New York, Monthly Review Press, 1967.
5. Also see, "The Growth and Decline of Import Substitution," *Economic Bulletin for Latin America,* New York, IX, No. 1, March 1964; and Celso Furtado, *Dialectica do Desenvolvimiento,* Rio de Janeiro, Fundo de Cultura, 1964.
6. Others who use a similar approach, though their ideologies do not permit them to derive the logically following conclusions, are Aníbal Pinto S.C., *Chile: Un caso de desarrollo frustrado,* Santiago, Editorial Universitaria, 1957; Celso Furtado, *A formaçao econômica do Brasil,* Rio de Janeiro, Fundo de Cultura, 1959 (recently translated into English and published under the title *The Economic Growth of Brazil* by the University of California Press); and Caio Prado Junior, *Historia Econômica do Brasil,* São Paulo, Editora Brasiliense, 7th ed., 1962.
7. See for instance Ramón Guerra y Sánchez, *Azúcar y Población en las Antillas,* Havana, 1942, 2nd ed., also published as *Sugar and Society in the Caribbean,* New Haven, Yale University Press, 1964.

8. Mario Góngora, *Origen de los "inquilinos" de Chile central,* Santiago Editorial Universitaria, 1960; Jean Borde and Mario Góngora, *Evolución de la propiedad rural en el Valle del Puango,* Santiago, Instituto de Sociología de la Universidad de Chile; Sergio Sepúlveda, *El trigo chileno en el mercado mundial,* Santiago Editorial Universitaria, 1959.

9. Woodrow Borah makes depression the centerpiece of his explanation in "New Spain's Century of Depression," *Ibero-Americana,* Berkeley, No. 35, 1951. François Chevalier speaks of turning in upon itself in the most authoritative study of the subject, "La formación de los grandes latifundios en México," Mexico, *Problemas Agrícolas e Industriales de México,* VIII, No. 1, 1956 (translated from the French and recently published by the University of California Press). The data which provide the basis for my contrary interpretation are supplied by these authors themselves. This problem is discussed in my "Con qué modo de producción convierte la gallina maíz en huevos de oro?" *El Gallo Ilustrado,* Suplemento de *El Día,* Mexico, Nos. 175 and 179, October 31 and November 28, 1965; and it is further analyzed in a study of Mexican agriculture under preparation by the author.

10. "Capitalism and the Myth of Feudalism in Brazilian Agriculture," in *Capitalism and Underdevelopment in Latin America,* cited in note 4 above.

8

Radical Theories of Development: Frank, the Modes of Production School, and Amin

David F. Ruccio and Lawrence H. Simon

I. INTRODUCTION[1]

The past four hundred years have witnessed the growth and global expansion of capitalism. In the minds of many, the development of capitalism is synonymous with the expansion of increasingly complex industrial, economic and social structures into ever wider areas of the world. At least since Adam Smith, bourgeois theorists of capitalism have triumphantly heralded this expansion as progressive and unilinear, limited only by the emergence in the twentieth century of socialist regimes. Insofar as there remain in the world today differences in levels of development and national wealth, these can be best overcome, according to orthodox theory, through the further growth of capitalism. The job of neoclassical development economics is to chart this path of growth for the so-called less-developed countries (LDCs).

The view from the left is very different. Where bourgeois theorists see a story of triumph and progress, radical theorists see one of domination and exploitation in both imperialist and neocolonialist modes on the one hand and struggles for independence on the other. Radicals are unanimous in rejecting the orthodox view as theoretically false and politically inadequate.

From afar, this radical approach might be thought to be a unified theoretical position that can be fairly easily differentiated from its orthodox opposite. To some degree this is true. But the left has also generated in the past two decades complex theoretical debates and opposing positions. Radical theorists differ, that is, concerning basic issues in their story. Is the develop-

Manuscript prepared for this volume.

ment of capitalism a necessary, if unfortunate, step in the path of develop-ment for any country? Are the economic structures that have developed in the various nations that were formerly colonies best characterized as capital-ist? If so, is it capitalism in the same form as developed in Europe and North America, or a new and indigenous form of capitalism? If not, then how should the economies of the LDCs be characterized?

While most radical analyses accept the existence of a world capitalism system, they differ on how to understand the basic dynamic of this system and on how to describe the relations between the more- and less-developed nations within this system. Again, while most, but not all, radical analyses question whether the present economic structures of LDCs will allow devel-opment, they differ as to how to characterize the barriers preventing growth. Radical interpretations also disagree as to how much is to be accepted from the theories of Marx and the Marxist tradition. The spectrum runs from what might be considered orthodox Marxist theories of development to theories that, while acknowledging the importance of Marx, in effect reject nearly all of his important claims about the status and development of the colonial world.

In this essay, we analyze three of the theories that have emerged as contending positions on the left. These three—Dependency Theory as formu-lated by Andre Gunder Frank, the Modes of Production school, and the theory of Samir Amin—by no means exhaust the radical perspective. This article, then, is not a survey of radical theories of development.[2] Rather, we hope that by looking in depth at three of the alternative views, the issues around which much of the debates have revolved will be clarified.

The three positions that we have chosen are not only major contenders in the debate, but they are related in important ways both historically and conceptually. Theories arise at least partly in reaction to other existing theo-ries that are judged inadequate by those seeking a new departure. The new theory takes up and recasts the challenge of the old one and is best under-stood in light of this challenge. A theory, then, has at least two tasks: a negative or critical one of arguing against its predecessors, and a positive or constructive one of providing an alternative account of the issues in dispute and of raising new questions. To understand a theory, then, requires placing it in the narrative of the debates in which it arose and developed.

The three theories we have selected have this relationship. Frank's work can be taken as the beginning of the modern debate on the left concerning development.[3] The Modes of Production school arises in direct response to what were seen as inadequacies in Frank's theory of underdevelopment. Amin's work represents an attempt to incorporate and synthesize into an encompassing theory of the world capitalist system various of the theoretical insights of Dependency Theory, the Modes of Production position, and more orthodox Marxist treatments.

This essay is intended to be, for the most part, an introduction to these three positions and, thus, is primarily analytic and expository. Its aim is to clarify the structure of the different theories and the issues of contention among them in order to allow those unfamiliar with the material a way into what has become a complex and sophisticated literature.[4]

The essay proceeds as follows. The second section presents Frank's theory of underdevelopment, focusing on the structure of his theoretical model and how it departs from the model of development in neoclassical economics. The third section is a discussion of two critics of Frank, Sanjaya Lall and Robert Brenner. Both Lall and Brenner are sympathetic critics, at least to the extent that they agree with Frank that the neoclassical position must be rejected and a radical alternative provided. Their criticisms illustrate some of the theoretical disagreements that Frank's version of Dependency Theory has generated.

Section four provides an analysis of the Modes of Production school. We analyze this position in terms of three distinguishable approaches: the articulation of modes of production, the colonial or peripheral modes of production, and the internationalization of capital. The focus of the discussion is not only on the basic claims of the three approaches, but also on the interrelations and differences among them. We also situate the overall Modes of Production position in the context of the general debate by analyzing the background and motivation for its emergence. In the fifth section, Amin's theory is presented. We end this section with a brief discussion of a recent reply by Amin to his critics in which points of contact and disagreement between his theory and the others we discuss are further clarified.

II. FRANK AND DEPENDENCY THEORY

Andre Gunder Frank is generally credited as the father of Dependency Theory.[5] *Capitalism and Underdevelopment in Latin America,* written in the early sixties and published in English in 1967, was the first important statement of the theory.[6] While Frank certainly had predecessors, as he readily acknowledges, his book can still be used to mark the opening salvo in the debate over Dependency Theory, in part because this book continues to be very influential and is widely cited by both exponents and critics of Dependency Theory. To understand the structure of Frank's argument, however, it is necessary to keep in mind its antecedents, both the positions Frank critized and the authors upon whom he relied in formulating his own position.

Frank's work grew out of a reaction to both orthodox neoclassical work on development and to the views of certain traditional orthodox Marxists, in particular, those prevalent among the Communist Parties in Latin America. According to Frank, both of these opposing positions shared in certain important regards theoretical theses that were faulty. Positively, Frank's views were influenced by the structuralist theory of Prebisch and others in Latin America and by the work of the so-called neo-Marxists, especially that of Paul Baran.[7] In fact, in the theoretical configuration of development economics Dependency Theory is perhaps best located on the continuum somewhere between orthodox structuralist theory and Marxism.

A central thesis shared, according to Frank, by both neoclassical and orthodox Marxist theories of development, and of which he was critical, was that capitalism was a normal and necessary stage of development. This conception of capitalism was part of a more general view of development as occurring through a series of stages. In addition, according to Frank, both of these positions accepted a general dualistic view of so-called Third World societies. Of course, these theses were expressed by each position in very different theoretical language and supported by antithetical theoretical arguments. And, needless to say, the implications each drew from these theses could not be more different. For the neoclassical, capitalism was the end of development, while for the Marxist, it was a necessary, if regrettable, stage to be transcended by socialism. But both agreed that any (nonsocialist) country that needed to develop had to do so within the framework of capitalism, and moreover, that the operations of the capitalist system (of course, conceived differently by the two positions) would lead to higher levels of development in the normal course of things.

In particular, Dependency Theory was defined against the prevailing neoclassical position.[8] That view starts from the assumption that the economies of all countries can be arranged on a scale from least to most developed (from backward to advanced, or from low-income to high-income, modified perhaps by the degree of oil reserves). Development is taken to be a unilinear process, and all nations have undergone and will continue to undergo essentially the same process. Presumably, according to this approach, at some point in the past all countries were at a stage of economic development that would now be considered undeveloped. For reasons generally taken to be extraneous to the theory, at some point certain countries began to develop economically, while others lagged behind or failed to develop at all. Different levels of development reflect different starting points and different growth rates. The presently undeveloped countries, then, have yet to undergo this process, and they should see their future in the past course of the presently more developed countries.

The orthodox measure of development is the accumulation of wealth (or "use-values"). According to this measure, most countries in the world are obviously relatively undeveloped in comparison to the so-called First World; but, at the same time, most countries have at least sectors of their economies that are relatively developed in comparison to the overall economy.

Neoclassical theory typically understands the condition of less-developed countries in terms of what is called a dualistic economy. According to the theory of dualism, an economy of an undeveloped nation has two sectors, one traditional and one relatively modern and developed. The two sectors are taken to be largely independent of each other. They may be linked during the transition to modern growth, however, in that the traditional sector may provide labor and an agricultural surplus to the modern sector. The modern sector, moreover, is intertwined in the world capitalist market, while the traditional sector is in effect precapitalist and more or less untouched by capitalist market relations. The dynamic of growth is due to trade and general economic activity, so the process of development of the whole economy is seen to involve the modernization of transformation of the traditional sector so as to bring it into the sphere of the market and thus expose it to the possibilities of trade and development offered by the free market.

Methodologically, neoclassical theory claims to present a model of economic backwardness and development that is based on empirical observation and certain theoretical assumptions about the nature of market activity and economic rationality. The market is taken as the central institutional structure that organizes economic activity and rewards efficiency. Individual actors in the market are taken to be rational, or at least capable of rational decision-making in light of given needs, desires, and possible rewards. Neoclassical theory is essentially methodologically individualist in that it seeks to understand economic development ultimately in terms of the market behaviors of individual actors. Instances where development has failed to occur are explained either in terms of the absence of certain necessary conditions or in terms of local conditions that distort the proper operation of the market mechanism, preventing actors from behaving rationally, or the like.

Frank's original formulation of Dependency Theory begins with a rejection of two of the central theses of this neoclassical dualism. First, Frank rejects the dualist model of the economies of the undeveloped nations in which there are two sectors, only one of which, the more developed, is capitalist. Rather, according to Frank, during the era of European capitalist expansion, most areas, even the geographically remote, were incorporated within the network of capitalist relations. As a result, all parts of the economies of undeveloped nations should be seen to be within the web of capitalism. Not to see them as part of the capitalist system is necessarily to misunderstand their nature and operation. Frank puts this claim forward as an empirical thesis: "A mounting body of evidence suggests, and I am confident that future historical research will confirm, that the expansion of the capitalist system over the past centuries effectively and entirely penetrated even the apparently most isolated sectors of the underdeveloped world."[9]

The second thesis of dualism that Frank rejects is that the present condition of the undeveloped countries is similar to some original, predevelopment stage of the presently developed nations. Rather, Frank asserts, despite certain surface similarities (noncomplexity, nonindustrialization, and/or poverty) between the present condition of the undeveloped nations and the reconstructed past of the now developed nations, neither the colonial past nor the present of the undeveloped nations resembles in any important respect the past of the developed nations. If we accept the assumption, which Frank seems to accept, that at some point in the past prior to the emergence and expansion of capitalism all countries were more or less the same developmentally (that is, that there was some kind of "original stage" the exact nature of which is never specified by Frank), then it follows that the present condition of the undeveloped nations is not original, primal, or traditional; rather, this state is itself a product of the historical development of capitalism on a world scale.

This point has two important implications. First, there is no single universal trajectory for development that is followed by all nations, for obviously the discrepancy between the more- and less-developed nations today is a result of at least two different developmental paths. Second, if we call the original, predevelopment stage one of undevelopment, then it is no longer correct to refer to the present condition of the less-developed nations today as undeveloped, since their present condition is itself a product of an historical, developmental sequence. Thus, Frank introduces a new term, "underdeveloped," to characterize the condition of the presently less-developed countries: "The now developed countries were never *under*developed, though they may have been *un*developed."[10]

Frank shows little concern for the condition he calls undeveloped. The only relevant history for Frank concerns the "development of underdevelopment," and this process only begins with the penetration of capitalism. What came before is of little concern to Frank, and he has a good theoretical reason, within his model, for this attitude. Whatever the conditions that characterized various areas, regions, or countries in their original, i.e., pre-capitalist, state, these conditions had little or no impact on subsequent development. Whatever the differences, if any, in their original conditions, all countries that are underdeveloped today are characterized by essentially the same conditions, so that the crucial variables explaining this present condition cannot include the original state.

Frank does discuss conditions in underdeveloped areas before the penetration of capitalism in explaining why some countries became developed and others underdeveloped. The kinds of conditions that enter into the explanation at this point, however, concern natural or physical factors such as natural resources, climate, soil fertility, and the like. They do not include facts about the economic and social structures that predominated in these areas. Thus, if underdevelopment is in the first instance a description of an economic and social condition, then the analogous original conditions, i.e., economic and social, do not enter crucially into the explanation. There is, however, one important historical case where Frank would admit that the original, precapitalist conditions do enter crucially into the explanation. This, of course, is the explanation of the original emergence of capitalism in Europe. But this case is, for the most part, an element of the story of the development of development, and not that of underdevelopment. It follows from what has been said that the process of development for Frank is the process of capitalist development, and that the history of development is the history of capitalism.[11]

Underdevelopment is a condition that characterizes the entire economy of a country, regardless of the different levels of sectoral development. It is a condition, moreover, that characterizes all the presently developing nations. This suggests (although by no means entails) that underdevelopment cannot be explained simply in terms of factors internal to the social and economic histories of the underdeveloped nations, for it seems highly unlikely that the histories of so many nations in different parts of the world with different initial conditions would have been such as to have led to the same outcome. Rather, what is suggested is that there is some common, external causal factor. The theoretical task that Frank undertakes is to identify this factor and incorporate it into a theory that explains the nature and development of underdevelopment.

To accomplish this task, Frank constructs a theoretical model that claims to show how the present condition of underdeveloped countries came about historically and is maintained today. This model employs certain theoretical concepts and posits the existence of certain entities or processes. The concepts are theoretical in the sense that their full meaning can only be grasped in the context of their role in the theoretical model. The posited entities or processes are theoretical in a somewhat different sense. First, their natures can be explained fully only in relation to the model and the theoretical concepts it uses. Second, they cannot be perceived or picked out independently of the theoretical model. They are observable, that is, only through the "lens" of the model. At the same time, the explanatory acceptability of the theoretical model depends, at least in part, on the acceptability of the theoretical concepts. As we shall see below, much of the critical reaction to Frank and, indeed, much of the debate concerning Dependency Theory revolves around the acceptability of various theoretical concepts and their utilization in explanations of development.

The key concept in this model is dependency, hence Dependency Theory. This concept is used to pick out and characterize the object of study, namely, the present condition of developing nations. That is, an initial distinction is assumed between developed and developing countries. What are initially identified as developing countries are supposedly picked out through a comparison with the developed countries in terms of certain indices, for instance, an index of wealth, both as to its level and distribution.[12] The so-called developing nations, Frank then suggests, are better considered as *under*developed rather than *un*developed in order to distinguish states of development historically produced from those that can be considered in some sense "original" conditions. These underdeveloped nations are then characterized as participating in a relation of dependency. It is because of their dependency relationship, which is to be elaborated in the model, that these countries are underdeveloped. That is, dependency causes underdevelopment.

Dependency relations, in Frank's view, require two parties, one dominant and the other dependent. For Frank, the central dependency relationship exists between the various countries of the developed world and those that are underdeveloped. Historically, the relationship was between a colony and the imperial power that conquered it. Today, it is more a matter of an underdeveloped country and those developed countries with which it has primary economic relations. Various names have been given to the parties to these relationships: metropolis/satellite, core/periphery, or center/periphery.

The metropolis-satellite relationship, to use the terms preferred by Frank, is one of dependency because of two features. First, the development of the satellite is dependent on the development of the metropolis, that is, on forces external to the satellite's economy and society. The suggestion in the model is that it is an asymmetrical relationship, with the development of the metropolis being for the most part independent, that is, determined by factors largely internal to the metropolitan economy and society. Thus, dependency in the first instance is a relation of unequal power. The metropolis has power over the course of development in the satellite, but not vice versa. It should be noted that this power need not be consciously realized or exercised, but might be (and generally is) the unintended result of structural relations and operations.

Frank sees the determining relationship as one-sided. Especially in his early work, he does not pay much attention to the reciprocal influence of the satellite on the metropolis. He has, that is to say, an insufficently dialectical understanding of the dependency relation. To say that the metropolis exercises greater power in the sense that Frank stipulates need not commit one to the denial that there is a sense in which the metropolis is also dependent on the satellite. The key to the relationship is control. The metropolis exercises greater power in that it has greater control within the relationship, in the way that a slavemaster who has control of slaves exercises greater power over those slaves, even while he or she may be very dependent on the slaves and, in general, on the master-slave relationship to reproduce him or herself as slavemaster.

The dependent development of the satellite is such as to disadvantage it further and exacerbate certain problems it experiences such as poverty and distorted development. The loss for the underdeveloped nation is twofold. Not only is it not in control of its own development, but it does not materially benefit from the relation of dependency. It is worth making this second point because a more sophisticated version of neoclassical theory might argue that developing countries do at times enter into dependency relations with developed nations due to certain types of market asymmetries, but that this dependency (here seen as just loss of control in some respects or to some degree) benefits the developing countries because it fosters development per se. It is this latter point that Frank denies. Dependency, for Frank, is a relation of exploitation, and, like "exploitation," "dependency" has a definite negative normative force as well as a descriptive role in Frank's theory.[13] It is also worth pointing out that the object of benefit or harm for Frank is the nation-state as such, rather than, for instance, classes. Frank does discuss the fact that certain classes, local ruling classes, can and do benefit, in the short term at least, from underdevelopment, but this benefit is understood against the backdrop of the harm done to the nation as a whole.

While the locus of dependency relationships in Frank's model is the nation-state and relations between nations, the scope of the theory is properly the world capitalist system. Nations are taken to be component parts of this system. To understand the development of underdevelopment in a particular country, it is necessary to place that country's history in the context of this larger system. It is important, according to Frank, to see capitalism as a world system and to understand its central structures. To fail to do so might well lead one to misidentify both the important structures within the underdeveloped countries and to misunderstand the nature of the dependency relation. Dependency, as we shall see, is explained in terms of its function within the larger system, and the theoretical model used in the explanation must, obviously, correctly characterize the system if the explanation is to be successful. A complete explanation of underdevelopment, then, would require nothing less than a full account of the origin, nature, and development of capitalism, for, as Frank writes, "one and the same historical process of the expansion and development of capitalism throughout the world has simultaneously generated—and continues to generate—both economic development and structural underdevelopment."[14]

By specifying that the scope of his theory is the world *capitalist* system, Frank has in effect raised the issue of the definition of "capitalism" that he is using. As various commentators have noted, Frank does not explicitly define "capitalism."[15] Nevertheless, given any number of remarks that he makes, it is a fairly straightforward task to discern how he uses the term. As we have said, Frank takes capitalism to be a world system, one that has existed since at least the sixteenth century. It has gone through three stages: mercantilist, industrial, and financial capitalism. What has remained constant through all the stages is a certain kind of exchange relationship characteristic of metropolis-satellite relations: "Whatever we may wish to say about its mercantilist, then industrial, then financial capitalist metropolis, in the peripheries of the world capitalist system the essential nature of the metropolis-satellite relations remains commercial, however 'feudal' or personal seeming these relations may appear."[16] If the periphery has been capitalist since the first European incursions, and if what has remained constant across the various stages is the nature of the exchange relations, then capitalism must be defined in terms of this relation.[17] Laclau fills out this definition attributed to Frank in the following way: Frank understands by capitalism "a) a system of production for the market, in which b) profit constitutes the motive of production, and c) this profit is realized for the benefit of someone other than the direct producer, who is thereby dispossessed of it."[18]

If capitalism is defined in terms of market exchange relations of a certain kind, we should specify more exactly what kind they are. As we have seen, according to Laclau's interpretation of Frank, the essential capitalist relation is a market exchange whereby profit is realized for the benefit of someone other than the direct producer. We have also seen that dependency relations in general for Frank involve power relations where one party is disadvantaged to the gain of the other. Third, we have noted that for Frank, the dependency relations that generate underdevelopment must be understood in terms of the capitalist world system. Putting these points together, we can conclude that, for Frank, the essential capitalist relation is a dependency relation and thus a relation of power. In other words, capitalism in the first instance is to be regarded as a system of power, power exercised through a particular form of relation, namely, a market exchange relation.

In what sense are capitalist market exchange relations relations of power? According to Frank, dependency relations in general and metropolis-satellite relations within capitalism in particular are best characterized as monopolistic and extractive. The metropolis exerts monopolistic control over economic and trade relations in the periphery. Monopoly domination within a market is, of course, a position of power. This position of power allows the metropolis to extract an economic surplus from the satellite. The appropriation of this surplus and its accumulation in and under the control of the metropolis is the central factor that deprives the underdeveloped nation of the ability to control its own growth and that thus leaves it dependent. The monopolistic, extractive relation was initially established by force of arms, but once it is in place, subsequent development perpetuates it through the structures of dependency and underdevelopment.

Two points should be noted about the monopolistic-extractive nature of the metropolis-satellite relation. The first is that any theory that attempts to conceptualize economic exchanges in what Frank considers the underdeveloped nations in terms of equivalent market exchanges necessarily, from his point of view, distorts the nature of what transpires. The outstanding theoretical issue is, of course, how to verify the existence of monopolistic market distortions and the "exploitative" transfer of surplus. This is a fundamental point of contention between neoclassical theories and Dependency Theory. In general, where a neoclassical theorist would see a free market and mutual advantage, Frank sees a structure of monopolistic relations and surplus transfer.

The second point to note is that Frank's concept of economic surplus is taken more or less directly from the work of Paul Baran. Frank appears to believe that Baran's concept is the same as that used by Marx in his analysis of "the surplus value created by producers and its appropriation by capitalists."[19] Many commentators have pointed out, however, that according to Marx's theory, the extraction of surplus takes place within the capital-wage labor relation within production, while for Frank, the extraction is a function of exchange relations in the market. The two concepts are, therefore, not the same. One difference to be noted in this context is that Marx emphasizes that for the purposes of his model he is assuming that market relations are exchanges of equivalents, while, as we have seen, Frank takes them to be monopolistic power relations involving the exchange of non-equivalents.

If Frank does conceive of capitalism in terms of a certain kind of market exchange relation, with production oriented towards the market, then three points should be noted that will be relevant to later criticisms of Frank. First, if the nature of the metropolis-satellite relationship remains a constant, then the analysis of the "development of underdevelopment" is, in a certain sense, ahistorical.[20] The central dynamic and structures are the same at all points in the history of the phenomenon. For Frank, the focus of his theory, therefore, is "the continuity and ubiquity of the structural essentials of economic development and underdevelopment throughout the expansion and development of the capitalist system at all times and places."[21] What is to be emphasized is continuity, not change.

Second, what defines the essential nature of an economic relation is its relationship to the larger system, and in particular, whether it is caught up in a commercial market exchange network that is connected to metropolitan development. Thus Frank can say, in the quotation given above, that however "feudal seeming" a relation may be, if it is part of such a market network, then the relation is capitalist. Among the things to be noted here is the implication for the theory-ladenness of the possible observations involved. Merely observing a relation in a supposedly theory-neutral way would not allow the correct characterization of the relation. A relation that might at first observation be "seen" as feudal is really not feudal. Only by viewing it in terms of the theory can the relation be "seen" correctly.

The third point to be noted in light of Frank's definition of capitalism is that he focuses on exchange relations and pays relatively little attention to the so-called relations of production. This emphasis is especially obvious in his early work. The concept of the relations of production is one that is traditionally prominent in many Marxist analyses. Therefore, some Marxist critics in particular take exception to Frank on this point. And as we shall see, the dispute over where the theoretical emphasis should be placed, on exchange or on production relations, is one of the key points in the Dependency Theory debates. In part the dispute is over what is to function as the key explanatory variable or, in terms of the theoretical model, over what is to be taken as an independent and what as a dependent variable.

In our discussion of dependency relations thus far we have focused on the form of the relation of metropolis to satellite at the level of nation-states. This relation is the primary one within Frank's model. However, the nation-

nation relation is not the only form of a metropolis-satellite relation for Frank. Rather, there is a chain of such relationships, all of which manifest the same form or structure. At the pinnacle of this chain is the nation-nation relationship of metropolis-satellite. But within the satellite itself, the structurally identical relationship is repeated on lower and increasingly local levels of the economy. The theoretical model, then, can be seen as a series of steps, each connection from step to lower step reiterating the same structural relations. As Frank puts it:

> It is a major thesis of this essay that this same structure extends from the macrometropolitan center of the world capitalist system "down" to the most supposedly isolated agricultural workers, who, through this chain of interlinked metropolitan-satellite relationships, are tied to the central world metropolis and thereby incorporated into the world capitalist system as a whole.[22]

There may seem at first to be real differences among the variety of metropolis-satellite dependency relationships; for instance, a nation-nation relationship seems very unlike that between an owner of a latifundium and a dependent sharecropper. Nevertheless, Frank maintains, they are essentially the same in structure, and it is their structure that determines their nature, despite the ready and apparent surface differences. This point, of course, can only be appreciated by "seeing" the relationships through the lens of the appropriate theory.

One last feature of Frank's theoretical model needs to be mentioned. The model has definite implications for the type of political developments and, in particular, for the nature of the class structure that one can expect to accompany the development of economic underdevelopment. It is necessary for Frank to speak to the issue of political development in order to provide some mechanism to account for how the policy of underdevelopment, as he calls it, is put into effect and maintained, especially after an underdeveloped colony achieves de jure independence, thus making the option to use the open coercion of an imperial power less available.[23]

Within the model, classes are understood in the first instance in terms of structural positions within a system of power relations. At each point in the metropolis-satellite chain, the structure of the chain creates certain objective interests, most important, the interest in controlling the monopoly relationship at that point in the chain so as to be able to benefit from the extractive power available at that position. The group that coheres around that interest is in effect the ruling class of that area, region, or nation. Since the ruling class at each point in the structure is dependent on the entire structure remaining more or less the same, so that the monopoly relationships can be maintained, each ruling class in effect bolsters every other ruling class. All ruling classes thus have an interest in perpetuating the development of underdevelopment, for that is precisely the structure that allows them to satisfy their interests as they find them. As Frank puts it:

> My thesis holds that the group interests which led to the continued underdevelopment of Chile [as a case in point] and the economic development of some other countries were themselves created by the same economic structure which encompassed all these groups: the world capitalist system. . . . It was in the nature of the structure of this system to produce interests leading to underdevelopment in the countries of the periphery, such as Chile, once they had already been effectively incorporated into the system as satellites.[24]

Frank does not explicitly address the question of why the same groups that were economically powerful were also politically dominant, so that they could implement politically the policies that would benefit them economically. Any attempt on the part of Frank to fill in this gap, either in terms of an instrumental version of the Marxist theory of the state, or in terms of a general theory of the convergence of economic and political elites, would only push the problem back one level.

The theoretical model sketched above is to be found in Frank's early work. His later work carries the model forward in most of its essentials, but there are a few points of theoretical development, especially in *Dependent Accumulation and Underdevelopment,* that deserve a brief mention.[25] In this book, Frank announces that he is responding to three criticisms of his earlier work. The three criticisms amount in effect to the charges that Frank did not pay sufficient attention to relations of production and thus overemphasized external as opposed to internal variables in his explanation of underdevelopment; that he was insufficiently historical and thus failed to appreciate and account for important differences across stages of the development of underdevelopment; and that he did not succeed in demonstrating the interconnections between metropolitan development and the dependent underdevelopment.[26] In response, Frank admits that a complete theoretical model of underdevelopment would have to pay more attention to the mode of production within the underdeveloped nation and to how it changes or does not change through the different stages of capitalist development. Furthermore, it would have to be more sensitive to the ways in which the dynamic of the development of underdevelopment can help to determine the nature of metropolitan development, which, of course, in turn helps determine the further course of the development of underdevelopment; or in a word, Frank admits that his model should be more dialectical. He thinks that these changes can be incorporated by refocusing the model more on the accumulation process seen from the point of view of the world system.

We cannot go into a thorough analysis of how Frank amends his theoretical model to account for these criticisms. It will have to suffice to say that while his focus in *Dependent Accumulation and Underdevelopment* is somewhat different from that of his earlier work in that more attention is paid to accumulation on the world scale, the essentials of his model still remain more or less as they were and as we outlined them above. Despite discussions of the accumulation process, his work still seems to focus on capitalism as, in the first instance, a process of exchange and not of a certain form of relations of production. Frank does in this later work use the concept of mode of production, but he offers no real analysis of the concept, and it seems to function less as an explanatory concept and more as a way of indicating awareness of historical difference. "Mode of production" as used by Frank allows him to mark off different ways in which dependent economies have been organized. But to the degree that the concept is focused on the organiza- tion of production, it remains subordinated to the notion of exchange rela- tions. Whatever the mode of production within the dependent country, the satellite is still considered to exist within the world capitalist system and thus in the last analysis to be capitalist. In the end, we believe that Frank's theoret- ical model and its explanatory force remains basically the same in his later work.

Before going on to discuss other positions in the Dependency Theory debates that developed out of or in opposition to Frank, it is worth examining some of the criticisms of Frank. In particular, we will look in detail at the arguments of two critics, Lall and Brenner. They can be seen as two repre- sentative positions critical of the original formulation of Dependency Theory by Frank. Lall concentrates on the adequacy of the concept of dependence. Brenner casts a wider net, questioning Frank's use of concepts such as capital- ism and class, and arguing that Frank has the order of explanation wrong. The arguments of a third critic, Laclau, will then figure in our discussion of the Modes of Production approach. While those are only three among the many critics of Frank, they raise interesting and important theoretical issues that help illuminate Frank's approach to development.

III. TWO METHODOLOGICAL CRITICS OF FRANK

Lall

Sanjaya Lall provides a somewhat limited but methodologically interesting criticism of Frank.[27] Lall's focus is the use of the concept of dependence. His concern, as a sympathetic critic of dependency theory, is that the central concept of the theory, that of a dependency relation, or as he puts it, depen- dence, has not been adequately formulated. In particular, Lall thinks that the concept sometimes seems to be defined in a circular or question-begging manner.

> Less developed countries (LDCs) are poor because they are dependent, and any characteristics that they display signify dependence. In such

tautologous definitions, "dependence" tends to be identified with features of LDCs which the economist in question happens to dislike, and ceases to offer an independent and verifiable explanation of the processes at work in the less developed world.[28]

Lall suggests two criteria that should be used to construct an adequate concept of dependence. The first criterion stipulates that the concept "lay down certain characteristics of dependent economies which are not found in nondependent ones." The second criterion stipulates further that the characteristics so designated "must be shown to affect adversely the course and pattern of development of the dependent countries."[29]

To understand what Lall's point is in suggesting these criteria, it is important to keep in mind a central thesis of dependency theory, namely, that dependence causes underdevelopment. If this thesis is interpreted as an ordinary causal claim, then its claim is that there is a correlation that supports a causal relation between two variables, the condition of being dependent and the condition of being underdeveloped. Now, if we are to verify this thesis, it must be possible to identify these two conditions independently of one another. If, as Lall suggests happens, the condition of being dependent is "identified with features of LDCs which the economist in question happens to dislike," then there is a considerable chance that the same characteristics used to identify one condition will be used to pick out the other. This is especially true given that dependency theory conceives of underdevelopment as a condition that is the result of and results in adverse effects. For example, if being poor is taken to be an essential characteristic of economies that are underdeveloped, then if "dependence" is defined in terms of, or picked out by, the state of being poor, it becomes true by definition that dependent economies are underdeveloped. But if this proposition is true by definition, it cannot be taken to be expressing a causal relation.

For the same reasons that it is necessary to identify the condition of being dependent independently of the condition of being underdeveloped, it is necessary to be able to differentiate dependent from nondependent economies. Again, consider the thesis, dependence causes underdevelopment. Assume that all economies in the world can be (roughly) categorized as either dependent or nondependent. Now, if the thesis is to have any explanatory merit, given our assumption, then it must be true that an economy is underdeveloped if and only if it is dependent. This is just to say that the condition of underdevelopment is caused by, and only by, the condition of dependence. What if, however, the characteristics used to pick out the condition of dependence were also true of some or all economies that are taken initially to be nondependent? If this were the case, then obviously the causal thesis could not be coherently applied and tested.

But this is just what Lall thinks is the case. He surveys a variety of attempts to differentiate dependent from nondependent economies, attempts that include the use of economic and noneconomic, static and dynamic char-

acteristics. In all instances, Lall concludes, the attempt fails. Whatever characteristic or set of characteristics is used, either it applies to some nondependent
economy as well as to dependent ones, or it fails to apply to all dependent
ones. Lall's conclusion is the strong one that

> the concept of dependence as applied to less developed countries is im-
> possible to define and cannot be shown to be causally related to a continu-
> ance of underdevelopment. It is usually given an *arbitrarily selective definition*
> *which picks certain features of a much broader phenomenon of international capitalist*
> *development,* and its selectivity only serves to misdirect analysis and re-
> search in this area.[30]

In our opinion, Lall's conclusion is a little strong, or at least a little
premature. We do find much of his analysis of the use of the concept of
dependence convincing as a criticism internal to Dependency Theory. Dependency theorists do need to pay more attention to the construction of their
concepts, especially that of dependence. However, even if all attempts so far
to construct an adequate concept have failed, that does not prove that the
project as such is wrong-headed and that all future attempts will fail.

An additional point should be made concerning Lall's criticism. Consider
again his claim that all attempts to construct a concept of dependence have
failed to provide a concept that applies to all, and only to, dependent economies. This claim, however, seems to presuppose that there is a way of initially
distinguishing all economies as either dependent or nondependent so as to be
able to determine whether a concept does or does not apply to them. In other
words, the denial of the adequacy of all concept candidates so far seems itself
to presuppose an adequate concept. This may be stating the point too
strongly, however. We might interpret Lall's claim in the following way:
There are certain economies, let us say those of the very poorest LDCs, that
everyone can agree initially are dependent.[31] Likewise, there are certain
economies that everyone can initially agree are nondependent. Let us attempt
to construct a concept of dependence by generalizing from what seem to be
the salient characteristics of these clear cases. Lall's claim, thus interpreted,
is that no concept that will be adequate can be constructed in this way. Again,
we feel that this claim has an a priori ring about it that Lall's argument, which
is essentially inductive, cannot substantiate.

Further, a determined dependency theorist has available the following
reply to Lall: "Even though my concept of dependence seems to you [Lall]
to pick out some economies that you consider to be nondependent, I disagree.
I have carefully constructed my concept and it is a coherent and convincing
one, stipulating conditions that if true, must demonstrate the existence of
dependence. Thus, I consider as dependent all economies to which it applies,
even those that you, given your initial intuitions, want to claim are nondependent. That is, I use my concept to overrule your (and perhaps my own)

intuitions. That is part of the way science progresses." Lall obviously has a reply to his critic, and the discussion goes on. We cannot follow it any further here. Lall's criticism is a methodologically important one, but not one that leaves the determined dependency theorist bereft of moves.

Brenner

Robert Brenner presents a more wide-ranging and extensive criticism of Frank than that of Lall. Brenner concedes that Frank's descriptions of the mechanisms of surplus transfer from the underdeveloped periphery to the developed core and of the resulting distortion of the economies of the periphery "clearly capture important aspects of the functioning reality of underdevelopment."[32] But in Brenner's opinion, while Frank's account may have descriptive adequacy, it fails to explain anything. In particular, it fails to explain the origins of underdevelopment. That is, Brenner rejects Frank's thesis that the development of underdevelopment is part of and necessitated by the development of capitalism in the metropolis.

Most of Brenner's argument is directed against the work of Sweezy and Wallerstein rather than Frank.[33] Since, however, Brenner sees Wallerstein's project of discovering the roots of development in the core as a continuation of and complement to Frank's work, the criticisms can be taken to apply to both theorists. The major problem Brenner has with the Frank–Wallerstein position has to do with the definition of capitalism it assumes. As we saw above, Frank (and Wallerstein) conceptualizes capitalism in terms of a system of power exercised through exchange relations and involving production oriented toward profit in the market. The essential relation marking an economy as capitalist, the point at which power is in the first instance exercised, is a certain type of market exchange within a world system of metropolis-satellite dependency relations.

According to Brenner, it follows from this conception of capitalism that the accumulation process is centrally concerned with the generation of absolute surplus value, value that is extracted by casting a wider and more intensive net over labor. It also follows from this starting point that the issue of the origins and development of capitalism primarily concerns the rise of a world commercial network and an expanding world market. In addition, Brenner argues that Frank and Wallerstein's model of capitalism leads them to understand class structure as determined in a rather mechanistic fashion by market relations. Market opportunities determine the nature of economic development in a given area, and in particular, the nature of production. The resulting requirements on production, in turn, determine the nature of the class structure. The classes that arise are structured by the dominant production process, and the production process that arises is the one best suited in a given area at a given time to allow the maximum extraction of absolute surplus value by the ruling class. This model and the explanation of both development and underdevelopment that it supports is, according to Brenner, theoretically inadequate and leads to empirically false explanations.

To appreciate why Brenner takes the Frank-Wallerstein position to be theoretically and explanatorily inadequate, it is necessary to contrast it with Brenner's understanding of capitalism. For Brenner, the defining and unique characteristic of capitalism is its tendency, not simply to develop, but to do so by way of expanding the productive forces. In other words, capitalism is a system of production involving, in particular, the extraction of *relative* surplus value.

> For capitalism differs from all pre-capitalist modes of production in its *systematic* tendency to unprecedented, though neither continuous nor unlimited, economic development—in particular through the expansion of what might be called (after Marx's terminology) relative as opposed to absolute surplus value.[34]

Expansion of productivity through technical innovation, Marx's revolutionary expansion of the forces of production, can occur only where it is possible to move labor in and out of the production process as best suits the available technology. Otherwise, the incentive for innovation would be lacking. But this form of labor mobility, according to Brenner, can only occur within a certain class structure, namely, one where labor is free wage labor that is at the mercy of market forces, in other words, where labor-power is a commodity. Thus, in Brenner's view, capitalism as a system of production oriented toward a specific form of accumulation (based on the extraction of relative surplus value) necessitates a specific class structure. But in contrast to the Frank-Wallerstein view, Brenner's position is that capitalism does not create the class structure it requires. Rather, capitalism can only exist within the confines of this class structure. The initial emergence of this class structure is thus a necessary condition for the emergence of capitalism, and the reproduction of this class structure is a necessary condition for the continued reproduction of capitalism. The problem of the origins of capitalism for Brenner, then, is not the development of a world market system as it is for the Frank-Wallerstein position. Rather, the problem for Brenner is the emergence of the necessary class structure, or in other words, the genesis of labor-power as a commodity.

Brenner's model of capitalism, then, leads to the result that the crucial explanatory variable in his account of underdevelopment is the class structure. Capitalism can exist only where the class structure accommodates it. And what ultimately determines the class structure are the outcomes of class struggles. The outcomes of class struggles, however, according to Brenner, cannot be determined in advance; it is not a matter of a mechanistic, deterministic process. Rather, in each instance under study, the particular conditions of class conflict, especially the opportunities available to the "ruling class" to exploit labor through extraction of either absolute or relative surplus value, must be analyzed in order to understand the possibilities inherent in the situation that could, but did not have to be, realized. Market opportunities do not determine class, as in the Frank-Wallerstein view. Rather, the outcomes of class struggle condition what kind of market relations are to be engaged in, for example, whether profit maximization is to be pursued. On Brenner's view, and contrary to Frank and Wallerstein, "neither economic development nor underdevelopment are *directly* dependent upon, caused by, one another. Each is the product of a specific evolution of class relations, *in part* determined historically 'outside' capitalism, in relationship with non-capitalist modes."[35]

Development and underdevelopment, thus, are explained by Brenner in terms of the particular opportunities for surplus extraction made possible by the different class configurations, free wage labor, in the case of development, and forced feudal or slave labor, at least initially, in the case of underdevelopment. In particular,

> the onset of a capitalist dynamic of development was thus, in the first appearance, made possible as an unintended consequence of class conflicts—conflicts in which the peasantry freed themselves from the extra-economic controls of the ruling class, while the latter secured ownership of the land. The resulting overall class structure of production and reproduction made possible an unprecedented degree of correspondence between the needs of surplus extraction and the *continuing development* of the productive forces through accumulation and innovation.[36]

Similarly,

> the development of underdevelopment was rooted in the class structure of production based on the extension of absolute surplus labour, which determined a sharp *disjuncture* between the requirements for the development of the productive forces (productivity of labour) and the structure of profitability of the economy as a whole.[37]

Brenner, then, presents a model of capitalism that contrasts with that of Frank, not so much in terms of the description of underdevelopment, as in the account of the origins of the structures that produce the conditions of underdevelopment. The two positions start off with different conceptions of capitalism. This initial difference leads to differences concerning the central dynamic of capitalism, in particular, the nature of the characteristic accumulation process. Given these differences, Brenner and Frank arrive at different conclusions about the importance of class structure as an explanatory variable. For Brenner it is central; for Frank it plays at best a minor explanatory role. It is important to reiterate that for Brenner, class structure is the outcome of class struggles, and the outcome of class struggles cannot be determined in advance; or at least, the outcome is a variable the determination of which falls outside the theoretical model in question.

We have, then, two contrasting models and an important difference in the form of explanation involved in each. How might we decide between them? We cannot give a complete answer to this question here. But it is instructive to summarize the nature of the criticisms that Brenner makes of the Frank–Wallerstein position. First, as we have seen, Brenner contends that the Frank–Wallerstein view is empirically inadequate. Brenner presents case studies of development in Poland, France, England, the Caribbean, and Virginia. In each case, Brenner argues, what happened historically can better be accounted for by his model of capitalism than by the Frank–Wallerstein model. On this level, joining the argument would require that both parties agree on some initial description of what actually occurred in each case history. Each side would then have to attempt to demonstrate in detail why its theoretical redescription and explanation of the history was superior to its rival. This process obviously does not admit of a clear way to establish the superior position, and it has the possible immediate problem of the two sides not agreeing even as to a common initial description of the subject matter.

The second form of criticism is based on conceptual analysis. Here the important claim made by Brenner is that the definition of capitalism used by Frank and Wallerstein is inadequate. The argument is that their definition gives a necessary but not sufficient condition for the existence of capitalism. Brenner admits that "there is no doubt that capitalism is a system in which production for a profit via exchange predominates." However, "production for exchange is perfectly compatible with a system in which it is either unnecessary or impossible, or both, to reinvest in expanded, improved production in order to 'profit.' "[38] The claim is that production for exchange for profit is compatible with, and indeed takes place in, systems that even Frank and Wallerstein would have to admit were not capitalist. They could reply, of course, by denying that such systems were capitalist or by claiming that it is a matter of degree, and therefore that once production for exchange for profit becomes the dominant relation, the claimed compatibility is no longer possible. A second criticism follows from Brenner's claim that there are problems with how Frank and Wallerstein understand some of their basic concepts. This charge is that the difficulties in correctly conceptualizing the object of study prevent Frank and Wallerstein from being able to raise certain questions that Brenner finds important. And in turn, not being able to raise certain questions further prevents Frank and Wallerstein from being able to confront and explain certain facts that Brenner holds as central to his account.[39] This charge, of course, could be parried by denying the importance of the questions and facts under contention.

The third form of criticism has to do with explanatory adequacy. Brenner makes a number of points in this regard. For example, the Frank–Wallerstein model, Brenner contends, assumes that the individuals who control the means of production have the motivation, the rationality, and the freedom to pursue profit maximization. That is, as Brenner interprets it, the model assumes "the extra-historical universe of *homo oeconomicus,* of individual profit maximizers competing on the market, outside of any system of social relations of exploitation."[40] But there are at least two related problems with this assumption. In the first place, this assumed universe is not some abstract, extra-historical realm; rather, it is the world of capitalism. The conditions specified by this model exist in, and only in, the capitalist market. Insofar as this model is used to explain the initial emergence of capitalism, and insofar as it assumes in its explanatory framework conditions that only existence within capitalism, it obviously begs the question.[41]

This is a familiar criticism, made first by Marx of Adam Smith. It is because Brenner finds Sweezy, Frank, and Wallerstein all guilty of this same fundamental mistake, as well as guilty of sharing "individualistic-mechanist presuppositions" with Smith, that he labels them "neo-Smithians." They are, however, neo-Smithians with a twist, or rather, an inversion, for "it has been their [Sweezy, Frank, Wallerstein] intention to negate the optimistic model of economic advance derived from Adam Smith."[42] Smith's model of economic development is inverted to become Frank's model of the development of underdevelopment. The result of this inversion, according to Brenner, is "an alternative theory of capitalist development which is, in its central aspects, the mirror image of the 'progressist' thesis they wish to surpass."[43]

The second problem with the assumption of rational profit-maximization is that it reflects the failure on the part of both Frank and Wallerstein to understand adequately the relations between individuals and social structures, in particular, class structures. In Brenner's view, the individual is much more produced by and constrained by class structures than Frank or Wallerstein seem to allow. This criticism is of a piece with Brenner's contention that Frank and Wallerstein do not accord class structure its proper explanatory role as a variable. As Brenner reads them, Frank and Wallerstein make class structure (reflected first of all in the relations of production) a consequence of the behavior of rational individuals in the market. For Brenner, this view has the relationship completely backwards. Individual rationality and behavior must be understood as conditioned and constrained by the existing class structure. Not to see the relation in this way, Brenner implies, is to have a fundamental mistake at the very basis of one's social theory.[44]

This discussion does not exhaust the criticisms Brenner makes of the Frank–Wallerstein model, to say nothing of criticisms made by other commentators in the debates over Dependency Theory.[45] The criticisms we have mentioned do reflect, however, some of the levels on which the issues are joined and some of the more methodological considerations that enter into the debates. We now proceed to examine some of the positions that have emerged out of these debates with Frank.

IV. THE MODES OF PRODUCTION SCHOOL

The debate concerning Dependency Theory entered a new stage with the emergence of the Modes of Production (MOP) school. The various approaches encompassed by this rubric represent both a criticism of the early forms of Dependency Theory, chiefly as represented by the writings of Frank (and, later, Wallerstein), and an extension of the basic problematic of Dependency Theory. The focus of the explanation of the persistence of underdevelopment is shifted by the MOP theorists away from what they understand to be the excessive emphasis in traditional Dependency Theory on a global scheme that exaggerates the role of external relations and markets. Instead, while not denying the importance of macro phenomena, relations between nations, and flows of commodities, they have focused on developing the concept of mode of production in an attempt to construct an alternative understanding of the phenomenon of underdevelopment. Despite the shift of focus, the object of investigation remains the specific forms of development of what is taken to be the periphery of the world economy. Moreover, the concepts of dependency and underdevelopment, although defined differently, are not themselves challenged. In this sense, the MOP school represents not a break from but, rather, an alternative formulation and extension of Dependency Theory itself.

Within the MOP school, three basic approaches can be distinguished. The "articulation of MOP" approach, as it has been termed, tends to explain the phenomenon of underdevelopment in terms of the relationships among and between the capitalist and other, noncapitalist modes of production existing within underdeveloped economies.[46] A second related approach, that of the "colonial or peripheral MOP," has sought to develop a set of concepts of modes of production that are specific to the colonial experiences and peripheral status of the developing countries.[47] According to this group of theorists, the concepts of modes of production that should be used to analyze the societies of the periphery are fundamentally different from those that have been used to investigate the countries of the center. Finally, there are MOP theorists who focus on what they call the "internationalization of capital" or the laws of motion of the capitalist mode of production.[48] In this view, international development (including development within specific nations) is analyzed in terms of the presumed dominance of the capitalist mode of production in the world economy. Each one of these approaches has staked out a different position in the dependency theory debate. The starting point in all cases is a concept of mode of production; however, they represent three alternative ways of constructing a theoretical model in terms of which an explanation of the past and present economic and social structures of developing countries can be generated.

Background

Although the work of many of the MOP theorists has been relatively well documented,[49] the theoretical sources of this attempt to analyze development by using concepts of modes of production are less well known. There are five major points that should be briefly elaborated. First, the various efforts to construct a theory centered on concepts of modes of production grew out of attempts to provide a link between Frank's relatively global model of metropolis-satellite relations and the ethnographic detail that emerged from detailed, especially anthropological, studies of developing countries. Many researchers found it difficult to relate the wealth of empirical detail generated in the course of field work to the overarching logic of patterns of surplus transfer between the core and periphery of the world economy that form the focus of Frank's model.[50] The concepts and conceptual strategies of a group of French anthropologists who analyzed African underdevelopment in terms of modes of production represented one attempt to bridge this gap between existing theory and empirical research.[51]

A second factor that gave rise to the proliferation of MOP approaches to development was the reaction against Frank's seeing "capitalism everywhere," that is, that commodity flows or markets were present and such markets were sufficient to characterize the society in question as capitalist. Laclau's New Left Review article is the locus classicus of this criticism of Frank's work.[52] Frank was accused of making all of the underdeveloped countries' social structures capitalist, from the sixteenth century onward, because he mistakenly identified markets or trade relations with capitalism. Laclau's alternative was to emphasize the primacy of the conditions of production over those of exchange.

To this end, Laclau proceeded to define a concept of mode of production as a combination of four factors: the pattern of ownership of the means of production, the form of appropriation of what he called an economic surplus, the degree of the division of labor, and the level of development of the forces of production.[53] In addition, Laclau distinguishes between a "mode of production" and an "economic system" to take account of the participation of precapitalist modes of production in a world capitalist economic system. An economic system is generally defined by Laclau as an articulated (or combined) set of different modes of production. In particular, the world capitalist system is not conceived to be a uniform production system, that is, a system with one exclusive mode of production. Rather, it is conceived to be an economic system in which both capitalist and noncapitalist modes of production coexist and which is characterized by the predominance of the capitalist mode of production. According to Laclau, Marxist theorists should attempt to understand underdeveloped countries in terms of the system of relations—the articulation—between the capitalist and other, noncapitalist modes of production, rather than in terms of Frank's homogeneous capitalist relations.

Third, the use of the concept of mode of production in Laclau's critique of Frank and as the basis of an alternative framework of analysis that displaces Frank's focus on commodity flows was itself predicated on a return to the work of Marx through the writings of Althusser and Balibar.[54] These two French theorists had taken up the project of reformulating the basic concepts of historical materialism. Among their primary concerns was to combat what they considered to be various non-Marxist forms of "essentialism" within the Marxist theoretical tradition.[55] In particular, the explanation of social phenomena in terms of an essential human nature or an economic determinism was criticized. Their effort to formulate a concept of mode of production, along with the concept of overdetermination, and to produce a nonessentialist Marxist social theory was central to the emergence of the concept of mode of production as an object of theoretical attention.

A fourth source of the MOP school was the reexamination of Marx's own analysis of the so-called original accumulation of capital and the transition from feudalism to capitalism. Marx's account of the emergence and development of some of the economic, political, and cultural conditions of capitalism in a noncapitalist, feudal setting is filtered through the Dobb-Sweezy "transition debate" to become an additional component of the MOP analysis of the transition to capitalism in developing countries.[56] The relevance of the transition debate is twofold. First, the MOP analysis of underdevelopment is concerned with the emergence, or lack thereof, of the capitalist mode of production in the developing countries and hence, implicitly or explicitly, with a comparison with the European experience. Second, once the idea of transition (e.g., to the capitalist mode of production) is analyzed, the combined existence of different, capitalist and noncapitalist modes of production during the period of transition becomes an object of theoretical attention.

Finally, the work of Hindess and Hirst deserves brief mention.[57] Although not explicitly addressed to the question of developing countries, theirs is arguably the most sophisticated attempt to construct a set of concepts of noncapitalist modes of production. Their analyses of primitive communal, ancient, slave, and feudal modes of production were particularly instructive. However, their subsequent rejection, based on both methodological and epistemological considerations, of the concept of mode of production has received much less attention in the MOP literature.[58]

These are some of the historical and theoretical conditions, among others, out of which the MOP school emerged and to which it has responded over time. We turn now to a brief summary of the three approaches that have used the concept MOP as their entry-point into the analysis of dependency and underdevelopment.

Articulation of Modes of Production

Laclau's critique of Frank announced the beginning of a Marxian reconceptualization of dependency theory based on the articulation of modes of production. Taking the concept of modes of production as their starting point, articulation of MOP theorists have sought to analyze the relations among and between the various possible capitalist and noncapitalist modes of production. The overriding objective has been, following Laclau, to produce a general theory of the articulation of modes of production within a capitalist economic system. The central focus of the articulation of MOP theorists is, in particular, the system of relations between the capitalist mode of production and the set of preexisting noncapitalist modes of production in the developing countries. A principal methodological concern in understanding this approach, then, is the constitution and use of the central concepts of mode of production and articulation within their theoretical model.

How can different capitalist and noncapitalist modes of production be combined or articulated in a single social formation within the context of ultimate capitalist development? In general, three alternative forms or models might be used to answer this question. The two salient variables of these models are the form of interaction and the degree of dominance by one mode of production over the others. One possibility is that the various modes of production are seen to exist alongside but essentially independent of one another. This position has traditionally been called "dualism" and Frank's original rejection of it is shared by the articulation of MOP theorists. A second answer is that the various modes of production in any particular society are interrelated under the dominance of one of these modes of production. One mode of production, for example, capitalism, would be understood to dominate the others in the sense of determining the nature of their existence—their reproduction over time, any changes they may undergo, and their eventual demise. A third possible model holds that the modes of production are combined in such a way that there is, in general, no dominant mode of production. Thus, there would be no general outcome of the articulation of modes of production in the sense of one mode necessarily "winning out" over all others. The only way to understand the particular outcome of articulation, for instance, capitalist development, would be in terms of the analysis of the specific factors involved in the concrete combination of modes of production in any particular society.

The second alternative (that of capitalist dominance) still admits of two possibilities that should be noted. On the one hand, the articulation of modes of production may be such that capitalism clearly and quickly overwhelms and determines the outcome of other modes of production. The result is that the transition to the exclusive existence of capitalism would be of relatively short duration. On the other hand, the transition to capitalism may be understood as a long and complex process, such that any society in transition can only be understood in terms of different stages of articulation between the capitalist and noncapitalist modes of production.

The first variation of this position of the general dominance of the capitalist mode of production is usually attributed to the early theorists of imperialism, writers such as Lenin and Luxemburg.[59] The articulation of MOP theorists, in contrast, adopt the second variation of the second alternative. Central to this latter view is an understanding of the transition to capitalism as long and problematic, and thus in need of detailed analysis in each case.

It is necessary, then, to understand the notion of articulation in this light. "Articulation," as it is used to analyze the combined presence of different capitalist and noncapitalist modes of production during the course of transition to capitalism, takes on the dual meaning of "joining together" and "giving expression to."[60] Modes of production are conceived to be articulated in a social formation such that (a) the development of each mode of production is closely connected with, in the sense of being both dependent on and/or determined by, the other modes of production; and (b) the way that one mode of production is manifested or expressed cannot be analyzed independently of how others are manifested.

Rey is one theorist who has attempted to produce a general theory of the relations among modes of production within a peripheral capitalist economic system using the concept of articulation.[61] His theory specifies three distinct and successive stages of articulation. In the first stage, the capitalist mode of production is "imported" into the noncapitalist peripheral society and proceeds to *reinforce* and, in some instances, to *create* noncapitalist modes of production. Second, capitalism "takes root" and *uses,* from its dominant position, the noncapitalist modes of production. Finally, at some point not yet reached by most developing countries, the capitalist mode of production *supplants* all noncapitalist modes of production: noncapitalism disappears. The often violent and prolonged nature of these stages of articulation in peripheral societies serves, in Rey's framework of analysis, to distinguish the articulation between capitalist and noncapitalist modes of production in the periphery from the articulation between capitalism and feudalism in Western Europe. Rey's unidirectional sequence of stages is more or less shared by all members of the articulation of MOP approach.

A more concrete, albeit schematic, example will serve to illustrate some of the salient features of this articulation of MOP approach and to compare it to the other two approaches discussed below. Postcolonial nineteenth-century Peru can be analyzed in terms of the articulation between capitalist and noncapitalist modes of production. In particular, Peruvian society during that period of time can be understood as comprising at least the primitive communal, feudal, and capitalist modes of production. The primitive communal mode of production was a more or less direct descendant of the precolonial Incan *ayllu* or clan-based community. The Peruvian hacienda can be conceptualized in terms of the lord-serf relations of the feudal mode of production. Finally, the incipient development of the capitalist mode of production within Peru could be found in the organization of the recovery of guano (bird droppings used as fertilizer) for eventual export to England.

Two aspects of the articulation between these capitalist and noncapitalist modes of production, while not exhaustive, illustrate the approach. First, the initial instance of capitalist development was a product of capitalist development in England; the capitalist mode of production did not emerge within any of the Peruvian noncapitalist modes of production. Guano was commercialized by British capital exports and served as a cheap raw material for further capitalist development in England. This form of capitalist export production led neither to the development of a domestic capitalist class nor to the expansion of the internal market for further capitalist development. Second, this form of dependent capitalist development served to reinforce the predominance of the feudal mode of production in the rural areas. For example, a combined strategy of debt, purchase, and forcible expropriation led to the destruction of the communal *communidades indigenas* and allowed the increased concentration of land in feudal latifundia. Neither capitalist agriculture nor capitalist industry developed to any significant degree at this time. The (noncapitalist) feudal mode of production was first created (in the colonial period), then reinforced (in the nineteenth century), and only gradually supplanted (well into the 1960s) by the development of the capitalist mode of production. The result of this articulation of modes of production was continued dependency and underdevelopment at the periphery of the world economy.

The articulation of MOP approach, then, is meant to provide a conceptual framework to analyze the interrelations between capitalist and noncapitalist modes of production as they manifest themselves in peripheral societies. The particular concern is to map out the development of capitalism from entry to hegemony where it was imposed initially from the outside. The central dynamic is the development of capitalism, understood in terms of the laws (or tendencies) governing its development and involving certain "needs" that come to be met by the noncapitalist modes of production—for instance, a need for a large pool of landless laborers. The development of the noncapitalist modes of production is explained in terms of their ability to satisfy the needs of capitalism. In turn, the development of the capitalist mode of production is understood to be enabled or hindered in terms of the ability of the noncapitalist modes of production to satisfy capitalism's posited needs.

It can be anticipated, then, that a major controversy resulting from such investigations into the articulation between the capitalist and noncapitalist modes of production has concerned the "needs" of capitalism during the course of reinforcing, using, and eventually supplanting noncapitalism. On one side, there are theorists who tend to stress the unchanging process of capitalist development.[62] Capitalism is inherently expansive according to these accounts; its internal dynamic forces it at all stages to engulf and inevitably destroy all noncapitalist forms of production. This conception of capitalist expansion results in a single general theory of the articulation between capitalist and noncapitalist modes of production. On the other side of the controversy, some argue that the capitalist mode of production involves different problems and contradictions according to its various forms and stages of development.[63] Therefore, the articulation between the capitalist and noncapitalist modes of production is founded on a changing pattern of capitalist expansion. For example, according to Bradby, "capitalism has different needs of precapitalist economies at different stages of development, which arise from specific historical circumstance, e.g., raw materials, land, labor-power, and at times of crisis, markets."[64] As a result of this latter mode of analysis, capitalism is considered inherently expansive, but there is no general theory of the forms of the system of relations between capitalist and noncapitalist modes of production.

Whether or not the stress is on the changing nature of capitalist expansion, the general conclusion of the articulation of MOP theorists is that the development of capitalism on a world scale involves, first, the creation and maintenance and, then, the breakdown of noncapitalist modes of production. However, at the same time that noncapitalist forms of production are understood to be dominated and at least tendentially supplanted by capitalism, an additional conclusion of the work of the articulation of MOP theorists is that the full, nondistorted development of the capitalist mode of production in the underdeveloped countries is itself blocked by its dependent relation to capitalism in the developed nations.

Thus, underdevelopment and dependency have somewhat different meanings in this framework compared to what we have seen in the case of Frank. For the articulation of MOP theorists, underdevelopment is caused by the persistence of precapitalist modes of production as they are reproduced in their articulation with the dominant capitalist mode of production. Full-fledged capitalist development is itself arrested by relations of dependency between core and periphery: On the one hand, the peripheral capitalist mode of production is imposed from the outside in the midst of preexisting noncapitalist modes of production, not a direct outgrowth of a Western European-like feudalism. The implication is that Western European feudalism provided a better "breeding ground" for capitalist development than did the noncapitalist modes of production that preexisted or that were subsequently created by colonial expansion in peripheral social formations. On the other hand, once in place, the peripheral capitalist mode of production is conceived to be reproduced in a dependent status vis-à-vis the capitalist mode of production in the center.

There has been an additional concern in the various attempts to analyze the articulation of MOP. It involves the thesis of the continued coexistence of the capitalist and noncapitalist modes of production and the portended eventual demise of those noncapitalist modes of production. According to Bradby, "the establishment of capitalism in a social formation necessarily implies the transformation, and in some sense the destruction of formerly dominant modes of production."[65] It is generally accepted that the societies or social formations of peripheral countries comprise both capitalist and noncapitalist modes of production at least at some stage in their history. Theorists differ, however, as to the manner and cause of the destruction of the noncapitalist modes of production. Are they destined to disappear because of pressures induced by the coexisting capitalist mode of production, or will their own developmental dynamic cause their destruction?

This debate parallels the earlier transition debate between Dobb and Sweezy over whether the demise of feudalism in Western Europe was caused by primarily internal factors (Dobb) or external factors (Sweezy). Wolpe formulates this distinction in the context of the articulation of modes of production in peripheral social formations by noting that "it is one thing to argue that precapitalist relations of production may be transformed into capitalist relations; it is quite another to assume that this is both an inevitable and necessary effect of the CMP [capitalist mode of production]."[66] In general, the dynamic of peripheral social formations that comprise both capitalist and noncapitalist modes of production has been analyzed in terms of the external relations—conflicts, tensions, etc.—among these modes of production. Social change is understood to occur as one mode of production, generally the capitalist mode of production, grows at the expense of other, noncapitalist modes of production. As a result, the sources of change internal to each mode of production have received scant attention.

However this controversy is resolved, the general thrust of the literature has been to argue that although these peripheral social formations comprise both capitalist and noncapitalist modes of production, the arrival of the capitalist mode of production from outside stamps these societies with its unique mark. The logic of articulation tends to be analyzed in terms of the functional needs of the reproduction of the capitalist mode of production. Thus, we have Quijano's characterization of this articulation as a "combination of capitalist and precapitalist relations of production, under the hegemony of the first and serving its interests. The movement of the whole configuration is directed by the first and, from this point of view, it is *fundamentally* capitalist but not homogeneously capitalist."[67]

To appreciate the appearance and further elaboration of the articulation of MOP approach, it is helpful to note the critical tension that exists between this approach and other frameworks of analysis. The articulation of MOP position in some ways agrees with, and at the same time is quite critical of, other frameworks in regard to certain key points. It has already been stated above that this approach was in part a response to Frank's original formulation of Dependency Theory in which peripheral societies were characterized as capitalist from the time they were first inserted into what he termed the capitalist world economy. In contrast to Frank's seeing capitalism everywhere, the articulation of MOP theorists have focused on the continued existence of various noncapitalist modes of production and their articulation with the capitalist mode of production. However, they have also taken a page from Frank's book by insisting that the capitalist mode of production was originally introduced from outside the periphery and that it continues to take its dynamic from the capitalist mode of production in the center. In this sense, the articulation of capitalist and noncapitalist modes of production in the developing countries is a different formulation of the original notion of dependency. As Foster-Carter has stated it, "the 'history of capital itself' *continues* to be 'written outside such social formations'."[68]

The articulation of MOP approach also shares with Frank and the remainder of the dependency theory school a criticism of the orthodox "dualist" conception of the developing countries. Arrighi, for example, has analyzed what orthodox economists understand to be the labor surplus economy (for instance, the Lewis model) as a *product* of capitalist development, not as some original state.[69] However, his criticism is distanced from that of Frank in the sense that Arrighi reconceptualizes what others consider to be dualism as a structured combination of capitalism *and* noncapitalism, as an articulated combination of modes of production.

Not surprisingly, a traditional interpretation of the Marxist theory of development has also been the object of criticism in the work of the articulation of MOP theorists. Two aspects of this critique deserve at least brief mention. First, many of the articulation of MOP theorists have argued against the notion of a necessary or inevitable succession of modes of production.[70] Thus, they react against the mechanistic-deterministic tendency often found in some traditional Marxist analyses that hold that there is a unique path of development for all countries. Articulation of MOP theorists maintain that the transition to capitalism in peripheral societies has noncapitalist origins different from those involved in the transition in Western Europe. This means that there is no single succession of stages of development in all countries.[71]

The criticism of traditional Marxist theories of development made by the articulation of MOP theorists often has a second aspect. The question here is whether the transition to capitalism in peripheral societies is fundamentally distinct from the transitions that have occurred elsewhere, especially in Western Europe. The traditional Marxist answer is taken to be that there is no fundamental distinction to be drawn here. The articulation of MOP theorists, on the other hand, argue that something different has been occurring in the peripheral transition to the capitalist mode of production. In particular, the development of capitalism in the periphery is seen as an *uneven* process taking place over an *extended* period of time. As we mentioned above in relation to Rey, the assumption here is that the European transition was, in contrast, relatively smooth and rapid. This attempt to analyze peripheral capitalist development as unlike the supposedly smooth, short development of capitalism in Western Europe is then used by Rey to argue that violence and other aspects of formal colonialism are inherent in the development of the capitalist mode of production in the periphery.

While critics of the articulation of MOP approach can agree that the development of capitalism in the peripheral countries is uneven and prolonged, they can also point out that it is evident that the transition to capitalism during, say, the period 1100–1850 in Western Europe was neither smooth nor of short duration. In support of their position, these critics can point out that the work of historians as diverse as Dobb and Pirenne has demonstrated the extended, often violent nature of the Western European transition to capitalism.[72] Therefore, without denying that there are certainly differences between the transitions to capitalism in the so-called core and periphery countries, critics of the articulation of MOP approach can maintain that it is probably mistaken to attempt to distinguish these transitions on the basis of their relative unevenness or the length of time over which they have been occurring.

In summary, the articulation of MOP theorists construct their understanding of the developing countries in terms of a system of relations between capitalist and noncapitalist modes of production. In particular, the concepts of dependency and underdevelopment are taken over from Dependency Theory and reinterpreted as the persistence of noncapitalist modes of production and the less than full development of the capitalist mode of production in that context. The articulation of MOP approach differs from specifically Frank-like interpretations of Dependency Theory, then, because of the focus on the relationship between capitalism and noncapitalism within the periphery. However, it still takes as given the notion, shared by Dependency Theory, that there are fundamentally different schemes of development that define a core and periphery of a world economy.

Peripheral Modes of Production

A second approach within the MOP school criticizes the specific set of concepts of modes of production that the articulation of MOP theorists have tended to use in their analyses. This alternative approach has sought to specify the concepts of "peripheral modes of production" or "colonial modes of production," a set of *sui generis* modes of production that are said to correspond better than the "classical" concepts of capitalist and noncapitalist modes of production to the conditions of underdevelopment and dependency in the peripheral countries of the world economy.

The modes of production picked out by these new concepts are considered to be qualitatively distinct from those that are used to analyze the development of capitalism in Western Europe and elsewhere. The operative assumption is that the forms of development in the core and periphery are fundamentally different and that different concepts must be used to understand these different forms of development. According to the peripheral MOP theorists, the fact that colonialism changed the precolonial pattern of development—in particular, the precolonial modes of production—in the colonized countries means that what is required is a separate set of concepts of modes of production with which to analyze their colonial and postcolonial experiences. This argument is best summarized by C. F. S. Cardoso:

> The specificity of internal colonial structures and of their historical genesis implies the inadequacy of such categories as "feudalism" to explain them. What is required is the elaboration of a theory of *colonial modes of production,* starting with the notion that such structures are *specific and dependent.* [73]

Here, then, the concept of mode of production is modified by the notion of dependency to produce a framework of analysis based on a set of concepts of peripheral or colonial modes of production. The presupposition seems to be that a mode of production that is affected to some more or less significant degrees by conditions external to the social formation where that mode of production is located is fundamentally different from an "independent" mode of production. For example, according to this approach, the existence of slavery in Brazil during the colonial period would make it a different mode of production, by virtue of its colonial ties with Portugal, from the slave mode of production of ancient Rome. Thus, despite what might at first appear as important similarities between the two cases, different concepts are needed in each case to conduct a proper analysis. This presumption that external influences serve as the criterion for a separate set of concepts of peripheral modes of production is also the origin of the well known Alavi-Banaji-et al. debate on India.[74]

Again, a more concrete example will help to illustrate this particular version of the MOP interpretation. Returning to the case of Peru, it will be remembered that our hypothetical articulation of MOP analysis utilized "classical" concepts of modes of production and conceptualized dependency in terms of the specific articulation among these modes of production. The present, alternative approach would drop the notion of different modes of production articulated in a single social formation. Rather, it would emphasize the colonial origins and general dependent nature of economic and social relations in Peru. Indeed, all of those relations that would be picked out by the articulation of MOP theorists as elements of the "primitive communal," "feudal," or "capitalist" modes of production would be understood as different aspects of a single peripheral mode of production, as distinct social relations that were specific to the peripheral status of the Peruvian social formation. It follows that one would not expect this peripheral mode of production to develop along the same path as the classical modes. This peripheral mode of production would generate a path of development fundamentally different from what would have existed in a nondependent setting. In relation to our example, the role of Peru's economy as a subordinate mode of production within the world capitalist system precluded the development of capitalism in Peru in the same form that it had emerged from nondependent, noncapitalist modes of production in the core countries. The peripheral status of this mode of production, not the articulation between capitalist and noncapitalist modes of production, explains dependency and underdevelopment in Peru.

It is interesting to note that the advocates of these concepts of *sui generis* modes of production for analyzing the developing countries tend to accept the use of the classical concepts of the modes of production of slavery, capitalism, etc. for the countries of the core. However, it would be difficult to argue that the modes of production of the colonizing countries, especially the capitalist mode of production, were less affected by colonialism than those of the colonized countries. Was the development of capitalism in Britain any less conditioned by the existence of colonial ties with India than the existing modes of production in India itself? If not, then why, on their theoretical assumptions, should the classical concepts be thought to be applicable to core countries across the precolonial, colonial, and postcolonial periods? And if these concepts of modes of production are not applicable across periods, how do we demarcate new and changing modes of production? There seems to be a problem of concept specification here.

This attempt to draw a sharp distinction between peripheral and classical modes of production does make it quite evident, however, that the focus of this form of analysis is on the external relations of domination that shape and otherwise determine what are conceived to be the subordinate modes of production of the peripheral countries. In this regard, then, the work of the peripheral MOP theorists is continuous with the earlier work of Frank. They agree with Frank that the dependency condition of the developing world is a result of the domination of economic forces (for the most part) outside the developing countries themselves. Where they differ from Frank is over how best to analyze the internal structures of dependency, whether, for instance, underdevelopment should be analyzed in terms of capitalist relations or whether it should be seen as the result of the logic of development of a different, peripheral mode of production.

Internationalization of Capital

The third major approach to the MOP analysis of dependency and underdevelopment focuses on the internationalization of capital as part of a world system that is to be understood in terms of the laws of motion of the capitalist mode of production. In many ways, Frank's most recent works on "world accumulation" reflect this new focus.[75] Attention is shifted away from the articulation between capitalist and noncapitalist modes of production and away from the specification of specific peripheral modes of production to an analysis of the structure and logic of development of the capitalist mode of production itself. According to the internationalization of capital theorists, the other two MOP approaches do not pay sufficient attention to the "real" dynamic determining world development, i.e., the capitalist mode of production. This mode of analysis presumes the dominance of the capitalist mode of production within the international economy; that is, it implies that the fundamental structure of the world economy is that of the capitalist mode of production and that the logic of world development reflects the laws governing that mode of production. In this way, the internationalization of the capitalist mode of production becomes the new demiurge, propelling the world economy forward and driving a larger and larger wedge between core and periphery.

This focus on the structure and effects of the capitalist mode of production on a world scale may be seen as either a critique or an extension of the two other MOP approaches surveyed in previous sections. It represents a critique to the extent that noncapitalist and peripheral modes of production are replaced by a single global capitalist mode of production. For example, units of production that would be analyzed as feudal or peripheral in the other MOP frameworks would be placed inside a single process of capitalist accumulation by the internationalization of capital theorists. On the other hand, it represents an extension insofar as some theorists argue that the historical period when the other modes of production approaches were applicable has passed. There may have been and probably were either noncapitalist or peripheral modes of production at one time in the developing countries, so they might argue, but these modes of production have been supplanted by a single capitalist mode of production on a world scale. Interpreted thusly, the various MOP approaches would represent a historical sequence at the level of theory that corresponds to the stages of development of the world economy.

However understood, whether as a break from or an extension of the other MOP frameworks, the basic unit of analysis of the internationalization of capital approach is the structure and movement of the capitalist mode of production. Partly in response to the debate between theoretical approaches that argued over the predominance of circulation (Frank) versus that of production (Laclau), the internationalization of capital theorists have defined capitalism in terms of a particular interpretation of Marx's three circuits of commodity-capital, money-capital, and productive-capital. In other words, capitalist production is conceived of as a *unity* of production and circulation. The focus is, in particular, on the global nature of these circuits as they transcend the confines of the nation-state. The symbol of this global process of accumulation is, of course, the transnational or multinational corporation. These corporations embody the logic of the third stage of the international expansion of the capitalist mode of production, intertwining the various parts of the world economy into a single entity and subordinating these parts to the needs of capitalist accumulation.

Within this framework, how is what appears to some as the articulation between capitalist and noncapitalist modes of production to be understood? Barkin responds:

We can examine the problems of the relationship between peasant and capitalist production by determining if and how surplus value is generated and the ways in which it is appropriated by different segments of the capitalist class. In this way, the complex productive structures within individual countries can be analyzed in terms of their particular contributions to the global process of articulation.[76]

The articulation *between modes of production* within peripheral social formations is replaced by a notion of *articulation within the capitalist mode of production* itself. According to Palloix,

> this new type of articulation characterizes the different chains of dependence in the self-expansion of capital, in particular with the underdeveloped countries, which is no longer an articulation of the capitalist mode of production at the centre with other modes of production, but an articulation within the world CMP [capitalist mode of production] itself, among differing processes of self-expansion of capital and increasingly accentuated differentiation of this expansion as between the centre and the periphery.[77]

To return once again to our Peruvian illustration, the internationalization of capital theorists would tend to explain Peruvian development in terms of the logic of the development of the capitalist mode of production on a world scale. No capitalist production was initiated within the Peruvian social formation during the colonial and immediate postcolonial periods because the global expansion of capitalism took the form of the extension of predominantly commercial relations. That is, Peru was a site for exports (of gold, sugar, etc.) to the core countries. In a second stage, the export of money-capital financed a certain development of infrastructure and involved Peru in a web of international debt relations. In neither of these stages was capitalist production itself initiated in Peru. Only with the internationalization of the circuit of productive-capital did Peru embark on a path of capitalist development per se. For some, it would be described as dependent capitalism, Peru occupying a subordinate position in the international division of labor; underdevelopment would be reproduced as a result. For others, this capitalist development, although incipient, would be characterized as a break from dependency, which was characteristic of the noncapitalist phases, and thus the end of underdevelopment. In both cases, the explanation of Peruvian (under)development is based on the effects of the development of the capitalist mode of production on a world scale.

Thus, while they all focus on the internationalization of the various circuits of capital, and therefore of the capitalist mode of production itself, the various internationalization of capital theorists reach different conclusions concerning the continued existence of dependency and underdevelopment. Basically, as exemplified in the preceding example, the positions are two. On the one hand, it is argued that the new international division of labor produced by the internationalization of the capitalist mode of production serves to perpetuate conditions of underdevelopment and the dependency of the peripheral countries on the core countries (where the multinational corporations are based).[78] Underdevelopment and dependency are no longer associated with the persistence of noncapitalist modes of productions, as they are with the articulation of MOP theorists, or with the dependent status of developing countries, as in the peripheral MOP approach; they are effects internal to the capitalist mode of production itself.

On the other hand, the analyses of, for example, Cypher and, even more so, Warren argue that underdevelopment is associated only with the continued existence of noncapitalist modes of production and that these are entirely supplanted by the expansion of the capitalist mode of production.[79] The expansion of the capitalist mode of production on a world scale, particularly within what others would term the periphery, induces a process of unqualified capitalist development. Here the break with the conclusions of Frank and other theorists of the "development of underdevelopment" or "dependent development" is virtually complete.

Even many of those who assume the first position and choose to retain terms such as "dependency" and "underdevelopment" tend to analyze the development of so-called Third World countries solely in terms of the logic of expansion of the capitalist mode of production. A typical statement is the following:

> International markets and economic power structures are increasingly determining the individual decisions made in ever more isolated parts of national economies, even when "noncapitalist" productive groups are involved, such as peasant producers in many Third World economies.[80]

Two factors appear to be lost here. Any dynamic inherent in the particular economic structure, capitalist or otherwise, of a developing country is overlooked in favor of international forces. Second, noncapitalist modes of production recede into the background or disappear completely; thus, we are faced with the collapse of the notion of articulation and an ironic return to Frank's original position, this time in terms of "seeing the capitalist mode of production everywhere."

V. AMIN

The various conceptualizations of dependency and underdevelopment analyzed in previous sections are synthesized and recast as a distinct version of Dependency Theory in the work of Samir Amin. Basically, Amin combines notions of the world capitalist system, the articulation of modes of production, and the internationalization of capital with a theory of unequal exchange. The result is a theory of development in which the core and periphery are conceived as complementary opposites within a world capitalist social formation. This relation between core and periphery promotes capitalist development in the former while blocking the same path of development in the latter. This conception of dichotomous economic development serves, in turn, as the basis of what Amin considers to be the central political contradiction of the world capitalist system.

Amin begins his theory of development with the presumption of a world capitalist system that is divided into two fundamentally distinct parts—a core and a periphery—that are functionally related. In a manner obviously consistent with Frank's approach, he argues that "the structures of the periphery are shaped so as to meet the needs of accumulation at the center, that is, provided that the development of the center engenders and maintains the underdevelopment of the periphery."[81]

Going beyond Frank, however, Amin realizes the importance of providing a more detailed analysis of the internal structures of the countries of the periphery. Amin shares with the articulation of modes of production theorists a structural explanation of the underdevelopment of the periphery in terms of the system of relations between the capitalist and various noncapitalist modes of production. In general, for Amin, "social formations are . . . concrete, organized structures that are marked by a dominant mode of production and the articulation around this of a complex of modes of production that are subordinate to it."[82]

The particular social formations of the world capitalist economy are analyzed in terms of the dominance of the capitalist mode of production and the subordinate existence of various noncapitalist modes of production. Finally, Amin follows the internationalization of capital theorists in analyzing the various parts of his world economy in terms of the globalization of the capitalist mode of production.

> The predominance of the capitalist mode of production is also expressed on another plane. It constitutes a world system in which all formations, central and peripheral alike, are arranged in a single system, organized and hierarchical.[83]

These three notions (world capitalist system, articulation of modes of production, and internationalization of the capitalist modes of production) are combined, as we show below, with a theory of unequal exchange to constitute Amin's particular theory of blocked development in the periphery.

Amin's work is characterized, then, by this synthesis of other Dependency Theory approaches to produce an alternative model of dependency and underdevelopment. His work is also characterized by the importance it places on history. This focus on history is thematic in at least two senses. First, much of Amin's published work—in fact, some would argue, the best of that work—consists of historical writing. His accounts of the different paths to capitalism in the social formations of the periphery, especially in Africa, are among the best available.[84] Second, Amin conceives of history as providing the "correct perspective" for carrying out the analysis of the developing countries. The terms of his own particular analysis are said to correspond to a perspective that emerges from the history of the developing countries.[85] Theories that have been generated from perspectives that represent the histories of the core countries—in particular, neoclassical and traditional Marxist theories of development—do not correspond, according to Amin, to the reality of the developing countries.

The basic terms of Amin's version of Dependency Theory are by now quite familiar: Concepts of modes of production, social formation, center, periphery, and the accumulation of capital seem to be borrowed more or less intact from other theorists and used to construct a theoretical model. This model is then deployed to explain the process of development of the world capitalist system. The particular use of such concepts would appear to make Amin's mode of analysis a straightforward Marxist one. However, at least two difficulties arise in this connection. On the one hand, commentators have noted the relative lack of precision in Amin's use of these concepts. Explicit definitions of concepts are rarely offered and, because of their shifting meanings from passage to passage, implicit definitions are difficult to construct. This is especially troublesome given the vastly different meanings of such concepts throughout the Marxian tradition. Thus, it is difficult to pinpoint exactly which interpretation of the concepts and method of Marxist theory is at work in Amin's writings. On the other hand, Amin self-consciously distances his analysis from that of Marx, if only because the latter's theory was limited by his perspective which, in turn, corresponded to the historical period in which he wrote. In this vein, Amin writes that

> in fact, the monopolies, the rise of which Marx could not imagine, were to prevent any local capitalism that might arise from competing. The development of capitalism in the periphery was to remain extraverted, based on the external market, and could therefore not lead to a full flowering of the capitalist mode of production in the periphery.[86]

The central element of Amin's model of the world economy is the relationship between the two groups of core and periphery countries as complementary opposites. These two poles are created by the history of capitalist expansion from the core. According to Amin, a core and periphery exist at all of the three stages into which he periodizes capitalist development: mercantilist, premonopoly/competitive, and monopoly/imperialist capitalism. However, the dichotomy becomes "hardened" in the third, imperialist stage:

From that point on, no country of the periphery or semiperiphery is capable of joining the core.

The reason for this hardening of the core and periphery is that Amin considers these two parts of the world economy to be governed by fundamentally different laws of development. The contrast is between *autocentric* and *extraverted* accumulation. "I maintain that the dynamic of the core is autonomous, that the periphery adjusts to it, and that the functions the periphery fulfills differ from one stage to another."[87]

Amin is quite specific in stating that autocentric accumulation does not mean autarchy. Rather, autocentric development is a result of the dynamic of development originating in the core itself. The nature of development in the core is such that it determines its own development as well as that of the periphery. The key relation making for a pattern of autocentric accumulation in the center is the balance between increases in productivity and wages.[88] This results in an expansion of the internal market and the balanced development of industries specialized in the production of both producer and consumer goods (or, in Amin's terminology, Departments I and II). This balance between changes in productivity and wages in the center is also supported by surplus transfers from the periphery on the basis of unequal exchange.

The periphery, on the other hand, is barred from achieving such a balance. Its pattern of accumulation is characterized as extraverted, deformed, and dependent. The pattern of accumulation is fundamentally different in the periphery where the coexistence of capitalist and noncapitalist modes of production means that there is no necessary relation between the levels of productivity and wages. Increases in productivity, even in the "modern" export sector, are not translated into corresponding improvements in wages because of the existence of a Lewis-like surplus labor force. The sources of this "surplus labor" are those parts of the economy in which noncapitalist relations are still strong. This imbalance between productivity and wages leaves the domestic market "limited and distorted," so that the key result is a link between production in the export sector and luxury goods consumption.

According to Amin, the peripheral economy is considered to be "disarticulated."[89] It should be emphasized that this concept of disarticulation is quite different from what it might mean for the articulation of modes of production theorists. "Articulation" and "disarticulation" in Amin's sense refer to the economic conditions that give rise to a balance or imbalance between changes in productivity and wages. The result of disarticulation, then, is that the possibility of autocentric accumulation in the periphery is blocked.

The three main "distortions" of the periphery with respect to the development of capitalism in the core that derive from this model of disarticulation concern the main sectors of economic activity. The peripheral economy is biased toward export production, service activities, and, in the choice of branches of industry proper, toward light industry with modern technology. This pattern of investment or accumulation reproduces what Amin calls the "marginalization of the masses," a level of unemployment that ensures a minimum wage in all sectors far below the level of productivity. This minimum wage serves, in turn, as the basis of a restricted internal market. The final result of this fundamentally distinct pattern of accumulation in the periphery is that development is blocked.

> None of the features that define the structure of the periphery is thus weakened as economic growth proceeds: on the contrary, these features are accentuated. Whereas at the center growth means development, making the economy more integral, in the periphery growth does not mean development, for it disarticulates the economy—it is only a "development of underdevelopment."[90]

Amin's conceptions of dependency and underdevelopment are thus quite clear: Underdevelopment means both that noncapitalist modes of production are reproduced and that the expansion of the capitalist mode of production is distorted in the periphery of the world economy. Insofar as these conditions are maintained, they continue to serve as the basis for the dependency of the peripheral countries on the core countries. In the end, the periphery does not have the power to control its own development.

The key mechanism in Amin's model whereby the two patterns of autocentric and dependent development are reproduced is the process of unequal exchange between core and periphery. Amin takes over and subsequently modifies Emmanuel's original theory of unequal exchange.[91] Emmanuel takes as given and bases his analysis on differences in real wages between center and periphery. Amin argues that the essential condition for unequal exchange is not merely wage differentials, but rather that these real wage differences are larger than productivity differences. The result, however, is the same as that in Emmanuel's model: The prices (of production) at which the goods of the center and periphery exchange are such that a surplus is transferred to the former from the latter. This surplus transfer means that there is an external drain on internally generated investment funds and the reproduction of a limited internal market. These results then serve to reproduce the general conditions of accumulation that, in turn, give rise to the wage-productivity differentials that are the basis of unequal exchange.

Given this relationship between the phenomenon of unequal exchange and the conditions that give rise to unequal exchange, a question immediately arises concerning the pattern of cause and effect between international prices and unequal wage levels. Amin responds:

> The question is pointless. Inequality in wages, due to historical reasons (the difference between social formations), constitutes the basis of spe-

cialization and a system of international prices that perpetuate this inequality.[92]

That is, once some initial wage-productivity differences between the core and periphery historically emerge, a pattern of unequal exchange is produced whereby these initial differences continue to be reproduced over time.

Amin's theory of unequal exchange, like that of Emmanuel and others, has elicited comments and criticisms from many quarters.[93] The most damaging criticism to his general model of the unidirectional transfer of a surplus from the periphery to the core concerns the real wage-productivity disparity between center and periphery. According to Amin, this transfer of surplus requires that production in the periphery be based on a higher rate of exploitation than that in the center. Amin's own equations bear this out. If this is so, critics respond, why is it the case, assuming as Amin does the full mobility of capital, that all production in the core is not transferred to the periphery? Amin's answer is twofold. First, capitalists respond to different profit rates, not to different rates of exploitation. And since Amin's model of unequal exchange assumes the existence of a single, general rate of profit across all industries, there is no apparent reason for capital to be shifted from the core to the periphery. Second, Amin has argued that the absence of a large domestic market in the periphery keeps industry in the core countries. This second response is less than satisfactory because there is no reason that the location of production must coincide with the location of the final market. His own assumption of the existence of international exchange shows this.

His first answer, concerning the difference between profitability and exploitation, is also beset with difficulties. On the one hand, Marx's theory of prices of production and a general rate of profit, which Amin says that he adopts, was part of Marx's attempt to analyze the dynamic nature of capitalist competition.[94] Marx used the concept of price of production as a *hypothetical equilibrium* to illustrate the ceaseless *movement* in the direction of the formation of a general rate of profit. Flows of capital between industries in response to unequal rates of profit so change the conditions of profitability that the hypothetical general rate of profit itself changes. This general rate of profit can be thought of as a shifting equilibrium, an elusive goal that is never reached. Its only purpose in volume 3 of *Capital* is to illustrate the dynamics of capitalist competition by momentarily abstracting from that movement. On the other hand, even assuming a general rate of profit *across* industries does not mean that the rate of profit is equal *within* each industry. The existence of a range of "efficiencies" among firms that make up each industry at any point in time implies that there will be a similar range of profit rates among those firms.[95] The competitive dynamic that forces less efficient producers within an industry to innovate, e.g., by moving to a location where rates of exploitation are supposed to be higher (in the periphery, according to Amin), is not brought to a standstill even if a general rate of profit is imposed across industries.

In general, then, the existence at a point in time of a set of prices does not ensure that the underlying conditions that give rise to those prices will be reproduced over time. In fact, the opposite conclusion is more likely, namely, that the existence of unequal prices of production will cause movements of capital within and between industries so that the conditions of profitability within those industries are changed. The nature of these changes in the conditions of profitability cannot, of course, be predetermined. However, there is no reason, even on the basis of Amin's assumptions, for such capital movements to unilaterally promote capitalist development in one set of countries (the core) and prevent such development in another group of countries (the periphery). Unequal capitalist development in both core and periphery, rather than the "development of underdevelopment," would be the more likely result.

Amin's model of the world capitalist economy starts with a fundamental distinction between core and peripheral patterns of accumulation. This relation of complementary opposites is reproduced over time by the mechanism of unequal exchange. The result, then, of Amin's economic analysis is that the development of capitalism on a world scale is radically dichotomized: While continuing apace in the core countries, the development of capitalism is substantially blocked in the peripheral countries. This underdevelopment means, for Amin, that noncapitalist modes of production continue to exist in the periphery and that the peripheral capitalist mode of production cannot serve as the basis for a process of autocentric development.

This model of economic development (and underdevelopment) serves, in turn, as the basis for Amin's analysis of what he considers to be the central contradiction of the world capitalist system, to wit, the conflict between what Amin calls the world bourgeoisie and the world proletariat. The implicit notion of contradiction in Amin's work is that of a pair of opposing forces, each of which is generated by complementary processes of accumulation within a single world capitalist system. The central nucleus of the world bourgeoisie is located in the core countries. Because of the existence of "superexploitation," within the periphery, Amin finds the central nucleus of the world proletariat there. Amin explains the superexploitation of the peripheral proletariat in the following manner:

> [Unequal exchange] means that the bourgeoisie of the center, the only one that exists on the scale of the world system, exploits the proletariat everywhere, at the center and at the periphery, but that it exploits the proletariat of the periphery even more brutally, and that this is possible because the objective mechanism upon which is based the unity that links it to its own proletariat, in an autocentric economy, and which restricts the degree of exploitation it carries out at the center, does not function at the extraverted periphery.[96]

According to Amin, the relationship between capitalists and workers in the core countries is characterized by a "social democratic alliance." Capitalists are said to benefit from the continued existence of profitable production while workers share both in increases in productivity at home and in transfer of surplus from the periphery. Workers in the periphery are subject to superexploitation. Therefore, the principal set of opposing interests that is the basis of the contradiction of the world system is between the world bourgeoisie (of the core) and the world proletariat (of the periphery).

Amin's framework of analysis has, of course, not escaped the criticisms of writers both inside and outside the Dependency Theory tradition.[97] His most recent, comprehensive reply, responding to the critical commentaries of Warren, Smith, and Brewer, serves to highlight the main elements of his interpretation of Dependency Theory.[98] Amin's points are basically three. First, he seeks to clear up what he considers a misinterpretation of his notion of the blocked development of the periphery. "Blocking" does not mean stagnation or the absence of change. Rather, capitalist development in the periphery is considered to be blocked because it "does not reproduce the model of that of the developed world."[99] What this means for Amin is that peripheral development is subject to periods of growth and crisis because of an external impetus, and that this uneven process continues to create inequality in the distribution of income.

Amin's critics would be hard-pressed to disagree with the notions that the developing countries continue to experience income inequalities and that economic crises are transmitted internationally. However, it is not clear how these phenomena serve to block peripheral development or serve as the basis of his radical dichotomy between the patterns of accumulation in the core and periphery. What this means is that Amin's conclusion concerning the complementary and opposite nature of the relationship between the core and periphery depends crucially on his presumption of such a dichotomy as the starting point of his analysis. Amin begins his investigation with, and thus ends that investigation with, the division of the world capitalist system into two groups of core and periphery countries.

This is Amin's second point. All attempts to deny, as a point of departure, this core-periphery dichotomy are fundamentally mistaken: "[T]he 'theory' which rejects the analysis of capitalist expansion in terms of centre and periphery stops at the threshold of the real questions."[100] This is not just one among other entry-points into an analysis of development for Amin, one which has its attendant consequences for the subsequent conclusions of that analysis. Rather, it is the entry point which is determined by "history." In this sense, Amin is merely reasserting that one of the defining characteristics of Dependency Theory—the presumption that there is a world system divided into a core and periphery—is also his and that this starting point is the correct one to analyze dependency and underdevelopment.

Finally, Amin reiterates, in the face of the protestations of his critics, the basic theses of his previous analyses. Unequal exchange, the social democratic alliance between workers and capitalists in the core, etc. remain his basic arguments. He also redefines the relationship of his framework of analysis to that of other versions of Dependency Theory. On the one hand, the modes of production debate is not "decisive" because it avoids an analysis of the insertion of noncapitalist modes of production into a "world system which can only be termed capitalist."[101] On the other hand, the work of Frank and Wallerstein continues to be valid. In particular, Amin reaffirms that "the development of some [countries] is the cause of the underdevelopment of others."[102]

It should be relatively clear from our and other summaries of Amin's work that both the starting point and end point of Amin's analysis of the world capitalist system is the fundamental dichotomy between the modes of accumulation in the core and in the periphery. Distinct processes of accumulation are posited at the beginning of his analysis and reproduced over time, through the mechanism of unequal exchange, so that the fundamental differences between these complementary opposite forms of development are present in his conclusions. In addition, the fundamental political contradiction of the world system—between the capitalists of the center and the superexploited workers of the periphery—corresponds exactly to this economic distinction between core and periphery.

The key mechanism that is both cause and effect of this dichotomy, unequal exchange, has been called into question above. Our point is not the substantive one that unequal exchange cannot or does not take place in international trade. Rather, our criticism indicates that the existence of unequal exchange, and the accompanying flows of profits among enterprises within and between industries, cannot ensure the reproduction of the two fundamentally distinct patterns of accumulation that are presumed in Amin's analysis. In addition, it is only the presumption of this essential economic dichotomy between core and periphery that allows Amin to make the fundamental political conflict of the world system that between capitalists located in the core countries and workers located in the periphery. To so reduce the political dynamic within the world system, if such a system can be presumed at all, serves only to "forget about" the other conflicts and contradictions that emerge in the course of world development.

VI. CONCLUSION

There is a wide variety of theories that serve as alternatives to orthodox, neoclassical approaches to development. We have presented three of those theories in this chapter: the Dependency Theory of Frank (and, by extension, Wallerstein), the Modes of Production school, and the approach elaborated by Amin.

All three theoretical approaches are explicitly put forward as dependency and/or Marxian alternatives to bourgeois development theory. Using different concepts, they arrive at conclusions in stark contrast to those put forward by bourgeois economists and other social scientists. Where bourgeois theorists see the development of capitalism as propelling a process of modernization from traditional or backward forms of economic and social organization to modern growth and development, the radical theorists see imperialist domination and exploitation. Thus, these radicals "see" a different reality in the currently less-developed or underdeveloped countries. The difference in the very names used to designate these "poor" countries by the alternative approaches—less-developed vs. dependent and/or underdeveloped—betray these different realities.

Orthodox and radical theorists arrive at different conclusions because their analyses of development start in different places; they have different conceptual "entry-points." Orthodox theorists tend to focus on individual decision-making and begin their analysis with a particular model of human behavior. In neoclassical theory, capitalist economic growth and development are understood in terms of individual utilities or preferences. Prices, the distribution of income, and all other economic phenomena are derived from this utility model of behavior. Individual utilities, taken as given within the model, are considered the principal factor determining the economic forces leading to development. From this perspective, the development of capitalism is generally understood to bring about an increase in individual freedom. This greater freedom, in turn, is seen to help guarantee the accumulation of wealth and social modernization by providing the incentives for rational market behavior. This is true for all countries in which capitalism takes root.

The radical approaches arrive at different conclusions because they start with different concepts. In the case of Frank (and Wallerstein), the circulation of commodities serves as the conceptual entry-point for the analysis of world capitalist development. Laclau and his followers begin with concepts of modes of production to describe and analyze development in the core and periphery of the world economy. Different and unequal national units within a world capitalist social formation is the starting point for Amin's theory of development. Many radicals have attempted to use all three standpoints, by synthesizing concepts of commodity and capital flows, modes of production, and the world capitalist system into a single framework of analysis. Thus, radical approaches tend to replace the model of human behavior of orthodox theory with one of a variety of different concepts (or a combination of them).

It is natural, then, that capitalist development will look very different to these radical theorists in comparison with the bourgeois outlook. Where the orthodox theorists see freedom, the radicals see unequal power relations. The orthodox notion of economic growth for all countries becomes, in radical theories, economic growth for some countries at the expense of growth for all the others. The orthodox theory of a unilinear process of development from traditional to modern societies is similarly challenged by radical theorists: Development occurs in the center while underdevelopment or dependent development occurs in the periphery. In this sense, capitalism is the problem, not the solution.

These radical theories are certainly alternatives to the orthodox approach to development, both in terms of their conceptual entry-points and the conclusions they generate about the process of development. However, they share with their orthodox opposite one crucial element: They tend to reduce the analysis of development to one decisive factor. That is, just as the neoclassical conception of development explains all social phenomena in terms of a particular model of human behavior (psychological utility), the radical theories we have presented tend to explain development in terms of international commodity circulation, the mode of production, or the world capitalist social formation, respectively. The result is that quite different theories end up agreeing on the methodological point that the rest of society can be explained in terms of one essential factor. What they disagree about, then, is what the factor is.

The difficulty with all such approaches is that they attempt to reduce the explanation of a complex and diffuse phenomenon—world devleopment in the past four hundred years—to an ultimately determining factor. One can be justifiably wary of whether any theory of this sort can provide an entirely convincing account.

Orthodox and radical approaches also share another key aspect. They are both directly and indirectly connected to political agendas. Radical theorists tend to be more upfront about their political interests. Orthodox theorists, concerned to claim the mantle of science, tend to shy away from stating explicitly the political dimensions and implications of their approach. Nonetheless, we should recognize that such contrasting theories of development will lead to significantly different consequences for the actual course of development.

NOTES

1. We would like to thank Charles Wilber, Kenneth Jameson, Vaughn McKim, and Rhoda Halperin for their helpful comments on an earlier draft of this material. The research on this article was supported in part by a grant from the Institute for Scholarship in the Liberal Arts of the University of Notre Dame.
2. For three recent attempts to survey this literature, see Anthony Brewer, *Marxist Theories of Imperialism: A Critical Survey* (London: Routledge & Kegan Paul, 1980); Gabriel Palma, "Dependency: A Formal Theory of Underdevelopment or a Methodology for the Analysis of Concrete Situations of Underdevelopment?," *World Development* 6 (July–August 1978): 881–924; and Keith Griffin and John Gurley, "Radical Analyses of Imperialism, the Third World, and the Transition to Socialism: A Survey Article," *Journal of Economic Literature* 23 (September 1985): 1089–1143.
3. What might be called the classic debate took place in the first decades of this century and largely involved issues of how to interpret and extend Marx's theory

to the questions of imperialism and the colonial world. The major figures included Lenin, Luxemburg, Bukharin, and Hilferding. The works listed in footnote 2 all discuss this material. Paul Baran's *The Political Economy of Growth* (New York: Monthly Review Press, 1957) preceded Frank's work by a decade and was very influential in setting the stages for the modern debate.

4. For discussions of a more critical nature focusing in particular on methodological issues, see two essays by the authors, "A Methodological Analysis of Dependency Theory: Explanation in Andre Gunder Frank" and "Methodological Aspects of a Marxian Approach to Development: An Analysis of the Modes of Production School," both in *World Development* 14 (February 1986): 195–209 and 211–222. Some of the material in the present article has been adopted from these two essays.

5. Fernando Henrique Cardoso, it should perhaps be noted, differs somewhat from this view. See his "The Consumption of Dependency Theory in the United States," *Latin American Research Review* 12 (1977): 7–24.

6. Andre Gunder Frank, *Capitalism and Underdevelopment in Latin America: Historical Studies of Chile and Brazil* (New York and London: Monthly Review Press, 1967, rev. ed. 1969). Frank's other major works include: *Latin America: Underdevelopment or Revolution* (New York and London: Monthly Review Press, 1969); *Lumpenbourgeoisie: Lumpendevelopment: Dependence, Class, and Politics in Latin America* (New York and London: Monthly Review Press, 1972); *World Accumulation 1492–1978* (New York and London: Monthly Review Press, 1978); *Dependent Accumulation and Underdevelopment* (New York and London: Monthly Review Press, 1979); and *Critique and Anti-Critique: Essays on Dependence and Reformism* (New York: Praeger, 1984).

7. For a discussion of the structuralist position, see Kenneth P. Jameson, "Latin American Structuralism: A Methodological Perspective," *World Development* 14 (February 1986): 223–232.

8. For example, Walt W. Rostow, *The Stages of Economic Growth* (Cambridge: Cambridge University Press, 1960). For a recent restatement of this orthodox approach, see Bruce Herrick and Charles P. Kindleberger, *Economic Development,* 4th ed. (New York: McGraw-Hill, 1983).

9. Frank, *Latin America: Underdevelopment or Revolution,* p. 5.

10. Ibid. (emphasis in the original); see also *Capitalism and Underdevelopment,* pp. 3–6.

11. This point should not, of course, be taken to imply that Frank does not admit the possibility or desirability of socialist development. Quite to the contrary. But socialist development is a relatively recent phenomenon and cannot be part of the explanation of underdevelopment.

12. As we shall see in our discussion of Lall's criticism of Frank below, this initial distinction is open to damaging criticism.

13. It should be noted that not all Dependency Theorists would agree with this last point. For instance, dos Santos defines "dependence" in the following way: "Dependence is a conditioning situation in which the economies of one group of countries are conditioned by the development and expansion of others. A relationship of interdependence between two or more economies and the world trading system becomes a dependent relationship when some countries can expand through self-impulsion while othes, being in a dependent position, can only expand as a reflection of the dominant countries, which may have *positive or negative* effects on their immediate development." (emphasis added) (T. dos Santos, "The Structure of Dependence," *American Economic Review,* Papers and Proceedings 40

[May 1970]: 231–236.) The trouble with this definition is that if in fact the dependency relation has positive effects on the development of the dependent country, then it is hard to see how the theory can serve the critical function that Frank, at least, wants to give it. Three possible replies to this point are (1) that the positive effects are *immediate* and not long-term, and that the long-term effects of dependent development are and must be negative; (2) that even if there are positive effects on development, as long as the dependent country is dominated from without and does not control its own development, there is a violation of national autonomy, if not sovereignty, and this is to be criticized; and (3) that the theory is not meant to be critical, but only descriptive. The problems with these replies are that the first makes it unclear why the short-term positive effects should ever be mentioned; the second reply, if it is intended to support a critical theory, requires an additional argument to the effect that the loss of autonomy is worse than the gain in economic development, and this would be a controversial claim; and the third reply is not accurate, at least in relation to Frank. This entire problem can be sidetracked by building the normative dimension into the concept of dependence from the beginning. Sanjaya Lall also makes the point that "dependence" as used by the Dependency Theory school has a definite normative dimension, namely, that the future development of the dependent economy is adversely affected by its being dependent. See Sanjaya Lall, "Is 'Dependence' a Useful Concept in Analysing Underdevelopment?" *World Development* 3 (November and December 1975): 799–800. For an additional discussion and critique of Frank's use of the concept of dependence, see Brewer, *Marxist Theories of Imperialism,* pp. 164 and 177–180.

14. *Capitalism and Underdevelopment,* p. 9. It should be noted that while Frank's view requires a complete account of the origins and development of capitalism, and he acknowledges as much, his early work only gestured at such an account. In more recent work, however, he has attempted to develop more fully this side of his project. See especially, *Dependent Accumulation and Underdevelopment* and *World Accumulation 1492–1789.* It should also be mentioned that Immanuel Wallerstein shares Frank's view of capitalism as a world system and more or less agrees with Frank's understanding of what capitalism is and how it works. Wallerstein's work has, of course, concentrated on the historical development of the capitalist world system, and in many ways the projects and perspectives of Frank and Wallerstein complement each other. Thus many of the points we make about Frank could easily be adapted to fit Wallerstein's work. See Wallerstein, *The Modern World System: Capitalist Agriculture and the Origins of the European World—Economy in the Sixteenth Century* (New York: Academic Press, 1974) and *The Capitalist World Economy* (Cambridge and Paris: Cambridge Univesity Press and Editions de la Maison des Sciences de l'Homme, 1979).

15. See for instance Ernesto Laclau, "Feudalism and Capitalism in Latin America," *New Left Review,* no. 67 (May-June 1971), p. 24; and Brewer, *Marxist Theories of Imperialism,* p. 160.

16. *Capitalism and Underdevelopment,* p. 20; also see pp. 14–15.

17. Brewer makes this point in *Marxist Theories of Imperialism,* p. 160.

18. Laclau, "Feudalism and Capitalism in Latin America," pp. 24–25.

19. This point is made by Laclau, ibid., p. 22, and Brewer, *Marxist Theories of Imperialism,* p. 160. This criticism is one to which Frank tries to respond in his later work; see *Dependent Accumulation and Underdevelopment,* p. xii.

20. *Capitalism and Underdevelopment,* p. 12.
21. Ibid., p. 6.
22. Ibid., p. 16.
23. See *Lumpenbourgeoisie: Lumpendevelopment,* p. 13.
24. *Capitalism and Underdevelopment,* p. 94. Also see *Dependent Accumulation and Underdevelopment,* p. 123.
25. *Dependent Accumulation and Underdevelopment.*
26. Ibid., p. xii.
27. The article under discussion is Lall, "Is 'Dependence' a Useful Concept?"
28. Ibid., p. 800.
29. Ibid., p. 800.
30. Ibid., pp. 808–809 (emphasis in the original).
31. Notice that even putting the point this way circumscribes the audience to which the claim is addressed, for only those theorists who are predisposed to be sympathetic to the concept of dependence in the first place will have any initial notions or intuitions concerning the use of the concept; but without such intuitions, it is impossible to agree or disagree with the initial distinction. Without initial notions as to concept boundaries, no economies are obviously dependent or obviously nondependent.
32. Robert Brenner, "The Origins of Capitalist Development: A Critique of Neo-Smithian Marxism," *New Left Review,* no. 104 (July–August 1977), p. 83.
33. In particular, Brenner cites Sweezy's contribution to *The Transition from Feudalism to Capitalism,* introduced by Rodney Hilton (London: New Left Review, 1976) and Wallerstein's *The Modern World System* and a series of subsequent articles listed in ibid., p. 29, footnote 7.
34. Brenner, "The Origins of Capitalist Development," p. 30 (emphasis in the original).
35. Ibid., p. 61 (emphasis in the original).
36. Ibid., pp. 82–83 (emphasis in the original).
37. Ibid., p. 85 (emphasis in the original).
38. Ibid., p. 32.
39. See ibid., pp. 31–32 and 68 for examples of this criticism.
40. Ibid., p. 58. There might seem to be an initial tension between the claim that the explanation generated by the Frank–Wallerstein model at the same time is deterministic and yet relies on the free choice of rational individuals. If the individuals are really free, surely it is possible that they won't choose to act as the model determines they do. This tension, we think, can be dissolved by two considerations. First, the explanation is deterministic, not in the strong sense of metaphysical necessity, but rather in the sense of a lawlike natural relation. Second, it is important that the free individuals involved are also rational, where this is a strong condition. Given their assumed motivation, profit maximizing, and their assumed rationality, the individuals really do have no choice. For an individual to fail to act in the way the model stipulates would mean either that one of the initial assumptions was violated, or that some other variable was involved that the model failed to take into account. Thus, if the model is correct and given the nature of human beings as assumed by the model, and the initial conditions, it follows that the behavior predicted by the model obtains.
41. Brenner makes this point in several ways and in several places, directed variously against Smith, Sweezy, Wallerstein, and Frank. See for examples, ibid., pp. 34, 45, 55, 58, 67, and 83.

42. Ibid., p. 27.
43. Ibid., p. 27.
44. Brenner also makes this criticism in various ways; ibid., pp. 48–50 and 79–82.
45. Among the other interesting critics see especially Palma, "Dependency."
46. The individuals whose work exemplifies the articulation of MOP approach include Laclau, Rey, Arrighi, and Bradby. The most comprehensive surveys of this approach are Aidan Foster-Carter, "The Modes of Production Controversy," *New Left Review,* no. 107 (1978): 47–77, and John G. Taylor, *From Modernization to Modes of Production: A Critique of the Sociologies of Development and Underdevelopment* (London: Macmillan Press, 1979).
47. C. F. S. Cardoso, Banaji, and Alavi are among those who have developed this particular interpretation of MOP analysis. See Foster-Carter, "Modes of Production Controversy," pp. 63–64, and Brewer, *Marxist Theories of Imperialism,* pp. 268–272.
48. The work of Palloix, Cypher, Warren, and Barkin is representative. Unfortunately, the tendency is to submerge this approach within a more comprehensive MOP school of thought; see, e.g., James M. Cypher, "The Internationalization of Capital and the Transformation of Social Formations: A Critique of the Monthly Review School," *Review of Radical Political Economics* 11 (Winter 1979): 33–49. Our brief survey is an attempt to demonstrate the specificity of this internationalization of capital intepretation of Dependency Theory.
49. For example, in the surveys by Foster-Carter, Taylor, and Brewer.
50. Palma is one who has commented on the problem of "operationalizing" the concepts of Frank's formulation of Dependency Theory; see his "Dependency."
51. The most famous are Rey, Meillasoux, and Terray.
52. Laclau, "Feudalism and Capitalism in Latin America," pp. 19–37.
53. Ibid., p. 33.
54. Many of the MOP theorists have acknowledged their intellectual debt to the work of Althusser and Balibar. A central text in this tradition is Louis Althusser and Etienne Balibar, *Reading Capital* (London: New Left Books, 1975).
55. Essentialism is defined by Althusser and Balibar as a form of analysis in which the relations among social processes are understood in terms of essence—phenomenon relations. It is more or less synonymous with reductionism and determinism. According to Althusser and Balibar, the two most common forms of essentialism in the Marxist theoretical tradition are economic determinism and theoretical humanism. In both cases, an essence (the economy or human nature) serves to ultimately determine all other aspects of society (politics, culture, etc.) as the phenomenal forms of that essence. See, in particular, Louis Althusser, *For Marx* (New York: Vintage, 1970). This critique of essentialism and the project of formulating a nonessentialist interpretation of Marxist theory have been extended more recently by Stephen Resnick and Richard Wolff, "Marxist Epistemology: The Critique of Economic Determinism" *Social Text,* no. 6 (Fall 1982): 31–72.
56. The debate was initiated by the publication of Maurice Dobb, *Studies in the Development of Capitalism* (New York: International Publishers, 1947). The actual debate between Dobb and Paul Sweezy in *Science and Society,* along with other contributions, was published as *The Transition from Feudalism to Capitalism.*
57. Barry Hindess and Paul Hirst, *Pre-Capitalist Modes of Production* (London: Routledge & Kegan Paul, 1975).
58. Barry Hindess and Paul Hirst, *Modes of Production and Social Formation: An Auto-Critique of "Pre-Capitalist Modes of Production"* (Atlantic Highlands, NJ: Humanities Press, 1977).

59. See Vladimir Ilyich Lenin, *Imperialism: The Highest Stage of Capitalism* (New York: International, [originally published in Russian: 1917] 1933) and Rosa Luxemburg, *The Accumulation of Capital* (London: Routledge & Kegan Paul [1913] 1951).

60. Cf. the discussion by Foster-Carter, "Modes of Production Controversy," p. 53.

61. Pierre-Philippe Rey, *Colonialisme, Neo-colonialisme, et Transition au Capitalisme* (Paris: Maspero, 1971), *Les Alliances de Classes* (Paris: Maspero, 1973) and, in English, "The Lineage Mode of Production," *Critique of Anthropology,* no. 3 (Spring 1975): 27–79. Rey's work analyzed by Barbara Bradby, "The Destruction of Natural Economy," in Harold Wolpe, ed. *The Articulation of Modes of Production: Essays from Economy and Society* (London: Routledge & Kegan Paul, 1980), pp. 93–127.

62. The classic example is Luxemburg, *The Accumulation of Capital.*

63. A position elaborated by Bradby, "Destruction of Natural Economy."

64. Ibid., p. 95

65. Ibid., p. 93.

66. Harold Wolpe, "Introduction," in Wolpe, ed., *Articulation of Modes of Production,* p. 41.

67. Anibal Quijano Obregon, "The Marginal Pole of the Economy and the Marginalised Labour Force," in Wolpe, ed. *Articulation of Modes of Production,* p. 255.

68. "Modes of Production Controversy," p. 23.

69. Giovanni Arrighi, "Labour Supplies in Historical Perspective: A Study of the Proletarianization of the African Peasantry in Rhodesia," *Journal of Development Studies* 3 (1970): 197–234.

70. Conceptions of historical development based on more or less inevitable successions of MOP are criticized by Umberto Melotti, *Marx y el Tercer Mundo* (Buenos Aires: Amorrortu, 1974).

71. Certainly many of Marx's oft-quoted summary statements on historical development can be interpreted as laying out an inevitable succession of stages; one example is the following: "In broad outline, Asiatic, ancient, feudal and modern bourgeois modes of production can be designated as epochs marking progress in the economic development of society" (Karl Marx, "Preface," *A Contribution to the Critique of Political Economy* [New York: International Publishers, 1970], p. 21.) However, Marx himself made clear that his objective was not to present "an historic-philosophic theory of the general path every people is fated to tread" (Karl Marx and Friedrich Engels, *Basic Writings on Politics and Philosophy,* Lewis S. Feuer, ed. [Garden City, NY: Doubleday, 1959], p. 440.) Stalin's interpretation, to take one example, is exactly such a "philosophy of history"; see his "Anarchism or Socialism?" and "Dialectical Materialism" in J. V. Stalin, *Works,* vol. 1 (1901–1907) (Moscow: Foreign Languages Publishing House, 1952).

72. Dobb, *Studies in the Development of Capitalism,* and Henri Pirenne, *Economic and Social History of Medieval Europe* (New York: Harcourt, Brace, and World, 1937).

73. Ciro Flamarion Santana Cardoso, "Severo Martinez Pelaez y el Caracter del Regimen Colonial," in Carlos Sempat Assadourian et al., *Modos de Produccion en America Latina* (Cordoba, Argentina: Ediciones Pasado y Presente, 1974), p. 86 (our translation).

74. Hamza Alavi, "India and the Colonial Mode of Production," in *Socialist Register* (London: Merlin Press, 1975) pp. 160–197, and Jairus Banaji, "For a Theory of Colonial Modes of Production," *Economic and Political Weekly* (Bombay) 7 (December 1972); see, also, the discussion by Brewer, *Marxist Theories of Imperialism,* pp. 270–272.

75. For example, *World Accumulation, 1492–1789* and *Accumulation, Dependence, and Under-development.*

76. David Barkin, "Internationalization of Capital: An Alternative Approach," *Latin American Perspectives* 8 (Summer and Fall 1981): 157.

77. Christian Palloix, "The Internationalization of Capital and the Circuit of Social Capital," in *International Firms and Modern Imperialism,* ed. Hugo Radice (New York: Penguin, 1975), p. 83.

78. See, e.g., Folker Frobel, Jurgen Heinrichs, and Otto Kreye, *The New International Division of Labour: Structural Unemployment in Industrialised Countries and Industrialisation in Developing Countries* (Cambridge: Cambridge University Pres, 1981).

79. Cypher, "Internationalization of Capital," and Bill Warren, *Imperialism: Pioneer of Capitalism* (London: New Left Books, 1980).

80. Internationalization of Capital," p. 158.

81. Samir Amin, *Unequal Development: An Essay on the Social Formations of Peripheral Capitalism,* trans. Brian Pearce (New York: Monthly Review Press, 1976), p. 104.

82. Ibid. p. 16.

83. Ibid., p. 22.

84. For example, *L'Economie du Maghreb,* 2 vols. (Paris: Editions de Minuit, 1966); *Le Developpment du Capitalisme en Cote d'Ivoire* (Paris: Editions de Minuit, 1967); *L'Afrique de l'Ouest Bloquee* (Paris: Editions de Minuit, 1971); and *Neo-Colonialism in West Africa,* trans. Francis McDonagh (New York: Monthly Review Press, 1973).

85. This point concerning the epistemological status of history in Amin's work, as well as the more general analysis of this section, shares much with the more extensive critical analysis of Amin's theory of development by Joseph Medley, "Economic Growth and Development: A Critique of Samir Amin's Conception of Capital Accumulation and Development," unpublished Ph.D. dissertation, University of Massachusetts-Amherst (May 1981).

86. Amin, *Unequal Development,* p. 199.

87. Samir Amin, "Crisis, Nationalism, and Socialism," in Samir Amin, Giovanni Arrighi, Andre Gunder Frank, and Immanuel Wallerstein, *Dynamics of Global Crisis* (New York: Monthly Review Press, 1982), pp. 168–169.

88. This model of autocentric and, below, of extraverted development is presented by Amin in summary form in "Accumulation and Development: A Theoretical Model," *Review of African Political Economy,* no. 1 (1974): 9–26, and explored at length in *Accumulation on a World Scale,* 2 vols. (New York: Monthly Review Press, 1975).

89. Similar concepts of "social articulation" and "social disarticulation" are used by Alain de Janvry (with Elisabeth Sadoulet), "Social Articulation as a Condition for Equitable Growth," *Journal of Development Economics* 13 (1983): 275–303.

90. Amin, *Unequal Development,* p. 292.

91. Arghiri Emmanuel, *Unequal Exchange: A Study of the Imperialism of Trade,* trans. Brian Pearce (New York: Monthly Review Press, 1972).

92. Amin, "Crisis, Nationalism, and Socialism," p. 151.

93. See, e.g., the comments by Charles Bettelheim published as Appendices I and III to Emmanuel, *Unequal Exchange,* and the recent survey article by David Evans, "A Critical Assessment of Some Neo-Marxian Trade Theories," *Journal of Development Studies* 20 (Janury 1984): 202–226.

94. This interpretation of Marx's theory of value is presented at length by Bruce Roberts, "Value Categories and Marxian Method: A Different View of Value-

Price Transformation," unpublished Ph.D. dissertation, University of Massachusetts-Amherst (September 1981).

95. Richard D. Wolff, "Marxian Crisis Theory: Structure and Implications," *Review of Radical Political Economics* 10 (Spring 1978): 50.

96. Amin, *Unequal Development,* p. 196.

97. See, for a representative sample, the following: Jonathan Schiffer, "The Changing Postwar Pattern of Development or the Accumulated Wisdom of Samir Amin," *World Development* 9 (1981): 515–537; Sheila Smith, "The Ideas of Samir Amin: Theory of Tautology," *Journal of Development Studies* 17 (October 1980) and "Class Analysis versus World Systems: Critique of Samir Amin's Typology of Underdevelopment," *Journal of Contemporary Asia* 12 (1982): 7–18; and John Weeks and Eliabeth Dore, "International Exchange and the Causes of Backwardness," *Latin American Perspectives* 6 (Spring 1979): 71–77.

98. Samir Amin, "Expansion or Crisis of Capitalism?" *Third World Quarterly* 5 (April 1983): 361–385.

99. Ibid., p. 365.

100. Ibid., p. 377.

101. Ibid., p. 376.

102. Ibid., p. 371.

9

The Modernization of Underdevelopment: El Salvador, 1858–1931

E. Bradford Burns

"What most strikes me on arriving from Europe is the absence of all extreme poverty," Mrs. Henry Grant Foote observed approvingly of El Salvador in the mid-nineteenth century.[1] The British diplomat's wife concluded that Southern Europe and the major cities of England suffered far worse poverty and human misery than the diminutive—and other observers would add "backward"—Central American republic. These first impressions of the country, to which Queen Victoria's government had posted Mrs. Foote's husband in 1853, were also her conclusions strengthened by eight years of residence there.

Her memoir revealed at least one explanation for the satisfactory quality of life: people enjoyed access to land. The large Indian population still possessed a part of its communal lands, ranked by Mrs. Foote as among the "most fertile" areas of El Salvador.[2] Those who chose not to live in the communities, she noted, "generally have their own little piece of land and a house on it."[3] The outskirts of the capital, San Salvador, seemed almost Edenic in her prose: "The environs of the city are very beautiful, being one mass of luxuriant orange and mango trees, bending beneath their load of fruit, and the cottages of the poor people are remarkably neat and clean, each surrounded by its own beautiful shrubbery of fruit trees."[4] These observations buttressed her conclusion of the ready availability of food. The simple society excluded sharp distinctions between rich and poor. The Englishwoman praised the practical modesty among the upper class, although its humility sometimes bemused her. At one point she chuckled: "One custom struck us as very peculiar in this state. Everyone, from President downwards keeps a shop, and no one

From *Journal of Developing Areas,* No. 18 (April 1984), pp. 293–316. © 1984 by Western Illinois University.

objects to appear behind his counter and sell you a reel of cotton, the wives and daughters officiating in the same capacity."[5] She left an incomplete although suggestive portrait of the new nation, characterizing life as bucolic, devoid of social and economic extremes.

Around the middle of the century, a small group of foreign travelers and diplomats, among them John Baily, E. G. Squier, Carl Scherzer, and G. F. Von Tempsky, visited El Salvador.[6] Their accounts corroborated Mrs. Foote's. Although those visitors considered the small nation to be overcrowded even then, they agreed that most of the population owned land, either individually or collectively. The large hacienda existed but did not monopolize the rural economy. Squier noted, "There is little public and unclaimed land in the state, and few large tracts held by single individuals."[7] He contrasted that aspect of land tenure favorably with the experience of other nations he knew. The Indians, who at midcentury comprised at least a quarter of the population, worked either their communal lands or individual plots. A large number of them exclusively inhabited a Pacific coastal area of 50 by 20 miles between the ports of La Libertad and Acajutla, "retaining habits but little changed from what they were at the period of conquest," according to Squier.[8] All the travelers lauded the generosity of nature and spoke of the abundance of food. Von Tempsky recalled that the Indian Village, Chinameca, he visited in 1855 was "well supplied with the necessaries of life."[9] Particularly impressed with the region of Sonsonate, Scherzer lauded the abundance, variety, and low price of food.[10] None mentioned either malnutrition or starvation.

The largely subsistence economy produced rather leisurely for the world markets. Indigo, traditionally a principal export, earned $700,000 of $1,200,-000 from foreign sales in 1851. Minerals, balsams, skins, rice, sugar, cotton, and cacao accounted for much of the rest.

Even though the foreign visitors waxed eloquent about some idyllic aspects of life as they lived and perceived it in El Salvador, not one pretended that the isolated nation was a rustic paradise. Problems existed. The visitors lamented the disease and political turmoil. Still, even if life did not mirror the ideal, a socioeconomic pattern that benefited many had emerged in the long colonial period and much briefer national period: food was produced in sufficient quantity to feed the population, the economy was varied, little emphasis fell on the export sector, the land was reasonably well distributed, the foreign debt was low, and the absence of the extremes of poverty and wealth spoke of a vague degree of equality. Having endured for some time, however, by the 1850s such characteristics were about to disappear. The El Salvador those foreigners observed was on the threshold of change and a rather rapid and dramatic change at that.

Over the course of three centuries, Spain had implanted its political, economic, social, and cultural institutions in its vast American empire with varying degrees of effectiveness. Those regions nearest the viceregal capitals or well integrated into imperial trade patterns bore the most vivid testimony to their successful implantation. Consequently, no matter what great distances might have separated Lima from Mexico City, the gold mines of Colombia from the silver mines of Bolivia, or the sugar plantations of Cuba from the cacao estates of Venezuela, similarities in economic and political structures outweighed inevitable local variations. Historiographic studies tend to dwell on the relative changelessness and continuity of some of those institutions over half a millenium. The institutions surrounding the use of land and labor are two useful examples; the concentration and authoritarian exercise of political power is another. Still, the metropolitan institutions did not fully penetrate every part of Spanish America. To the degree they did not, those regions remained marginal to international trade and isolated from the primary preoccupations of the crown. Fusing Iberian, Indian, and African cultures and institutions, such regions remained nominally subordinate to a distant monarch but for practical purposes more responsive to local conditions.

More regional diversity existed in Spanish America during the period when the colonies obtained their independence, 1808–1824, than there would be at the end of the century. The reasons for the rapid homogenization during the nineteenth century are not difficult to find. Many of the elites in all the newly independent governments had embraced or would embrace the ideas that sprang from the European Enlightenment. They admired French culture, while they looked to England for their economic vigor. As the nineteenth century waxed, their collective desire grew to create in the New World a replica of Europe north of the Pyrenees. To emulate the "progress" the elites believed characteristic of their model nations, they needed capital. They obtained it through loans, investments, and trade, all three of which linked them ever more closely to North Atlantic capitalism. Marvelous advances in communication and transportation facilitated the growing conformity forged by common goals and trade patterns. One major consequence was that as the new nations neared the first centenary of their independence, the institutional patterns of Latin America reflected a more striking similarity than they had after more than three centuries of Iberian domination. To achieve conformity required certain areas and nations, those that once had been marginal to Spanish interests and thus most superficially incorporated into European commercial patterns, to change dramatically. A predominately export-oriented economy linked to international capitalism became the dynamo propelling that profound, rapid change. In certain cases, radical transformation—almost revolutionary in some instances—challenged the stereotypes of "changelessness" and "continuity" often applied to the entire area.

One of the new nations, El Salvador, provides a striking example of the rapid and profound change of a once-neglected outpost of the Spanish empire. Further, its experience with progress or modernization accompanied by the increasing impoverishment of the majority of the inhabitants illustrates how a Latin American nation could modernize without developing.[11]

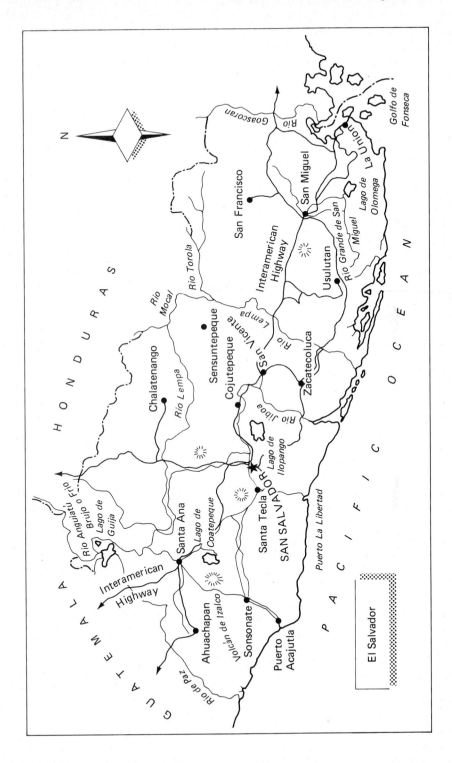

Spanish institutions had imperfectly penetrated El Salvador. Throughout the colonial period that small area bore a closer resemblance to its Indian past than to any of the bustling centers of colonial Spanish America. Like the other Central Americans, the Salvadorans remained geographically isolated and largely self-sufficient. As Adriaan C. van Oss convincingly argued, the Central Americans had "turned their backs on the coasts and thereby on intensive commerce with the motherland."[12] Yet, within the short span of three decades, roughly between 1860 and 1890, El Salvador acquired the economic, political, and social institutions characterizing the rest of Latin America. These included a dynamic and modernizing export sector based on monoculture and the predominance of the large estate producing for foreign trade; a subservient, impoverished, landless rural labor force; concentration of economic and political power within the hands of the principal planters who exercised it from a single dominant city, the capital, which, if it fell short of duplicating its urban model, Paris, nonetheless contained districts reflecting the architectural influence of nineteenth-century Europe; and a political understanding and tolerance between an increasingly professional military and politicoeconomic elites. In a number of fundamental aspects, El Salvador became nearly indistinguishable from the other Spanish-speaking nations. The process by which that formerly isolated and singular state acquired institutions characteristic of the rest of Spanish America as well as the consequences of that process merit study.

For three centuries Central America formed part of the Spanish empire before it fell briefly under Mexican rule. A shaky confederation, the United Provinces of Central America, emerged in 1824 but crumbled under political rivalries a decade and a half later. In 1839, some of the leading citizens of San Salvador declared the independence of El Salvador, although the vision of a greater Central American fatherland remained constant in El Salvador. Promulgating a constitution in 1841, the Salvadorans embarked on a tempestuous political journey. The population of the new republic, estimated in 1855 to be 394,000, consisted largely of Indians and mestizos with a small minority of whites, blacks, and mulattoes (see table 1). Most of the population lived in the countryside.

The economic structures characteristic of the long colonial past remained intact during the first half of the nineteenth century. El Salvador continued to export in small quantities marginal products of limited demand. The Spanish mercantilist legacy rested lightly on the region because of its isolation and economic insignificance. The land-use patterns accommodated both Spanish and Indian practices. The Indian villages held the land they needed; the traditional Indian communities survived. The haciendas, the large estates owned by Spaniards and their descendants, also existed. In the early nineteenth century, there were approximately 440 haciendas averaging close to 2,000 acres each.[13] They accounted for one-third of the land area. The Indian

TABLE 1   **Estimates of the Population of
El Salvador, 1821–1930**

YEAR	POPULATION
1821	250,000
1855	394,000
1878	554,000
1882	612,943
1892	703,500
1900	783,433
1910	986,537
1920	1,178,665
1930	1,353,170

SOURCE: Jeffry Royle Gibson, "A Demographic
Analysis of Urbanization: Evolution of a System
of Cities in Honduras, El Salvador, and Costa
Rica" (Ph.D. diss., Cornell University, 1970), p.
80.

communities produced food for local consumption. So did the haciendas, but
they also grew the principal export crops, foremost of which was indigo.

Indigo production required both a regular and a seasonal labor force. The
haciendas drew their workers from neighboring Indian communities. They
also slowly but steadily encroached on Indian lands. The control of the
political institutions of the new republic by a small merchant and planter class
complemented those trends. The new national elite fully understood the
importance to their own prosperity of controlling land and labor. No longer
did a distant Spanish crown thwart them. For the time being, however, certain
other realities inhibited their economic expansion. The frequent wars in
Central America, a scarcity of capital and credit, a disruption of trade routes
and patterns, and the lack of any products in high demand in foreign markets
caused a general economic decline throughout much of the first half of the
nineteenth century. Those political and economic realities enforced a kind of
balance between the Indian communities and the haciendas. Both seemed to
provide satisfactory, if very modest, life styles. Such was the El Salvador
described by Foote, Squier, Von Tempsky, Scherzer, and Baily.

After 1858, new socioeconomic patterns took shape. Greater political
stability and closer contact with the North Atlantic nations, principally the
United States, France, and Great Britain, partially explain the emergence of
the new patterns. Very importantly, the elite found a new crop, coffee, that
the country could grow and profitably sell abroad. More than anything else,
concentration on the growth and export of that single crop altered old institutions. Before the end of the century, the new coffee estates became the base
of economic production, political power, and social organization. The coffee
planters emerged as the powerful economic, political, and social elite.

Instrumental in initiating the challenge to the old system, President Gerardo Barrios (1858–1863) directed the fledgling nation's first steps toward modernization and change. A trip through Europe in the early 1850s had influenced him profoundly. In one letter back to El Salvador, he proclaimed his mission: "I urgently needed this trip to correct my ideas and to be useful to my country. . . . I will return to preach to my fellow countrymen what we Central Americans are and what we can become."[14] He did. He informed the legislative assembly in 1860 that he intended to "regenerate" the nation.[15]

In a pattern already becoming familiar throughout Latin America, those who would "regenerate" their society advocated rather uncritically the models provided by the leading capitalist nations of the North Atlantic. Their agrarian, industrial, and technological advances awed the Latin American elites. Those nations seemed to have found the sure road to "progress," a gloriously nineteenth-century notion for which the current social science concept "modernization" is synonymous. In the minds of the elites, "to progress" came to mean to recreate the European model in Latin America. Carried to its extreme, it even signified the encouragement of European immigration to replace the Indian and African peoples of the New World. Within a broad Latin American perspective, Barrios was by no means unique in either his discovery of Europe or his hope of recreating his nation in its image. Within the narrow confines of bucolic El Salvador, however, he seemed to be something of a visionary ready to deny the past in order to participate in an alluring if uncertain future.

Barrios characterized the nation he governed as one that was "backward," "destitute," and "misgoverned," and into which he believed he introduced "progress."[16] Both a military commander and the owner of a medium-sized estate, the president represented the nascent middle class in his lifestyle, outlook, and aspirations. His government vaguely encompassed a liberalism characteristic of later nineteenth-century Salvadoran politics. He favored individual liberties, opposed dictatorial rule, and sought to end the neofeudalism dominating the countryside. He succeeded in accelerating a rural shift from neofeudalism to neocapitalism. In a not unfamiliar pattern in nineteenth-century Latin America, however, liberty during the Barrios years—as thereafter—smiled exclusively on the elites, and authoritarian rule remained the practice despite rhetoric to the contrary.

A devoted francophile, President Barrios incorporated Liberal and Positivist ideas into his policies to turn his country from its Iberian and Indian past to a closer approximation of a rapidly changing Western Europe. In 1860, the first program he announced for his government included these five goals: promotion of agriculture, industry, and commerce; introduction into El Salvador of the progress that distinguished other nations; encouragement of immigration; reform of the educational system in accordance with the latest European ideas; and construction of roads and ports to facilitate international communication and transportation. Such goals typified the modernizers of nineteenth-century Latin America. Soon after the announcement of his program, the president promulgated the nation's first civil code and a new educational plan, both of which inevitably drew on the latest European models. In true Positivist fashion, Barrios believed the government should play a direct role in encouraging exports.[17] The most immediate results of his policies were to facilitate the growth of capitalism and to promote foreign commerce. Indeed, exports doubled between 1860 and 1862[18]

Barrios appreciated the incipient agrarian and commercial changes already under way in El Salvador. In 1853, steamship service had been inaugurated between El Salvador and California. Six years later, the government began to pay a subsidy to the Pacific Mail Steamship Company to service the Salvadoran ports. As one immediate consequence, sugar and rum exports rose, a trend Barrios applauded. United States diplomats stationed in San Salvador also spoke enthusiastically about the rising export trade facilitated by the steamships.[19] President Barrios not only encouraged the growth of crops with an international demand but favored land and labor laws complementary to such agrarian enterprise.

Understanding the importance of coffee on the world market and the suitability of El Salvador's rich volcanic soil to produce it, the president promoted its production.[20] Farmers had first started to grow small amounts of coffee for local consumption in the eighteenth century. Governmental encouragement of its production dated from 1846, without noticeable results. Barrios assumed a vigorous role in its promotion in order both to diversify exports and to increase national income. Under his direction, coffee exports had their modest beginnings. In his presidential address to the legislative assembly on 29 January 1862, he emphasized the impetus his government gave coffee, predicting (incorrectly) that within two years El Salvador would be the major coffee producer in Central America.[21]

In the decades after Barrios (really even including the Conservative government of Francisco Duenas, 1863–1871),[22] the Liberals articulated a program of goals focusing on the modernization of the transportation and communication infrastructures, the expansion of coffee exports, the adoption of European models, and the strengthening of governmental power. Never loath to use force to implement their program, they extended their authority from the presidential palace to the most remote hamlet.

The relatively complex process of coffee production engendered a series of crises in the traditional neo-Hispanic and neo-Indian institutions that had adequately served a society whose economy leisurely grew indigo and food crops.[23] The eventual triumph of coffee, a kind of victory of modern capitalism, necessitated new institutional arrangements.

Coffee production differed significantly from indigo, traditionally the primary export. The indigo plant grew without need of a great deal of care or investment. Within a year, the farmer could harvest it, although the amount of pigment increased if harvest could be delayed two or even three years. Indigo production required a small permanent work force supplemented during the harvesting and processing, both of which were relatively uncomplicated. Coffee could be grown under a variety of conditions on lands ranging from a small plot or a few acres to vast extensions of land. Small coffee planters seemed to flourish in some parts of Latin America. Colombia provided a useful example. In El Salvador, however, the growing and most especially the processing of coffee took place on medium-sized and large estates. Care, conservation, and fertilizing of the land and preparation of the coffee, including drying, processing, and sacking, required considerable capital and a large permanent work force generously augmented during the harvest season. Coffee planters waited three to five years for the first harvest. They required considerably more capital, patience, and skill than the producers of indigo. Those requirements severely limited the number of coffee growers but particularly the number of processors. Handsome profits, however, reimbursed the few who met the requirements.

The lure of a lucrative market prompted those planters who could bear the financial burden to expand their estates, which grew at the expense of communal landholdings and small landowners. The shift in landowning patterns fundamentally altered the lifestyle of the majority. The governments enthusiastically encouraged this change: they facilitated the concentration of land into fewer and fewer hands. Thus, in the decades between 1860 and 1890, the landholding patterns came to resemble the commercial capitalistic models characteristic of plantation economies elsewhere in the world. The first step was to label the Indian communal lands as retrograde, antiprogressive. They stood accused of the heinous crime of delaying or even preventing modernization. In short, they preserved the "backward" past. President Barrios initiated the legal attack on the *ejidos,* landholding communities, and the *tierras communales,* municipally owned and worked lands. His policies forced part of those lands onto the market, just as ambitious entrepreneurs sought more acres for coffee trees.

An official governmental land survey in 1879 revealed that only a quarter of the land still belonged to the villages.[24] The government of President Rafael Zaldivar (1876–1885) promptly oversaw the disposal of those remaining lands. Zaldivar proudly wore the modernizing mantle of Barrios, demonstrating his admiration for his predecessor by erecting an imposing mausoleum for him. An editorial in the *Diario Oficial* in early 1880 summarized the official attitude toward the communal lands, revealing once again the ideological continuity of the governments after 1858:

> On the one hand, we see virgin fertile lands that are calling for the application of capital and labor to reap the wealth that is promised; while

on the other, we see the majority of the inhabitants of our villages content to grow crops of maize and beans that will never raise this miserable people above their sorry position. They will remain in the same wretched state they endured in colonial times. . . . The government is determined to transform the Republic, to make each one of the villages, yesterday sad and miserable, into lively centers of work, wealth, and comfort.[25]

Action followed. In early 1881, the government abolished the tierras communales. With far-reaching consequences, the decree denounced ancient practices to declare unequivocally the economic policy in vogue for some decades dramatically enforced after 1881: "The existence of lands under the ownership of *Communidades* impedes agricultural development, obstructs the circulation of wealth, and weakens family bonds and the independence of the individual. Their existence is contrary to the economic and social principles that the Republic has accepted." A year later, a law dissolved the ejidos for the same reason: they were "an obstacle to our agricultural development [and] contrary to our economic principles."[26] The communidades and ejidos bore the blame, according to official thinking, of thwarting "progress," meaning, of course, the expansion of coffee culture. In both cases, the lands were divided among community members. Such actions disoriented the Indian and folk populations, which had little concept of private ownership of land. Quite the contrary, they identified the community and the land as one: the land existed for the commonweal of the group. The community cared for the land in an almost religious fashion. Cooperation rather than competition governed the economic behavior of those populations. In the government's judgment, the Indians and rural folk obviously were not prepared to contribute to El Salvador's capitalist future.

Once the communal lands were distributed into small plots, the coffee planters set about acquiring the land. Experience proved that it was easier to befuddle and buy out the new, small landowner than the well-entrenched and tradition-oriented community.[27] The emerging rural class system, increasingly characterized by a small group of wealthy coffee planters and processors on the one hand and a large body of ill-paid laborers on the other, contrasted sharply with the more equalitarian structures of rural El Salvador prior to 1860.

Export patterns altered radically during the same decades. From the colonial period into the early 1880s, El Salvador had enjoyed varied agrarian production and export: maize, indigo, tobacco, sugar, cacao, coffee, cotton, and tropical fruits. The midcentury invention of synthetic dyes doomed the most important of those exports, indigo. Coffee more than made up for its demise. The export statistics tell the tale. In 1860, coffee composed but 1 percent of the exports; in 1865, 8 percent; and in 1870, 17 percent. In 1875, for the first time, the value of coffee exports exceeded indigo exports, quite a change from 1865 when the value of indigo exports amounted to 15 times that of coffee. Table 2 indicates the changing nature of El Salvador's exports during the critical 1864–1875 period. In 1879, coffee accounted for 48.5 percent of the total value of all exports. By 1910, it accounted for $4,661,440 of exports totaling $5,696,706. Indigo by then earned only $107,936 on the world markets. During the decade of the 1880s, El Salvador became virtually a monoagricultural exporting nation, its economic prosperity largely dependent on the purchase of coffee by three or four nations, which, in turn, supplied investments, technology, and manufactured goods in quantities commensurate with the profits from coffee sales.

The domination of the national economy by coffee obviously affected the rural folk, the overwhelming majority of the population. The expanding coffee estates continued to dispossess vast numbers of them of their lands. They, then, depended on the coffee plantations for work and, to the relief of the coffee planters, formed a sizable pool of unemployed and underemployed who could be hired at meager wages. At the same time, the increasingly unstable position of larger numbers of the rural population created discontent and unrest among them. The rural poor protested their deteriorating situation. Major uprisings occurred in 1872, 1875, 1880, 1885, and 1898. The planter-dominated governments addressed the problem of maintaining order not only to assure tranquillity but just as importantly to insure a docile and plentiful labor supply. Threatening fines, arrests, and punishments, the Vagrancy Laws of 1881 required the populace to work. The Agrarian Law of 1907 further regulated the rural working class, while it authorized the organization of a rural constabulary to provide the physical protection the landowners demanded. Agricultural judges—in a fashion somewhat reminiscent of the Spanish *repartimiento* system—made certain that the labor force was available when and where the planters needed it. The new rural police enforced the judges' decisions, intimidated the workers, protected the planters, and guaranteed the type of rural order the planters believed essential to their prosperity. They already had closely identified national well-being with their own.

By the end of the century, coffee had transformed El Salvador. The landowning structures, the land-use patterns, and the relationship of the workers to the land were radically different. Whereas in 1858, there existed a reasonable balance between large estates, small landholdings, and ejidos, by 1890, the large estate dominated. The increasing accumulation of capital in a few hands strengthened the coffee estate, improved coffee processing, and further facilitated coffee exportation.

A tiny but significant group of capitalists appeared by the end of the century. Foreign immigrants, who invariably married into the leading Salvadoran families, played a disproportionately important role among them. They skillfully combined their wider knowledge of North Atlantic capitalism with local needs. A small number of Salvadoran capitalists from both the upper and middle classes and the local representatives of British capitalists

TABLE 2 **Value of Exports, 1854–1875** (In Silver Pesos)

YEAR	TOTAL VALUE OF EXPORTS	VALUE OF INDIGO EXPORTS	PERCENTAGE OF EXPORTS	VALUE OF COFFEE EXPORTS	PERCENTAGE OF EXPORTS	VALUE OF ALL OTHER EXPORTS	PERCENTAGE OF EXPORTS
1864	—	1,129,105	—	80,105	—	—	—
1865	2,765,260	1,357,400	49.0	138,263	1.5	1,369,597	49.5
1866	2,463,437	1,548,000	64.3	197,075	8.1	682,362	27.6
1867	3,056,388	1,979,850	64.7	275,075	9.1	801,463	26.2
1868	3,521,020	2,131,500	60.5	528,153	15.0	861,367	24.5
1869	3,906,100	2,447,550	62.7	507,793	13.0	950,767	24.8
1870	3,902,041	2,619,749	67.1	663,347	17.0	618,945	15.9
1871	3,896,588	2,308,317	59.2	662,420	17.0	925,851	23.8
1872	3,763,838	2,786,574	74.0	489,299	13.0	487,965	13.0
1873	3,521,096	1,808,037	51.2	1,056,329	30.0	662,730	18.8
1874	3,949,858	1,721,378	43.5	1,342,952	34.0	885,528	22.5
1875	5,070,172	1,160,700	22.9	1,673,157	33.0	2,236,351	44.1

SOURCE: Rafael Menjivar, *Acumulacion Originaria y Desarrollo del Capitalismo en El Salvador* (San Jose, Costa Rica: Editorial Universitaria Centroamerica, 1980), p. 35.

joined them. Some of them controlled the processing and/or export sectors of the coffee industry, highly lucrative and strategic enterprises. Their interests obviously intertwined with those of the coffee planters.

Political stability accompanied economic growth and change. Beginning with the government of Barrios in 1858 and ending with that of General Antonio Gutierrez in 1898, the chiefs-of-state stayed in office longer then their predecessors. In that 39-year time span, 7 presidents governed for an average of 5.7 years each, more than double the time the chiefs-of-state between 1839 and 1858 had served. Five of the presidents had military backgrounds. Force dislodged each president from office. The administration of Tomas Regalado, 1898–1903, marked a transition. General Regalado came to power through force, regularized his position through election, served the constitutional four-year term, and then stepped down from the presidency at the end of that term.[28]

The coffee elites had codified the political rules for their domination in the Constitution of 1886. It remained in force until 1939, the longest lived of El Salvador's many constitutions. Suppressing communal landownership, it emphasized the inviolability of private property. Within the classic framework of nineteenth-century liberalism, the document valued the individual over the collective. It enfranchised literate male adults, a minority in a land where illiteracy prevailed. Characterized as authoritarian and elitist, it served the planters handsomely during the half-century it was in force, defining the political boundaries of the "modern" state they sought to create.[29] It contributed significantly to the new political stability.

Increasing political stability, rising exports and income, economic growth, and a careful attention to the servicing of foreign debts nominated El Salvador as a candidate for foreign loans used to purchase a wide variety of consumer items the coffee class fancied, to introduce foreign technology, and to modernize the economy. Not unnaturally, a government in the service of the planters favored investment in and modernization of the infrastructure servicing the coffee industry. Renovation of two important ports, La Libertad and Acajutla, was completed in the 1860s. The first bank opened its doors in 1872, and they multiplied in number during the decade of the 1880s. The republic entered the railroad era in 1882 with the opening of a modest 12-mile line between Sonsonate, a departmental capital and one of the principal commercial centers, and Acajutla. The line facilitated the export of the varied local products, among which coffee was rapidly becoming the most important. English loans in 1889 promoted the expansion of an incipient railroad system that also fell under English administration.

British investments accompanied loans and together they assured Britain's economic preeminence. Besides railroads, mining attracted British capital. In 1888, the English established the Divisadero Gold and Silver Mining Company and the following year, the Butters Salvador Mines. The British began to enter the banking business in El Salvador in 1893.

The coffee interests also appreciated the importance of a modern capital, the symbol of their prosperity, as tribute to their "progressive" inclinations, and the focal point of their political authority. By the end of the century larger numbers of the richest families were building comfortable, in some cases even palatial, homes in the capital. They broke some of their immediate ties with the countryside and the provincial cities to become a more national elite centered in San Salvador.

A sleepy capital of 25,000 in 1860, San Salvador boasted of no pretentions. A visitor in the mid-1880s remembered: "There is very little architectural taste shown in the construction of the dwellings or of the public buildings . . . the streets are dull and unattractive. . . . The public buildings are of insignificant appearance."[30] It compared unfavorably with the cities of similar size in Latin America. Sensitive to that reality, the newly prosperous coffee elites resolved to renovate the capital, expunging the somnolent past in favor of the envisioned vigor of the future. The city took on new airs as the center of a booming economy. By 1910, the population numbered more than 32,000. The central streets had all been paved and electricity illuminated the city. An excellent drainage system insured the good health of the inhabitants. A series of new buildings, among them a commodious headquarters for the governmental ministries, a cathedral, and a market, added to the modernity. The elites boasted of attractive homes in the capital. The new and beautiful Avenida de la Independencia combined with ample parks and plazas to provide grace and spaciousness to the city. The modern, still somewhat quiet capital made a favorable impression on visitors. Above all else it spoke of—and symbolized—the prosperity that coffee afforded the nation.[31]

The very restricted democracy fostered by the Constitution of 1886 functioned smoothly in the early decades of the twentieth century. From 1903 to 1931, each president was elected in the approved fashion—selected by his predecessor and ratified by a limited electorate—and served for the constitutional mandate of four years. The politicians respected the doctrine of "no reelection." Peaceful selection and rotation of presidents contrasted sharply with the violence characteristic of the change of governments in the nineteenth century. The preponderance of civilian presidents was also unique. Of the eight men elected to the presidency during the 1903–1931 period, only one was a military officer, General Fernando Figueroa (1907–1911).

The prosperity and power of the coffee planters reached their culmination during the years 1913–1929, an economic and political period referred to as the Melendez-Quinonez dynasty because of the two related families that held the presidency. Those families ranked among the largest coffee producers. When an assassin felled President Manuel Enrique Araujo in 1913, Vice-President Carlos Melendez assumed the presidency as the constitution provided and then won the presidency in his own right during the elections the following year. In 1919, his brother, Jorge Melendez, succeeded him for four years, followed by his brother-in-law, Alfonso Quinonez Molina, for another quadrenniel. This tightly knit family political dynasty demonstrated the ease incumbent presidents enjoyed in manipulating elections to select their successors. It further illustrated the increasingly narrow political base of the coffee planters. Indeed, fewer and fewer men controlled the thriving coffee industry, particularly the processing and export. During the dynasty, perhaps more than at any other period, those linked to coffee exports were able to monopolize both economic and political power. One obviously enhanced the other. Wealth conferred the prestige that facilitated political manipulation. In turn, their control of the government complemented their economic interests. During those years, the planters successfully held the small but aggressive urban middle class at bay, repressed or manipulated the impoverished major-ity—both the rural masses and the growing urban working class—and neu-tralized the military, from whose ranks had arisen so many of the nineteenth-century presidents.

The actual exercise of political power by the coffee class forged a unique chapter in Salvadoran history: prolonged civilian rule. When General Figue-roa, a constitutionally elected president, left the presidential palace in 1911, civilian politicians occupied it for the succeeding two decades, a remarkable record, never equaled before or since. Of course the economic strength, politi-cal influence, and social domination of the coffee elites had been a reality since the last decades of the nineteenth century. From the beginning of their rise to economic and political power in the 1860s and 1870s they had enjoyed amiable relations with the military. The planters counted on the military to support a political system complementary to coffee exports. Economic pros-perity, after all, facilitated the modernization and professionalization of the army. The easy shift from military to civilian presidents manifested the harmonious relations between the planters and the officers.

The army had won its laurels on the battlefield. Nearly a century of international struggles—the frequent wars against Guatemala, Honduras, Nicaragua, and assorted foreign filibusters—and of civil wars created a strong and reasonably efficient army, perhaps the best in Central America. A prudent government pampered the military. A military academy to train officers func-tioned sporadically. In 1900, the third such school, the Escuela Politecnica Militar, opened, only to be closed in 1927. Five years later the government inaugurated the Escuela Militar, still functioning. Thus, for most of the years of the twentieth century, a professional academy existed. In 1909, the govern-ment contracted with Chile for a military mission to improve the training of officers. The Escuela Politecnica Militar and the Escuela Militar provided a reasonable-to-good education for the cadets and fostered the corporate inter-ests of an officer class. Increasingly the academy drew its cadets from the urban middle and lower middle classes, two groups enthusiastically advocat-ing the modernization of the country.[32] While the officers' concept of mod-ernization tended to parallel that of the planters, it also emphasized the need for up-to-date military training and equipment, manifested a growing faith in industrialization, and responded to the vague but powerful force of nationalism.

In 1910, the government reported that its army consisted of an impressive 78 staff officers, 512 officers, and 15,554 troops on active duty (a figure that seems to be inflated).[33] Percy F. Martin, in his exhaustive study of El Salvador in 1911, reported: "The Government . . . have [sic] devoted the closest care and attention to the question of military instruction, and the system at present in force is the outcome of the intelligent study of similar systems in force in other countries, and the adaptation of the best features existing in each. A very high *esprit de corps* exists among the Salvadoran troops, and, for the most part, they enter upon their schooling and training with both zeal and interest."[34] The government favored the officers with good pay, rapid promotion, and a host of benefits. Martin marveled at the comforts provided by one of the officers' clubs: "For the use of officers there exists a very agreeable Club, at which they can procure their full meals and all kinds of light refreshments at moderate prices: while the usual amusements such as drafts, cards, billiards, etc., are provided for them. So comfortable is this Club made that officers, as a rule, find very little inducement to visit the larger towns in search of their amusements."[35] A contented military was the logical corollary to planter prosperity.

The further solidification of the corporate interests of the military was encouraged by the establishment in 1919 of a periodical for and about the military and in 1922 of a mutual aid society, the *Circulo Militar.* More than an economic association, it encouraged the moral, physical, and intellectual improvement of its members. One knowledgeable visitor to Central America in 1928 claimed that El Salvador had the best-trained army in the region.[36]

Peace and order at home combined with increasing demands for coffee insured a heady prosperity for the planters and their government. With the exception of an occasional poor year, usually due to adverse weather, production moved upward after 1926 toward an annual harvest of 130,000,000–140,000,000 pounds, as table 3 illustrates. After 1904, El Salvador produced at least one-third of Central America's coffee, its closest competitors being first Guatemala and second Costa Rica. After 1924, Salvadoran production surpassed that of Guatemala to hold first place in quantity (and many would add quality) in Central America. The elites and the government became increasingly dependent on income from coffee production.

A significant change in El Salvador's international trade pattern also took place. In the nineteenth century, El Salvador sold much of its exports to the United States and bought most of its imports from Europe. In the twentieth century, that triangular pattern became increasingly bilateral due to a closer trade relationship with the United States, which bought more Salvadoran exports than any other nation and began to furnish most of its imports as well.

Growing U.S. investments in El Salvador further linked the two nations

TABLE 3   Coffee Production, 1924–1935

YEAR	POUNDS
1924–1925	95,020,000
1925–1926	101,413,000
1926–1927	66,139,000
1927–1928	149,474,000
1928–1929	134,042,000
1929–1930	143,301,000
1930–1931	165,347,000
1931–1932	105,822,000
1932–1933	141,096,000
1933–1934	127,869,000
1934–1935	130,073,000

SOURCE: Edelberto Torres Rivas, *Interpretacion del Desarrollo Social Centroamericano* (San Jose, Costa Rica: Editorial Universitaria Centroamerica, 1973), pp. 284–85.

economically. Prior to the opening of the twentieth century, U.S. investments had been practically nonexistent. In 1908, they totaled a modest $1.8 million, but they rose rapidly thereafter: $6.6 in 1914; $12.8 in 1919; and $24.8 in 1929. While these sums were insignificant in terms of total U.S. investments abroad, which in Latin America alone accounted for over $1.6 billion by the end of 1914, they represented a sizable proportion of the foreign investments in El Salvador by 1929. U.S. investors consequently began to exert influence over the Salvadoran economy. The pro-U.S. attitudes of the presidents of the Melendez-Quinonez dynasty greatly facilitated the penetration of North American interests into El Salvador, while World War I reduced the British presence.[37]

The coffee planters and their allies exuded confidence. Coffee prices, land devoted to coffee production, coffee exports, and coffee income all rose impressively after 1920. At no time from 1922 through 1935 did coffee represent less than 88 percent of the total value of exports. During three of those years, 1926, 1931, and 1934, it accounted for 95 percent. The amount of land producing coffee increased from 170,000 acres in the early 1920s to 262,000 acres in the early 1930s. Meanwhile, coffee growing and processing concentrated in ever fewer hands with no more than 350 growers controlling the industry by the mid-1920s. The largest enjoyed annual incomes of $200,000.[38]

Ruling from their comfortable and modern capital, the planters and their allies were creating an impressive infrastructure of roads, railroads, and ports as well as a telegraphic and telephone communication network. The plantations, the government, and the army were efficiently run. In their own terms, the elites were highly successful. Still, they nurtured visions of further change. Some fretted over the dependence on coffee for prosperity and talked of the need to diversify agriculture. A few experimented with cotton as an alternate export. Others spoke in terms of industrialization, and limited amounts of capital did support an incipient manufacturing sector. The elites even discussed the extension of democratization and the inclusion of the lower classes in the political process. It was the talk of a contented minority that wanted to perfect their political and economic systems. Benefiting from the great changes wrought by transforming a largely peasant and subsistence economy into a plantation and export economy, the coffee elites assumed that their own prosperity reflected the well-being of the nation they governed.

While the shift to coffee culture may have created an aura of progress around the plantation homes and the privileged areas of the capital, it proved increasingly detrimental to the quality of life of the majority. One U.S. observer contrasted the lifestyles of the classes in 1931:

> There is practically no middle class between the very rich and the very poor. From the people with whom I talked, I learned that roughly ninety percent of the wealth of the country is held by about half of one percent of the population. Thirty or forty families own nearly everything in the country. They live in almost regal splendor with many attendants, send their children to Europe or the United States to be educated, and spend money lavishly (on themselves). The rest of the population has practically nothing. These poor people work for a few cents a day and exist as best they can.[39]

This grim observation was by no means novel. After a tour of Central America in 1912, Charles Domville-Fife concluded that "there are more comparatively poor people in this country [El Salvador] than there are in some of the larger states."[40] An academic study of the 1919–1935 period speaks of "recurrent food shortages" and "economic desperation" among the masses in a period of high living costs and low wages.[41] The cost of basic foods skyrocketed between 1922 and 1926: corn prices, 100 percent; beans, 225 percent; and rice, 300 percent. The importation of those foods, once negligible, became significant in 1929.[42]

An analysis of the class structure in 1930 suggests the concentration of wealth: it categorized 0.2 percent of the population as upper class.[43] An accelerating rate of population increase accentuated the problems of poverty. The population reached 1,443,000 by 1930. The vast majority was rural. Yet, only 8.2 percent could be classified as landowners.[44]

The very changes that facilitated the concentration of land into fewer hands also precipitated the social and economic disintegration of the life style of the overwhelming majority of the Salvadorans. The changes squeezed off the land those who grew food for their own consumption and sold their surpluses in local market places. The relative ease of access to land—hence, food—depicted by the five travelers in the 1850s was no longer accurate after

1900. The dispossessed depended on seasonal plantation jobs. Some began to trickle into the towns and capital propelled by rural poverty and the search for urban jobs, which either did not exist or for which they were unprepared. The extent of the new social and economic disequilibrium was not immediately appreciated. Impressive economic growth masked for a time the weakness of the increasingly narrow, inflexible, and dependent economy.

As is true in such overly dependent economies, events in distant marketplaces would reveal local weaknesses. By the end of the 1920s, the capitalist world teetered on the edge of a major economic collapse whose reverberations would shake not only the economic but also the political foundations of El Salvador.

With his term of office nearing an end in 1927, President Quinonez picked his own brother-in-law, Pio Romero Bosque, to succeed him, a choice with significant consequences. Don Pio, as Salvadorans invariably refer to him, turned out to be more liberal, less conventional, and highly unpredictable in comparison with his three predecessors of the Melendez-Quinonez dynasty. He entered office riding high on the wave of coffee prosperity, but the international financial crisis that began in 1929–1930 soon tossed his government into a trough of economic troubles, testing all his skills in navigating the ship of state.

The dynamic sector of the economy suffered the vicissitudes common to nations dependent on the export of a single product. In an indictment before the Legislative Assembly, Minister of Finance Jose Esperanza Suay pointed out the cause of the nation's economic plight: "The coffee crisis that this year [1929] has alarmed everyone clearly indicates the dangers for our national economy of monoculture, the domination coffee asserts over agrarian production."[45] El Salvador may have been an efficient coffee producer, but it was not the only one. In fact, exporters were beginning to outnumber importers. The economic prosperity of at least ten Latin American nations, of which Brazil was by far the most important, also depended on coffee sales. At the same time, a few African areas were producing coffee for export. Demand fell while supplies remained constant or even increased in some instances. Consequently the price dropped drastically. In 1928, El Salvador sold its coffee for $15.75 per hundred kilograms—in 1932, for $5.97. The financial consequences for El Salvador can readily be perceived in an economy in which coffee constituted 90 percent of the exports and 80 percent of the national income. Not surprisingly therefore, government revenues plummeted 50 percent between 1928 and 1932. El Salvador witnessed the highest index of rural unemployment in Central America. Small coffee growers suffered severely. Their loss of land through bankruptcy and foreclosure—an estimated 28 percent of the coffee holdings—augmented the estates of the large landowners. The problems revealed a modernized but underdeveloped economy, one that readily responded to foreign whims but failed to serve Salvadoran needs.

The planters' reaction to the mounting problems exacerbated the nation's economic woes. They increased the amount of land devoted to coffee in an effort to make up for falling prices. The consequences of that trend were as obvious as they were disastrous: the economy depended more than ever on coffee, more peasants lost their land, rural unemployment rose, and food production for internal consumption declined.[46]

President Romero Bosque tried valiantly to ride out the economic storm. Politically he fared better. Practicing the liberal ideology he preached, he permitted the full play of those liberties authorized by the Constitution of 1886 but hitherto suppressed. His administrative talent and his unimpeachable honesty impressed his fellow countrymen. He determined to make honest men of politicians. He turned on his less-than-scrupulous predecessors and even sent Quinonez into exile. Those actions heightened his popularity despite the economic crisis.

To the amazement of all and the consternation of the professional politicians, Don Pio decided to hold an honest presidential election in 1931. Contrary to all previous political practices, the president advanced no candidate. It was indeed an historical first. Since no political parties existed, a few hastily organized to take advantage of the unprecedented opportunity to electioneer.

The six new parties represented the interests of the working, professional, middle, and planter classes and thereby reflected the social changes overtaking El Salvador.[47] A small but vocal urban working class had emerged in the 1920s, flexing its muscle in several important strikes. The presidents of the dynasty flirted occasionally with that potential source of political power. Their policies gyrated from wooing the workers to repressing them. In 1925, some workers and intellectuals, with the assistance of communist leaders from Guatemala, founded the Communist party of El Salvador. In the excitement of preparation for the 1931 election, a Labor party also emerged. It nominated Arturo Araujo, who enjoyed a genuinely popular following. The candidate sought to distance himself from his more radical supporters, the foremost of whom, Agustin Farabundo Marti, was busy organizing rural labor, an activity guaranteed to disturb landlords and arouse the suspicion of the military.

To avoid any of the international influences among the Labor party members, most notably of communism, Araujo turned to the ideas of Alberto Masferrer to enhance his party's program. An intellectual, philosopher, and writer, Masferrer dominated Salvadoran letters.[48] The strongest voice of the newly invigorated nationalism in El Salvador, he criticized the institutions that had been shaped by the coffee class and called for greater social justice. In Patria, the prestigious and lively newspaper he founded on 27 April 1928, Masferrer protested against the presence of foreign companies, the lack of decent housing, and the high cost of living. He advocated industrialization and the protection of national resources from foreign exploitation. He denounced those "who have the souls of a checkbook and the conscience of an account ledger," those who kept "the people in misery, who kill by hunger thousands of persons, and who cause more than half the workers to die due to lack of food, shelter, or rest before they reach the age of thirty."[49] Both the extreme left and right verbally assaulted Masferrer. The right labeled him a dangerous Bolshevik, criminal agitator, and subversive. The left attacked him as a demagogue, traitor, and right-wing socialist.

For his campaign, Araujo adopted Masferrer's program of *vitalismo,* the "vital minimum" that the philosopher defined as "the sure and constant satisfaction of our basic needs."[50] Thus, Araujo campaigned for the nine major points advocated by vitalismo, among them: hygenic, honest, and fairly remunerated work; medical care, potable water, and decent sanitation; a varied, adequate, and nutritious diet; decent housing; sufficient clothing; expedient and honest justice; education; and rest and recreation. Within the context of Salvadoran society in late 1930 and early 1931, Araujo ventilated some "revolutionary" views. Vitalismo, he declared, would be financed by transferring funds from the military budget to social expenditures. One can but speculate about the reaction to such a proposition within the confines of those comfortable officers' clubs.

Masferrer himself held some unconventional ideas about the role of the military within Salvadoran society. That fully one-sixth of the national budget went to the army in 1929 disturbed him. It was not productive investment; it did not contribute to national development. "For a country that no longer fights wars, our army is extraordinarily expensive. . . . And, if there are no longer any wars to fight, why should the state maintain such a burdensome institution?" he asked.[51] The army could serve much more useful national goals if it added to its traditional roles of protection from foreign invaders and the maintenance of internal order those of building and maintaining roads, providing water to the villages, improving the health of the inhabitants through sanitation campaigns, protecting the forests, and helping the population in times of natural disaster.

Araujo also heeded Masferrer's call for land reform. The philosopher advocated the nationalization of the land and its redistribution.[52] He classified the landowning system as well as the relations between the landlords and rural workers as "feudal": "The lord in this case is the landowner, he who gives and takes, he who permits the worker to reside on his lands or expels whoever does not obey or please him."[53] Araujo planned to have the government buy the land from the rich and redistribute it to the poor.

With its platform firmly buttressed by the ideas of Masferrer, the Labor party aroused the enthusiasm of large numbers of people who viewed its program as the means to solve the deepening economic difficulties and to create a more just society. For his running mate, Araujo chose a military man, General Maximiliano Hernandez Martinez. The general had borne the presidential standard of the small National Republican party before he joined forces with Araujo. First as a presidential candidate and later as a vice-presidential candidate, Martinez appealed to the popular classes on social issues.

Honoring his promises, Don Pio remained impartial during the selection of presidential candidates and the campaign. The elections took place in early January 1931. Araujo won. He confronted an impossible task. Somehow he had to reconcile the vast differences among the Labor party, the coffee planters, the military, and the newly emergent middle class. He had to accomplish his miracle in the midst of the worst—and what would be the longest—economic crisis in modern Salvadoran history. The problems cried for bold action; an irresolute president proved to be incapable of acting. He ignored the "vital minimum" program that he had supported during the campaign. His inaction confounded and then alienated his followers. Frustrations mounted daily; unrest resulted.

On 2 December 1931, the military responded to the crises precipitated by economic collapse and political unrest. The soldiers turned out of office the first and thus far only freely elected president, who fled the country after less than one year in office. The military coup was the first in 33 years—since November 1898, when General Tomas Regalado seized power—and the first staged by professional army officers who did not come from the dominant socioeconomic class.[54] Three days later the military junta turned power over to the constitutional vice-president, General Hernandez Martinez, who also had served as minister of war.[55] His exact role in the coup d'etat still remains unexplained. Invested with power, he governed energetically for the next 13 years, a record of political longevity in El Salvador.

Most sectors of society greeted the military seizure of power with relief. It had become painfully apparent to all that President Araujo, immobilized by the economic debacle and the inability of the national institutions to respond to new demands, could not govern. The majority thought the young officers who carried out his overthrow would be able to resolve the crises threatening to destroy the nation. Rightly or wrongly, the populace put trust and hope in those officers. The Marxist student newspaper *Estrella Roja* congratulated the military on the coup d'etat. It reiterated the belief that the incompetence of Araujo "imposed a moral obligation on the military to remove him from office." The newspaper quickly pointed out, however, that the coup itself could resolve few of the nation's fundamental problems:

> Pardon our skepticism. We do not believe that the coup will end the Salvadoran crisis which is far more transcendental than a mere change of government. The crisis has deeper roots than the incapacity of Don Arturo. It results from the domination of a capitalist class that owns all the land and means of production and has dedicated itself to coffee monoculture.[56]

Although no profound institutional changes were forthcoming, Araujo's downfall represented something more than "a mere change of government." It initiated new alliances and a sharing of power. In short, it ended the coffee planters' monopoly of economic and political power.

The economic collapse alone had not triggered the coup. The causes of the political change also included the growing social, economic, and political complexities engendered by incipient industrialization and growing urbanization, more intensive nationalism, the roles played by immigrants, an urban proletariat, an expanding middle class, and professional military officers in an increasingly varied society, improved transportation and communication, and efforts to diversify the economy. Further, any explanation of the coup must take into account the inability of President Araujo to govern, an unfortunate reality in the country's first democratic experiment, which may have revealed as much about institutional structures as it did about the chief executive.

The demands on the government varied, and while some could be reconciled, others could not. The rural folk looked to the communal past for a solution to their plight. They wanted the government to return land to them. The planter elites obviously favored the present land distribution and the export economy from which they had extracted so many benefits for such a long period. The expanding middle class and the professional military thought in nationalistic terms that included a reduction in the level of dependency, a wider sharing of social benefits, and industrialization. Their solutions to the crises lay in the cities. Urban growth had been slow, and, as table 4 shows, the populations of the five largest cities remained relatively small. Urban dwellers accounted for only 15 percent of the population. Yet, they provided many of the leaders advocating innovations.

The events of 1931 brought to a close a dynamic period in the history of El Salvador during which the coffee planters had gained economic and political ascendancy to dominate the nation. Stresses during the preceding decade demonstrated the increasing difficulty the coffee planters experienced in governing the nation. The brief political experiment under Don Pio and Don Arturo had been sufficient to prove that a functioning, pluralistic democracy would not work to the planters' best advantage. They lost their political monopoly. The coup in 1931 signified that they would not regain it. They understood by then that they would benefit most from an authoritarian government managed by the military and complementary to some of the

TABLE 4 **Populations of the Five Largest Cities, 1930**

CITY	POPULATION
San Salvador	89,385
Santa Ana	39,825
Santa Tecla	20,049
San Miguel	17,330
Sonsonate	15,260

SOURCE: Gibson, "A Demographic Analysis of Urbanization," p. 338.

goals of the middle class, which wanted access to the national institutions and upward mobility. Those groups worked out a suitable arrangement to the exclusion of the rural masses and the urban working class. They divided the tasks of government after 5 December 1931: the military exercised political power, while the landowners, in alliance with sympathetic bankers, merchants, exporters, and segments of the urban middle class, controlled the economy. Each respected the other. General Martinez succeeded in reestablishing oligarchical control, although he could not return the nation to the status quo ante 1931. El Salvador was entering a new phase of history.

During the 1858–1931 period, El Salvador reshaped its institutions in order better to export coffee; modernization had taken place, producing some of the advantages its advocates had predicted. There were more and better roads, a modest railroad system, efficient ports, and a capital city with sections boasting all the amenities of its European or U.S. counterparts. Almost everything connected with the export of coffee and the life styles of the elites seemed up-to-date, indistinguishable from what one might find in the capitals of the major industrial nations. Impressive growth had taken place. The statistics measuring population, coffee production, and foreign investments had risen impressively, and, until 1929, so had national income. An observer could conclude that certain aspects of national life had progressed in the course of seven decades, that the "progressive" El Salvador of 1931 differed considerably from the "backward" nation Barrios had resolved to "regenerate" in 1858.

National life was different, but not always in a positive way. Quite another legacy of growth and progress was the nation's acute dependence on the export of a single product, coffee, for its prosperity. Monoculture and plantations were some of the results, and they dominated the economy. The efficient production of coffee did not extend to foodstuffs. The countryside fed the population less adequately than before. By the end of the 1920s, El Salvador began to import food, not because the land could not feed the people—the hoary excuse of overpopulation has been disproven—but rather because the planters used it to grow export crops.[57] On several levels, the nation had lost control of its own economy. By 1931, El Salvador confronted a series of political and economic crises, the consequences of the type of modernization its governments had imposed.

The perceptive observations of two commentators, widely spaced in time, reveal the basic difference separating the El Salvador of the end of the 1850s from that of the end of the 1920s. Mrs. Foote had lived among a well-fed population. Large estates, small farms, and communal lands coexisted. The relatively varied export sector had played a significant but not the dominant role in the economy. The critical eye of Alberto Masferrer viewed quite a different situation. He assessed the state of Salvadoran society in 1928 in this way:

There are no longer crises; instead, there are chronical illnesses and endemic hunger. . . . El Salvador no longer has wild fruits and vegetables that once everyone could harvest, nor even cultivated fruits that once were inexpensive. . . . Today there are the coffee estates and they grow only coffee. . . . Where there is now a voracious estate that consumes hundreds and hundreds of acres, before there were two hundred small farmers whose plots produced corn, rice, beans, fruits, and vegetables. Now the highlands support only coffee estates and the lowlands cattle ranches. The cornfields are disappearing. And where will the corn come from? The coffee planter is not going to grow it because his profits are greater growing coffee. If he harvests enough coffee and it sells for a good price, he can import corn and it will cost him less than if he sacrifices coffee trees in order to grow it. . . . Who will grow corn and where? . . . Any nation that cannot assure the production and regulate the price of the most vital crop, the daily food of the people, has no right to regard itself as sovereign. . . . Such has become the case of our nation.[58]

In vivid contrast to Mrs. Foote's earlier observations, Masferrer saw a hungry population with limited access to the use of land, a population whose basic need for food was subordinated to the demands of an export-oriented economy. The "progress" charted by the Salvadoran elites had failed to benefit the overwhelming majority of the citizens.[59] Prosperity for a few cost the well-being of the many.

The contrasts between Foote's and Masferrer's observations suggest that little or no development had taken place, if one measures development by a rising quality of life index and the maximum use of resources, natural and human, for the well-being of the majority. Thus, the contrasts provoke serious questions about the wisdom of the type of modernization and economic growth El Salvador pursued after 1858, since neither addressed the needs of the majority of the Salvadorans. Rather, they left a legacy of poverty, dependency, and class conflict that succeeding generations of generals, politicians, and planters have not been able to resolve.

NOTES

1. Mrs. H. G. Foote, *Recollections of Central America and the West Coast of Africa* (London: Newby, 1869), p. 101.
2. Ibid., p. 84.
3. Ibid., p. 61.
4. Ibid., pp. 54–55.
5. Ibid., p. 60.
6. John Baily, *Central America: Describing Each of the States of Guatemala, Honduras, Salvador, Nicaragua, and Costa Rica* (London: Saunders, 1850); E. G. Squier, *Notes on Central America, Particularly the States of Honduras and Salvador* (New York: Harper, 1855); Carl

Scherzer, *Travels in the Free States of Central America: Nicaragua, Honduras, and San Salvador,*
2 vols. (London: Longman, 1857); G. F. Von Tempsky, *Mitla: A Narrative of Incidents
and Personal Adventures on a Journey in Mexico, Guatemala, and Salvador in the Years 1853–
1855* (London: Longman, 1858). In a much later and certainly more scholarly
study, David Browning tends to confirm the main theses of these more impressio-
nistic travelers: *El Salvador: Landscape and Society* (Oxford: Oxford University Press,
1971).

7. Squier, *Notes on Central America,* p. 326.
8. Ibid., p. 331.
9. Von Tempsky, *Mitla,* p. 424.
10. Scherzer, *Travels in the Free States,* vol. 2, pp. 148, 195–96.
11. For a series of useful case studies of the effects of the penetration of international
    capitalism upon the local economies during the nineteenth century, see Roberto
    Cortes Conde, *The First States of Modernization in Spanish America* (New York: Harper,
    1974).
12. Adriaan C. van Oss, "El Regimen Autosuficiente de Espana en Centro America,"
    Mesoamerica (Guatemala) 3 (June 1982): 68.
13. Browning, *El Salvador,* pp. 85, 87.
14. Letter of General Gerardo Barrios, Rome, 21 November 1853, printed in the *Revista
    del Departamento de Historia y Hemeroteca Nacional* (San Salvador) 11 (March 1939): 42.
15. That speech is printed in Joaquin Parada Aparicio, *Discursos Medico-Historicos Sal-
    vadorenos* (San Salvador: Editorial Ungo, 1942), p. 222.
16. Address to the General Assembly, 29 January 1862, printed in Italo Lopez Vallecil-
    los, *Gerardo Barrios y su Tiempo,* vol. 2 (San Salvador: Ministerio de Educacion, 1967),
    p. 219.
17. Gary G. Kuhn, "El Positivismo de Gerardo Barrios," *Revista del Pensamiento Cen-
    troamericano* (Managua) 36 (July–December 1981): 88. For a more general statement
    on Positivism in El Salvador see Patricia A. Andrews, "El Liberalismo en El
    Salvador a Finales del Siglo XIX," ibid., pp. 89–93.
18. Kuhn, "El Positivismo," p. 87.
19. ". . . the commerce of the Central American States has wonderfully increased, and
    especially within fifteen years and since the establishment of the line of steamers
    from Panama. This has introduced and established regularity, certainty, and dis-
    patch in their communication with the rest of the world. It has organized and
    maintained a mail service and secured a rapid, sure, and safe mode of commercial
    intercourse and exchange. In the interests which are thus growing up into impor-
    tance, [sic] and wealth and commanding influence will be found the means of
    counteracting the unfortunate results of their political systems, and those interests
    must soon be powerful and widespread enough to be able to finally put down the
    political system which retards or hinders their development. . . . Since the estab-
    lishment of the Panama Company's Steamers, the Revenues from the Custom
    House in . . . Salvador have more than quadrupled. The foreign commerce of all
    the Republics, which, previous thereto, was in the hands of a few who could
    afford to import cargoes around Cape Horn, has been opened to all. . . . The growth
    of California and the States on the Pacific has opened new courses for their trade"
    (James R. Partridge to Secretary of State, 22 April 1865, Diplomatic Dispatches
    from U.S. Ministers to Central America, General Records of the Department of
    State, National Archives of the United States of America). "The Republic of

Salvador, though territorially much the smallest of the five Central American States, is *first* in the amount of exports and only *second* in population. It has three seaports on the Pacific, La Union, La Libertad, and Acajutla, at all of which the Panama Railroad Steamers stop twice a month, up and down, and at which American vessels land and receive freight and passengers. In the other Central American States these steamers land only at one port" (A. S. Williams to Secretary of State, 27 March 1867, ibid.).

20. Lopez Vallecillos, *Gerardo Barrios,* pp. 216–18, 127–28.
21. Ibid., pp. 216–17.
22. This interpretation of the Duenas administration rests on the assessments of Derek N. Kerr, "La Edad de Oro del Cafe en El Salvador, 1863–1885," *Mesoamerica* (Guatemala) 3 (June 1982): 4, 7, as well as on the diplomatic dispatches of A. S. Williams. In particular, see his dispatches of 12 January and 8 February 1969, to the U.S. Secretary of State, Diplomatic Dispatches from U.S. Ministers to Central America, General Records of the Department of State, National Archives of the United States of America.
23. For an understanding of the negative effect the introduction of coffee culture had on the peasantry of Costa Rica and Guatemala, see Mitchell A. Seligson, *Peasants of Costa Rica and the Development of Agrarian Capitalism* (Madison: University of Wisconsin Press, 1980); and David J. McCreery, "Coffee and Class: The Structure of Development in Liberal Guatemala," *Hispanic American Historical Review* 56 (August 1976): 438–60.
24. Browning, *El Salvador,* p. 190.
25. Ibid., p. 173.
26. The quotations from the Law for Extinction of Communal Lands, 26 February 1881, and the Law for the Extinction of Public Lands, 2 March 1882, are found in William H. Durham, *Scarcity and Survival in Central America: Ecological Origins of the Soccer War* (Stanford, CA: Stanford University Press, 1979), p. 42.
27. This trend was almost universal throughout Latin America. For the general discussion consult E. Bradford Burns, *The Poverty of Progress: Latin America in the Nineteenth Century* (Berkeley and Los Angeles: University of California Press, 1980), particularly pp. 132–54. For specific discussions of El Salvador see Browning, *El Salvador,* particularly pp. 146, 147, 167, 173, 175, and 214; Alastair White, *El Salvador* (Boulder, CO: Westview, 1982), p. 93; and Rafael Menjivar, *Acumulacion Originaria y Desarrollo del Capitalismo en El Salvador* (San Jose, Costa Rica: Editorial Universitaria Centroamericana, 1980), pp. 123–27.
28. Jorge Larde Y Larin, *Guia Historica de El Salvador* (San Salvador: Ministerio de Cultura, 1958), pp. 32–43.
29. Rafael Guidos Vejar, *El Ascenso del Militarismo en El Salvador* (San Salvador: UCA/ Editores 1980), p. 65.
30. William Eleroy Curtis, *The Capitals of Spanish America* (New York: Harper, 1888), 180–81.
31. Percy F. Martin, *Salvador in the XXth Century* (London: Arnold, 1911), pp. 256–75.
32. The role of the military in El Salvador, 1858–1931, and the relations between civilian politicians and military officers adhere in general terms to the broad observations made by Edwin Lieuwen concerning the behavioral pattern of the

military throughout Latin America in the nineteenth and early twentieth centuries. See his *Arms and Politics in Latin America* (New York: Praeger, 1961), pp. 17–35. Vejar provides the details and some general conclusions for the study of the Salvadoran military in the nineteenth and early twentieth centuries in *El Ascenso del Militarismo.*

33. Martin, *Salvador,* p. 86.

34. Ibid., p. 87.

35. Ibid., p. 88.

36. Arthur J. Ruhl, *The Central Americans* (New York: Scribner's, 1928), p. 174.

37. Rafael Menjivar covers the topic and statistics of growing U.S. investments in *Acumulacion Originaria,* pp. 55–81.

38. The statistical data in this paragraph are drawn largely from Everett A. Wilson, "The Crisis of National Integration in El Salvador, 1919–1935" (Ph.D. diss., Stanford University, 1969), pp. 108–41.

39. Major A. R. Harris, U.S. Military Attache to Central America, 22 December 1931, National Archives of the United States, R. G. 59, File 816.00/828, as quoted in Thomas P. Anderson, *Matanza: El Salvador's Communist Revolt of 1932* (Lincoln: University of Nebraska Press, 1971), pp. 83–84.

40. Charles W. Domville-Fife, *Guatemala and the States of Central America* (London: Francis Griffiths, 1913), pp. 285–86.

41. Wilson, "Crisis of National Integration," pp. 29, 115, 128.

42. Ibid., pp. 126–127; Durham, *Scarcity and Survival,* p. 36.

43. Alejandro R. Marroquin, "Estudio Sobre la Crisis de los Anos Trenta en El Salvador," *Anuario de Estudios Centralamericanos* 3 (1977): 118.

44. Ibid.

45. Quoted in ibid., p. 121.

46. Vejar, *Ascenso del Militarismo,* pp. 102, 100.

47. These parties were the Partido Evolucion Nacional (National Evolution party), representing the most conservative and economically powerful groups; the Partido Zaratista (party of Alberto Gomez Zarate), grouping together the urban supporters of Zarate who favored the policies of the "Dynasty"; the Partido Constitucional (Constitutional party), sharing much of the conservative philosophy of the National Evolution party and appealing largely to the same groups; the Partido Fraternal Progresista (Progressive Fraternal party), directed by a general and enjoying military support, appealed to the rural workers in a paternalistic way; Partido Nacional Republiciano (National Republican party), also directed by a general, Maximiliano Hernandez Martinez, and uniting professionals, students, workers, and some coffee growers; and the Partido Laborista (Labor party), appealing to the urban and rural workers as well as to smaller farmers. Ibid., pp. 113–14.

48. Hugo Lindo, "El Ano de Alberto Masferrer," *Inter-American Review of Bibliography* 29 (July–September, 1969): 263–77. His biographers tend to be uncritical. One, Matilde Elena Lopez, characterized him as Central America's "broadest thinker," one of the "most illustrious men of the continent," and a "revolutionary." *Masferrer: Alto Pensador de Centroamerica: Ensayo Biografico* (Guatemala City: Editorial del Ministerio de Educacion, 1954), p. 9.

49. Quoted in Marroquin, "Estudio Sobre la Crisis," p. 144.
50. Alberto Masferrer, *Patria* (San Salvador: Editorial Universitaria, 1960), p. 83. The first edition of *El Minimum Vital* appeared in 1929. This essay draws on Masferrer's newspaper discussions of his idea and on the definitive textual edition: *Minimum Vital y Otras Obras de Caracter Sociologico* (Guatamela City: Ediciones del Gobierno, 1950), pp. 179–210.
51. Masferrer, *Patria,* p. 219.
52. Ibid., 189–90.
53. Quoted in Marroquin, "Estudio Sobre la Crisis," p. 145.
54. Vejar, *Ascenso del Militarismo,* p. 12.
55. There is no doubt that Maximiliano Hernandez Martinez is a controversial figure in Salvadoran historiography, generally denounced as an "eccentric"—if not "insane"—dictator. Two scholars of twentieth-century Salvadoran history, Everett A. Wilson and Robert V. Elam, suggest that some revisionist assessments of Martinez may be in order. Wilson concludes, "There are several indications that Martinez, in spite of the notorious eccentricity and brutality of his long regime, presided over significant national reconstruction in the early 1930's" ("Crisis of National Integration," p. 233). Elam emphasizes, "Perhaps no president in this nation's history began with a broader base of support than that enjoyed by Maximiliano Hernandez Martinez in 1932" ("Appeal to Arms: The Army and Politics in El Salvador, 1931–1964" [Ph.D. diss., University of New Mexico, 1968], p. 45).
56. Vejar, *Ascenso del Militarismo,* p. 131.
57. A major theme of William H. Durham, *Scarcity and Survival in Central America,* is that if Salvadorans would make more efficient use of their land, they would be able to feed themselves well.
58. Masferrer, *Patria,* pp. 179–82.
59. The Salvadoran situation amply illustrates the theme of the impoverishment of the majority as Latin America "progressed" or "modernized" in the nineteenth century set forth in Burns, *The Poverty of Progress.* For an economist's view of that theme, consult Robert E. Gamer, *The Developing Nations: A Comparative Perspective* (Boston: Allyn and Bacon, 1976). Another useful economic analysis, but with a contemporary emphasis, is: David Felix, "Income Distribution and the Quality of Life in Latin America: Patterns, Trends, and Policy Implications," *Latin American Research Review* 18, no. 2 (1983): 3–34.

PART THREE

ECONOMIC DEVELOPMENT IN A REVOLUTIONARY WORLD: TRADE AND DEPENDENCY

The developing economies are integrated into a global system that is indeed very different from the world in which the industrialized countries grew. A most obvious change is the existence of the modern industrial states themselves. One of the major hurdles for the Third World, then, is to compete with mature economies that have a running head start in manufacturing, finances, and technology.

The concept of *relative bargaining power* helps us to understand these asymmetries in the global trade system. Trade is a bargain, a deal struck between two or more agents each having something to offer the other. The *terms of trade,* or the *prices* each can command, depend upon the relative bargaining power of agents in the transaction. There are both supply and demand determinants of bargaining power and the consequent prices. One must consider the product being offered and whether there are alternative sources of supply. The oil-exporting nations are an example of those most able to set prices due to a supply monopoly, whereas many agricultural exporters are subject to wide market swings and have little bargaining leverage.

One also must take account of demand considerations. Is the product a vital input in production, necessary for basic consumption, or perhaps seen as crucial to national security concerns? These are cases where, due to strong demand conditions, the seller has the greater bargaining power to determine price.

More important than supply and demand in assessing relative bargaining power is who determines and controls the rules of the game. Because the industrial countries have a longer history in trade, particularly one in which the now developing countries were their colonies, the First World has considerable power in setting the rules of the game. The articles in this section focus on this asymmetric nature of the global trade system, highlighting the origins and consequences of this imbalanced bargaining structure.

We open with Lance Taylor questioning the premises of both the Third World's New International Economic Order (NIEO) and the First World's proposals for export-led development. The institutional framework within which international transactions take place militates against success of either strategy. Rather he argues that underdeveloped countries will have to opt for internally oriented strategies.

Asymmetric bargaining structure is clearly evidenced in global financial institutions, in particular the International Monetary Fund (IMF). Sidney Dell argues in "Stabilization: The Political Economy of Overkill," that the expressed attempts at even-handedness by the IMF have in fact resulted in inequality of burden sharing among borrowers in the First and Third World. The historical roots for such imbalance may be found in the origins of the IMF at Bretton Woods. The IMF was not conceived to deal with Third World financial problems, but rather was designed specifically to cope with short-run balance of payments difficulties in industrial economies. Thus by imposing short-run solutions on the long-term structural problems of the Third World, the IMF is administering the wrong medicine and may in fact be exacerbating the disease. Moreover, we should note that except for the presence of a fairly weak Latin American contingent and seven African and Asian countries, the remainder of the Third World was unrepresented when these policies were formulated. The rules of the game were set without their participation, and they now must accept the consequences.

In his article on Nicaragua, E. V. K. Fitzgerald describes the attempt to design and implement a demand management policy which combines stabilization with economic justice in a mixed economy.

The most serious problem facing Third World countries is the international debt crisis. Frances Stewart analyzes the debt problem and possible solutions from the perspective of the major interests involved. Any lasting solution must reverse the negative basic transfer, from Third World to First World countries, and reduce the net present value of the debt. Any such solution must take into account the bargaining position of different borrowing countries.

The major orthodox prescription for growth is to utilize the structure of world markets and gear the economy to export production. In theory, the world economy will absorb all that can be produced at the appropriate market clearing price. Thus, not limited by small domestic demand, production for global markets affords the possibility of an ever-expanding economic pie. Growth, growth, and more growth means plenty of benefits for all, and distributional tensions borne of scarcity need never surface. This strategy of export-led growth has been successfully pursued by the "Gang of Four"—Hong Kong, South Korea, Singapore, and Taiwan (they also had some redistributive policies). In the last selection, however, Cline raises an intriguing practical case against export-led growth for all nations. He argues that the Gang of Four model involves a fallacy of composition. That is, while individual poor countries might thrive by export-led growth, if everyone followed suit, in the aggregate they would encounter sharp protective resistance to the resulting flood of exports. Quite simply, if everyone jumps on the export boat, they'll all sink in a sea of protectionism.

10

Back to Basics: Theory for the Rhetoric in North-South Negotiations

Lance Taylor

The hurricane's eye hovering over the North-South conflict is about to move away. The kindly Brandt Report heralded its arrival in early 1980[1]. . . . As the storm rises, it is wise to contemplate the South's failure in the previous round. Northern negotiators in 1980 could justifiably draw a sigh of relief— they had just repulsed Southern claims to stabilize raw material prices, provide debt relief, leash the multinationals, reduce trade barriers, transfer technology, and effect sundry other modifications in the world balance of economic power. A New International Economic Order (NIEO) had been trumpeted by the South a decade earlier; in the final analysis, the old order was hardly touched.

What went wrong with the NIEO proposals—were they just repulsed by a bit of Northern stonewalling, or was the whole design fundamentally flawed? If, as seems likely, there were significant defects in the theory underlying NIEO, how can they be changed? Finally, what strategies of co-operation and conflict would a more realistic view of the difficulties faced by the very heterogenous economies of the 'South' imply? The best place to begin the reassessment is with the basic linkages in the international economy, those of commodity trade.

To a first approximation (modified later) the iron law of trade for poor countries is that they are hewers of raw materials and drawers of oil for the industrialized world. The trade patterns imposed by colonialism and the South's own lack of technical mastery when it was integrated into the world system under Pax Britannica last century persist—most Southern nations export commodities whose sales abroad will at best expand as rapidly as the

From *World Development,* Vol. 10, No. 4 (1982), pp. 327–335. Copyright © 1982 by Pergamon Press, Ltd. Reprinted by permission.

North's aggregate demand.[2] Growth in industrialized countries is determined by their own interactive policies, unaffected by any Southern action except the occasional OPEC shock. Thus the South finds its export balance both out of its own control and structured to lag macroeconomic disturbances in the rest of the world. Even productivity gains in export sectors do Southern economies no good—because their sales volume is determined by the level of Northern economic activity, cost-saving improvements just get transformed into a lower price. This perverse behavior of the export terms of trade lies at the heart of NIEO reasoning; its misinterpretation was the major intellectual error underlying the ill-fated 1974 proposals of the United Nations Conference on Trade and Development (UNCTAD) for commodity price control.

One last implication of the South's export dependence regards its own rate of growth. The required investment can be financed by saving from three main sources—incomes generated in non-export sectors, profits in exports, and capital flows from the North and OPEC which by accounting necessity must be absorbed in the form of a deficit on commodity trade.[3] Since in most Southern countries saving from sectors not linked to trade (mainly services and some parts of industry and agriculture) will not expand rapidly, the success of their investment programmes is determined from abroad. That is, export profits depend on output policy in the North and (as will be shown later) each poor country's trade deficit is largely set by Northern hands.

* * * * * *

The view of international trade just sketched has a distinguished history—in one variant or another it represents the vision of several economists whose writings in the 1950s laid the conceptual foundations for the NIEO proposals and UNCTAD. For present purposes it suffices to consider the particular formulations of Raul Prebisch (the first head of UNCTAD), Ragnar Nurkse, and the still very active Princeton economist, W. A. Lewis.

Prebisch stressed the negative effect of productivity increases on the South's terms of trade that was mentioned earlier, and went on to hint that the long-term outcome would be a steady decline in the region's purchasing power and prospects for growth. The empirical evidence suggests that the master pushed his theory too far. Over the century preceding 1950 the terms of trade faced by raw material exporting economies and/or the countries and colonies that now make up the Third World were on average stable (but fluctuated greatly from time to time). Since 1950, the South's terms of trade may have declined, though how much this apparent tendency was perturbed by the commodity booms of the Korean War and the mid-1970s remains unclear.[4]

There are enough other things going on in the world economy that affect the terms of trade to make a direct test of Prebisch's hypothesis against the 'facts' (or roughly constructed numerical approximations thereof) largely irrelevant. His logic was sound, though he overestimated the importance of his particular chain of economic links. What does matter is his recognition that the South was dealt a bad hand in the trading game, bad enough so that tinkering in commodity markets is not going to affect its long-run fate. Misperception of this idea led Prebisch's successors at UNCTAD to propose their integrated commodity scheme, a resounding failure that had much to do with dragging other, more sensible NIEO proposals down.

The story goes as follows. In the early 1970s UNCTAD econometricians were working on models of price-stabilizing commodity buffer stocks. Such agencies are supposed to enter commodity markets as buyers when supplies are high and prices low, and as sellers when markets are tight. With enough resources (both money and physical inventories of the commodity in question), a buffer might help stabilize price when market responses are calm.[5] Moreover, a system of linked buffer stocks could presumably save money if fluctuations in the markets for its constituent commodities were not directly related. Buying cheap in one market could be financed by selling dear in another, and everyone would be better off from more stable prices all around.

The UNCTAD technicians computed that a system of stocks valued at $6 billion (in 1974 prices) could give perceptible market stabilization; later and fancier statistical work put the figure nearer $10 billion. But the main point is that this money was only supposed to buy a reduction in price fluctuations. The *level* of a commodity's terms of trade would not be affected, and Prebisch's long-term dilemma would not be addressed at all. Of course, Northern negotiators feared that the hidden agenda for UNCTAD was to set up commodity cartels on the basis of the buffer stocks. OPEC was riding high at the time, and prospects for cartels in copper, bauxite, coffee and even highly competitive staples such as sugar glittered in its reflected light. Market realities soon put them back into the shadows. UNCTAD left pushing a $6 billion Rube Goldberg scheme, thinly disguising a quest for market dominance that Prebisch had already shown could not work. Small wonder that after 5 years of negotiation, the best UNCTAD could get was 400 million 1979 dollars in advanced country 'pledges' (not monetary commitments) to apply as a down payment on raising capital for its $6 billion holy grail.

* * * * * *

Reflection on this fiasco suggests that details of economic structure narrowly limit the means by which poor countries might improve their lot. General problems already mentioned are lack of buoyant export markets and dependence on a trade deficit to generate savings supply. To these might be added the fact that almost all countries are dependent on imports to supply key capital goods. Jet airliners are a frivolous example—how many countries are in a position to manufacture those? The same point applies to a whole range of machinery and equipment. Its implication is that a closed or 'autarkic' development strategy is impossible for most economies of the world.[6] Besides these universal aspects of dependence, specific groups of countries are hampered by additional problems as well. Some examples are as follows.

Mineral (including petroleum) exporters. Here, the problem is that a mineral extraction sector employs few people and generates little internal demand. At the same time, the foreign exchange it provides may be ample. The trick is to turn the dollars into internal economic growth and diversification. Attempts to increase domestic capacity via investment will typically put pressure on industries producing goods that cannot be imported, the prime example being construction. The price of construction services (or any other non-tradable good) will rise relative to those for imports and exports. Resources will be drawn away from production of tradables, and the economy will find itself specialized in its primary export and non-tradables. At the same time, the Central Bank will find it difficult to prevent transformation of at least some foreign exchange into domestic currency, so that inflationary pressures will build up unless free imports are allowed. The outcome (the Venezuelan disease) will be a highly unbalanced economy, devoid of agricultural and industrial production capacity and know-how. When the flow of dollars from mineral extraction abates, there are poor prospects for future growth.[7]

Food exporters. Few Third World economies export food (a major change from the situation before World War II), although many devote land to exports which could otherwise support grain production. In either case, an increase in export prices will enrich the rural sector. In poor countries, most of the initial rise in income will be devoted to food purchases. Even if food production goes up along with prices, the surplus available for export may stagnate or fall. Unless unpopular internal income redistribution policies are pursued, a country with these problems will benefit little in its balance of payments from improved terms of trade.[8]

Countries with a lagging agricultural sector. Even if foreign trade difficulties are not relevant, agricultural performance strongly constrains growth prospects in poor countries. For example, an increase in investment demand should in principle generate additional employment and growth. However, a large share of the wage payments received by newly employed workers will be directed toward food. If agricultural supply lags, the outcome will be rapid food price increases and frustration of the initial impetus toward economic expansion. After a time, the food price pressure will lead to rising wages and cost-push inflation. Until growth targets are curtailed or food output goes up, stagnation and inflation together will bedevil a country of this kind.[9]

Countries with unequal income distributions. The analysis here hinges around the notion that if income is highly concentrated, there is likely to be a low level of aggregate demand. On the other hand, income redistribution toward workers and the poor in general would lead to much higher demand levels for wage goods. Capacity utilization would rise in those industries, investment would be stimulated, and unless other barriers were to arise a higher overall growth rate could result. The catch is that the profit rate (or even absolute profits) may fall. Capitalist resistance is at least a major reason why growth gains from income redistribution are infrequently observed.[10]

Oil importers. Oil shocks affect rich and poor countries alike. The price of a key raw material goes up, and sooner or later the outcome will be an increase in final output prices. If wages are more or less fixed in money terms, the real purchasing power of labour incomes will fall. Aggregate demand and capacity utilization will decline; investment in consequence may be cut back, leading to slower growth. The outcome is again stagflation, which standard fiscal and monetary policies will be powerless to offset.[11]

* * * * * *

Most poor countries fall into one or more of the foregoing cages. How can they break out? In recent years, liberal commentators have stressed export-led growth. If an economy learns to sell products for which demand in the North grows fast, it should have no problems in maintaining both imports and aggregate demand. Moreover, access to international capital markets will be easy, so foreign saving will be in ample supply to support high levels of investment and growth. Roughly, this is the strategy that has been followed by the so-called New Industrializing Countries (NICs). The leading lights are the economists' Gang of Four—South Korea, Taiwan, Hong Kong and Singapore—plus others such as Mexico and Brazil. In effect, all these economies give their exporters large incentives to perform, and seem to have reaped rapid GNP growth rates (upwards of 8%/year) therefrom. They are the paradigm for most North Atlantic economists who dispense conventional wisdom and policy advice to the Third World.[12]

No doubt, exports can be an engine of growth. But the historical and geographical uniqueness of the NICs raises doubts as to how universally it can be applied. Singapore and Hong Kong are city-states that catapulted entrepot trade into prosperous manufacturing enterprise. The model has been around since the Phoenicians, but has never spread. South Korea and Taiwan were given land reform by the Japanese and Americans, so that their agricultural bottlenecks were straightened out. Moreover, they benefited from lavish foreign aid and preferential access to their mentor countries' markets during their initial growth push in the 1960s. To date, they maintain more than usually constricted political regimes, in contrast to the more open politics but extremely unequal distributions of income in Mexico and Brazil. These latter two large countries have based their export success on manufacturing sectors that were highly protected for many years, as well as on abundant natural resources.

More countries may become NICs, but the foregoing review suggests that they may be peculiar in various ways. Also, along Prebisch lines, not all countries in the South can have exports to the North which grow more rapidly than the market as a whole is going to expand. The NIC club is necessarily exclusive; the more countries that enter, the more difficult it is for those left behind to join.

Faced with such prospects, most nations in the Third World may have to opt for internally oriented, or as Nurkse put it, 'balanced' growth strategies.[13] In terms of our basic model, countries must strive for both production of their own capital goods and generation of their own internal supplies of saving. If followed through, this process may prove painful for presently dominant classes in several ways. Small-scale agriculture and non-luxury consumer goods production are less dependent on imported machines than are processes making goods favoured by large landowners and the urban bourgeoisie; a substantial income redistribution may be implied. Mineral production and other cheap sources of foreign exchange may be curtailed; the loss would show up rapidly in reductions in the range and quality of consumer imports. A substantial increase in food production can in some cases be achieved by frankly capitalist methods (as in the 'Green Revolution') but land reform provides an alternative route. And finally, the whole balanced growth strategy is always in danger of being suffocated by small internal markets and the lack of efficiency that often leads carefully nurtured infant industries never to grow up. South–South trade and joint Southern efforts to open Northern markets could help alleviate such problems. Discussion of the practicality of these options is best preceded by analysis of another set of issues—how money and financial institutions constrain Southern independence in international trade.

* * * * * *

To appreciate the world financial market, one must begin with the key currency country at the top. For most of the time since the 17th century, a single country with its financial centre has dominated the bankers' world. Generation of a payment surplus (fed by interest income) to finance other countries' deficits, massive ability to export capital goods, and possession of the financial centre were defining characteristics of the dominant economies during the eras of Pax Britannica (from the Congress of Vienna until the period between the World Wars) and Pax Americana (which lasted roughly until the Nixon shocks of 1971). By contrast, requiring a trade deficit to provide saving, lacking capacity to produce sophisticated structures and machines, and possession of a weak currency are key indices of underdevelopment, as we have already seen. The position of the poor countries did not change during the 1970s in this regard. The interesting development was dissipation of the regalia of economic fame.

Roughly speaking, the situation today is that the financial system still centres in New York and London, but competitors ranging from Zurich to offshore operations specializing in fast financial intermediation and tax avoidance manipulate an ever growing trade. Capital goods production is dispersed all the way from Boeing in Seattle to sweatshop operations in the NICs. The trade surplus is concentrated on the Western shore of the Persian Gulf, though Japan and (decreasingly) West Germany still assume the finance capital exporter's role. Despite any more or less conspiratorial interpretation one may place on the Saudi–American special relationship, the first oil shock loosened the international financial game. Improbably, Third World countries took some advantage of the situation, as we will see later.

For the non-oil-exporting countries of the South as the passive participants, the main question is how the North may react to what promises to be a long succession of oil shocks. The North's (more specifically the Americans') options are basically two—accept the loss in real purchasing power that an oil price increase entails and run a recession, or else allow price increases (ratified by money creation) to erode the real price of oil away. The choice here is very delicate since all internal political factions are involved. As Michal Kalecki suggested long ago, Northern capitalists may welcome a degree of recession for the discipline it brings to the labour market, but fear the socially disruptive effects of inflation like the plague.[14] Northern workers lose much in recession, while Persian Gulf rentiers dislike the progressive reduction in value of their dollar-denominated bonds that inflation brings.

The measure of success for the inflationary gambit is the interest rate for international loans. In the economists' 'long run' the real interest rate (defined as the market rate less the rate of inflation) ought to equal the average rate of profit on capital investment world-wide. In practice, as Keynes observed, the long run arrives only when we are all dead; meanwhile the real interest rate can fluctuate and even stay negative for extended periods of time.

By and large, the North ran a fast enough inflation to keep the real interest rate low or negative for most of the 1970s (exact estimates inevitably vary, depending on choice of price index). At the same time, recession and half-hearted conservation measures reduced oil imports and the North's overall trade deficit to less than OPEC's surplus on current account. Since the sum of trade deficits and surpluses world-wide must be zero, the non-OPEC South had to run an overall deficit to counter the oil exporters' 'gains'.

* * * * * *

Why the quotation marks on 'gains'? One reason, already noted, is that mineral-rich countries face a difficult task in translating their foreign exchange wealth into diversified internal development. In their different ways, Venezuela and the Shah's Iran turn this observation into a cliché. More fundamentally, a trade deficit is in principle a gain for a country able to transform it to more rapid investment and growth. One defence of the current system, popular on the Boston–Washington axis these Reagan months, is that the international capital flows triggered by OPEC surpluses allowed the NICs to do their thing. Access to virtually limitless loans at negative real interest rates is just the shot in the arm that peripheral capitalism is asserted to need.

Regrettably, this particular line of reasoning is pocked with flaws. Bankers are not unlike sheep crossing a highway; at times they follow the leader in offering loans beyond all prudent sense. The financial crises induced by excessive lending to Turkey, Peru and Indonesia during the late 1970s are cases in point. (This is not to say that authorities in these and other countries should not have put their own finances in order, but that international banks cheered them down the primrose path.) On the other side of the Eurocurrency trade, no loans at all may be available to countries that are not 'credit-worthy' by New York and London consensus. A system that allocates large but ultimately finite volumes of funds to 170 sovereign nations at negative lending rates cannot be cleared by price. Arbitrary (that is, politically and ideologically based) grants of the borrowing privilege must finally be made.[15]

With actual institutions, international loans (and borrowers' trade deficits) are allocated in two ways. The normal channel begins with the money centre banks, recipients of OPEC deposits in the first instance. Each bank lends according to its own market knowledge, previous commitments, home government pressures, and so on. But especially for poor countries another agency sets standards of creditworthiness and (at times) organizes packages of loans. This agency is the International Monetary Fund (IMF). It has replaced commodity schemes as the focus of Third World attention on the international economic scene.[16]

* * * * * *

Along with its next-door Washington neighbour, the World Bank, the IMF was conceived at the 1944 conference in Bretton Woods, New Hampshire, that set the rules governing international finance until the Nixon shocks. The Fund was charged with regulating monetary relationships among nations with the understanding that a country would alter its exchange rate only when its balance of payments fell into 'fundamental disequilibrium'. In practice, this diagnosis came to be associated with a large deficit, and the main remedy was devaluation of the local currency (leading to an increase in the relative domestic prices of tradable goods). Though Keynes and others at Bretton Woods urged that countries with payments surpluses be forced to adjust (presumably by appreciating their exchange rates or increasing their lending abroad), political reality and bankers' conventional wisdom left surplus economies well free of the Fund's writ.

Countries that belong to the Fund pay in quotas in gold or foreign exchange. When faced with payments difficulties, a country can draw on 'tranches' of an amount up to six times its quota, as well as gain access to other pots of foreign exchange that the IMF collects from time to time (e.g. an 'oil facility' after the first shock, a 'trust fund' for poor borrowers, and so on). The trick is that a country only gets these resources subject to steadily increasing 'conditionality' or control over its economic policy decisions by the Fund.

Sooner or later after a country gets in balance-of-payments difficulties as perceived by the world's lenders, a mission from the IMF will arrive. The visit is consummated when the Finance Minister signs a 'letter of intent' to change his policy mix. The reward is the right to draw on higher tranches of the country's quota, plus other Fund facilities as may apply. The amount of the IMF loan is usually only a few hundred million dollars. More important than the money is the seal of approval it brings. Armed with the letter of intent (and sometimes quiet knowledge of phone calls from the IMF country economist to New York), the Finance Minister usually finds that he can borrow what he needs.

Between nations, the purpose of these exercises (letters of intent signed each year can be counted in the tens) is to allocate payments deficits across the world. Though diffuse and subtle, political criteria clearly play a role in determining which countries are offered Fund assistance at conditions they can accept, and which are not. Detailed case studies are the only means to obtain understanding here.[17]

For present purposes, the more interesting question is what happens within an economy after a Fund visit, or what policy changes does conditionality impose? The menu is selected from a limited number of items available in a macroeconomic model that the IMF has retained for many years.[18] The key assumptions are that the level of output is fixed by 'full employment' of resources, while the price level will follow in the short run from costs as determined by the wage level and exchange rate. By an accounting equation that describes the balance sheet of the banking system, any rise in the money supply (the banks' main liability item) must be balanced by increases in loans to the government or private firms, or else by higher foreign exchange reserves (banks' loans and foreign exchange holdings are their principal assets). The final assumption is that demand for money follows from the 'needs of trade' as predicted by the multiplication: value of trade = (price level) $\times$ (level of output).

To apply the model, make projections of output and the price level; then you have money demand. Put a limit on government borrowing from the banking system, and assume that private-sector borrowing follows a stable relationship with GNP. From the balance sheet of the banking system, the change in foreign reserves 'must' be determined as a residual item. Or, in other words, if government borrowing from the banking system is restricted, then the balance of payments will improve. Just to help matters along, a devaluation is usually prescribed. The result is that domestic import and export prices go up; presumably exports will respond by rising, while imports will fall. Finally, restriction of wage levels will help hold traded goods price inflation down. A corollary will be a shift in the income distribution toward profits, stimulating investment and leading to more growth in the medium run.

* * * * * *

This package sounds coherent, and for the balance of payments it often succeeds. The problem is that the Fund model has the mechanisms wrong. The money crunch that results from restricting government spending drives up interest rates, and constricts investment demand. Moreover, in poor countries with underdeveloped infrastructure for both commercial activities and finance, firms have large working capital commitments. When interest rates rise, the costs of financing this working capital increase, and will be passed along in prices. The consequences are lower output levels (from lower investment demand) and inflation—monetary contraction is stagflationary in the short run. This aspect of how real economies function is routinely ruled out by the Fund's (and all monetarists') full-employment assumption.

On the side of devaluation, the price increases that it causes reduce the real purchasing power of wages and lead to lower consumption demand. This effect is multiplied if imports initially exceed exports, the usual case. The gain of purchasing power enjoyed by exporters from devaluation is more than offset by the loss of importers and further demand contraction ensues. The fall in economic activity that comes from interest rate increases and devaluation leads to lower imports and an improved trade balance—these are the channels via which the Fund package 'works'. At the same time, investment and growth prospects for the future decline, while the income distribution shifts against wages. There is even inflation until higher foreign exchange and interest rate costs work themselves through the system. Medium-term wage repression becomes necessary to round out the low inflation and surplus balance-of-payments positions that are the hallmarks of financial grace.[19]

* * * * * *

The bind that these policies impose upon progressive Third World governments becomes strikingly clear. Income redistribution with adequate growth requires foreign resources; both growth and distribution are the immediate casualties when an increasing payments deficit leads a country to run foul of the Fund. Even non-progressive governments pursuing expansionist policies face a similar fate. The only countries escaping IMF tutelage are slow growers, those who can pursue largely autarkic development strategies, and the NICs. As darlings of the capital markets NICs paradoxically transform export expansion into widening payments deficits since their sales abroad make them good credit risks. The strategy has led to external hiccups (Brazil had trouble borrowing for most of 1980, but re-entered Eurocurrency markets with a flourish after good exports in early 1981) and at least one internal crash

(Iran). In any case, the NIC option may soon be foreclosed. Trade preferences in industrial country markets for the existing crew are being wound up, and it is hard to imagine that they will be extended much more widely abroad.

The slow growing and/or autarkic countries follow balanced growth strategies of the kind described earlier. Their policy options would be wider if more foreign resources came their way. Exerting pressure for more dollars is the one tactic upon which almost all poor countries agree. Their chosen approach is to call for large increases in their IMF quotas (which bring voting rights) and overall resources of the Fund. More foreign exchange available to the Fund would permit its members bigger deficits, while greater Third World voting power in the Board of Governors might induce the staff to recommend policies involving less monetary and exchange rate overkill.

Were world financial markets better disciplined, countries espousing such heretical notions might soon be whipped into line. In fact, a more liberal Fund may possibly arise. The fair omen is a recent large increase in the Saudi Arabian quota, in response to a contribution of at least $10 billion. The foul sign is American intransigence regarding Fund packages with light conditionality. The hope must be that there will be enough liquidity in the IMF to convince diehard staffers and Governors that harsh conditionality has ceased to make sense. Paradoxically, world recession may help on this front. But more important is the fact that the diehards are losing their theoretical strength—the intellectual attack by Third World economists on the Fund is beginning to have its effects. In the best of worlds, poor countries would not be squeezed from financial markets in the 1980s, precisely because they could have recourse to a born-again IMF.

Whether such hopes are realized depends very much on the abilities of Southern negotiators, as well as the economists who can keep up an intellectual critique. It also bears recalling that the North carries its monetary weapon in reserve. The key currency countries can always create enough money to make the real gains from Third World or OPEC receipt of dollar-denominated IMF loans or oil sales arbitrarily small. Pumping up inflation is not politically costless for the North. The point is just that power over hard currency issue can counter growing Southern power in the management of the Fund.[20]

* * * * * *

Similar ambiguities plague Southern efforts to improve their lot in other aspects of the world system. In commodity trade, for example, the rules regarding tariff policy are set by another agency left over from the post-World War II international design, the General Agreement on Tariffs and Trade (or GATT). The spirit of the GATT is that tariff barriers should be lowered and that countries should not discriminate against each other in attempting to pursue beggar-my-neighbour strategies in trade. The practice has been for the North grudgingly to allow the South some freedom to

subsidize non-traditional exports and also to grant discriminatory trade preferences to favoured clients (e.g. from the US to East Asia and South America
and from the Common Market to ex-colonies). But the trade barriers lowered
under these generalized systems of preference can always be raised again;
indeed the free-traders in the Reagan administration seem determined to do
just that. The South has little power to influence the domestic political considerations via which such decisions of the transnational companies whose
multi-country operations completely bypass the concepts of national sovereignty upon which the GATT rules are based.[21] Of course the transnationals
keep both their headquarters and their basic political allegiance squarely in
the North.

This line of argument rapidly becomes tedious; other examples of inherently inferior Southern bargaining positions can easily be found. One conclusion is that Third World countries should train large corps of lawyers; one
criticism of UNCTAD's present management is that the only thing it knows
how to do is talk. Yet the major lesson from the South's possible success in
changing the course of the IMF is that the economists' critique had to be
combined with financial market loosening as well as the Saudis' economic
clout.

We come full circle to Nurkse's vision with which we began. Until
Southern countries gain control of their own economic destinies, via production of capital goods and income-elastic exports, their dependent position is
certain to persist. Small gains are always feasible at the negotiating table, but
the experience of the 1970s shows that major realignments in the international system are not going to be talked into effect. What *is* feasible for most
countries is an inward-looking balanced growth strategy, delinked from
Northern pressures to the maximum possible extent. South–South trade
financed by a rejuvenated IMF and relaxation of NIC restrictions on imports
from their poorer neighbours would help greatly toward these ends. But in
the final analysis each country has to go it alone, to make its own way out
of the structural cage in which it now finds itself. The NIEO failures showed
how tightly Southern countries are bound. The successes will come only
when they break their constraints.

NOTES

1. The official title is *North–South: A Program for Survival* (Cambridge, Massachusetts:
   MIT Press, 1980). Willy Brandt chaired the responsible Commission on International Development Issues, with funding from various sources.
2. In fact, as Lewis pointed out in his Nobel Prize lecture in 1979, the relevant
   elasticity is about 0.8—a 1% increase in the growth rate of OECD economies will
   increase Southern export growth by about 0.8%. W. A. Lewis, 'The slowing down
   of the engine of growth', *American Economic Review*, Vol. 70 (1980), pp. 555–564.
3. This theorem in accounting states that the only way one country can receive
   resources from another is by selling less than it buys. Under present financial

market arrangements, the recipient country becomes indebted to its benefactor, and there is a corresponding capital flow. The monetary units in terms of which this flow is measured turn out to be very important, as we will see later. The key point is that the North as a whole can pay its debts to OPEC by creating dollars, marks or yen while the South with its assorted soft currencies can only accommodate capital inflows by building up dollar-denominated debt.

4. For a succinct review of the numbers and their interpretation, see David Evans, 'International commodity policy: UNCTAD and NIEO in search of a rationale', *World Development,* Vol. 7 (1979), pp. 259–279. The best statement of Prebisch's own views is his paper 'Commercial policy in the underdeveloped countries', *American Economic Review,* Vol. 49 (1959), pp. 251–273. A sympathetic and widely quoted formalization comes from Edmar Bacha, 'An interpretation of unequal exchange from Prebisch-Singer to Emmanuel', *Journal of Development Economics,* Vol. 5 (1978), pp. 319–329.

5. How much good a buffer stock could do when markets are chaotic and buyers panicky is another question. For example, econometric simulations show that a reserve of about 20 million tons would be enough to stabilize world wheat markets in 'most' circumstances. But market commentators suggested that stores three or more times this large would have been necessary to damp the price increases during the mid-1970s food crisis. A buffer stock's resources are likely to prove too small just when its services are really required.

6. The possible exceptions are very large countries rich in natural resources. The very size of their economies means that they can support substantial markets in virtually all commodities, while natural resource wealth obviates dependence on raw material imports. Of the currently well-off nations, only the US and the Soviet Union were able to follow largely autarkic growth trajectories, and even they depended on raw material exports at crucial junctures. In present circumstances, Brazil, Mexico, India, China and Indonesia might be in a position to follow autarkic strategies, though all lack some natural resources.

7. Difficulties faced by mineral exporters have flickered in and out of professional economists' attention for years. They are in at the moment, though the best analysis is as yet unpublished. A good descriptive paper comes from the World Bank's Development Research Center: Alan Gelb, 'Capital importing oil-exporters: adjustment issues and policy choice'. From the same Center on theory see Sweder van Wijnbergen, 'Inflation, employment and the Dutch disease in oil-exporting countries'; as well as an MIT dissertation essay by Youssef Boutros-Ghali, 'Single export systems and the dependent economy model' (1981).

8. This problem has long been noted by specialists on Argentina, which exports wheat and beef, its wage goods. It has recently been stressed by Graciela Chichilnisky, an Argentinian teaching in England. For an abbreviated presentation of her model, see G. Chichilnisky and L. Taylor, 'Agriculture and the rest of the economy: macro connections and policy restraints', *American Journal of Agricultural Economics,* Vol. 26 (1980), pp. 303–309.

9. This inflationary dilemma has long been stressed by Latin American writers. The canonical paper is by Prebisch's colleague, Osvaldo Sunkel, 'Inflation in Chile: an unorthodox approach', *International Economic Papers,* No. 10 (1960). For more formalized versions, see Chichilnisky and Taylor, *op. cit.* (1980); and Eliana A. Cardoso, 'Food supply and inflation', *Journal of Development Economics,* Vol. 8 (1981), pp. 269–284.

10. This model is often proposed by Indian economists as an explanation of the relatively slow growth in their economy. See, for example, Deepak Nayyar, 'Industrial development in India: some reflections on growth and stagnation', *Economic and Political Weekly* (Bombay), Special Number (August 1978). An analytical version appears in the unpublished paper by Amitava Dutt at MIT, 'Stagnation, income distribution and monopoly power' (1981).

11. This chain of consequences is by now very familiar. A recent, elegant restatement focused on poor countries is given by Sweder van Wijnbergen, *Oil Price Shocks and the Current Account* (World Bank, 1981).

12. The literature is enormous, at times ecstatic. For a clear-headed presentation by advocates, see Jagdish Bhagwati and T. N. Srinivasan, 'Trade policy and development', in R. Dornbusch and J. A. Frenkel (eds), *International Economic Policy: Theory and Evidence* (Baltimore: Johns Hopkins University Press, 1979).

13. Ragnar Nurkse, *Patterns of Trade and Development* (Stockholm: Almquist & Wicksell, 1959).

14. Michal Kalecki, 'Political aspects of full employment', from his *Selected Essays on the Dynamics of the Capitalist Economy* (London: Cambridge University Press, 1971); reprinted from *Political Quarterly* (1943).

15. A parallel situation is that of fishermen in a large sea. Each small boat's captain does not realize that his catch reduces the stock available for all the rest. Unless each fisherman's take is somehow limited, the final outcome may be enough fishermen to make the fishery disappear. In financial markets, the OPEC surplus will persist but late or ill-favoured claimants for loans may be forced to the wall.

16. The following brief discussion of the role of the IMF can be supplemented by the excellent review paper by Edmar L. Bacha and Carlos F. Diaz-Alejandro, 'Financial markets: a view from the semi-periphery', Discussion Paper No. 367, Economic Growth Center, Yale University (January 1981).

17. Think of Jamaica's return to financial respectability and the Fund's good graces after the election of Edward Seaga last fall; loans from Venezuela and socialist good wishes had not been enough to keep the more radical Michael Manley afloat. For a critical review of IMF actions in this and other cases, see Issue 2 for 1980 of *Development Dialogue,* published by the Dag Hammarskjold Foundation, Uppsala, Sweden. The issue presents the proceedings of a conference of moderately leftist economists in Tanzania, which generated an Arusha Initiative for reconstructing the Fund, as well as most other aspects of the world financial system. Several more orthodox country analyses appear in William R. Cline and Sydney Weintraub (eds), *Economic Stabilization in Developing Countries* (Washington, D.C.: Brookings Institution, 1981), which reports the proceedings of a conference among Washington policy-makers and centrist academics sponsored by the US Department of State.

18. The structure of the Fund model was set out in print by J. J. Polak, the institution's chief theorist, almost 25 years ago: 'Monetary analysis of income formation and payments problems', *IMF Staff Papers,* Vol. 6 (1957), pp. 1–50. The practice is described in a speech made in 1967 by the head of the IMF Latin American section, E. Walter Robichek, 'Financial programming exercises of the International Monetary Fund in Latin America'. This presentation is a key text used by the IMF Institute, the Fund's educational wing.

19. How the IMF medicine really works has been known to practising economists in poor countries ever since the Fund began. As is often the case, there was a long

lag between economic perception and its elaboration into a consistent theoretical view. For Fund economics, this task was finished only in the past few years. For a doctrinal history and a formal presentation, see Lance Taylor, 'IS/LM in the tropics: diagrammatics of the new structuralist macro critique', in Cline and Weintraub, *op. cit.* (1981); or else in *Structuralist Macroeconomics* (New York: Basic Books) (in press).

20. In principle, IMF issuance of its own reserve currency or special drawing rights (SDRs) could be managed in such a way as to give money creation privileges to the Third World. This possibility has been roundly rejected by industrialized countries, as one might surmise. The Arusha conferees [*Development Dialogue, op. cit.* (1980)] come out in favour of a commodity-based world monetary system. Such schemes have been floated for at least a century, are universally considered eccentric, and will not be sanctioned by everybody who is anybody in the financial world.

21. Well over half of Third World manufactured exports take the form of intra-company trade. The presiding transnationals can easily set their internal prices to take profits where convenient while still satisfying all GATT provisions regarding non-discriminatory trade.

11

Stabilization: The Political Economy of Overkill

Sidney Dell

1. INTRODUCTION

In the course of his remarkable essay on stabilization plans in the Southern Cone of Latin America, Diaz-Alejandro (1981) suggests that these plans were a case of 'overkill', in the sense that the economic retrenchment that they brought about went much further than was strictly necessary in terms of what could have been regarded as reasonable objectives.

The term 'overkill' used by Diaz-Alejandro could well be used much more generally to describe the national and international programmes of adjustment adopted in the 1970s and early 1980s. The following discussion deals first with international aspects of this process of 'overkill', and later with some of the national aspects.

2. INTERNATIONAL ASPECTS

(a) The Distortion of Priorities

The purposes of the International Monetary Fund (IMF) are set out in the first of its Articles of Agreement. Six such purposes are defined, including international monetary co-operation, the expansion and balanced growth of international trade, the promotion of exchange stability and of a multilateral system of payments, the mitigation of disequilibrium in balances of payments and the provision of resources to facilitate the correction of such disequilibrium.

The fundamental objectives underlying these 'purposes' are described in

The views expressed in this paper are those of the author and not necessarily those of the United Nations Secretariat. This paper was originally presented to a Conference on IMF Conditionality held by the Institute for International Economics in March 1982. It has been published in John Williamson, ed., *IMF Conditionality* (Washington, D.C.: Institute for International Economics, 1983). Distributed by MIT Press.

Article I (ii) as being 'the promotion and maintenance of high levels of employment and real income and . . . the development of the productive resources of all members as primary objectives of economic policy'. Further reference to these 'primary objectives' is made in Article I (v) which lays down that the correction of maladjustments in the balance of payments should be undertaken 'without resorting to measures destructive of national or international prosperity'.

The international community seems to have strayed quite far from these 'primary objectives of economic policy'. In a situation of increasingly inadequate effective demand, growing underutilization of productive capacity and soaring unemployment, the pressure continues for even greater reductions of demand, which are likely to increase the volume of idle capacity and unemployment still further. The singlemindedness of the attack on inflation[1] seems to have gone beyond the point at which tradeoffs with other objectives are even considered, so that monetary restriction has almost become an end in itself. This is a distortion of IMF priorities, as well as the priorities of Article 55 of the United Nations Charter and of the International Development Strategy drawn up under that Charter.[2]

There is irony in the fact that the first industrial country to express any sense of alarm about the current situation is precisely the one that, throughout the post-war period, had maintained the strongest orthodoxy in fiscal and monetary matters, and that on past occasions had invariably resisted proposals for economic expansion that might carry with them the smallest risk of inflation. On the insistence of Chancellor Schmidt, the Washington communiqué of 6 January 1982 contained the following warning: 'The chancellor referred to the danger of a worldwide depression.'

In the circumstances, it might have been expected that world leadership would be concerned at the present time with charting a programme of economic recovery and with seeking international co-operation in such a programme. In fact, however, the IMF management takes the position that:

> The fight against inflation must continue to concentrate heavily on demand management for although the increase in oil prices was earlier an important contributing factor, oil prices have recently softened and the major impulse behind inflation in both industrial and developing countries has come from expansionary financial policies mainly associated with large budgetary deficits and from a complex of cost-push factors and expectations (Dale, 1982).

This statement exemplifies the fundamental error of much current thinking about the world economy as well as about the problems faced by individual countries, industrial and developing.

It is interesting to examine this statement in the context of the United States, whose economy is still so large in relative terms as to play the leading role in determining the level of activity of the industrial countries as a whole and hence, to a considerable extent, of the developing countries as well.

In April 1982 unemployment in the United States was at a level of approximately 9% and rising. There was idle productive capacity in every sector of the economy and the rate of utilization of capacity had fallen to a level of 70% or lower in manufacturing industry. If it is true that current financial policy in the United States is expansionary as a result of the large budget deficit, why is it that output is not rising? Why, on the contrary, has real GNP been falling at a rate of no less than 4.5% per annum for the past 6 months? And if real income, and hence real demand, is falling, what sense does it make to say that the fight against inflation is essentially a problem of demand management?

The mistake here is two-fold. In the first place, a budget deficit *per se* tells us nothing about whether aggregate demand is excessive or not. It is only when we consider the budget deficit in conjunction with other demands on private saving—namely gross investment and net exports—that we can tell whether aggregate demand is excessive. This, of course, is just as true of developing countries as of industrial countries.

Secondly, under conditions of substantial unemployment and excess capacity, one must distinguish between that part of a budget deficit which is an automatic response to the low level of business activity, leading to reduced government revenues and higher government transfers, and the rest of the deficit which would add to demand even at a high level of employment. Despite the ascendancy of monetarism, the US Department of Commerce continues to estimate the high employment budget deficit at regular intervals, and not long ago it issued a revised series going all the way back to 1955. Unfortunately the Department has over the years progressively raised the percentage of unemployment used as a basis for defining the concept of high employment, so that that percentage now stands at 5.1, a level that seems much too high. Nevertheless, even at this level, the high employment budget was in surplus in the United States in 1979, 1980 and the first three quarters of 1981, while the deficit in the fourth quarter of 1981 was equivalent to considerably less than 1% of GNP—well within the order of error of the estimates. Now if the high employment budget was balanced or in surplus throughout the period from 1979 to 1981, it can hardly be said that inflation in the United States during that period was due to 'expansionary financial policies mainly associated with large budgetary deficits'. Clearly the source of inflation must be sought elsewhere. Even for 1982, available projections indicate that the expansionary thrust of the deficit, adjusted for the level of employment, is likely to be small or negligible.

Although the notion of a high employment budget deficit cannot be transferred mechanically to developing countries because of conceptual problems connected with the definitions of unemployment and excess capacity, it is just as true in these countries as in the industrial countries that at reduced levels of activity budget deficits increase because of the associated declines in government revenue. Consequently the expansionary thrust of a budget deficit in a developing country, as in an industrial country, cannot be assessed without allowing for the level of economic activity.

It has been necessary to dwell upon this matter because it is typical of the errors of diagnosis that so often lead to the disorientation of stabilization programmes and hence to the process of overkill. Deflationary policies, however essential they may be in cases where balance-of-payments disequilibrium is due primarily to excess demand, should not be regarded as a panacea for all problems. Nor should the explicit injunction of Article I (v) be forgotten, i.e. that measures to restore external equilibrium should not be 'destructive of national or international prosperity'. In many cases measures that carry the obvious risk of being destructive of national prosperity are nevertheless considered indispensable in overcoming inflation, or in restoring external balance, or both. Moreover such measures are commonplace not only in countries where balance-of-payments support is being sought, but in many other countries also.

Some comfort is derived from the recent slowing down of cost inflation, as though this single measure of economic health could be given priority and ascendancy over all others. No one ever doubted that with sufficient determination it would be possible to cut back the level of business activity to the point at which demand inflation would be eliminated and cost inflation at least slowed down. The question was rather that of determining whether it was really necessary to burn down the house in order to discover roast pig; and whether there was not some better way of doing things that would give higher priority to 'national and international prosperity' and somewhat less importance to the rate of increase in prices.

That is not to say that inflation is a matter that can be neglected. On the contrary, it is clear that inflation can seriously distort the development process by encouraging the use of resources in socially undesirable ways and by intensifying inequity in the distribution of income. But if the real problem is cost-induced inflation, and the remedy applied is demand deflation, the cure is likely to prove worse than the disease. Instead of reducing social tension it is likely to aggravate it, and even if the cost inflation is slowed down temporarily, the benefits are likely to last only as long as demand is maintained at subnormal levels.

A permanent solution to the problem of cost inflation cannot be obtained by seeking to play on the fear of rising unemployment among those who try to protect themselves against increases in the cost of living by demanding higher wages. Where a cut in living standards is unavoidable, price stability in a democratic society depends on general agreement as to the way in which the burden should be shared. Intimidation through unemployment is likely to make any long-lasting agreement on burden-sharing more difficult to achieve, not less.

The ultimate futility of the deflationary approach becomes particularly clear in the prospects for the world economy foreseen by the adherents of this approach. After a decade of stagnation their programme of action calls for little but further stagnation for some time to come, so as to ensure that the inflationary psychology is broken. Such stagnation seriously prejudices the adjustment process, since adjustment is always easier in an expanding economy. But the real danger is more fundamental. Sooner or later persistent deflation, whether monetary, fiscal or both, is bound to cause a crisis of confidence, and it is this that Chancellor Schmidt no doubt has in mind in speaking of the danger of depression. If such a depression were to come, it would be the first to be brought about deliberately, on the misguided view that this is the only way of dealing with inflation.

(b) The Problem of Symmetry

The Fund continues to insist that the origin of a balance-of-payments deficit, whether internal or external, has no bearing on the adjustment measures required. On this view, the only valid question is whether a deficit is temporary or persistent; and if it is persistent there is only one way of dealing with it.

In taking this position, the Fund appears to shrug off its responsibility for ensuring that the burden of adjustment is distributed equitably and efficiently among countries. Since the underlying principle seems to have been forgotten, it is, perhaps, worth restating it—and, in fact, putting it in the terms in which it has been advanced in the past by some of the industrial countries that are now most insistent in pressing for unilateral adjustment by deficit developing countries.

The need for equity and efficiency in the distribution of the burden of adjustment was advanced with particular emphasis by Paul Volcker, representing the United States Government in the Committee of Twenty at Deputy level. The *Economic Report of the President* for January 1973 sets out the essential elements of the case argued before the Committee by Volcker as well as the text of a memorandum on this matter submitted to the Committee in November 1972.

The point was made that there had been nothing in the Bretton Woods system to assure compatibility of the balance-of-payments objectives of various countries, and that the breakdown of the system could be attributed to the failure to induce the adjustments required to achieve equilibrium. In the light of this experience the US proposals for a new system were designed 'to apply equivalent incentives for adjustment evenhandedly to all countries' [*Economic Report of the President (1973)*, pp. 161–162].

Symmetry in the adjustment process was seen as partly a question of equity, in the sense of sharing the political and economic costs of adjustment. But it was also necessary for efficiency:

> If countries on both the deficit and the surplus side of a payments imbalance follow active policies for the restoration of equilibrium the process is likely to be easier than if the deficit countries try to bring about adjustment by themselves. Deficit countries would in any case be unable to restore equilibrium unless surplus countries at least followed policies consistent with a reduction of the net surplus in their payments positions (ibid., pp. 124–125).

The US view as to what was the main shortcoming in the adjustment process was not, of course, shared by the European countries, which regarded the asymmetry between the reserve centre and the rest of the world as the crucial problem, and asset settlement as the solution to that problem. But as Williamson (1977) has pointed out, there was no necessary contradiction between these two approaches and it would have been possible to construct a system that incorporated both. Unfortunately the system (if system it can be called) that actually emerged incorporates neither approach.

(c) The Parallel of the 1980s and 1970s

The combined current account deficit of net oil-importing developing countries rose from $30 billion in 1978 to $80 billion in 1981. As against this increase of $50 billion, their bill for oil and interest payments alone increased by close to $70 billion. In fact, despite the world recession, the net oil-importing developing countries achieved a remarkable improvement in their exports, and actually moved into surplus on their non-oil trade accounts (De Larosière, 1981). This refutes the assertion often made that the developing countries did not adjust after the first oil crisis. They certainly did adjust, and on an impressive scale. The deterioration in their current account that occurred in 1979–1981 despite these significant efforts of adjustment was due entirely to factors beyond their control—namely the further rise in oil prices and the new upsurge in interest rates.

In January 1974, at a time when many countries were facing large deficits in their balances of payments resulting mainly from a deterioration in terms of trade, the Managing Director of the IMF presented a note to the Committee of Twenty in which he indicated that oil-importing countries would, in the short run, have to accept the deterioration of the current account of the balance of payments, since:

> Attempts to eliminate the additional current deficit caused by higher oil prices through deflationary demand policies, import restrictions, and general resort to exchange rate depreciation would serve only to shift the

payments problem from one oil importing country to another and to damage world trade and economic activity (IMF, 1974, pp. 25–26).

Subsequently, in its communiqué of 13 June 1974, the Committee of Twenty noted:

> As a result of inflation, the energy situation, and other unsettled conditions, many countries are experiencing large current account deficits that need to be financed. . . . Sustained co-operation would be needed to ensure appropriate financing without endangering the smooth functioning of private financial markets and *to avert the danger of adjustment action that merely shifts the problem to other countries* (emphasis supplied) (Committee of Twenty, 1974, p. 221).

These were the considerations underlying the decision to establish an oil facility to provide balance-of-payments support at low conditionality in 1974–1975. Any Fund member drawing on the oil facility was required 'to co-operate with the Fund in order to find appropriate solutions for its balance-of-payments problem'. This requirement of co-operation with the Fund was the same as that applicable to the compensatory financing facility, but the character of the conditionality involved was quite different. Under the relevant decisions of the Executive Board on this matter[3] member countries drawing on the oil facility were required to avoid 'competitive depreciation and the escalation of restrictions on trade and payments'; and to pursue 'policies that would sustain appropriate levels of economic activity and employment, while minimizing inflation'.

One would have thought that similar considerations and objectives would have been applied to the situation in 1981–1982. Here again, the upsurge in oil prices of 1979–1980, coupled with general inflation, had a major effect on the balances of payments of a large number of countries. And once more, as in 1974–1975, it was important that deficit countries should not adopt policies that would merely aggravate the problems of other countries. But while in 1974–1975 the emphasis of the Fund was on avoiding restrictive policies and on sustaining 'appropriate levels of economic activity and employment', in 1981–1982 the resources provided by the Fund bring with them all the rigours of upper-credit-tranche conditionality, generally involving severe economic retrenchment. The deflation brought about by the adjustment process is thereby superimposed on, and reinforces, the primary deflation resulting from business recession in the industrial countries.

It is apparent that in the view of responsible Fund authorities the situation in the 1980s is quite different from that prevailing in the 1970s and is therefore not susceptible to the same treatment. The reasons for this view are, however, not altogether clear. At times it appears to be suggested that the surpluses of the oil-exporting countries are likely to be more persistent in the

1980s than in the 1970s.[4] On the grounds that persistent imbalance calls for adjustment regardless of its character and origin, therefore, it is argued that a much greater effort of adjustment is required in the 1980s than in the 1970s.

The expectation that the oil surpluses will be more persistent in the 1980s is, however, open to question. While the recent decline in the real price of oil is no doubt attributable to a substantial extent to the slackening of business activity, there appears to be evidence also of increased capacity for the supply of oil as well as, in the words of the Interim Committee 'a break in the previous close link between economic growth and oil consumption' (IMF, 1981, p. 200). In addition, the import demand of OPEC countries associated with development and defense has shown tendencies to increase faster than expected. A continuation of recent downward trends in oil prices, and in the relationship between oil consumption and GNP in the industrial countries, together with further expansion in the import demand of OPEC countries would eliminate the OPEC current account surplus in the near future. Relevant also is the fact that the long-term component of the financing of OPEC countries' current account surpluses has been increasing significantly. For all these reasons there are grounds for doubting whether the evolution of the balance-of-payments positions of the OPEC countries in the early 1980s calls for a greater degree of adjustment by deficit countries than occurred in the 1970s—and the latter, as shown earlier, was itself quite impressive.

(d) The Burden of Unilateral Adjustment

The downward pressure of the adjustment process on non-oil developing countries in 1980–1981 was much heavier than necessary in the circumstances in which these countries found themselves. In analysing the situation of these countries in October 1979 the Interim Committee stated that

> It was especially important, in the Committee's view, that the industrial countries, in the design of their economic policies, pay particular attention to the economic needs of developing countries. In this connection, a wide range of policies was seen to be relevant, including the reduction of protectionist measures; the opening of import markets to exports of manufactures and commodities from developing countries and of capital markets to outflows of funds to such countries; and measures to give new impetus to the flow of official development assistance, which had stagnated in recent years (IMF, 1980b, p. 153).

The fact that protectionist measures were actually intensified, that the flow of official development assistance continued to stagnate and that private capital flows levelled off added greatly to the burdens imposed on the developing countries. Moreover the particular mix of fiscal and monetary policies employed by the industrial countries, without regard to international consequences, in dealing with inflation, aggravated the imbalance still further by steeply raising the interest cost of foreign borrowing from both private and public institutions, including the Fund, the World Bank and the regional development banks.

Here again the policy stance of the IMF is inconsistent. On the one hand it seeks to encourage export supply in the developing countries through adjustment of exchange rates and other 'outward-looking' policies. On the other hand it advocates further reductions in aggregate demand, and hence in the demand for imports, in the industrial countries that provide the principal markets for the additional export supplies thus generated. The Fund has been outspoken on the subject of protectionism, but its admonitions in this respect are more than nullified by its insistence that the industrial countries balance their budgets at low levels of employment and maintain or strengthen their policies of monetary restriction. After all, it is precisely the low level of employment that encourages protectionism.

Further inconsistency can be seen in the emphasis placed by the IMF on the need for governments to create market and other incentives for structural change while at the same time recommending deflationary policies that destroy any inducement to incur the risks of the investment in the new capacity that would be required.

(e) The Doctrine of Persistence

The logic of the IMF's position is, of course, that if the protectionism and other policy developments in the industrial countries mentioned earlier appear to be of a persistent character, there is no choice for the deficit countries but to adjust accordingly. In fact the doctrine of persistence would appear to imply that even if the policies pursued by one group of member countries were of a deliberately 'beggar-my-neighbour' character, and looked like continuing indefinitely, and if other countries encountering consequential deficits were to seek balance-of-payments support, the IMF would be compelled to insist on whatever degree of adjustment was called for in the circumstances, as a condition of providing such support. But does this not raise the question whether the IMF thereby becomes, albeit unwillingly, an accomplice in the 'beggar-my-neighbour' policies in question?

It should be noted further that under current conditions of long-lasting business stagnation, the line to be drawn between persistent and temporary imbalance becomes indeterminate. In the past, deficits caused by slackening of import demand owing to a business recession in major markets would have been regarded as coming unequivocally within the category of 'temporary' and therefore eligible for financing without adjustment. This was because recessions had hitherto been of relatively brief duration, and self-reversing. At the present time, however, recessions are not necessarily 'temporary'. As far as is known, it has not yet been suggested that a country should be declared ineligible for compensatory financing if its export shortfall is due to a decline in import demand in other countries resulting from a downturn in business activity that is expected to persist. Yet this is the logic of the IMF position, and it would also be required if the wording of the decision establishing the facility, which is intended only for cases of temporary shortfalls, were taken literally.[5] For the time being, efforts to neutralize the intent and effectiveness of the facility are taking the form of proposals to tighten the regime of conditionality that is applied.

Thus a new situation may be approaching in which all deficits are considered to be of a character that calls for adjustment, and in which even the compensatory financing facility becomes otiose.

(f) The Basis of Conditionality

But what is it that requires the Fund to insist on stringent upper-credit-tranche conditionality regardless of whether a borrowing country is responsible for the deficit confronting it, and regardless even of whether the factors contributing to the deficit (such as protectionism) are compatible with the Fund's own 'purposes' and 'primary objectives'?

Originally the imposition of conditions on a potential borrower was considered to be justified largely in terms of the need to ensure prompt repayment of drawings so as to safeguard the revolving character of the Fund's resources. Thus Article I (v) provides for 'making the general resources of the Fund temporarily available to [members] under adequate safeguards'.

But, as Killick (1981, p. 3) has pointed out, 'the stringency of conditionality has sometimes seemed disproportionate to the need to safeguard the repayment of Fund credits—credits which in the past have often been small relative to a country's total foreign exchange obligations'. There is, moreover, no method of correlating the conditions imposed with the capacity to repay, if only because circumstances can change drastically over the period of the loan. For example, no matter how severe the conditions imposed on a primary producing country may be, the capacity to repay will inevitably deteriorate if the price of its principal export falls significantly, as happens not infrequently.

The World Bank and regional development banks have not hitherto made demands on borrowing countries of the type characteristic of Fund programmes, and yet no-one imagines that repayment of their loans is less assured than of the loans made by the Fund. It is true that the projects for which financial support is obtained from the multilateral banks are appraised so as to determine that they will yield a return adequate to service the loans. But this does not provide any guarantee that foreign exchange will in fact be available in the amounts and at the times required. In practice, repayment to the multilateral banks is ensured not by project appraisal but by the fact that no country would willingly risk the drastic consequences for its access to all forms of credit that would result from a default to any of these banks. And the same consideration applies to repayments to the Fund, whether or not the loans involved carry upper-credit-tranche conditionality.

In justifying its policies on conditionality, the IMF now relies relatively less on the idea that this will safeguard the revolving character of its resources and relatively more on its responsibility, under Article V.3(a), for assisting members 'to solve their balance-of-payments problems in a manner consistent with the provisions of this Agreement'. Moreover Article IV. 3(a) requires the Fund to 'oversee the international monetary system in order to ensure its effective operation'. While this provision is included in the Article concerning exchange arrangements, its significance may be regarded as being of a general character.

(g) The Fund's Mandate

Thus the IMF may be said to have a general mandate for watching over the international monetary system and for seeking viable and consistent balance-of-payments policies among its members. In carrying out this mandate, the Fund has at its disposal resources calling for various levels of conditionality. However, as shown elsewhere (Dell, 1981, pp. 29–30), the low-conditionality resources happen, at the present time, to constitute an abnormally low proportion of the total, because of the particular method that members have adopted for enlarging access to the Fund's resources—that is, by increasing access as a percentage of quota rather than by increasing quotas themselves. The effect of this is that, of the cumulative 600% of quota available to members for drawings, only 25% is provided at low (first-credit-tranche) conditionality; whereas if quotas had been increased six-fold, which would have been the normal way of proceeding, first-credit-tranche conditionality would have applied to the equivalent of 150% of current quotas.

All this does not, however, mean that the Fund lacks discretion in determining the stringency of conditions to be applied, even if it is established that a source of imbalance is 'persistent'. As we have seen, the compulsion on a member to repay its drawings on the Fund is not derived from the provisions of the stand-by arrangement but is based on the profound interest of sovereign governments in maintaining their creditworthiness not only with the Fund but with all other potential creditors.

Nor do the more general responsibilities of the Fund in relation to the international monetary system require it to impose conditions on a deficit country that ignore the degree of responsibility of that country for the imbalance arising. On the contrary, the Fund has an implied responsibility *not* to act in a manner that appears to condone behaviour on the part of other countries that is incompatible with the Fund's 'purposes' and with 'primary objectives of economic policy'. In particular, the Fund has an obligation to do all it can to assist a member that is suffering the effects of events beyond its control or of injurious policies pursued by other members.

The Fund has itself pointed out that the effort of non-oil developing countries to adjust to increased oil prices 'is hampered by the slowing in the pace of industrial activity in the rest of the world, as well as by protectionist barriers to certain types of their exports to the industrial countries' (IMF, 1980b, p. 51). An additional obstacle mentioned by the Fund is the effect of unusually high rates of interest on external debt. As noted earlier, this resulted from the particular constellation of domestic fiscal and monetary policies employed by the industrial countries in attempting to deal with inflation, without regard to international repercussions.

In the light of these findings, the idea that the Fund's options are limited to a determination whether a deficit is temporary or persistent is farfetched. The Fund cannot, of course, supply more resources than are available to it. But, subject to that constraint, there is much that the Fund can do to lighten the burden of adjustment, and avoid the application of severe and peremptory measures, especially of a deflationary character.

Developing countries must, of course, adjust to irreversible changes—this issue is not in dispute. But in determining the appropriate policy mix, including the amount of balance-of-payments support to be provided, the conditions required for the provision of that support, and the period over which adjustment should be programmed, it is important to distinguish between those elements of a balance-of-payments deficit for which a developing country is itself responsible and those elements that are due to factors beyond its control.

(h) A Possible Solution: Liberalization of CFF?

This is not a revolutionary idea. At one time levels of activity had to be cut back even where external imbalance was due to a temporary decline in foreign demand for exports. The introduction by the IMF of the compensatory financing facility (CFF) and later of the oil facilities indicated clear recognition of the principle that it is improper to force standard adjustment policies on member countries in circumstances for which they are not responsible. What is now proposed is an extension of that principle to all external sources of disturbance in the balance of payments.

Indeed, the Fund is itself well aware of the shortcomings of CFF and has taken a number of steps to improve its coverage and relevance. The facility was established in 1963, but only 57 drawings, totalling SDR1.2 billion were made under the restrictive provisions that applied during its first 13 years. A turning point was the liberalization of the facility in 1975. From January 1976 to December 1981 there were drawings totalling SDR5.9 billion under the facility; these accounted for 32% of total drawings by non-oil-exporting developing countries during that period (Goreux, 1980, pp. 2–3, updated by the IMF).

Important as the liberalization of December 1975 was, the facility was still subject to major shortcomings. Although CFF drawing rights were increased progressively from 50 to 75% and later to 100% of quota in any one year, even the latter amount was in many cases insufficient to finance the full amount of export shortfalls, especially if they persisted over periods longer than a year. Moreover the reasoning that had been applied to export shortfalls was still not applied to import overages resulting from factors beyond the control of particular countries. In May 1981 a first and very limited step towards the latter objective was taken by the Fund when it agreed to extend financial assistance at low conditionality 'to members that encounter a balance of payments difficulty produced by an excess in the cost of their cereal imports'. As in the case of export shortfalls, the Fund must be satisfied that the source of difficulty is short-term in character and is 'largely attributable to circumstances beyond the control of the member'.[6]

It thus took no less than 18 years for the Fund to reach the conclusion that the logic that it had introduced with respect to export shortfalls in 1963 was applicable also to import overages. And even then, in 1981, the step forward that was taken was extremely limited and inadequate in scope.

There is nevertheless still hope that the next stages of the process of liberalization can be accelerated and that the low-conditionality facility of the Fund will be enlarged so as to be applicable to all imports and so as to provide drawing rights that are much larger in relation to potential shortfalls and overages than they are today.

If this were done, the Fund would have at its disposal, at last, an array of facilities that would allow it to adjust the volume and conditions of the balance-of-payments support that it provides to the circumstances of each case, including particularly the degree of responsibility of the country concerned for the difficulty encountered.

It has been suggested by William Dale, Deputy Managing Director of the IMF (1982), that what he calls 'pure intermediation' by the Fund is unnecessary because there is no longer any uncertainty about the adequacy of finance for that purpose. The implication here, presumably, is that 'pure intermediation' is a function of the commercial banks only. In that case, however, the only countries entitled to have access to 'pure intermediation' would be those that the commercial banks deem to be creditworthy in their terms—the industrial countries together with a minority of developing countries, as matters now stand.

As noted earlier, if the Fund had enlarged access to its resources by raising quotas instead of by increasing drawing rights as a percentage of existing quotas, the volume of resources available to members on first-credit-tranche terms would have been six times as large as they are under the method actually employed. The Interim Committee and the IMF management have stated repeatedly that the correct method of enlarging Fund resources is by increasing quotas. The Fund authorities must therefore see a role for a much increased volume of first-credit-tranche resources, whether one calls it 'pure intermediation' or anything else.

3. NATIONAL ASPECTS

(a) Even-handedness or Discrimination?

The IMF approach to the balance-of-payments problems of developing countries starts out from three basic assumptions. The first of these is that there is sufficient flexibility in the economies of these countries to permit them to respond to standard adjustment formulae without undue cost. The second is that by and large the problems are of a short-term character that can and should be handled within a relatively short time-frame. The third is that within the framework of appropriate government policies it is generally best to rely on market forces to bring about the requisite adjustment.

These basic assumptions are considered equally valid for all members of the Fund, and even-handed treatment of Fund members therefore requires that stabilization programmes should be of roughly similar design regardless of what countries are involved. This does not, of course, mean that the content of programmes has to be the same from country to country: obviously the degree of devaluation, if any, required in a particular case will depend on the circumstances of that case, and similar considerations apply to all other stabilization measures involved. On the other hand, given the degree of balance-of-payments pressure and the factors responsible for that pressure in any particular country, the stabilization measures required would be approximately the same regardless of whether the country were developed or developing.

This may seem to imply even-handed treatment of Fund members, but it is not necessarily so in practice. Indeed even-handed treatment as seen from the standpoint of the lender can and frequently does involve inequality of burden-sharing among borrowers. This can be illustrated by a hypothetical case involving two countries suspected of having overvalued exchange rates, one of which is completely dependent on primary commodities for its export revenues while the other obtains most of such revenues from sales of diversified manufactures. Standard purchasing power parity calculations may show the degree of devaluation required to be the same in both cases. But the burden of such devaluation will be much greater for the exporter of primary commodities than for the exporter of manufactures because of the much smaller responsiveness of exports to be expected in the former case: in fact, the impact on primary exports may be perverse. In that case the entire burden of correcting the disequilibrium falls on imports and hence on the curtailment of domestic consumption or investment or both. The country exporting manufactures, on the other hand, may find itself in a position to correct its external balance entirely through an increase in exports and hence in the level of business activity. If unutilized labour and capital are available, such a country may actually be able to improve its situation even from the standpoint of domestic consumption and investment.

More generally, any approach to stabilization policies that overlooks the much lower mobility of resources in developing than in developed countries is bound to discriminate against the former if standard formulae are applied to purely monetary measures of internal and external disequilibrium. Moreover, correction of present imbalances calls for structural adjustment over periods longer than traditional Fund programmes. While the need for medium-term structural adjustment has been accepted in principle in statements by the Interim Committee and the IMF management, it is unclear how far the requirements of such adjustment are recognized in practice. The very fact that adjustment is programmed over a longer period would appear to imply a less rigorous and demanding programme of stabilization than if the same degree of adjustment had to be achieved within a shorter period. It has nevertheless been stated by the Fund that on average resources are now being provided at a much more exacting level of conditionality than they were in the mid-1970s, and that while, in the mid-1970s, approximately three-quarters of the resources provided by the fund to its members were at low conditionality, three-quarters of current new lending commitments involve upper-credit-tranche programmes.[7]

Finally, the effort to induce developing countries to rely on market forces in the adjustment process contrasts oddly with the steady increase in the number of products exported by developing countries that have been removed from the influence of market forces through restrictive measures adopted by the industrial countries.

If free market conditions were the key to development, there would be no dichotomy between developed and underdeveloped economies, since government intervention in the latter economies is a relatively recent phenomenon, following accession to economic independence. There is not a single industrial country that did not employ vigorous protection at some stage in its history. Among the much applauded newly industrializing countries (NICs), the most important have highly regulated economies. Even so highly industrialized a country as Japan, the miracle economy of the century, continues to this day to protect its industrial development in a variety of ways. While Japan is under great pressure to dismantle this protection, the important lesson of Japan for the developing countries and for the Fund is that properly managed protection, so far from being an obstacle to growth, is an indispensable instrument in promoting growth.

Where there is a case against regulation, it depends not on any inherent superiority of market forces, but on the much simpler consideration that many developing countries do not have the administrative resources required for extensive or detailed regulation and control; and that even where such resources do exist, it is often difficult to ensure that regulation and control are exercised in the interests of the public at large and not merely in the interest of the regulators and controllers. But that does not mean that developing countries should do away with all controls—only that they should limit themselves to those key controls that they are able to operate efficiently.

(b) The Capacity for Adjustment

Mention was made earlier of inter-country differences in the elasticity of supply of exports as a factor in explaining differences in the effectiveness of adjustment. This is one example—perhaps the most important—of a more general differentiation between countries in their capacity for adjustment. For example, countries differ considerably in the extent to which they can compress imports without suffering adverse effects. On the one hand some countries are better equipped than others in terms of the availability of skills and resources for developing substitutes for imports. On the other hand, while in some countries imports may include a substantial share of non-essentials that can be readily restricted without serious economic injury, in others they may consist entirely of essential foodstuffs, raw materials and equipment, the curtailment of which would have damaging effects on basic consumption, investment or production.

In the UNDP/UNCTAD study (Dell and Lawrence, 1980) it was found that much of the inter-country variation in performance during the 1970s could be attributed to differences in the capacity for adjustment. It was also suggested that adjustment programmes and policies should be adapted to the particular capabilities for adjustment of each country. Mention has already been made of the potentially very different effects of devaluation in various countries, depending on the responsiveness of actual or potential exports to such a step in the short and medium term. Similarly, a cost-benefit analysis of general measures to improve the trade balance by cutting consumption would yield one set of results in a country in which exported goods were not consumed domestically and imported consumer goods consisted mainly of basic foodstuffs, and a different set of results when a substantial proportion of exportables was consumed domestically and there was a wide range of imported consumer goods.

(c) Exchange Rate Policies

Perhaps the greatest difficulties in relation to stabilization programmes have arisen in the area of exchange rate adjustment. It is here that the effect of government intervention in the economy is particularly visible. Moreover, the effect of that intervention is usually to bring about a decline in domestic consumption[8] and a shift in the distribution of income. In many cases, in fact, it is precisely the fall in real income and the shift in income distribution that are the main goals of exchange rate adjustments, especially where supply and demand elasticities in foreign trade are relatively low.

It is not uncommon for exchange rate adjustments exceeding 50% to be proposed, often on the basis of the crudest purchasing power parity calculations. It is not merely that the data themselves have serious shortcomings. There is also the problem of determining the composition and weighting of the two price or cost series to be compared, for which there is no unique solution. No doubt in extreme cases the need for exchange rate adjustment is clear enough on the basis of any reasonable grouping of the available data. But establishing the required direction of change is not the same thing as determining the precise degree of adjustment needed.

More serious, however, is the fact that, as Kaldor has pointed out, it cannot be taken for granted that the internal distribution of income, which is the outcome of complex political forces, can be effectively changed by devaluation. A large-scale devaluation may well be followed by a price upheaval that ends up by reproducing, at a much higher level of prices, the same price and cost relationships as had prevailed before the devaluation (Kaldor, 1982).

A study of Tanzanian experience in the 1970s for the UNDP/UNCTAD project showed that Tanzania had resisted devaluation on the grounds that any attempt by that country to raise its share of export markets for primary commodities would have provoked retaliation; and that there was a preference for using import controls and selective indirect taxation for limiting imports since those were the instruments of choice in the overall planning process. On the other hand, devaluation was regarded as far too unselective a means of demand management that would tend to shift income from the relatively poor producers of food to the relatively richer exporters of cash crops, which was inconsistent with Tanzania's social objectives and the goal of raising food production. Tanzania nevertheless devalued in 1971 and 1975 when absolute cuts in domestic export prices or major export subsidies would otherwise have been needed.

Devaluations in Zambia in 1976 and 1978 were designed to maintain the profitability of the mining companies in the face of rising external costs (equivalent to 60–70% of total costs) and falling copper prices. The difficulty seen in the devaluation strategy, however, was that to the extent that it succeeded, it tended to increase excess supplies and, hence, depress prices still further, thereby making it necessary to undertake recurrent devaluations.

Doubts about the effectiveness of the exchange rate weapon are, however, not limited to low-income primary producing countries. Brailovsky (1981) has studied the impact of exchange rate changes during the 1960s and 1970s in a group of 13 countries, of which seven are among the leading industrial country exporters of manufactures—Canada, France, the Federal Republic of Germany, Italy, Japan, the Netherlands and the United Kingdom—while the remaining six are the more successful exporters of manufactures among the developing countries—Argentina, Brazil, Hong Kong, the Republic of Korea, Mexico and Singapore.

The data presented by Brailovsky suggest that changes in nominal exchange rates resulted in relatively small changes in real exchange rates during the periods examined, and it is therefore not surprising that they account for only a small proportion of the shifts in market shares. The main impact of changes in nominal exchange rates was on rates of domestic inflation rather than on real exchange rates.[9]

(d) The Role of Monetarism

Despite a certain eclecticism to be found in the published IMF literature, most Fund programmes are established within a common framework. According to members of the Fund staff, 'In this framework there is a fairly well-defined relationship between money, the balance of payments, and domestic prices, in which the supply of and demand for money play a central linking role' (Khan and Knight, 1981, p. 3).

A distinction is often drawn between what is called the new monetarism and the old monetarism, and between their respective prescriptions for stabilization. The important point, however, is not the differences but the similarities, particularly the incorrect diagnosis of problems, and the consequent shortcomings of would-be remedial programmes.

(e) The Case Against Monetarism

This is not the place to elaborate on the case against monetarism—there is an abundant and growing literature [see particularly Hicks (1975, 1976) and Kaldor (1964, 1978, 1981)] in support of the propositions that:

   (a) Correlations between the supply of money and levels of expenditure do not indicate the direction of causality, even if there is a time lag between the former series and the latter.

   (b) While narrow definitions of the money supply are not very useful for most purposes, broad definitions are arbitrary, and money supply broadly defined is surrounded by a halo of liquid assets that are not included but are nevertheless close substitutes for assets that *are* included.

   (c) It is not the money supply, however defined, that is relevant to spending decisions but liquidity in the widest sense, including not only money but money substitutes. And liquidity in this widest sense is not under the control of the monetary authorities.

   (d) In a credit economy, the fact that a substantial proportion of bank money is idle breaks the link between the total quantity of money and that part of it which is circulating. In so far as monetary controls are effective at all, it is the rate of interest that is important and not the total quantity of money, however defined.

(e) If output is below capacity levels, it is likely that an increase in money supply will be non-inflationary and that the effect will be a rise in output.

(f) Goodhart's law: any measure of the money supply that is used as a basis for an attempt at official control quickly loses its meaning.

(g) It is not incorrect to group all forms of inflation together as being induced by a single factor—an increase in the money supply. In deciding on the remedy for inflation, it is essential, as noted earlier, to distinguish between demand inflation and cost inflation, and to adapt the remedies accordingly.

Perhaps the most important single economic reason why the management of national economies is in disarray throughout the developed as well as the developing world at the present time is that problems of cost inflation are being attacked by measures to deflate demand even in situations where economies are operating at 20% or more below capacity. As Killick (1981, p. 28) concludes on the basis of replies to questionnaires addressed to IMF staff, 'it appears on this evidence that the Fund is no less likely to require demand restraint even in countries in which its own staff does not believe excess demand to be a principal cause of the payments problems'. Demand deflation, if taken far enough, will ultimately have an impact on cost inflation—there is no dispute about this. What is in question is the need for the heavy social and economic costs that are involved.

(f) The Policy of Sackcloth and Ashes

As Diaz-Alejandro (1981, p. 125) has pointed out in examining the stabilization plans of the Southern Cone countries of Latin America:

> Even in cases where excess demand was a plausible explanation for the high rates of inflation during the preplan period, its explanatory power declines as the months go by and excess capacity and foreign exchange reserves pile up. Remaining fiscal deficits and/or high rates of increase in the money supply provide weak explanations under conditions of declining output and of shrinking real credit and cash balances. Excessive trade union power can hardly be blamed when real wages collapse and union leaders are jailed, or worse.

Despite continuing retrenchment, inflation rates were not brought down below the 15–20% level. The situation became one of 'overkill', in the sense that reductions in aggregate demand went beyond what was required to make room for an expansion in the production of exportables and of those importables and non-traded goods benefiting from the new constellation of relative prices. The curtailment of demand brought with it severe weakness in capital formation as reductions in public investment were accompanied by lack of confidence on the part of the private sector. Diaz-Alejandro suggests that the process of 'overkill' cannot be fully explained without reference to the authorities' wish to discipline the labour force by creating a soft labour market.

The situation thus described is characteristic of many countries in other parts of the developing, and, indeed, of the developed world. In some developing countries stabilization programmes in the 1970s induced declines in real wages of the order of 20–40% over relatively short periods (Dell and Lawrence, 1980, p. 64). It should be noted that programmes of this type were by no means limited to countries entering into stand-by arrangements with the IMF. The wave of exaggerated economic retrenchment was and is an almost world-wide phenomenon, and in many cases where adjustment policies of great severity were applied under stand-by arrangements, the government itself was at least as keen to cut back as the IMF mission involved. Moreover, as is well known, in a not inconsiderable number of cases ministries of finance and central banks welcomed the support given by IMF missions to policies of retrenchment that the former were having difficulty in persuading other sectors of the government to accept.

Is evidence of the type cited earlier relevant? Williamson (1982, pp. 4–5) points out quite correctly that a comparison of 'what is' with 'what was' is 'conceptually inappropriate' if one is trying to assess policy results and economic performance. What is implied here, however, is that alternative methods of adjustment were available that would not have involved so large a reduction in real income, and in some cases perhaps no reduction at all. Such methods would have required correct identification of the sources of cost inflation and the mobilization of the social consensus required to slow down and ultimately halt the struggle between social groups to safeguard their respective shares of real income. Given such social consensus, the need for demand deflation would have been correspondingly reduced, devaluations, where they occurred, could have been much less drastic, and the fall in real wages would have been correspondingly smaller. In cases where idle resources could be shifted to exportables facing open markets abroad, the adjustment process could even have been carried out without loss of output and income—as did in fact occur in countries such as Brazil and the Republic of Korea where access to the international capital market made it possible to escape the standard deflationary remedies, at least for a time. More recently, in the face of mounting debt and soaring interest rates in the international market, even Brazil has felt compelled to deflate.

As to why the sackcloth and ashes approach to adjustment was preferred, the reasons lie more in the realm of politics than of economics. Many governments, developing as well as developed, were seeking radical solutions to what they regarded as long-standing problems of income distribution and trade union militancy, and came to the conclusion that their goals were too far from existing realities to be realized through the normal processes of negotiation and compromise required for the attainment of social consensus.

At the international level the radical solution envisaged by developed countries takes the form of reducing, so far as possible, the transfer of concessional resources to developing countries and relying on market incentives to generate the flows of private capital required to supplement the domestic efforts of these countries and provide them with balance-of-payments support when needed. Under this concept, the role of the Bretton Woods institutions is to support the basic thrust of the aforementioned strategy by cooperating more closely with the private sector, and negotiating the kind of stabilization programmes that would help deficit countries to attract balance-of-payments support from the only source capable as matters stand of providing it in the volume required—namely the commercial banking system.

This strategy, of course, leaves out all those countries that are unable to attract large-scale commercial bank loans *under any conditions.* For them the Fund is the lender of both first and last resort. Thus the concept of the Fund as primarily a stimulus to and guarantor of the creditworthiness of developing countries, and only a residual provider of balance-of-payments support in its own right, is completely unacceptable to the low-income countries that have no other source of such support available to them. The strategy is also unwelcome to other developing countries, if only because the country limits for lending set by commercial banks for prudential reasons do not, in the aggregate, reflect an appropriate measure of the borrowing capacity of the countries concerned, especially under conditions of artificially high interest rates.

(g) Pinpoint Targetry

One advantage of monetarist theories is that they make it possible to devise straightforward performance criteria in the form of precise monetary targets that can be readily monitored by the IMF. This creates an objective basis for determining whether member countries that have entered into stand-by arrangements with the Fund are performing sufficiently well to establish an entitlement to successive phased drawings on the lines of credit established by the Fund under these arrangements.

Killick (1981, p. 25) finds that 'In economic terms, by far the strongest evidence of a stereotyped approach is the almost ur.'versal inclusion of ceilings on bank credit, which in many cases are the chief test the government must pass', though he notes also that 'there is a considerable diversity as to the form which these take' to suit local conditions. Almost all stand-by arrangements include limits on the amount of new bank credit which could be extended to both the public and private sectors.

The fact is, however, that neither the developed nor the developing countries have had much success in achieving quantitative monetary targets, even when they have set the targets for themselves. The Governor of the

Bank of England (Bank of England, 1978, pp. 36–38) has reported that from 1974 to the beginning of 1978 the mean error of forecasts of the public-sector borrowing requirement (PSBR) made at the beginning of each financial year in the United Kingdom was of the order of 3 billion pounds sterling: the average annual level of the PSBR from 1974/1975 to 1977/1978 was £8.2 billion. For this and other reasons the Governor was sharply critical of procedures requiring a particular numerical target to be reached by a particular date: 'Firm deadlines can force one either to adjust too fast to an unforeseen trend developing late in the period, or to appear to accept a failure to reach one's target.'

Similar problems have arisen in the United States. As reported by Governor Henry Wallich (1980, pp. 12–13) of the Board of Governors of the Federal Reserve System:

> Since mid-1974, a whole collection of standard money-demand functions used routinely in econometric models has misperformed on a large scale by overpredicting the amount of money that would be demanded at given levels of income and interest rates. By late 1979 this overprediction amounted to anywhere from 9 to 17 percent of M-1A or M-1B, or something like $35–70 billion. This overprediction of the amount of money required made the Federal Reserve's targets, which seemed quite restrictive, turn out relatively unrestrictive. . . . The uncertainties inherent in this approach underline the advisability of stating money-supply targets in terms of a range rather than of a single number.

Wallich suggests further that 'it may be risky to become irrevocably committed to a numerical set of targets'. And he points out that the most successful countries in conducting noninflationary monetary policies have been the Federal Republic of Germany and Switzerland and that both these countries have been 'quite relaxed about their adherence to [money supply] targets'.

Incidentally, the Federal Reserve study prompted Wallich to conclude further that 'monetary restraint, however steady, cannot quickly bring down inflation nor interest rates. The most plausible view is that the main impact of monetary restraint on prices occurs with a two-year lag.' This is not a very promising time horizon even for stabilization programmes based on IMF extended arrangements, let alone for standard one-year programmes.

(h) The Breakdown of Stand-by Arrangements

The IMF is, of course, not 'irrevocably committed' (to use Wallich's phrase) to precise monetary targets. Killick (1981) reports that on the average as many as one-third of the Fund's stand-by arrangements are amended as a result of minor deviations from targets that are regarded as temporary or reversible, or that result from unexpected changes in circumstances.

More serious, however, are the many cases in which credit ceilings are exceeded, or other targets breached, by margins that cannot be dealt with by waivers. Here the member government automatically loses its right to draw outstanding instalments of its line of credit without, as Sir Joseph Gold (IMF, 1969, p. 533) has pointed out, the need for a decision by, or even notice to, the Executive Board.

The government always has the option in such cases of negotiating a new understanding with the Fund, but there is no guarantee that such negotiations will succeed or that the new targets will be more easily achieved than the previous ones. Moreover, in many cases some of the damage done by the breakdown of the agreement may be irreversible, especially if it leads to a general loss of confidence and the government is forced into costly alternative courses of action.

The frequency of breakdowns indicates in itself that there is something wrong with the system of pinpoint targetry. Can so many governments all be guilty of incompetence or mismanagement? In some cases, the time lags involved in the preparation of the necessary statistics are such that the negotiators on both sides are unaware that the targets under discussion are already out of date and impossible of achievement. Even where this is not the case, the aforementioned experience of the United Kingdom and the United States indicates that reliance on precise quantitative targets is full of pitfalls, and that the errors of estimation may be of very large orders of magnitude.

These shortcomings would be serious even if it were clear that monetary targets were the right targets on which to concentrate. But this is not necessarily the case even if the primary objective is demand management: where demand is excessive it may be much more important and effective to raise taxes than to restrict credit. In the many instances in which improvements in the balance of payments depend primarily on structural change, monetary targets may be at best of limited importance and at worst entirely irrelevant.

A good example of destabilizing error resulting from the uncertainties of forecasting is to be found in the experience of Peru in 1978–1979. Peru was compelled to negotiate for an IMF stand-by in the third quarter of 1978, and had to accept stringent obligations to deflate the economy—less severely than the unrealistic agreement of December 1977 had provided, but still harsh enough.

Yet if one examines the balance-of-payments projections agreed upon as a basis for the stand-by negotiations, it is immediately apparent that had the negotiators known that the price of copper would recover from 58 cents/lb in July 1978 to 90 cents/lb in March 1979, they would have realized that that fact alone would come close to restoring external balance without any cutting down of the economy at all. By April 1979, the Peruvian balance of payments was so strong and the inflow of capital so massive that the Financial Times was reporting 'an embarrassingly large inflation-inducing surfeit of dollars'.

Mistakes of forecasting are, of course, unavoidable and a case of this kind underlines the dangers of pinpoint targetry. A more important source of concern is that here was a case in which the projected external imbalance was largely due to a temporary and reversible factor—namely the low price of copper. The cost to Peru in terms of lost output and investment was out of all proportion to the magnitude of the external problem that had been encountered. It is disquieting that the economy of a country such as Peru—which by developing country standards has relatively diversified exports—can still be at the mercy of the volatility of a single commodity. And it is alarming that such a country can find itself compelled to endure lasting damage to its economy on account of circumstances that are reversible, through an inability to mobilize balance-of-payments support on a scale sufficient to avoid such damage.

4. CONCLUSION

A number of forward-looking steps have been taken. The Fund (1980a, p. 42) has stated that:

> In view of the size of the current deficits and of the difficulties that may arise in private intermediation, the Fund must be prepared, when necessary, to lend in larger amounts than in the past. Also, the structural problems faced by many countries may require that adjustment take place over a longer period than has been typical in the framework of Fund programs in the past. Further, lending by the Fund must reflect the sort of flexibility, with an awareness of the circumstances of members, that is called for in the Executive Board's current guidelines on conditionality.

More recent developments, notably the severe tightening of conditionality, raise some doubts as to whether the promise of that statement is being or will be realized. The concept of unilateral adjustment, with one group of countries at best neutral towards, and at worst frustrating, the adjustment process of the other group, is not an acceptable basis for IMF supervision of the international monetary system. There is a pressing need for the Fund to reconsider its position on this basic issue.

Furthermore, care should be taken to avoid overkill in determining the degree and character of adjustment needed in stabilization programmes. This will require setting aside monetarist doctrines that lead to mistakes in the diagnosis of problems and in the specification of solutions, especially where problems of structural adjustment over the medium term are involved.

One useful device for dealing with some aspects of both these problems would be to liberalize and enlarge the compensatory financing facility with the objective of applying the same kind of regime to imports as to exports. This would have the effect of providing the Fund with an array of facilities at low and high conditionality that would make it possible to design stabilization programmes in a manner that would be more responsive to the particular situations of individual countries.

NOTES

1. It may be noted that the purposes of the IMF, as stated in Article I, did not, even after the amendments adopted in 1969 and 1978, include the elimination or reduction of inflation. Inflation is relevant to the IMF purposes to the extent that it contributes to balance-of-payments disequilibrium.
2. Article 55 of the United Nations Charter calls for the promotion of 'higher standards of living, full employment, and conditions of economic and social progress and development'.
3. Executive Board decisions 4134-(74/4) of 23 January 1974 and 4241-(74/67) of 13 June 1974 as recorded in International Monetary Fund, *Annual Report* 1974, pp. 108 and 122–123. I am indebted to Mr. Alexandre Kafka, Executive Director of the IMF, for this point.
4. Alternative scenarios through the mid-1980s explored in the Fund's *World Economic Outlook* published in June 1981 assumed that the real price of oil would either remain steady or continue to increase, so that the current account surplus of oil-exporting countries would either decline from $96 billion in 1981 to some $50 billion by 1985, or remain approximately unchanged. No consideration was given to the possibility that the real price of oil might decline.
5. Executive Board decision No. 6224-(79/135) provides in part that requests for drawings on the compensatory financing facility will be met when the Fund is satisfied that 'the shortfall is of a short-term character and is largely attributable to circumstances beyond the control of the member'.
6. *IMF Survey* (18 June 1981). The use of the word 'short-term' appears unnecessarily restrictive. It is implicit in the wording of Article I (v) cited earlier that the balance-of-payments difficulties for which Fund financing is appropriate may be characterized as 'temporary' (i.e. likely to be reversed in due course) rather than as merely 'short-term'.
7. *IMF Survey* (9 February 1981, p. 35).
8. Even if the fall in domestic consumption is unavoidable, the perception of the general public may be that a government that devalues is responsible for the decline in living standards.
9. Brailovsky defines the real exchange rate as the weighted average of the ratio between domestic and foreign prices, both converted to a common currency, the weights corresponding to the area composition of trade.

REFERENCES

Bank of England, *Quarterly Bulletin,* Vol. 18, No. 1 (March 1978).

Brailovsky, Vladimiro, with the assistance of Juan Carlos Moreno, 'Exchange rate policies, manufactured exports and the rate of inflation' (Mexico: Institute for Industrial Planning, 1981), mimeo.

Committee of Twenty, *International Monetary Reform: Documents of the Committee of Twenty* (Washington, D.C.: IMF, 1974).

Dale, William B., 'The financing and adjustment of payments imbalances', paper presented to a conference on IMF Conditionality held by the Institute for International Economics in March 1982: it will be published in a Conference volume edited by John Williamson.

De Larosière, Jacques, Address to the 1981 Annual Meetings of the Fund and Bank, *IMF Survey* (12 October 1981).

Dell, Sidney, *On Being Grandmotherly: The Evolution of IMF Conditionality* (Princeton, New Jersey: International Finance Section, Princeton University, 1981).

Dell, Sidney and Roger Lawrence, *The Balance of Payments Adjustment Process in Developing Countries* (New York: Pergamon Press, 1980).

Diaz-Alejandro, Carlos F., 'Southern Cone stabilization plans', in William R. Cline and Sidney Weintraub (eds), *Economic Stabilization in Developing Countries* (Washington, D.C.: Brookings Institution, 1981).

Economic Report of the President (Washington, D.C.: U.S. Government Printing Office, 1973).

Goreux, Louis M., *Compensatory Financing Facility,* IMF Pamphlet Series No. 34 (Washington, D.C.: 1980).

Hicks, Sir John, 'What is wrong with monetarism', *Lloyds Bank Review* (October 1975).

Hicks, Sir John, 'The little that is right with monetarism', *Lloyds Bank Review* (July 1976).

International Monetary Fund, *International Monetary Fund* 1945–65, Vol II (Washington, D.C.: 1969).

International Monetary Fund, *World Economic Outlook* (Washington, D.C.: 1980a).

International Monetary Fund, *Annual Report* 1980 (Washington, D.C.: 1980b).

International Monetary Fund, *Annual Report* 1981 (Washington, D.C.: 1981).

Kaldor, Lord, *Essays on Economic Policy,* Vol. I. Chaps. II.6 and II.7 (London: Duckworth, 1964).

Kaldor, Lord, *Further Essays on Applied Economics,* Chaps. I.1 and II.8 (London: Duckworth, 1978).

Kaldor, Lord, *Memorandum of Evidence on Monetary Policy to the Select Committee of the Treasury and Civil Service* (London: H.M. Stationery Office, 1981).

Kaldor, Lord, 'The role of devaluation in the adjustment of balance of payments deficits', report to the Group of Twenty-Four (1982).

Khan, Mohsin and Malcolm D. Knight, 'Stabilization programs in developing countries: a formal framework', *International Monetary Fund Staff Papers,* Vol. 28, No. 1 (March 1981).

Killick, Tony, 'IMF stabilization programmes' (London: Overseas Development Institute, 1981), mimeo.

Wallich, Henry, 'Federal reserve policy and the economic outlook', address to the Chesapeake Chapter of Robert Morris Associates (3 December 1980), mimeo.

Williamson, John, *The Failure of World Monetary Reform* 1971–74 (London: Nelson, 1977).

Williamson, John, 'On judging the success of IMF policy advice', paper presented to a Conference on IMF Conditionality held by the Institute for International Economics in March 1982: it will be published in a Conference volume edited by John Williamson.

12

Stabilization and Economic Justice: The Case of Nicaragua

E. V. K. Fitzgerald

The theme of this paper is stabilization policy, a term which has unfortunately earned itself a bad name in development economics in the past few years. In Latin America, however, stabilization policy has been a constant feature of economic debate at least since independence, precisely because of the effect of the world trade cycle on export earnings, and thus the need for politically sovereign governments frequently to adjust domestic economic policy to an exogenously determined balance of payments.

The modern debate on stabilization in Latin America really starts, however, in the Great Depression of the 1930s, when for the first time there was a general reaction against the principles of "sound finance" and an attempt to implement a strategy of counter-cyclical monetary intervention and import-substituting industrialization. Monetarism, of course, had been the current orthodoxy since the previous century, when it was felt by bankers (and Marx, incidentally) that the effect of the downswing of the trade cycle was to reduce wages to reasonable proportions, eliminate inefficient enterprises and restore profitable capital accumulation—the effect transmitted from center to periphery by the gold standard. It should also be remembered that the rest of what is now called the Third World was then largely colonized and thus part of enclosed currency areas. In other words, Latin America had developed, long before the present decade, a definite attitude toward stabilization based on the premise that industrialization and real wage maintenance were more important objectives than price stability or a fixed exchange rate.

In the present debate about stabilization, when the principles of "sound finance" are again popular not only with international bankers but with certain governments in the Continent, the disagreement starts not so much with the correct policy but with the causes of the problem. Briefly, the

From *Debt and Development in Latin America*, Kwan S. Kim and David F. Ruccio, eds. (Notre Dame, Ind.: University of Notre Dame Press, 1985), pp. 191–204. Reprinted by permission.

debtors' story is about the depression in the world economy, deterioration in the terms of trade, the need to sustain investment in production and social infrastructure, and rising interest rates. Just as briefly, the creditors' story is about irresponsible government borrowing, failure to adjust domestic policies to external realities, lack of business confidence and shortages of funds. But whatever the causes, and however much debt rescheduling the bankers can be persuaded to accept (for they too wish to avoid default), some sort of stabilization policy has to be adopted to bring imports into line with exports and to restore a country's credit-worthiness. Again, no person would disagree that the only solution in the long run is to expand exportable production and achieve higher world prices, although there might still be debate as to how this is to be managed.

In the short run, stabilization policy must act on demand; even in the long run, in a situation of supply constraint (particularly of imported producer goods but also often of food), demand must be kept roughly in line with the expansion of production capacity. The orthodox package of demand control is well known (budget cuts, real wage decline, devaluation, etc.) and is correctly criticized by all those concerned with issues of economic justice for having a greater impact on the incomes of the poor than on the rich and of sacrificing development to profitability. The bankers reply that this may well be so, but profitability must be restored if accumulation is to start on a balanced basis and full employment is to be achieved. The weakness of the critics' position is that they have very little to offer as an alternative for short-term demand management, which is what counts at any given moment. Moreover, when popular governments do gain power,[1] they often run into situations of balance of payments deficits and soaring inflation, which undermine their support among the very poor whom they are seeking to help.

It is this problem that I wish to address here. Is it possible to design and implement a demand management policy which combines stabilization with economic justice in a mixed economy? By "economic justice" in this context I do not mean anything very complex and Rawlsian; rather, my premise is that the real incomes of workers, artisans, and peasants should not fall in the process. In other words, the problem is to formulate a realistic alternative to IMF-style policies.

To put the same question in another form, why is it that popular governments seem to have so much trouble with finance? This is not only a problem in mixed economies; for even the socialist countries, when they decide to decentralize and restore a degree of enterprise initiative and consumer choice, seem to run rapidly into severe macroeconomic disequilibria and require a stabilization policy as well. Yugoslavia is a good example of this.

It is my contention that such an "economically just stabilization policy" is possible in principle. This belief is based on the approach to macroeconomic analysis developed by Kalecki, which itself derives from the tradition of the classic pillars of political economy, and which is more suitable to the peculiar economic structure of Latin America (and much of the semi-industrialized Third World for that matter) than either Keynes or Friedman. This approach places income distribution and price formation at the center of the stage, but works from the supply side, so that the fundamental determinant of the standard of living of workers and peasants is the supply of basic needs (or "necessities" as Kalecki calls them); if these basic needs are secured, then the effect of macroeconomic adjustment will automatically fall on the supply of other commodities. If, in turn, adequate profits are sustained (through price policy) and investment is stimulated (through the import of capital goods), there is no reason why production should suffer either. Of course, the necessary demand constraint will fall particularly on the middle class in the nonproductive sectors, such as commerce and services, which absorbs a very large slice of the pie in Latin America but does very little to justify it.

1. BASIC NEEDS

I do not wish to dwell too long on the characteristics of the Nicaraguan economy, but rather to explain the sort of stabilization policy problems that faced the government in the first years after the revolution in 1979. I shall take the story up to mid-1983 because since then the increase in insurgency financed and supported by the present United States administration has forced Nicaragua into what is virtually a war economy. Very different considerations come into play about resource allocation and foreign finance under such conditions, even though macroeconomic disequilibrium is clearly just as undesirable, if not more so.

The economic situation in July in 1979, when the Sandinistas took power after a popular rebellion against Somoza, was critical. Gross domestic product (GDP) in that year fell by one-third, industry had been bombed and looted, crops had not been sown for the 1979–1980 harvests, cattle had been slaughtered, airplanes and ships stolen, wages left unpaid, hospitals destroyed and foreign debtors unpaid. The cost of the war was estimated by the United Nations to exceed 1 billion dollars, in an economy with a national income of little more than double that figure.[2] Somoza had run up an external debt of 1.6 billion dollars in the previous few years, but there was little evidence of productive investments; the funds had been used to finance capital flight, and only 3 million dollars were left in the reserves from these loans and the bumper 1978–1979 export harvest of cotton, coffee, and sugar.

The nationalization of the properties of Somoza and his "cronies" gave the new government direct ownership of about one-quarter of material production (that is, about one-half of big business in the country), all the banks, and most of the transportation system. To this was added strict state control over foreign trade because of the foreign exchange shortage, and over wholesale trade in basic consumer goods to avoid speculation. On the other hand, the private sector controlled (and still controls) three-quarters of production, almost all retail commerce, housing, and so on.[3] As we shall see, there was not only a commitment to maintain private productive enterprise so long as it contributed to development goals, paid fair wages, etc., but also to provide a positive stimulus to small farmers, artisans, and local organizations of social services such as health and education. On the international scene, political non-alignment was matched by trade and aid relations with all areas of the world economy. This is what the Sandinistas call a "mixed economy"; in terms of comparative economic institutions, it might be compared with, say, Mexico.

Finally, because the movement of Sandino and the resistance to Somoza had been essentially a "national liberation struggle," a clear strategic aim was to reduce economic dependence on the United States, but without going to the other extreme, as Cuba was forced to do. Nicaragua is lucky in that, since 1959, Latin America had developed very rapidly, so other semi-industrialized economies such as Mexico and Brazil were in a good position to help economically. Similarly Europe, the Arab world, Japan, etc., provided the possibility of trade and finance independent of the United States, but without excessive commitment to the socialist bloc which would be incongruent with geopolitical realities and inappropriate to the development needs of Nicaragua.

In this sort of situation, even with considerable foreign aid, it would not have been possible simply to expand the economy in a "Keynesian" fashion to restore income levels, because of the domestic supply constraints. Moreover, as income redistribution towards the poor was obviously necessary (otherwise why have a revolution?) some differential action was needed; but simply raising wages would be highly inflationary (as the Chilean experience had shown[4]) and would not benefit the really poor in the so-called informal sector. While credit to industry and agriculture had to be raised (with particular emphasis on small farmers for the first time, which had a considerable redistributive effect) to restore production, and the budget had to be expanded rapidly in response to the new health and education programs, some sort of stabilization policy was necessary to contain inflation. However, with three-quarters of the economy in private hands, it was not possible to control incomes or prices directly.

The only way to secure popular living standards was through the supply itself of basic needs, by removing them from the impact of market forces. That is, it was necessary to make access to food, clothing, housing, health, education, public transport, and so on independent of the actual monetary income of the family. If people's only access to basic needs is through the market, and you cannot control everybody's income, a stabilization policy will naturally fall most severely on the poorest. So the first stage in the stabilization policy, strange as it may seem, was to secure basic needs and not to adjust wages upwards.

Guaranteeing the food supply to the population is a problem of production and distribution. The main supply of staple items such as corn and beans, cheese and tomatoes, comes from small peasant farmers. There is a dilemma between low prices (which help the urban poor) and high ones (which help the peasants) which can only be resolved by higher productivity. Thus, the land reform program had to include the allocation of fertile lands to small farmers (in service cooperatives for the most part) and investment in irrigation on state farms—both in order to raise food output. Therefore, from the start, the economic plans included national food security as a key objective.[5]

The other problem is distribution: if distribution is left to the market in times of shortage, food prices will rise and the urban poor above all will suffer. But the dangers of rationing or state retailing are also considerable because of the bureaucratization that they entail. In the case of Nicaragua, it would also be politically and economically impossible to set up a chain of state stores replacing all the small shopkeepers. What was done, then, was to establish a minimum quota per capita for basic products (sugar, cooking oil, etc.) which is supplied through the neighborhood private shops; the shopkeeper receives from the state warehouses the amount that corresponds to the population of his area (about a thousand people on average) and the neighborhood committees see that he adheres to the rules. Other goods, and the surplus of basic products, are sold through the open market.[6]

The next step was taken in education, where the Literacy Crusade in 1980 reduced illiteracy from over 60 percent to approximately 12 percent; since then, the program has been continued in the form of adult education organized at the local level. At the moment, out of a population of 3 million persons, Nicaragua has one million participating in one form of education or another. This educational effort is largely independent of market forces, although private (religious) schools are still important in secondary education. The health system is not based on large hospitals and doctors but, rather, on local sanitation and preventive medicine centered on the family itself. The main cause of death in Nicaragua has traditionally been child gastroenteritis; this has been reduced enormously by teaching mothers simple methods of rehydration. Polio has been eliminated, and malaria controlled through mass sprayings and annual medication campaigns. These are all essentially community affairs. Similarly, the housing programs (after a false start with apartment buildings) are based on the "site and services" system where the local authority opens dirt streets and installs electricity and water connections to housing plots. Families then build their own houses, buying basic materials at a fixed price from the state and gradually improving the house over the years.

In sum, the "basic needs program" is based on popular organization. Politically and socially, the advantages of this are obvious; but economically too this has the effect of mobilizing underutilized labor without a large capital cost, raising living standards directly without paying inflationary wages.

From the point of view of stabilization, this also protects popular living standards from market forces. This is *real* supply-side economics.

2. EXTERNAL BALANCE

The second step in the stabilization policy was to reduce as much as possible the exchange content of consumption, so as to release imports for exportable production and investment. The main objective of cutting consumption in a stabilization policy for a small developing economy is the reduction of imports to reduce the trade deficit. Normally this is done by cutting total consumption. However, an alternative is to reduce the import content of consumption itself, even if this requires changes in traditional patterns. There is a belief among many development economists (particularly of the structuralist ECLA—Economic Commission on Latin America—school) that the consumption of the poor (food, clothing, etc.) contains less foreign exchange than that of the rich (televisions, automobiles, etc.) Even though this is clearly true for some items, it became rapidly obvious in Nicaragua that popular consumption also relies heavily on foreign exchange. For example, beer bottles are imported from Guatemala, the tops from Canada, the hops from Europe, and so on. However, in cigarettes it was possible to eliminate cellophane in the wrappings and substitute tobacco stems for the filters. Again, housewives come to shop with a basket instead of receiving paper bags.

This process has been repeated throughout the consumption system, although it can sometimes have unexpected results. Imports of drinking glasses were halted to encourage use of local pottery; but the informal sector immediately started to fashion glasses out of bottles, thereby creating a bottle shortage. Imports of packaged soups were halted on the grounds that this was a middle-class luxury, until a delegation of agricultural workers pointed out that when peasant women are working on the harvest there is no time to prepare supper in the evening. Planners often forget these things. Another example is the ranking of basic needs themselves. In the case of Managua, for example, we put housing further up the list than public transport; the inhabitants of the barrios had the opposite opinion. This is simply because senior planners have their own cars and are shocked by informal housing which is "home" to someone else.

Having established basic needs consumption and reduced import content as much as possible, it was nonetheless necessary to cut non-basic consumption to the very minimum as the cutting edge of the stabilization program. The problem, of course, is to define non-basic consumption in order to act on it from the supply side, apply taxes, and so on. Imports of cars and televisions with official exchange supplies were quickly eliminated; taxes were raised on gasoline, and eventually rationing was introduced. However, the Ministry of Finance wanted beer, rum, and cigarettes defined as non-basic in order to raise taxes and reduce the fiscal deficit; the trades unions were of the opposite opinion. The effect of this, particularly the import controls, was to reduce sharply non-basic consumption to less than half the pre-1979 level, while basic consumption was restored to its previous level by 1981. Nonetheless, this basic consumption was more equally spread than before, so that urban employees in particular did not feel any great improvement, in marked contrast to the peasantry and the urban poor. One inevitable result has been that the competition in the market for the limited amount of free foreign exchange has pushed the parallel rate skywards.

In general, the effect of supply restraint without direct control over private sector incomes has inevitably been inflationary; but the inflation is differential—a combination of controlled prices for basic consumption goods and services and market-clearing prices for the rest. This is the monetary side of the "real" redistribution of income through differential access. Logically, if a different supply pattern is imposed on the existing income distribution in a market economy, price adjustment must take place.

The consumption policy obviously has a negative impact on the middle and upper classes, who are the beneficiaries of an "orthodox" stabilization policy but not of this sort of economic justice. This can, as in the case of Cuba, have as a consequence the emigration of key producers, technicians, and professionals. Therefore, an attempt has been made to give incentives to these people in the form of vehicles, housing, and so on—creating the problem that this tends to generate the sort of hierarchy known as "nomenklatura" in socialist countries. One of the major sources of internal opposition to the present government in Nicaragua is precisely this urban middle class in the commercial and services sectors, who have been badly hit by this stabilization policy. Someone has to bear the burden of a reduction in consumer demand, or in the case of Nicaragua, of a limited expansion after a war: in Nicaragua, this "someone" has been the better-off non-producers. (In other cases, such as that of Costa Rica, it has been the poor who bear the burden.) These are the political costs of economic justice. In consequence, the government has tried to explain to producers and professionals why they cannot expect any great improvement in their standard of living; as a whole, their reaction has been positive.

The planners felt that once a consumption policy had been worked out, the next task would be the balance of payments: if basic needs and foreign exchange could be arranged, then the financial balances could be safely worked out without endangering the "real side" of the economy. This, incidentally, turned out to be also the basis for effective economic planning in a mixed economy. In technical terms, foreign trade is the "Department One" of the economy while basic needs is the "Department Two," both of which must be brought into line for an effective economic plan.[7] The first task was to restore the level of export volume, particularly from agriculture, even though world prices had been declining; long-term restructuring towards semi-industrialized natural resource exports would depend upon heavy investments that would not bear fruit until the second half of the decade.

Naturally enough, there was a tendency to turn land over to food crops, so the land reform program had to emphasize restored productivity in cotton, coffee, sugar, and meat on the large farms, both state and private. Cotton posed a particular problem because of the ecological damage the existing system meant in terms of pesticides, etc., even though it is the most profitable crop for the country in terms of net foreign exchange earnings. Fortunately, with the help of an American volunteer entymologist, it was possible to discover a way of spraying around the edge of the cotton fields and killing off the bugs early on; this saved both foreign exchange and human lives, not to mention maintaining the ecological balance.

Recovery of meat production was very difficult because of the slaughter of the herds in 1979; it will take a decade to restore the previous level. In this case and that of sugar, moreover, the level of domestic demand began to rise dangerously, threatening export earnings and requiring domestic rationing. Generally speaking, however, the government managed to get export volumes up to something approaching pre-1979 volumes by 1983. Meanwhile, however, world prices had weakened and, more seriously, the prices of imported inputs and machinery had risen by over one-half. Thus, instead of a balance of about 600 million dollars in exports and imports, there was an export income of about 500 million dollars and imports of 900 million dollars, so that a deficit of 400 million dollars had to be financed internationally.

As stated above, the new government inherited from Somoza a debt of 1,600 million dollars and virtually no reserves. The servicing of that debt would have involved paying some 500 million dollars, which was quite impossible. There was a morally very strong position for refusing to pay at all; but this would have meant severing connections with the Western banking system, which was contrary to the strategy of nonalignment. The banks, more from a fear of the bad example to other countries than from altruism, agreed to an unprecedented restructuring on the basis of a five-year grace period on principal and a flat 7 percent interest rate meanwhile, the differential with the prime rate being capitalized.[8]

The next step was to negotiate new finance. By 1980 it was very clear that the United States government was not going to help and would put heavy pressure on the World Bank and the Inter-American Development Bank as well. The World Bank produced a very favorable report in 1981 ("The Challenge of Reconstruction"[9]) but since January 1982 did not make a single new loan, on the ostensible grounds of "inappropriate macroeconomic policy." The interesting development was that the major source of external finance since 1979 has in fact been Third World countries such as Mexico, Argentina, and Brazil, and Western Europe. The socialist countries have provided about one-quarter of all foreign aid. If we compare the case of Nicaragua with that of Cuba, for example, the Cubans had to choose between the USA and the USSR, and once they were cut off from the former, the latter was the only choice. In the case of Nicaragua, twenty years later and with a far less sophisticated economy, the choice of trading and financial partners is far wider, and the possibility of truly non-aligned international economic relations is possible.[10]

Every year, among donations, trade credits and development project loans, it has been possible to obtain the 400 million dollars or so necessary to balance the external accounts. About half of these resources have gone into essential supplies such as medicines, food, fertilizers, and spare parts; but the other half has gone into investment projects. This is because this deficit on external account is clearly not sustainable in the long run. The development projects emphasize the resolution of this problem through the industrialization of natural resources. On the export side, we may mention expansion of sugar (to be sold to socialist countries at fair prices), renovation of the coffee plantations, expansion of burley tobacco, the development of processed fruit and vegetables, exploration for new gold deposits, re-equipment of the fishing fleet and the sawmills, and the expansion of traditional crops such as cotton and sesame. All these projects are already financed and under way; they should come on board before the end of the decade.

The perils of import-substitution are well known in Latin America, so the strategy here has been to concentrate on basic needs (particularly food) and energy. Here we may mention irrigated grains (corn and beans), African palm oil, cotton spinning and textile mills (Nicaragua exports raw cotton and imports cloth at present!), on the one hand, and the generation of geothermal and hydroelectric power to substitute for imported oil, on the other. The geothermal is very interesting because it is based on tapping the heat of volcanoes for steam-driven turbines with Italian technology.

Thus, the long-term solution to stabilization is from production, and not just demand restraint. However, this will not be sufficient unless there is some improvement in the external terms of trade, particularly access to developed country markets at "just" prices—that is, prices which enable reasonable wages to be paid and leave enough to finance further expansion, once the imported inputs have been purchased. The present prices set by the world economy (that is, imposed by the developed economies) are not sufficient to allow this. This is not just a problem for Nicaragua, but for Latin America and the whole Third World, which is why the proposed New International Economic Order is so important. It is worth noting that this is essentially based on the concept of the "just price" discussed by Aquinas several centuries ago!

3. FINANCIAL BALANCE

The last step in stabilization was to construct and apply the internal financial balances that would be consistent with basic needs, on the one hand, and the external account, on the other. This, in a small way, was an innovation in planning technique, and derived in part from work done by Richard Stone at Cambridge in recent years. The method is based on the integration of the "sources and uses of funds" for the whole financial system with the national accounts upon which the annual economic program itself is based. The basic needs program determines the extent of government expenditure, while production targets the amount of domestic credit. Foreign finance, recuperation of credit from the previous year's agricultural cycle and savings deposits are the main sources of finance, along with a limited amount of monetary expansion in line with economic expansion and international inflation. Given these sources, and the need for production and investment credit in the economic program, the permissible government budget deficit emerges as a remainder.

Thus, the total supply of finance is kept in line with the expansion of the economy and the availability of external resources. In principle, therefore, it will not be inflationary. The point here is that a "monetarist" policy can be applied as long as the basic balances of the economy are controlled beforehand. Given the requirements of finance within the plan for production and investments (in both the public and private sectors), the permissible government deficit to be financed by the Central Bank is the residual. Once the minimum budget consistent with basic needs requirements is met, then the targets for fiscal income are derived, framing tax and tariff policy for the next year. This oversimplifies the procedure somewhat, as a process of mutual adjustment in the targets has to be undertaken to achieve the proper balance, but this is the basic logic.

4. CONCLUSION

Taking the first years of the Sandinista revolution as a whole, how successful has the policy been? As the figures in the Appendix indicate, GDP had recovered to about 85 percent of its pre-revolutionary level by 1983; this represents a considerable effort considering that the real volume of imports was 20 percent below its 1977 level and several sectors, such as fishing, mining, and construction, were seriously affected by military conditions, while the livestock sector still needed more time to recuperate from the 1978–1979 slaughtering. As the tables indicate, real export volume in 1983 was still below the historical level, but in fact in real terms (in 1980 prices) the trade gap had been gradually moving into balance between 1980 and 1983, though this was not reflected in the balance of payments because of the dollar price movements. In other words, if the prices of 1983 had been the same as those in 1977, there would only have been a modest deficit on current account, which could have been covered by normal development loans for the import of capital equipment.

Turning to the balance of internal demand, we see a rapid recovery of investment, which reached 1978 levels by 1981, but which had to be scaled back a bit to accommodate the expansion of military construction from 1982 onwards, which is not shown in the national accounts. With partial recovery of national income, a closing real trade gap, and rising investment, consumption was bound to suffer. Public consumption (that is, goods and services used by the government, mainly for health, education and other social services) has obviously expanded rapidly as part of that basic needs program: the real level in 1983 was nearly three times that of 1977. Private consumption, therefore, although it recovered initially between 1979 and 1980, began to decline rapidly thereafter to make room for the other demand categories; in 1983 it was barely two-thirds of what it had been in 1977. Given that basic consumption (food, clothing, etc.) was maintained, what was actually happening was a drastic decline in non-basic consumption, as we have explained above.

In sum, this is the logic of a stabilization program with economic justice.

EDITORS' NOTES

1. "Popular governments" may be defined as governments that draw their support from, and intend to benefit, the majority of the population: industrial and agricultural workers, peasants, and low-income urban groups.
2. See the report by the United Nations Economic Commission on Latin America, *Nicaragua: Repercusiones Económicas de los Acontecimientos Políticas Recientes* (August 1979).
3. See E. V. K. Fitzgerald, "The Economics of Revolution," in Thomas W. Walker, ed., *Nicaragua in Revolution* (New York: Praeger, 1982).
4. See Alain de Janvry's paper, this volume.
5. See Solon Barraclough, *A Preliminary Analysis of the Nicaraguan Food System* (Geneva: UNRISD, 1982).
6. See CIERA, *Distribución y Consumo Popular de Alimentos en Managua* (Managua: CIERA, 1983) and *La Situación del Abastecimiento* (Managua: CIERA/MIDINRA, 1983).
7. This model is developed more formally in E. V. K. Fitzgerald, "Planned Accumulation and Income Distribution in the Small Peripheral Economy," in K. Martin, ed., *Readings in Capitalist and Non-Capitalist Development* (London: Allen and Unwin, forthcoming).
8. See the references in the report by the International Monetary Fund, *Recent Multilateral Debt Restructurings with Official and Bank Creditors,* Occasional Paper 25 (December 1983).
9. World Bank, *Nicaragua: The Challenge of Reconstruction,* Report No. 3524–NI (October 9, 1981).
10. See Michael E. Conroy, *External Dependence, External Assistance, and "Economic Aggression" Against Nicaragua,* Helen Kellogg Institute for International Studies Working Paper No. 27 (July 1984).

Appendix

Gross Domestic Product (Millions of Cordobas at 1980 Prices)

	1977	1978	1979	1980	1981	1982	1983
G.D.P.	29,353	27,050	19,902	21,892	23,052	22,779	23,683
Gross Fixed Investment	6,831	2,897	-1,266	3,364	5,201	4,302	4,351
Fixed	6,183	3,431	1,203	2,883	4,694	3,801	3,830
Inventories	648	-534	-2,469	481	507	501	521
Consumption	23,805	22,841	17,640	22,488	20,665	19,424	19,904
Public	2,351	2,843	3,045	4,107	4,658	5,446	6,286
Private	21,454	19,998	14,595	18,381	16,007	13,978	13,618
Basic	—	10,000	—	10,587	10,905	10,362	10,920
Non-basic	—	9,998	—	7,794	5,102	3,616	2,698
Exports of Goods and Services	6,800	7,413	8,484	5,039	5,789	5,323	5,800
Imports of Goods and Services	8,083	6,101	4,956	8,999	8,603	6,269	6,372

Trade Balance (Millions of US Dollars)

	1977	1978	1979	1980	1981	1982	1983
Export (f.o.b.)	636.2	646.0	615.9	450.4	499.8	405.8	432.0
Imports (c.i.f.)	761.9	593.9	360.2	887.2	999.4	775.5	807.0
External Terms of Trade (change)	15.6	—	-3.8	3.6	-20.5	-14.4	-12.2

General Price Index (Annual Change)

1977	1978	1979	1980	1981	1982	1983
11.4	4.6	48.2	35.3	23.9	24.8	31.0

SOURCE: UN/ECLA based on Nicaraguan national accounts.

13

The International Debt Situation and North–South Relations

Frances Stewart*

1. INTRODUCTION

Little progress has been made on major North–South issues during the past few decades. This lack of progress has occurred despite a consensus among many observers (most recently exemplified in the Brandt Commission Reports) of a mutual interest in both North and South in various reforms. Deeper analysis of the nature of the interests involved in North–South relationships explains why this is so. The mutual interests identified by those advocating reform are of a very general type, while the sort of interests that determine government attitudes towards negotiations and reform tend to be rather nationalistic and those of particular powerful pressure groups, which dominate any 'general' interests. An example of this occurs in relation to trade, where the general interest in free [trade] is evident, especially among consumers, but particular producer groups (workers and managers/owners) often succeed in securing protection. Examples in other areas abound: for instance in relation to the arms trade, or to the world food situation.[1]

In order to make progress in identifying obstacles to reform in North–South relationships and in formulating proposals with more likelihood of success, it is necessary to examine the particular interests involved in each of the major issues, and how they would be affected by various reforms. It is not sufficient to identify some general interests in reforms. However, this is not to argue that because particular interests are so important there is no room

*This is a revised version of a paper written for the North–South Roundtable on Money and Finance. I am very grateful for comments from Stephany Griffiths-Jones, Michael Lipton and Paul Streeten.

From *World Development*, Vol. 13, No. 2 (1985), pp. 191–204. Copyright © 1985 by Pergamon Press, Ltd. Reprinted by permission.

for imagination or creativity in analysis or action. Rather imagination is needed, but it must be consistent with the underlying interests. In the absence of any vision, the world may muddle through more or less efficiently, with occasional catastrophes. Imaginative ideas which bear no relationship to underlying interests will not change this, as we have seen in connection with the Brandt proposals. However, where visionary ideas build on the underlying interests, changes may be achieved which produce substantial improvements. The Bretton Woods system was an example of this; Marshall aid another. In both, the interests of the US economy coincided with a system which promoted world welfare. It is this matching of interests and vision which has been lacking in proposals for North–South reforms in recent years, and which is needed in future analysis.

The debt situation has recently become of critical importance to the stability of the world economy, as well as to the prospects of particular countries. Like other North–South issues, it has long been a subject of discussion, with a profusion of proposals for change. As with other issues, most of the proposals have come to little. This paper will examine the debt issue from the point of view of the particular interests involved, in order to permit a greater understanding of current developments and to identify which reforms incorporate a sufficient element of particular interests to be worth pursuing with a reasonable chance of success.

Section 3 of this paper defines the major actors involved in the debt situation and considers their objectives and likely responses. But before doing so it is helpful to understand the evolution of the debt situation and, in particular, why what appeared to be a stable situation with capital flowing from North to South has developed into a crisis situation in which capital is flowing, in many instances, from South to North.

2. BACKGROUND ANALYSIS

A fundamental concept necessary for understanding the evolution of the debt situation, and the reaction of different actors to it, is the 'basic transfer'. The basic transfer of a country is defined as the net foreign exchange inflow (or outflow) associated with its international borrowing. This basic transfer consists of the difference between the net capital inflow and interest payments on existing debt. The net capital inflow is the difference between the gross inflow and amortization on past debt. The size (and sign) of the basic transfer is very important because it represents the foreign exchange the country is gaining, in the period considered, from international capital flows.

The net capital inflow, Fn, may be expressed as a rate of increase of total foreign debt, so that if total foreign debt accumulated over the past is D, and d is the percentage rate of increase of this debt, then,

$$Fn = d.D.$$

Interest payments on past debt are equal to the average rate of interest, r, times the outstanding debt, D, so that interest payments consist of $r.D$. The basic transfer is the net capital inflow less interest payments, or

$$d.D - r.d = (d - r)D. \tag{1}$$

The basic transfer will therefore be positive or negative according as $d >$ or $< r.$[2]

When a country first accumulates foreign debt, the rate of increase, d, may be very high since the base is very small and foreign borrowing forms such a small proportion of total finance. But as foreign finance comes to form a high proportion of total finance, d naturally starts to fall. Ultimately a limit to the rate of increase in foreign-owned capital is set by the rate of increase of the total capital stock, at the point at which foreign finance forms such a high proportion of total finance that either the national government or the foreign lenders do not wish to increase the proportion further. Hence any country where foreign borrowing is a significant source of finance can expect to have a rapid rate of increase in the stock of foreign capital initially, but subsequently some slowdown is inevitable. A slowdown in d can therefore be expected in the normal course of events without any special factors. However, the rate of increase of foreign debt may also slow down sharply (and even become negative) for a variety of special reasons, such as world recession, or a loss of confidence in the country's repayment capacity. Capital flight by local residents for political or other reasons (e.g. because they believe the currency is likely to be devalued) may also create, or magnify, a negative basic transfer.[3] As the passage of time elapses from when substantial borrowing first starts, the rate of amortization rises, which requires a higher gross inflow (or rollover) to maintain a given net inflow. This in itself does not necessarily cause a slowdown in the net inflow, but it gives rise to the possibility of sharp fluctuations in the net inflow, making confidence factors more important. Whether or not these confidence factors do cause a significant reduction in d depends on many factors. Three are especially relevant to the analysis: first, the debt situation of the country resulting from its own past borrowing and the burden this imposes on the country's foreign exchange position. Secondly, a country's past development strategy which determines its potential to earn the necessary foreign exchange to service the debt. Both these factors influence beliefs about its servicing and repayment capacity. Thirdly, the world environment with respect to markets, commodity prices and capital flows may change in such a way as to lead to change in d. While the last factor is common to all borrowing countries, the first two differ between countries, explaining why some countries have suffered more from withdrawal of confidence than others.

The other element determining the basic transfer is the interest rate payable on past debt. This depends on the type of debt incurred (official or private), since different interest rates are payable on different types of debt; on the course of world interest rates, and the extent to which debt has been incurred on a variable interest basis; and on the margin the country has to pay over and above LIBOR.

As is well known, after being very low in real terms for most of the 1970s, interest rates rose sharply and have remained high (with some fluctuations) in the 1980s. The impact of the rise in interest rates was made worse—especially for some countries—by the increase in the proportion of private debt as a percentage of the total, and the increasing proportion of debt subject to variable interest rates, as indicated in Table 1.

The proportion of debt subject to floating interest rates varies substantially among countries. Low income countries—with only a small amount of borrowing from financial markets—have a very low proportion which did not increase during this period. Latin American countries have the highest proportion, rising from 23.8% in 1973 to 62.0% in 1982. Interest rates on average rose from 6.6% in 1973 to 11.0% in 1982 for all debt, and from 9.0% to 13.1% on debt from private creditors.

The basic transfer changed from being substantially positive in most cases to a low, or in some cases negative, figure because of the coincidence of a number of factors:

(i)   a natural slowdown in d as foreign borrowing proceeded;
(ii) a rise in the average value of r because of rising interest rates, an increasing proportion of private debt, and an increasing proportion of debt subject to floating interest rates;
(iii) a slowdown in private flows because of confidence factors, arising from the world economic situation and the build up of debt in particular countries;
(iv) capital flight by residents anticipating crisis measures.

That the basic transfer should become negative after an initial period of sustained borrowing when it was positive is not surprising, nor unreasonable. Borrowing with interest implies that the total to be repaid, if added up, will exceed the sum initially borrowed. However, the emergence of a negative basic transfer can nonetheless create problems, especially in certain circum-

TABLE 1   **All Borrowing Countries**

YEAR	PRIVATE DEBT* AS PROPORTION TOTAL	DEBT WITH FLOATING INTEREST AS % TOTAL
1973	34.6	11.6
1978	45.6	27.0
1982	49.0	37.5

*Includes only publicly guaranteed debt.
SOURCE: World Bank, World Debt Tables, 1983–4.

stances. Very high interest rates may—as they appear to have done recently—bring on a situation of negative balance prematurely. If countries whose basic transfer is negative are still patently underdeveloped as compared with lending countries, then the world resource flows implied contradict the direction which would appear desirable, involving poorer countries running trade surpluses, producing more than they consume, while richer countries may consume more than they produce. This situation may all the same be acceptable to countries whose past development strategies have made it relatively easy for them to achieve a trade surplus (as for example, Taiwan today). But countries whose past strategies have been heavily import-substituting may find the switch to achieving a trade surplus very difficult, consequently facing acute foreign exchange problems and being forced to undertake deflationary policies to achieve the trade target required by the basic balance. The situation is likely to be more unacceptable if it occurs—as is likely for reasons given above—at a time when there is an unfavourable international environment, making a turn-around in the trade position particularly difficult.

It is important to distinguish those cases where the basic transfer has become zero or negative because of the underlying situation—*viz.* slowdown in d to below the ruling rate of interest—from those cases where short-run confidence factors have been responsible for a sudden, but quite possibly temporary, fall in d. In the first type of case, the basic transfer is likely to be negative over the medium term, while in the second type a reversal of the adverse confidence factors may again produce a positive basic transfer. Countries in the first category are more likely to take a hard look at adjustment costs and to bargain toughly on adjustment conditions and rescheduling. Since they cannot expect a positive basic transfer even over the medium term, default becomes an option. In contrast, countries whose basic transfer is negative only because of temporary factors will be more anxious to reach a solution which involves a continued flow of finance. In practice, it may be difficult to disentangle these two situations, since a negative medium-term transfer is likely to produce adverse confidence factors.

The expression above describing the determinants of the basic transfer facilitates an analysis of the various ways in which the debt situation may be transformed. Any improvement, from the point of view of debtor countries, requires a change in the basic transfer. This may be achieved by increasing the net flow (raising d) or reducing interest payments (r). The net inflow may be expressed as the difference between the gross inflow and amortization. Suppose g expresses the gross inflow as a proportion of existing debt and a, amortizations. Then the basic transfer may be rewritten:

$$(g.D - a.D) - r.D, \text{ or}$$
$$(g - a - r)D. \tag{2}$$

Historically, when the debt burden became too great, 'the burden was reduced in two ways: (i) bankruptcies and defaults which had the effect of reducing both amortization and interest payments; (ii) inflation (with fixed interest rates) reduced the value of r in terms of d (since r was fixed in money terms and d rose with inflation).

Today, both these methods of reducing the debt burden have been largely eliminated. Sovereign lending has made bankruptcies and defaults much rarer, and short-term borrowing and floating interest rates on longer term loans have reduced the significance of inflation in lowering the burden of debt.

By ruling out both these possibilities, countries today have been put in a straitjacket which may not be acceptable when the basic transfer becomes negative over a prolonged period and the costs of adjustment are high. The IMF provides short-term assistance which is relevant to countries where the negative basic transfer is of a short-term nature, but does not help solve the problem of countries where it is long-term. It is the latter countries for which some 'solution' to the debt problem is essential, if they are not to take radical action unilaterally.

The next section of this paper will consider the objectives and interests of the various actors involved in the debt situation and in potential solutions.

3. MAJOR ACTORS IN THE DEBT SITUATION

There are four main categories of actors:

(a) the international banks;
(b) governments of borrowing countries;
(c) governments of countries where the major banks have their headquarters;
(d) international institutions.

As we shall see, there are important subgroups within these categories. It should be noted that none of the categories consists of *individuals*. Individuals may influence the decisions of institutions, but institutions are the effective actors. This is one reason why the normal analysis of mutual and general interests, which defines interests at the level of individual welfare, is often irrelevant to action.

(a) International Banks

These are the banks which have been responsible for much of the lending to the Third World. They need to be subdivided into two groups:

Bi: banks whose loans to LDCs form a large proportion of their total loans, in many cases exceeding their capital;
Bii: banks whose loans to LDCs are of subsidiary importance to their activities.

Table 2 illustrates the significance of loans to the Third World for some major banks.

Bi: The major interest of this category of banks is two-fold: first to avoid any major default or appearance of default—hence the anxiety to avoid a situation in which loans become nonperforming while delayed amortization, which does not get classified as default in the same way, is more readily accepted. In general these banks would prefer to extend new credit and maintain interest payments, rather than having interest unpaid. The second objective of these banks is to maximize profitability, but this is less important than the avoidance of default.

This group of banks will: (i) pressurize others to take action to help avoid defaults (including their own governments, international institutions and governments of LDCs); (ii) extend loans themselves, even if not justified on 'economic' grounds, to avoid default; (iii) be prepared to sacrifice the profita-bility objective, as indicated by the recent 'softening' of terms on margins and rescheduling, if this is judged necessary to avoid default; (iv) treat countries differently according to the size of the stake involved in each country, but still be unwilling to see any default because of its possible significance as a precedent; (v) have an interest in ensuring *joint* action so that their own finance is not threatened by the action of other banks. Therefore, they have an interest in using international institutions to secure this.

Bii: the second category of banks has rather different interests. Being less involved, their survival does not depend on avoiding default. Consequently, their concerns are (i) to maximize yields; and (ii) to withdraw their loans wherever they consider them unsafe. Their interests, therefore, may come into conflict with the first category of banks, since in the desire to maximize returns and withdraw from insecure situations, the second category could precipitate a crisis which would threaten the major bank. Hence this category of banks may be pressured by the major banks or international institutions to stay in the LDCs, despite their wishes (as with the 7% solution).[4]

TABLE 2   **Debt Exposure of Major Banks**

BANKS	LATIN AMERICAN DEBT AS % EQUITY, 1983 (1)	EXCLUDING MEXICO, END 1983 (2)
Citicorp	195	124
J. P. Morgan	136	96
Bank of America	164	87
Chase Manhattan		147
Midland	189	213
Lloyds	164	228

SOURCE: (1) ICBA, *Banking Analysis.*
(2) de Zoete and Bevan, quoted in *Financial Times* (31 May 1984).

(b) Borrowing Country Governments

There are important differences between countries which lead to differences in response to the debt situation. These differences include the following.

(i) Differences in the balance of debt borrowed from official and private institutions. While it is the private debt situation which is primarily relevant to countries' attitudes towards this type of debt, their attitudes may also be influenced by possible implications for official flows of finance, where countries rely heavily on these. A tough stance towards private debt might trigger off retaliatory action on official finance. This possibility may be ignored where official finance is insignificant, either in total or in terms of current net flows.

(ii) Prospects for the basic transfer, as defined above. Where the basic transfer is large and positive, countries are unlikely to take action which might threaten it. But where the transfer is small or negative, a tougher negotiating position is likely, especially, as noted above, if the situation is expected to persist over a period of years.

(iii) The foreign exchange and trade position. If the foreign exchange position is strong and has been achieved by expansion of export earnings rather than drastic cuts in imports and deflation, then irrespective of the basic transfer, a country is not likely to bargain toughly on debt. A debt crisis involves a foreign exchange crisis. An adverse balance on debt, however, often causes a foreign exchange crisis. But a country which expects that it will be able to achieve the required turn-around on the trade balance without excessive deflation is less likely to negotiate strongly on debt than one where the required trade surplus appears to be achievable only by sustained reductions in expenditure (contrast, for example, S.Korea and Mexico).

(iv) The potential for others to retaliate on non-debt issues in reaction to action on debt. Countries which are heavily dependent for exports and/or imports, or other factors, on countries most seriously affected by their actions on debt will tend to be more cautious than countries which are more independent. For example, because of oil exports and food self-sufficiency, Venezuela and Mexico are less likely to worry about trade retaliation than Brazil whose exports (of steel and orange juice) are particularly vulnerable to possible US action.

(v) Attitudes towards Fund programmes may be influenced by the potential size of Fund finance as compared with the finance a country would gain by postponing payments on debt servicing. Where the latter greatly exceed the former, the country has little to gain in the way of import finance from reaching a speedy agreement with the Fund, especially if a Fund programme is unlikely to produce a substantial net inflow of finance from other sources. Hence countries in this position will tend to weigh the costs of Fund programmes more heavily than those where they gain substantial finance for imports by concluding a programme.

(vi) Internal politics. Even where the 'objective' circumstances are identical, internal politics may differ leading to different reactions. Internal politics may differ with respect to the attention paid to local public opinion, demonstrations etc., and also with respect to the dependence of the regime on foreign support. The political bases of the various regimes and how they would be affected by different strategies are of major importance in determining country reactions. Internal politics are themselves affected by past strategies, including past policies towards debt, but it would be too complex and lengthy to discuss the taxonomy here.

(vii) Because of the *regionalization effect*—i.e. that lack of confidence in one country can lead to a general lack of confidence in countries in the same area—neighbouring countries, especially if heavily indebted themselves, have an interest in how a country treats its debt situation. Consequently, they may take action, as in the Argentinian situation in the first half of 1984, when loans were advanced to Argentina by major Latin American countries to prevent non-payment of interest. Regional cooperation may also be sought to coordinate action, to present a wider front to creditors. This could be of significance to the outcome because a major influence on bank reaction is the extent of their involvement. While loans to any one country may be insignificant, added together they may become of major importance. This factor is obviously of greater relevance to smaller countries, such as Costa Rica, Ecuador or Bolivia, which have already shown greater eagerness for coordinated action than some of the major debtors.

(c) Governments of Countries where the Banks Have Their Headquarters

An overriding objective of these governments is to prevent the collapse of a major bank, which could threaten the stability of their financial systems. But they also wish, as a subordinate objective, to maintain interest payments from borrowing countries. In order to achieve the overriding objective, such governments are prepared to put pressure on borrowing governments and international institutions, and to extend finance themselves. This has been illustrated by the US administration's activities in recent years—e.g. with respect to the Mexican situation in 1982 and the Argentinian situation in 1984, and also in supporting an increase in the IMF quota and a widening of the General Agreement to Borrow (in contrast to the niggardly attitude towards the

World Bank and IDA). Perhaps surprisingly, in view of the heavy involvement of UK banks, the UK government has adopted a much more passive role.

These governments, of course, represent trading nations as well as financial headquarters. Their trading strategy does not always seem to support their financial objectives—by giving way to protectionist pressures, for example, they make it more difficult for borrowing countries to meet their interest obligations, while world recessions, by depressing export markets generally, has been a major cause of the debt servicing problem. However, protectionist sentiment has remained for the most part sentiment, rather than action, and the US has led the world, via its budget and trade deficit, in resuscitating world demand, so that the contradictions may not be as real as they appear. Nonetheless, US monetary policy, involving very high interest rates, has been a major factor threatening the stability of the debt servicing and has thus contradicted the government's objective of maintaining financial stability.

The US government, like that of borrowing countries, is subject to many internal political pressures, often of a contradictory nature, which help explain the contradictions in policy stance.

(d) International Institutions

These institutions—notably the IMF, the Bank for International Settlements (BIS) and the World Bank—are the creatures of the governments which control them, and do not have a genuine independent existance. However, their officials take their own line, trying to push member governments to follow, while in the short run they have some independence of action. But if their policies conflict in a major way with those that the powerful governments want, then they will be pushed to one side and alternative mechanisms devised.

The BIS is more obviously a creature of governments than the IMF and has played an interesting role in recent years, permitting governments to bypass the slow and stringent Fund procedures when they seem to be getting in the way, without actually abolishing them. If default is threatened because the borrowing countries have run out of cash, and they are unable to come to speedy accommodation with the Fund, the BIS can provide short-run bridging finance, and can help maintain pressure on the banks to extend credit and deadlines.

The IMF is concerned with short- and medium-term adjustment policies so as to produce a stable financial system: its interest in financial flows is (i) to secure the necessary finance while adjustment takes place, but (ii) only if the country is following the adjustment prescribed by the Fund.

The Fund's concern with securing adjustment (which reflects the objectives of the controlling countries over the medium term) means that it cannot act as 'lender-of-the-last-resort' providing near-automatic short-term finance, because if it did so its ability to enforce conditionality would be lessened. Hence emergency finance has to be sought elsewhere (from governments themselves and the BIS). Thus the existence of more than one international institution to deal with the situation is necessary to achieve the twin objectives of the major lending countries—to prevent short-term financial collapse, while securing the adjustment policies which will ensure repayment over the medium term.

The international institutions have the role of countering the Prisoner's Dilemma aspect of international debt. Some coordination among banks is necessary, and to the extent that private cartels are prohibited, public institutions have to play that role. The Fund 'seal of approval' does this, but there is no mechanism for ensuring that individual banks respect it to the point of extending credit to countries they consider a bad risk. Hence it is only a partially satisfactory solution. There is a need for either more public finance (e.g. through the Fund) or some better way of enforcing cooperation from the private banks.

4. POLICY RESPONSES AND REFORM

It was argued above that powerful particular interests are the main determinants of policy in both North and South. Section 2 described the evolution of the debt situation which has led to a position in which many countries have a negative basic transfer over the medium term. Putting these arguments together, in combination with the analysis of major interests involved in the debt situation presented in the last section, makes it easier to predict policy responses and assess the feasibility and desirability of various reforms.

Two types of policy response that are often discussed are *default* and *rescheduling,* the first being unilateral action by debtor countries, while the second is agreed between debtors, banks and governments. Both concepts need further clarification since both may cover a variety of measures, with different implications.

Default may involve: (a) 100% default with complete and apparently permanent termination of all payments of interest and amortization; (b) moratorium on payments of amortization, for varying lengths of time; (c) moratorium on payments of interest, for varying lengths of time; (d) moratorium on payments of interest and amortization; (e) write-down of total service payments to some proportion of exports, GNP or some other level, which may or may not be temporary, and may or may not be compensated for later by higher payments.

Rescheduling, involving banks and borrowing countries, leads to a rearrangement of the timing of payments (amortization and sometimes interest); so far it has always involved *higher* total payments with less payable immediately and more in the future.

It is helpful to consider all these possibilities in terms of the way in which they affect the net present value of the debt (NPVD). Any given debt may be expressed as a stream of payments of interest and amortization which, when discounted at the ruling interest rate, gives an NPVD.

From the point of view of the debt burden of countries, there is a crucial distinction between those measures which reduce the NPVD and those which increase it, or leave it unchanged. All the varieties of default involve a reduction of NPVD, in the extreme case (100% default) reducing it to zero, while the other cases (moratorium, write-down) reducing it by varying amounts. In contrast, rescheduling, as practiced, involves increasing the NPVD by varying amounts, depending on the precise conditions, while relieving the immediate liquidity problem. Thus it may reverse a negative transfer in the immediate future, while leading to a greater negative transfer in the medium term, by which time the country might be in a better position to pay.

Countries with prospects of a negative basic transfer over the medium term have a strong motive to reduce the NPVD of their debt obligations, if necessary by unilateral action, until such time as the basic transfer becomes positive. But this does not imply 100% default. In many cases, a quite modest write-down or reduction in service payments would achieve the required turn-around in the basic transfer. This would represent a much more attractive option for most countries than 100% default since the implications for other aspects of North–South relations (e.g. trade, aid) would be much less serious. Moreover, 100% default would also prevent a positive basic transfer, by reducing capital inflow to zero, for an indefinite period, and could lead to very strong reactions including the possibility of military action. Write-down of some sort may be a temporary device until such a point as international interest rates fall and the basic transfer becomes positive.

The major banks (and HQ governments) have a strong motive to avoid creating a situation in which major write-off occurs. Hence their adoption of rescheduling and support for IMF programmes. But these policies, since they do not reduce the NPVD, may leave the countries with a negative basic transfer, reduced in the short term but increased in the longer term. They do not, therefore, represent a permanent solution in many cases, as is becoming apparent with the experience of those countries which have had to undergo a series of rescheduling operations and IMF programmes. So long as the negative basic transfer remains, the possibility of unilateral action to reduce the NPVD also remains. A satisfactory medium-term solution must (a) alter the terms of the debt so that the basic transfer becomes positive; (b) reduce the NPVD; and (c) improve the foreign exchange earning capacity of the country so as to meet the required debt servicing (albeit at reduced rates).

Possible solutions may be analysed in terms of expression (2) above, describing the determinants of the basic balance, *viz.* $(g - a - r) D$ where g, a and r are defined as a stream of payments over time.

A large number of proposals for reform have been put forward.[5] These may be briefly categorized as follows:

(1) Insurance for commercial banks' portfolios. This scheme (associated with Wallich[6] among others) would be financed by both governments and the banks. The main objective would be to stabilize financial flows, possibly encouraging additional lending as a result of the reduction in risk. The reform would make little contribution to reducing the NPVD. A variant of such schemes is to insure bank deposits.

(2) Lender-of-the-last-resort facilities, suggested by Lipton and Griffith-Jones.[7] This is a contingency plan whereby some central institution (IMF, BIS, or some other body) would provide finance for banks in difficulties due to LDC inability to repay. The main burden of the scheme would be borne by supporting governments. The scheme, like the insurance scheme, would help secure financial stability.

(3) Central bank discounting of commercial bank loans with LDCs. The scheme (put forward by Lever)[8] would help stabilize bank lending, by reducing banks' liquidity problems. It would not, it appears, reduce LDC obligations.

(4) Exchange of LDC debt for ownership of assets in LDCs. Such a scheme would provide a temporary relief from payment obligations, but at the cost of alienating assets at a low price. In the longer run, the new debt burden would be at least as great as the old.

(5) Proposals to 'cap' interest rates, limiting LDC debt servicing obligations to payment capacity (e.g. some fixed proportion of export earnings). Interest capping has been proposed by Solomon of the New York Federal Reserve Bank, Bailey (US National Security Council) as well as by a number of developing countries.[9] The precise implications for LDC debt burden would depend on whether the net effect was to stretch out the total, while leaving the NPVD unchanged, or to reduce the NPVD.

(6) Debt restructuring proposals (these abound, see e.g. those of Kenen, Rohatyn, ul Haq).[10] The 'cap' might be one feature of such restructuring. There are a great variety of schemes involving various terms and institutional forms. All require the transformation of existing debt into longer term maturity, with lower interest rates, and some element of debt relief, as compared with the existing burden.

The various schemes are intended to fulfill different types of objectives. The first three are primarily designed to secure greater financial stability. New capital flows (and reduced withdrawal) are likely to be encouraged, and some reduction of risk premia might result. The negative basic transfer might be temporarily reduced, as g rises, but the NPVD is likely to increase as a result, so that the long-run problem might become worse.

The last four types of schemes assist the current payments position by reducing the short-run servicing costs (reducing interest and amortization payments in the short run.) In so doing they will also contribute to increased confidence and reduced instability. Whether they will lead to a reduction in the NPVD depends on whether long-run service payments rise to compensate for short-term reductions (as with rescheduling exercises). The gross inflow of funds may be reduced by such schemes, where they involve substantial reductions in the NPVD and the commercial banks bear a high proportion of these losses. But the increased confidence—in particular the reduced likelihood of unilateral and substantial defaults—will work to increase the inflow.

Table 3 summarizes some of these effects. For countries with a negative basic transfer over the medium term, only schemes that reduce the NPVD are likely to be sufficient to avoid unilateral action. Hence while the first three categories—insurance, lender-of-the-last resort and Central Bank discounting—could be attractive from the point of view of the Northern interest in financial stability, they are not likely to be sufficient to avoid more radical action by some Southern governments. The next three solutions—'cap' proposals, debt for equity and high interest compensation schemes—offer relief in the short term, but at the possible expense of greater payments in the future. However, whether this is so or not depends on the precise details of the schemes; they could be devised so as to reduce the NPVD. The debt-into-equity proposal is likely to meet overwhelming hostility from Third World governments. The final set of schemes offers a permanent reduction of amortization and interest. These schemes therefore should be more attractive to borrowers than unilateral action. When considered on their own, they involve losses for the banks and the HQ governments, but in terms of the opportunity cost (*viz.* unilateral action by borrowers) they offer gains. This type of scheme, therefore, potentially provides for a genuine identity of interest in reform between powerful groups among lenders and borrowers. It is on this category that attention should be focused.

If the present situation persists (high r, low g) it is likely that unilateral action will secure a *de facto* solution on these lines, as indicated by statements from a number of important borrowing countries (Argentina, Venezuela, the Philippines, for example). The multi-year rescheduling agreed with Mexico in September 1984 in some respects represents such an *ad hoc* settlement. However, a generalized negotiated *de jure* solution would be preferable from many points of view:

TABLE 3

SCHEME	VARIABLE AFFECTED	EFFECT ON NEW FLOWS	EFFECT ON NPVD	EFFECT ON FINANCIAL STABILITY	BURDEN SHARING	COMMENT
1. Insurance (Wallich)	Raise g	Positive in short run	Small	Positive	Little burden: Northern govts.	Inadequate—does not reduce NPVD. Unlikely to raise g much
2. Lender of last resort (Lipton, Griffith-Jones)	Raise g	As above	Small	Positive	Northern govts.	As above; deals with financial instability
3. Discount banks loans by Central Banks (Lever)	Raise g	As above	Small	Positive	Little; mainly Northern govts.	As above
4. Exchange debt for equity	Mainly timing	Little	Could increase NPVD	Probably positive	Banks could lose now; gain later	LDC hostility likely
5. High interest compensatory fund at IMF	Reduce r, temporarily	None	Little; depends on terms	Small, positive	Govts. temporarily	Temporary solution
6. 'Cap': reducing current interest to be compensated later (Solomon)	Affects timing, may not affect total of any variable	Could be negative	None, unless later comp. is small	Probably positive	Banks, temporarily and possibly HQ govts.	Helps current situation. May worsen future

(i)   It would prevent the lurch from crisis to crisis, which is having negative effects on world trade, financial confidence and capital flows.

(ii) The process of negotiations would offer the chance of combining some conditionality and adjustment with a solution to the debt problem.

(iii) *Ad hoc* resolution will only secure a solution for countries in a strong bargaining position—*viz,* those with negative basic transfers and which have borrowed enough to have a significant effect on major banks. The *ad hoc* solution would exclude other countries which have major problems but are in a weaker position to enforce a solution by threatening unilateral action. A generalized solution is needed to extend the benefits to countries in a weak position to bargain individually.

The next section of this paper will provide a tentative classification of countries' debts and bargaining positions.

5. COUNTRY CLASSIFICATION

The earlier analysis suggests big differences in countries' policy responses and negotiating strengths according to their particular circumstances. One critical factor is whether the basic transfer—over the medium term—is expected to be positive or negative. Another factor is the relative significance of official and private capital. A country's importance to the banking community—in terms of the magnitude of outstanding debt—is the major determinant of negotiating strength. (There are many other relevant differences—some noted above—for example, with respect to past development strategy and trading potential, but these will not be explored here.)

There is a substantial statistical problem in classifying countries. The World Bank provides systematic data on public guaranteed debt of more than one year's duration. But nonguaranteed private debt is often very large, as is debt of less than one-year term. For example, at the end of 1982 publicly guaranteed and official debt accounted for 73% of total debt (of more than one year) in Latin America,[11] with private nonguaranteed debt at $64 b, as compared to $135 b of publicly guaranteed debt incurred in financial markets. At the end of 1982, short-term bank debt amounted to 13.5% of total debt in Algeria, 48.5% in Argentina, 34.8% in Brazil, 57.2% in S. Korea and 59.9% in the Philippines.[12]

In many countries, the quantities are unknown. The Argentinian case provides an (extreme) example: the Minister of Finance stated in April 1984: 'We still don't know the debt; there were no registers in the central bank . . . with most loans we could not identify the purpose, the amount, the interest or the grace period.' According to a report in the *International Herald Tribune*, more than one hundred officials were searching through stacks of paper piled six feet high.[13]

AMEX has compiled comprehensive statistics for 24 major debtor countries.[14] Of the 24, 19 countries had a negative basic transfer from bank loans (including short-term and non-guaranteed loans) in 1982 and 1983. Some details are provided in Table 4. Another two countries (Nigeria and the Philippines) had a negative transfer from the banking sector in 1983, but not in 1982.

Countries where the negative transfer was very large (over 50%) of imports in that year were Argentina, Chile, Ecuador, and Mexico, while it was of significant magnitude (over 20% of imports) in Costa Rica, Ivory Coast, Sudan, Venezuela and Yugoslavia, and in Nigeria and the Philippines in 1983. If the negative transfer is expected to continue, these countries have a strong motive for bargaining for improved terms.

In a few of the countries with a negative transfer on bank borrowing, this was outweighed by positive official balance. This would give governments and multilateral institutions some leverage in preventing excessively hard bargaining. This was the case—among the 21 countries—for Cameroon, S. Korea, Peru, Sudan and Tunisia.

Table 4 indicates the significance of each country to the banking system, in terms of the amount of bank debt they account for as a proportion of the total in the AMEX sample. Brazil and Mexico are by far the most significant, with over 20% in each case. Argentina, S. Korea and Venezuela each account for over 5%. Algeria, Chile, the Philippines, Turkey and Yugoslavia account for between 2.5 and 5%. The remaining countries are of minor significance to the banking system.

Putting these factors together (see Table 5), we find that based on these figures, Mexico, followed by Argentina, is in the strongest position to strike a good bargain, having both motive and bargaining strength. Venezuela, Chile, Yugoslavia and the Philippines are in the next rank, in terms of a combination of motive and potential power. Brazil, Algeria, Turkey and S. Korea were next in order, according to these 1982 figures.

This identification of particular countries is, of course, very tentative. In the first place, it turns on just two (and in one case one) year's figures. Policy responses depend on the prospects over a period of years. Secondly, as stated above, there are many other dimensions determining bargaining stance and strength, which have not been taken into account. Nonetheless, the fact that the final shortlist in fact includes countries that have bargained toughly, and have in some cases secured apparently good terms, provides some support for the methodology adopted.

The World Bank data are more comprehensive in terms of country coverage, but much less in terms of debt. Table 6 lists a further 30 countries which had negative transfers on financial markets, including only publicly guaranteed debt, and debt of over one-year's duration. The size of the negative

TABLE 4 Countries With Negative Transfer* (Among 24 Major Debtors)

COUNTRY	(1) (2) BASIC TRANSFER ON BANK DEBT $M. 1982	1983	(3) TRANSFER 1982 AS % IMPORTS 1982	(4) TRANSFER ON OFFICIAL ACCOUNT 1982, $M.	(5) OVERALL TRANSFER 1982 (BANK + OFFICIAL) $M.	(6) BANK DEBT AS % TOTAL 24 COUNTRIES JUNE 1983
Algeria	−1853	−859	−17.9	+250	−1603	2.9
Argentina	−5600	−2414	−104.9	−21	−5621	6.7
Brazil	−1644	−2526	−7.9	+54	−1590	21.3
Cameroon	−69	−53	−9.4	+211	+142	0.3
Chile	−3533	−1539	−100.1	−167	−3700	3.3
Colombia	−559	−100	−10.2	+211	−348	1.9
Costa Rica	−333	−400	−39.8	+75	−258	0.1
Ecuador	−1207	−752	−60.7	−297	−1504	0.9
Ivory Coast	−492	−524	−22.6	+211	−281	0.6
S. Korea	−321	−2094	−13.2	+592	+271	6.6
Mexico	−8553	−1706	−73.4	+1350	−7203	24.1
Morocco	−611	−639	−1.5	+503	−108	1.2
Peru	−161	−627	−4.5	+162	+1	1.1
Sudan	−260	−193	−20.2	+392	+132	0.4
Thailand	−792	−558	−9.3	+543	−249	1.5
Tunisia	−172	−19	−5.0	+178	+6	0.4
Turkey	−986	−245	−11.2	+561	−425	2.5
Venezuela	−4265	−5904	−34.1	−9	−4274	6.2
Yugoslavia	−3168	−4198	−23.6	−149	−3317	4.2
Positive, 1982; Negative 1983						
Nigeria	+1753	−876	+12.8 (−20.6)†	+108	+1861	2.1
Philippines	+36	−2029	+0.4 (−25.1)‡	+224	+260	4.6

NOTES: *24 countries covered by AMEX study. Countries included in the study which had positive basic transfer, 1982 and 1983, were Indonesia, Malaysia and Uruguay.
†Figure in brackets for first half 1983.
‡Figure in brackets for whole 1983.

SOURCE: Cols. 1, 2, 3, 4, 6: AMEX Bank Review Special Papers 'International Debt Banks and the LDCs' (10 March 1983).
Col. 4: World Bank, *World Debt Tables*, 1983–84.

TABLE 5   **Ranking of Countries' Bargaining Position and Strength**

MOTIVE SIZE OF NEGATIVE TRANSFER:	OVERALL TRANSFER INCLUDING OFFICIAL FLOWS	SIGNIFICANCE TO BANKING SYSTEM
Over 50% imports, 1982		
Argentina	Negative	**
Chile	Negative	*
Ecuador	Negative	—
Mexico	Negative	***
20–50%		
Costa Rica	Negative	—
Ivory Coast	Negative	—
Sudan	Positive	—
Venezuela	Negative	**
Yugoslavia	Negative	*
Nigeria (1983)	Negative	*
Philippines (1983)	Negative	*
5–20%		
Algeria	Negative	*
Brazil	Negative	***
Cameroon	Positive	—
Colombia	Negative	—
S. Korea	Positive	**
Thailand	Negative	—
Tunisia	Negative	—
Turkey	Negative	*

***: highly significant accounting for over 20% of debt to 24 countries.
**: significant accounting for 5–20%.
*: of some significance (2.5–5.0%).
—: not significant (below 2.5%).
SOURCE: Table 4.

transfer would be likely to be greater with more comprehensive coverage, and a greater number of countries would have a negative overall balance. None of these countries were of major significance to the world banking system, each accounting for a half per cent or less of total outstanding debt.

6. CONCLUSIONS

The accumulation of debt, by some countries, together with high interest rates, has led to a position of negative basic transfer. Where countries are facing foreign exchange problems, and where IMF assistance is relatively small in relation to needs while Fund programmes require substantial cuts in public expenditure and real wages, such countries are likely to negotiate

TABLE 6   **Other Countries With Financial Markets, 1982; Publicly Guaranteed Debt of More Than One Year Maturity**

COUNTRY	TRANSFER ON FINANCIAL MARKETS AS % IMPORTS, 1982	OVERALL TRANSFER*	% OF WORLD DEBT†
Trinidad & Tobago‡	−1.3	—	0.2
Gabon‡	−9.4	—	0.2
Sierra Leone‡	−1.7	—	0.01
Bolivia‡	−9.1	—	0.5
Hungary	−6.7	—	0.04
Israel	−1.2	—	2.2
Benin§	−2.0	+	0.1
Ethiopia‡	−0.7	+	0.01
Gambia‡	−1.9	+	0.01
Kenya	−6.0	+	0.3
Liberia‡	−1.4	+	0.07
Malawi	−6.9	+	0.07
Mauritius	−0.3	+	0.07
Niger‖	−6.0	+	0.09
Swaziland‡	−1.1	+	0.01
Tanzania¶	−0.6	+	0.03
Togo‖	−2.2	+	0.09
Uganda¶	−0.4	+	0.01
Zaire§	−0.7	+	0.5
Fiji‡	−0.5	+	0.02
W. Samoa	−3.8	+	0
Guyana‡	−1.9	+	0.05
Haiti	−0.6	+	0.03
Honduras‡	−2.1	+	0.1
Jamaica‡	−5.6	+	0.2
Nicaragua‖	−12.3	+	0.4
Egypt‡	−1.3	+	0.2
Jordan‡	−0.9	+	0.09
Syrian Arab Rep‡	−0.2	+	0.11
Pakistan	−1.1	+	0.15

NOTES: *Includes official flows and suppliers' credits.
†World debt on financial markets including only publicly guaranteed debt of more than one year.
‡Imports for 1981.
§Imports for 1977.
‖Imports for 1979.
¶Imports for 1980.

SOURCE: World Bank, *World Debt Tables*, 1983–84.

toughly on debt and consider taking unilateral action if these negotiations do not succeed. At the same time, the big borrowers form such an important element of total bank finance that neither the banks nor the HQ governments can afford to face any major defaults. This is a situation where there is an identity of interests—*in an operational sense*—among the major actors in achieving reforms which will make the burden of debt tolerable to the debtors, while avoiding large-scale defaults. Schemes which involve lowered interest rates and extended terms with lower amortization would achieve this. Proposals to limit service payments to a given proportion of exports are a special case of this type of scheme. Some such solution will probably be achieved in an *ad hoc* way, without any international negotiations. However, a more formal and across-the-board scheme would be preferable because it would avoid the uncertainties involved in *ad hoc* solutions, and would extend the benefits of renegotiations of debt to the many countries which are not in a position to negotiate a solution for themselves. Moreover, debt restructuring may be associated with internal policy reforms. If the Fund and others wish to retain some conditionality, they should support debt reform, for otherwise the countries will come to recognize that reneging on debt is less expensive—in terms of political, economic and social costs—and brings in more foreign exchange, than negotiating Fund programmes.

NOTES

1. Frances Stewart, 'Global negotiations and North–South relations', (Committee for Development Planning, December 1983).
2. This approach to analysing financial transfers was developed by Domar in his analysis of the burden of domestic debt. See E. Domar, *Essays in the Theory of Economic Growth* (Oxford University Press, 1957). It was applied to foreign direct investment in developing countries by Paul Streeten—see P. Streeten, *The Frontiers of Development Studies* (Macmillan, 1972), p. 209.
3. There is evidence that this has been of major magnitude in some countries. The BIS estimated that Latin Americans 'had spirited $55 billion in the six years to 1983—almost a third of the region's increase in borrowing during the period'. (*Guardian,* 19 June 1984.)
4. This was the exercise conducted by the IMF and the major banks at the end of 1982, when the Fund coordinated the activities of all lenders to Mexico, securing an agreement that they would increase their lending by 7%.
5. A detailed summary of many of these schemes, together with references is contained in 'The Debt Crisis and the World Economy'. Report by a Commonwealth Group of Experts (Commonwealth Secretariat, 1984), Appendix 2.2. *AMEX Bank Review* Vol. 11, No. 5, (19 June 1984), also provides a useful survey of proposals.
6. See H. Wallich, 'Insurance of bank lending to developing countries' (Group of Thirty, 1984).
7. See M. Lipton and S. Griffith-Jones 'International lenders of the last resort: are changes required?', Background Paper (Commonwealth Secretariat, May 1983).

8. *The Economist* (July 1983).
9. R. Solomon, Senate Banking Committee Hearings (May 1984); M. Baily, *Business Week* (10 Jan. 1983); limitation of debt services to a predetermined proportion of export earnings was one of the demands in the Consensus of Cartegna, signed by 11 Ministers of countries in Latin America, June 1984.
10. F. Rohatyn, *Business Week,* (28 Feb. 1983); P. Kenen, *New York Times* (6 March 1983); Mahbub ul Haq, paper for North–South Roundtable on Money and Finance (September 1984).
11. World Bank, *World Debt Tables,* 1983–84.
12. *AMEX Bank Review* (15 September 1983), Vol. 10, Nos. 8/9.
13. Quoted in *International Herald Tribune* (10 April 1984) and by F. Khilji in M.Sc. Thesis (Oxford, 1984).
14. *AMEX Bank Review,* Special Papers, 'International debt, banks and the LDCs', No. 10 (March 1984).

14

Can the East Asian Model of Development Be Generalized?

William R. Cline

1. INTRODUCTION

Export-oriented growth is the fashion today among development analysts. Exhaustive cross-country studies have documented the inefficiencies of the inward-looking strategies popular in the 1950s and 1960s (Little *et al.*, 1970; Krueger, 1978). Recognizing that new converts among policy-makers may err in the direction of excessive stimulus to exports, Bhagwati and Krueger (1973) have nevertheless argued that resulting distortions would be less severe (and more favourable to growth) than those that arise under regimes of import substitution.

Events of the last two decades have tended to vindicate export optimists, as several developing countries have achieved rapid export growth. Economy wide growth appears to have been closely related to export performance (Balassa, 1978), in part because of the efficiency-stimulating influence of international competition. Experience has cast doubt on the export pessimism that was dominant earlier and led to the model of import-substituting industrialization in the first place (Nurkse, 1953; Prebisch, 1959).

There is, however, a current running counter to the new emphasis on exports among academics and policy-makers. That current is the phenomenon of neoprotectionism in industrial countries. The 1970s saw the tightening or new imposition of trade barriers affecting developing country exports of manufactures such as textiles, clothing, footwear, television sets and ship-building. A major shortcoming of the Tokyo Round of trade negotiations completed in 1979 was its failure to reach agreement on a 'safeguards' code limiting the enactment of quotas or voluntary export restrictions on imports causing domestic dislocation.

Reprinted with permission from *World Development*, Vol. 10, No. 2. Copyright 1982, Pergamon Press, Ltd.

Without invoking a new spectre of export pessimism, it may reasonably be asked whether the recent emphasis on export-oriented growth has sufficiently taken account of the constraints on international market demand. Most studies have concentrated instead on the side of export supply, and specifically on the impact of developing country policy regimes on that supply.

This paper examines whether one version of export-oriented growth, the East Asian model, could be generalized among developing countries without violating plausible constraints on the absorptive capacity of industrial country markets. This analysis is of course an acid test. The East Asian "Gang of Four" (G-4)—Hong Kong, Korea, Singapore and Taiwan—have pursued strategies relying extremely heavily on exports. Nevertheless, the test is not unfair, considering the regularity with which policy-makers and academics extol the virtues of the G-4 model and at least implicitly urge its emulation [World Bank (1979), p. 68; Hughes (1980), p. 27; and, despite their caveats, Banerji and Riedel (1980)]. Indeed, some analysts have cited the merits of the East Asian export model not only for growth but also for the achievement of equitable income distribution through emphasis on labour-intensive exports (Fei *et al.*, 1979). The issue at stake, however, is whether advice to follow the G-4 model involves a fallacy of composition, in that while individual developing countries might thrive by doing so, in the aggregate they would encounter sharp protective resistance to the resulting flood of exports.

2. METHOD

The method of this study is one of comparative statics. Using a 1976 base, the analysis calculates the levels of manufactured exports from developing countries that would have occurred in that year if all developing countries had experienced the same intensity of exports in their economies as was experienced by Hong Kong, Korea, Singapore and Taiwan, after adjustment for normal inter-country differences associated with size and level of development. These hypothetical levels of developing country exports are then compared to industrial country apparent consumption, at the sectoral level, to determine how high the resulting import penetration ratios would have been. Using an arbitrary threshold ratio of imports (from developing countries) to apparent consumption in the industrial country, it is then possible to calculate the portion of LDC exports that would be presumptively infeasible because of a likely protective response.

The hypothetical levels of trade under a uniform G-4 regime among developing countries are calculated as:

$$X_{ijk}^a = \beta_j X_{ijk} , \qquad (1)$$

where X_{ijk} is the 1976 value of exports of manufactured good k from developing country j to industrial country i, X_{ijk}^a is the same concept but at its hypothetical G-4 level, and β_j is an expansion factor relating the hypothetical level of exports to the actual level.

The expansion factor β_j is calculated on the basis of cross-country patterns of the level of manufactured exports in relation to GDP,[1] as estimated in Chenery and Syrquin (1975) for the period 1950–1970. Their estimates relate the share of manufactured exports in GDP to the logarithms of *per capita* income and country population, and to the squares of these variables. Defining as λ_j the ratio of a country's actual GDP share of manufactured exports to the level predicted by the Chenery-Syrquin pattern, the expansion factor β_j is calculated as:

$$\beta_j = \frac{\lambda^{G4}}{\lambda_j}, \tag{2}$$

where λ^{G4} is the average of λ for Hong Kong, Korea, Singapore and Taiwan. The term λ^{G4} shows how much the manufactured export propensity under the G-4 regime exceeds the standard international propensity for countries of the size and *per capita* income of the G-4 countries. Equation (2) states that if a country's manufactured exports are at the level that would be expected given its *per capita* income and size ($\lambda_j = 1.0$), the country's expansion factor to reach a hypothetical G-4 level is merely the ratio of actual exports in the East Asian countries to the exports they would be expected to have according to international norms. If the country itself has atypically high (low) exports, with $\lambda_j > (<)$ 1.0, the country's expansion factor is lower (higher).

The estimate represented in equation (1) assumes that the product composition and industrial country market composition remain unchanged for a particular developing country as it expands its exports to the G-4 level. But because manufactured exports of developing countries tend to be concentrated already in certain sensitive sectors such as textiles and clothing, it is likely that the scope for market accommodation of export expansion at the margin would be greater if the extra exports had a product composition that was more diversified. Therefore, as an alternative set of estimates, the hypothetical G-4 exports are also calculated as:

$$X^b_{ijk} = X_{ijk} + (\beta_j - 1)X_{ij}\phi_{ik}, \tag{3}$$

where X_{ij} is the total base value of manufactured exports from developing country j to industrial country i, and ϕ_{ik} is the base period share of sector k in the total manufactured imports of country i from all sources.[2] Thus, variant 'b' assumes that at the margin the product composition of the developing countries' exports is homogeneous with the general composition of imports into the market in question. This variant implies a sacrifice of some of the gains from comparative advantage in return for greater likelihood of continued market access.[3]

It is worth noting that neither variant applies the product composition of the exports of the G-4 countries themselves. Their exports are heavily concentrated in products that already face stiff protection, such as textiles, clothing, footwear and television sets. Thus, the analysis assumes a generalized move to the level, but not the product composition, of East Asian manufactured exports.

Given estimates of sectoral import penetration ratios into the industrial country markets, $Z_{ik}^L = M_{ik}^L / C_{ik}$, where Z_{ik}^L is the import penetration ratio for imports from all developing countries into industrial country i in sector k, M_{ik}^L is the corresponding total of imports from all developing countries in the country and sector, and C_{ik} is the corresponding value of domestic apparent consumption (output minus exports plus imports), the levels of developing country import penetration under a G-4 regime are calculated as:

$$Z_{ik}^a = Z_{ik}^L \frac{X_{ik}^a}{X_{ik}}; Z_{ik}^b = Z_{ik}^L \frac{X_{ik}^b}{X_{ik}}, \tag{4}$$

where X_{ik}, X_{ik}^a and X_{ik}^b are the original, variant a, and variant b levels of total manufactured imports from developing countries into country i in sector k (for example, $X_{ik} = \Sigma_j X_{ijk}$).

The estimates of import penetration from developing countries under a G-4 regime provide the basis for inferences about the market feasibility of generalizing the East Asian export model of development. Using a threshold of 15% penetration, the analysis later examines the product sectors in which developing countries would be likely to overburden the political-economic absorptive capacity in major industrial country markets by exceeding this threshold. The frequency of such sectors, and more meaningfully their combined weight in the total of developing countries' manufactured exports, cast light on whether the G-4 regime is infeasible.

The analysis is solely focussed on market prospects, and does not treat additional factors such as a possible worsening in the terms of trade of developing countries if they all tried to pursue the East Asian export strategy. Even on the issue of market access there is no pretense that the analysis involves a rigorous investigation of the causes of protection [as in Caves (1976) and Fieleke (1976)]. Nevertheless, simple rules of thumb such as the 15% penetration ratio do provide a useful point of departure for a general evaluation of market access. Although no unique level of the penetration ratio can be identified as the critical level where protection occurs, the penetration ratio is generally regarded as one of the most important indicators of potential protectionist response.[4]

It might be that the total import penetration ratio from all sources instead of only developing countries would be more relevant as a criterion for protective response.[5] Because developing countries have little free importation of their own that they can impede in retaliatory moves, and perhaps because of their small size and bargaining strength relative to major industrial countries, it seems reasonable to consider a given degree of import penetration more likely to trigger protection if the suppliers are from developing countries than if they are from developed countries. In any event, even a total penetration ratio (for all suppliers) of 15% is sufficiently high to suggest jeopardy to market access. Thus, the use of import penetration from developing countries alone probably tends to understate the incidence of sectors in which problems of protective response would be likely to be encountered under the G-4 regime.

Another issue concerns the offsetting role of industrial country exports. High imports from LDCs would induce high respending by the developing countries on exports from the North. It is unlikely, however, that this extra source of employment in the industrial countries would offset the protectionist pressures arising from higher import penetration. Because extra imports would tend to be in different sectors from extra exports, the implications for labour dislocation are more appropriately drawn from the gross import changes rather than net trade changes. To be sure, the more the developing countries consciously diversified their new exports into sectors in which industrial countries would also gain exports, moving toward a pattern of intra-industry trade similar to that among industrial countries, the more weight the derived expansion of industrial country exports would have in stemming protectionism.

3. DATA

The trade data used in the calculations are from the United Nations commodity trade data tapes for each of the importing industrial countries examined (Canada, France, Germany, Italy, Japan, United Kingdom, US). These data, at the five-digit level of the Standard International Trade Classification, are converted to four-digit categories of the International Standard Industrial Classification (ISIC).[6] Eighty manufacturing categories are included (ISIC 3111–3909 excluding 3530, petroleum refining). Developing countries in the analysis include all countries in Africa except South Africa, Asia excluding Japan, Oceania except Australia and New Zealand, and Latin America and the Caribbean. Import penetration ratios in the base period are derived from the estimates of import data at the four-digit ISIC level, combined with estimates of the corresponding domestic production and trade in the industrial country markets examined [see Cline (1980)]. The LDC penetration ratios refer to imports from developing countries divided by apparent consumption (domestic production plus total imports minus total exports in the sector). For estimates of expected shares of manufactured exports in GDP based on the Chenery-Syrquin patterns, the calculations apply World Bank data on *per capita* income, population, and manufactured exports (World Bank, 1977, 1978) and the US wholesale price deflators (International Monetary Fund, 1978).

4. EXPORT EXPANSION

Tables 1 and 2 report the estimates of the extent to which LDC exports of manufacturers would expand if the export strategies of all developing countries had resembled those of the East Asian G-4 in the base year 1976. Table 1 shows that on average the G-4 had manufactured exports 4.4 times as high as would have been expected based on cross-country norms, whereas major Latin American countries had as low as one-fifth the expected levels and a broad grouping of 66 developing countries (excluding the 13 listed individually) exported less than half the amount expected based on these norms. The final column of the table shows the multiple by which a developing country's manufactured exports would have to expand in order to resemble the G-4 pattern. These multiples are high, indicating approximately a 20-fold increase for some Latin American countries and nearly a 10-fold increase for the broad

TABLE 1   **Manufactured Export Shares in GDP and Expansion Factors, 1976**

| | GDP Share (%) | | | EXPANSION |
COUNTRY	ACTUAL (A)	CROSS–COUNTRY NORM* (B)	RATIO [(A)/(B)] (C)	FACTOR TO G-4 BASE† (D)
Hong Kong	60.8	12.0	5.07	—
Korea	28.1	6.2	4.53	—
Singapore	48.6	12.6	3.86	—
Taiwan	37.4	8.8	4.25	—
G-4	—	—	4.43	—
Argentina	2.4	10.5	0.23	18.80
Brazil	2.0	6.8	0.29	14.92
Colombia	2.5	6.3	0.40	11.02
Mexico	1.5	7.6	0.20	22.53
India	3.0	< 0‡	—	0‡
Indonesia	0.4	0.6	0.70	6.27
Israel	13.3	15.7	0.85	5.19
Malaysia	7.5	7.8	0.96	4.58
Pakistan	5.2	1.2	4.44	0.99
Other developing countries	—	—	0.47§	9.42

*Based on Chenery and Syrquin (1975), p. 39. Data for 1976 from World Bank, *World Development Report,* 1978 and 1979.
†From equation (2), equals 4.4 divided by column (C) for all except G-4 countries. Exports of G-4 countries remain unchanged in calculations.
‡Cross-country equation predicts negative value (because of a negative coefficient on the square of the logarithm of population, applied to India's large population). Hypothetical exports set equal to zero.
§Based on export-weighted ratio of actual to predicted manufactured exports for 66 other developing countries.

grouping of 'other' developing countries. The exception is India, whose large population causes a predicted negative value of manufactured exports according to the cross-country regression norm (although the estimates force India's hypothetical exports to zero).

Table 2 shows the hypothetical expansion of LDC exports by industrial country market. Overall, generalization of the East Asian export model would multiply LDC manufactured exports seven-fold. This expansion would imply a rise in the LDC share of the market for manufactured imports from 16.7 to 60.6% for all seven industrial countries, and from 27.0 to 74.4% in the United States. These estimates alone are sufficient to cast serious doubt on the feasibility of a generalized move to the G-4 export strategy. The non-oil developing countries have only approximately 16% of the combined GDP of industrial and non-oil developing countries, and it is highly implausible that they could capture 60% of the industrial countries' markets for imports without provoking serious protective responses.

5. IMPORT PENETRATION

The impression of difficulty of market access is strengthened by the estimates of import penetration ratios that would result from a mass shift by developing countries to the East Asian model of export-led growth. Table 3 shows the estimated ratios of LDC import penetration into four industrial country markets, for those sectors in which LDC penetration would exceed 15% of the market (excluding a number of sectors with penetration over 15% but of only minor importance, sectors having a share of less than 1% in both total and LDC-supplied manufactured imports in 1976). As shown in the table, a large number of important product sectors would have LDC penetration ratios above the threshold of 15% under the G-4 scenario. Moreover, in several sectors the LDC import penetration ratios reach improbably or impossibly high levels. Thus, under variant 'a' in which the product composition is held the same as in the base period, several food sectors show imports from LDCs in excess of the entire domestic market. And approximately half of the sectors shown indicate LDC penetration ratios above 30%, so that the pattern is one of frequent incidence of very high penetration rather than one of only modest excess above the 15% threshold chosen.

Diversification of product composition eliminates most cases of penetration ratios over 100%, but still leaves a high frequency of high penetration sectors, causing higher penetration in non-traditional sectors. Thus, in variant 'b' in which the increment in LDC exports would be distributed across sectors in proportion to base period imports from all sources (instead of base period LDC supply), penetration ratios decline for traditional sectors such as foods but rise for non-traditional sectors such as chemicals and office machinery.

Out of 80 four-digit ISIC categories under the G-4 scenario (with base period product composition) LDC penetration ratios exceed the threshold of

TABLE 2 Exports of Manufactures* From Developing Countries to Seven Industrial Countries: Actual and Hypothetical (1976)

MARKET	ACTUAL ($BILLION) (A)	PER CENT OF MANUFACTURED IMPORTS (B)	HYPOTHETICAL G-4 BASIS ($BILLION) (C)	PER CENT OF MANUFACTURED IMPORTS (D)	RATIO [(C)/(A)]
Canada	1.81	5.8	11.15	27.4	6.15
France	4.20	9.2	37.09	47.7	8.83
Germany	7.29	12.0	55.54	51.0	7.62
Italy	2.84	10.7	26.13	52.4	9.19
Japan	8.17	35.5	48.84	76.7	5.98
United Kingdom	5.60	13.9	37.43	51.9	6.68
US	21.30	27.0	166.54	74.4	7.82
Total	51.23	16.7	382.72	60.6	7.47

*ISIC 3111–3909 excluding 3530, petroleum refining.

TABLE 3 Sectors* with LDC Import Penetration of 15% or More Under East Asian Export Model† (1976 Base, %)

ISIC	PRODUCT	US			Germany			United Kingdom			Japan		
		ACTUAL	CASE A	CASE B	ACTUAL	CASE A	CASE B	ACTUAL	CASE A	CASE B	ACTUAL	CASE A	CASE B
3111	Meat	—	—	—	3.4	42.2	25.2	6.5	82.8	60.2	5.0	39.6	110.1
3112	Dairy products	—	—	—	—	—	—	0.1	0.4	18.0	—	—	—
3113	Fruits, canned and pres.	1.7	15.0	9.0	11.3	87.0	49.1	4.7	35.0	22.7	6.7	25.4	43.0
3114	Canned fish	17.4	199.0	117.9	3.5	30.0	24.6	2.0	16.1	17.5	15.6	74.3	74.2
3115	Vegetables, animal fats	3.9	30.8	14.9	19.9	206.7	53.9	13.5	92.2	33.0	4.8	37.1	25.0
3116	Grain mill prod.	10.7	126.0	37.5	26.7	304.8	58.2	4.5	41.8	17.8	7.6	76.3	40.0
3118	Sugar factories	13.7	131.0	54.1	—	—	—	27.4	264.7	59.6	16.3	139.6	120.1
3119	Confectionary	12.9	135.5	49.4	17.8	171.4	48.6	10.9	98.6	27.5	5.0	47.1	24.5
3121	Foods n.e.s.	16.3	185.5	58.3	26.1	271.7	65.0	22.9	189.5	47.8	5.3	50.2	29.0
3140	Tobacco	3.7	37.4	17.6	2.4	26.2	9.4	8.9	55.2	25.6	1.1	9.8	17.0
3211	Textiles, spinning and weaving	3.5	19.0	19.5	10.1	90.6	49.3	8.8	48.7	34.1	6.8	49.0	40.0
3214	Carpets	—	—	—	21.1	156.1	56.6	4.6	29.7	16.8	—	—	—
3220	Apparel	9.5	31.6	38.1	13.3	40.4	49.0	16.3	29.5	42.7	8.2	15.5	39.1
3231	Tanneries	18.2	225.3	87.0	8.8	77.4	47.9	22.2	119.9	44.9	7.8	16.4	33.5
3240	Footwear	9.7	55.9	61.2	2.4	7.1	32.2	3.7	14.0	18.4	3.8	6.1	19.9
3311	Wood mills	2.2	10.9	25.3	—	—	—	5.3	34.1	34.4	1.4	5.5	21.2
3320	Furniture, non-metal	1.5	11.1	17.0	—	—	—	—	—	—	—	—	—
3411	Pulp, paper, paperboard	0.1	0.9	32.3	0.3	2.9	29.7	0.4	4.0	47.8	0.1	0.8	20.0
3511	Industrial chemicals	1.0	11.7	26.1	0.5	5.0	17.8	1.5	14.0	21.0	1.3	10.5	36.8
3522	Medicines	—	—	—	—	—	—	—	—	—	1.3	4.5	26.8
3529	Chemical prod. n.e.s.	1.1	10.4	15.6	—	—	—	2.3	20.2	32.9	1.5	9.4	36.6
3551	Tires and tubes	0.9	2.6	26.9	0.5	0.7	21.6	—	—	—	—	—	—
3559	Rubber n.e.s.	4.0	15.5	23.9	1.4	4.0	23.1	2.5	6.9	17.3	—	—	—
3560	Plastics n.e.s.	3.6	16.8	22.4	1.2	3.9	28.8	2.3	5.5	33.4	—	—	—
3710	Iron, steel	0.6	5.8	16.5	0.4	3.8	16.0	—	—	—	—	—	—
3720	Non-ferrous metals	3.4	34.0	30.5	7.4	64.2	39.5	7.5	54.5	35.2	5.4	46.3	41.0
3819	Metal prod. n.e.s.	—	—	—	0.5	1.6	16.9	—	—	—	—	—	—

TABLE 3 *(Continued)*

ISIC	PRODUCT	US			Germany			United Kingdom			Japan		
		ACTUAL	CASE A	CASE B	ACTUAL	CASE A	CASE B	ACTUAL	CASE A	CASE B	ACTUAL	CASE A	CASE B
3823	Metal and woodworking mach.	—	—	—	3.0	13.7	352.0	0.2	0.8	23.9	3.6	3.9	332.2
3824	Special industrial mach.	0.2	2.4	19.4	0.3	2.4	23.6	0.2	1.9	23.2	—	—	—
3825	Office, computing mach.	1.9	14.4	29.1	1.7	3.7	29.6	1.4	10.5	48.8	0.9	10.0	29.6
3832	Radio, TV	6.1	36.5	43.1	2.7	6.6	24.1	2.2	5.5	21.9	2.0	4.0	17.4
3841	Ship building	—	—	—	—	—	—	0.4	3.9	19.6	—	—	—
3843	Motor vehicles	0.2	4.3	37.4	1.0	15.1	60.3	0.2	1.5	22.3	—	—	—
3845	Aircraft	—	—	—	0.4	3.3	36.2	3.2	27.1	27.7	0.0	0.1	70.5
3851	Scientific equipment	—	—	—	1.4	10.2	44.6	2.7	20.9	47.6	1.1	2.0	70.5
3852	Photographic, optical prod.	0.8	2.2	17.2	7.0	13.0	87.6	1.1	3.4	28.7	1.5	3.6	42.2
3853	Watches, clocks	11.8	39.7	77.1	8.2	16.5	52.2	10.3	22.3	62.6	2.7	3.3	30.2
3901	Jewelry	11.8	63.0	88.2	28.3	170.6	139.3	24.7	201.4	239.4	28.2	165.0	171.2
3909	Manuf. n.e.s.	5.2	23.9	32.3	17.0	74.7	83.1	5.8	17.2	28.9	—	—	—

*Excluding those with less than 1% share in both LDC and total supply to the market . . . indicates that penetration ratios are below 15%.

†Case a: product composition same as in base period.

Case b: incremental LDC exports have same product composition as total non-oil imports into the market in the base period.

291

15% in 43 sectors in the US, 41 in Germany, 44 in the United Kingdom, and 33 in Japan. After taking account of the relative importance of these high-penetration sectors in overall imports, the conclusion is even stronger that the bulk of the market would be vulnerable to closure of access because of high import penetration. Table 4 shows the percentage of total manufactured imports included in sectors with LDC penetration exceeding 15% for four industrial countries. These figures show the great bulk of these markets being oversaturated with LDC supplies under the East Asian export model. Approximately 80% of the prospective value of the LDC export market in these industrial countries would be in products with LDC penetration exceeding the 15% threshold, and therefore of dubious feasibility in terms of market access.

This finding is remarkably uniform across the four industrial countries. Moreover, the results remain unchanged by use of the product diversification strategy (variant *b*), indicating that the level of LDC exports is so high under the G-4 scenario that even diversification cannot avoid a high incidence of high import penetration.

Table 4 reports in parentheses alternative figures for a more restricted case in which only a limited group of newly industrializing developing countries expand their manufactured exports to G-4 dimensions (Argentina, Brazil, Colombia, Mexico, Indonesia, Israel, Malaysia). The alternative calculations apply equations (1)—(3) only to these seven developing countries, leaving the manufactured exports of all others unchanged at their 1976 levels. This variant addresses the possible critique that the basic analysis is highly unrealistic because the great bulk of developing countries, especially those at low income levels, are unlikely to follow the East Asian export model. With-

TABLE 4   **Percentage of Total DC Market for Manufactured Imports From LDCs Represented by Sectors With LDC Import Penetration Ratios Above 15%**

		East Asian Export Model	
MARKET	1976 ACTUAL	VARIANT *a* (LDC PRODUCT COMPOSITION)†‡	VARIANT *b* (HOMOGENEOUS MARGINAL PRODUCT COMPOSITION)‡§
US	16	80 (71)	85 (63)
Germany	32	81 (72)	79 (48)
United Kingdom	37	85 (68)	82 (37)
Japan	26	75 (65)	81 (36)

†Equals $\sum_{ie*} \phi_i^L$ where i is sector i, * is the set of sectors with LDC penetration above 15% and ϕ_i^L is the share of sector i in base period imports from LDCs.

‡Figures in parentheses: G-4 expansion applied to Argentina, Brazil, Colombia, Mexico, Indonesia, Israel, Malaysia only.

§Equals $(1/\beta) \sum_{ie*} \phi_i^L + (1 - 1/\beta) \sum_{ie*} \phi_i^T$ where β is the ratio of expanded to base imports from LDCs, ϕ_i^T is the share sector i in base period imports from all sources, and other notation is as in note †.

out necessarily accepting this critique, the alternative analysis indicates the dimensions of the problem if that model is followed by seven NICs, most of them countries that have already adopted aggressive policies favouring manufactured exports. In this more limited scenario, LDC exports of manufactures multiply by a factor of 4.2, instead of 7.5 in the basic model. As the figures in the parentheses show, even in this more restricted case, the fraction of LDC manufactured exports into industrial countries that exceed the 15% penetration threshold remains quite high. In variant a, this measure of potential protection difficulty is relatively close to the figure in unrestricted generalization of the G-4 model across all developing countries. In variant b, the figures in parentheses show that potential market resistance would be much lower if only seven NICs followed the G-4 model and they did so using product diversification. Even in this case, however, penetration into the US market would exceed 15% for a relatively high fraction of imported manufactures from developing countries (63%). In short, even if only a limited number of NICs were to follow the G-4 model, there could be substantial risk of protectionist response.

Another alternative to the basic analysis would be to apply a penetration threshold for imports from all sources, rather than from developing countries alone. Limited sensitivity analysis suggests that this approach would not significantly alter the basic estimates.[7]

6. QUALIFICATIONS

Several qualifications of these results warrant discussion, although none should fundamentally change the conclusions of the analysis. The cross-country norms do not include a variable for natural resource endowment, and it is possible that export differences between the East Asian economies (especially the city-state, island economies of Hong Kong and Singapore) and much more resource-abundant economies such as those in Latin America could be explained by such a variable. In that case, the estimated expansion of manufactured exports under the G-4 model would be smaller, because the East Asian countries would not lie so far above the cross-country patterns, nor the resource-abundant countries so far below it.

A dynamic analysis might reach different conclusions than this comparative static analysis. For example, if the protection rule were that serious risk of protection would only arise if the annual increase in imports exceeded some rate considered likely to provoke excessively abrupt adjustment, it might be that even the high penetration ratios associated with generalization of the East Asian model could be accommodated by industrial countries if two to three decades were allowed for the adjustment process. However, Cable and Rebelo (1980) have found the level of the import penetration ratio to be more important in explaining protection than the rate of change in penetration. More broadly, it seems unlikely that dynamic formulations of the problem would reach different conclusions from those found here. For example, the fact that the market in industrial countries would grow along with income would not reduce the estimated import penetration ratios even with a time dimension in the analysis, because GDP levels in developing countries (and therefore the base for their manufactured exports) would also be growing over time, probably more rapidly than income and markets in industrial countries. Moreover, the experience of the Multifibres Agreement gives little cause for optimism that adjustment will be accepted if it is phased in over a long time period.

Industrial country exports would rise, as developing countries earn more foreign exchange by moving toward G-4 export intensities, and the analysis here makes no allowance for possible alleviation of protectionist pressure through the opening of new export jobs. However, if North–South trade continued to be mainly inter-industry (along Heckscher–Ohlin lines) as contrasted with intra-industry (as is more frequent in North–North trade, explained in part by greater dominance of product differentiation and less influence of differing relative factor endowments), the new export jobs would tend to be in sectors different from those losing jobs to imports, and the resulting reduction of protectionist pressure would be limited.

Market price effects of developing country export expansion would tend to moderate this expansion long before the higher export propensities of the East Asian countries became generalized. The outward shift in supply would cause relative prices for the exports to decline, causing a new equilibrium with a smaller increase in the quantity supplied than expected at constant prices. However, this qualification reinforces the policy conclusion: the developing countries *en masse* cannot expect to imitate the G-4 export results.

South–South trade might take up much of the increase in developing country exports, reducing the pressure on markets in the North. The strategy of South–South linkage has received increasing attention as growth in the industrial countries has slowed (Lewis, 1980). However, it could be even more unrealistic for a typical developing country to wager that the markets of Brazil and India would be open to manufactured imports from the South, than to place the same bet with respect to US and European markets. Moreover, past trade propensities suggest that the bulk of the new trade would be North–South.[8]

7. CONCLUSION AND POLICY IMPLICATIONS

The simulation exercise presented here indicates that generalization of the East Asian model of export-led development across all developing countries would result in untenable market penetration into industrial countries. Generalization of the G-4 export strategy would require LDC exports of manufactures to rise seven-fold, implying a surge in their share of industrial country manufactured imports from approximately one-sixth to approximately three-fifths. Using an LDC import penetration ratio of 15% as a threshold beyond which protective response would be expected, fully four-fifths of the industrial country markets for manufactured exports from LDCs would be vulnerable to probable protective action in the face of the flood of LDC exports caused by a general adoption of the East Asian export model.

These findings suggest it would be inadvisable for authorities in developing countries to rely in their long-term plans upon the same kind of export results that have been obtained by the four East Asian countries. To the extent that these countries have distorted incentives in favour of exports, and there is some evidence that at least Korea has done so (Frank *et al.*, 1975), other developing countries would do well not to imitate these export-biased policies. To the extent that the G-4 countries have merely followed open-trade policies and realistic exchange rates (as seems to have been the case especially in Hong Kong with its free-market orientation) other developing countries would be well advised to adopt similar policies (on grounds of general efficiency), but ill-advised to expect free-market policies to yield the same results that were achieved by the East Asian economies, which took advantage of the open-economy strategy before the export field became crowded by competition from other developing countries, and did so when the world economy was in a phase of prolonged buoyancy.

The findings of the study should not be interpreted to favour a closed-economy strategy or discouragement of exports. On the contrary, in many developing countries trade liberalization still has far to go. Several Latin American countries in particular could raise their manufactured exports substantially without even reaching cross-country norms, let alone export dimensions of the East Asian variety, and one strongly suspects that in many such cases liberalization of the trading and exchange rate regimes would lead to more rapid export growth.

The analysis of this study does mean that it is necessary to consider the aggregate market implications of export-oriented growth as an increasingly popular development strategy. It is seriously misleading to hold up the East Asian G-4 as a model for development because that model almost certainly cannot be generalized without provoking protectionist response ruling out its implementation. Elevator salesmen must attach a warning label that their product is safe only if not overloaded by too many passengers at one time; advocates of the East Asian export model would do well to attach a similar caveat to their prescription. More broadly, development planners adopting the increasingly popular strategy of export-led growth must take into account the probable capacity of the international market to absorb the resulting increases in exports from their own and like-minded developing countries.

NOTES

1. Other criteria could be used instead, such as the percentage of labour force employed in the production of manufactured exports. However, the criterion relating

manufactured exports to GDP has the advantage that the Chenery-Syrquin cross-country patterns can be used for normalization to remove the influences of developmental level and country size.

2. The first two elements of the final right-hand term give the total increment of exports from the country, and the final element distributes the increment across sectors.

3. If there were reason to believe that some industrial countries would be more receptive than others to an expansion in manufactured exports from developing countries, the market-country composition could also be varied from the base year profile.

4. In their empirical study of British protection, Cable and Rebelo (1980), p. 48, found the import penetration ratio to be the single most important explanatory variable.

5. For purposes of comparison, the discussion later examines the sensitivity of the results for the US if, instead of the 15% threshold for imports from developing countries, the analysis uses a threshold of 25% import penetration from all sources.

6. For details see Cline (1980).

7. Using a threshold of 25% penetration by imports from all sources the percentage of hypothetical (G-4) US manufactured imports from developing countries in sectors exceeding the threshold falls from 80% (Table 4) to 71% (with base period product composition).

8. Nevertheless, there may be some bias in the calculations here toward overstating the portion of increased LDC exports that would be directed toward markets in the North as opposed to the South. Proportionate expansion of exports to all destinations [equations (1) and (3)] has the implicit consequence of causing a larger proportionate rise in the LDC share of import supply in markets in the North than in this share for markets in the South. The reason is that additional export earnings would cause imports into the South to rise proportionately more than imports into the North, and with equal proportionate rises in the LDC-supplied imports for both North and South, the LDC share of manufactured imports would rise proportionately more in the North than in the South. (The greater proportionate rise of total manufactured imports in the South may be seen as follows. Table 2 implies that manufactured imports into the North would rise by 108% in the G-4 scenario. In contrast, the hypothesized 647% rise in LDC exports of manufactures would, when spent on imports, cause a rise of about 160% in their manufactured imports, given the current 4 to 1 ratio of LDC imports to exports in manufactures, and abstracting from non-manufactured trade.) An alternative approach would be to assume that the proportionate rise in LDC supply shares in imports is identical in markets of both the North and South. Using GATT (International Trade Center, 1980) data on manufactured trade, referring to a narrower range of goods than considered here, the consequence would be that the share of LDCs in import markets would rise from 7.7 to 33.8% in the South and from 6.2 to 27.2% in the North, compared with a rise to 21.9% in the South and 32.9% in the North as implied by the calculations in this study. (I am indebted to Jean Waelbroeck for this point.) Nevertheless, even this alternative approach would cause a 5.7-fold rise in LDC exports of manufactures to the North, and as was shown in the analysis of the more limited, NIC-based scenario (Table 4, parentheses) even a four-fold rise in these exports would be likely to cause market absorption problems. Moreover, under current conditions of LDC protection, it is not necessarily more realistic to assume that the increase in

the share of LDCs in the supply of manufactured imports would be identical in the markets of North and South; instead, the larger rise in markets in the North (implicit in the calculations here) could be more meaningful.

REFERENCES

Balassa, Bela, 'Exports and economic growth: further evidence', *Journal of Development Economics,* Vol. 5, No. 2 (June 1978), pp. 181–189.

Banerji, Ranadev and James Riedel, 'Industrial employment expansion under alternative trade strategies: case of India and Taiwan: 1950–1970', *Journal of Development Economics,* Vol. 7, No. 4 (1980), pp. 567–577.

Bhagwati, Jagdish and Anne O. Kreuger, 'Exchange control, liberalization and economic development', *American Economic Review* (May 1973).

Cable, Vincent and Ivonia Rebelo, 'Britain's patterns of specialization in manufactured goods with developing countries and trade protection', World Bank Staff Working Paper No. 425 (October 1980).

Caves, Richard E., 'Economic models of political choice: Canada's tariff structure', *Canadian Journal of Economics,* Vol. 9, No. 2 (May 1976), pp. 278–300.

Chenery, H. and M. Syrquin, *Patterns of Development* 1950–1970 (London: Oxford University Press, 1975).

Cline, William R., 'Estimates of penetration in industrial country markets by manufactured exports of developing countries', mimeo (Washington, D.C.: Brookings Institution, 1980).

Fei, John C. H., Gustav Ranis and Shirley W. Y. Kuo, *Growth with Equity: The Taiwan Case* (New York: Oxford University Press, 1979).

Fieleke, Norman S., 'The tariff structures for manufacturing industries in the United States: a test of some traditional explanations', *Columbia Journal of World Business,* Vol. 11, No. 4 (Winter 1976), pp. 98–104.

Frank, Charles R., Jr., Kwang Suk Kim and Larry E. Westphal, *Foreign Trade Regimes and Economic Development: South Korea,* Vol. 7 (New York: Columbia University Press, 1975).

Hughes, Helen, 'Achievements and objectives of industrialization', in J. Cody, H. Hughes and D. Wall (eds), *Policies for Industrial Progress in Developing Countries* (New York: Oxford University Press, 1980), pp. 11–37.

International Trade Centre, UNCTAD/GATT, 'Analysis of actual and potential trade flows between developing countries' [ITC/TD/16(C), October 1980].

Krueger, Anne O., *Foreign Trade Regimes and Economic Development: Liberalization Attempts and Consequences* (Ballinger, 1978).

Lewis, W. Arthur, 'The slowing down of the engine of growth', *American Economic Review,* Vol. 70, No. 4 (September 1980), pp. 555–564.

Little, I., T. Scitovsky and M. Scott, *Industry and Trade in Some Developing Countries: A Comparative Study* (Paris: OECD, 1970).

Nurkse, Ragnar, *Problems of Capital Formation in Underdeveloped Countries* (New York: Oxford University Press, 1953).

Prebisch, Raul, 'Commercial policy in the underdeveloped countries', *American Economic Review* (May 1959).

World Bank, *World Development Report,* 1977; 1978; 1979 (Washington, D.C.: World Bank, annually).

PART FOUR

AGRICULTURAL INSTITUTIONS AND STRATEGY

Agricultural institutions assume a critical role in the development strategy of a nation. They provide the output of food and raw materials for the whole population, supply capital and labor to the nonagricultural sectors, and in agricultural-export economies are a source of foreign exchange. In light of this central position of agriculture, the fact that the sector systematically suffers crisis and decline is indeed serious. The crisis assumes three dimensions: stagnation, increasing inequality, and marginalization. Stagnation refers to the low level of productive activity in the sector, that is, declining output relative to rising demand. There also is found increasing inequality, a distributional crisis wherein the share of the poorest farmers in the agricultural pie is shrinking to the benefit of wealthy landowners. Finally there is evidence of marginalization. Marginals are those who are forced outside the dominant capitalist system by the power of agricultural concentration. On the margin, these people must eke out a meager existence from the dregs of the feudal-capitalist order.

The authors in this section deal with the causes of stagnation, increasing inequality, and marginalization in the agricultural sector and offer alternative policy recommendations.

Lofchie and Commins utilize a competing paradigms approach. They describe the political economy school's theory of the underdevelopment of agriculture as premised upon the concept of agrarian dualism. Agrarian dualism pits the small peasant farmer against the reign of large capitalist estates. The surplus is drained from the peasantry, marginalizing small farmers and forcing them to work on the larger estates. Linked into the capitalist system, the larger estates squeeze the rural sector for profits that in turn benefit industrial centers. Benefits are drawn away from agriculture; stagnation is thus the result of structural neglect.

In contrast, the orthodox school offers a theory of comparative advantage as an explanation of stagnation and marginalization. It looks at reasons for market failure in the agricultural sector. The orthodox economists stipulate that too much competition, highly elastic products, and a stronger market in refining rather than leaving agricultural products raw are contributing causes to the rural crisis. Lofchie and Commins broaden the scope of possible explanations to include environmental constraints. They point out that the fragility of the soils and the quickly progressing processes of desertification and deforestation rule out food aid as a viable long-run policy option to mitigate rural problems. Although the effects of food aid—targeting food to the neediest, the provision of nutrients, and price stabilization—are in the short run beneficial, the long-run costs of corruption, disincentives, bureaucratic red tape, and the burdens such aid places on the marginal farmer outweigh the benefits. Instead, Lofchie and Commins' guidelines for the future include empowering the peasantry, paying attention to small farmers through changes in land tenure and greater access to credit, and increasing sensitivity to environmental constraints.

Griffin and Ghose focus on the distributive aspects of the rural crisis. They contend that stagnation is not due to inadequate growth but to inappropriate patterns of agricultural growth. Thus the stagnation problem has distributional roots. The pattern of ownership biased against small farmers is evidenced by the concentration of landholdings in the hands of the wealthy and by a government technology policy favoring capital over labor. With an increase of food prices, a natural consequence of inflationary growth policies, the poor farmer benefits little and is hurt by the general price increase, while the large estate owner is able to command monopoly profits.

Griffin and Ghose advocate redistributional policies of land reform and the creation of additional rural employment. The employment programs should focus not on a large number of work-relief positions, but on quality projects leading to the construction of durable assets to become the property of those who build them. It is admitted by the authors that such a program would necessitate a major redistribution of political power and government advocacy of the peasant farmers—seemingly unlikely events.

One problem with the orthodox free market approach to land reform as described by Lofchie and Commins is that it must assume the existence not only of a market, but also of microeconomic decisionmakers identical to any other type of production unit. Schejtman, in "The Peasant Economy: Internal Logic, Articulation, and Persistence," illustrates how, because production is based in the family and not in a neutrally organized business unit, decisions are made on the familial criterion of kin group well-being and not on the economic efficiency motive of pure profit maximization. Thus, in adverse situations where commercial enterprises might choose to close operations, the peasant economy pursues a different, though entirely rational, logic. The article concludes with a brief analysis of the forces outside the peasant economy that work toward its break-up, recovery, or persistence.

In the final selection, Joseph Stiglitz argues that a special theory of peasant economy is not needed to understand either peasant behavior or the nature of agricultural institutions in Third World countries. Rather, he argues that the theory of rural organization based on rational peasants in environments where information is imperfect and costly provides a simple explanation for a wide variety of phenomena such as sharecropping and the interlinkage of credit and land markets.

15

Food Deficits and Agricultural Policies in Tropical Africa

Michael F. Lofchie and Stephen K. Commins *

Hunger is the most immediate, visible, and compelling symptom of a continent-wide agricultural breakdown in tropical Africa. The crisis of food deficits has now become so perennial and so widespread that it can no longer be understood as the outcome of particular political or climatic occurrences such as wars, ethnic strife, or drought. Sub-Saharan Africa is the only region in the world where food production *per capita* has declined during the past two decades. As a result, the average calorie intake *per capita* has now fallen below minimal nutritional standards in a majority of African countries. By current estimates, approximately 150 million out of Africa's 450 million people suffer from some form of malnutrition originating in an inadequate supply of foodstuffs. This abysmal picture is further highlighted by the fact that the Food and Agricultural Organisation of the United Nations recently indicated that no fewer than 28 African countries were faced with food shortages so critical that further famine might occur imminently.[1] This stark reality challenges fundamentally our earlier assumptions about the possibility of economic development.

There is every indication that food shortages will become more rather than less severe during the next decade. By 1980, Africa had already become heavily dependent upon food imports, at a time when grain prices were rising and African governments faced acute shortages of foreign exchange. Grain

*Michael F. Lofchie is Professor of Political Science at the University of California, Los Angeles, and acknowledges the support received from his Department and the African Studies Center. Stephen K. Commins is Co-ordinator of the Food and Agriculture Project of the African Studies Center, and acknowledges the support of the St. Augustine by-the-sea Episcopal Church for sabbatical leave during 1981. Both authors wish to thank the Episcopal Diocese of Los Angeles for a grant from the Presiding Bishop's Fund for World Relief.

Reprinted from the *Journal of Modern African Studies,* Vol. 20, No. 1 (March 2, 1981) by permission of Cambridge University Press.

imports tripled during the 20 years between 1960 and 1978, but due to price increases, especially during the 1970s, their cost multiplied nearly 12-fold. If current trends continue, Africa's demand for food imports will triple again by 1990, when sub-Saharan countries will be forced to import approximately 17 million tons of grain annually, simply to maintain 1975 levels of consumption. Even this staggering volume of imports would do nothing to reduce the tragic gap between average consumption *per capita* and the amount of food required to provide minimal nutritional standards. A further 13 million tons of imports would be required to alleviate this deficit.[2] Even the most optimistic estimates, which foresee some recovery in the productivity of the food-producing sector of African agriculture, envision the need for a doubling of food imports during the decade of the 1980s.

Food deficits on such a massive scale are a sobering entry point for Africa's third decade of independence. The problem is much deeper than the failure of an agricultural continent to feed itself. It is present in the environmental degradation that afflicts not only the semi-arid areas of western and eastern Africa, but also the high rainfall regions of Zaïre, Zambia, and the West African coast. Desertification, the conversion of once arable soil to desert-like infertility, can be observed in every African country across the equatorial belt from Senegal to Somalia. Soil loss on so appalling a scale reflects both the pressure of increasing population to land ratios, and the imprudent use of capital-intensive temperate-zone technologies on fragile tropical soils. Generations of accumulated wisdom and historically evolved agricultural systems are now rendered largely irrelevant by greatly increased production requirements, and by the pressures of outside markets and political forces.

Africa has been the scene of a bewildering kaleidoscope of experimental strategies for agricultural development. It has become a continental proving-ground for policies ranging from socialist collectivism to free-market individualism, with countless approaches somewhere on the continuum between the two. It would require an encyclopedic inventory of research even to compile the literature on world hunger, and this would not begin to touch on such sensitive theoretical concerns as the determinants of successes or failures of rural development efforts.[3]

The causes and remedies of food deficits in Africa have been the subject of a wide-ranging debate.[4] This article examines certain of the principal schools of thought which participate in this debate, and assesses the remedial policies which each suggests. Our objective is to help clarify some of the contending analytic viewpoints, to call attention to the bewildering complexity of the problem, and to suggest a framework within which future rural development policies may be considered. It is useful for our purposes to begin with a discussion of two major contending approaches. These might best be identified as the theory of underdevelopment and the theory of comparative advantage. We will then consider the factor of environmental deterioration, and the impact of international food-aid policies, particularly those of the United States.

THE THEORY OF UNDERDEVELOPMENT

The best known and, by a wide margin, most widely discussed analysis of poverty and agricultural failure in Africa is found in the complex of theories concerned with underdevelopment. It would not repay us here to summarise at length the differing analyses of such prolific theoreticians as Paul Baran, André Gunder Frank, Samir Amin, Argihiri Emmanuel, Walter Rodney, and Immanuel Wallerstein.[5] It may suffice to extract from this protean array of literature a common core of presuppositions which bears most directly on the problem of food deficits, and on the failure of the food-producing sector of African agriculture to provide adequately for the continent's population.

The point of departure from the theory of underdevelopment is the view that the root causes of Africa's economic problems, like those of other developing areas, lie in the nature of the continent's relationship with the global economic system. Underdevelopment theorists normally begin with the presupposition that the world can be divided into the core and the periphery. The core consists of those few countries, principally in North America and Western Europe, which, during the past five centuries, have been able to develop advanced capitalist economic systems. The periphery consists of those countries in Africa, Latin America, Asia, and elsewhere, commonly referred to as the 'developing areas', whose economies are, in fact, desperately underdeveloped. The theory of underdevelopment asserts that the core countries have been able to achieve advanced forms of capitalism at least in part because of their capacity to exploit—that is, extract an economic surplus from—the periphery. The peripheral countries, conversely, are poor because their wealth has been drained off to sustain the process of economic growth in the core. In a nutshell, the economic surplus which might have been used to generate development in peripheral areas is used instead to finance further enrichment of already affluent nations.

Peripheral countries find it virtually impossible to transform their status in the world system. For they are highly dependent on the core for capital, technology, and for markets for their products. Moreover, the policies of these countries are formulated by élites, sometimes referred to as 'comprador', whose decisions advance the interests of western capital. Although theorists of underdevelopment sometimes acknowledge a degree of mutual independence between core and periphery, they view this as highly asymmetrical because the core countries have far greater discretion over the terms of their participation in the global economic system. The peripheral countries, precisely because they are so poor, are politically as well as economically weak, and must generally accept the terms of trade they are confronted with as a set of 'givens' over which they have little or no control.

The theory of underdevelopment attempts to explain the reasons for the failure of the agricultural sector of developing areas to generate an adequate supply of locally needed food items. It is believed that since the economies of the developing areas are fundamentally shaped by their dependence upon the global economic system, there is a pronounced tendency to favour export agriculture over the production of food crops for domestic consumption. Dependency gives rise to a pronounced dichotomy between the export sector and the food-producing sector; the striking contrast between the two has given rise to the concept of 'agrarian dualism'. For export production is often carried on in large, plantation-sized farms which are highly favoured in terms of agricultural inputs, whereas food crops for local consumption are grown on peasant farms which are badly deprived of needed agricultural supports.

The export-oriented plantations have benefited from a host of support-ive inputs not typically available to peasant farmers. They have access to agricultural-extension services which can help to introduce and sustain scien-tific methods of production, including high-yield seeds, pesticides, and ad-vanced irrigation technologies. They also benefit from the availability of highly developed infrastructures to deal with the transportation, packaging, and storage of their products. Export agriculture is additionally buoyed by a host of private firms and government agencies which provide 'soft' services such as credit, insurance, market analyses and, most importantly, which handle the actual sales transactions to foreign purchasers or commodity ex-changes.

The peasant sector, where much of the country's supply of foodstuffs is produced, contrasts fundamentally with the export plantations. Units of pro-duction are small in scale, and thus are not in a position to take advantage of modern agricultural technologies. As a result the most common instrument is the hand-held hoe; less frequently, some form of animal-drawn cultivation. Almost never, except in the rarest cases of successful peasant co-operatives, is there any complex machinery. Peasant agriculture is also starved of other vital inputs. Agricultural-extension services are conspicuous by their inade-quacy, with the result that there is little or no provision of scientific inputs for the production of locally consumed food crops. Modern varieties of seeds, fertilisers, and pesticides are, similarly, far less commonly available than in the plantation or export areas. Feeder roads tend to be woefully inadequate, as well as other important elements of infrastructure, such as facilities for the storage or preservation of food grains. There are few systematic efforts to organise the supply of food items from the countryside to urban centres, or between different rural areas, with the result that an appalling proportion of the food which is produced goes wasted for want of access to markets. In sum, the shortage of foodstuffs in Africa can be traced directly to the systematic structural neglect of the food-producing sector.

This theory of the roots of Africa's food crisis has proved to be highly compelling because of its sweeping synthesis of historical, political, and eco-nomic factors. But its very all-inclusive generality is also the source of consid-

erable doubt about its ultimate utility. For although the theory does illuminate important structural pathologies in African agriculture, it can be deeply
criticised on a variety of grounds. Some of the more general judgments are
fairly well known.[6] These include: a tendency to challenge the crudely moral-
istic oversimplification involved in a bimodal division of the world between
exploitative core and exploited periphery; a growing realisation that the very
term 'periphery' is so broad that it impedes an understanding of the considerable economic and political differences between countries in the developing
world; and, among some thinkers, a strong conviction that the notion of
'comprador' is inadequate as a conceptualisation of class domination in
Africa.

It has recently been argued that the theory of underdevelopment also
fails to understand the nature of the African peasantry, and the overriding
cultural factors which limit their food production.[7] Other critics have called
attention to the need for a more sophisticated classification than dependent
versus non-dependent countries, and for a far more probing treatment of the
class factors which inhibit or facilitate food production on the African continent. In the last analysis, a theory which uses identical terms to explain
skyrocketing food imports both in Nigeria and Tanzania is seriously lacking
in persuasiveness.

Our principal concern is with the limitations of the theory of underdevelopment as it pertains to a strategy of rural development. Here, its shortcomings are particularly acute. A conspicuous feature of the theory's strong
condemnation of the global trading system is a call for withdrawal from
external markets—a process sometimes referred to as economic closure—and
those who lay heavy stress on the exploitative aspects of world trade for
underdeveloped countries are especially likely to suggest this as a remedy.
The difficulty with this approach is that it leaves a host of critically important
practical questions unanswered, especially those that have to do with the
acquisition of foreign exchange. While it is absolutely true, as dependency
theorists point out, that the terms of world trade have shifted steadily against
agricultural countries, it is woefully inadequate to suggest that the solution
is to withdraw from world markets, because those who choose to do so must
necessarily forgo, or reduce substantially, their stocks of innumerable essential commodities. The theory of underdevelopment is regrettably silent on
how countries which pursue a policy of closure can equip themselves with
the scientific and technological wherewithal of the modern world.

A second shortcoming in the rural strategy of the theory of underdevelopment is its unqualified reliance upon collectivised agriculture. Agrarian socialism tends to be viewed as an integral accompaniment of the policy
of closure. The argument advanced for this position by a number of theorists
is that unless the capitalist relations of production in the countryside are
dissolved, it would be impossible to reorient agricultural production away
from world trade towards the cultivation of foodstuffs for local consumption.
Capitalist farmers would continue to be attracted to the higher levels of profit

available in western markets, and their influence over the local state would enable them to influence agricultural policy in such a way as to facilitate production for export.

Our reservation concerning socialist agriculture is essentially pragmatic, and has to do with the fact that it has generally proved incapable of sustaining high levels of agricultural production.[8] For this reason, country after country in Eastern Europe and elsewhere has abandoned collectivised farming in favour of private farming, mixed forms of production, or locally controlled co-operatives. Whatever its attractive theoretical merits, agrarian collectivism in Africa has been consistently unable to transform production levels in the countryside. Indeed, those countries which have sought to implement rural socialism, most conspicuously Tanzania, find themselves today in the midst of calamitous agricultural crises, and they must import enormous volumes of foodstuffs in order to avert starvation in the countryside. The great irony of socialist agriculture in Africa is that it has tended to exacerbate the very dependency it was intended to remove; it has necessitated heightened levels of financial and material dependence on western donors.

In the last analysis, the greatest value of the theory of underdevelopment may lie in the fact that it sounds a persuasive warning about the pitfalls of uncritical dependence upon world trade. It demonstrates graphically the results of a world economy in which relatively affluent nations can afford to outbid local consumers for the use of local agricultural land. However, the theory does not demonstrate the viability of a strategy of 'withdrawal' and, indeed, it does not even rebut theories of rural development which call for poorer countries to remain involved in world markets as a partial solution to their food crises.

COMPARATIVE ADVANTAGE

The major alternative to dependency theory is found in the principle of comparative advantage, the view that countries can maximise their economic potential by specialising in the production of commodities at which they are most efficient in terms of such inputs as capital and labour. This concept was originally suggested in the writings of David Ricardo nearly 200 years ago. For Ricardo, the notion of comparative advantage was a powerful argument for free trade since an unrestricted flow of products between countries would enable them to use their productive resources most efficiently:

> It is quite important to the happiness of mankind that our own enjoyment should be increased by the better distribution of labor, by each country producing those commodities for which by its situation, its climate and its natural or artificial advantages, it is adapted, and by their exchanging them for the commodities of other countries, as that they should be augmented by a rise in the rate of profit.[9]

This kind of specialisation, according to Ricardo, would not only lead to more wealth for all nations, but to the greatest possible improvement in living conditions for their people. He believed strongly that comparative advantage must work to the benefit of all concerned, and that the poorer governments would only worsen their economic position by withdrawing from world markets—indeed, there is a strong implication in Ricardo's work that the least-developed nations would be particularly well advised to specialise narrowly in their range of products, since this would enable them to trade in world markets on the most advantageous possible terms.[10]

Writers who followed Ricardo have expanded and altered some of his theoretical ideas, but the basics of the argument have remained the same.[11] Perhaps the most significant addition has been the expansion in the number of factors of production which need to be taken into account to determine a country's comparative advantage. Ricardo gave almost exclusive emphasis to labour as the measuring rod of efficiency in any sphere of production. More contemporary authors have argued the need for land and capital to be taken into account, as well, before a country's comparative advantage can be accurately established. Significantly, however, two of the major premises of Ricardo's thought have remained intact. Modern theorists of comparative advantage tend not to question either his assumption of the mobility of labour between spheres of production, or his conviction that poor and rich countries alike would improve their economic well-being by participating freely in world markets.

Agricultural economists who accept the doctrine of comparative advantage tend to see no fundamental problem in economies which are characterised by agrarian dualism. They see the heavy structural emphasis on export crops as the natural and beneficial consequence of the operation of free-market forces. William O. Jones, for example, has stated that:

> The great African production of coffee, cocoa, tea, peanuts, palm oil, and cotton occurred because these crops could be sold; that is, because consumers in Europe, North America, and elsewhere manifested an economic demand for these commodities, and because a marketing system was developed to communicate the character and magnitude of this demand to African farmers. As a consequence, African producers were able to enjoy more nonfarm goods such as textiles and utensils, than they had before.[12]

According to this perspective, it would be a grave mistake to shift away from export crops to food production as a means of solving the problems of food deficits. If such inputs as capital, land, and labour are more effectively utilised when allotted to the production of export crops, it would, from the standpoint of comparative advantage, be economically imprudent to shift these resources to food production. For the income generated by the sale of export crops, such as coffee, cocoa, or tea, would make it possible to purchase far greater amounts of wheat and corn than could have been produced domestically with the same inputs.

Perhaps the most important contemporary proponent of the theory of comparative advantage for developing countries is Hollis Chenery, an economist with the World Bank. His influence has been based partly on his willingness to challenge certain of the more extravagant claims sometimes advanced by other economists. In particular, Chenery questions the classical assumption that specialisation of production for foreign trade promotes economic growth. He demonstrates a distinction between analyses of comparative advantage (trade theory) and of economic development (growth theory). In his most recent work, Chenery associates himself with a number of important economists, including Joseph Schumpeter, who believe that 'comparative advantage is a static concept that ignores a variety of dynamic elements'. The elements Chenery refers to, including especially the stimulus that exports provide for the growth of the industrial sector, would be of critical importance for a country seeking overall expansion of its economic system.[13]

For the political leaders of developing countries who require practical guidance in making decisions about how best to allocate their own scarce resources, growth theory would appear to have decisive advantages. It is, for example, far more concerned than is the theory of comparative advantage with changing relationships 'over time among producers, consumers and investors in related sectors of the economy'. Indeed, if there is one single point of differentiation between growth theory and trade theory, it is the greater concern in growth theory for the expansion of multiple sectors of the economy, not simply the export sector. Chenery is particularly emphatic on this point:

> [development requires] much more emphasis on the sequence of expansion of production and factor use by sector than on the conditions of general equilibrium. Growth theory either ignores comparative advantage and the possibilities of trade completely, or considers mainly the dynamic aspects, such as the stimulus that an increase in exports provides to the development of related sectors. . . . With this different point of view, growth theorists often suggest investment criteria that are quite contradictory to those derived from considerations of comparative advantage.[14]

For Chenery, it is axiomatic that a developing country's best long-term economic interests lie in balanced, multi-sectoral development. Present market forces, which comparative advantage would rely upon to promote this purpose, are inadequate, since they do not reflect future patterns of consumption and demand.

Given the force of this critique it is rather surprising that Chenery nevertheless continues to advocate a positive rôle for the concept of comparative advantage in the development process. His argument on this point is carefully modulated: if comparative advantage can be modified by taking into account some of the important differing assumptions of growth theory, it can serve as an influential principle of planning. Four such assumptions would need to be incorporated into the theory, namely:

(a) factor prices do not necessarily reflect opportunity costs with any accuracy; (b) the quantity and quality of factors of production may change substantially over time, in part as a result of the production process itself; (c) economies of scale relative to the size of existing markets are important in a number of sectors of production; and (d) complementarity among commodities is dominant in both producer and consumer demand.[15]

By accepting these assumptions, rather than the more pristine doctrine of pure comparative advantage, a developing country can carefully plan its economic policies so as to achieve a judicious balance between emphasis on foreign trade and other strategies which are more likely to promote multisectoral development.

Chenery's contribution is of immense value to development scholars. For it establishes the principle that participation in the global trading economy may not by itself enable a developing country to allocate its resources in such a way that the growth of complementary sectors of its economy is promoted. We would identify this principle, for the sake of brevity, as 'market failure', and Chenery's theoretical concern about this is well substantiated by the unfortunate experiences of a number of African economies. For countries which have pursued an aggressive strategy of emphasis upon export agriculture have often experienced failure in its bitterest form. Their earnings from agricultural exports have fallen far short of national needs, and they have been consistently unable to enter the world market to acquire food grains on anything even remotely resembling an adequate scale.

The reasons for this market failure are worth identifying. Contrary to early expectations which saw tropical exports as scarce, high-demand goods, available from only a limited number of suppliers, whereas food grains produced in the temperate zones would be available in abundance, the exact opposite has turned out to be the case. The production of tropical export crops is now an enormously competitive field with new suppliers constantly entering the market,[16] sometimes in response to only modest upward fluctuations in price. Indeed, the market is so competitive that the entry of a single new producer, or the harvest of a bumper crop in one country, can depress prices below their previous level. Coffee provides an excellent example of this situation. African suppliers such as Kenya, Tanzania, Ethiopia, Uganda, and the Ivory Coast compete intensely for market shares against not only each other, but also a host of producers in Latin America, notably Brazil and

Colombia. The dominant tendency for the past decade has been for conditions in the world coffee market to depress prices, and to hold them relatively constant at low levels.

This tendency is strongly reinforced by the nature of the market confronted by tropical producers. For the real market does not consist of large numbers of consumer nations bidding competitively against one another for tropical commodities, but rather of a handful of powerful multinational trading corporations. Companies such as General Foods, Nestles, Lipton, and Brooke Bond often occupy an oligopolistic or, not infrequently, a monopolistic position in the market.[17] If tropical commodities appear expensive on the shelves of western supermarkets, the reasons have less to do with the rate of return to producer countries than with the ability of these processing and trading firms to engage in the time-honoured tradition of purchasing cheap and selling dear. Part of what enables them to do so, in addition to their commanding position in the market-place, is the high degree of elasticity of demand for the products they provide, because this can be used to gain bargaining leverage against the producer nations.

The market strength of the large trading companies—or, more precisely, the weakness of the tropical producers—is further reinforced by such factors as the elasticity of consumer demand and the ready availability of synthetic or substitute products. Since tropical agricultural products are not day-to-day necessities, individual purchasers can quickly alter their consumption patterns in response to price fluctuations. This tends to have a continuously depressing effect on the market. The easy availability of alternatives—synthetic chocolate for cocoa, a coffee-chicory mixture for whole coffee, herb and spice teas for authentic tea, or soft drinks for any of these—has a similar effect. The cumulative impact of these factors has been to make it almost impossible for producers in the developing world to gain price leverage in the international marketplace. As a result, tropical agriculture seems perilously unlikely in the future to do any better than it has in the past in generating the levels of foreign exchange necessary to finance a sustained programme of food imports.

Further doubt is cast on the wisdom of any strategy based on the continuation of export agriculture, and the import of food crops, by the nature of the world market for basic grains. Temperate-zone food exporters, in clear contrast to tropical crop exporters, benefit from a highly buoyant market for their products. Countries which can export wheat, corn, rice, and other grains are dealing in day-to-day necessities, and they can be confident that prospective customers do not have substitutes or alternatives readily at hand. Moreover, the world market for these crops is virtually monopolised by the United States, Canada, Australia, and Argentina, the great wheat exporters who can choose from a host of anxious consumer nations in both the developed and developing worlds. They can also depend upon a steady and expanding market for their goods. Not only are massive importers such as China and

Russia constantly entering this market to negotiate long-term, high-volume purchase agreements, but there is a rapidly increasing demand for food grains among middle-income developing countries and in Eastern Europe.

The poorer developing nations enter the market for food grain only with the greatest difficulty. They lack adequate reserves of foreign exchange, and in any case these are often committed in large measure to other vital purposes, such as petroleum imports, the financing of foreign debts, and the purchase of raw materials for factories. Because the grain needs of African countries often fluctuate widely from one year to the next, it is impossible to predict import levels over an extended period of time. And since African economies are typically small in scale, their grain purchases do not begin to compare with those of the Soviet Union and China. As a result, they are compelled to enter what amounts to an international grain 'spot market'. This can be disastrous, as it was during the early 1970s when the famine-struck countries of the Sahel had to enter the international grain market at a moment of critical scarcity, just as soaring purchases by the Soviet Union had driven prices to record levels.

It would therefore appear than an undiluted comparative advantage approach to development is a risky strategy at best. Danger of 'market failure' places many developing countries in a highly vulnerable position, especially given their weakness in the international marketplace. Inability to provide basic foodstuffs for the local population is all-too-common a result of government decisions which rely heavily on export commodity strategies. Nevertheless, the basic principle of comparative advantage has validity in that Africa does possess highly varied resources and production factors which, at least potentially, would enable a number of countries to compete very effectively on world markets. A strategy of comparative advantage could have considerable utility only if it were incorporated into a broader approach to agricultural development, one that reflected sensitivity to other important political, economic, and environmental considerations.

ENVIRONMENTAL CONSTRAINTS[18]

In considering the broad framework for strategies of agricultural development in Africa, it is essential to consider the continent's particular environmental constraints. Although these have been well explored in a number of books,[19] the relationship between environmental deterioration and agricultural stagnation is still too often ignored in the formulation of appropriate strategies. The task of doing so is formidable, for Africa is a continent of micro-environments, with great ecological changes often occurring over very short distances. Such variations make environmentally conscious agricultural planning extraordinarily difficult and complex. Yet the necessity for such a strategy is tragically illustrated by the fact that the planned introduction of certain exogenous crops, and of new agricultural techniques, has already led to ecological disasters which, in themselves, make efforts at future development even more daunting.

Underlying the basic difficulties of agricultural production in tropical Africa is the general fragility of most of the soils. African soils vary greatly in depth and initial nutrient content, reflecting differing influences of parent material, vegetation, and climate. But as a general rule, the soil cover of sub-Saharan Africa is not readily suitable for on-going agriculture. The problem, in a nutshell, lies in the fact that 'sandy soils deficient in important elements preponderate over clay and limestone soils and there are proportionately fewer young, rich alluvial soils than on any other continent'.[20] The principal exceptions are in northern Africa, where the Nile food plain and the lowland regions of the western Mediterranean countries can sustain intensive agriculture over extended periods. Sub-Saharan Africa is not so fortunate. Its soils tend to be highly weathered, relatively poor in humus, and very susceptible to such damaging processes as erosion and leaching.

To understand the nature of the environmental constraints on African agricultural development, it is useful to begin by recalling that the continent was once highly forested, with a rich cover of trees protecting and nurturing the soils beneath. Under this historical condition, in so far as it can be presently reconstructed, its tropical soils were rich and fertile. For the humus content of the soil—which is of vital importance in providing nutrients for plant life, and in retaining moisture near the surface—was constantly replenished by leaf litter from the canopy of trees. Wherever the forest cover has been removed, whether through natural causes such as fires, or as a result of human habitation, the effect has been to set in motion a disastrous cycle of rapid ecological deterioration: without a covering blanket of trees, the soil no longer benefits from the continuous replenishment of its humus content. And, since tropical soils have a high level of micro-organic activity, the residual humus in the topsoil tends to be rapidly depleted by the process of microbial decay. African tropical soils are so unstable in this respect that they can lose their arability almost completely in a matter of years.

Deforestation has other negative consequences as well. Without a layer of humus near the surface, rainfall penetrates rapidly downwards into the subsoil, leaching the surface of many available nutrients, thereby drastically diminishing its utility for agricultural purposes. In areas where the previous cover consisted of savannah grassland, a comparable cycle of decay can be discerned. The richness of these regions was often reflected, in the past, in the dark, highly organic texture of the surface soils. However, if the natural vegetation of savannah grasses is removed for agricultural or grazing purposes, the soils are also exposed in a rapid process of nutrient removal by a combination of microbial activity and downward leaching due to heavy precipitation.

The tendency for rainfall to penetrate rapidly downwards often leads to an even more serious ecological malaise, because the sub-surface water dissolves the laterite found in many African soils. When the water evaporates, as between heavy rains, these metal deposits precipitate out, leading to the formation of a stone-like pan beneath the surface of the soil. Once underway, this condition is extremely difficult, if not impossible, to reverse. Deep ploughing, sometimes suggested as the only possible corrective, has not proved to be a solution; this action merely brings fragments of the encrusted iron pan to the surface where they must be laboriously removed by hand. Moreover, without a top blotter of leaf litter or savannah grasses, the first heavy rains merely repeat the cycle. Downward penetration of water once again sends sub-surface metallic deposits into solution, and evaporation then recapitulates the formation of the sub-surface pan.

Contemporary Ivory Coast furnishes a sad example of the ecological and agricultural ramifications of the unplanned removal of the forest cover.[21] The timber resources of the nation's rainforest, once one of the lushest in West Africa, are being rapidly dissipated to help boost the country's exports. As recently as 25 years ago, the Ivory Coast's forests covered approximately 12 million hectares. This has now shrunk to about one-third of that area, and the pace of felling timber is such that little, if any, woodland may remain by the end of the century. Without the protection of the forest canopy, the soils in many southern areas have been exposed to severe processes of nutrient removal, laterisation, and erosion, rendering them virtually useless for agricultural purposes. These vast regions have also lost most of their capacity to retain moisture, depleting the underground reserves and leading to severe water shortages. Even more ominously, these changes have drastically disrupted rainfall patterns in the Ivory Coast's northern neighbours, Mali and Upper Volta. The contemporary intensification of drought conditions in these societies is, in part, traceable to the ecological disruptions in the Ivory Coast.

In the past, traditional patterns of cropping were developed which were adaptive to the difficulties of tropical environment.[22] For example, the forested areas were, in effect, closed communities where plants and animals constantly replenished the nutrients in the soil through their death and decay. Successful farming required that the canopy of forest and bush be continued in some fashion to allow for a return of nutrients to the earth. In dried, more savannah-like areas, 'shifting cultivation' evolved as the major agricultural technique: old fields whose fertility was depleted were simply abandoned for varying periods of time (up to 20 years) and new fields were opened up. Shifting cultivation generally differed from 'crop rotation', whereby extended land-use was sustained by changing what was planted on a given piece of land from one year to the next, although inevitably both systems tended to overlap regions of Africa.

It would be unrealistic to portray traditional agricultural systems as models of pristine harmony, but there is considerable reason to believe that they did work reasonably well when compared with much that has occurred since the colonial era. Since population densities were low, there was little need for intensive cultivation and, therefore, little hardship involved in practising agricultural methods which required farm areas to be left fallow for long periods. Perhaps more importantly, low population pressure meant that very few communities suffered from land scarcity; virtually all members of society could be assured of access to some arable land.

Since land was relatively abundant, traditional methods of agriculture were not accompanied by the extreme socio-economic inequalities that have become commonplace today. Class formation, where it did occur, was of limited proportions, and there were few glaring divisions between landless and landed populations. This probably meant that when calamities of deprivation did occur, they tended to be the result of natural disasters, such as drought or flood, rather than maldistribution in the economic system. Under these conditions, deprivation would have been more equally shared among all members of society. To the extent that the extensive starvation which accompanies contemporary food shortages is a result of social structures characterised by wide gaps between wealth and poverty, this particular aspect of food deficit was, in all likelihood, far less common then than now.[23]

European rule contributed to the decay of Africa's agricultural resources in at least two distinct ways. One was through the imposition of export requirements which involved the introduction of crops and methods of cultivation that were not well suited to the African soil base. Cotton, groundnuts, and tobacco have proved particularly destructive. Their introduction necessitated clearing large areas of the original cover of forest and brush, thereby depriving the soil of its principal source of organic replenishment. These three crops are also especially damaging in that they tend to absorb unusually large quantities of nutrients from the top-soil, thereby contributing to a particularly rapid decline in arability. Moreover, unlike the original cover of forest, grasses, and scrub, these crops are harvested annually, a practice that leaves the ground bare between growing seasons. Stripped of its cover, the top-soil is especially susceptible to erosion and laterisation. The cumulative result has been to launch an apparently irreversible cycle of deterioration, and to convert large areas of Africa from a humanly suitable milieu to desert or semi-desert in less than a century's time.

The second effect of European rule was more indirect and had to do with rapid population growth. The introduction of bio-scientific medicine eventually led to lower death rates and increasing numbers of people. By the early decades of this century, there were simply more people in the rural areas of much of Africa than could be supported by traditional methods of shifting cultivation which required that large amounts of land be left unutilised at any given time. Land areas which had been allowed to regenerate during periods of extended fallow, now had to be cultivated annually with all-too-apparent results in terms of declining soil fertility. Levels of production that could formerly be sustained without the need for exogenous supports, now required greater and greater amounts of fertilisers and other purchased inputs.

This has had the effect of tying Africa's rural food producers ever more closely to the urban cash economy, a dependence which can seriously exacerbate the problem of food scarcity in the countryside.

The growth of population has also meant greatly increased pressure on Africa's remaining forest reserves. Vast areas have been cleared to make way for agricultural production, a process which has sometimes occurred even where soil fertility and other determinants of production are so favourable that only the most marginal sort of agriculture can be sustained. Forested areas are also denuded as a result of the insatiable demand for charcoal, still the continent's most common cooking fuel and, increasingly, an important source of export earnings for certain countries. The cumulative result of all these pressures is that the forest canopy which was once a major part of the African geographical environment, an invaluable ecological resource, may well have been irretrievably lost.

The portentous implication of environmental deterioration in Africa is that it rules out a return to earlier systems of agricultural production as a solution to the on-going crisis of food shortages. Not only would these systems be completely incapable of sustaining today's levels of population, but they were, in any case, dependent upon ecological sources of soil replenishment which are no longer part of the natural environment. An agricultural restoration, if it is to occur, will necessarily depend upon artificial methods of providing humus and nutrients to the soil. But the lessons which can be drawn from environmental deterioration are, nevertheless, too important to be overlooked. For even the most agro-scientific approaches to agricultural recovery are unlikely to remedy the crisis of food shortages in the absence of an ecologically conscious response to economic activities which continue to damage the environmental milieu. Under present conditions, it is not at all difficult to envision a future in which agro-scientific programmes to rebuild production are dwarfed by the magnitude of the agricultural consequences of environmental damage. Already heavily dependent upon food imports from abroad, Africa conveys an unmistakable impression of a continent moving even further in that direction.

FOOD AID

The most common response to the problem of food deficits in Africa has been to import what is most urgently needed from abroad, frequently in the form of food aid. As an immediate remedy for critical emergencies, this 'solution' cannot be faulted. Even the most vocal critics of corruption, waste, and inefficiency in food-aid programmes acknowledge that they save lives. If starvation is the result of short-term causes, such as drought, war, or blight, food aid can provide a breathing space until more basic remedies can be introduced, or until natural recovery occurs—as a result, this type of assistance has been virtually immune to fundamental criticism. Of course, some reforms have been suggested in order to improve the delivery of food to the truly needy through the elimination of programmatic abuses.[24] This approach can be of great value, especially when the budgets for such relief work are under political attack in donor countries. But it should not be allowed to obscure the more basic question; namely, do food-aid programmes contribute to the persistence, or even worsening, of the very problems they are intended to alleviate?

The issue is enormously complex. For food assistance can clearly be of some concrete benefit in less-developed countries.[25] It can be targeted specifically towards the most deprived and disenfranchised groups within a society, and can thus provide a modest safety net for the poorest of the poor, a social stratum that has proved maddeningly elusive to a host of other governmental and international development agencies. Food-aid programmes which provide essential nutrition for such vulnerable groups as refugees, women, and children have an especially compelling moral claim to continued support. Moreover, they can provide tangible resources for other, more all-inclusive development projects. Food aid may be employed, for example, to encourage price stabilisation and grain storage, development tasks that are of great importance in rural areas which are affected by cyclical instability in the availability of food supplies. Food aid has sometimes been linked effectively to the improvement of rural infrastructures through 'food for work' projects which employ food recipients as labourers for the construction of roads, irrigation systems, and reclaimed land. And, in a context where foreign assistance is declining in real terms, food aid can free scarce governmental resources for other social services.

None the less, serious questions about the ultimate impact of food aid remain. As the Presidential Commission on World Hunger noted in its final report:

> At best, there is an inherent contradiction between food which increases the dependency of recipients upon donors, and measures to increase purchasing power and basic food production within developing countries themselves. . . . In some cases, food aid undermines the efforts of recipient nations to develop a more self-reliant base of their own. Food aid has also enabled some recipient governments to postpone essential agricultural reforms, to give low priority to agricultural investment, and to maintain a pricing system which gives farmers inadequate incentives to increase local production required for greater self-reliance in basic foodstuffs.[26]

Comments such as these have helped dispel the mystique of food aid, and have paved the way for searching criticisms about its nature and impact, as well as the policy motivations of the donors. The 'Food for Peace' programme of the United States, PL 480, has been the subject of intense scrutiny since it is by far the largest single food-aid scheme in the developing world and, as such, has provided a model for many others. Numerous critics have pointed out, for example, that this programme had its origins in domestic pressures within America, especially the need to solve the problem of growing domestic food surpluses by creating foreign markets for grains. Others have singled out the tendency for food aid to be awarded on the basis of political and military criteria, rather than the needs of the people themselves.[27]

Food aid has also lent itself to serious abuse within the recipient countries.[28] It has provided a source of enrichment for corrupt élites who somehow manage to spirit away an appalling amount of the food intended for the hungry, and who cheat relief organisations by charging exorbitant sums for transportation and storage. Politicians have also taken advantage of assistance programmes by demanding bribes to allow relief organisations to operate, by using food relief as a source of patronage, and by threatening to withhold food relief from potentially disaffected groups. Moreover, food-for-work projects are clearly of much greater benefit to well-to-do landowners—whose holdings increase substantially in value from infrastructural improvements—than to landless and destitute families. Indeed, food-relief programmes have been the subject to such a wide variety of forms of corruption that they have helped to widen the gap between rich and poor in virtually every country in which they operate.

The most serious criticisms of food assistance, however, focus on its tendency to act as a long-term disincentive for local agricultural production.[29] Most of what is imported is distributed through the national marketing network, and so often competes directly with locally produced foodstuffs. As a result, in country after country, the availability of concessionally priced food from abroad has fundamentally undermined the price structure of locally produced food items, and has contributed to the further decline of agricultural economies already buffeted by drought, input shortages, and political disruptions. The aid administrators have been chronically unable to remedy this problem. Motivated by the need to make food available as quickly as possible to needy persons, often under extremely difficult conditions, they have not had the opportunity or the authority to introduce methods of distribution that would conserve the economic basis of local agriculture. Even such targeted programmes as food-for-work and maternal-child care are now generally acknowledged to have a measurable disincentive effect on local agricultural production.

As a result, some peasant farmers have actually been driven off the land by this kind of external assistance. Marginal agriculturalists who might otherwise have been able to survive economically have, on occasion, been unable to compete in the market-place with heavily subsidised wheat or rice. Driven from their plots by cheap foreign grains, as well as by the conditions which induced the initial shortages, such farmers have frequently been compelled to join the ranks of those who depend for their survival upon food assistance.

In this way, food aid can set up a permanent cycle of deterioration. It can increase the number of dependent persons by diminishing the market for locally produced goods; it can result in the establishment of a price structure which makes it difficult, if not impossible, for peasant producers to recover economically; and it can compete directly against the donor capital that is needed to improve transportation and storage. These tendencies may help explain why so many food-assistance programmes which were initially intended only to provide short-term emergency relief have become more or less indelible features of the rural economic landscape.

An equally serious long-term issue is the destruction of initiative at the local level. Peasants who are economically exploited by corrupt food-aid administrators, or who are victimised when assistance programmes are manipulated for political purposes, are hardly likely to emerge as eager participants when called upon to involve themselves in development projects for economic reconstruction. Food aid has also been observed to generate a mentality of dependence. A report on an agro-forestry project in Upper Volta graphically depicts this problem:

> So extensive has this food aid mentality permeated the way of life, that rather than act as an incentive to community improvement, food aid has the opposite effect. It is an assurance that despite bad labor practices that lead to eroded and exhausted soil and marginal harvests, there will be food to eat, there will be food aid. Food aid is an argument *against* the idea that land reclamation and sound agricultural practices are necessary.[30]

It is nearly impossible to discredit the arguments of those who feel that food aid is an unfortunate part of an international system of dependence that casts Africa in the role of a continent of begging bowls.

In the final analysis, food aid is not a solution for human misery and malnutrition in Africa. It is essentially a dead-end approach, an entry into a morass of complexities from which there is no apparent exit. Rather than being easily administered—enjoying local political support and targeted towards specific recipient populations—food-aid programmes have become bureaucratic and political nightmares for both planners and project administrators. The ease with which such assistance can be dissipated or spoiled makes for stresses and strains in the body politic that are enduring and difficult to locate—when someone cares to try. And far from alleviating the misery of hunger the net result may be to contribute to its continuation. As a short-term necessity in situations of dire emergency, food aid may well be the only answer; as a strategy for agricultural development it is no solution at all.

The ultimate irony of food-assistance programmes, however, may well lie in the fact that there are often adequate local foodstuffs available in other districts of the recipient country. These are typically prevented from reaching needy areas by a lack of administrative capacity, and by inadequacies in infrastructure and marketing mechanisms. If the resources and human energies allotted to these programmes could be channelled towards improving the country's own systems of economic management, transportation, storage, and distribution, this would undoubtedly do more to alleviate hunger on a long-term basis than any quantity of external food assistance.

CONCLUSION

It is clear that no single theoretical perspective adequately explains the decline of food production in Africa, and that there is no single policy which is likely to resolve it. The morass of historical, environmental, and economic factors is so complex as to render the efficacy of any solution problematic. Underdevelopment theory, for example, is helpful in analysing the impact of colonialism and the international economic system on Africa, but it falls far short of suggesting workable solutions. The alternatives it presents presuppose massive and radical changes not only in Africa, but in the West as well. Since theorists of underdevelopment tend to believe that the impoverishment of the less-developed world will continue so long as capitalism determines the international market behavior of western nations, they tend to remain aloof from discussions of specific projects and policy remedies. For all of its complex historical analysis, then, the theory of underdevelopment in its raw form reduces to an almost absurdly simple policy prescription: end global capitalism.

Much the same can be said of the doctrine of comparative advantage. Since those who hold this position tend to explain any shortages—including food deficits—in terms of governmental interference with the operation of free-market forces, the solution they prescribe tends towards an equally simple, and equally unworkable, remedy: eliminate state-imposed barriers to the operation of the market. Theorists of both underdevelopment and comparative advantage share a disquieting trait in common: they tend to treat evidence of the failure of their strategy as proof of the need for ever greater applications. Thus, in the former, the remedy for failure of socialism becomes—apply more socialism. Just as, in the latter, the solution for the failure of free-market approaches becomes—free the market further.

Both of these approaches tend to be equally insensitive to Africa's immense environmental problems. Workable strategies of agricultural development should take into account the highly delicate and already badly disrupted state of the ecological basis of African agriculture. This would entail working out an extremely difficult balance between the retention of those traditional agricultural systems which can be defended on environmental grounds, and the introduction of modern agricultural practices which would be more responsive to the growing food requirements of rapidly increasing populations. On a continent where about one-half of the land can be classified as arid or semi-arid, the introduction of annual crops can be disastrous. Yet socialist and free-market oriented agricultural planners alike all too often see the remedy for Africa's food deficits in terms of the creation of large-scale, capital-intensive farms.

Additionally, western aid programmes have often run counter to the needs of African peasants, and have thus inhibited rather than encouraged greater local food production. Government-to-government assistance runs a very great risk of supporting corrupt and venal régimes and, to this degree, can be held partly accountable for the growing mood of cynicism and disillusionment with African leaders. This mood had been well expressed by the Ghanaian novelist Ayi Kwei Armah:

> How long will Africa be cursed with its leaders? There were men dying
> from the loss of hope, and others were finding gaudy ways to enjoy power
> they did not have. We were ready here for big and beautiful things, but
> what we had was our own black men hugging new paunches scrambling
> to ask the white man to welcome them onto our backs. These men who
> were to lead us out of our despair, they came like men already grown fat
> and cynical with the eating of centuries of power they had never struggled
> for, old before they had ever been born into power, and ready only for
> the grave.[31]

Yet so long as external assistance is given on a government-to-government basis, it is almost impossible to conceive of an aid project which would by-pass an entrenched régime to deal with the agricultural needs of food producers at the local level.

. . . . . .

This article has examined four approaches to Africa's food deficits. Combining their positive features we would suggest a series of critically important reforms which can best be understood as broad guidelines for future agricultural development in Africa. These might include:

(1) Genuine empowerment of the peasantry in order to enable rural
    producers to affect the political process, the character of the
    marketplace, and the administration and implementation of
    foreign aid. This would be essential in preventing their
    exploitation by political élites, and in reversing national policies
    which subordinate peasant needs to the interests of the urban
    privileged. It could be facilitated by links with trade unions and
    rural-based co-operatives. One of the most important problems
    confronting peasant movements in Africa is to overcome
    rural-urban conflicts over food policies. The realisation of power
    by the peasantry would assist in the creation of effective

channels of communication with government agencies, and with organisations representing the interests of urban-based social classes.

(2) Land-tenure policies which prevent 'the sharks eating the fishes' and which, thereby, preserve the positive features of small-scale peasant agriculture. The shortcomings of both socialist and free-market strategies are instructive on this point. The efforts of governments to create collective agriculture have not only led to the coercion and brutalisation of the peasantry, but to a sharp downward spiral in agricultural production. Large-scale agricultural projects promoted by capitalist interests have also done more harm than good by creating massive numbers of landless and unemployed persons. Small-holder schemes sustained, in part, by governmental limitations on land acquisition and support for agricultural improvements, show great promise in avoiding both these pitfalls.

(3) Freer access to commodity markets through by-passing the large firms which presently dominate the international marketplace in Africa's major export products. Without this major external change, internal reforms that lead to greater security of land tenure and increased peasant participation will lose much of their long-term effectiveness. The theory of comparative advantage has much positive merit for developing countries in Africa, but even a carefully planned emphasis on export crops will continue to be disastrous unless there are real prospects of improved price levels for these products. The paramount objective of this reform would be to avoid the extremes of autarky and dependence in international markets, and to generate new and more equitable modalities for trade, transfer of technology, and investment.

(4) Agricultural policies that are more fully influenced by sensitivity to environmental constraints. Far too much of the planning for African agriculture has separated environmental from developmental issues. The result has been agricultural policies which devastate the land and drastically diminish its value as an economic resource for future generations. The measurements of economic output should be revised to incorporate such criteria as long-term sustainability. This might be expected to lead to a fundamental reappraisal of the value of such crops as groundnuts, cotton, and tobacco, as well as agricultural projects which include a much greater emphasis on reforestation.

Reordering paradigms and practices will be a formidable task. Yet the compelling reality of Africa's increasing food deficits requires nothing less than fundamental changes in these areas. To the extent that previous policies have failed to alleviate the severe shortages, a continuation of existing practices seems an exercise in futility. Models of agricultural reform which do not take these guidelines into account offer only the prospect of an ever deepening crisis.

NOTES

1. *Times* (Los Angeles), 9 March 1981.
2. United States Department of Agriculture, *Food Problems and Prospects in Sub-Saharan Africa: the decade of the 1980's* (Washington, D.C., 1981) pp. 1–8.
3. See, for example, Nicole Ball, *World Hunger: a guide to the economic and political dimensions* (Santa Barbara and Oxford, 1981).
4. E.g. Kenneth Anthony et al., *Agricultural Change in Tropical Africa* (Ithaca, 1979), and 'The Roots of Famine', in *Review of African Political Economy* (London), 15–16, 1979, pp. 1–74; Raymond Hopkins and Donald Puchala (eds.), *The Global Political Economy of Food* (Madison, 1978); Radha Sinha, *Food and Poverty: the political economy of confrontation* (London, 1976); Lester R. Brown, with Erik P. Eckholm, *By Bread Alone* (New York, 1974); and Susan George, *How the Other Half Dies: the real reasons for world hunger* (Montclair, 1977).
5. Cf. Paul Baran, *Political Economy of Growth* (New York, 1957); Samir Amin, *Unequal Development* (New York, 1976); Immanuel Wallerstein, *The Modern World System: capitalist agriculture and the origins of the European world economy in the sixteenth century* (New York, 1974); Walter Rodney, *How Europe Underdeveloped Africa* (Dar es Salaam, 1972); Argihiri Emmanuel, *Unequal Exchange* (New York, 1972); and André Gunder Frank, *Dependent Accumulation and Underdevelopment* (London, 1978).
6. Nicola Swainson, *The Development of Corporate Capitalism in Kenya, 1918–1977* (London and Berkeley, 1980); Richard L. Sklar, 'The Nature of Class Domination in Africa', in *The Journal of Modern African Studies* (Cambridge), 17, 4, December 1979, pp. 531–52, and 'Postimperialism: a class analysis of multinational corporate expansion', in *Comparative Politics* (New York), October 1976, pp. 15–92.
7. Goran Hyden, *Beyond Ujamaa in Tanzania: underdevelopment and an uncaptured peasantry* (London and Berkeley, 1980).
8. René Dumont, *Socialism and Development* (New York, 1973), especially chs. 2 and 4.
9. *Works and Correspondence of David Ricardo,* edited by Pierro Sraffa, Vol. 1 (Cambridge, 1962), 'On the Principles of Political Economy and Taxation', p. 132.
10. Ibid., p. 135.
11. We are indebted to Rhys Payne, 'Economic Development and the Principle of Comparative Advantage', University of California, Los Angeles, 1980, for a sweeping survey of the relevant theories.
12. William O. Jones, *Marketing Staple Food Crops in Tropical Africa* (Ithaca, 1972), p. 233.
13. Hollis Chenery, *Structural Change and Development Policy* (Oxford, 1979).
14. Ibid., p. 275.
15. Ibid.
16. Barbara Dinham and Colin Hines, *Agribusiness in Africa* (London, 1982).
17. Ibid.

18. We are indebted to the helpful comments of Dean Freudenberger, Jerry Moles and Antony Orme in the preparation of this section.

19. Antoon de Vos, *Africa, the Devastated Continent?* (The Hague, 1975); Paul Richards (ed.), *African Environment: perspectives and prospects* (London, 1975); and Michel Frederic Thomas and G. W. Whittington (eds.), *Environment and Land Use in Africa* (London, 1969).

20. De Vos, op. cit., p. 20.

21. Howard Schissel, 'Forest Cover Blown', in *The Guardian* (London), 29 April 1981.

22. William Allan, *The African Husbandman* (Edinburgh, 1965), and A. T. Grove and F.M. G. Klein, *Rural Africa* (Cambridge, 1979).

23. Jean Suret-Canale, *French Colonialism in West Africa* (New York edn., 1971); Richard W. Franke and Barbara H. Chasin, *Seeds of Famine: ecological destruction and the development dilemma in the West African Sahel* (Montclair, 1980); Robin Parsons and Neil Palmer (eds.), *Roots of Rural Poverty in Central and Southern Africa* (Berkeley, 1977); and Colin Bundy, *The Rise and Fall of the South African Peasantry* (London, 1979).

24. Report of the Presidential Commission on World Hunger, *Overcoming World Hunger: the challenge ahead* (Washington, D.C., 1980); Mark Schomer, 'Can Food Aid and Development Aid Promote Self-Reliance?', Bread for the World Background Paper No. 28, 1978; Brown, op. cit.; and Hopkins and Puchala (eds.), op cit.

25. Christopher Stevens, *Food Aid and the Developing World: four African case studies* (London, 1979), and S. J. Maxwell and H. W. Singer, 'Food Aid to Developing Countries: a survey', in *World Development* (Oxford), 1979, pp. 225–47.

26. Presidential Commission on World Hunger, op. cit. p. 140.

27. Frances Moore Lappe, Joseph Collins, and David Kinley, *Aid as Obstacle* (San Francisco, 1980); Denis Goulet and Michael Hudson, *Myth of Aid* (New York, 1971); Jack Nelson, *Hunger for Justice* (1980); and George, op. cit.

28. Betsy Hartmann and James Boyce, *Needless Hunger: voices from a Bangladesh village* (San Francisco, 1979); Barry Newman, 'Graft and Inefficiency in Bangladesh Subvert Food-for-Work Program', in *Wall Street Journal* (New York), 20 April 1981; and Geoffrey Lean, 'Scandal of UN's Food Aid in Africa', in *The Observer* (London), 17 June 1979.

29. Lean, op. cit.; Alan Riding, 'US Food Aid Seen Hurting Guatemala', in *New York Times,* 6 November 1977; and Tony Jackson, 'Statement Before the Committee on Development and Cooperation of the European Parliament', Brussels, 1 April 1980.

30. October 1980 description of the Church-funded Agro/Forestry Project in Ouahigouya, Upper Volta, which has been operational since 1979.

31. Ayi Kwei Armah, *The Beautyful Ones Are Not Yet Born* (New York edn. 1969), p. 79.

16

Growth and Impoverishment in the Rural Areas of Asia

Keith Griffin with the assistance of Ajit Kumar Ghose

The non-socialist countries of South, Southeast and East Asia have experienced rapid growth for about a quarter-century. Indeed the sustained growth of domestic product in Asia has been faster than at any other time in the recorded history of the region. Furthermore, the rates of growth have exceeded, sometimes by large margins, the rates of growth experienced by the now industrialized countries during the period of their accelerated expansion approximately a century ago.[1] Of course when one examines individual countries it readily becomes apparent that experience has varied widely.

At one extreme are Bangladesh and Nepal where growth rates have been well below those of the other countries of the region: in Bangladesh during 1960 to 1973 the rate of growth was only 2.0% per annum and in Nepal during the period 1950–1973 it was 2.3%. At the other extreme are two countries, Taiwan and South Korea, which enjoyed spectacular rates of growth from 1950 to 1973 of 9.3 and 7.7% per annum, respectively. Even India, widely believed to have experienced persistent stagnation, grew nearly 4% a year during the period under review. All the other Asian countries grew faster than this, often considerably faster.

Population growth also was rapid, however. Even so, only in Bangladesh did output per head fail to rise: in the 13 years after 1960 GDP *per capita* in Bangladesh declined 0.7% a year. Elsewhere, during 1950 to 1973 it rose, sometimes dramatically as in Taiwan and South Korea, where it increased 6.0 and 5.1% a year, respectively, and sometimes moderately, as in Nepal, Sri Lanka and India, where it increased 0.6, 1.7 and 1.8% a year, respectively. The growth rate of *per capita* output was such that average incomes would double in 32 years in Indonesia, in 25 years in the Philippines and in about 20 years

Reprinted with permission from *World Development*, Vol. 7, No. 4/5. Copyright 1979, Pergamon Press, Ltd.

in Thailand. The achievements of the last two or three decades in Asia clearly are remarkable, particularly when set against the pessimism of the years immediately after the end of the Second World War.

Despite these impressive aggregate growth performances, development has been highly uneven. Some sectors, regions and classes have benefited considerably more than others and a vocabulary has been invented which attempts to describe both those who gain and those who lose from the process of uneven development as well as the remedies for it. Thus for example the gainers sometimes are described as the 'lower-middle classes'[2] or the 'urban class'[3] while the losers are the *lumpen proletariat* or those who obtain a livelihood in the 'informal sector'.[4] The remedy, depending on the writer, consists of 'integrated development', or a 'basic needs' strategy or simply an 'alternative development'.[5]

One manifestation of uneven development, about which there seems to be a consensus, is the crisis of poverty in the rural areas of Asia. That a crisis exists no longer is widely disputed. What is in dispute is the nature of the crisis.

1. ALTERNATIVE VIEWS OF THE RURAL CRISIS

At least five views or explanations of the crisis have been put forward. To some extent these different views overlap and therefore are complementary, but the emphasis placed on each varies considerably and these differences in emphasis are associated with substantial differences in the perception of the nature of the fundamental problem.

TABLE 1   **Percentage Annual Growth Rates of GDP and GDP per Capita, 1950–73**

	GDP	GDP PER CAPITA
Bangladesh	2.0	−0.7
Burma	4.7	2.7
India	3.9	1.8
Indonesia	4.4	2.2
Malaysia	5.1	2.1
Nepal	2.3	0.6
Pakistan	6.0	2.8
Philippines	5.9	2.8
South Korea	7.7	5.1
Sri Lanka	4.1	1.7
Taiwan	9.3	6.0
Thailand	6.7	3.5

NOTE: In the cases of Bangladesh and Pakistan the data refer to the period 1960–73.

SOURCE: IBRD, *World Tables* 1976 (Washington: 1976).

(a) Random Shocks

First, there is the view that a major problem in the rural areas, perhaps *the* major problem, arises from cyclical instability of food supplies. Those who hold this view are less concerned about the average level of production than about fluctuations around the average. That is, they are concerned primarily with the question of 'food security'. The World Food Council, for example, has given high priority to creating internationally controlled stocks of food for use in emergencies, particularly wheat, while the United Nations Disaster Relief Office has been created to provide assistance during such emergencies.

Fortunately, emergencies have been absent from Asia for the last three years. Three successive good harvests have enabled countries to rebuild their domestic stocks of grains and, in fact, food stocks in India are the largest they have ever been, viz., 18 million tons in January 1978. There is no room for complacency, however. In the early years of the present decade Asia was afflicted by a series of natural disasters, e.g., severe damage from typhoons in the Philippines, serious drought in Maharashtra and Bihar and massive floods in Andra Pradesh and Bangladesh. The 1974 floods in Bangladesh, for instance, covered about 40% of the country's land, i.e. 22,042 square miles. The economic losses were estimated by the Planning Commission to be $580 million, of which a fall in agricultural output accounted for $300 million and damage to rural infrastructure another $80 million. The immediate consequence of the disaster was a need to spend $132 million on imported grain and $199 million on rehabilitation.[6] Disasters on this scale clearly are unusual, but random shocks of this type can be expected to occur at irregular intervals.

The hardship arising from a given decline in production evidently is smaller the more average levels of output exceed nutritional requirements and the more equal is the distribution of income. The great problem in Asia is that some of the countries subject to the greatest instability of food supplies, Sri Lanka, Indonesia and Bangladesh, also have a low *per capita* availability of food. As a result, these Asian countries are doubly afflicted, by a low average level of production and by relatively high variation around the average.

Table 2 contains a measure of instability of food supplies (or, strictly speaking, cereal supplies) for our 12 countries. In constructing this indicator we first estimated the trend rate of growth of cereal production plus imports minus exports, i.e. of the total amount of cereals potentially available for domestic consumption.[7] Next we calculated the annual percentage deviation of cereal availabilities from the trend. Finally, we calculated the average of the absolute value of these annual percentage deviations. This last figure is our indicator of instability. The period covered is 1961 to 1976, except in the case of Taiwan where it is 1961 to 1970 because of the limited availability of data.

TABLE 2   Foodgrain Instability in Asia (Average Percentage Deviation From Trend)

Bangladesh	6.5
Burma	4.9
India	4.6
Indonesia	7.6
Malaysia	4.6
Nepal	4.1
Pakistan	5.6
Philippines	3.1
South Korea	4.9
Sri Lanka	8.7
Taiwan	4.7
Thailand	8.6

It can be seen from the table that instability is highest in Sri Lanka and Thailand and lowest in the Philippines and Nepal. In no country is average instability as high as 9% and in over half the countries it is less that 5%. These data suggest that instability as such is relatively modest and is unlikely to be the sole cause of the agrarian crisis. Indeed our indicator probably exaggerates the degree of instability of foodgrain consumption because it does not take into account changes in domestic stocks. These stocks, in most instances, probably move in a contra-cyclical direction and thereby help to offset fluctuations in production and foreign commerce.

Random shocks and unfavourable episodic phenomena are more likely to be significant for particular regions of a nation than for the nation as a whole. This does not imply that the shocks are not serious for the people affected, but it does imply that only rarely will the entire population of a country be affected. If a large part of South and Southeast Asia is experiencing a crisis, this must be due to secular rather than random occurrences.

(b) High Population Densities and Growth Rates

A second explanation for the crisis in the rural areas of Asia is that demographic phenomena constitute a major obstacle to the reduction of poverty in the countryside. In fact this probably is the most popular of the explanations concerned with trends rather than fluctuations in Asian agriculture. There are, however, two separate hypotheses. The first is that high population densities are associated with low rates of growth of agricultural output and hence with low rates of growth of income in rural areas. The second hypothesis focuses not on population densities but on the rate of growth of population, postulating an inverse association between the rate of demographic increase and the rate of growth of agricultural production.

These hypotheses can readily be tested and the data necessary to do so have been assembled in Table 3. Two alternative measures of density have been provided. Column 1 contains data on population density per square kilometre in 1960 (D) for all 12 of our countries while column 2 contains data on population density per square kilometre of agricultural land in 1970 (Dag) for the 11 countries for which data are available. The rate of growth of population (P) is reported in column 3. Two measures of agricultural growth rates are provided: the rate of growth of gross agricultural production (G) in column 4 and the rate of growth of agricultural production *per capita* (Gpc) in column 5.

In an attempt to discover whether high population densities are an obstacle to agricultural growth six regression equations were estimated. The results were as follows:

	VARIABLES	COEFFICIENT OF CORRELATION
(1)	G and D	-0.1025
(2)	G and D,	
	excluding Bangladesh	0.2196
(3)	Gpc and D	-0.2318
(4)	Gpc and D,	
	excluding Bangladesh	0.2133
(5)	G and Dag	0.3582
(6)	Gpc and Dag	0.3407

First, there was a negative correlation between population density per square kilometre (D) and both measures of agricultural growth (G and Gpc) when all 12 countries were included. [See equations (1) and (3).] Second, the inverse correlation disappeared when Bangladesh was dropped from the sample. [See equations (2) and (4).] That is, the negative association is attributable entirely to one country with an exceptionally high population density and exceptionally low rates of growth of agricultural output and agricultural output per head. Third, the correlation between population density per square kilometre of agricultural land (Dag) and both measures of agricultural growth is positive for the 11 countries for which data are available. [See equations (5) and (6).] Note, however, that this correlation does not include Bangladesh. Fourth, none of the coefficients of correlation are statistically significant. The conclusion of this analysis, therefore, is that there is no evidence of a strong direct negative effect of population density on the growth performance of the agricultural sector. If high densities inhibit growth, the retarding effects must be both too weak and too subtle to be detected by a simple correlation analysis.

A similar analysis was conducted in an attempt to discover whether a rapid rate of growth of population is an obstacle to agricultural growth. The results of the four regression equations were as follows:

	VARIABLES	COEFFICIENT OF CORRELATION
(7)	G and P	0.6013
(8)	G and P, excluding Bangladesh	0.7427
(9)	Gpc and P	0.2031
(10)	Gpc and P, excluding Bangladesh	0.3698

First, there is a positive association between the rate of growth of agricultural output (G) and the rate of growth of population (P), whether or not Bangladesh is included in the sample. [See equations (7) and (8).] That is, the faster does the population increase, and hence presumably the labour force, the faster does agricultural production expand. Moreover, second, these coefficients are statistically significant and thus are unlikely to have arisen by chance. Third, there also is a positive association between the rate of growth of agricultural output per head (Gpc) and population growth, whether or not Bangladesh is included. [See equations (9) and (10).] Fourth, the last two coefficients, however, are not statistically significant. The conclusion seems to be, therefore, that there is no direct connection between population growth and the growth of *per capita* agricultural output but there may be a positive connection between population growth and the rate of growth of gross agricultural output. This is more or less what one would expect if the productivity of labour on the margin is positive.

Our results provide no support to those who believe that demographic phenomena are at the heart of the rural crisis. Equally, when birth rates begin to fall, as they now appear to be in several Asian countries including India, our results would not lead one to expect that this would make a dramatic difference. The origins of the crisis in rural Asia are to be found not in demography but more likely in the structure of the economy.

(c) Stagnation of Agricultural Production

Not so many years ago it was widely believed that agricultural production in Asia was undergoing a 'green revolution' as a result of the introduction of higher yielding varieties of rice and wheat. Today this optimism has all but vanished and been replaced by the view that production has been stagnant. Indeed this stagnation is the third explanation for the agrarian crisis and at least implicitly provides the rationale for the emphasis placed on the need to accelerate agricultural growth by so many international agencies, including

TABLE 3   Demographic Characteristics and Agricultural Growth

	(1) POPULATION DENSITY PER SQ. KM., 1960 (D)	(2) POPULATION DENSITY PER SQ. KM. OF AGRICULTURAL LAND, 1970 (DAG)	(3) PERCENTAGE ANNUAL RATE OF GROWTH OF POPULATION, 1950–73 (P)	(4) PERCENTAGE ANNUAL RATE OF GROWTH OF AGRICULTURAL OUTPUT, 1950–73 (G)	(5) PERCENTAGE ANNUAL RATE OF GROWTH OF AGRICULTURAL OUTPUT PER CAPITA, 1950–73 (GPC)
Bangladesh	339	n.a.	2.8*	1.7*	−1.1*
Burma	30	143	2.0	2.4	0.4
India	136	301	2.0	2.8	0.8
Indonesia	62	426	2.1	3.2	1.1
Malaysia	24	304	2.9	4.0	1.1
Nepal	65	276	1.8*	1.4†	−0.4†
Pakistan	57	258	3.2*	4.8*	1.6*
Philippines	92	369	3.0	3.4	0.4
South Korea	250	1337	2.4	4.7	2.3
Sri Lanka	151	520	2.5	2.3	−0.2
Taiwan	295	1610	3.1	3.9	0.8
Thailand	50	234	3.0	4.3	1.3

NOTES: *1960–73
†1961–73

SOURCE: IBRD, *World Tables 1976* (Washington: 1976) and Government of Pakistan, *Statistical Pocket Book of Pakistan 1971* (Karachi: 1971), for population density in Bangladesh.

the Food and Agriculture Organization of the United Nations, the International Fund for Agricultural Development and the International Food Policy Research Institute.

It should be said right away that the new view is closer to the truth than the old. Like every generalization, however, the new view simplifies reality and in this case the simplification often is misleading. More important, the policy inference drawn by the stagnationists, viz. accelerate production by all available means, is simple-minded and possibly harmful.

As a glance at the last column in Table 3 will show, in only 3 of our 12 countries has there been a negative trend rate of growth of agricultural output per head. Moreover, 2 of these countries, Nepal and Sri Lanka, are rather small—in our sample only Malaysia is smaller—and their performance would have little influence on an all-Asia average. The third country, Bangladesh, is large and has been declining at a rapid rate. The point to note in this case, however, is that aggregate *per capita* income has been declining in Bangladesh, not just agricultural production per head. That is, the stagnation in agriculture is part of a process of overall stagnation and decline. Despite these qualifications about the significance of the experience of Nepal, Sri Lanka and Bangladesh for the rest of Asia, there is no doubt that in the 3 countries concerned the stagnation of agricultural production is a major cause of the agrarian crisis.

In the other 9 countries, however, agricultural output per head has been rising since 1950. In Burma and the Philippines the rate of growth has been slow, only 0.4% per head per year, but elsewhere it has been at least twice as rapid: 0.8% in India and Taiwan, 1.1% in Indonesia and Malaysia and as much as 2.3% in South Korea. In Asia as a whole, during the period 1950–73, the annual rate of growth of agricultural production per head was between 1.5% in South Asia and 2.0% in East Asia.

Growth rates such as these evidently do not describe a situation of stagnation. Furthermore, given these figures it is hard to imagine that the agrarian crisis in Asia could have been caused by an insufficiently rapid increase in agricultural output. On the contrary, in several respects the pace of expansion has been surprisingly fast. One must dig deeper to find the roots of the problem.

(d) Increasing Relative Inequality

It seems possible, fourth, that the agrarian crisis has little to do with growth rates, either national or sectoral, but instead is primarily a distributive crisis. That is, growing inequality in the distribution of income may be the major problem. Certainly there is a great deal of evidence, fragmentary and of uncertain reliability though it may be, that inequality has been rising in most parts of Asia.

Some authors emphasize the disparities between urban and rural incomes and argue that these disparities have tended to increase over time.[8]

There is no doubt that average incomes in urban areas are higher, often substantially higher, than in the countryside. In the Philippines, Thailand, Malaysia, India, Bangladesh and Sri Lanka (including the plantation sector) average incomes in rural areas are a half or less of those in urban areas; in Indonesia and Pakistan rural incomes are about a third lower than urban ones. Only in Taiwan and South Korea are there narrow rural-urban income differentials. Moreover, it is only in these last two countries that one can be certain that the disparity is declining rapidly. Elsewhere it probably is increasing.

Within the countryside there are unmistakable signs of growing regional inequality. For example, in India average incomes have been rising much more rapidly in the wheat growing than in the rice growing regions. Between 1956–57 and 1973–74 the average annual *per capita* rate of growth of agricultural production was 3.16% in Punjab/Haryana (a wheat producing region) and only 0.79% in West Bengal and 1.01% in Tamil Nadu (rice producing regions). In other countries regional disparities arise not from cropping patterns but from differences in technology or geography. It is commonly observed throughout Asia that the irrigated areas have enjoyed a faster rate of growth of incomes than the unirrigated and dry farming regions. Similarly, for obvious reasons, the plains and river valleys have grown more rapidly than the upland regions.

Even within geographically homogeneous regions, however, intra-regional inequalities have tended to increase. It is a remarkable feature of Asian agriculture that the institutions, policies and technologies associated with the so-called green revolution often have had a noticeable class bias which has accentuated the initial inequality in the distribution of income.[9]

An unequal distribution of income in rural areas almost always is associated with an unequal distribution of land. Of the 12 countries in our sample, only 2 have had major redistributive land reforms, namely Taiwan and South Korea. It is significant that these are the only 2 countries in which there is no evidence of an agrarian crisis. In most of the other countries two things seem to be happening simultaneously. First, the proportion of the rural population that is without land is rising rapidly. That is, small farmers and tenants, or the children of such people, are being transformed into a landless labour force. Second, inequality in the distribution of land among those who have access to it is increasing more often than not. Data on the distribution of land are difficult to obtain and often are not very reliable, but for what they are worth the data assembled in Table 4 indicate that the distribution of land as measured by the Gini coefficient has become substantially more unequal in Bangladesh, India, Indonesia, Sri Lanka and Malaysia, has remained largely unchanged in the Philippines and South Korea and has become more equal in Thailand. (In the case of Thailand the reduction in inequality is due to spontaneous colonization and land clearance which led to a rapid expansion of the area under cultivation.)

The available evidence on the distribution of money income in rural areas is broadly consistent with that on land distribution. The figures are

TABLE 4   **The Gini Coefficient of Land Distribution**

COUNTRY	YEAR	COEFFICIENT
Bangladesh	1960	0.47
	1974	0.57
India	1961	0.59
	1970	0.63
Indonesia	1960	0.47
	1974	0.57
Malaysia	1960	0.44
	1971	0.54
Philippines	1960	0.52
	1971	0.51
South Korea	1963	0.30
	1974	0.32
Sri Lanka	1962	0.35
	1970	0.41
Thailand	1963	0.46
	1971	0.41

SOURCES: *Sri Lanka:* E. L. H. Lee, 'Rural Poverty in Sri Lanka, 1963–73' in ILO, *Poverty and Landlessness in Rural Asia* (Geneva: 1977), p. 171, and refers to paddy land only. *All other countries:* T. Onchan and L. Paulino, *Rural Poverty, Income Distribution and Employment in Developing Asian Countries: Review of Past Decade* (Bangkok: Kasetsart University, 1977) as reported in Fu-chen Lo, Kamal Salih and Mike Douglass, *Uneven Development, Rural-Urban Transformation and Regional Development Alternatives in Asia* (Nagoya, Japan: United Nations Centre for Regional Development, 1978).

reproduced in Table 5. It can be seen that of the 8 countries for which we have data, the distribution of money income as measured by the Gini coefficient improved in only two. These are Bangladesh and Pakistan. The period covered by the two observations for Bangladesh, however, is very short and there are numerous indications that since the middle 1960s the distribution of income in rural areas has become far worse.[10] As regards Pakistan, the Gini coefficients suggest that rural inequality declined between 1963 and 1968 and then remained stable. Other evidence, in contrast, shows that inequality (as measured by the proportion of the rural population in poverty) probably increased after 1968 or 1969 and that by 1971–72 inequality had once again become as great as in 1963.[11] Thus one should be unusually cautious when interpreting the data in Table 5 for these two countries. Rural inequality almost certainly has increased in India, Malaysia and the Philippines. It may also have increased in Sri Lanka, Thailand and Indonesia, although comprehensive data on Indonesia are lacking. Trends in income distribution in the rural areas of Burma and Nepal are unknown.

Table 5 indicates that the degree of inequality in South Korea has re-

TABLE 5 The Distribution of Household Income in the Rural Areas of Asia (Gini Coefficients)

Bangladesh	
1963–64	0.35
1966–67	0.33
India	
1953–57	0.31
1960	0.45
1964–65	0.37
1967–68	0.48
Malaysia	
1957–58	0.35
1970	0.46
Pakistan	
1963–64	0.36
1966–67	0.33
1968–69	0.30
1969–70	0.30
1970–71	0.30
Philippines	
1961	0.41
1965	0.43
1971	0.47
South Korea	
1966	0.31
1970	0.31
1971	0.31
Sri Lanka	
1969–70	0.35
1973	0.37
Thailand	
1962–63	0.44
1970	0.45

SOURCE: Shail Jain, *Size Distribution of Income: A Compilation of Data* (Washington: World Bank, 1975).

mained unchanged since 1966. This probably is correct: the reduction in inequality in the South Korean countryside occurred earlier during the period of land reforms following the Korean War.[12] Unfortunately we have no data on the distribution of income in the rural areas of Taiwan. National data, however, show that inequality fell sharply after the land reforms in the early 1950s. Moreover, inequality began to fall again after 1961 and it is probable that the distribution of income in Taiwan (both nationally and in the rural areas) is the most equal of all the countries included in our sample.[13]

It should be noted, however, that the data in Table 5 refer to the distribution of money income and take no account of possible changes in relative prices. Yet we shall see below that in all the Asian countries considered, the relative price of food rose and since the poor spend a higher than average proportion of their income on food, they suffered more than any other group. The implication of this finding is that the data in Table 5 understate the deterioration in the distribution of real income in the 6 countries where inequality is reported to have increased or remained constant and overstate the improvement in income distribution in the two countries where inequality is reported to have diminished.

In conclusion, it seems safe to assume that except in countries which have had a radical redistribution of land, the degree of inequality in rural Asia has not diminished significantly and in most countries has increased.

(e) Absolute Impoverishment

Indeed there is evidence supporting the even stronger proposition that in many areas the absolute standard of living of a significant minority of the rural population has declined. That is, despite the growth of *per capita* income and *per capita* agricultural output large numbers of people in Asia have experienced absolute impoverishment. This, then, is the fifth characteristic of the agrarian crisis.

The evidence is far from conclusive but there are scattered indications that the poorest people often are becoming poorer. In some areas, for example, it is evident that real wage rates for agricultural activities have declined. This is true for such widely scattered places as the Philippines, Indonesia, Bangladesh, the plantation sector of Sri Lanka and parts of India. Again, many knowledgeable observers are convinced that rural unemployment has increased in almost every country in Asia except Taiwan and South Korea, although it is impossible to prove this with quantitative information. More solidly based are data on the rapidly increasing proportion of landlessness and the rapid growth of a rural wage-earning labour force. This is especially noticeable in South Asia. Finally, many studies suggest that the proportion of the rural population below some (rather arbitrary) poverty line has tended to increase.

The claim that poverty has been rising during a period of unusually rapid growth may seem rather paradoxical to many readers. Hence it is worthwhile to review some of the evidence in more detail. We shall concentrate on two studies in which attempts have been made to trace changes in the overall incidence of rural poverty.

2. THE PROBLEM OF INCREASING POVERTY

The first study, sponsored by the International Labour Office, consisted of detailed examinations of trends in rural poverty in 6 countries (Pakistan, Bangladesh, Sri Lanka, Malaysia, Indonesia and the Philippines) and in four states of India (Punjab, Uttar Pradesh, Bihar and Tamil Nadu).[14] Several approaches were adopted in order to detect from the readily available data what has been happening to standards of living in the rural areas. In some cases it was possible to focus on particular classes or homogeneous occupational groups, e.g. plantation workers or landless agricultural labourers. In other cases, estimates were made of changes in the real income of particular fractiles of the income distribution, say, the bottom 20%. In yet other cases a 'poverty line' was constructed and calculations were made of changes in the proportion of the rural population in poverty.

Whatever the approach used, the general conclusion of the study was that there was no evidence that the very poor in Asia were becoming less poor and considerable evidence that in many areas they were becoming further impoverished. This can best be illustrated by considering some of the results obtained when poverty lines were constructed. The device of a poverty line has several disadvantages, but for our purposes it has the great merit of allowing one to see immediately what has been happening to the overall incidence of poverty in rural areas.[15]

Let us take four countries as examples: Malaysia, the Philippines, Pakistan and Bangladesh.

(i)   In the Malaysian case the poverty line was drawn at 97.4 Malaysian dollars per household per month at 1965 prices. In 1957 approximately 40% of the rural population of the country had an income less than this. By 1970 the proportion had risen to 47%, i.e. the incidence of rural poverty increased by about 17% in 13 years.[16]

(ii) The poverty line in the Philippines was drawn at 434 pesos per family per year at 1965 prices. In 1956–57 about 10% of the rural population was below this line, whereas roughly 12% fell below the line in 1970–71, a rise in the incidence of poverty of about 20%.[17]

(iii) In Pakistan the poverty line was constructed in such a way that it was consistent with the level of income sufficient to yield food consumption satisfying 95% of the estimated caloric requirements. Observations are available for 6 years in the period 1963–64 to 1971–72. As can be seen in Figure 1, there is no trend in rural poverty in Pakistan one way or the other. The incidence of poverty appears to have declined until around 1968-69 and to have risen thereafter. At the end of the period the proportion of the rural population in poverty was approximately the same as at the beginning.[18]

(iv)   The poverty line used for Bangladesh was Tk23.61 *per capita* per month in 1963–64 prices. This corresponds to a level of income sufficient to yield food consumption satisfying 90% of the estimated caloric requirements. There are four observations covering the period 1963–64 to 1975. The proportion of the rural population in poverty was 40% in the initial year, rising to a peak of 79% in 1973–74 and then falling somewhat to 62% in 1975. The incidence of poverty, however, was more than 50% greater at the end of the period than at the beginning.[19]

The second study was undertaken at the World Bank by Montek Ahluwalia.[20] It covered 14 states in India for the period 1956–57 to 1973–74. Unlike the ILO study, Ahluwalia used the same poverty line for calculating the incidence of rural poverty in each state, viz. Rs15 per person in 1960–61 rural prices. The justification for using this level of income as the dividing line between the poor and the non-poor is that it has been adopted by the Planning Commission and therefore is widely used and recognized in official documents.

We comment at length in the next section on Ahluwalia's findings and the conclusions he draws from them. Here we merely select 5 states where trends in the incidence of poverty from 1960–61 onwards are highly significant in a statistical sense. These states are Andhra Pradesh, Assam, Bihar, Madhya Pradesh and West Bengal. They include states from all over India and provide a good illustration of what has been happening in that vast and varied country.

(v)   In Andhra Pradesh, unique among the states of India, the incidence of poverty actually declined. In 1960–61 about 50% of the rural population was deemed to be poor, whereas by 1973–74 only 39.8% were so classified. In other words, the incidence of rural poverty in Andhra Pradesh declined by about 20% over the period.

(vi)   In Assam, in contrast, the proportion of the rural population in poverty increased from 25.6% at the beginning of the period to 39.3% at the end. That is, the incidence of poverty rose by more than a half.

(vii)   In Bihar there was a steady and sharp increase in poverty from 41.5% of the rural population in 1960–61 to 70.9% in 1967–68.

The following year the incidence of poverty declined to about 59% and remained constant for the rest of the period. Comparing the first year with the last the incidence of poverty increased by 40%.

(viii) A broadly similar pattern occurred in Madhya Pradesh, except that the fluctuations were not as great and the trend rate of increase in poverty was fractionally slower.

(ix) In West Bengal the incidence of poverty doubled between 1960–61 and 1967–68, i.e. from 40.4 to 80.3% of the rural population. Thereafter it declined steadily but by 1973–74 it was still 63% higher than in the initial year.

To summarize the 5 Indian cases, there was a statistically significant rise in poverty in 4 out of 5 states. The arithmetic average of the incidence of poverty was 40.3% in 1960–61. This increased to 51.2% in 1973–74. That is, despite the decline in poverty in Andhra Pradesh, on average the incidence of rural poverty in the 5 states taken as a whole increased by more than a quarter in 13 years. By any standards this is an alarming rate of impoverishment. Moreover, even in Punjab/Haryana, a region which experienced very rapid growth, there was no measurable tendency for the incidence of poverty to decline. Indeed, taken at its face value, poverty in Punjab/Haryana increased from 18.8% of the rural population in 1960–61 to 23.0% in 1973–74, but the underlying trend was not statistically significant.

The trends in poverty for all 9 cases discussed are depicted in Figure 1. An index of the incidence of rural poverty has been calculated for each case

FIGURE 1

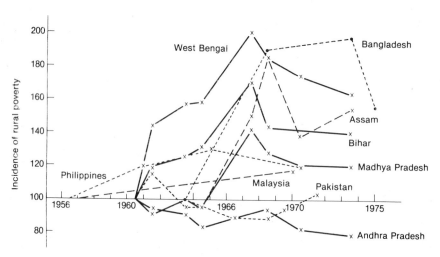

using the initial year as the base of 100. It can be seen in Figure 1 that both the base year and the terminal year vary from case to case. Moreover, as indicated in the text, the definition of the poverty line is not uniform, except in the Indian cases, and of course the initial incidence of poverty varies considerably from one case to another. Thus the trends are not directly comparable in quantitative terms. The most that can be said is that over the (different) periods considered the incidence of poverty in, say, Malaysia increased much less rapidly than, say, in Assam. Qualitatively, however, the figure provides a good description of the general direction in which things are moving in rural Asia. As can readily be seen, the direction is unfavourable and the speed of deterioration often is rapid.

Some corroborating evidence is available from FAO's estimates of the extent of malnutrition, although the period covered is rather short. The data for 9 Asian countries are presented in Table 6. In only 1 of the 9 countries, namely Indonesia, did either the absolute number or the proportion of the population that is malnourished decline during the period 1969–71 to 1972–74. In all the other countries the absolute number of malnourished persons increased. In 4 countries (Bangladesh, Philippines, South Korea and Thailand) the relative incidence of malnourishment remained unchanged and in South Korea, indeed, malnourishment is not a serious problem. In the other 4 countries, i.e. Burma, India, Nepal and Pakistan, the incidence of malnutrition rose from already high levels.

Considering the 9 countries as a whole, the number of malnourished persons rose from 251 million in 1969–71 to 291 million in 1972–74, i.e. the number increased by 40 million people. Those suffering from malnutrition in these 9 countries thus rose by 15.9%, a rate of growth far in excess of population increase. This result is entirely consistent with our view that poverty in rural Asia has been rising. The period covered in Table 6, however, is one in which production increased relatively slowly, as can be seen in the last column of the table. One might be tempted, therefore, to attribute the rise in poverty and hunger to agricultural stagnation. In the next section we hope to demonstrate that in general this hypothesis is not correct.

3. RURAL POVERTY AND AGRICULTURAL GROWTH

We showed earlier that with few exceptions agricultural output per head in Asia has been rising. It follows from this that a general decline in agricultural output or in agricultural value added *per capita* cannot be the cause of the growing impoverishment we have identified. Average incomes in rural areas have been rising, not falling, yet a significant minority of the rural population in Asia has experienced a decline in their standard of living.

Despite the fact that the growth of agricultural output per head has been positive, many authors believe that none the less it has been too slow to alleviate poverty. If only the rate of agricultural growth could be accelerated

TABLE 6   **The Incidence of Malnutrition, 1969–74 (Number of Individuals and Percentage of the Total Population)**

| | Number in Thousands | | Percentage | | PERCENTAGE CHANGE IN |
	AVERAGE 1969–71	AVERAGE 1972–74	AVERAGE 1969–71	AVERAGE 1972–74	AGRICULTURAL OUTPUT, 1969–71 TO 1972–74
Bangladesh	25,723	27,026	38	38	−2.6
Burma	5272	6555	19	22	2.8
India	141,214	175,162	26	30	1.7
Indonesia	40,619	38,742	34	30	14.8
Nepal	3033	3499	27	29	2.7
Pakistan	14,508	17,223	24	26	6.9
Philippines	13,161	14,550	35	35	10.5
South Korea	1255	1332	4	4	3.8
Thailand	6434	7095	18	18	11.4

SOURCES: FAO, *Fourth World Food Survey* (Rome: 1977); FAO, *The State of Food and Agriculture* (Rome: various issues).

further, such authors claim, then poverty would begin to disappear. This doctrine of a close connection between changes in the incidence of rural poverty and the agricultural growth rate is exactly analogous to the now discredited 'trickle down' theory which postulates a close connection between the growth of GNP and the incidence of national poverty. This new doctrine we shall call 'trickle down modified', or TDM for short.

The most forceful advocate of TDM is Montek Ahluwalia of the World Bank. In a paper entitled 'Rural Poverty and Agricultural Growth in India', Ahluwalia claims that 'at the all India level there is very strong evidence to suggest that agricultural growth, within the existing institutional system, tends to reduce the incidence of poverty'.[21] Moreover, after examining 14 states he claims that his 'findings provide substantial confirmation at the state level of the hypotheses . . . that improved agricultural performance, even within the existing institutional constraints, will tend to reduce the incidence of rural poverty'.[22]

Ahluwalia defines the rural poor as those below a monthly consumer expenditure level of Rs15 per person in 1960–61 prices. He uses the National Sample survey data available for 9 of the 17 years in the period 1956–57 to 1973–74 for 14 states. It is apparent from inspecting his data, however, that inclusion of the two observations from the 1950s, namely 1957–58 and 1959–60, tends to obscure the rising incidence of rural poverty that occurred in many states of India from about 1960. Accordingly our estimates of trends in poverty are based on Ahluwalia's data for the somewhat shorter period of 14 years extending from 1960–61 to 1973–74.

We have calculated two measures of the changing incidence of rural poverty. First, we estimated the percentage increase in rural poverty from the average of the years 1960–64 to the average for 1970–74. This estimate is reported in column 1 of Table 7. The data indicate, for instance, that over the period examined rural poverty declined by 0.9% in Punjab/Haryana and rose by 7.5% in Orissa. Note that according to this measure rural poverty rose in all but 2 of the 14 states and in half the states the increase was greater than 5%.

Second, we also estimated the trend rate of change in rural poverty by fitting a trend line to all the observations for the period. As is explained in the note to Table 7, Rajasthan was excluded because of poor quality of some of the data. The estimates for the remaining 13 states are reported in column 2 of the Table. It can be seen that only in Andhra Pradesh was there a trend toward diminishing poverty. In all the other states there was a tendency for rural poverty to increase. In some states, e.g. Assam and West Bengal, the trend was extraordinarily rapid, whereas in others, notably Tamil Nadu and Kerala, the trend was rather slow. In 5 cases the estimated trend was statistically significant at the 5% confidence level. In 4 of the cases, viz. Assam, Bihar, Madhya Pradesh and West Bengal, the trend was toward increasing poverty while in one case, viz. Andhra Pradesh, the trend, as we have seen,

TABLE 7 **Rural Poverty and Agricultural Growth**

	(1) CHANGE IN POVERTY (RP_1) (PERCENTAGE INCREASE)	(2) POVERTY TREND (RP_2) (% PER ANNUM)	(3) PER CAPITA AGRICULTURAL GROWTH TREND (AG) (% PER ANNUM)	(4) PER CAPITA FOOD PRODUCTION TREND (FG) (% PER ANNUM)
1. Andhra Pradesh	−15.2	−2.5	−0.6	−1.6
2. Assam	40.9	7.6	−0.1	−1.3
3. Bihar	22.6	4.6	1.3	−0.1
4. Gujarat	1.8	1.5	0.9	0.8
5. Karnataka	12.9	3.8	0.8	1.1
6. Kerala	3.8	0.7	0.9	0.4
7. Madhya Pradesh	23.9	4.5	−1.1	−0.3
8. Maharashtra	3.2	1.1	−3.3	−4.7
9. Orissa	7.5	1.7	2.7	−0.8
10. Punjab/Haryana	−0.9	1.6	3.2	5.5
11. Rajasthan	9.7	*	−0.3	0.2
12. Tamil Nadu	1.0	0.3	1.0	0.5
13. Uttar Pradesh	1.5	2.1	1.4	1.1
14. West Bengal	26.0	6.1	0.8	0.9

NOTE: *No attempt was made to estimate a poverty trend for Rajasthan because the figure for 1967–68 was improbably low. That is, according to the official data the incidence of rural poverty is reported to have risen from 11.8% in 1967–68 to 41.4% in the following year.

SOURCES: Estimates computed from Montek Ahluwalia, *op. cit.*; Perspective Planning Division, Planning Commission, Government of India, *Studies on the Structure of Indian Economy and Planning for Development* (New Delhi: May 1977), mimeo.; Government of India, *Indian Agriculture in Brief* (various issues).

was toward decreasing rural poverty. In the other 8 cases the estimated trend in a statistical sense was not significantly different from zero.

Table 7 also contains estimates of the trend rate of growth of agricultural output *per capita* [column (3)] and of the trend rate of growth of food production *per capita* [column (4)] over the period 1956–57 to 1973–74. In 5 of the states there was a tendency for *per capita* agricultural output to decline and in 6 states there was a tendency for *per capita* food production to decline. Growth experience varied widely. For example, *per capita* food production rose 5.5% a year in Punjab/Haryana and declined 4.7% a year in Maharashtra. This wide range of experience is a great advantage when it comes to testing the TDM doctrine, as we shall now proceed to do.

If the TDM hypothesis is correct one would expect to find an inverse association, hopefully statistically significant, between some measure of the trend in rural poverty and some measure of the trend rate of growth of output. In an attempt to discover whether this inverse association exists we estimated 4 regression equations. The results were as follows:

	VARIABLES	COEFFICIENT OF REGRESSION	R^2
(1)	RP_1 and AG	-0.69	0.006
(2)	RP_1 and FG	-0.62	0.009
(3)	RP_2 and AG	0.04	0.001
(4)	RP_2 and FG	0.07	0.004

First, when the percentage change in poverty from 1960–64 to 1970–74 (RP_1) was used as the dependent variable, there was an inverse association with the trend rate of growth of output, whether this was measured as the rate of growth of total agricultural production *per capita (AG)* or as the growth of food production *per capita (FG)*. In both cases, however, the regression equation explained less than 1% of the variation in rural poverty [see the R^2s of equations (1) and (2)] and in neither case was the coefficient of regression significant.

Second, when the dependent variable was defined as the percentage annual trend rate of growth of rural poverty (RP_2), the sign of the coefficient of regression became positive when either AG or FG was used as the independent variable. That is, the nature of the association was the opposite of what the TDM hypothesis would lead one to expect. The explanatory power of equations (3) and (4) was very low—less than one half of one per cent of the variation in RP_2 was explained by the variation in either AG or FG—and, as before, the coefficient of regression was not significant.

It should be clear from this statistical exercise that there is no evidence whatever, let alone 'very strong evidence', that agricultural growth tends to reduce the incidence of rural poverty. The connection between the two is approximately zero. The defenders of TDM could of course argue that the

FIGURE 2

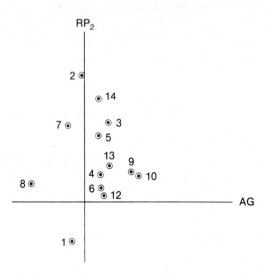

relationship is non-linear and therefore that our linear regression equations may be misleading because they overlook this possibility. Inspection of scatter diagrams, however, would provide no support for those who might be tempted to clutch at this straw. One such scatter diagram is reproduced above to reassure the sceptical reader. (The numbering of the observations corresponds to the number of the state in Table 7.) It can be seen at a glance that there is no systematic tendency for the incidence of rural poverty to decline as the rate of growth rises.

4. POVERTY, HUNGER AND FOOD PRICES

One of the consequences of poverty is hunger. Although the growth of *per capita* incomes in Asia, and even of agricultural output, sometimes has been impressive, the problems of poverty and hunger have not been solved. Incremental incomes have tended to be distributed very unequally and the living standards of the lowest income groups either have remained unchanged or have deteriorated. The problem often has not been one of inadequate growth but of an inappropriate pattern of growth.

An important aspect of this inappropriateness is the failure of food supplies to keep up with the expansion of demand. As can be seen in Table 8, food output per head, with few exceptions, either has been declining or has grown at a slow rate. Incomes per head, on the other hand, as we saw in Table 1, have been rising in all countries except Bangladesh, often quite rapidly. Given the positive and frequently rather high income elasticities of demand for food in most Asian countries,[23] the aggregate demand for food has increased quite rapidly and has generally outstripped supply.

TABLE 8   **Food Output Per Capita 1974–76**
(Index: 1961–63 = 100)

Bangladesh	90
Burma	92
India	96
Indonesia	110
Malaysia	144
Nepal	91
Pakistan	115
Philippines	106
South Korea	127
Sri Lanka	89
Taiwan*	116
Thailand	108

NOTE: *In the case of Taiwan the figure refers to the period 1969–71.

SOURCE: FAO, *Production Yearbook* (various issues).

As a result, in countries which are net importers of food, there has been some tendency for their dependence on imported food supplies to increase. This has occurred, for instance, in Bangladesh, South Korea, Sri Lanka and Taiwan. In India and the Philippines import dependency has remained ap-

TABLE 9   **Net Trade in Cereals, 1961–63 to 1974–76**

	INDEX OF NET TRADE IN CEREALS (1961–63 = 100)	Net Trade as a Percentage of Domestic Output of Cereals [Imports (−) and Exports (+)]	
		1961–63	1974–76
Net importers			
Bangladesh	216	−5.8	−10.1
India	153	−4.8	−5.4
Indonesia	152	−8.0	−7.0
Malaysia	130	−64.9	−45.4
Pakistan	103	−8.6	−4.7
Philippines	160	−10.2	−9.6
South Korea	383	−12.0	−32.8
Sri Lanka	153	−64.1	−72.1
Taiwan	431*	−9.8	−34.0*
Net exporters			
Burma	7	+22.4	+1.3
Nepal	24	+5.3	+1.1
Thailand	188	+16.6	+21.3

*Refers to 1968–70.

SOURCE: FAO, *Production Yearbook* (various issues); FAO, *Trade Yearbook* (various issues).

proximately constant, while in Indonesia, Malaysia and Pakistan it has declined. Countries which are net exporters of food have tended to experience falling exportable surpluses. The great exception is Thailand, where the proportion of cereal output sold abroad has increased sharply. In Burma and Nepal, in contrast, exportable surpluses have declined dramatically, although the official figures for Burma may exaggerate the fall somewhat because of smuggling.

Rising food imports and falling exports have not been sufficient to bridge the gap between demand and domestic supply and as a result the relative price of food has been tending to rise throughout Asia. This can be seen in Table 10.

The data in the table show that in all 12 countries food prices have increased at a faster rate than other prices. The significance of this is apparent when one remembers that more than half of the expenditure of an average consumer in most of these countries is on food.[24] The price index of all items is thus strongly influenced by the index of food prices. Unfortunately, indices of prices of items other than food are not available, but it is clear that these prices lagged considerably behind food prices. One important implication of these differential movements in food and non-food prices, as previously mentioned, is that changes in the distribution of money incomes actually understate changes in the distribution of real income. This arises from the fact that the lower is the level of total household expenditure per head, the higher is the proportion spent on food. As a result, in countries where the relative price of food is rising, a reduction in inequality in the distribution of money

TABLE 10 **Consumer Price Indices of Food and All Items, 1973 (Base: 1963–65 = 100)**

	FOOD	ALL ITEMS
Bangladesh	308	292
Burma*	194	182
India	236	221
Indonesia*	1308	1266
Malaysia	150	139
Nepal†	192	177
Pakistan	230	214
Philippines	308	255
South Korea*	305	266
Sri Lanka	177	165
Taiwan‡	131	121
Thailand	185	159

NOTES: *The base is 1965–67 = 100.
†The base is 1964–66 = 100.
‡The base is 1961–63 = 100 and the final period is 1968–70.
SOURCE: United Nations, *Statistical Yearbook* (various issues).

income is necessary in order to keep the distribution of real income un-changed.

It is noteworthy that South Korea and Taiwan have not been immune from a rising relative price of food, yet in these two countries inequality has not increased and the incidence of rural poverty has declined. That is, a phenomenon which has tended to impoverish the poor in most countries has not done so in two.

The reason has to do with the structure of the rural economy in the two groups of countries. If food prices are increasing faster than other prices, those who produce food for sale will gain at the expense of wage earners, producers of non-food items and even small farmers who grow some food but who have to supplement household supplies by purchases in the market. In other words, the major beneficiaries of rising food prices are those farmers who have a marketable surplus. The distribution among the agricultural popula-tion of the gains and losses from rising food prices therefore is crucially dependent on the pattern of land distribution and the institutional structure of the rural economy. If the agricultural sector is characterized by a relatively egalitarian distribution of land and a virtual absence of landlessness and wage labour, then a rise in the relative price of food is likely to contribute to the prosperity of the agricultural population as a whole, including the very poor. Broadly speaking, this is what happened in South Korea and Taiwan.

In most of the other Asian countries, however, the distribution of land is unequal, the incidence of landlessness and near-landlessness is quite high and rising and a significant section of the agricultural population consists of wage labourers. In this situation a rise in the relative price of food is of benefit to only a small group of large farmers; the real income of all the others, i.e. of those who are net buyers of food, is gradually squeezed by rising food prices. In consequence the distribution of real income tends to become worse and the extent of poverty and hunger tends to increase.[25]

5. THE CAUSES OF IMMISERIZING GROWTH

Many of the Asian nations thus have a structural predisposition in favour of immiserizing growth. Major reasons for this are, first, the concentration of productive wealth, particularly landed wealth, in a few hands; second, partly as a consequence of the first, a high degree of inequality in the distribution of income; and, third, the control by a small segment of the population of the instruments of the state and the use of this control to further their own economic interests. Initial inequality in wealth, income and political power, in the absence of broad and deep institutional reforms, tends to be self-perpetuating and in fact often is cumulative. A high proportion of new asset formation is done by those who already have some wealth, and hence if the ownership of the stock of capital is unequally distributed, new investment tends to accentuate the initial maldistribution. Moreover, the savings capacity of households depends on their economic surplus, i.e. the difference between their actual income and minimum subsistence requirements, and this surplus rises more than proportionately with a rise in income. High income groups therefore have a potential for accumulation which exceeds by a wide margin the potential of low income groups. Admittedly this potential seldom is exploited fully, and some low income households such as small peasant landowners and shopkeepers have been known to save a surprisingly large fraction of their income, but the advantage of the upper income groups nevertheless is real and considerable. This advantage, finally, is reinforced by state expenditure, tax and price policies, as we shall see.

The important exceptions to the above generalizations obviously are South Korea and Taiwan. In both these countries redistributive land reforms and other measures helped to create a more egalitarian distribution of wealth. Income inequality was diminished not just once-for-all, but in the case of Taiwan, cumulatively and institutions were devised or reformed to ensure that the benefits of growth were widely shared. The state intervened in economic processes to a considerable extent, but this intervention had the effect of reducing poverty rather than increasing it.

In the majority of countries, however, the mechanisms for allocating resources, and the institutional and political structures through which they operate, are heavily biased against the poor. It is commonly recognized that in most Asian countries there has been a socially undesirable substitution of capital for labour in agriculture, particularly on farms owned by large land-lords, and that this is due to government policies which have created a set of incentives favoring labour displacing mechanization. Low and even negative real rates of interest, overvalued currencies combined with import quotas and foreign exchange licensing systems, and international aid programmes which subsidize imported equipment have resulted in a set of relative factor prices which discourages the use of labour and encourages so-called progressive farmers to mechanize or 'modernize'.

This view undoubtedly is correct as far as it goes, but it is possible to go further. First, there is no such thing as 'the' price of a factor of production in rural areas: different groups of people often face radically different sets of relative factor prices. In a formulation which we find helpful, price 'distortions' are intimately related to the concentration of economic and political power.[26] Particular emphasis is placed on the monopoly of land and the oligopsonistic features of the labour market. Clearly, control of land does not *ipso facto* give a landowner control over labour, but in conditions commonly encountered in Asia, monopoly and monopsony frequently go together. That is, monopolistic landlords in fact typically face a less than infinitely elastic supply of labour.[27] One ought usually to expect that the higher the degree of monopoly in the land market, the lower will be the wage rate. This will occur for two reasons. First, the greater is land concentration, the more likely it is that landowners will cease to be price takers in the labour market. Furthermore, second, the greater is land concentration, the more labour is likely to be on offer at any and all wage rates. Naturally, conditions will vary from one locality to another, and within localities the bargaining strength of different persons will vary, with the result that the price paid for the 'same' factor of production—land, labour, finance capital—will differ markedly from one person to another.

Second, the customary approach of the economist of viewing markets in isolation often is misleading. Within the village economy, particularly in South Asia, factor and commodity markets are interlinked in such a way that the imperfections of markets viewed in isolation are reinforced. For example, a single landowner may enter into a transaction to supply a villager with some land (say, on a crop-sharing basis), production credit, some material inputs, a homestead, consumption loans, and employment on his self-operated holding; in addition the landowner may undertake to market the tenant's share of the output. Most economists would treat this not as a single relationship between two individuals but as a multiplicity of exchanges through independent and competitive markets. To each exchange there would correspond a price determined by the forces of supply and demand operating in the market.

In reality, however, prices frequently have little to do with supply and demand in single markets or with opportunity costs. Thus a landowner may supply credit 'free' to his tenant, and then recoup the loss by charging a higher rent for land or by obtaining a high share of the crop for himself. A casual labourer may be given a free advance on consumption (in cash or in kind) by his employer and in return work at a lower wage rate than those not given an advance. A farm servant may be provided with a rent-free homestead in return for a certain number of additional days of work by members of his household. In situations such as these, wage, rental and interest rates, and even the price paid to a tenant for his marketed surplus, cannot be understood unless the entire relationship between the transactors is taken into account.

A number of economists have begun to examine the way in which markets interlock in rural areas. Perhaps the most prominent are Krishna Bharadwaj, K.N. Raj, Amit Bhaduri, Pranab Bardhan and Ashok Rudra.[28] There is some dispute about whether these market and production relations are capitalist or feudal (or semi-feudal). There is also a dispute about the effect of inter-related factor markets on incentives to innovate. It seems to us, however, that little is gained by describing these relations as feudal; the agricultural systems of the Asian countries we are considering are essentially capitalist. Moreover, there is little evidence to support those who argue that landowners are inhibited from introducing new technology because of linkages between credit markets and sharecropping arrangements. Interlinkages of markets are important not because they signify feudalism or discourage technical change but because they increase the control of landowners over the available resources and enable them to appropriate a larger share of the economic surplus. The interlinkages are associated with 'personalized' markets and the absence of arms-length trading; the interlinkages increase the large landowners' ability to manoeuvre, e.g. enabling them to avoid controls on interest rates, rents, maximum crop shares or minimum wages by introducing offsetting changes in other prices; and it is likely that dominance in one market interlinked with another facilitates some control in that second market.

Third, many of the prices that matter in the agricultural sector, particularly the prices of material inputs and staple crops, are 'political' prices, not prices determined exclusively by economic forces. Government intervention in market processes through taxes, subsidies, quotas and rationing is widespread and to comprehend the set of relative prices that results one needs a theory of politics and the state as much as a theory of economics. It is only in this way, for example, that one can explain the fact that in India the price of rice (a crop grown mainly by smallholders) is below the world level while the price of wheat (a crop often grown by large landowners) is substantially above the world level.

Finally, many resources are allocated by the state bureaucracy either at a price below a market clearing price or at no charge at all. Examples include subsidized credit provided by state banks, water supplied by public irrigation systems at nominal cost and extension services provided free of charge. In cases such as these rationing and other non-price allocating devices must be employed, and the crucial question becomes who has access to the institutions which produce and deliver these services and on what terms. A literature on 'access' is beginning to emerge, but much more research needs to be done on this important topic.[29] None the less, the studies that are available strengthen the view that allocations by the state typically benefit the middle and upper-income groups rather than the poor.

(a) The Pattern of Growth

The pace and pattern of growth are strongly affected by the types of technical innovations that are introduced and by the institutional arrangements for spreading the benefits and costs of change. Three specific technical innovations have been prominent in rural Asia in recent years—the introduction of higher yielding varieties of rice and wheat, the spread of irrigation and the introduction of tractors—and it has been shown that in each case innovation has been accompanied, at least in some regions, by greater inequality and poverty. Let us consider briefly each of these in turn.

At first glance it is hard to imagine that the use of new seeds to grow higher yielding grain varieties could lead to increased poverty. On the contrary, improved varieties should have multiple benefits and negligible costs. The seeds being highly divisible, new varieties should be accessible to all farmers, large and small alike, and hence the innovation should spread quickly. Rice and wheat being important 'wage goods', the increased supply of grains should result in lower costs of food and higher real incomes, particularly for the poor who spend a large proportion of their income on food.

Moreover, the use of the new varieties should be accompanied by additional demand for labour and consequently more employment opportunities or higher wages, or both, in rural areas.

Unfortunately, in practice the results have been neither so favourable nor so simple; the introduction of new varieties set in motion a complex sequence of events which has harmed some groups and helped others.[30] For example, the seeds (particularly in the case of rice) were most readily adopted in the irrigated plains and valleys and turned out to be unsuitable in the uplands and in rain-fed agricultural areas. As a result, the innovation has not spread as widely as originally was hoped and regional inequalities have tended to be accentuated. Moreover, even where the varieties are suited to the local natural environment, there is a persistent tendency for the large farmers to be represented disproportionately among the innovators and for the small farmers to be excluded, to innovate only partially or to lag behind. Part of the reason for this is that the new varieties are relatively intensive in working capital and the small farmers have less access to credit markets and have to pay a higher average price for whatever credit they receive. In addition, most policies and public institutions in the rural areas, e.g. the extension service, favour large farmers. Finally, the increase in yields associated with the introduction of the new varieties has been rather modest yet the new varieties have been accompanied by a much greater use of labour-displacing mechanization. This combination of circumstances has been severely disadvantageous to the large and growing number of landless labourers and probably is the single most important reason for the growing impoverishment in parts of Asia.

In many regions inadequate or unreliable sources of water are a more serious obstacle to increasing agricultural output than the scarcity of fertile land or the limited availability of suitable varieties.[31] One would naturally expect, therefore, that investment in irrigation would provide a good return on capital, create employment opportunities and benefit the farming community as a whole.

Once again, however, these expectations have not always been realized. For instance, a study of a tank and channel public irrigation scheme in the Hambantota District of Sri Lanka concluded that 'if we take equity of distribution as one of the criteria for evaluating irrigation organization, the records leave us no doubt that the big landowners were often able to exercise manipulative power to obtain more water for themselves, though their activities also brought them into conflict with one another. And if we take productivity of water and stability of the system as criteria, then again it seems that the system . . . was ineffective because it never succeeded in securing timely irrigation'.[32] Inequality and inefficiency of the kind discovered in Sri Lanka are common features of public irrigation schemes in Asia although they are not unique to them; similar problems also arise in the case of private investment in irrigation.

Let us consider the situation in Tamil Nadu, India. Half the electric pump-sets and 30% of the diesel pump-sets in India are located in Tamil

Nadu.[33] Thus the experience of this state is of general interest. Yet the conclusions of a study in the North Arcot District of the state are disconcerting. Private irrigation with pump-sets has had a greater effect on rice production than have improved varieties. Pump-sets 'have enabled those farmers who have been able to install them on good wells to appropriate communal groundwater, to cultivate large acreages and to increase multiple cropping. Their reliable and often abundant water supply makes adoption of HYVs and the use of other inputs less risky and more profitable for them. But, as the water-table drops in consequence, their less fortunate neighbours without pump-sets find that the old lift technology of the kavalai becomes gradually more marginal, or that they cannot afford to deepen their wells. The land of some of the poorer and smaller cultivators thus goes out of irrigated cultivation while multiple cropping is extended on the land of the richer and larger cultivators'.[34] In this manner the larger and richer landowners benefit considerably from investment in irrigation, but at the expense of the poor and small farmers. Moreover, the new technology seems not to generate many net additional employment opportunities for wage labourers: 'In the many villages which are saturated with population, pump-sets may do little to alleviate the plight of the landless. . . .'[35] Consequently the poorer landowners, tenants and landless labourers have tended to lose out to the richer landowners in both relative and absolute terms.

It is almost universally recognized that the introduction of tractors and other labour-saving equipment reduces the demand for labour and consequently employment and wage rates. It has frequently been claimed, however, that when tractors are accompanied by the introduction of improved varieties, employment actually rises substantially. Unfortunately, this proposition appears not to be true, as can be seen by examining the evidence from Bangladesh.

The effects on employment and output of the two different types of technical change emerge clearly from a careful study of 459 farms in Bangladesh. The farms were first divided into two groups of comparable size. In the first group traditional varieties of rice were cultivated while in the second group higher yielding varieties were planted. Each of these major groups was then subdivided into farms which used bullock power and those which used a tractor/power tiller. Thus 4 different combinations of seed variety and source of power could be examined.

The data in Table 11 refer to the aman season of 1975. For ease of comparison the data are presented in index number form with farms cultivating traditional varieties with bullocks constituting the base. The aman season is the main rice growing season in Bangladesh and it is in this period that the effects of technical change are likely to be most significant.

It is evident from the table that the new varieties do indeed have higher yields than the traditional ones. A switch from old to new varieties on farms using bullock power results in a rise of output per acre of about 42%. A

TABLE 11   **Bangladesh: Labour Intensity and Yields in Rice Farming: Aman Season 1975**

	LABOUR INPUT PER ACRE	OUTPUT PER ACRE	NUMBER OF FARMS
Traditional varieties			
Bullock farms	100.0	100.0	243
Tractor/power tiller farms	92.3	94.7	18
Higher yielding varieties			
Bullock farms	127.8	142.1	156
Tractor/power tiller farms	99.6	131.6	42

SOURCE: Compiled from data in Iftikhar Ahmed, 'Technical change and labour utilisation in rice cultivation: Bangladesh', *The Bangladesh Development Studies* (July 1977), Tables III and IV, p. 362.

broadly similar rise occurs on farms using mechanical sources of power. What is noteworthy in Bangladesh is that the use of tractors and power tillers actually reduces yields whether of traditional or higher yielding varieties. The reason for this, evidently, is that the introduction of tractors/power tillers is essentially a labour-saving rather than a land-augmenting technical change.

This can readily be seen by looking at the first column of the table. The introduction of the tractor/power tiller on farms growing traditional varieties reduces employment by about 8% while the introduction of mechanical power on farms growing higher yielding varieties reduces employment by about a quarter. In contrast, the switch from traditional to higher yielding varieties, whatever the source of power, results in an increase in employment: on bullock farms the increase is about 28% and on tractor/power tiller farms about 8%.

The evidence thus is clear. The introduction of mechanical innovations in Bangladesh, viz. tractors and power tillers, reduces both output and employment. Moreover, what is true of Bangladesh is likely to be equally true in other parts of Asia. In the increasingly labour-scarce economies of East Asia, i.e. South Korea and Taiwan, investment in such equipment undoubtedly is appropriate. But the growing use of labour-saving machinery in the labour-abundant economies of South and Southeast Asia is inappropriate and must account in part for the rising poverty in those areas, particularly among the landless labour class.

The patterns of technical change in rural Asia that have been underlined are reinforced by other components of the growth process to produce an overall pattern of growth which in most countries is biased against the poor. Let us quickly list some of these components.[36] First, there is the generally low level of private net investment and, second, its concentration in the urban areas. Third, most private investment, wherever it is located, takes the form of relatively capital-intensive projects which provide few employment opportunities either in the construction stage or during the period of normal operation. Fourth, state investment also tends to be located disproportionately in urban areas and, fifth, to be highly capital-intensive. Sixth, the state further aggravates poverty and inequality through its expenditure policies on social welfare. That is, the benefits of expenditure on health, education, social security and public housing tend to accrue predominantly to middle and upper-income groups; often the distribution of benefits from such programmes is even more unequal than the distribution of income.

Finally, there is population growth. Given the initial inequalities in wealth, income, institutional structures and political power and given that the pattern of economic growth is biased against the poor in numerous ways, rapid population growth certainly makes matters worse rather than better. It does this, however, not by reducing the aggregate rate of growth of output or of output per head nor, as we have seen, by reducing the rate of growth of agricultural output or of agricultural output per head. The primary effect of rapid demographic expansion is to lower the share of labour in national produce and thereby to increase inequality in the distribution of income.[37] That is, population growth increases the supply of labour relative to land and capital and given a low elasticity of substitution between factors of production, tends to raise the share of rent and profits in total income. This would not affect the distribution of income among households if productive assets were equally distributed, but since they are not, population growth tends inevitably to be a disequalizing force. It is in this sense that population expansion is one of the causes of immiserizing growth.

6. POLICY IMPLICATIONS

It has been shown that inequality, poverty and hunger can increase, and indeed have increased, even in countries which have experienced rising income per head and greater food output per head. The view that the benefits of overall growth automatically will 'trickle down' to the lowest income groups within a reasonable period of time no longer is tenable by informed observers. Moreover, there is considerable doubt that a switch in emphasis from aggregate to sectoral growth rates will make much difference. That is, an acceleration in the rate of agricultural growth as such is unlikely to be sufficient to reduce the incidence of rural poverty. The view that we have labelled 'trickle down modified' finds little support in the data we have examined. On the contrary, our analysis indicates that if a government wishes to reduce rural poverty significantly within, say, one generation, it will have to introduce measures which attack the problem directly.

By now it should be obvious that the most direct way of reducing rural poverty is by redistributing productive assets, notably cultivable land, water rights, forest and plantation enterprises, livestock, mechanical equipment and major structures. Such a 'land reform' is certainly the fastest and in some instances perhaps the only way to improve the standard of living of the very poor. South Korea and Taiwan have shown what can be done within the context of a capitalist system with private property. China has demonstrated the possibilities within a collectivist, socialist system. In order to be meaningful the minimum redistribution in the other Asian countries should include the free provision to every rural family of title to a house site and allotment suitable for raising poultry (chickens, ducks, geese) or other small animals (such as rabbits) and for growing some staples plus vegetables and fruit. It is especially important that landless labourers should be provided with this minimum productive base.

Measures to redistribute income should be regarded as complementary to a redistribution of wealth, not as a substitute for it. The remarkable thing in fact about conventional means of redistributing income, i.e. government tax, subsidy and expenditure policies, is their ineffectiveness. Decades of experience in the welfare states of Europe have underlined the difficulty of raising the share of the poor in the national income in the absence of major structural reforms. The impossibility of confining the benefits of public policies to designated groups—the problem of 'leakages'—in combination with the self-stabilizing properties of the price system conspire to limit severely the amount by which an initial pattern of income distribution can be altered by policy instruments of the type normally used by governments.[38] In addition, in many parts of Asia, it is difficult for the government even to touch the poor with its programmes, let alone confine the benefits of its programmes to them. Just as national income flows trickle down only slowly to the poor, if at all, so too, the relatively much smaller flows of income and expenditure consciously manipulated by governments trickle down only slowly, if at all, to the poor.

The creation of additional employment opportunities in rural areas is one way both of directing new income flows predominantly toward the poor and of generating a net increase in output. It should be recalled, however, that in many regions, particularly where multiple cropping is practiced, there is relatively little year-round unemployment or even pronounced seasonal unemployment. What is primarily required, therefore, is not more jobs for the unemployed but better jobs (i.e. more productive and higher income earning jobs) for those already employed.

In a great many countries, with the notable exception of China, rural employment schemes have been little more than a form of outdoor relief hastily improvised in times of harvest failure and famine. Organization has been inefficient, resources have been wasted on a vast scale, few permanent additions have been made to the stock of capital assets in the countryside and only an insignificant contribution has been made to alleviating poverty. In practice the poor would have gained more had they been given the money spent on the programmes rather than the jobs.

If rural employment programmes are to make a permanent contribution to reducing poverty two things should occur. First, the focus of the schemes should switch from charitable relief of distress to the construction of durable assets. That is, the schemes should come to be viewed as a means of deploying labour to accelerate investment. Second, the assets created by such schemes should become the property of the labourers who construct them. In a collectivist agricultural system this happens more or less automatically in most cases,[39] but in a capitalist system the value added generated by the use of new assets rarely accrues to the workers. If the asset is paid for and owned by a private capitalist, the net income accrues to him as profit or rent. If it is owned by the state and its services provided free of charge, as is often the case, 'externalities' are generated and usually these are captured by property owners. For example, the benefits of a public highway or of soil conservation works or of drainage and irrigation facilities are reflected in part in a higher price of land, in higher returns to farmers and in higher rents charged by rentiers.

On the other hand, in many cases one could combine capital formation with progressive income redistribution by ensuring that the assets are constructed by the poor, e.g. landless labourers, and that upon completion ownership of the assets is transferred to a cooperative consisting solely of those who supplied their labour. The purpose of the cooperative would be to manage the assets and charge for their use, distributing part of the income to the members and retaining part to finance future capital accumulation. In this way the productive base of the poorest households could be strengthened on a continuing basis.

The sorts of reforms just discussed, and other policies favouring the poor implicit in earlier sections of this paper, evidently require major changes in political power and in institutions. It would be unrealistic to expect that the radical transformation of society entailed by a development strategy oriented toward the eradication of poverty could occur peacefully. Those who gain from the *status quo* surely would fight to prevent the loss of their privileges while the poor, if shown a reasonable prospect of victory, equally surely would fight for their newly promised rights.[40]

Assuming there really is a change in orientation, it is necessary to enquire into the implications for the administration of development. In most Asian countries, and India is a prime example, rural development is conceived and implemented within a framework of highly centralized planning or policy formation. Typically, there is a one-way flow of orders and ideas from the centre in New Delhi, Manila, Jakarta or Islamabad to, ultimately, the official on the lowest rung of the administrative ladder, say, the Village Level Worker. There is little vertical consultation even within the administrative services, let alone between representatives of the mass of the rural population and the government. As a result the system of administration is inflexible and incapable of adapting to local conditions in the countryside. In practice the emphasis is placed on the avoidance of risk and error, on following bureaucratic procedures. The inevitable outcome is a slow moving and conservative apparatus which does little to help the poor.

This administrative structure is incompatible with anti-poverty oriented rural development. If the political forces in control of the state are determined to have the latter, the former must go. In essence what is required is that government should be brought closer to the majority of the people while the mass of the people should be brought into a position to influence government. That is, one must decentralize from the top and organize the bottom.

There is, of course, no single level at which all planning should occur. Some tasks, e.g. general export policy, should be planned at the centre and others, e.g. the construction of a village school, should be planned and implemented locally. The important thing is that an institutional hierarchy should be created which permits activities to take place in units which are large enough to exploit whatever economies of scale may exist yet small enough to ensure flexibility and responsiveness to the needs of local people.[41] It is in this light that proposals for, say, Block level planning in India should be examined. A Block, i.e. a unit of approximately 100,000 persons, may be too small for some purposes and too large for others. There is nothing intrinsically good or bad about a Block as such. It all depends on whether there is a coherent institutional hierarchy and how the Block fits into it.

Having said this, however, it remains true that in most of Asia effective action in rural areas would be encouraged if much more emphasis were placed on small groups and organizations.[42] China has its production teams, South Korea its Saemaul Undong and Taiwan its small groups to manage irrigation works. Similar institutions are needed elsewhere.

Investment planning is a case in point. The centralized planning procedures existing at present are biased in favour of large projects designed to high engineering standards, amenable to sophisticated cost-benefit analysis and perhaps suitable for foreign financing. Anti-poverty focused rural development, however, requires a great many small, labour-intensive investment projects that are dispersed throughout the countryside. These projects cannot be identified, designed and appraised at the centre; of necessity projects of the type required must be identified locally and their desirability and feasibility determined there. This in turn implies that plans for rural development should be made locally, by those who will implement them, benefit from them and bear the major cost of them.

Government, of course, has a major role to play in helping rural people to plan their own activities, to articulate their demands and to become organized. The poor are unlikely to organize themselves spontaneously; some outside stimulus normally will be necessary and government can assist the process by at least being tolerant of rural peasant movements and better still by encouraging and supporting local organizations. Under favourable conditions a large number of such organizations could emerge. Some may form around a piece of technology, as with irrigation cooperatives; some may be interest groups, including women's organizations (a group, incidentally, which is especially disadvantaged in South Asia); and some may be class based groups, such as unions of landless labourers or plantation workers, small farmers associations, etc.

Ideally, these organizations should have their own funds and be independent of government yet have ready access to it. The government, in turn, should regard local organizations as partners in rural development, sources of ideas, places where priorities can be hammered out, recruitment grounds for 'bare-foot' doctors and engineers, peasant leaders and local government personnel. In this way it should be possible to approach the ultimate objective in which planning for the poor becomes planning by the poor.

NOTES

1. See W. Arthur Lewis, *Growth and Fluctuations* 1870–1913 (London: George Allen and Unwin, 1978).
2. Michal Kalecki, *Essays on Developing Economies* (Harvester Press, 1976). Ch. 4.
3. Michael Lipton, *Why Poor People Stay Poor: Urban Bias in World Development* (London: Temple Smith, 1977).
4. See for example ILO, *Employment, Incomes and Equality: A Strategy for Increasing Productive Employment in Kenya* (Geneva: 1972), Ch. 13.
5. See ILO, *Employment, Growth and Basic Needs* (Geneva: 1976).
6. Frank Long, 'The impact of natural disaster on Third World agriculture', *The American Journal of Economics and Sociology* (April 1978), p. 155 who cites *A Report on 1974 Flood Damages* by the Bangladesh Planning Commission (1974).
7. The estimating equation was Tons = a + b Time. An alternative equation of Log Tons = α + β Time was also used which produced broadly similar results but slightly higher estimates of instability.
8. See, for example, Michael Lipton, op. cit.
9. See Keith Griffin, *The Political Economy of Agrarian Change* (London: Macmillan, 1974).
10. See, for example, A. R. Khan, 'Poverty and inequality in rural Bangladesh', in ILO, *Poverty and Landlessness in Rural Asia* (Geneva: 1977).
11. See S. M. Naseem, 'Rural poverty and landlessness in Pakistan', in ILO, ibid.
12. E. L. H. Lee, 'Egalitarian peasant farming and rural development: the case of South Korea', *World Development,* Vol. 7, Nos. 4/5 (April/May, 1979), pp. 493–517.
13. The Gini coefficients for the overall distribution of income in Taiwan are as follows:

1953	0.58
1959–60	0.45
1961	0.47
1964	0.33
1972	0.28

See Shail Jain, *Size Distribution of Income: A Compilation of Data* (Washington: World Bank, 1975).

14. ILO, *Poverty and Landlessness in Rural Asia* (Geneva: 1977). A summary of the study is contained in Keith Griffin and Azizur Rahman Khan, 'Poverty in the Third World: ugly facts and fancy models', *World Development* (March 1978). For a detailed study of Indonesia see Ingrid Palmer, *The Indonesian Economy since 1965* (London: Frank Cass, 1978).

15. For a discussion of the advantages and disadvantages of poverty lines see Keith Griffin, *International Inequality and National Poverty* (Macmillan, 1978), pp. 141–143.

16. E. L. H. Lee, 'Rural poverty in West Malaysia, 1957–70', in ILO, *Poverty and Landlessness in Rural Asia,* op. cit.

17. A. R. Khan, 'Growth and inequality in the rural Philippines', in ILO, ibid.

18. See S. M. Naseem, op. cit.

19. See A. R. Khan, 'Poverty and inequality in rural Bangladesh', loc. cit.

20. Montek Ahluwalia, 'Rural poverty and agricultural growth in India', a paper presented to the IBRD-sponsored Workshop on Analysis of Distributional Issues in Development Planning (Bellagio, Italy: 22–27 April 1977). (A revised and somewhat more cautiously worded version was published as 'Rural poverty and agricultural performance in India', *Journal of Development Studies,* Vol. 14, No. 3 (April 1978).

21. Ibid., p. 29.

22. Ibid., p. 26.

23. FAO estimates of the income elasticity of demand for cereals (not food as a whole) are as follows:

Burma	0.1
India	0.4
Indonesia	0.5
Malaysia	0.2
Pakistan (including Bangladesh)	0.4
Philippines	0.5
South Korea	0.4
Sri Lanka	0.6
Taiwan	0.1
Thailand	0.2

See FAO, *Agricultural Commodities—Projections for 1975 and 1985* (Rome: 1967), p. 32.

24. For example, the percentage of total consumption expenditure on food and drink was as follows:

Pakistan (including Bangladesh) (1970–71)	52.9
Philippines (1968)	59.8
Sri Lanka (1969–70)	58.2
Thailand (1962–63)	45.6

See ILO, *Household Income and Expenditure Statistics, No. 2, 1960–1972, Africa, Asia, Latin America* (Geneva: 1974), p. 107.

25. For an elaboration of the argument see Amartya Sen, 'Starvation and exchange entitlements: a general approach and its application to the Great Bengal Famine', *Cambridge Journal of Economics,* Vol. 1, No. 1 (March 1977); and Keith Griffin, *International Inequality and National Poverty,* op. cit., Ch. 8.

26. Keith Griffin, *The Political Economy of Agrarian Change,* op. cit.

27. For evidence that the supply of village labour is inelastic even in densely populated areas such as West Bengal see Pranab Bardhan, 'Aspects of the rural labour market in West Bengal: an analysis of household survey data, 1971–73', ILO World Employment Programme Research Working Paper (March 1978). Bardhan's results do not of course demonstrate that individual landowners face an inelastic supply of labour, but they are consistent with this view. His results certainly are inconsistent with the commonly held alternative view of surplus or infinitely elastic supply of labour.

28. See, for example, Krishna Bharadwaj, *Production Conditions in Indian Agriculture,* University of Cambridge Department of Applied Economics, Occasional Paper 33 (Cambridge University Press, 1974); Amit Bhaduri, 'A study in agricultural backwardness under semi-feudalism', *Economic Journal* (March 1973); Pranab Bardhan, 'Variations in extent and forms of agricultural tenancy: analysis of Indian data across regions and over time', *Economic and Political Weekly* (11 and 18 September 1976).

29. Bernard Schaffer, 'Official providers: access, equity and participation', mimeo. (Institute of Development Studies, University of Sussex, October 1977); also see the special issue of *Development and Change,* Vol. VI, No. 2 (1975).

30. For an attempt to sort out the benefits and costs see Keith Griffin, *The Political Economy of Agrarian Change,* op. cit.

31. This argument is carefully developed in Shigeru Ishikawa, *Economic Development in Asian Perspective* (Tokyo: Kinokuniya Bookstore Co., 1967).

32. John Harriss, 'Problems of water management in Hambantota District', in B. H. Farmer (ed.), *Green Revolution? Technology and Change in Rice-Growing Areas of Tamil Nadu and Sri Lanka* (London: Macmillan, 1977), pp. 368–369.

33. Barbara Harris, 'Alternative technologies', in B. H. Farmer (ed.), ibid., p. 386.

34. Robert Chambers and B. H. Farmer, 'Perceptions, technology and the future', in B. H. Farmer (ed.), ibid., p. 416.

35. Ibid., p. 418.

36. For a slightly lengthier discussion see Keith Griffin, 'Increasing poverty and changing ideas about development strategies', *Development and Change* (October 1977), pp. 497–499.

37. For a discussion of some of these issues in the Indian context see R. H. Cassen, *India: Population, Economy, Society* (London: Macmillan, 1978).

38. For a more detailed discussion see Keith Griffin, *Land Concentration and Rural Poverty* (London: Macmillan, 1976), pp. 8–10.

39. Thomas Balogh has recommended that public works schemes should be 'linked' to the creation of cooperative or collective institutions. See his 'Agricultural and economic development', *Oxford Economic Papers* (1961).

40. Thus in 1977 and 1978 'there have been a series of violent crimes . . . by upper caste Hindus against Untouchables in rural areas of states in north, south and central India. . . .' The Untouchables had been allocated land under Mrs. Gandhi's government during the emergency but after Janata came to power there was an

attempt by the upper castes to reclaim their land. 'Local authorities have shown a reluctance to bring influential offenders to court and the police have often cooperated'. It was not until April 1978 in fact that the first upper caste Hindus were sentenced to life imprisonment for murder. (See the report in *The Times* (London), 20 April 1978.)

41. For a discussion of the institutional hierarchy for rural development in China see Keith Griffin, *International Inequality and National Poverty,* op. cit., Ch. 9.

42. This point has been stressed in P. B. Krishnaswamy, *Micro-Macro Links in Planning* (Australian National University, Development Studies Centre Monograph No. 9, 1977).

17

The Peasant Economy: Internal Logic, Articulation, and Persistence

Alexander Schejtman

INTRODUCTION

Until very recently, studies on economic development, agrarian structure and the agricultural economy in Latin America, whatever the school of theory to which their authors subscribed, failed to perceive peasant agriculture as a specific and distinct form of organization of production.

Under the approaches derived, to a greater or lesser extent, from nineteenth-century liberalism and the Ricardian school of political economy, the peasantry was a socio-cultural remnant of the past-whether termed feudal, pre-capitalist or traditional—destined to disappear fairly rapidly as a result of the growth of commercial agriculture and manufacturing; for that reason, it merited no more consideration as a form of production than that involved in analysis of the mechanisms which encourage or hinder its 'modernization'.

For neo-classical economists, the peasant family unit did not constitute a specific object of analysis as distinct from the agricultural enterprise (or, for these purposes, from any other production unit), since as far as the behaviour of the producer was concerned, the differences they observed could all be attributed to different scales of production and differences in the relative availability of factors. For that reason, decisions concerning what, how and how much to produce were considered to be governed, in both cases, by the tendency for the ratio between the marginal productivity and the price of each of the 'factors' used to become uniform; in other words, the allocation of resources was governed by a single type of operating logic.

The persistence of the peasantry—or, more precisely, the fact that the substantial fall in numbers forecast by political economy seems unlikely to

From *CEPAL Review,* No. 11 (August 1980), pp. 115–134.

occur within a time scale of significance for social analysis and for the formulation of development strategies—as well as the inability of neo-classical analysis to account for a number of salient features of the behaviour of the peasant producer,[1] have led in the past decade to the emergence of an extensive literature devoted to re-examining the terms in which the peasant question has traditionally been tackled in economic analysis.

Two landmarks may be observed in this process of re-examination. First, a number of critiques have been made since the mid-1960s of the dualist propositions of various schools of thought, both those founded on the traditional-modern dichotomy and those drawn up in terms of the dichotomy between feudalism and capitalism. Second, a tendency has emerged to analyse the peasant economy as a *sui generis* form of organizing production, based on the 'rediscovery' of the writings of the so-called 'Russian populists' of the 1920s, and particularly those of A. V. Chayanov and his Organization of Production school.[2]

The criticism of dualism was a factor in the abandonment of the view of peripheral societies as split into two sectors: the traditional, pre-capitalist, semifeudal or feudal sector, regarded as a relic of a colonial past, and the modern, dynamic or capitalist sector, whose task was to 'absorb' and transform the former in its image and likeness.

In opposition to this approach there arose the view that both sectors had been formed by a single historical process, and that they were articulated within a global whole of which both formed an integral part, each accounting for the other. This involved abandonment of the idea of backwardness, and implicit or explicit acceptance of the possibility that peasant forms might persist or even be created as part of a dynamic of capitalist development.

The second of the landmarks mentioned earlier—the study of peasant economy, which is also the fundamental purpose of this article—represents an effort to study an important part of the peripheral economies which, having been described as 'traditional', had suffered from neglect in analysis or had simply been assimilated to a single allegedly universal rationality corresponding to that of the 'maximizer' of the neo-classical type.

The central part of the present article falls within the context of this latter objective. It constitutes an attempt to combine in a single formulation the contributions of various writers to describing the peasant economy, in an effort to demonstrate both the theoretical legitimacy and the empirical importance of this conceptualization in the formulation of development strategies for countries with a substantial peasant sector.

In addition to analysing the peasant economy as a specific form of organizing production—the principal purpose of the article—we shall in the second part sketch the contrast between the main features of peasant agriculture and those characteristic of commercial or capitalist agriculture. The article concludes with a few considerations on the nature of the insertion or articulation of peasant agriculture within the economy as a whole.

I. THE SPECIFIC CHARACTERISTICS OF THE PEASANT ECONOMY

The concept of the peasant economy encompasses that sector of domestic agricultural activity in which family-type units engaged in the process of production with the aim of ensuring, from one cycle to another, the reproduction of their living and working conditions, or, to put it another way, the reproduction of the producers and the unit of production itself. Achieving this objective means generating, firstly, the means of subsistence (biological and cultural) of all members of the family, active or not, and secondly—over and above those needs—a fund designed to pay for the replacement of the means of production used in the production cycle and to deal with the various eventualities which may affect the existence of the family group (illness, expenses for formal occasions, and so on).

The operating logic applied to the productive resources available, in other words the logic which governs the decisions concerning what, how and how much to produce and what to do with the product obtained, falls within the framework of the objectives described above, and gives the peasant economy its own rationality which is distinct from that of commercial agriculture. The latter, in contrast, decides what, how and how much to produce in such a way as to maximize rates of profit and accumulation. In this regard, then, we would appear to be faced with two specific and distinct forms of social organization of production.[3]

If one postulated the existence of a universal rationality as regards criteria for the allocation of resources, and if one considered that differences in behaviour between the various types of unit should be attributed exclusively to differences of scale and of resource availability, one would have to classify as purely 'irrational' a number of basic, recurrent and empirically observable phenomena in areas where the peasant economy prevails.

By way of illustration we might mention some of these phenomena, which point to the existence of a specific peasant rationality different from the commercial rationality.

An evaluation of the economic results achieved by peasant units over one or more cycles, using conventional 'factor cost' concepts, will show in the vast majority of cases that these units systematically incur losses. In other words, when the costs of this type of unit are evaluated, using market prices to impute land rent, current wages to estimate the cost of family labour used and market prices to impute the value of inputs which are not purchased in the market, with monetary costs actually incurred being added to this total, and when in valuing the product the goods sold are added to those consumed on the spot, valued at market prices, the difference between the value of the product and the cost thus calculated is very often negative. This type of result, which would seem to suggest that "half of mankind is today engaged in productive activity which registers a continuous deficit, is, nevertheless, a sort of *reductio ad absurdum* "[4] and constitutes "an instructive example not of the stupidity or philanthropy of peasants, but of the mistakenness of the belief that there is only one economic rationality in all places and at all times."[5]

The ability of peasant units to sell their livestock at prices which would in many cases signify losses (even with respect to his current costs) for an efficient commercial producer further testifies to the existence of two different ways of valuing resources and products in the two types of economy.

Another phenomenon of this type may be observed in the readiness of the peasant tenant to pay rents (in cash or in kind) which are generally higher than those prevailing in capitalist forms of letting, without any non-economic pressure necessarily being applied. In neo-classical terms, one might say that the peasant is prepared to pay as land rent more than the estimated value of the 'marginal product of the land' or, in the case of purchases of land, to pay for it more than the value of the expected rent, discounted at the internal rate of return on capital which encourages an entrepreneur to invest.[6]

Similarly revealing is the presence in some areas of peasant units which, while possessing productive resources in similar quantities or proportions, cultivate their land with different levels of intensity.[7] This would appear to reveal inefficient or irrational practices on the part of some of these producers, who would seem to have rejected voluntarily an economic 'optimum' of the neoclassical type. The same judgment would apply to situations of multiple cropping (or multiple activity), or where staple products occur exclusively despite the possibility of increasing the product through specialization or through inclusion of commercial products involving speculation or risk.

The examples given above are far from exceptional in areas of peasant agriculture, and by no means exhaust the number of empirical observations suggesting the existence of a type of rationality which is distinct from the commercial rationality and is determined by factors of a historical and structural nature, both within and outside the units of production, which will be examined below in some detail.

1. The Family-based Nature of the Production Unit

The peasant unit is at the same time a unit of production and a unit of consumption where household activity is inseparable from production activity. In this unit, decisions relating to consumption are inseparable from those which relate to production, and when production is embarked upon little or no use is made of (net) wage labour. This characteristic, which provides an explanation for many others, has been recognized as being of central importance by all writers who have dealt with the subject of the peasant economy; they have even pointed out that, in many cases, the nuclear or extended nature of the family is an integral part of a production strategy for survival.

As early as 1913 studies may be found which highlight the phenomenon mentioned above and define peasant units as "consumer-labour enterprises, with the consumer needs of the family as their aim and the labour force of the family as their means, with no or very little use of wage labour".[8] T. Shanin, one of the classics of rural sociology, regards the peasant unit as "characterized by a nearly total integration of the peasant family's life and its farming enterprise. The family provides the work team for the farm, while the farm's activities are geared mainly to production of the basic consumption needs of the family plus the enforced dues to the holders of political and economic power".[9] J. Tepicht shares this view: "in our model the grounding in the family signifies a symbiosis between the agricultural enterprise *(ferme)* and the household economy (*ménage*)".[10] Chayanov states that "in the family economic unit, which makes no use of hired labour, the composition and size of the family is one of the main factors in the organization of the peasant economic unit".[11]

The division of labour within the family unit is effected on the basis of differences of age and sex, and is frequently governed by custom as regards men's work and women's work. The implications of this attitude to work are analysed below.[12]

2. The Irrevocable Commitment to the Family Labour Force

The entrepreneur can regulate the labour force in his unit of production at will—if we leave aside legal restrictions—as the market dictates. In contrast, the head of the family in a peasant unit takes as his starting point the family labour force available and has to find productive employment for all its members. S. H. Franklin, in an important study on the European peasantry[13] highlights this commitment as the central feature of the peasant unit: "The head of the peasant unit *(chef d'entreprise)* lacks the freedom of action (of the capitalist entrepreneur) to regulate the labour force. His labour force is made up of his relations ("kith and kin") . . . and engaging and dismissing them in accordance with the dictates of some external regulatory mechanism would be at once inhuman, impractical and irrational. Inhuman because only in exceptional circumstances is it possible to find alternative job opportunities. Impractical because the members of his labour force, as members of the family, have a right to a share in the ownership of the means of production . . . Irrational because the objectives of the undertaking are first and foremost genealogical, and only secondarily economic, since the task of the *"chef"* is to maximize the labour input rather than profit or any other indicator of efficiency".[14]

Figure 1 clearly shows the implications of this feature, as well as others which will be referred to later, but which Franklin seems to have missed.

The shaded areas in the graph include sets of observations on the intensity of labour (hours per year per hectare) for units of different area with different numbers of standard labour units.[15] The ranges should be read as follows: the (shaded) upper set includes observations on units covering less than 10 hectares; the next on units of between 10 and 20 hectares, and so on

FIGURE 1

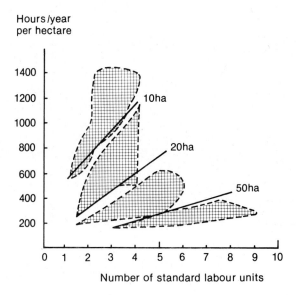

SOURCE: S. H. Franklin, op. cit., p. 17, where he cites the results of a field study by Van Deeren (1964).

until the last, which includes observations on units covering more than 50 hectares.

It may be noted that what Franklin calls the "labour commitment of the *chef d'enterprise*" is reflected in the fact that, for a given range of areas, there is a tendency to raise the number of working days per hectare as the number of labour units increases. In contrast, what is not given sufficient prominence by Franklin is that for each level of size and number of labour units there is a whole range of labour intensities per hectare which tends to be broader as the size of the unit declines. This, as we shall see below, suggests that among the units in a single area category and with the same number of labour units, the number of consumers per labour unit may vary.

3. Labour Intensity and Chayanov's Law

The intensity with which factors are used—given a certain availability of factors and a certain technological level—is determined by the degree to which requirements for the reproduction of the family and the unit of production, including debts or undertakings to third parties, are met.

Generally, and all other things being equal, there will be a tendency to intensify labour as the ratio of dependents to labour units rises. In other words, for equal resources (land and means of production), the number of working days per hectare will tend to rise with the ratio between consumers who have to be supported and family labour available. On the other hand, if the amount of land available increases, the number of working days per hectare will tend to fall, all other things being equal. In this regard, it may be said that within the technology range characteristic of the peasant economy, the dominant form of substitution is between land and labour (operating in both directions), in contrast to commercial agriculture, where the dominant substitution is that which tends to occur between capital and labour and between capital and land.[16]

The 'rules' for intensification mentioned above can be represented more clearly using a simplified graphic model (Figure 2)[17] where resources (land, means of production, labour force, and so on) and technology are of a given magnitude and are common to all the family units represented, with variations only in the number of the consumers which each unit must support. These consumers are represented in terms of an 'average consumer', in standard consumer units (Uc) into which the different age and sex groups of the family members have been converted. This variable (Uc) is represented in the graph as a downward projection of the horizontal axis. The horizontal axis proper (Uc) indicates the available family labour, standardized and expressed in man-hours per year.

If we assume that available working days are greater than $\overline{OY}$, which is the point of greatest intensity (or the point where the marginal product of labour, measured in terms of grain, would become zero), the minimum point of intensity (man-hours per year per unit of area) will depend on Uc, increasing in the same direction as Uc. For Uc = 4, the hours of labour will be $\overline{OX}$; for Uc = 5 they will rise to $\overline{OZ}$, and so on up to $\overline{OY}$ for Uc = 9, where the minimum intensity required and the maximum intensity possible will coincide.

In this case (Uc = 9), the product required to satisfy consumption by this unit is equal to $\overline{OC}$, which is the maximum possible in the light of the land, means of production and technology available. For all the other cases (Uc $\leqq$ 8) the minimum acceptable intensity would be determined, in the sense, for example, that a family with Uc = 4 has to perform at least $\overline{OX}$ working days; but beyond this point, and up to $\overline{OY}$, determination of the specific level of intensity—what Chayanov calls the "self-exploitation of the labour force"—would be established on the basis of the ratio between the satisfaction of needs which exceed minimum needs and the shortage of additional labour required to meet them.[18] It is unnecessary to point out that when resources are insufficient (Uc > 9 in the example), not only will the intensity used be the maximum possible, but in addition it will be necessary to seek additional employment in order to secure an income which will ensure the reproduction of the family and the unit of production, or else face its deterioration or break-up.[19]

Since in general the situation of peasant units is at or near the point of

FIGURE 2

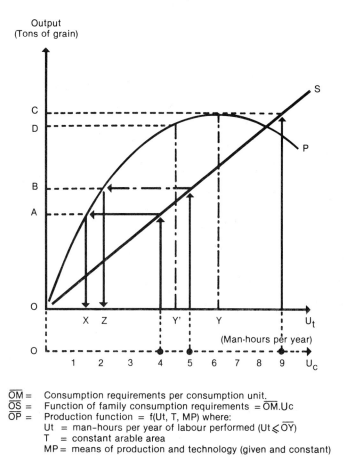

OM = Consumption requirements per consumption unit.
OS = Function of family consumption requirements = $\overline{OM}.Uc$
OP = Production function = f(Ut, T, MP) where:
Ut = man–hours per year of labour performed (Ut $\leqslant \overline{OY}$)
T = constant arable area
MP = means of production and technology (given and constant)

Fuente: Schejtman, A., op. cit., 1975.

maximum intensity, the margin for subjective considerations regarding the marginal utility of products and the marginal disutility of effort, which are of central importance in Chayanov's argument, is narrow enough to be irrelevant in practice and to permit determination of the level in terms which lead one to consider that the peasant unit tends to seek to raise its income as much as possible, regardless of the effort involved:[20] "In contrast to the capitalist, who does not commit funds if he is not assured of a rate of profit at least in proportion to them, and also in contrast to the wage earner, who for each hour of overtime will demand as much as, or more than, he demands for ordinary working hours, the 'personnel' of a family farm are prepared to contribute additional labour to raise their overall income, which [given the operation of the law of diminishing returns—A.S.] will be remunerated at a lower price, reducing the average value of their collective 'pay' ".[21]

4. The Partially Market-oriented Nature of Peasant Output

Peasant economy ceases to be a 'natural' economy, or one of on-the-spot consumption, or self-sufficiency, from the moment when a varying proportion of the material requirements for its reproduction, whether inputs or final consumption goods, must be acquired in the market, using money. For this purpose, the family unit is forced to join the market for goods and services as a supplier of products and/or of labour power.

However, in contrast to a United States farmer or any other kind of family undertaking of a commercial nature, the family unit generally comes to market in its capacity as a producer of use values (to use the classical terminology) and not of products which have been defined *a priori* as commodities, unless elements of external compulsion so dictate. In other words, the decision concerning what to produce is not based on the marketability of the product, but on its role in supporting the family and the production unit.

Frequently, even the manner of selling what has been produced reflects this feature of the peasant economy. Thus, when the product or products sold are the same as those which feature in the basic diet (maize, beans, wheat and so on), the peasant does not, at the time of the harvest, identify how much will be sent to market and how much will be consumed on the spot, but takes out for sale small parts of what has been harvested as the need arises for purchases and payments. Only on an *ex post* basis is it possible to reconstruct how much has been sold and distinguish it from what has been consumed on the spot. Only the presence of external constraints—either of an ecological nature (such as the fact that cultivation of basic grains is impossible)[22] or of a socioeconomic nature (such as the existence of land earmarked by law for a specific purpose)—or the existence of advances or borrowings which give the creditor power to make decisions concerning the crops will prevent the full expression of the partially market-oriented nature of peasant output.

Obviously, the more the peasant unit depends on purchased inputs and goods for its reproduction, the greater (other things being equal) will be the role which market considerations play in decisions on what and how to produce.

It may be deduced from the above that we do not subscribe to the characterization of the peasant economy as a 'simple mercantile economy' adopted by various writers,[23] since, although we agree that the aim of this type of economy is to reproduce its component units, we feel that the internal operating logic is not a purely market-oriented logic, such as that which would be applied by a Western farmer or craftsman. At the same time, to quote Tepicht, in the context of the theory from which the description "simple mercantile economy" has been taken, the latter "is but the embryo of the capitalist economy", while the 'historical vocation' of the peasant economy appears to be, very different from this role, in so far as this type of economy persists not only in many formations of a capitalist type, but even in those of a socialist type, as will be emphasized below.[24]

5. The Indivisibility of the Family Income

At the beginning of the article it was pointed out that when evaluating the results of the economic activity of peasant units, conventional economic analyses 'discovered' deficit situations in most cases. This was the result of applying to such units accounting categories identical to those applied to commercial agriculture, where rent, wages and profit are an objective reality. For this purpose, the analyses imputed market values to the effort made by the peasant and his family within their own unit, conferring on him the dual character of entrepreneur and wage earner and thus creating a schizoid being who, if he pays himself the current wage in his capacity as a wage earner, is guilty of irrational or philanthropic behaviour as an entrepreneur, since he not only fails to secure the average profit but suffers systematic losses in the 'capital' advanced; if, on the other hand, the average profit is imputed to him as remuneration for his entrepreneurial activities, he is cheating himself as a wage earner, by failing to allocate himself even a reproduction wage.

In contrast to this fiction, which we feel throws no light on the motivations of the peasant as a producer, the important categories are those which have an objective existence or which are capable of being objectified on the basis of the concrete behaviour of the units.

In this regard, the result (and the aim) of the economic activity of the family unit is the total family income (gross or net, in cash and in kind) derived from the joint efforts of its members, in which it is not possible to separate the part of the product attributable to rent from that attributable to wages or profits.[25]

6. The Non-transferable Nature of a Portion of Family Labour

One of the special features of the peasant unit is that it makes use of labour power which would not be in a position to create value in other production contexts. We refer both to the work of children, old people and women and to the unsystematic use of the spare time of the head of the family and his adult children of working age. This is one of the reasons for the ability of the family unit to bring products to the market at prices markedly lower than those required to stimulate commercial production.

According to Tepicht, peasant labour "is composed of at least two *qualitatively different* parts, both because of the nature of the forces it uses (some transferable to other economic sectors and others not), and because of the natural character of its products and the labour remuneration which is concealed in the prices at which they can be sold".[26] In other words, "what the peasant unit is in a position to produce with marginal forces in exchange for a marginal payment requires a completely different estimate by society (the market) if one considers the labour force required for this type of output".[27]

This is so much so that even in countries with centrally planned economies one may observe that, in collective units, the ratio between payments per working day devoted to livestock raising and payments per working day devoted to crop farming is greater than 1, whereas the implicit ratio (as indicated by the prices of the products concerned) in the peasant units is substantially less than 1.[28]

This ability to make use of the marginal labour force (that is to say, to convert it into products) may also be extended to land in the sense that areas which are marginal for commercial agriculture because of their extremely low productive potential—in other words, areas which are not even regarded as resources by commercial agriculture—can nevertheless support the peasant family, since the family regards any element which is capable of contributing to a net increase in the family income as a resource for as long as its reproduction requirements remain unsatisfied and there exists a margin within which its labour can productively be intensified.

A. Warman refers very lucidly to this phenomenon: "the peasant family in a capitalist society is first and foremost a unit which produces using unpaid labour. The labour of children and women, which is the object of very limited circulation as a commodity in capitalist Mexico, is one of the most important components of the peasant product. Women and children contribute thousands of working days which are invested in the independent production of peasants, in addition to performing work which is not strictly productive but which reduces outgoings and makes it possible to continue living with incomes which in statistical terms would be not just insufficient, but downright ridiculous".[29] Elsewhere he writes that "looking after livestock demands more energy than it yields, but this energy is distributed over a longer period and in units of low intensity which can be entrusted to people who cannot fully participate in labour during the critical period because they have little physical energy (such as children or old people) or who carry out other occupations at the same time (such as women). Owning livestock proves to be rational: it is like borrowing energy which is paid back with interest, but in instalments which can be paid by those without a full-time occupation in farming".[30]

7. The Special Type of Risk Internalization

For an entrepreneur, at least in theoretical terms, the risk or uncertainty which attach to the profits that can be derived from alternative applications of his capital are viewed in the decision-making process as probability functions which prompt him to seek at least a degree of proportionality between profit and risk. In the case of the peasant, his vulnerability to the effects of an adverse result is so extreme that, following Lipton[31], it seems appropriate to take the view that his behaviour as a producer is guided by a kind of 'survival algorithm' which leads him to avoid risks despite the potential profits which would arise if he accepted them. Lipton states that, while a well-off American farmer may prefer a 50% probability of obtaining US$ 5,000 or US$ 10,000 to the certainty of obtaining US$ 7,000, an Indian farmer who is offered a choice between a 50% probability of X rupees or 1,000 rupees and the certainty of 700 rupees per year, with which he can barely feed his family, cannot put X much below 700.[32]

The way peasant units thus internalize risk and uncertainty is another of the reasons that help to explain the persistence of cropping methods which, though they generate lower incomes, lessen the variability of the expected values of output. These considerations also explain why peasants will not consider growing certain crops which produce a higher yield per unit area, but which are subject to substantial variations in prices or involve a complex marketing mechanism.[33]

8. Labour-Intensive Technology

The need to take maximum advantage of the most abundant resource (the labour commitment referred to in the previous paragraph) and the existence of unfavourable terms of trade for peasant products in the overall or local market give rise to a tendency to reduce the purchase of inputs and means of production to the lowest possible level. As a result, the intensity of means of production per worker, or of purchased inputs per unit of product or per working day, are generally well below those of commercial or capitalist agriculture. In this regard, the decision on what to produce seems to be guided by the criterion of maximizing labour power per unit of product generated and/or minimizing purchased or hired inputs and means of production.

9. Membership of a Landgroup

In contrast to an agricultural enterprise, the peasant unit cannot be viewed as a unit separate from other similar units, but always appears as part of a larger grouping of units with which it shares a common territorial base:[34] what A. Pearse defines as the landgroup, which consists of "a group of families forming part of a larger society and living in permanent interdependence interaction, and propinquity by virtue of a system of arrangements between them for the occupation and productive use of a single land area and the physical resources it contains, from which they gain their livelihood".[35] J. Tepicht, for his part, calls this social context the "protective shell of the family economy".[36]

The very reproduction of the peasant family unit depends in many cases on the complex system of non-market exchanges conducted with a greater or lesser degree of reciprocity within the landgroup. Even the survival or decline of the family units frequently depends on the degree of cohesion which the landgroup maintains in the face of limitations on its scope for survival, generally arising from the development of commercial agriculture.

In fact, as is emphasized below, the penetration and development of market relations progressively weaken the role of the landgroup in the cycle of social reproduction of the family units, with the result that this reproduction occurs on an increasingly individual basis, which is unquestionably less secure.

Despite the crucial importance which the landgroup has had and continues to have in accounting for the persistence of the peasantry, and despite the importance it should have when any rural development strategy based on the peasantry is being drawn up, there has very often been a tendency to restrict analysis of the peasant economy to analysis of the family unit. A. Warman, in contrast, emphasizes that "it is obvious that the family cannot remain in a position to produce without capital and without opportunities to accumulate and cannot subsist without reserves or savings, in an environment dominated by capitalist relationships, without the support of a larger grouping which furnishes conditions of stability in this contradictory situation. In the case of Mexico, the larger grouping takes the form of the agrarian community, in which one may observe on a broader and more complex, though still partial, scale the production relations of the peasant economy".[37]

10. Commercial Agriculture: Principal Contrasts

By way of concluding this first chapter it seems appropriate to outline the principal features of commercial agriculture so that we can contrast them, albeit in general terms, with those which have been highlighted as being characteristic of the peasant economy.

A description of this sector does not call for a very detailed conceptual effort, since—given the level of abstraction in this chapter—its principal features are only too well known; reference has already been made to some of them when contrasting them with those of the peasant economy. Accordingly, it will be sufficient to point out that in commercial units there is a clear separation between capital and labour power, and that as a result profit, wages and even land rent are categories which are the objective expression of relations between owners of means of production, landowners and sellers of labour power.

Kinship relations are completely divorced from production relations; in other words, what we have called the commitment to the labour force does not exist.

The relations between units are regulated by universal market laws in which there is no place for exchanges based on reciprocity, or, to put it another way, on considerations of community and kinship.

Production is exclusively market-oriented (though for some crops a margin is left to allow for internal consumption or use as inputs within the unit), in the sense that decisions on what and how to produce are completely unrelated to what the producers and their families consume.

Considerations of risk and uncertainty arise strictly in terms of probabilities, in the sense that they are internalized in the decision-making process as ratios between magnitudes of profit expected and probabilities associated with each magnitude.

The principal aim of production, and accordingly the criterion used to determine what to produce, how much, how and for what purpose, is to secure at least average profit, which is destined for accumulation (and, of course, consumption by the entrepreneurs).

The contrast between the two forms of social organization of production referred to is represented diagramatically in Table 1.

II. ARTICULATION AND BREAK-UP OF PEASANT AGRICULTURE

So far we have restricted ourselves to analysing the rules which govern the internal operation of the peasant economy, and the differences which emerge from a comparison with those applying to commercial agriculture. We will now consider the way in which these characteristics influence the position of the peasant economy in the national society of which it is part.

1. The Concept of Articulation

We consider the concept of articulation of different forms of social organization of production—the peasant and the capitalist forms—to be of central importance in classifying the phenomena which we wish to examine.

By articulation we mean the relationships (or system of relationships) which link the sectors in question one with another and with the rest of the economy, forming an integrated whole (the economic system) whose structure and dynamics are determined by (and in turn determine) the structure and dynamics of the parts.[38]

Articulation takes the form of exchanges of goods and services (or values) between sectors: exchanges which are characterized by their asymmetry[39] (or lack of equivalence), and which lead to transfer of surpluses from the peasant sector to the rest of the economy, as a result of a form of integration in which the peasant economy sector is subordinated to the remaining elements in the structure (capitalist agriculture and the urban-industrial complex).[40]

Although this articulation is expressed or becomes visible at the level of

TABLE 1

	PEASANT AGRICULTURE	COMMERCIAL AGRICULTURE
Purpose of production	Reproduction of the producers and the production unit	Maximization of the rate of profit and capital accumulation
Origin of the labour force	Basically the family and, on occasion, reciprocated loans from other units; exceptionally, marginal quantities of wage labour	Wage labour
Commitment of the head to the labour force	Absolute	Non-existent, apart from legal requirements
Technology	Very labour-intensive; low intensity of 'capital' and of purchased inputs	Greater capital intensity per labour unit and higher proportion of purchased inputs in the value of the final product
Destination of the product and origin of inputs	The market, in part	The market
Criterion for intensification of labour	Maximum total product, even at the cost of a fall in the average product. Limit: nil marginal product	Marginal productivity $\geq$ wage
Risk and uncertainty	Assessment not based on probabilities; 'survival algorithm'	Internalization based on probabilities, in the search for rates of profit proportional to risk
Nature of the labour force	Makes use of non-transferable or marginal labour	Uses only transferable labour on the basis of skills
Components of net income or product	Indivisible family product or income, realized partially in kind	Wage, rent and profit, exclusively in the form of money

the market relations between sectors—in the markets for products, inputs, labour and even land—the terms of this exchange, or its asymmetrical nature, cannot be explained at this level, but originate in differences at the level of the process of production, i.e., the level of the forms of production or differences in the operating logic specific to each of the sectors.

We shall first consider the main forms of articulation, and then examine how the nature of each form may be 'explained', in the final analysis, in terms of differences in the process of production.

2. Articulation in the Market for Products

An initial form of articulation, or, to express it differently, of exploitation of peasant agriculture, is that which arises in the market for products to which the peasant comes to sell part of his output and to buy inputs and final goods which he requires for his reproduction. There the terms of trade, or the relative prices of what he buys and what he sells, are and always have been systematically unfavourable to him. Regardless of the fact that the terms of trade may record improvements in a specific period and with respect to a base year, there is a sort of 'primordial' undervaluation of peasant products which is inherent in the very structure of relative prices (as between peasant production and capitalist production), formed over generations, on which the reproduction of the economy as a whole is crucially dependent because of the well-known relationship between food prices, wage levels and the rate of profit.[41]

Although the extent of inequality in exchange—in other words, the magnitude of the surplus transferred from the peasant sector to the rest of society through the above-mentioned mechanism—can rise or fall depending on the greater or lesser bargaining power (social power in the market) which each party can exert in the market relationship, its origin lies in the internal logic of production in each sector, and not in the market relationships, although this is where it is expressed.

The 'secret' which makes unequal exchange possible is to be found in the readiness of peasant agriculture to produce at prices lower than those which a capitalist producer would require in order to do so in the same conditions, since while it is sufficient for the former to meet the requirements for the reproduction of the labour force employed and the fund for the replacement of the means of production used, the latter sector requires in addition a profit which is at least equal to the average profit in the economy.

If, to simplify, we assume that the labour force employed in the two cases is the same, that the cost of its reproduction is covered by wages, that the inputs purchased are the same in both cases and that the peasant's replacement fund is equal to the entrepreneur's depreciation, the difference in the prices at which each will be prepared to produce will be the average profit, if they pay the same rent, or the profit plus land rent if both own the land.[42]

"The small peasant landowner behaves neither like the owner of property nor like the capitalist entrepreneur. As a matter of principle he is obliged to produce regardless of conditions on the market, or he will fail to survive. Immediately he *contents himself with the equivalent of a wage,* without raising the question of rent, or even the question of profit. The small peasant behaves exactly like a wage-paid piece-worker."[43]

This is precisely why peasant agriculture may be found in areas (marginal lands) and in lines of products where capitalist undertakings would be uneconomic.

This is the phenomenon which lies at the very foundation of the formation of the price systems, and particularly of the historical process of formation of relative prices between agriculture and industry, which have made possible a systematic transfer of surpluses from the peasantry to other sectors through the medium of exchange.

This situation does not apply only to the peripheral countries, since it arises in any economy (capitalist or socialist) where there is a substantial sector involving family producers, even the "farmer" type, whose product —to quote G. J. Johnson, referring to the United States—is supplied to society at 'bargain prices': "A cynic might even say that the family farm is an institution which operates in order to encourage the families of farmers to provide quantities of labour and capital at rates of return which are substantially lower than the norm in order to supply the economy as a whole with agricultural products at bargain or sale prices".[44] This is why over long periods the rise in agricultural productivity in many developed countries has not been accompanied by proportional increases in the incomes of farmers, in contrast to what happens in the remainder of the economy.[45]

This asymmetry exerts pressure for the intensification of family agriculture, which, in the "farmer" type, usually takes the form of overinvestment and, in the peripheral peasant type, that of more intensive self-exploitation of family labour.[46]

State subsidies, either provided directly through the medium of low prices for inputs and products and credit at low interest rates, or implicitly through the financing of infrastructure for which the beneficiaries are not charged, represent no more than a form of partially compensatory recognition of this phenomenon.[47]

3. Articulation in the Labour Market

Another area where articulation is expressed is the labour market, particularly, though not exclusively, the market for agricultural day-labourers, who can be engaged by the commercial sector at wages lower than their cost of survival or reproduction.

If no peasant economy sector existed, the wage bill would have to be sufficient at least to guarantee the sustenance and reproduction of the labour employed, in other words the sustenance, over time, of the labour force required by the process of accumulation and growth. If an average rate of profit prevailed in both sectors (agriculture and industry), this would lead to higher agricultural prices, with the consequent chain reaction on wages, profits and accumulation.

The fact that a substantial proportion of the labour force employed in commercial agriculture (and even in urban-industrial activities) originates from or is more or less directly linked with the peasant economy, and that its conditions for reproduction are in part generated in the peasant economy, permits a reduction of the wage bill by means of the dual mechanism whereby wages paid per day worked are lower than in other sectors, while payment is made only for days actually worked, however low this number may be, regardless of the fact that this may by no means cover the annual subsistence of the worker himself, and still less that of his family. The viability of capitalist agriculture is frequently due to the fact that it is possible to pay wages lower than the reproduction cost of the labour, especially in areas where the differential land rent (in the Ricardian sense) is very low or non-existent.[48]

Temporary rural migrations from areas of peasant agriculture to areas of commercial agriculture merely confirm this interdependence.

Similarly, in the case of the sale of labour power, the possibility of a non-equivalent exchange—in other words, the possibility of paying less than the reproduction cost of the labour employed—is a phenomenon which, although it is expressed in the labour market, and although it may appear to depend exclusively on the bargaining power between the parties, has its origin in the conditions of production and reproduction of the peasant economy.

The above is connected not only with the fact that subsistence is assured in part by the peasant economy itself, but also with the fact that the amount of labour power supplied by the peasants, as well as the wage levels they are prepared to accept, are determined by the production conditions characterizing the unit to which they belong. In this regard, the further the peasant is from obtaining the level of income (in cash and in kind) required for reproduction in his own unit, the greater will be the number of days he is prepared to work in exchange for a wage, and the higher the level of intensity with which he is working his plot of land, the lower will be the wage necessary to attract him away from it, in accordance with the phenomenon of diminishing returns.

The diagram [Figure 3], which is of course an oversimplification of real conditions, helps to clarify the above: Here we are comparing two production units (A and B), whose average and marginal product curves (AP' and BQ', AP and BQ), in this example indicate greater availability of land in unit B. Let us assume that magnitude $OC \times OM$ is equal to the net reproduction income. Unit A, with the maximum possible intensity (in other words, using

OP working days and with nil marginal productivity), does not achieve the reproduction income, since $OC \times OP < OC \times OM$. It will therefore be sufficient to offer a wage equal to OS ($= RT$) so that the peasant will work away from the plot for at least PR working days (assuming that the family labour available is greater than OR) so as to ensure that $(OC \cdot OP) + (PR \cdot RT) = (OC \cdot OM)$. In contrast, the peasant on unit B, who can achieve the reproduction income on his own plot ($OC \cdot OM = UK \cdot OU$) by working OU days, will not be prepared to sell labour power unless the wage offered is greater than UK.

The two articulation mechanisms described (product market and labour market), though significantly different in form, nevertheless have a common basis: the peasant unit's capacity and readiness (for structural, not philanthropic reason) to undervalue its working time with respect to the patterns established by the rules of operation of the capitalist sector, either as labour power proper, or as labour power materialized in the products which it places on the market.

This capacity is the source both of the peasantry's strength, in the sense of a force working for its persistence, and of its weakness, in the sense of a force working for its break-up.

4. Break-up, Recovery and Persistence

As was pointed out in the introduction, all the schools of thought which derive from liberalism (liberals proper, rationalists, positivists, marxists and so on) postulated the transitional nature of the peasantry, which was regarded as a segment of society doomed to disappear—some of its members converted

FIGURE 3

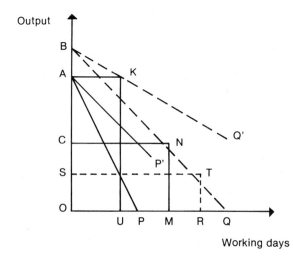

Working days

into *bourgeois,* the rest converted into proletarians—as a result of the vigour of capitalist development. Peasantries in specific societies were considered cultural and/or social relics from former times.

Although it is true that the relative importance of the peasant sector, as a segment of the population, has been declining, nevertheless in the peripheral countries the peasantry remains one of the largest groups, since it rarely accounts for less than a third of the working population. If this is a mere transitory phase, it must be recognized that the transition has been very lengthy. What is more, in some societies the influences working for its disappearance have been checked, to some extent, by others which are not only preventing its disappearance but even, in specific areas and circumstances, creating peasant forms of organization of production where they did not exist previously.

From the political and economic policy viewpoint, and bearing in mind the above considerations, it seems more sensible to abandon the assumption of transitoriness and take the view that for the foreseeable future (and for a period relevant in terms of policy formulation) the peasantry will persist. Consequently, it is necessary to undertake an analysis of the forces working to ensure its persistence, and those fostering its break-up, so that they can be taken into account in the formulation of development strategies and policies designed to ensure that the peasant sector plays a role commensurate with its potential.

In the discussion below, break-up of the peasant form will be understood to mean the process which leads to the progressive narrowing down of options which would permit the family unit to survive using its own resources: in other words, loss of the ability to generate a volume of output which is equivalent to the fund for family consumption and the fund for the replacement of inputs and means of production.

Recovery will be understood to mean those processes which reverse the above-mentioned trend, as well as those which lead to the creation of peasant units in areas where they did not exist before.

In general terms, the forces working in favour of the persistence, recovery or break-up of the peasant sector act on, and have their basis in, the basic network of relations between and within sectors (between the peasant and the rest of society), which we have defined as a form of articulation which subordinates the peasant form to the national economy and society, and whose principal features have already been described. In other words, these forces help to intensify, redefine or restrain the elements of asymmetrical symbiosis of a structural nature which have been encompassed here under the concept of articulation through subordination. In this sense these forces can be viewed as superstructural elements, which affect and are affected by the structure defined as articulation.

For descriptive purposes, these forces may be grouped on the basis of their origin, and a distinction may be drawn between those which stem from the State and its policies; those generated by the action of the intermediary persons or institutions, or brokers, that represent a link between the peasantry and the rest of the economy; those generated by the conscious actions of the commercial sector; and those which derive from the dynamics of demographic and ecological factors.

(a) Action by the state. Since the State is an expression of the correlation of social forces at each moment in time, its action cannot fail to be a blend of contradictory forces, even if the resultant of these forces is the maintenance of the conditions of reproduction of the social whole and, consequently, the maintenance of the type of articulation to which we have been referring.

In general, policies which involve subsidies to the peasant sector,[49] such as credit at preferential rates, support prices, the establishment of minimum wages (especially if compliance is monitored), and so on, are actions which tend to limit or check the break-up of the peasant unit by making possible terms of trade, in various areas, better than those which would be achieved in free market conditions.

Agrarian reform and new settlement are also, at least in theory, policies which impede the break-up of peasant units, and even encourage their creation through the subdivision of larger geographical units and the development of complementary legislation and action to protect the units created.

In contrast to the above-mentioned actions, public investment in irrigation, or in improving communications and prospects for the export of produce, has frequently led to increased imposition on the resources of the peasant sector—both directly, through appropriation of the areas in question by commercial agriculture, and indirectly, through accentuation of the (asymmetrical) trade relations in the process of reproduction of the peasant economy—and have thereby increased its vulnerability.

(b) Action by intermediary elements. Here we are referring to the various types of mechanism for intermediation which link the peasantry to the rest of the economy and permit the extraction of surpluses at the level of relations of distribution and exchange. In general, these intermediary persons and/or institutions make use both of the possibilities opened up by the specific operating logic of the peasant economy and of those derived from the lesser bargaining power of units from that sector and the intermediaries' monopoly (sometimes on a very small scale) of the channels through which this sector is linked to society as a whole.

The functions of the intermediary elements have been classified by A. Warman as follows:

(i)   Material adaptation of products, involving a sort of scaling down of what reaches the peasant sector as a product, and a scaling up of what leaves the peasant sector for the rest of the economy;

(ii) 'conversion of symbols', involving 'translation' into the peasant language of the external norms of trade and accounting, in other words, converting units of weight, quality standards and so on into generally accepted terms;

(iii) the physical movement of the products which enter or leave the peasant economy from and to the external world;

(iv) the mobilization of finance by means of which the peasant can be more fully integrated in the market for consumer goods or inputs, to a greater extent than would be possible if he sold his products or labour power himself.

These types of function make it possible to extend market relations in the process of reproduction of the peasant economy and to integrate it in the rest of the national (and international) economy. In order to fulfil this function, the intermediary element "is located between two modes of production, handles two types of language, two types of social relationship and economic rationality, and guides the flow of capital towards the dominant mode. He himself obtains a profit from all his acts, equally when he converts weights into kilos and when he lends money for the sowing of onions . . . His success depends on his flexibility and diversification, on his being able to sell seven different things and accept a chicken in payment".[50] Each of the functions described involves the appropriation of surpluses, and in this regard contributes to the break-up of the peasantry; however, to the extent that the persistence and reproduction of the peasantry depend on exchange through the medium of trade, the intermediary elements contribute to its survival, although they exact a high price.

(c) Action by enterprises responsible for processing and intermediation. Although strictly speaking this phenomenon should be included among the structural components of articulation, we have decided to highlight it separately since it is a recent tendency in the organization of agricultural production. We refer to the phenomenon of the contracts commonly drawn up between large agro-industrial or agri-business enterprises and the peasants of specific regions.

These contracts reflect a tendency on the part of capital to abandon direct control of land and the processes of primary production and replace them by financial and commercial control of a huge network of small and medium-sized 'independent' producers, either by creating a sort of peasantry economically attached to them or by "attaching" a pre-existing group of peasants, who can be induced to work on advantageous conditions which—for the reasons already indicated—business agriculture would not accept. This is particularly true in situations where the process of break-up of the peasantry can only be halted by exploring avenues for labour intensification which involve the partial or total abandonment of traditional farming patterns and their replacement by market-oriented patterns with high unit values.

(d) The dynamics of demographic and ecological factors. Natural growth in the peasant population, which is appreciably greater than the expansion of the already inadequate capacity of the remaining sectors to absorb that growth productively, is reflected in increasing pressure on land, or, to put it another way, a deterioration in the land/man ratio, not only in the sense of an arithmetical fall but in the no less important sense of a decline in the productive potential of the existing land.

In general, this is a force which contributes to the break-up of the peasantry, since fragmentation—which is the result of the subdivision of plots as a consequence of population growth—is an inescapable sign of a rise in the fragility or vulnerability of the peasant economy and a prelude to its disappearance.

The existence of possibilities of working outside the plot can help to defer the impact of this tendency through 'subsidization' of the continued existence of the unit with incomes obtained outside it. Within the peasant segment, the above-mentioned forces give rise to a process of differentiation or polarization, in which a minority of the units succeed not only in preventing break-up but even turn the intensification in market-oriented relations to their account and achieve a certain amount of accumulation.

Another section achieves a sort of equilibrium between the various forces and succeeds in maintaining its conditions of reproduction over time with a greater or lesser degree of security.

For the majority, however, the dynamics of break-up—which takes the form of a progressive loss of their ability to support themselves—are inexorable and can be alleviated only by the possibility, which is not always available, for the producer or the members of his family to obtain incomes from outside the plot.

In socioeconomic analysis of the peasant sector, and in the diagnoses which precede the formulation of a strategy for its development, it is of crucial importance to recognize the type of heterogeneity to which the processes of differentiation indicated here can lead.

In other words, we may, for the purposes of description, stratify the peasant segment as a function of the magnitude of a specific variable within a continuum (land, output, and so on). The important distinction is whether or not internal conditions exist for the support of the production unit and/or the landgroup.

This criterion can be used to distinguish at least three important categories within the peasant agriculture sector:

(i)   the infrasubsistence segment, or 'poor peasant' segment, made up of those units which need incomes from outside the plot in order to attain a minimum subsistence income. This appears to be the segment recording fastest relative growth in Latin America;[51]

(ii)   The stationary, "simple reproduction" or "average peasant" segment, made up of that part of the peasantry whose product is sufficient to cover the fund for family consumption and the fund for the replacement of inputs and means of production, from one cycle to another;

(iii)   the surplus-producing or 'rich' peasant segment, made up of those units which, with their resources, more or less systematically generate a surplus over and above what is required for the reproduction of the family and the production unit, although they cannot always convert it into accumulation. Whether or not this stratum will lose its peasant status—in other words, whether or not it will become involved in a process of accumulation founded on the systematic engagement of non-family labour on a substantial scale—will depend on conditions which it is beyond the scope of this paper to analyse.

NOTES

1. Reference is made to several of these features in section 1.1.
2. The impact of Chayanov's writings on Western literature made itself felt surprisingly late, even though one of his articles, containing the most important part of his contribution to theory, was published in 1931 by the University of Minnesota Press in a group of papers edited by P. Sorokin, C. Zimmerman and C. Galpin (A. V. Chayanov, "The Socioeconomic Nature of Peasant Farm Economy", in *A Systematic Source Book in Rural Sociology*). Nevertheless, neither anthropologists nor economists seem to have become aware of Chayanov's importance until the mid-1960s. Eric Wolf, who quotes the text mentioned above, was one of the first to take up the essence of Chayanov's argument, in his book *Peasants* (New Jersey, Prentice Hall, 1966) (pp. 14 and 15). In the same year, D. Thorner, B. Kerblay and R.E.F. Smith published—in addition to a biographical analysis of the writer and an assessment of his contributions to theory—two of his most important works (see A. V. Chayanov, *The Theory of Peasant Economy* (Richard D. Irwin, Inc., Illinois, 1966)). It was after the publication of this book that Chayanov's work became widely known both in the English-speaking world and in Latin America.
3. We shall speak here of forms of organization of production (or, more briefly, forms) in order to avoid a debate on whether or not the peasant economy is a mode of production in the sense in which the term is used in historical materialism. Although such a debate might be of importance as regards some of its theoretical implications, it is not germane to the purposes of the present article, which are limited to showing that what is involved is a form of production which is different

from the commercial form and is governed by its own rules. Those interested in the debate can consult, for example: R. Bartra, *Estructura agraria y clases sociales en México* (Ed. Era, Mexico City, 1974), who considers peasant agriculture as a simple market mode. This view is shared by M. Coello, "La pequeña producción campesina y la ley de Chayanov", *Historia y sociedad,* No. 8, Mexico City, 1975. J. Tepicht, *Marxisme et agriculture: le paysan polonais* (Paris, A. Colin, 1973), pp. 13–46, regards it as being a mode in its own right. A. Warman adopts a similar position in . . . *Y venimos a contradecir* (Mexico City, La Casa Chata, 1976), chap. VI.

Among the critics of the "mode of production" approach, see H. Bernstein, "Concept for the Analysis of Contemporary Peasantries" (mimeo, to be published shortly in M. J. Mbiling and C. K. Omari, *Peasant Production in Tanzania,* University of Dar es Salaam) or, following a different argument, G. Esteva's article "La economia campesina moderna" (photocopy supplied by the author), 1979. In P. Vilar, "La economia campesina", *Historia y sociedad,* No. 15, Mexico City, 1977, we find a notable critique of the validity of the concept of the peasant economy. The *Journal of Peasant Studies* (JPS), London, has published a large number of articles on the subject of the peasant mode (or form); see, for example: J. Ennew, P. Hirst and K. Tribe, " 'Peasantry' as an Economic Category", *JPS,* vol. 4, No. 4 (July 1977); M. Harrison, "The Peasant Mode of Production in the Work of A.V. Chayanov", *JPS,* vol. 4, No. 4 (July 1977); D. E. Goodman, "Rural Structure, Surplus Mobilization, and Modes of Production in a Peripheral Region: The Brazilian North-East", *JPS,* vol. 5, No. 1 (October 1977), and C. D. Scott, "Peasants, Proletarianization and the Articulation of Modes of Production: The Case of Sugar-cane Cutters in Northern Peru, 1940–1969", *JPS,* vol. 3, No. 3 (April 1976).

4. W. Kula, *Théorie économique du système féodal,* quoted by R. Bartra, op. cit., 1973, p. 36.
5. J. Tepicht, op. cit., 1973, p. 36.
6. A. Schejtman, "Elementos para una teoria de la economia campesina: pequeños propietarios y campesinos de hacienda", *El Trimestre Económico,* vol. XLII(2), No. 166, Mexico City, April-June 1975; republished in *Economá Campesina* (Lima, DESCO, 1979).
7. In areas where the amount of land is very limited, this phenomenon may not be manifested very clearly. However, when the peasant unit faces no major limitations on its choice of desirable scales (as in the humid tropics, or in areas with extensive stretches of previously unfarmed land which has not yet been appropriated by large landowners), differences of scale may be observed which cannot be explained in terms of the availability of other complementary resources (labour force, tools, and so on) but must be attributed to objectives different from those which enter into the definition of economic 'optima'.
8. T. Shanin, "A Russian peasant household at the turn of the century", in T. Shanin, ed., *Peasants and Peasant Societies* (Harmondsworth, Middx., Penguin, 1971), p. 30, quoting a Russian encyclopaedia published in 1913.
9. Ibid.
10. Tepicht illustrates this by citing a region of Algeria (Zeribe) where a study of 'the joint property type' (of the old extended families) indicates an almost complete absence of 'mixed' situations of joint production activity and separate kitchens, or vice versa. Either the couples join together in work in the fields and at the table, or they separate and become modernized both in the fields and at the table (even if they live under the same roof). Op. cit., pp. 23–24.

11. Chayanov, 1974, op. cit. Chayanov even comes to see in the family structure (size, ages, sexes) the principal element of economic differentiation; we do not share this view, as is indicated below at the beginning of the section on differentiation.

12. The great flexibility which may be observed in this symbiosis between the undertaking and the family is illustrated by A. Warman with reference to the Zapata period: "as access to the land controlled by the *hacienda* became more difficult, the extended family gained strength as the most efficient unit for securing an independent supply of maize and raising wage incomes to cover subsistence for the peasants. It was the only form of organization which made it possible to survive and maintain the men in fighting condition". Op. cit., 1977, p. 307.

13. S. H. Franklin, *The European Peasantry* (London, Methuen, 1969).

14. The expression "maximize the labour input" is ambiguous; strictly one should speak of maximizing the input of *productive* labour, that is labour which generates increases in net income, and not labour in general.

15. We assume that "standard labour units", which is the variable used by Franklin, implies that the various categories of worker in the unit have been reduced to a homogeneous unit, using criteria which are unfortunately not clear.

16. J. Tepicht, op cit., pp. 24 and 26.

17. Taken from A. Schejtman, op. cit.

18. A. V. Chayanov, op. cit., 1974, p. 84.

19. A. Warman (op. cit., 1976, p. 326) sets out this 'law' as follows: "Once subsistence requirements have been met, the peasant stops producing. Firstly, the diminishing returns from the more intensive activity mean that any additional income over the subsistence minimum demands a disproportionate increase in activity. Secondly, incorporation in the capitalist market means that any rise in income leads to a rise in the transfer of surpluses". Warman also introduces the problem of subordination, to which we shall refer below.

20. J. Tepicht, op. cit., p. 41.

21. Ibid., p. 35.

22. An interesting example of an ecological constraint is furnished by certain forms of co-ownership of livestock observed in the Mexican humid tropics, where, as a result of the fact that the peasants find it impossible to continue with agriculture based on felling, clearing and burning—because the pressure of numbers on the land does not permit renewal of the plant cover required for this practice—a system of co-ownership has arisen between private stock raisers and *ejidatarios*, whereby the former concentrate on fattening and the latter on breeding. The cattle belong to the stock raiser, and the *ejidatarios* are entitled to half the calves (normally the females) and to the milk, in exchange for the use of their pastures and their care of the livestock under the co-ownership agreement. In these circumstances, the milk, which is sold or is made into cheese for sale, comes to play part of the role of maize, and the female calves the role which livestock normally plays in peasant agriculture: a savings fund and an illusory form of accumulation.

23. See footnote 3 for author references. The term "simple" is used by these writers to describe a situation where there is no accumulation of surpluses nor any increase in the production capacity of the units over time.

24. J. Tepicht, op. cit., p. 18.

25. See A. V. Chayanov, 1966, op. cit., pp. 2–5, and J. Tepicht, op. cit., p. 36. Perhaps the only virtue of the fiction referred to above is to show that peasant units are

prepared to supply their products at prices below those which a capitalist producer would demand in order to pay current wages and rents and obtain at least the average profit. However, the reasons why this occurs are totally obscured by this form of evaluation or calculation. R. Bartra, in his study on Mexican agrarian structure (Bartra, op. cit., pp. 58–66), makes use of the categories of wage, rent and profit in the manner indicated.

26. J. Tepicht, op. cit., pp. 39–40.
27. Ibid., p. 38.
28. Ibid., pp. 36–37.
29. A. Warman, op. cit., p. 310.
30. Ibid., p. 298.
31. M. Lipton, "The Theory of the Optimizing Peasant", *Journal of Development Structures*, vol. IV (April 1968), pp. 327–351.
32. Ibid., p. 345.
33. An intuitive approach, corroborated by some empirical evidence, indicates a certain correlation between the value (and degree of liquidity) of the assets the peasant owns and his ability to take risks, either by adding crops and/or techniques which, although more profitable, are also more risky than the traditional ones, or by specializing in some of the traditional crops instead of maintaining the pattern of a larger number of crops occupying small areas, which is characteristic of the poor peasant. In this regard, livestock destined for breeding, the principal form of saving, fulfils the function of insurance against poor harvests or the adverse result of a risk taken, so that those who possess most livestock are most prepared to introduce innovations in cropping patterns or methods. A. Schejtman, *Hacienda and Peasant Economy,* degree thesis, University of Oxford, 1970, chap. IV.
34. We have avoided the term "rural or local community" which is used so frequently in the literature, since it implicitly contains the idea that the group in question shares common interest, which is not always the case, and raises "an empirical problem which should not be introduced into the definition" of these groupings. D. Lehman, *On the Theory of Peasant Economy* (photocopy provided by the author), p. 15; and H. Mendras, quoted by J. Tepicht, op. cit., p. 22.
35. A. Pearse, *The Latin American Peasant* (London, Frank Cass, 1975), p. 51. This is identical to the concept used by Warman in *Los campesinos hijos predilectos del régimen* (Mexico City, Nuestro Tiempo, 1972), p. 145, when he speaks of a "group which shares a common territorial base".
36. J. Tepicht, op. cit., p. 20.
37. A. Warman, op. cit., 1976, p. 314; see also p. 325.
38. This concept is used by many writers in a sense very close to that given it in this paragraph. Examples are J. Bengoa, "Economia campesina y acumulación capitalista", *Economia campesina,* op. cit., pp. 251–286; R. Bartra, op. cit., pp. 79–87; A. Warman, op. cit., pp. 324–337; G. Oliver, *Hacia una fundamentación analitica para una nueva estrategia de desarollo rural* (photocopy) (Mexico City, CIDER, 1977), pp. 176–199.
39. The term "asymmetry" was used by Warman (op. cit., 1976, p. 325), in a sense similar to that which we are using here, in order to contrast (symmetrical) relationships within the peasant community with those which arise between that community and the rest of society. "In the peasant mode of production the internal relationships are oriented towards symmetry, towards reciprocity, in order to

make it possible to ensure the subsistence of the families, the smallest efficient units in the grouping. The community is the context through which flow the relationships of reciprocity which play the role of redistributing resources, flexibly transmitting the use of the means which make agricultural production, the basic activity of this mode, possible. Among the different peasant communities the symmetrical relationship is realized through the direct exchange of complementary goods by the producers themselves. In order for the resources to be exchanged symmetrically, they must be under the independent command and control of the peasants, whether or not they are formally recognized as their possessions." We shall see below when analysing the phenomenon of peasant differentiation, how the loss of independent control over their conditions of reproduction leads to the emergence of asymmetrical relationships even within the landgroup.

40. In order to define this form of articulation, some writers have adopted the term "subsumption", which encompasses the concepts of integration and subordination (G. Esteva, op. cit., p. 4).

41. J. Tepicht, "Economia contadina e teoria marxista", *Critica marxista*, No. 1, Rome, 1967, p. 76.

42. Land rent (imputed or actually paid) will have to be added to profit if we compare a peasant landowner with an entrepreneur landowner, since while the former would be prepared to overlook the value of this rent, or (to express it more clearly) to view it as an integral part of his total 'reproduction' income, the latter will demand a return equivalent to that on his other capital.

43. K. Vergópoulos, "Capitalismo disforme", in S. Amin and K. Vergópoulos, *La cuestión campesina y el capitalismo* (Mexico City, Nuestro Tiempo, 1975), p. 165. Chayanov made exactly the same observation: ". . . we take the motivation of the peasant's economic activity not as that of an entrepreneur who as a result of investment of his capital receives the difference between gross income and production overheads, but rather as the motivation of the worker on a peculiar piece-rate system which allows him alone to determine the time and intensity of his work". Op. cit., 1966, p. 42.

44. Quoted by J. Tepicht, op. cit., 1967, p. 74.

45. "As an example one might cite the case of French agriculture after the last world war. Denis Cespède has shown very clearly the transfers of agricultural values to the benefit of the industrial sector. Between 1946 and 1962, agricultural productivity rose from 100 to 272, while nonagricultural productivity rose from 100 to 189.2. Nevertheless, over the same period the per capita income of the active population rose from 100 to 167.8 for agriculture, while for the non-agricultural sectors it increased from 100 to 205.4. Let us note in passing that starting in 1937 a similar situation arose in the United States, where average annual growth in the productivity of agricultural labour substantially exceeded that of industrial labour: 3.8% compared with 1.4% for the years 1937–1948, and 6.2% against 3% for 1948–1953." K. Vergópoulos, op. cit., p. 169.

46. See G. J. Johnson, "The Modern Family Farm and its Problems", in *Economic Problems of Agriculture in Industrial Societies* (London, Macmillan, 1969).

47. In order to gain a vivid idea of what would be involved if this asymmetry were to be completely corrected, one need simply observe what happened in the urban-industrial world when the oil-producing countries decided to cease subsidizing the energy which they were selling to the industrialized countries at prices lower

than production costs in absolute terms. Oil, like land, is a non-renewable resource (though this applies in a more relative sense to the latter), and can command absolute rent. The fact that, in agriculture, this rent has declined, and even disappeared in many cases, is no more than the result of the subordination of agriculture to the requirements of urban-industrial development.

48. We make this qualification because in areas with high differential rents which can be appropriated by the entrepreneur landowner, he is in a position to secure extraordinary profits which enable him to compensate both for the unfavorable price relations and for the payment of wages equivalent to the reproduction cost of the labour.

49. We are using the term "subsidies" in the sense that the prices or values involved are more favourable to the peasantry than those to which they would be subjected in the market without State intervention. In no case are they subsidies in the sense of a return of the impositions arising from the structural relations which are expressed in the price system.

50. A. Warman, op. cit., 1976, p. 332.

51. It need barely be noted that rural workers who are landless or, rather, who are not attached to a family unit which possesses land, are not regarded as peasants in the sense in which this term has been used here.

18

The New Development Economics

Joseph E. Stiglitz *

1. INTRODUCTION

For the past 15 years, I have been attempting to construct a consistent view of less developed economies and the development process, to identify in what ways they are similar and in what ways (and why) they are different from more developed economies.[1] I cannot present even a summary of these views here. What I have been asked to do is to present one piece of that perspective, that relating to the organization of the rural sector, and to explain why I (or someone else) should "believe" these theories, or at least, why they are more plausible than several widely discussed alternative theories.

There are five central tenets of my approach:

1. Individuals (including peasants in the rural sectors of LDCs) are rational, that is, they act in a (reasonably) consistent manner, one which adapts to changes in circumstances.

2. Information is costly. This has numerous important implications: individuals do not acquire perfect information, and hence their behavior may differ markedly from what it would have been if they had perfect information. When individuals engage in a trade (buying labor services, extending credit, renting land or bullocks), there is imperfect information concerning the items to be traded; thus, transactions which would be desirable in the presence of perfect information may not occur. Similarly, certain contracts, e.g. performing certain services at a certain standard, may not be

*I am indebted to A. Braverman and R. Sah for helpful discussions. Financial support from the National Science Foundation is gratefully acknowledged.

From *World Development,* Vol. 14, No. 2 (1986), pp. 257–265. Copyright © 1986 by Pergamon Press, Ltd. Reprinted by permission.

feasible, especially if it is costly to ascertain, *ex post,* whether or how well those services have been performed.

3. Institutions adapt to reflect these information (and other transaction) costs. Thus, institutions are not to be taken as exogenous, but are endogenous, and changes in the environment may lead, with a lag, to changes in institutional structure.

4. The fact that individuals are rational and that institutions are adaptable does not, however, imply that the economy is (Pareto) efficient. The efficiency of market economies obtains only under the peculiar set of circumstances explored by Arrow and Debreu. These include a complete set of markets and perfect information, assumptions which, if questionable in more developed economies, are clearly irrelevant in LDCs. With imperfect information and incomplete markets, the economy is almost always constrained Pareto inefficient, i.e., there exists a set of taxes and subsidies which can make everyone better off (See Greenwald and Stiglitz, forthcoming).

5. This implies that there is a *potential* role for the government. That is, the government could effect a Pareto improvement if (i) it had sufficient knowledge of the structure of the economy; (ii) those responsible for implementing government policy had at least as much information as those in the private sector; (iii) those responsible for designing and implementing government policy had the incentives to direct policies to effect Pareto improvements, rather than, for instance, to redistribute income (either from the poor to the rich or vice versa, or from everyone else, to themselves), often at considerable loss to national output. Informational problems, including incentive problems, are no less important in the public sector than in the private; the fact that we have studied them well in the latter does not mean that they are not present in the former. The consequence of these remarks is to make us cautious in recommending particular government actions as remedies for certain observed deficiencies in the market.

2. THE BASIC OUTLINES OF THE THEORY OF RURAL ORGANIZATION

In this section, I wish to outline what the general approach presented above says about the economic organization of the rural sector. There are a wide variety of institutional arrangements observed in different LDCs. One set that has been of longstanding interest to economists is sharecropping. Earlier views of sharecropping held that it was an inefficient form of economic organization: the worker received less than the value of his marginal product, and thus he had insufficient incentives to exert effort. The question was, how could such a seemingly inefficient form of economic organization have survived for so long (and why should it be such a prevalent form of economic organization at so many different places at different times?). For those who believe in even a modicum of economic rationality, some explanation had to be found.

One explanation that comes to mind is that peasants are more risk averse than landlords: if workers rented the land from the landlords, they would have to bear all of the risk. Though workers' risk aversion is undoubtedly of importance, it cannot be the entire explanation: there are alternative (and perhaps more effective) risk-sharing arrangements. In particular, in the wage system, the landlord bears all of the risk, the worker none. Any degree of risk sharing between the landlord and the worker can be attained by the worker dividing his time between working as a wage-laborer and working on his own or rented land.[2]

The other central part of the explanation of sharecropping is that it provides an effective incentive system in the presence of costly supervision. Since in a wage system, the worker's compensation is not directly related to his output, the landlord must spend resources to ensure that the worker actually works. In a sharecropping system, since the worker's pay depends directly on his output, he has some incentives to work. The incentives may not be as strong as they would if he owned the land (since he receives, say, only half the product); but that is not the relevant alternative. Sharecropping thus represents a compromise between the rental system, in which incentives are "correct" but all the risk is borne by the worker, and the wage system, in which the landlord who is in a better position to bear risk, bears all the risk but in which effort can only be sustained through expenditures on supervision. This new view (Stiglitz, April 1974) turns the traditional criticism of sharecropping on its head: it is precisely because of its incentive properties, relative to the relevant alternative, the wage system, that the sharecropping system is employed.

The contention that the rental system provides correct incentives is, however, not quite correct. The rental system provides correct incentives for effort decisions. But tenants make many decisions other than those involving effort; they make decisions concerning the choice of technique, the use of fertilizer, the timing of harvest, etc. These decisions affect the riskiness of the outcomes. For instance, many of the high-yielding seed varieties have a higher mean output, but a greater sensitivity to rainfall. Whenever there is a finite probability of default (that is, the tenant not paying the promised rent), then tenants may not have, with the rental system, the correct incentives with respect to these decisions. Of course, with unlimited liability, the worker could be made to bear all of the costs. But since the tenant might be unable to pay his rent even if he had undertaken all of the "right" decisions, and since it is often difficult to ascertain whether the individual took "unnecessary" risks, most societies are reluctant to grant unlimited liability, or to use extreme measures like debtor prisons, to ensure that individuals do not take unnecessary risks.[3] Hence, in effect, part of the costs of risk taking by the tenant is borne by the landlord.[4] With sharecropping, both the landlord and the tenant face the same risks.[5]

Thus, sharecropping can be viewed as an institution which has developed in response to (a) risk aversion on the part of workers; (b) the limited ability (or desire) to force the tenant to pay back rents when he is clearly unable to do so; and (c) the limited ability to monitor the actions of the tenant (or the high costs of doing so).

The general theory has been extended in a number of directions, only three of which I can discuss here: cost sharing, interlinkage, and technical change.

In many situations, there are other important inputs besides labor and land, such as bullocks or fertilizer. How should these inputs be paid for? Clearly, if the worker pays all of the costs, but receives only a fraction of the benefits, he will have an insufficient incentive to supply these other inputs. Cost sharing is a proposed remedy. If the worker receives 50% of the output, and pays 50% of the cost, it would appear that he has the correct incentives: both benefits and costs have been cut in half.[6]

But in fact, though cost shares equal to output shares are common, they are far from universal. How do we explain these deviations from what seems both a simple, reasonable rule, and a rule which ensures economic efficiency? To find the answer, we again return to our general theoretical framework, which focuses on the role of imperfect information. First, it is clear that the landlord may want the tenant to supply more fertilizer than he would with a 50-50 rule, if increasing the fertilizer increases the marginal product of labor, and thus induces the worker to work harder. Remember, the central problem of the landlord is that he cannot directly control the actions of his worker; he must induce them to work hard. The reason that sharecropping was employed was to provide these additional incentives.

But if a cost-sharing arrangement can be implemented, it means that the expenditures can be monitored; and if the expenditures can be monitored, there is no necessity for engaging in cost sharing; rather the terms of the contract could simply specify the levels of various inputs. But workers typically have more information about current circumstances than the landlord (in the fashionable technical jargon, we say there is an asymmetry of information). A contract which specifies the level of inputs cannot adapt to the changing circumstances. Cost-sharing contracts provide the ability and incentives for these adaptations, and thus are more efficient contracts than contracts which simply specified the level of inputs.[7]

Another aspect of economic organization in many LDCs is the interlinkage of markets: the landlord may also supply credit (and he may also supply food and inputs as well). How can we explain this interlinkage? Some have claimed that it is simply another way that landlords exploit their workers. We shall comment later on these alternative explanations. For now, we simply note that our general theory can explain the prevalence of interlinkage (both under competitive and noncompetitive circumstances). We have repeatedly noted the problem of the landlord in inducing the worker both to work hard and to make the "correct" decisions from his point of view (with respect to choice of technique, etc.) Exactly analogous problems arise with respect to lenders. Their concern is that the borrower will default on the loan. The probability of a default depends in part on the actions taken by the borrower. The actions of the tenant-borrower thus affect both the lender and the land-lord. Note too that the terms of the contract with the landlord will affect the lender, and vice versa: if the landlord can, for instance reduce the probability of default by supplying more fertilizer, the lender is better off. The actions of the borrower (both with respect to effort and the choice of technique) may be affected by the individual's indebtedness, so that the landlords (expected) income may be affected by the amount (and terms) of indebtedness. There appear to be clear and possibly significant externalities between the actions of the landlord and the actions of the lender. Whenever there are such externalities, a natural market solution is to internalize the externality, and that is precisely what the interlinkage of markets does.[8]

Thus, interlinkage is motivated by the desire for economic efficiency, not necessarily by the desire for further exploitation of the worker.

Interlinkage has, in turn, been linked to the incentives landlords have for resisting profitable innovations. Bhaduri[9] has argued, for instance, that land-lords-cum-creditors may resist innovations, because innovations reduce the demand for credit, and thus the income which they receive in their capacity as creditors. Braverman and Stiglitz[10] have shown that there is no presumption that innovations result in a reduction in the demand for credit. Credit is used to smooth income across periods, and under quite plausible conditions, innovations may either increase or decrease the aggregate demand for credit. But they argue further that what happens to the demand for credit is beside the point.

The central question is simply whether the innovation moves the economically relevant utilities possibilities schedule outward or inward. The utilities possibilities schedule gives the maximum level of (expected) utility to one group (the landlord) given the level of (expected) utility of the other (the workers). The economically relevant utilities possibilities curve takes into account the information problems which have been the center of our discussion thus far, for instance, the fact that with sharecropping, individuals' incentives are different from what they would be with costless monitoring. The utilities possibilities schedule with costless monitoring might move one way, the economically relevant utilities possibilities schedule the other. Thus, for instance, there are innovations which, at each level of input, increase the output, but which, at the same time, exacerbate the incentives-monitoring problem. Such innovations would not be socially desirable. Landlords would resist such innovations, as well they should, though from an "engineering" point of view, such innovations might look desirable.

The consequences of interlinkage for the adoption of innovations, within this perspective, are ambiguous. There are innovations which would be adopted with interlinkage, but would not without it, and conversely; but the effect of the innovation on the demand for credit does not seem to play a central role.

Though the landlord correctly worries about the incentive-monitoring consequences of an innovation, one should not jump to the conclusions either that the landlords collectively make decisions which maximize their own welfare, or that the landlord always makes the socially efficient decision. The landlord, within a competitive environment, will adopt an innovation if at current prices (terms of contracts, etc.) it is profitable for him to do so. Of course, when all the landlords adopt the innovation, prices (terms of contracts) will change, and they may change in such a way that landlords are adversely affected.[11] In a competitive environment landlords cannot resist innovations simply because it is disadvantageous to them to do so. (By contrast, if they are in a "monopoly" position, they will not wish to resist such innovations, since presumably they will be able to capture all the surplus associated with the innovation.)

But just as the market allocation is not constrained Pareto efficient (even assuming a perfectly competitive economy) whenever there are problems of moral hazard, so too the market decisions concerning innovation are not constrained Pareto efficient. (We use the term constrained Pareto efficient to remind us that we are accounting for the limitations on information; we have not assumed the government has any information other than that possessed by private individuals.) Though in principle there exist government interventions which (accounting for the costs of information) could make everyone better off, whether such Pareto improving interventions are likely to emerge from the political process remains a moot question.

3. ALTERNATIVE THEORIES

In this section, I wish to present in summary form what I view to be the major competing approaches to understanding the organization of economic activity in the rural sector.

In many respects, I see my view as lying between other more extreme views. In one, the peasant is viewed as rational, working in an environment with reasonably complete information and complete and competitive markets. In this view, then, the differences between LDCs and more developed countries lies not so much in the difference between sophisticated, maximizing farmers and uneducated rule-bound peasants, as it does in differences in the economic environments, the goods produced by these economies, their endowments, and how their endowments are used to produce goods. In this view, sharecropping is a rational response to the problems of risk sharing; but there is less concern about the incentive problems than I have expressed; with perfect information and perfect enforceability of contracts, the sharecropping contract can enforce the desired level of labor supply and the choice of technique which is efficient. These theories have had little to say about some of the other phenomena which I have discussed: interlinkage, technical change, cost sharing. Interlinkage might be explained in terms of the advantages in transactions costs, but if transactions costs were central, one should only have observed simple cost-sharing rules (with cost share equalling output share).

By contrast, there are those who view the peasant as irrational, with his behavior dictated by customs and institutions which may have served a useful function at some previous time but no longer do so. This approach (which I shall refer to, somewhat loosely, as the institutional-historical approach) may attempt to describe the kinds of LDCs in which there is sharecropping, interlinkage, or cost sharing. It may attempt to relate current practices to earlier practices. In particular, the institutional-historical approach may identify particular historical events which lead to the establishment of the sharecropping system, or the development of the credit system. But this leaves largely unanswered the question of why so many LDCs developed similar institutional structures, or why in some countries cost shares equal output shares, while in others the two differ. More fundamentally, a theory must explain how earlier practices developed; and to provide an explanation of these, one has to have recourse to one of the other theories. Thus, by itself, the institutional-historical approach is incomplete.

Still a third view emphasizes the departures from competitiveness in the rural sector, and the consequent ability of the landlords to exploit the workers. In some cases, workers are tied to their land; legal constraints may put the landlord in a position to exploit the worker. But in the absence of these legal constraints, one has to explain how the landlords exercise their allegedly coercive powers. In many LDCs there is a well-developed labor market. Many landlords need laborers at harvest time and at planting time. The worker chooses for whom he will work. It is important to recognize that the exploitation hypothesis fails to explain the mechanisms by which, in situations where there are many landlords, they exercise their exploitative power.[12] More generally, it fails to explain variations in the degree of exploitation over time and across countries. The fact that wages are low is not necessarily evidence of exploitation: the competitive market will yield low wages when the value of the marginal product of labor is low.

The exploitation hypothesis also fails to explain the detailed structure of rural organization: why cost shares are the way they are, or why (or how) landlords who can exploit their workers use the credit market to gain further exploitative capacity.

There may be some grain of truth in all these approaches. Important instances of currently dysfunctional institutions and customs can clearly be identified. Institutional structures clearly do not adapt instantaneously to changed circumstances. Yet, as social scientists, our objective is to identify the systematical components, the regularities of social behavior, to look for general principles underlying a variety of phenomena. It is useful to describe the institutions found in the rural sector of LDCs, but description is not enough.

Therefore, I view the rationality hypothesis as a convenient starting point, a simple and general principle with which to understand economic behavior. Important instances of departures from rationality may well be observed. As social scientists, our objective is to look for *systematic* departures. Some systematic departures have been noted, for instance in the work of Tversky, in individuals' judgments of probabilities, particularly of small probability events; but as Binswanger's 1978 study has noted, departures from the theory appear less important in "important" decisions than in less important decisions. Many of the seeming departures from "rationality" that have been noted can be interpreted as "rational" decision-making in the presence of imperfect information.

I also view the competitiveness hypothesis as a convenient starting point.[13] Many of the central phenomena of interest can be explained without recourse to the exploitation hypothesis. Some degree of imperfect competition is not inconsistent with the imperfect information paradigm: the imperfect information paradigm provides part of the explanation for the absence of perfect competition; it can help identify situations where the landlords may be in a better position to exploit the workers. Moreover, to the extent that imperfect information limits the extent to which even a monopoly landlord can extract surplus from his workers, the imperfect information paradigm can provide insights into how he can increase his monopoly profits. The theory of interlinkage we have developed can thus be applied to the behavior of a monopolist landlord.

There is one other approach that has received some attention that is, in fact, closely related to the one I have advocated: the transactions cost approach, which attempts to explicate economic relations by focusing on transactions costs. Information costs are an important part of transactions costs (though information problems arise in other contexts as well). My reservations concerning the transactions cost approach lie in its lack of specificity: while the information paradigm provides a well-defined structure which allows one to derive clear propositions concerning, for instance, the design of contracts, the transactions cost paradigm does not. Thus, the transactions cost approach might provide some insight into why cost sharing is employed, but not into the terms of the cost-sharing agreement. The transactions cost paradigm might say that economies of scope provide an explanation for why the landlord also supplies credit, but it does not provide insights into when the landlord-cum-creditor would subsidize credit, or when he would "tax" it. Moreover, while the information paradigm identifies parameters which affect the magnitude of the externalities between landlords and creditors, and thus enables, in principle, the identification of circumstances under which inter-linkage is more likely to be observed; the transactions cost paradigm can do little more than to say that there are circumstances in which the diseconomies of scope exceed the economies, and in these circumstances there will not be interlinkage.

4. CRITERIA FOR EVALUATING ALTERNATIVE THEORIES

In the previous section, I discussed briefly some of the major competing hypotheses. In this section, I wish to outline a set of criteria for evaluating a theory, and to apply these criteria to these alternative theories. No novelty is claimed for the criteria; no attempt is made to provide a general epistemological theory.[14] These are presented more in the spirit of a "working man's" criteria.

We can divide the criteria into two groups: internal and external. The internal criteria include:[15]

(a) *Internal consistency:* Are the axioms (underlying assumptions) mutually consistent, and do the conclusions follow from these assumptions?

(b) *Simplicity:* In general, the fewer the assumptions required to explain the given phenomena, the better.

(c) *Completeness:* The assumptions of the model should be as "primitive" as possible. Thus, in macroeconomics, a theory which explains unemployment in terms of wage rigidities is, in this sense, incomplete: it leaves open the question of why wages are rigid.

The external criteria include:

(a) *Verifiability* (or falsifiability): The theory should have at least some implications which are verifiable or falsifiable, in principle; that is, it should at least be possible to design thought experiments under which some of the implications of the theory could be rejected.

(b) *External consistency:* Are *all* the implications of the model consistent with observations? Note that among the (obvious and direct) implications of the model are those that directly follow from the assumptions; thus, if an assumption itself can be falsified, the model will not possess the property of external consistency. Friedman's contention that a theory should only be judged by the validity of its conclusions is, in this view, wrong. Theories whose assumptions seem unreasonable, i.e., whose assumptions themselves can be falsified or whose assumptions have other implications which seem unacceptable (i.e., can be falsified) should be rejected. *Some* of the implications of many "bad" theories may be correct; indeed, probably no theory that has received any attention has *all* of its implications inconsistent with (at least some interpretations of) the data. But a good theory should have no implication which is inconsistent with observations.

(c) *External completeness:* The theory should have something to say about as many regularities that have been observed in the area of study as possible. Thus, a theory which explains both why there is sharecropping as well as the determinants of the shares is better than a theory which simply explains why there is sharecropping. This is closely related to the criteria of:

(d) *Specificity:* A good theory should make as many specific predictions concerning particular phenomena as possible.

(e) *Predictive power:* A good theory should not only be consistent with regularities which have already been noted, but should suggest new regularities which have not yet been noted.

(f) *Generality:* The same general hypotheses should be able to explain phenomena in widely different contexts.

I now want to review the performance of the alternative theories in terms of these basic criteria. The imperfect information paradigm does well, I would argue, on all of the criteria. The work in this area has been marked by an attempt to state clearly the assumptions, and to derive its conclusions from the assumptions: it does well on the criterion of internal consistency. Similarly, it does well on the other two internal criteria: the assumptions are simple and are reasonably primitive. Though in most work, the information technology is taken as given, in some ongoing research (see e.g., Braverman-Stiglitz, forthcoming), even this is taken to be endogenously determined. The theory provides specific predictions which are verifiable, and indeed has something to say about virtually every aspect of rural economic organization. It makes predictions concerning a variety of regularities that should be found in LDCs, but unfortunately, these have not been subjected to rigorous testing. At the same time, there is no well-agreed upon regularity that seems inconsistent with the theory.

One of its most attractive properties, however, is that the information paradigm provides a general framework which is applicable to both developed and less developed economies. The concerns about effort and choice of technique which are central to sharecropping reappear, in somewhat modified form, in the analysis of labor and capital markets in more developed countries. It shares this property with the "rational peasant, with perfect markets and complete information" paradigm. But the latter theory fails to provide a good account of the differences between developed and less developed economies.

But my major objection to the rational peasant model with full information and complete markets (as with the corresponding theories of developed economies) is that it is inconsistent with many observations and it fails to provide explanations of others.

It does not explain why sharecropping is employed (with perfect information, there are a variety of equivalent contractual forms; if sharecropping were employed, the contract would specify the amount of labor to be supplied).

It fails to explain cost sharing, and in particular why cost shares should differ from output shares.

It assumes that there is a complete set of risk markets; it is clear that individuals cannot purchase insurance against many important risks and that this has important consequences for their behavior.

In most small villages, it is not reasonable to assume that if a landlord offered a rupee less to his wage laborers, he would obtain no workers. In many situations, there appear to be workers who are willing to work at the going wage, but fail to obtain employment: there appears to be involuntary unemployment, a phenomenon which seems inconsistent with the classical competitive models.

This theory can be adapted to make it at least seem to explain the phenomena under study and to make it seem less inconsistent with the facts:[16] indeed, our imperfect information paradigm can be thought of as one such adaptation. But we would argue that it is a fundamental alteration, one which affects our views of economic relations under a wide variety of circumstances. When a theory provides predictions which are inconsistent with the facts in a wide variety of circumstances, and when it fails to provide explanations of important regularities, what is needed is not an *ad hoc* modification of the model on a case-by-case basis, but rather a basic reformulation: the imperfect information paradigm provides such a reformulation.

The transactions cost approach represents another attempt to modify the basic theory in a consistent way. As we have commented above, information costs are a particular form of transaction costs, and I find many aspects of the transactions cost approach attractive.[17] But the theory fails on several of the critical external criteria: to the extent that the theory relies on unobservable transaction costs, it often seems to fail the test of falsifiability; just as the present set of economic relations is justified by current (unobservable) transaction costs, changes in the nature of economic relations are "explained" by reference to similarly unobservable changes in transaction costs. The theory also fails the test of specificity of predictions and of external completeness: as we noted, while it may provide an explanation for why sharecropping is employed, it cannot explain the nature of the cost-sharing arrangements and has little to say about other items of the sharecropping contract.

By contrast, the exploitation theory fails on both the internal and external criteria for judging theories. There is not a clearly stated set of primitive assumptions from which the conclusions logically follow. For instance, if the structure of economic relations is determined by the attempt of landlords to exploit their workers, what determines the limits on their capacities to do so? The theory fails to explain why sharecropping provides a better method of exploitation than other forms of contractual arrangements; it fails to explain why cost sharing enhances the ability of the landlord to exploit his workers. It fails to explain the circumstances under which cost shares would exceed output shares. And it fails to explain why providing credit enhances the ability of the landlord to exploit the peasant. When there are many landlords in a community, it fails to explain how they can act collusively together. The experience with cartels in other areas is that it is hard to maintain collusive arrangements voluntarily when the number of participants becomes more than a few. If this is true here, then the theory only provides an explanation of the structure of economic relations within communities with a limited number of landlords; if this is not true in LDCs, why?

To the extent that the theory relies on the notion of power which cannot be independently quantified, the theory is not falsifiable: one can always account for differences in the terms of the contract over time or geographically in terms of differences in power.[18] To the extent that the theory fails to provide answers to these questions, it is seriously incomplete.

5. CONCLUSIONS

The theory of rural organization which is based on rational peasants in environments in which information is imperfect and costly provides a simple explanation for a wide variety of phenomena in LDCs. It represents an important application of a more general paradigm, what I have referred loosely to as the "Imperfect Information Paradigm" which has been useful in explaining phenomena under a wide variety of settings, under competition, oligopoly, and monopoly, in labor markets, capital markets, insurance markets, and product markets. The richness of social phenomena is such as to make it unreasonable to expect any theory to explain all of the observed variations in institutions and behavior. But a theory should at least be able to explain the important regularities. Here, we are concerned with explaining sharecropping, both its widespread use, and the form it takes; it should explain cost sharing, with cost shares frequently differing from output shares, and the interlinkage of credit and land markets. This our theory does, and the competing theories fail to do. There is a rich set of further predictions emanating from our theory which have yet to be tested. Whether, when these tests are performed, the theory will still stand, or whether it will have to be modified, or abandoned, remains to be seen.

NOTES

1. For two surveys of certain aspects of this work, see Stiglitz (1982b, 1985).
2. See Stiglitz (April 1974).
3. Indeed, such extreme measures may have deleterious incentive effects, discouraging risk taking.
4. See Johnson (1950); Allen (1985).
5. This aspect of sharecropping has been emphasized by Johnson (1950), and by Braverman and Stiglitz (1982a). See also Stiglitz and Weiss (1981).
6. See Heady (1947).
7. See Braverman and Stiglitz (1982b).
8. See Braverman and Stiglitz (1982a). This problem is discussed in the more general information theoretic literature under the rubric of the multiple principle-agent problem. The externalities which we have discussed here arise in virtually all moral hazard problems. See Arnott and Stiglitz (1984).
9. See Bhaduri (1973).
10. Braverman and Stiglitz (forthcoming).
11. If the innovation, at the current prices, increases the demand for workers enough, then the terms of the contracts may shift sufficiently in workers' favor to make landlords worse off. This is analogous to what, in more simple contexts, is referred to as a Pigou land-saving innovation.
12. Note that recent advances in repeated games have shown how collusive outcomes can be attained even in non-cooperative settings. Thus, landlords in rural economies where mobility is limited and in which there are only a few landlords in any community may well act collusively. The circumstances in which these noncooperative collusive arrangements work well has, however, not been well studied.
13. Indeed, with limited labor mobility, in small villages the labor markets are unlikely to be perfectly competitive; at the same time, the landlord is far from a labor monopolist. The real world is probably better described by a model of "monopolistic competition" than either of the polar models, monopoly or perfect competition.
14. Similarly, this is not the place to provide an evaluation of alternative theories (e.g., the theories of Karl Popper).
15. This list is not meant to be exhaustive. An important criterion in other contexts is *robustness;* the conclusions of the theory should not be sensitive to small perturbations in the assumptions.
16. When the theory gets complicated by these *ad hoc* modifications it loses the property of simplicity, which was originally one of its main virtues.
17. It is sometimes suggested that, once transactions costs are accounted for, equilibrium with rational peasants will have all the standard efficiency properties that economies with no transactions costs have. This is another example where the conclusion does not follow logically from the assumptions; the conclusion is arrived at by reasoning by analogy. Transactions costs (including information

costs) are "like" other production costs. Why, once these are appropriately accounted for, should not the economy still be efficient?

Unfortunately, it turns out that, in general, economies with imperfect information (or incomplete markets) are not constrained Pareto efficient (where the term "constrained" Pareto efficient simply reminds us that we have appropriately taken into account the transactions costs (information imperfection, incomplete markets). (See Greenwald and Stiglitz, forthcoming.) The formalization of Adam Smith's invisible hand conjecture is one of the great achievements of modern economic theory; the Fundamental theorem of economics, like any other theorem, depends on the assumptions. The assumptions concerning perfect information, no transactions costs, and complete market markets are not innocuous assumptions, but are central to the validity of the result. Information costs may, in some respects, be like other costs of production, but the differences are sufficiently important to invalidate the Fundamental Theorem of Welfare Economics.

18. Thus, "power" is to the exploitation theory what transactions cost is to the transactions cost model.

REFERENCES

Allen, F., "The fixed nature of sharecropping contracts," *Journal of Public Economics* (March 1985), pp. 30–48.

Arnott, R., and J. E. Stiglitz, "Equilibrium in competitive insurance markets." Mimeo. (Princeton University, 1984).

Bhaduri, A., "Agricultural backwardness under semifeudalism," *Economic Journal* (1973).

Binswanger, H. P., "Attitudes towards risk: Experimental measurement evidence in rural India," *American Journal of Agricultural Economics,* Vol. 62, No. 3 (August 1980), pp. 395–407.

Binswanger, H. P., "Attitudes towards risk: Implications and psychological theories of an experiment in rural India," Yale University Economic Growth Center DP 286 (1978b).

Braverman, A., and J. E. Stiglitz, "Sharecropping and the interlinking of agrarian markets," *American Economic Review,* Vol. 72, No. 4 (September 1982a), pp. 695–715.

Braverman, A., and J. E. Stiglitz, "Moral hazard, incentive flexibility and risk: Cost sharing arrangements under sharecropping," Princeton University, Econometric Research Center Memorandum No. 298 (1982b).

Braverman, A., and J. E. Stiglitz, "Cost sharing arrangements under sharecropping: Moral hazard, incentive flexibility and risk," Mimeo. (Princeton University, 1985).

Braverman, A., and J. E. Stiglitz, "Landlords, tenants and technological innovations," *Journal of Development Economics* (forthcoming).

Greenwald, B., and J. E. Stiglitz, "Externalities in economies with imperfect information and incomplete markets," *Quarterly Journal of Economics,* (forthcoming).

Heady, E., "Economics of farm leasing system," *Journal of Farm Economics* (August 1947).

Johnson, D. Gale "Resource allocation under share contracts," *Journal of Public Economics* (April 1950), pp. 111–123.

Newbery, D., and J. E. Stiglitz, "Sharecropping, risk sharing, and the importance of imperfect information," paper presented to a conference in Mexico City, March

1976 and published in Ja. A. Roumasset *et al.* (Eds.), *Risk, Uncertainty and Development* (SEARCA, A/D/C, 1979), pp. 311–341.

Newbery, D., and J. E. Stiglitz, *The Theory of Commodity Price Stabilization* (Oxford University Press, 1981).

Newbery, D., and J. E. Stiglitz, "The choice of techniques and the optimality of market equilibrium with rational expectations," *Journal of Political Economy,* Vol. 90. No. 2 (April 1982), pp. 223–246.

Stiglitz, J. E., "Rural-urban migration, surplus labor and the relationship between urban and rural wages," *East African Economic Review,* Vol. 1–2 (December 1969). pp. 1–27.

Stiglitz, J. E., "Alternate theories of wage determination and unemployment in LDCs: The labor turnover model," *Quarterly Journal of Economics,* Vol. 87 (May 1974), pp. 194–227.

Stiglitz, J. E., "Incentives and risk sharing in sharecropping," *Review of Economic Studies,* Vol. 41 (April 1974), pp. 219–255.

Stiglitz, J. E., "The efficiency wage hypothesis, surplus labor and the distribution of income in LDCs," *Oxford Economic Papers,* Vol. 28, No. 2 (July 1976), pp. 185–207.

Stiglitz, J. E., "Some further remarks on cost-benefit analysis," in H. Schwartz and R. Berney (Eds.), *Social and Economic Dimensions of Project Evaluation* (IDB, 1977); Proceedings of the Symposium on Cost-Benefit Analysis, IDB, Washington, D.C., March 1973, pp. 253–282.

Stiglitz, J. E., "Alternative theories of wage determination and unemployment: The efficiency wage model," in Gersovitz *et al.,* (Eds.) *The Theory and Experience of Economic Development: Essays in Honor of Sir W. Arthur Lewis* (London: George Allen & Unwin, 1982a), pp. 78–106.

Stiglitz, J. E., "Structure of labor markets and shadow prices in LDCs," presented at World Bank Conference, February 1976, in R. Sabot, (Ed.) *Migration and the Labor Market in Developing Countries* (Boulder, CO: Westview Press 1982b), pp. 13–64.

Stiglitz, J. E., "The wage-productivity hypothesis: Its economic consequences and policy implications," paper presented to the American Economic Association (1982).

Stiglitz, J. E., "Economics of information and the theory of economic development," *Revista de Econometria* (forthcoming).

Stiglitz, J. E., and A. Weiss, "Credit rationing in markets with imperfect information," *American Economic Review,* Vol. 71, No. 3 (June 1981), pp. 393–410.

Tversky, A., "Intransitivity of preferences," *Psychological Review,* Vol. 76 (1969), pp. 31–48.

PART FIVE

INDUSTRIAL INSTITUTIONS
AND STRATEGY

Industrialization always has been considered the basis of economic development. Klaus Esser proposes an industrial strategy for Latin America based on the achievement of "inward-directed growth" through the creation of capital and mass consumer good industries, the continuance of selective import substitution, and a selective and dynamic policy aimed at gaining market positions in First World countries. He further underscores the economic, social, and political conditions which must be met if such a strategy is to be carried out successfully. In particular, Esser emphasizes that the systematic effort required to apply this strategy, the imbalances to which it gives rise, and the obstacles in its path require it to be based upon the participation, motivation, and creativity of society as a whole.

In the second selection, R. B. Sutcliffe reexamines his earlier work as a member of the dependency school about the relationship between development and industrialization. Four of the arguments—that industrialization is necessary to meet human needs, that Third World countries in general are not succeeding in industrializing, that capital-intensive technology is desirable, and that industrialization requires more autarky—are all found to be in need of considerable modification. However, he also argues that the proposed alternatives such as agricultural first development and emphasis on intermediate technology are for the most part unacceptable. Part of the problem, he argues, is insufficient concern for the human consequences.

In the final selection, Frances Stewart criticizes the methodology of social cost-benefit analysis (SCB) as a means of assessing alternative projects in underdeveloped countries. She argues that any ranking of "socially desirable" projects depends on the values of the analyst. When specifying the practical definitions of "social" welfare, "social" objectives, and "social" costs, Stewart shows that a weighting system for values necessarily underlies any SCB. To illuminate the role of conflicting values in project selection Stewart suggests the use of class analysis.

For Stewart a class is an interest group with common values. In terms of SCB, for each alternative set of values (or for each class) there is a corresponding different set of "shadow prices" and therefore a different rank-order of projects. Consequently, the choice between projects will ultimately depend on whose values the policy-maker is taking. Use of government values as a proxy for social values, as widely advocated in the current literature, is found unacceptable since governments typically represent certain class interests. Thus, Stewart concludes, SCB is primarily an instrument of class struggle rather than a practical tool for achieving a social welfare optimum.

19

Modification of the Industrialization Model in Latin America

Klaus Esser

I. INSUFFICIENT INHERENT MOMENTUM WITHIN THE INDUSTRIALIZATION PROCESS

The decline in exports of raw materials consequent upon the world economic crisis was followed by a need to substitute domestic production for imports. Originally, when import substitution was still a spontaneous process, it represented a defensive strategy. Even in its dirigistic phase—from the end of the Second World War—it never developed into a comprehensive and aggressive industrialization strategy. "Industrialization" in Latin America meant the introduction of technical progress not into all sectors of the economy but only into the modern branches of industry and the export-oriented sectors: mining, agriculture, and trade.

Unlike East Asia (Japan, South Korea), Latin America retained its pre-industrial economic and power structures. Consequently, the region had to rely on the "modern sector of the economy" in seeking high rates of growth. The models of development were dual or unbalanced based on the premise that the momentum of the modern sector would gradually dislodge the traditional structures. However, in many countries opportunities for import substitution were exhausted as early as the 1960s, and insufficient action was taken to mitigate internal imbalances and thereby increase domestic demand. Sectoral, regional, and social imbalances—the heterogeneity within and among the various sectors—were soon found to form a critical barrier to the inherent momentum of the industrialization process.

The shape of industrialization was determined from the outset by the attitudes of upper and middle-class consumers. The increasingly marked

From *CEPAL Review*, No. 26 (August 1985), pp. 101–114.

concentration of incomes which reflected the economic, social and political imbalances resulted in the premature imitation of consumption patterns typical of the industrialized countries, in particular the United States. It steered industrial development towards consumer durables, including cars, and sectors in which development depended on investment by transnational companies; for many years only scant importance was attached to labour-intensive exportable consumer goods and indeed to capital goods. This type of industrialization did not absorb an adequate fraction of the quickly expanding labour force and resulted in a rapid increase in foreign participation, which later was frequently excluded from deliberations on industrialization strategy.

Industries under foreign control (the motor vehicle, chemicals and pharmaceutical industries, for example) experienced a period of vigorous growth as long as the—mostly small—domestic markets remained unsaturated. In many instances, assembly and packing plants were commissioned, but the subsequent transfers of resources (profits, payments for technologies) represented a constant drain on the balance of payments. The national private sector has largely continued to produce simple consumer goods, demand for which has expanded only sluggishly, especially since the mid-1960s, because of the stagnation in agriculture, the strong concentration of income, and the absence of government corrective policies.

Growth in the agricultural and industrial sectors was largely ascribable to a few large companies, while small and medium-sized national firms were neglected, their development even being hampered by the economic policy pursued. However, an industrialization process confined to large companies implied that there was no alternative to importing foreign technologies. This productivity was further aggravated by the fact that the technological and industrial options selected by the industrialized countries (large-scale technologies, armaments industry) were emulated in an increasing number of sectors.

Medium-sized and even small countries likewise spent many years trying to press ahead as far as possible with an import-substituting type of industrialization. Despite its inadequate geographical size, Chile, for example, opted for an industrialization path looking to heavy industry and forward integration. Even countries such as Uruguay sought to establish a motor vehicle industry, thereby overlooking the advantages of industrial specialization. Such industries tied up considerable financial resources but did little to accelerate the industrialization process because expansion in the industries manufacturing intermediate products remained inadequate and intra-industrial demand limited; moreover, they soon became obsolete owing to the limitations of national technological capacity. Only the larger countries were capable of substituting domestic production for some of the more complex import items, thus developing an industrial apparatus with increasingly clear vertical and horizontal linkages.

In Brazil, the economic and political influence of the groups predominating within the pre-industrial sector was nullified, and industry came under pressure to step up its competitiveness. Since the mid-1960s, moreover, Brazil's domestic market had proved to be sufficiently large to afford industrialization a further boost: by means of government investment in the basic and capital goods industries and also investment by foreign groups in the development of fully integrated motor vehicle complexes and industries producing consumer durables and showing considerable intra-industrial demand. Since the mid-1970s, Brazil has also become an internationally significant exporter of manufactures. It owes its exceptional position in Latin America, however, to its size and potential, and also to massive commitments by multinational groups; social, sectoral and regional imbalances here are certainly no less pronounced than in the other countries.

Although imports continued to expand (both despite and on account of the import-substituting industrialization strategy), and the evolution of the terms of trade was perceived to be critical in Latin America, virtually all countries in the region have relied on exporting their large-scale and well-diversified natural resources to back up their industrialization process. Export business is transacted by foreign and, to an increasing extent, domestic mining and petroleum companies, and also via certain segments of agriculture, which has undergone thorough modernization only in the large countries. Because of the significance of agriculture in export business, and by extension, the power held by landowners, the efforts made to remove the structural obstacles to industrialization in the agricultural sector have remained scant, and more and more compromises have had to be made in economic policy. In some small and medium-sized countries in particular, it was not long before signs of stagnation emerged because the excessive emphasis placed on import substitution precluded any industrialization based on natural resources, and more specifically on agriculture, a strategy which would have entailed an export-oriented approach.

Some of the proceeds from exports accrued to a stratum of society whose position had never been challenged in the past but which combined imported consumption patterns with limited production know-how. Substantial sums were also invested in the public sector of the economy, where the bureaucracy was quick to adopt the values and demand pattern of the weak private-sector bourgeoisie. Even as early as the mid-1950s, dependence on a few exports had resulted in a shortage of foreign exchange reserves, though this conduced to a general feeling of export pessimism rather than to any change in favour of exporting manufactures. Latin America was slow in emulating the shift of emphasis in world trade toward manufactures during the period of rapid expansion on the world market which lasted from 1955 until 1980.

Whereas in Japan, South Korea, and Taiwan massive redistribution measures, including agrarian reforms, were instrumental in securing high rates of saving, in Latin America a degree of concentration of wealth and income by far higher than in virtually any other region of the world led to consumerism in relatively narrow population strata, to squandering of resources and—in periods of crisis or more attractive interest levels abroad—to a massive flight of capital. Whereas in the industrialized countries the financial infrastructure was established parallel to and on the basis of the industrialization process, in Latin America no mobilization of domestic capital based on the expansion of the financial infrastructure occurred because of the excessively easy access to cheap foreign capital. The capital inflow from abroad even partially took the place of savings formation at home.

The exogenous causes of the shortage of resources, and indirectly also of capital formation within the region, should not be underestimated; undoubtedly, however, these would not necessarily have represented an insurmountable obstacle to a dynamic industrialization process if suitable conditions had been created and enterprise-oriented strategies pursued. It is significant that the "light exports" of agricultural products and petroleum of Argentina and Venezuela were precisely those which made it possible to retain an extensive growth model over a period of decades, whereas the competitiveness of the economy, and of industrial exports in particular, remained extremely low in relation to the level of industrialization. Capital is indeed an important factor in development, but it is by no means sufficient in itself. Precisely because the export of raw materials and an influx of capital from abroad paved the way for a succession of "soft options", the deployment of capital remained relatively inefficient. Institutional and microeconomic factors, and in particular the low level of performance of government and industrial firms, together with the lack of cooperation between these, did much more to hamper the industrialization process than any shortage of capital.

II. THE 1970s: THE ROAD TO CRISIS

The problematic elements of the Latin American industrialization model outlined above were compounded in the 1970s by factors which at the outset could be ascribed largely to the region's power structures and economic strategies but subsequently to changes in the world economy:

- The oil price rises triggered off substitution programmes, most of which entailed large-scale projects having a long gestation period and requiring extensive imports and foreign financing. It was soon found that dams (such as that of Itaipú) were too large and ecologically questionable; that nuclear programmes were financially demanding and technologically unpredictable; and that a scheme like Brazil's alcohol programme were not only costly but also antisocial because of its displacement of small farmers. In some cases, significant substitution effects could be achieved, but the programmes concerned always exacerbated the existing economic and social imbalances, prevented the implementation of alternative schemes—some of which might have made for a drastic reduction in energy consumption—and increased foreign debts.

■ The upswing in imports and external financing was also ascribable to the greater emphasis attached to expanding the basic and capital goods industries in the large and some of the medium-sized countries. The oil-exporting countries (Mexico, Venezuela) set out to develop their petrochemicals and steel industries, but the projects concerned made only slow progress because the financial and, in some instances, technological strain exceeded the resources of the companies concerned, most of which were State-owned. Had these projects been executed as originally planned, they would also have necessitated extensive exports, though the world market situation had not been adequately considered at the design stage. Admittedly, a number of countries succeeded in greatly expanding their capital goods industries: between 1978 and 1981 self-sufficiency in capital goods rose to 80% in Brazil, 70% in Mexico and Argentina and 40 to 45% in Columbia and Peru, but only to 10% in Chile. Large sums were also invested in the expansion of mining companies, many of which had been nationalized in the 1960s and 1970s with a view to increasing exports.

■ After the seizure of power by the armed forces, Brazil and Argentina in particular began to develop large-scale military-industrial complexes for security reasons and also in pursuit of their objective of becoming major powers (armaments and nuclear programmes, aircraft construction, including aluminium industries). While Brazil made every effort to become internationally competitive and rapidly increased its exports of military equipment, Argentina's military-industrial complex remained inefficient. Nonetheless, the country succeeded in evading the monetarist experiment, in obtaining major subsidies for its basic industry, which was similarly controlled by the military, in ensuring that the domestic private sector was given preference over foreign direct investment, and even in keeping alive obsolete industrial companies. Not only did its efforts contribute little to increasing exports; they also tied up an enormous amount of capital and entailed extensive importing of armaments. "Military strength" resulted in a general neglect of other objectives, in particular the upgrading of efficiency by means of industrial specialization.

■ In the countries of the Southern Cone (Argentina, Chile, Uruguay), where opportunities for import substitution were almost exhausted as early as in the mid-1950s because of the length of time which this strategy had already been pursued (a tendency which had political implications inasmuch as the population was relatively well organized), the military governments opted for monetarist economic policies. Placing their trust in market forces, they proceeded to generally liberalize imports and capital markets; however, no adequate support was forthcoming for the adjustments to the needs of the world market which companies made by specializing within the agricultural and industrial sectors, and during the second phase in particular (1978 and 1981), the pressure to adjust became unrealistic in the wake of the "monetary approach to the balance of payments" advocated by the modern monetarist school. These economic policies resulted in the loss of a social consensus on basic aspects of development, further exacerbation of existing economic and social imbalances, drastic contraction of domestic markets, de-industrialization tendencies, and a tremendous increase in speculative capital movements, flight of capital and external indebtedness.

Latin America's foreign debts have mainly endogenous causes which were bound to result in a crisis in the wake of the changes taking place in the world economy. At a time of international adjustment, the countries of the region persisted in pinning their hopes on a high rate of growth. The cumulative effects of overconcentration on the modern sector, an inadequate technological basis for the industrialization process and poor export performance were adversely compounded in the 1970s by various factors: this applies as much to the above-mentioned gigantomania in connection with substitution projects in basic industries and the energy sector—which were not infrequently supported by international financing institutions—as to the subordination of the industrialization process to notions of security policy and military interests. It also holds good when one considers the attempts made, in particular in Mexico, to pursue a twofold policy of implementing major heavy industry projects and at the same time expanding the likewise import-intensive consumer durables industry, including integrated motor vehicle complexes. In Brazil too, where a large measure of import substitution was achieved in this manner, the procedure in question resulted in a high level of external indebtedness. It is virtually impossible to trace the underlying economic considerations that explain how, despite the austerity programme introduced in the OECD countries, the traditional obstacles to demand for consumer goods could be removed, thus enabling large quantities of goods to be imported. The irresponsible allocation of loans by the international banking system is undoubtedly as unsatisfactory an explanation for Latin America's adopting such a course of action as any reference to increased exports. The combined impact of all these factors meant that the economies of the region were much more severely affected than those of the industrial countries or the countries of Asia; it resulted in "derailment".

III. STABILIZATION WITH CREATIVE TRANSFORMATION

Even assuming that its liquidity problems will be alleviated and its debts partially cleared—courses of action which are hardly avoidable, though there are no signs of their being accomplished in the foreseeable future—the region faces a fairly protracted period of limitation of its external financing facilities. It will not be able to recover from its decline before the early 1990s. Technocratic attempts at stabilization are at present having the effect of making domestic markets contract, while in the light of foreign trade problems it is becoming increasingly necessary for economic policies to focus on expanding exports. The action possibilities open to governments for halting the "downward spiral", preventing the further obsolescence of the production apparatus, and combating mass poverty are proving to be inadequate while this "stabilization without creativity" persists. As has been apparent in some countries of the region for many years, concentration on short-term policies creates an inexorable and growing need for stabilization.

Many governments are still hoping that the traditional "growth-cum-debt" pattern can be resumed and repeated. They base their action on the familiar concepts of concentrating excessively on economic growth, improving the climate for foreign direct investment, and overcoming assumed shortages of capital by raising yet more funds abroad. But since stabilization is not accompanied by standard-setting economic and social reforms, these concepts are encountering growing political resistance. The coincidence of various factors (internal and external imbalances, foreign indebtedness, saturation of the industrialized countries' markets and the protectionism to which these countries are resorting in order to facilitate the technological modernization of their industries, the third technological revolution, etc.) has brought Latin America to a turning-point. The long period of low growth should therefore be used to bring about a creative transformation.

If the region is to overcome the recession, regain its industrial momentum, and adjust to the changes in world economic conditions, a more complex strategy will be required. The objective here cannot be to "catch up" with the industrialized countries; instead, the region must try to avoid their mistakes—which are having increasingly serious repercussions, particularly with respect to the environment—and to link elements of "catching up" and "closing the gap" with original solutions which, wherever possible, anticipate new developments in certain sectors and may even enable the region to "overtake" the industrialized countries in some areas. What is needed is a skillful and flexible combination of elements such as the following, the relative importance of which may well vary through time:

■ development of domestic markets to permit "inward-directed growth" via the mass-produced consumer and capital goods industries. This will require above all prompt action to minimize growth-inhibiting imbalances and reinforce the technological foundations on which industrialization is based;

- continuance of import substitution, though now with a view to reducing imports selectively and preventing a further rise in domestic costs, widespread inefficiency, inadequate profitability, and limitation of opportunities for private-sector investment, phenomena which import substitution has provoked in the past;
- establishment of clear-cut objectives for the division of industrial labour within the region, especially in high-technology research and the motor vehicle and capital goods industries;
- an aggressive but selective policy of forging links with the industrialized countries, not with a view to highly subsidized export trade in manufactures, wherever this might be possible, but concentrating instead on industrial linkages which would enable the region to acquire strategically important market positions and shares.

A strategy which seeks to combine elements of both inward-looking and outward-directed industrialization such as this presupposes reforms in the following five fields in particular:

1. Industrialization is a macrosocial problem and calls for increasing homogeneity of structures. The manoeuverability of societies in Latin America would be markedly enhanced if nonindustrial production methods in the "traditional" sector were phased out and social, sectoral, regional and ecological imbalances were reduced. Agricultural reforms in particular are long overdue in many countries of the region and are an imperative necessity if economic and social growth is to become more balanced, the rapidly growing urban population is to be fed, industrialization speeded up, and politically stable development achieved. What is required is a skillful combination of elements of structural and technological reform, a feature which agricultural reforms have customarily lacked in the past. This would entail:

- selective measures to change tenancy and ownership structures and introduce ecologically acceptable forms of reallocating and consolidating farmland, where possible without disrupting modern export-oriented holdings;
- a radical change in the agro-technological base in the traditional sectors of agriculture and the grouping of small farmers in co-operatives with a view to largely excluding the middleman from trade in mass-produced consumer goods (this being essential if prices are to be raised *and* the urban population is to be catered for at reasonable cost);
- selective strengthening of the input and output sectors of agriculture (metal-working, chemicals; biogas and other decentralized energies; agricultural banks); in some instances, in particular where artificial fertilizers

and insecticides are concerned, agreements with industrially advanced neighbouring countries would be an advantage.

It is important to ensure that the adverse financial and ecological effects of the agricultural policies pursued in the industrialized countries are precluded in this region. Evaluation of the industrialized countries' experience and knowledge of new methods applicable in bioecologically-oriented agriculture are therefore essential. The aim here must be to develop an agricultural sector in which the consumption of costly energy, artificial fertilizers and pesticides, and thus the level of government subsidization, is kept as low as possible. It is not to give priority to the development of the agricultural sector but to speed up the pace of industrialization which, in the small and medium-sized countries in particular, will not be possible until modern technology and modern production methods are introduced in the agricultural sector.

2. Although industrialization requires concentration of the population and the emergence of centres of economic agglomeration, the processes of urbanization and economic concentration, proceeding almost unchecked as they did in the region in the absence of government counteraction, soon generated marginalization tendencies and had a deleterious effect on the economy as a whole. Political, administrative, and financial decentralization would counteract the urban agglomeration process and the neglect of the hinterland and of "absolute poverty", and change the features of the industrialization process. Stimulating regions and communities to act on their own responsibility and initiative and encouraging self-help organizations are instrumental in invigorating and expanding the non-durable consumer and capital goods industries, thereby broadening the basis for industrialization and rendering it more independent.

The objective of tapping neglected regional and local potential via decentralized development is not to initiate a process of "self-centered regionalization" or "regionally centered development" but rather to counterbalance concentrations of population and agglomeration (as has recently been done in Spain), if possible *without* obstructing the development of national industrial cores or diminishing their international competitiveness. Advantage must be taken of the many attempts made and initiatives launched to develop regional circuits. Although special schemes such as that designed to assist the North-East of Brazil are justifiable, emphasis should initially be placed on the elimination of intraregional economic and social imbalances rather than on financial compensation to offset the discrepancies between rich and poor regions such as is customary in the industrialized countries. Priority should be attached in this context to strengthening financial authority at the regional and local levels and to developing small towns ("agro-urban centres") in the hinterland.

In this decentralization endeavour, much depends on ensuring that the municipal level is geared to the concept of self-help. Experience in Latin America has shown that even countries which have made some progress in industrialization cannot imitate the industrialized countries in the provision of a national social security system and must in any case avoid the cost explosion which has occurred in the OECD welfare states. Furthermore, the burden on central government must be eased wherever possible so that it can concentrate on the major tasks of guiding and controlling the industrialization process. The State should stimulate, guide and monitor, but provide only subsidiary support for local self-reliance. Developing countries will therefore differ from industrialized countries in the distinction which they must make between individual responsibility and social security, especially in view of the extreme importance of moulding together into small, uncomplicated, closely-knit communities a population which has become individualized in the wake of migratory processes and is held together, if at all, by an unstable family structure, and in which distrust is the predominating social sentiment. The public interest can only become a generally meaningful value if society is organized from the bottom up: in small groups, especially self-help groups to combat poverty, and community structures at the local level.

3. Dynamic industrialization is inconceivable without mastery of technology. The technological development of industry, for its part, in turn presupposes an appropriate mentality: no industrial revolution can take place without a revolution in value systems. In Latin America, however, industrialization began in a society in which, despite numerous adjustments, traditional values still predominate. The countries of the region selected the capital investment option, but accepted the rent-seeking attitude of the investors. At the same time, they neglected the most important factor of development, namely, the creation of satisfactory resources in terms of human capital.

Perhaps the most important cause of the dependence incurred by the incorporation of technology was the shortage of technical skills. The education and training system reflects the imbalances prevailing in the economic field: the lower strata of society have the doubtful privilege of undergoing an extended period of education during which they learn little or nothing about self-help and technology. Except in Brazil, the size of the skilled workforce has remained limited, and the scant provision made for training is normally concentrated in special institutions (SENA, etc.). The universities produce large numbers of intellectuals who understand little of industrialization and, because of the social inequities and obstacles to their own careers, set their sights on political change. The domestic and foreign private sector prefers to recruit its highly qualified employees from foreign or national private colleges.

Priority needs to be given to an education and training offensive to generate basic and versatile skills and promote a generalized mastery of technology, including the new technologies. Only such an offensive would make it possible to reinforce self-help capacity among broad population groups, to ensure understanding of various technological levels and the combination of these, to develop selected key technologies, to establish a dynamic innovation system with a high level of technological flexibility, and, finally, to create a "national technological culture."

At this stage, rapid adaptation and imitation of technologies is more important than basic research. "Technological independence" cannot be achieved within the foreseeable future, but this time-span can certainly bring a continual reinforcement of "technological autonomy", which ought to be directed towards ensuring a rapid increase in productivity, in particular by means of the new key technologies. The path towards the commercialization of adapted or imitated technologies can be shortened, especially if it is possible for industry and research institutes to work in close co-operation. However, intensive and continuous co-operation between the universities and industry will not be possible until profound reforms have been implemented in the long-since dysfunctional university sector. A measure of the stature of the new democracies in the region will be whether or not they can be successful in implementing reforms such as these, which do not represent a primarily financial problem.

4. The international learning process is tending towards the view that dynamic industrialization is possible only if an autonomous industrial and technological core can be created and constantly strengthened. "Industrialization" implies the creation of a national industrial core, in particular in the capital goods industry, which possesses the technological competence to modernize the entire production sector to an increasing extent out of its own resources. This core can only develop from a sustained and co-ordinated commitment on the part of government, industry, and research institutions. A country which relies exclusively on the free forces of the market is in effect consolidating its state of backwardness and will be largely negatively affected by the new technologies. It may even be said that an import-substituting industrialization which does not seek to establish a technologically competent industrial core and to promote technical progress in all sectors can at best aspire to earn such large amounts of foreign exchange revenue from its exports of raw materials that it is able to advance in step with the technological state of the art in the industrial countries by virtue of constant imports of capital goods.

It is astonishing that technological competence within the State and national companies in the countries of Latin America has remained so low. Little effort was made over a period of decades to back up industrial development by establishing independent technological expertise. Technological and entrepreneurial capacity for adaptation and imitation remained limited, and, economic linkages were slow to multiply. Industrialization failed to develop sufficient momentum of its own because import substitution was based on foreign technologies and, in many dynamic sectors of industry, on foreign direct investment. It was not until the 1970s that the institutional conditions for importing and developing technology were improved in the larger countries. But even now, only Brazil has the ability to ensure the rapid incorporation of technology and, in a few sectors only, to achieve autonomous technological development.

The only developing countries which can undergo a process of dynamic industrialization are those which succeed in incorporating traditional *and* new technologies strictly in accordance with their needs and on a low-cost basis. A "forward-looking strategy" at technological level is required before it is possible to incorporate several generations of technology simultaneously, to make "development leaps", to develop constructive relations with foreign companies, to proceed beyond complementary foreign trade in at least some selected fields, and to enter the international technology race. For all developing countries, however, a minimum level of technological competence is essential if advantage is to be taken of the opportunities offered by both old and new technologies and national control over the development process is to be gradually extended.

5. How many technologically competent firms, how many national firms that are internationally competitive are operating on the economies of large countries such as Mexico or Argentina? This question is even more legitimate when viewed in the context of comparison with the countries of East and South-East Asia, where the industrialization process in many cases is of much more recent date. The propelling force of industrialization in market economies, i.e., the private companies, which take most of the decisions on production and investment, remains undeveloped. Even in Brazil the industrial bourgeoisie drops into third place behind government and foreign capital in many key sectors. Given this situation, it not uncommonly happens that too little attention is paid to the functions which the private sector should perform in industrialization, in developing technology, and in exporting manufactures. This is particularly true with respect to the following:

- the development of a small group of large, efficient, national companies with diversified production, innovative capacity, and financial management systems, which are instrumental in ensuring active integration into the world market and may come to resemble multinational groups;
- the emergence of technologically up-to-date small and medium-sized enterprises such as those which play an important role in the OECD countries as subcontractors—rendering the larger companies more competitive—and also in the innovation process;
- the restructuring of labour-intensive small and medium-sized firms in traditional sectors of industry which have an entrepreneurial and em-

ployment potential that has so far remained largely untapped and which have been slow in fulfilling their functions in the fields of production, distribution, and provision of services.

IV. OBJECTIVES AND INSTRUMENTS OF A COMPLEX INDUSTRIALIZATION STRATEGY

The implementation of such a concept is dependent on whether or not the new democracies can succeed in strengthening the autonomy of the State and at the same time can upgrade its capacities for concertation, monitoring, and control. Because political will is not clearly agglomerated and administrative capacities are inadequate, in many instances governments have so far not even been successful in indicating a clear course for the public sector to adopt. Countries such as Argentina are largely "undermanaged"; they show evidence of accumulated institutional deficits which could only be remedied over a space of years because of vested interests and considerations of party politics. Decisions on industry policy or regional policy, for example, are often taken without reference to the criteria of economic profitability. Inspection and evaluation exercises cannot suffice to direct attention to more efficient and less costly options. Of particular importance is the lack of modern systems of "bonuses and sanctions" both in the public sector and in relations between government and enterprise, such a system being required for any transition to the phase of "intensive industrialization."

However important stable macroeconomic conditions may be, macroeconomic control alone is not sufficient—as is evident in the industrial countries too—to manage the technological upheaval and its profound social implications. Indeed, macroeconomic steering must be complemented by enterprise-oriented policies which single out areas of emphasis in a number of selected fields. The establishment of clear focal areas and the creation of sufficient negotiating authority to have these consolidated are much more important than the still popular formulation of comprehensive macroeconomic and sectoral plans, for example. The various spheres of policy (industrial policy, regional policy, etc.) should be directed towards consolidating these focal areas, reconciling apparently contradictory elements therein, correcting the imbalances which continually emerge in the wake of economic growth, and smoothing the path for industrialization.

Industrial policy should be directed towards strengthening the national industrial core and upgrading international competitiveness. It should be concentrated on a few areas having favourable prospects for development, and be selectively designed so as to support a small group of modern entrepreneurs. In the field of the new spearhead technologies, attention must be directed towards the high-volume, standardized product path in a small group of strongly export-oriented foreign companies, and also towards the rapid diffusion to virtually all fields of the economy, using medium-sized national enterprises as vehicles, of the innovations in the computer industry (this having the currently most important key technology) as well as in the information and communication industry. The development of such medium-sized national firms could be supported by means of fixed-period protection and promotion programmes. An over-complicated network of policies and instruments such as tends to impose too much strain on both the public administration and the entrepreneurial sector could be avoided by establishing an efficient development bank which would support industrial and technological change with inter-company linkage contracts, participations and consultancy programmes.

The capital goods industry should be given top priority. Its expansion should focus not on large-scale projects requiring considerable capital and imports but wherever possible on the intelligent deployment of modern technologies. This is likely to be feasible wherever governments and companies can agree on "technological grading", for example. Whereas the neoliberal experiments have frequently led to an upturn in import business, both government purchasing and private-sector demand should in the future look more towards domestic sources of capital goods. The State should place obstacles in the way of channelling investment towards projects in which economic profitability is of only secondary importance. Despite positive effects on the overall economy, tax incentives for investment in construction should be eliminated in the interest of supporting readiness to commit venture capital. In addition, structural change should be promoted directly, for example through cheap loans to companies which have excelled by virtue of innovation effort or export expansion.

Further concentration on the basic industry sector would in any case be extremely difficult to finance, would provide the region with excess capacity, and would represent an erroneous path of specialization for many small and medium-sized countries, even within a context of regionalization. The process of consolidation should advance hand-in-hand with a gradual elimination of subsidies, especially in industries which are stagnating or in decline in the industrial countries. The consumer goods industry should concentrate in future on mass-produced consumer goods rather than on complex durables. Here, the objective should not be to widen the range of products but to increase demand by standardizing products, limiting production to a few models and types only, and introducing other measures to bring down costs, many of which would also reduce energy consumption and would be more acceptable from the environmental viewpoint (e.g., a move away from the principle of producing disposable articles). In weak industries, restructuring programmes such as those introduced in Southern Europe should be launched. Restrictions on the development of the basic industry sector and consumer durables should be paralleled by restrictions imposed for several years on the extension of material infrastructure; despite grave problems of indebtedness, in some countries there has been but little evidence of this.

In technology policy the primary need at this stage is to optimize technologies imported from the industrial countries: for example, to place greater emphasis than hitherto on acquiring technologies on the basis of licenses and other forms of co-operation not involving capital participation, and then adapting the technologies thus acquired to specifically national needs. The technologies selected should be amenable to broad-based diffusion in the agricultural sector, the agroindustries, and industries producing mass consumer goods and capital goods. Here, the scope for action open to governments and companies could best be maximized by means of a series of relatively small but technology-intensive investments. Modern production and information technologies, precisely because of their flexibility, make it possible to manufacture in small series on a viable basis. Assuming a predominance of clear-cut, smaller projects carried out mainly by domestic firms and financed with domestic funds, demand for imported capital and goods would decline and exports of industrial goods expand. In addition, this would be instrumental in reducing the problems encountered in the employment and environmental fields.

It appears important to emphasize that it would not suffice to establish a small technologically modern export sector. The aim should be to bring about a general improvement in the efficiency of the economy, in the level of technology it relies on, and in the quality of workmanship and service, so that more and more sectors may become increasingly competitive. Specialization, selectivity, and flexibility are possible, especially if they can draw on a generally modern industrial apparatus. An aggressive export orientation calls for efficiency in a constantly expanding domestic market. The government can support the establishment of a broad technological base by providing favourable conditions for investment, by introducing reforms in the education and training system, by making effective use of the media, by introducing new technologies in the public administration and by taking suitable measures in government procurement policy, investment financing, and external economic relations.

Of decisive importance is the implementation of strategies to build up a core of medium-sized enterprises which are equipped with modern technologies and prepared to operate on competitive markets. In many countries there is no shortage of firms which, given a suitable bonus and sanction system, could develop into agents of change. Even a small group of "new companies" can exert pressure to adapt on larger companies, many of which show weaknesses from the viewpoints of research and development and export business; such a group can also be instrumental in modernizing small and medium supply firms, and can furthermore introduce modern concepts of labour relations. Only a new entrepreneurial core such as this can pave the way for the transition to "intensive industrialization". It is the only agent capable of supporting that type of industrialization which the new technologies render economical in its inputs of energy, materials, and capital investment. As soon as this core offers sound prospects, it will contribute towards mobilizing residual capital and bringing back capital expedited elsewhere.

The employment problem can be alleviated only in the event that various factors can be made to coincide: a high rate of economic growth accompanied by dynamic inward expansion; better-balanced distribution, to be brought about primarily via structural reforms in the agricultural sector and the creation of intermediary organizations; the juxtaposition of various technological levels, in particular a combination of high-level and low-level technologies in the industrial sector, such as is found in China; and in addition a redistribution of the volume of labour and expansion of the education and training process. Furthermore, short-term special programmes to reduce unemployment are indispensable (small dams, rural road construction, housing, social services, reafforestation programmes). Infrastructure and production-oriented measures of this type, which would not infrequently obviate the need for major projects heavily dependent on external financing, ought to absorb more than 20% of the labour force in many countries, thereby substantially alleviating the employment problem. The programmes should be transformed into local programmes as soon as possible. Finally, it is essential that population growth be drastically curtailed. Most Latin American experts agree that the problem of absolute poverty or pauperization is financially and organizationally soluble, even during a period of recession such as this, provided the countries concerned make sufficient effort to solve it; the problem, it is claimed, remains unsolved for want of political attention.

Apart from the social costs involved, the price paid for industrialization in ecological terms is extremely high, even in the earlier stages of the process. But neither the public nor governments are as yet sufficiently aware of the need to protect the environment. Despite the catastrophic conditions prevailing in some areas of agglomeration, very little is spent on environmental protection. Road traffic is largely responsible for air pollution. Rail networks could be developed with little external assistance, incorporating road-and-rail links for example, or in combination with a network providing bicycle tracks, of which there are very few at present. In addition to consideration of such energy-conserving, less environmentally offensive, and lower-cost transport systems, importance should also be attached to regionalizing the automotive industry, thereby permitting its thorough modernization, and likewise to introducing speed restrictions such as those imposed in almost all industrialized countries. The aim in the industrial sector in this respect should be not only to extend the inspection and monitoring systems (ex-post environmental protection) but also to examine industries *before* they develop with a view to ensuring their environmental compatibility. At least those of the industrialized countries' environmental and nature conservation policies which are not excessively expensive could be emulated in the short term. If ecological disasters are to be avoided, a number of projects will have to be abandoned.

The low level of progress towards integration made in past decades can be ascribed primarily to the fact that although relatively weak countries have endeavoured to form regional associations, the larger countries have set virtually no store by regional markets, regarding national industrialization as their priority. It was not until the mid-1970s that it became evident that they would likewise have to rely on an intraregional industrial division of labour in order to achieve economies of scale, and that regional co-operation was indispensable in view of the pace of technological innovation. As can be seen from the example of the European Community, the fragmentation of an industrial area cannot be remedied simply by establishing a customs union. What is needed is a joint strategy in the fields of science, technology, and industry. Research and development programmes have been but few in number to date in Latin America, this omission being particularly grave in the field of the new key technologies.

More realistic than an integration model which is overambitious in terms of political and planning possibilities is a form of regionalization which takes account of the growing discrepancies in levels of industrialization. The determining factor here is the interest felt by the larger countries in having stable regional markets for their manufactures, providing, of course, that their supply capacity is sufficiently advanced to permit production at world market price levels. Close co-operation among the industrial agglomeration centres within the region will have spill-over and spread effects that will benefit the other countries, which are unable to develop so differentiated an industrial structure and have to seek niches for their exports by resorting to industrial specialization. The process of negotiation between the advanced and the less advanced countries will determine whether traditional forms of the division of labour can be dispensed with or can be gradually displaced.

Latin America has to overcome its "export pessimism" in a situation wherein the multilateral trade order set forth in GATT is exposed to progressive erosion, protectionism among the industrial countries is becoming yet more pronounced, and the new information and organization technologies are rendering the trade position of the region even more difficult. In the case of labour-intensive industrial goods in particular, the developing countries' export opportunities are diminishing in consequence of technological innovation. This consideration lends substance to the call for "technological development leaps". Active relations with the industrial countries will become indispensable, their nature being dependent on the level of industrialization achieved and also on amenability to the continuing furtherance of the industrialization process. The region should enter upon an emulation race which is backed by active but selective policies in the fields of trade, foreign investment, technological and scientific co-operation and development financing. In many cases, "counter-trade" will be inevitable during the initial period; the decisive factor, however, is arrival, step by step, at a high level of efficiency, creativity, and competitiveness on the basis of technological modernization throughout a large part of the production apparatus.

Such a complex strategy can be implemented effectively only if the fronts shaping domestic politics, which were stiffened during the 1970s, become more relaxed and it proves possible to bring together social and political forces in the interests of a "social project". The resolve to co-operate is much more in evidence today in many countries, and, providing adequate governmental co-ordination is forthcoming, could really afford scope for broad-based "social pacts". This is all the more probable in the light of the fact that those strata which tended to reject the concept of industrialization have forfeited political power by siding with backward-looking military officers, by engaging in experiments with monetarism, and also as a result of deteriorating terms of trade and the technological developments taking place in the industrial countries (high-fructose corn syrup, single-cell proteins, etc.).

A broad-based consensus is also required because the *leitbild* of a technology-based growth model—its image as a guide—is indeed problematic. Technological dependence is virtually inevitable during the course of a somewhat protracted learning process. The new technologies have properties which do not only imply economies in input factors, low maintenance costs, and versatility; it should be recalled in particular that they will do little to contribute towards overcoming the employment problem. The social consequences of innovation leaps, as indeed in the industrial countries too, are not of a solely positive nature, and supporting measures are also required to counteract the new imbalances. If the complex industrialization strategies are to solve such problems, they presuppose participation; participation is the essential element ensuring that sufficient motivation, creativity, and human effort is forthcoming to guarantee that such strategies can be successfully carried out.

20
Industry and Underdevelopment Re-examined*

R. B. Sutcliffe

I

In my book entitled *Industry and Underdevelopment,* written for the most part fifteen years ago, I argued the following positions:

I: that the industrialization of countries was (according both to pure theory and to historical experience) necessary to eliminate human poverty and satisfy human needs with rising standards of living; only a small number of areas or countries could, due to super-generous natural endowments, escape this logic;

II: that up to the present only a privileged few countries had industrialized successfully, and that it did not look from the evidence as if the underdeveloped countries were undergoing the process at all, or at best they were undergoing it at a very slow pace;

III.   that successful modern industrialisation in general requires the use of large-scale units of production to take advantage of economies of scale; and also the use of modern technology which usually means relatively capital-intensive techniques. This is one of the advantages of being a latecomer. Nonetheless many qualifications to this were made and a cautious welcome was

*School of Economics and Politics, Kingston Polytechnic. I am grateful to other contributors to this volume for comments on an earlier draft, especially to the editors, to David Evans and to Martin Bell; and to Kaighn Smith for help with the numbers.

From *Journal of Development Studies,* Vol. 21, No. 1 (October 1984), pp 121–133. Copyright © 1984 by Frank Cass & Co. Ltd.

given to certain versions of intermediate technology and forms of technological dualism;

IV: that because there was something in the existence of, or policies of, industrialised countries which prevented the independent industrialisation of the underdeveloped ones, such a process was only possible if these latter could immunise themselves against the damaging effects of contact with the industrialised countries; and this, with many qualifications, suggested the need for a fairly high degree of economic autarky which quite possibly could only be achieved through socialism in the underdeveloped countries; this was combined with a generally positive evaluation of the economic aspects of the Soviet, and often also the Chinese, model of industrialisation.

These positions, I think, coincide with or overlap a range of positions which have become a kind of orthodoxy throughout a large part of the development economics profession, especially on the socialist and nationalist left. This orthodoxy includes various theories which have come to be known under the collective title of 'dependency theory'.

All these ideas have been more widely discussed during the period since I did the reading for my book. Now, on reflection, I find that just about all of them require at least a good deal of critical modification, and some of them more of a thoroughgoing revision. In this article I will briefly explain why, referring to a number of the more controversial and interesting writings on the subject in the last few years. These include: Michael Lipton's *Why Poor People Stay Poor;* Fritz Schumacher's *Small is Beautiful;* Frances Stewart's *Technology and Underdevelopment;* Arghiri Emmanuel's *Intermediate or Underdeveloped Technology?*; Gavin Kitching's *Development and Underdevelopment in Historical Perspective,* and Bill Warren's *Imperialism, Pioneer of Capitalism.* All of these are works which have in some way managed to have an impact on discussion within the field of development economics by changing the terms of the existing debate. They have all, therefore, forced economists working in the field of development to re-examine old positions.

II

Gavin Kitching's stimulating book gives a good summary of the traditional and almost universally accepted argument for industrialisation as a necessary step towards the elimination of human poverty. It is based on the expanding variety of human needs as material standards rise, and as such it is incontestable, almost axiomatic. But, more than before, I think it needs some quite strong qualifications.

The argument is a theoretical one. It assumes that more or less any conceivable evolution of consumption preferences for some distance above the mere subsistence level of income involves a rising share of industrial goods. In principle, it could be objected, these goods could be supplied for any given population by the production and exchange of other non-industrial goods and services as long as the levels of productivity and the terms of trade of the non-industrial sectors allow it. In other words, in principle a nation of bee-keepers, or of bankers, or of masseurs, or of airline pilots could have a high standard of living. And of course non-industrial workers in industrialised countries often do have a high standard of living. That there should be a whole nation of such people, however, is scarcely possible—it could occur only for small countries extraordinarily well endowed by nature. In any case, for one nation to live like that implies industrialisation somewhere else to provide inputs to the primary production or services. So this whole line of argument is not really one against industrialisation in general, only in some very special places.

Another objection to the standard pro-industrialisation argument is less often made but is, in my view, much more important. The theoretical argument for industrialisation as a route to satisfying human needs does not prove that real historical or present-day industrialisations in fact do supply human needs well. Conceivable ideal industrialisation will satisfy needs; but 'actually existing industrialisation' (to adapt a phrase of Rudolph Bahro) may not. And I contend that in most cases it does not.

It is surely a fact that the standard, universally accepted *theoretical* defence of industrialisation has never been the main motive for any actually existing industrialisation. Real-world industrialisations have not been motivated directly by the desire to satisfy human needs in general. In cases where industrialisation has been fostered by state authorities then this has usually been done as a means of increasing the military might of the nation against others, or to augment the power of the ruling group within their own country. Hence a very great part of industrial output during the process of industrialisation has taken the form of goods which in no way meet human needs but rather create the means to destroy or intimidate human beings.

Also, even if the irreducible nature of human tastes dictates a high proportion of industrial output it does not follow that either the total amount of industrial goods which have been produced, or their composition between different products, are consonant with satisfying human needs. In other words some very radically different structure of industrialisation might in principle have met human needs better. No doubt it is reaction against the deficiencies of actually existing industrialisation which has partly fuelled the popular argument for 'basic needs' strategies; and some of these are very rejecting of industrialisation in a way that I do not intend to be.

The frequent non-congruence in practice between actual industrial output and the fulfilment of human needs illustrates one way in which important truths can be obscured by economists' excessive concentration on industrialisation as a process in the life of *nations* (the abstract) rather than of *people* (the concrete)). Another problem with this national emphasis is geographical.

Even in the most industrialised of nations there are areas of economic back-wardness where industrialisation and its effects have not penetrated. Usually, of course, in the industrialised countries there are no longer large numbers of people living in 'pre-industrial conditions' in those areas because the original inhabitants have long since migrated to the more industrialised areas (urbanisation). Historically, too, industrialisation was accompanied by an-other form of migration—international migration from the slower or non-industrialising areas to the faster industrialising areas—particularly of course from Europe to North America. This form of migration has—for racist and other reasons—become much more difficult in the modern epoch. Therefore international migration is now largely ruled out as a method of spreading the 'benefits' of industrialisation to a wider proportion of the world's population. This is perhaps one reason why it does make some sense to emphasise the polarisation of developed/industrialised and underdeveloped/non-industri-alised areas today as a polarisation of *nations* rather than as one of the forms of intra-national polarisation which have been common to all industrialisa-tions.

On the other hand, to see the polarisation between nations as the main and invariable feature of modern economic change can be extremely mislead-ing. It passes over the fact that some industrial growth has taken place in the underdeveloped countries and that important processes of polarisation have been taking place within them; and this is related to patterns of world indus-trial growth which, because of the growing internationalisation of the capital-ist economy, are less comprehensible in terms of nations than they were in the past.

The dependency/national polarisation approach used to be taken to imply that all nations as at present constituted ought, if they want to enrich themselves to European levels, to undergo a parallel process of national industrialisaion. At best this argument could only apply to broad *regions* since, although the economies of scale argument is often taken much too far, there are enough technical economies of scale to mean that it is inconsistent for very small nations (of which there are very many in the Third World) both to want to enrich themselves and to want to undergo a complete industrialisa-tion within their own borders. It is almost certain, and no longer widely denied, that some processes of industrialisation which have actually occurred (measured in terms of the composition of GDP and so on) behind high tariff walls have led not to national enrichment but to some national impoverish-ment. Political decentralisation in general seems to me to be desirable, but not with every decentralised unit aiming to construct an industrial replica of the superstates within its own borders.

The most ardent proponents of rapid industrialisation will often admit that actually existing industrialisations may leave something to be desired in their meeting of human needs; but, they argue, at any event they have created the *potential* for those needs to be met more effectively. This argument is related, I think, to the question of the relative valuation of the consumption of different generations. It tends to value the consumption of future generations highly relative to the present one (and the present one highly relative to past ones). Even in general philosophical terms this balance of interest would be hard to justify to those whose needs are not met today. It can only be defended by arguing that to ignore the interests of the unborn will (by storing up crisis and disaster) in fact cause more long-run suffering for the living than valuing their consumption relatively low. But in any event such decisions are never in the real world taken by society as a whole according to rational philosophical argument. They are taken by ruling classes and elites (often assisted by economists and other intellectuals). And those who are relatively privileged today will be likely to act as if they value the consumption of future generations more than the consumption of present ones (themselves excepted). Those who starve today would no doubt evaluate differently. But by definition they do not have the power.

Of course it can be argued, again theoretically, that it is possible to conceive a rapid industrialisation and the restriction of today's consumption taking place in a much more egalitarian manner than they have in practice. Thus high levels of investment *could* be financed with less poverty and deprivation today. (In general terms this is the argument associated with the left opposition in the Soviet industrialisation debate.) This is correct in theory, but there is no example of it in practice, which suggests that the political conditions for it are at very best extremely difficult to attain and may be altogether unattainable *(Skouras, 1977)*. If the inevitable political concomitants of rapid industrialisation are what has been observed then this is surely an argument if not for less rapid industrialisation then at least against the adventuristic industrialisation targets so beloved of planning bureaucrats and politicians.

To sum up, a theoretical argument for industrialisation based on human need is obviously valid in theory. But it is not proved by existing or past industrialisations. Most people involved in the theoretical discussion can see themselves as beneficiaries of past industrialisations. But more knowledge of the costs paid by the victims of all the capitalist and non-capitalist industrialisations of the past ought to make us very wary of the application of the theoretical argument to industrialisation in the present. Economists should therefore devote more attention to the quality of industrialisations as they affect the lives of living human beings. So far industrialisation has been more historically progressive in theory than in practice.

III

Although I shall not keep alluding to them, the points made in the previous section have some relevance to evaluating the quantitative data on the recent industrialisation of underdeveloped countries. I accept that the available evidence on this suggests a faster rate of industrial growth in the underdeveloped countries than I had expected at the time of writing *Industry and Underdevelopment.*

According to the World Bank statisticians, the aggregate rate of growth of both industrial and manufacturing output have been over three per cent a year for 34 low-income countries and over six per cent a year for 59 middle-income countries over the two decades 1960–81 *(World Bank, 1983)*. These rates have been higher than for the industrialised capitalist countries and so the share of the underdeveloped countries in the world's manufacturing output (excluding high-income oil producers and East European planned economies) has risen a little—from 17.6 per cent in 1960 to 18.9 per cent in 1981 (calculated from World Bank [*1983*]). Their share of world exports of manufactures rose from 3.9 per cent to 8.2 per cent in the same period. To view this slightly differently the developing countries' share of the manufactured imports of all industrial countries rose from 5.3 per cent in 1962 to 13.1 per cent in 1978 *(World Bank, 1982)*. According to the World Bank figures, the share of the GDP of low-income countries arising in the industrial sector rose from 25 per cent in 1960 to 34 per cent in 1981. For manufacturing the rise was only from 11 to 16 percent. The record is much more modest for this group if India and China are omitted (and it is China which really makes the difference). For the remaining countries the share of industry rose from 12 to only 17 per cent; and for manufacturing, from nine to 10 per cent. In the middle-income group the changes were from 30 to 38 per cent for industry, and from 20 to 22 percent for manufacturing alone *(World Bank, 1983)*.

As everyone has to acknowledge, the performance of different countries has varied very much. A very high proportion of the aggregate growth, especially of manufactured exports, has been concentrated in a very few countries indeed. These are the ones generally known as the Newly Industrialised Countries (NICs).

Of course, it is a debatable point how much significance should be attached to this qualification. The optimists argue that the NICs are an *example* which any underdeveloped country could have followed with the right policies. They imply that there is no overall problem of markets for potential competitively produced manufactured exports. Some of those who do acknowledge that the potential market is limited argue that the NICs, through good fortune or good policy, did relatively better than other countries, but do not rule out the possibility that the benefit could be more evenly spread if not much greater in the aggregate. Among the more orthodox pessimists, other than those who seek spuriously to deny the success of the NICs, most regard them as *exceptions* to the general failure of the underdeveloped countries to industrialise. There has certainly been some polarisation between the NICs and other developing countries, even though this phenomenon may not be as clear as is often supposed, since there are some near-NICs and not-so-near-NICs.

Despite the NICs there is little evidence that more than a handful of countries have in the last two or three decades been passing through an equivalent process of industrialisation to that which transformed the structure of society and the level of labour productivity in, say, nineteenth-century Europe or twentieth-century Japan.

Such a qualitative structural change is of course hard to measure. But it was some approximation to it which I was trying to achieve by proposing in *Industry and Underdevelopment* a multi-dimensional definition of an industrialised country. It would be only honest to admit that I started from a preconception about which countries could be regarded as industrialised and which could not. I then looked for a quantitative basis for the presupposed qualitative difference between these two classes of countries. The 'test' of industrialisation I arrived at was a three-part one: industrialised countries were defined as those with 25 per cent or more of GDP in the industrial sector; with 60 per cent of industrial output in manufacturing; and with 10 percent of the population employed in industrial activities. The reasons for this definition are not worth repeating here. I reiterate it because I want to look at the results which would be obtained by applying the same 'tests' today (most of the figures used in the book were from the mid-1960s) *(Sutcliffe, 1971: 16–26)*.

Under the definition the countries which were 'industrialised' at the time of writing *Industry and Underdevelopment* were the expected countries of Western Europe, Eastern Europe, North America, Japan and Australasia with the addition of Argentina, Hong Kong and Malta. No doubt Singapore would have figured in them too had I been able to obtain the appropriate figures. On the borderline were Uruguay, Israel, Yugoslavia and Portugal.

Since then, according to the latest figures, all the borderline cases have crossed the line and are now industrialised according to these criteria. The only countries to have passed the combined test since then are South Korea and probably Taiwan. An examination of other candidates, including NICs and near-NICs, suggest that most of them are not even approaching the fulfilment of the three criteria of the definition and this is usually because industrial employment is not expanding as a share of the population, though on the first two criteria alone (the sectoral structure of output) many of them would 'pass'.

I believe that these results call into question some of the optimistic conclusions drawn from the aggregate statistics by writers such as Bill Warren. A number of other statistical points also tend to deepen my scepticism of the 'optimistic' perspective.

First, there remains a vast difference between the level of manufacturing output per head of population in the most retarded of the advanced industrialised countries and even the most statistically industrialised of the underdeveloped ones. So while the definitions based on sectoral shares and the labour force show South Korea to be as industrialised as the UK the difference between the two countries' levels of manufacturing output per head (1978 figures) is between $621 and $2,667. In a number of Third World countries (of which South Korea is an example) real structural change has been taking place which in relation to the patterns followed historically by the presently advanced industrialised countries is 'premature'.

Part of this may be a statistical illusion due to differences between domestic and world relative prices. But I believe that many countries have in a real sense structurally industrialised at a much lower level of labour productivity than was the case in the advanced countries. Of the NICs only Singapore has a level of manufacturing output per head higher than some industrialised countries; and that is an unfair comparison given that Singapore is a city-state without a hinterland or rural sector. Singapore's statistics can prove very little; other individual cities in the Third World might show similar results if they could be statistically isolated from their hinterlands (for example, Sao Paulo).

Second, in a number of cases the noted structural shifts in the composition of output are more apparent than real since they result not from a rise in industry so much as a fall in agriculture. In the last 15 years agricultural performance in many underdeveloped countries has been notoriously bad. Out of the World Bank's low-income category 23 out of 33 countries have experienced a decline in food output per head during the 1970s *(World Bank, 1982: Table 1)*. This tragic phenomenon produces a pattern of structural change which appears to be the same but in reality differs from that of successfully industrialising countries. "Industrialism" here is a sign not of economic advance but of economic decline.

Third, statistics produced by UNIDO suggest another important phenomenon. In aggregate they show a fairly fast rise in industrial output in underdeveloped countries between 1955 and 1979 (around seven percent, which squares with the World Bank figure). But they also show (in contrast to the received wisdom) that industrial employment has also grown quite fast *(UNIDO, 1982)*. Putting these two figures together, however, does not amount to a double success story because it implies a low increase in industrial productivity—of less than two percent a year. Yet everyone points to evidence of the adoption of high productivity modern techniques in many industries (and this is in fact widely regarded as a problem in itself). If that is really happening then these aggregate figures imply that some of the remarkably high increase in industrial employment has been in occupations which have extremely low levels of labour productivity.

There could be two reasons for this. One is that the product mix of new employment has been towards relatively low productivity industries. But this is unlikely since the UNIDO figures show that the aggregate figures are replicated in virtually all separate industries. So we cannot conclude that the phenomenon has been due to the unbalanced growth of any particular industry. The other possible reason is that the increase in employment has taken place in low productivity techniques. This may be connected with widespread observations that there is in underdeveloped countries a large sector of very primitive small-scale workshops which are very far from modern factory industry. This is seen by various economists as a form of disguised unemployment, or as part of the 'informal sector'. Again, however, it is hard to believe that this phenomenon, although it surely exists, shows up in aggregate statistics for industrial output and employment since statistics for these kinds of activities are notoriously elusive. If they were included in full then the tendency for slow productivity growth in industry would be even more marked; it may even become productivity decline. While a mystery remains, these speculations suggest once again that not all statistical industrialisation represents economic progress in the normally accepted sense.

The available statistics suggest to me that both extremes in the argument over the industrialisation record of the Third World are wrong: both Warren's optimistic view that industrialisation, the equivalent of the process which transformed the advanced countries, is now taking place quite rapidly in the underdeveloped ones; and the orthodox dependency view that hardly anything significant is happening. The truth seems not to be midway between the two but more complex and ambiguous than either. A form of industrialisation has been taking place in quite a widespread manner. But in many countries it is composed of different elements which are not homogeneous and do not unambiguously represent economic modernisation.

In many countries what seems to be happening is that modern industry is growing at high and rising productivity levels and at the same time small-scale, more primitive industry survives at low, possibly declining productivity levels, but provides a meagre living for a growing share of the people. What may be occurring therefore is a process of internal polarisation, one which is more complex and more extreme than I envisaged when writing *Industry and Underdevelopment* and one which is very different from what took place in the successful industrialisations of the past.

IV

Heated debates have raged over the last ten years or so about the related questions of choice of techniques, economies of scale, urban bias and so on. On this collection of questions economists have tended to range themselves in two rival camps: those who favour rapid industrial development, extol modern technologies, reject (or ignore) the notion of urban bias and so on; and those who favour rural development, think urban bias has been significant and damaging and favour the use of intermediate (or appropriate) technology. Harking back to earlier debates on related subjects Kitching *(1982)* and Byres *(1979)*, have described parts of this discussion as one between populists and anti-populists, the latter by implication being on the side of historical progress, the former being largely backward-looking.

The socialist tradition in the last century has by and large rejected the kinds of arguments which are today produced by such writers as Schumacher and Lipton. Just as Marx and Engels are supposed to have vanquished the Utopian socialists, Lenin defeated the Narodniks and (dare one add?) Stalin triumphed over Bukharin, so today populists are widely seen by socialists as the remnants of a losing tradition. On the whole I think this was the position adopted in my book, though with some reservations. Today I regard those reservations as much more important. But the debate is one which takes place at so many levels that it is hard to disentangle them into some coherent threads.

Socialist orthodoxies usually contain a strong belief in the idea that the use of the most advanced techniques will maximise the surplus and thereby the rate of development, and that such techniques are becoming increasingly large-scale and capital-intensive. However, despite many obstinate attempts to deny it (such as that recently by Emmanuel *[1982]*), there is convincing evidence that in many activities less capital-intensive techniques may be surplus-maximising, that not all technical progress implies growing minimum scale of production, and that better directed research can result in more appropriate techniques *(Stewart, 1978; Kaplinsky, 1982)*. Such newly discovered techniques can sometimes not only be economically and technically efficient but can also possess other virtues.

The choice of techniques debate has seldom broken out of a neo-classical mould. It is usually posed as a discussion about maximising output or the rate of growth of output. So far it has not fully incorporated work on technology which sees the choice of technique as much more than a technical, economic choice. From the point of view of the choosers (whether they be capitalists or state bureaucrats) technological choice is often determined by questions of control and discipline of the labour force within the production process. Machine-paced operations may be chosen not for their superiority in terms of technical efficiency but for their ability to enforce labour discipline. From the point of view of the worker the nature of technology can determine much of the character of her or his life. Of course, many labour-intensive technologies are associated with the most inhuman forms of exploitation and wage slavery. But also many capital-intensive technologies, especially of mass, assembly-line production, are associated with the loss of human independence and control by the worker.

If we are to consider industrialisation not from the point of view of the nation-state or other inhuman abstractions but from the point of view of its relationship with real human beings alive, and to be born, then these points are every bit as important as the ones concerned with the maximising of output and growth (which also of course indirectly affect real people's lives). This is why I think that the populists, intermediate technologies and the like have introduced a crucial set of considerations into the debate on industrialisation.

This does not mean that I agree with all that they say. But I think that it is important for economists to admit that the questions they raise are necessary dimensions to the problems of industrialisation and the choice of technology which are excluded from the usual economists' debate. Unfortunately the reason that they are excluded is that they represent in some form the interests of those who stand to be the victims of the industrialisation process. These are usually the groups in society that do not have an audible voice. When they do the practical choice of technology becomes a different question. The reason, for example, why the level of productivity in the German motor industry is higher than in the British surely has a lot to do with the ability of British workers' trade unions to defend themselves against the consequences of advanced technologies. And it is hard to imagine that Soviet industrialisation would have occurred in anything like the way it has if the political voices of the working class had not been so completely stifled.

I think that the consequences of this argument is that in political systems which are basically exploitative, be they capitalist or 'socialist', the existence of elements of workers' democracy may, by constraining technological choice, slow down the process of industrialisation. But that does not mean that there is a trade-off between democracy and industrialisation, at least not in any simple sense. It is part of the job of economists who are concerned both with democracy and with long-term economic progress to search for ways of transcending this trade-off. One element of this would surely be intermediate technology—not conceived of as a traditional technology designed to preserve traditional ways of life which can be oppressive to those condemned to lead them (especially to women) as more modern forms of tyranny, but rather conceived as modern forms of technology which allow endurable labour processes. This would only make sense in a humane and democratic form of society which hardly exists today anywhere on earth. But that fact does not seem to me to justify economists collaborating in making choices which are only rational in the context of societies in which it is the beneficiaries, and not the victims, of industrialisation who take all the decisions.

There is nevertheless an unsatisfactory aspect to the view of many of the populists and appropriate technologists—their failure to distinguish between different classes of victim in the industrialisation process. Traditional or rural exploiters tend not to be sufficiently distinguished from those whom they exploit today. This can be particularly true of Michael Lipton's *(1977)* notion of urban bias which elides class distinctions within rural (and urban) society as Terry Byres *(1979)* quite convincingly argues. On a different plane, it is worth reminding ourselves that a humane concern for the victims of actually existing industrialisation can easily slip into a defence of preindustrial privilege and exploitation, an opposition to radical change of any kind, and a defence of the values and modes of life of villages which are so often especially reactionary and oppressive.

It has often been said that it is necessary to accept (for *whom* to accept we may ask?) the suffering attendant on processes like industrialisation in the interests of material progress which will pave the way for a better life for future generations. If ever this view was justified it no longer is today. Partly this is because the advanced nature of technology means that (at least if research and development work is radically re-directed) the potential choices are far wider than they were in the nineteenth century. The resources and technology surely now exist to resolve all the principle material problems of humanity. We live in potential affluence; the potential is unrealised for reasons which are basically political.

V

The main source of unease I have tried to draw attention to is the tendency among economists on various sides of the debates about industrialism to which I have briefly referred, to ignore the problem of the victims. This has been especially evident, I think, in the generally positive evaluation among economists, especially socialists, of the industrialisation of the Soviet Union, a process mainly directed towards increasing the military power under the control of a dictatorial group and one in the course of which millions died or suffered unbelievable torments. Often these things are either passed over; or else there is a rather blithe assumption that somehow all the economic success of the Soviet Union could be repeated without its political aspects. This has generally been the line of those who support the positions of the left opposition on industrialisation during the 1920s debate and after.

I have always believed that in some sense Stalinism held back rather than advanced the development of the Soviet Union by imprisoning the creative human endeavour of the majority of its citizens. But I do not think that means that economically the same process would have been possible in a more humane environment. The kind of nationalist industrialisation which took place in the Soviet Union in some ways required the politics which went with it. A more humane and democratic process could have occurred only in the context of a much more open, less nationalistic and militaristic environment—a fact which supporters of the left opposition then and now have too often forgotten.

The cult of Soviet success has combined with the analysis of dependency theory to produce the notion that the most appropriate road to industrialisation in the Third World today is via a non-capitalist route which would of necessity be relatively autarkic. This was a major theme of *Industry and Underdevelopment* and others have developed it more explicitly. I now believe that it is the wrong way round to look at the relation of socialism and industrialisation. It sees socialism not so much as an end defined in terms of social justice and individual fulfilment, but as a means to effect separation from the international capitalist economy. It becomes a theory of 'socialism in one country' in many countries. Socialism is devalued, as it is in practice so often in the real world, into a euphemism for nationalism and perhaps for dictatorship as well. It loses a central element of the nineteenth-century socialist tradition which is its internationalism—the idea that material and political problems in the world as a whole will only be resolved by a combined struggle of the oppressed in the advanced and the backward parts of the world because their exploiters are internationalised. The internationalism of capitalism was seen in that tradition as something to be built on rather than something to be reversed.

However, the reaction of Warren and others to the deficiencies of nationalist socialism seems to me to be equally wrong. Warren and Emmanuel reassert Marx's surely invalidated expectation that capitalism was capable of developing the whole world in the image of the advanced countries and that the working class would then inherit an advanced planet. Just as much as the advocates of the non-capitalist road to industrialisation, such arguments imply a conception of historical progress in which the suffering of victims is seen as inevitable and ultimately justified. Growing inequality can be interpreted as a necessary element in a process of development which would enable the problems of the majority of people to be resolved in the future. Emmanuel argues that:

> if capitalism is hell there exists a still more frightful hell: that of less developed capitalism . . . if [capitalist] development does not *ipso facto* lead to the satisfaction of 'social needs', it nonetheless constitutes, via the political struggles made possible by a certain pluralism inherent in the higher phase of the industrial revolution, a much more favourable framework for a certain satisfaction of these needs than those of past class regimes *(Emmanuel, 1982: 105)*.

I think that the experience has substantially invalidated these ideas that capitalist development has created and can still create the material preconditions for socialism which requires merely political struggle at the right moment in history (but not yet!) *(Auerbach, 1982)*. The economic structure of advanced capitalism is inappropriate in very many ways as a material basis for a socialist society. It is inappropriate to a very great extent in terms of the products it produces (armaments, far too many motor cars, planned obsolescent goods and so on). It is even more inappropriate in terms of the forms of participation in the labour process possible with the favoured technology (over-centralisation, de-skilling, etc.). It is in many ways a totalitarian, alienating experience which does not create, even destroys, the values which could help to build a truly socialist society. Capitalist development has helped to create a view of socialism which is centralised, statist and bureaucratically controlled from above—a necessary measure until the "cultural level of the people" can be raised.

I believe that it is at least possible to contemplate a process of economic development and industrialisation in the poor countries which would have less of these deficiencies of actually existing industrialisation, capitalist or 'socialist'. Socialist thinking on these questions needs to recapture some of its Utopian traditions.

As a caste development economists have been a very privileged stratum during the years since 1945. We have found it easy to earn very high salaries and live interesting and even exotic working lives. I do not think that this disentitles us from having views about the world. But it does disentitle us from recommending that the material suffering of anyone alive today should be regarded as acceptable in the interests of the abstraction of human progress. It should oblige us to contribute to the search for a more humane road to economic development than the rocky path represented by actually existing industrialisation.

REFERENCES

Auerbach, Paul, 1982, 'From Menshevism and Post-Revolutionary Adventurism to Stalinism and the New Industrial State', Kingston Polytechnic School of Economics and Politics *Discussion Paper in Political Economy,* No. 39.

Byres, T.J., 1979, 'Of Neo-Populist Pipe-Dreams: Daedalus in the Third World and the Myth of Urban Bias', *Journal of Peasant Studies,* Vol. 6, No. 2.

Emmanuel, A., 1982, *Appropriate or Underdeveloped Technology?,* Chichester: John Wiley.

Kaplinsky, R., 1982, 'Fractions of capital and accumulation in Kenya', Institute of Development Studies, University of Sussex, Brighton, mimeo.

Kitching, Gavin, 1982, *Development and Underdevelopment in Historical Perspective: Populism, Nationalism and Industrialisation,* London and New York: Methuen.

Lipton, Michael, 1977, *Why Poor People Stay Poor: A Study of Urban Bias in World Development,* London: Temple Smith.

Schumacher, E.F., 1973, *Small is Beautiful: Economics as if People Mattered,* New York: Harper & Row.

Singh, Ajit, 1979, 'The 'Basic Needs' approach to development *vs.* the New International Economic Order: the significance of Third World industrialisation', *World Development,* Vol. 7, No. 6.

Skouras, Thanos, 1977, 'The Political Concomitants of Rapid Industrialisation' (Thames Papers in Political Economy), Thames Polytechnic, London.

Stewart, Frances, 1978, *Technology and Underdevelopment,* London: Macmillan.

Sutcliffe, R.B., 1972, *Industry and Underdevelopment,* London: Addison Wesley.

UNCTAD, 1978, 'Recent trends and developments in trade in manufactures and semi-manufactures of developing countries and territories: 1977 review'. Report by the UNCTAD Secretariat, Geneva.

UNIDO, 1982, *Yearbook of Industrial Statistics,* Vienna: UNIDO.

Warren, Bill, 1980, *Imperialism: Pioneer of Capitalism,* London: Verso.

World Bank, 1982, *World Development Report,* Washington, D.C.: IBRD.

World Bank, 1983, *World Development Report,* Washington, D.C.: IBRD.

21

A Note on Social Cost-Benefit Analysis and Class Conflict in LDCs

Frances Stewart

Social cost-benefit analysis is a technique of project evaluation designed to ensure that projects are selected in accordance with their *social* or *national* profitability. The two terms appear to be used interchangeably by most analysts. As UNIDO [21] puts it, "the object of social choice is to maximize social gains" (p. 27), and this will be achieved by selecting projects according to their *national economic profitability.* The UNIDO Guidelines are intended to describe the rules one has to apply to arrive at national economic profitability. Similarly, the Little-Mirrlees Manual [12] is concerned to "produce a practical method of analysis which could be systematically applied and which would, we believe, measure social benefit better than a profitability analysis" (p. 37).

In developed countries techniques of social cost-benefit analysis (SCB) were originally introduced, and have since been mainly used, for evaluation of projects in the public sector, in which the output is largely unmarketed, and for which therefore some method of choice, other than the market, is essential. In contrast, the techniques as developed for LDCs[1] are mainly concerned with *marketed* inputs and outputs.[2] Here the techniques are not primarily concerned to measure the normally unmeasured (though some attempt is also made to allow for various externalities), but to correct the measures provided by the market so that they coincide with social and not simply private valuation. Shadow prices[3] are to be used, which measure the social costs and benefits associated with different projects, and then social welfare may be maximized by maximizing the net present value of the stream of benefits, net of costs.

Although it is possible—as shown by the vast amount of literature on

Reprinted with permission from *World Development,* Vol. 3, No. 1 (1975), Pergamon Press, Ltd.

these questions—to disagree about the precise methodology of SCB (for example whether it is better to use world prices and a shadow wage rate or domestic prices and a shadow exchange rate; how one should take externalities or risk into account), it might seem difficult to object to the *intention* of SCB and, taken *very* broadly, its methodology. As Layard [8] puts it:

> The basic notion is very simple. If we have to decide whether to do A or not, the rule is: Do A if the benefits exceed those of the next best alternative course of action, and not otherwise. If we apply this rule to all possible choices we shall generate *the largest possible benefits,* given the constraints within which we live. *And no-one could complain at that.*[4]

It would seem *logically* perverse to object to maximization of benefits, or maximization of social welfare, as the aim of social choice. It also appears obvious that, in many developing countries, market prices do not correctly represent social evaluation of the resources used. For example, wages in the modern sector often exceed the opportunity cost of labour. Heavy and uneven protection means that domestic prices overstate the foreign exchange costs of resources used. Unsatisfactory income distribution makes market demand a poor guide to social gains. One could go on. The simple point, which is the basis of the need for SCB, is that it is difficult to claim that market prices produce the correct results.

All this seems unexceptionable: as Layard says, "no-one could complain at that." But the argument has skated over a major problem and raised a central puzzle. The puzzle is why, for marketed inputs and output, market prices, if incorrect, should not be altered, rather than using incorrect prices and relying on SCB to bring about the correct results. After all, a change in market prices affects all projects; SCB normally only affects a minority of cases. The problem arises in the definition and derivation of *social* welfare, *social* objectives, and *social* costs (all concepts which are logically related). Or, put in Layard's terms, what do we mean by "the largest possible benefits"? Light is shed on the puzzle from further analysis of the problem: we shall therefore discuss this first and return to the puzzle at the end.

The benefits of a project, that is its contribution to social welfare, can only be assessed once one knows what social objectives are and what weight is to be attributed to them. Suppose one is comparing two projects, both of which involve spending the same amount of foreign exchange, and which have the following consequences (as illustrated in Table 1). It is at once clear that the figures, as they stand, comparing the projects are incommensurable. Market prices would give one set of values and one solution. SCB experts might argue that this should be rejected as giving insufficient weight to, e.g., urban employment, or savings. SCB analysis would therefore give its own weighting, as shown in shadow prices. These prices are in part derived from (relatively) value-free facts. But most of the shadow prices of SCB depend

TABLE 1

CONSEQUENCES	PROJECT A	PROJECT B
Output	+10,000 shoes p.a.	+100,000 bushels of wheat p.a.
Employment:		
urban	+100	—
rural	—	No additional employees. Extra utilization of employed and self-employed
Incomes:		
urban middle class	+500 Rs	+50 Rs
urban working class	+1,000 Rs	—
rural landlords	—	+1,000 Rs
rural peasants	—	+500 Rs
Savings:		
urban	+100 Rs	—
rural	—	+500 Rs

NOTE: Figures are (obviously) fictional.

on values as well as facts. Thus it may be a known fact that employment of an additional urban worker will, indirectly, reduce agricultural output by a known (in physical quantities) amount, but valuation of these physical quantities, in terms commensurable with other items in the calculation, or of the effects on consumption and savings of an extra urban employee, all depend on values as well as facts.

It is here that the key question arises. In any society there are individuals, groups and classes with different interests, and objectives.

Differences in objectives and their weighting, here described as values, arise from differences in tastes, and differences in interests. Differences in tastes (which form the basis of much of the analysis of individual and social preference in welfare economics) suggest an individualistic analysis, in which each individual is regarded as having a set of preferences, and the task of the social welfare function is to produce a set of orderings consistent with the individual orderings.[5] In contrast, differences in interests suggest a class analysis; individuals' differing interests arise in large part from their membership of a class—i.e., from their relationship to the modes of production, because, e.g., they are peasants, or because they are industrial workers—not because of their unique characteristics as individuals. Not all relevant classifications are strictly economic. For example, generations may, for some purposes, form a common interest group, so may bachelors, or large families. A class, or interest group, may be defined as having common values. The preference ordering of any individual is then an amalgam of his individual tastes and his preferences as determined by his interests, i.e., as deriving from membership of one or more interest groups. Since individual tastes are themselves largely determined by environment, and indeed by the class to which individuals belong, the distinction between tastes (individually determined) and interests (class determined) can be overemphasized.

To each set of values, there corresponds a set of shadow prices—i.e., those prices which would contribute most to the objectives. If used for project evaluation, a different set of projects would be chosen according to whose values, and hence which shadow prices, were being used. The choice between projects A and B [in Table 1] illustrates the point. The weighting given to the different consequences of two projects, and consequently which project gives maximum benefits, depends on whose values one is taking, as illustrated in Table 2.

The absolute value of the figures in the table is arbitrary and unimportant. But the sharp difference in ordering is not. It shows that to select projects in such a way that net benefits are maximized is meaningless as a criterion of selection, until one has defined whose benefits one is talking about. Conflicts which arise depend on the extent to which different interests are differently affected by the projects being compared, and the extent to which the weighting of different classes does in fact differ. In the above example, though the figures differ, the ordering of all the urban classes is the same, and so is that of the rural classes. But it would be easy to devise examples in which the ordering of, e.g., the employed urban and the unemployed urban differed. Some overlap of interests has been allowed for in attributing the weights. For example, it is assumed that the urban middle classes have some interest in maintaining urban employment and working class incomes (so as to reduce threats of various kinds from the unemployed upon their security and conscience), and that the urban unemployed have some interest in maintaining rural (peasant) incomes and employment, because this represents an alternative opportunity for them, and because they have family interests in the rural areas. Obviously, the weighting differs from society to society and depends on the links between different parts of the productive structure, which is a product of the history of the political economy.

The table has chosen one class structure to illustrate potential conflicts. Other class structures are possible. So are other dimensions of conflict. For example, different generations (both among those alive, and also among those not yet born) have different interests and objectives. Race, religion, tribe and caste provide other possible sources of conflict. Whatever dimension is chosen it is clear that weighting attributed to different objectives depends on the characteristics of those making the valuation. There is no objective function or social welfare function independent of a *prior* weighting decision: this prior decision, which since it is prior cannot emerge from the social welfare function itself, is that of how to weight the weightings among conflicting classes, groups or individuals in society.

TABLE 2

	Urban			Rural	
	MIDDLE CLASS	WORKING CLASS		LANDLORD	PEASANTS
Weighting given: by to		EMPLOYED	UNEMPLOYED		
Employment:					
urban	10	10	70	—	10
rural	—	5	5	—	10
Incomes:					
urban middle class	65	—	—	—	—
urban working class	5	85	20	—	10
rural landlord	—	—	—	70	—
rural peasants	—	—	5	—	60
Savings:					
urban	20	—	—	—	—
rural	—	—	—	30	10

Weighting chosen to add up to 100.

Value of project* according to:	A	B
Urban middle class	40,500	3,250
Urban working class:		
employed	86,000	Zero
unemployed	27,000	2,500
Rural landlords	Zero	85,000
Rural peasants	11,000	35,000

*Assuming weighting is calculated so that weights may be applied by straight multiplication of values given in Table 1.

Methods of SCB do, of course, recognize the need to elucidate social values. The UNIDO Guidelines spend some time in describing the equi-welfare curves that enable one to arrive at the (socially) correct weighting of different objectives.[6] But this attempt misses the point since there is no single set of curves, but a number of sets according to whose valuation is being used, as illustrated in the diagram below. The problem is really not one of information at all, though lack of information may misleadingly make it appear so.

Suppose *PP* is the production possibility curve. For the urban population the best position would be U: for the rural population it is R. How can we say that either position maximizes *social* welfare, or even that some intermediate position maximizes social welfare, since which intermediate position one chooses depends on how one weights the objectives of the rural as against the urban sector; and such weighting is a question of values.

There is a connection between this problem and the debate, starting with the Kaldor-Hicks criterion [7,6], as to what constitutes an increase in economic welfare: if one could unambiguously define an increase in economic welfare, this definition would provide a basis for SCB. Indeed the Kaldor-Hicks criterion provides the explicit basis for exercises in SCB which do not use distributional weights—see Harberger [4]. However, none of those contributing to the debate succeeded in this since the criteria depend on the assumption that the question of distribution of costs and benefits has been dealt with satisfactorily, *independently* of the criteria,[7] and it is precisely this

DIAGRAM 1

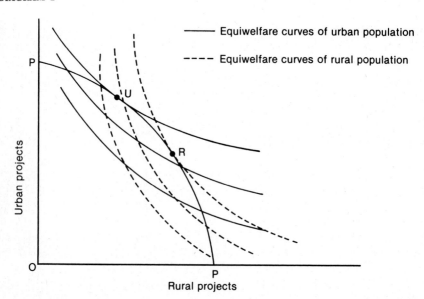

Rural projects

question of distribution that lies at the heart of the problem of definition of social welfare.

Subsequent attempts to replace the rather crude (and sometimes inconsistent[8]) bribery/compensation criteria with a social welfare function,[9] that in theory ordered all social states (like the UNIDO equi-welfare curves) failed to provide a solution to the question. They failed in two respects: first, purely logically Arrow showed that it was impossible, on quite unrestrictive assumptions, always to produce a *consistent* ordering. Moreover, and of greater relevance for our purpose, advocates of social welfare functions never clarified the key question with which we are concerned, namely, *who* should determine society's preferences, which as we have seen is crucial to the outcome.

However SCB is only meaningful if social values are established. Hence despite the manifold and well-established difficulties, advocates of SCB require a method of establishing values. Both LM and UNIDO solve the problem by looking to the Government to establish the values. They do so in two ways: by asking them directly, and by performing a sort of revealed preference exercise on the Government's choices, deducing the values it places on different objectives by its decisions on projects differently affecting the different objectives.[10]

There is an information problem about ascertaining the Government's values, especially since Governments are not monolithic, not consistent, and circumstances change. The revealed preference approach poses particular problems because behavior alone does not reveal the assumptions about constraints, and the actions of others, that were being made, when the observed decisions were made.[11] For example, Governments may act in one particular way, not because that is their preferred course of action, considering their own action in isolation, but because they assume (rightly or wrongly) that by acting in this way they will induce certain behavior in others. Hence, their action does not reveal their preferences as between possibilities open to them, as the theory of revealed preference assumes, but rather it constitutes an amalgam of preferences and assumptions about the consequences of action. However, though these are major problems in ascertaining Government values, they are not of central concern here. Here we are concerned with the principle of taking Government decisions and values to represent social values.

We have argued above that there is no correct weighting of conflicting values, and no objective definition of social welfare. To use Government values may be justified in two ways: one is simply by definition, defining social welfare and social values as what the Government wants. This either means that Governments, like Kings of old, and the Pope of new, can do no wrong, or that social welfare loses its prescriptive value. Few would accept that Governments can do no wrong (more, perhaps, that Governments can do no right): if this is the basis of SCB then it is a weak one. But if we accept that Governments are not necessarily right, and persist in claiming that social welfare is by definition that which Governments want to maximize, it is perfectly possible to question social welfare maximization as an aim. To return to Layard's quotation: if maximization of benefits means maximization of benefits as defined with reference to Government objectives, then we may certainly complain at that.

Much of the above may be agreed on. But it may be argued that decisions have to be made: while it is true that it is impossible to draw up a "correct" social welfare function, Governments represent the whole community and are in the best position to fulfil an impossible task—to draw up or elucidate a sort of general will, from the mass of conflicting interests. This is the second type of justification for using Government values, and depends on a theory of Governments as being above the fray, impartial, if sometimes misguided, brokers between the different interests in society. Governments are assumed to resemble Plato's Guardians (the UNIDO Guidelines actually refer to them as "guardians of public policy"), whose only concern is the good of all.[12] Here the earlier distinction between differences in values arising from differences in tastes, and differences arising from differences in interests becomes important. While it may be reasonable to expect Governments to decide how differences in tastes, based on individual differences, may best be resolved, it is not reasonable when it comes to conflicts in interests. Suppose, for example, some people would like their policemen to be dressed in blue, others in red, and yet others black, and all agree that a *single* colour is to be preferred. Choice of colour, it might be argued, can be left to the Government, since a decision must be made. But when we come to differences in interests this is not so, because the Government itself is part of the class and interest struggle. Representing a single interest (or an alliance of interests), their weighting of social objectives does not represent some sort of attempt at synthesis of the national interest, but rather primarily the interests on which they depend for their power.[13]

There are two distinct, but related questions; both need different treatment in conflict or class societies, and in no-conflict homogeneous societies. The first question is the conceptual one: that measurement of benefits (or social welfare) generated by a project cannot be separated from the distributional consequences, and that there is no single correct measure; the measure depends on the point of view adopted. The second question is pragmatic: accepting that we cannot establish a uniquely correct "social" view, should we turn to the Government, as *deus ex machina,* to do the impossible and provide one? While this would be a reasonable line to take if Governments were disinterested arbiters, in a class and conflict society, where Governments are part of the system, taking Government values to represent "social" values means taking the views of the particular class constellation represented by the Government. In homogeneous societies both problems tend to disappear: the conceptual question, which essentially arises out of the problem of how to weight the interests and views of different parts of society, disappears where there is no conflict. The general will can then be identified as the will of all. Similarly in such societies, Governments can be argued to be the best interpreters of social values. This is to say no more than that it is easy to identify what to do in homogeneous societies. But in conflict societies, the problem becomes acute: conflicts mean that there is a problem in identifying social values, while in such societies Governments generally are actively engaged in the conflict. Social cost-benefit analysis, in so far as it implies that social welfare maximization or national welfare maximization is meaningful (and also possible) in conflict societies, is highly misleading, and sometimes dangerously so, since it dresses up one set of activities—those of taking the objectives of one section of society, normally those represented by the Government, and showing how they may be more efficiently fulfilled—as another, that of maximizing the benefits to society. The former being a meaningful (and possible), but for many an undesirable, objective: the latter being meaningless and therefore impossible, though desirable.[14]

One way of defending SCB from these charges is to argue that SCB merely provides the technology or methodology of rational decision making. There is no need to take Government values. One can, if one likes, take any values one likes—one's own, those of the political opposition, etc. SCB does not claim to provide a unique or objective assessment of the net benefits of projects, but simply a method of assessment which will give different results according to the assessor. While this is in one sense true, it is a specious argument for three reasons. In the first place, the manuals are explicitly addressed to Governments: "The Government requires a methodology for comparing and evaluating alternative projects. . . . This volume is concerned with the formulation of such a methodology."[15] Secondly, the language adopted suggests, if it does not imply, the objectivity of the analysis, as if there were a well-defined social welfare function, which correctly represented *the* interests of the society. Thus the Guidelines argue[16] that "Projects should therefore be formulated and evaluated in such a way as to single out for implementation those that contribute most to *the ultimate objectives of the country.*" (My emphasis.) The Guidelines show how to arrive at "the optimal welfare point" (p. 124). In the third place, the way in which a set of values is translated into shadow prices depends on the power of the decision maker.[17] If the volumes were really intended to provide a general decision-making framework for any individual or class, then this area would require serious attention. In fact, it is ignored, and the only power limitations discussed are those of the Government.

Regarding SCB as a method of translating Government objectives into reality brings us back to the puzzle mentioned earlier: if that is the correct view of SCB, why does the Government not use more direct means, particularly the price and tax system, to achieve its objectives. One reason why SCB is used is that for some things it is a more efficient instrument than other possibilities. The price and tax system may not be able to discriminate as finely (in time or by commodity) as project selection. For externalities, the price system tends to be a clumsy instrument, which is why SCB was initially devised in developed countries to deal with those cases where prices do not operate at all, or efficiently. But SCB for developing countries is intended to deal with marketed outputs, where, often, the price system does present an efficient alternative: indeed since it is likely that SCB will only deal with a minority of projects, the price system, which extends to all projects, would seem to be a more efficient instrument. The SCB analysts are aware of this puzzle and pose and answer it in the following terms:

> One could, of course, retort by asking why if the guardians of public policy do not like the income distribution (e.g., if they disapprove of the existing inequality), they do not reform it directly. Once the distribution is reformed, the project evaluator can simply treat the money prices offered as guides to welfare without worrying about income distribution. This retort, while not uncommon, is somewhat hollow, since there are constraints—political, economic and social—that prevent such reforms of income distribution, and given these limitations the exercise of project evaluation cannot be based on the notion that all appropriate income redistributions have already been carried out. (UNIDO, *Guidelines,* pp. 22–23.)

Little-Mirrlees pose, and answer, a similar question in similar vein:

> In the previous Chapter we raised the question whether a Government seriously wants to raise the rate of investment at the expense of current consumption, if it does not raise taxation when it can, and if it does not take other steps to see that public savings, including those of public enterprises are as high as reasonably possible. Of course governments want to stay in power. There is a limit to the extent to which they will try to squeeze more savings from the public even if it is believed on ethical grounds that a greater provision should be made for investment and growth, and thus for consumption in the future. This raises a very important point. The most important and normal way for a government to hold consumption in check and so increase savings is taxation; and taxation is notoriously unpopular. ([12], p. 42.)

Both answer the question in terms of *constraints* on Government action which prevent it going as far as it would like by the use of normal instruments. But why, then, should these constraints be removed by the introduction of SCB? If a Government's political supporters prevent it from raising taxation as much as it might like, this is surely because those who pay the taxes dislike, and are strong enough to resist, the cut in real income implied, not because they have taken a particular dislike to the form (taxation) which the cut takes. In the first instance, ignorance may prevent any public outcry against the use of SCB to achieve objectives which have been successfully thwarted as far as other instruments are concerned. But if the use of SCB is equally effective in achieving the objective, then it is likely to be subject to the same constraints as other instruments. Why should the *instrument* used influence the possibilities?

If the net effects are identical it seems unlikely, in the long run when the veil of ignorance has been eliminated, that constraints will be removed simply by the introduction of new tools. The unpopularity of taxation is not irrational but a consequence of its effects and will be shared by any other instrument, including SCB, which has the same effects. The possibilities of using SCB to achieve objectives such as income redistribution, where other tools are ruled out because they are unpopular, thus must rest on some peculiarities of SCB, as compared with other tools.

First, SCB has, to date, applied, and is likely to apply, to only a small minority of cases. Hence the over-all effect on interests is likely to be marginal as compared with more direct methods. Its use depends on its marginality, or ineffectiveness. As soon as it becomes more than a marginal instrument, it will be subject to the same constraints as other instruments.

Second, SCB is optional and not mandatory. With most systems of taxation, once a system (and rates) have been established, its enforcement is subject to the country's legal system. There has never been the same sort of legal enforcement of SCB. Governments may go against the recommendations of SCB with legal impunity. This means that it is easier to establish it as a system, than to change the tax system, because it is always possible, when the time comes, to ignore the recommendations. The third London Airport provides an example.

Third, SCB, as an instrument, does not always have identical effects with the alternative instruments. Partly, this is because it only applies to a small number of cases, so the impact is much smaller—i.e., the same point as that above. For example, it may be politically attractive to put a high weight on redistribution of income in SCB, thus getting credit for pursuing the objective, while not actually meeting any costs to speak of, because of the small number of cases. But there are also cases where SCB involves a *different* distribution of costs and benefits from the alternative instruments. The premium put on savings is a good example. Raising savings by extra taxation involves placing the burden of reduced current consumption on current taxpayers, generally the employed and the richer members of society. Using SCB to achieve extra savings means that those whose consumption is cut are those who would be employed if no premium were put on savings, but are not if a premium is placed on savings and capital-intensive projects therefore selected. The burden is thus borne by the unemployed. The different class burden explains why a Government may be subject to constraints in the use of one instrument—taxation—but not another—SCB.

SCB is thus used as an instrument, rather than other instruments, because Governments do not represent the "social" interest, but their own class interests, and yet wish to appear to represent the "wider" social interests. SCB is used either because Governments do not wish the impact to be effective (reasons one and two above), or because they want a different class distribution of the costs and benefits than would be achieved by the use of more direct instruments (reason three). The answer to the puzzle thus supports the general analysis of this paper. SCB does not show Governments stepping outside their normal activities to represent the interests of all; rather, it is another instrument in the class struggle.

NOTES

1. In UNIDO[21] and Little and Mirrlees.[12]
2. Little-Mirrlees, p. 31.
3. Sometimes described (e.g., by Little-Mirrlees) as social accounting prices.
4. Layard,[8] p. 9. My emphasis.
5. See Arrow[1] and Sen.[17]
6. Though this does seem a somewhat clumsy device, since once one had enough knowledge about social objectives to draw up the curves one would not need the curves to tell one what to do.
7. Little's[11] criteria recognize the central importance of distribution by combining the Scitovsky criteria with the additional requirement that the distributional implications must be acceptable. But again this leaves completely unanswered our central question: who is to determine what is acceptable?
8. See Scitovsky[16] and Samuelson.[15]
9. See Bergson.[3]
10. A revealed preference exercise on other non-SCB decisions has also been suggested,[22] though this is a bit odd if it is assumed that SCB allows the Government to attain objectives, which it cannot obtain in its absence. Seton[20] uses this method to establish the weights the Government gives to income distributional objectives.
11. See Sen.[18]
12. Plato spends considerable time delineating the very stringent conditions in which the Guardians must be chosen, educated and live if they are to represent the general interest, and not sectional interests: so that "the whole State will grow up in noble order and the several classes will receive the proportion of happiness which nature assigns to them." (Book IV, p. 420.) They "may not touch or handle silver or gold." They should have no property beyond what is absolutely necessary. Even laughter was to be banned.
13. Some recent analyses show how interests dominate Government in a number of developing countries. Beckford[2] shows how the interests of the plantation companies are pursued in plantation economies by apparently "independent" Governments. Leys[9],[10] (for Kenya) and Harris[5] (for India) analyze and explain Govern-

ment action in terms of the interests they represent. For developed countries see Milliband.[13]

14. This does raise the interesting question of whether one can desire something which is meaningless.

15. Introduction to the Guidelines, UNIDO, p. 1.

16. Again in the Introduction.

17. This point is explored in Sen.[18]

REFERENCES

1. Arrow, K. J. (1951) *Social Choice and Individual Values,* Wiley.
2. Beckford, G. L. (1972) *Persistent Poverty, Underdevelopment in Plantation Economies of the Third World,* Oxford University Press.
3. Bergson, A. (1938) "A Reformulation of Certain Aspects of Welfare Economics," *Quarterly Journal of Economics.*
4. Harberger, A. C. (1971) "Three Basic Postulates for Applied Economics: An Interpretative Essay," *Journal of Economic Literature.*
5. Harris, N. (1974) *India-China-Underdevelopment and Revolution,* Delhi.
6. Hicks, J. R. (1940) "The Valuation of Social Income," *Economica.*
7. Kaldor, N. (1938) "Welfare Propositions of Economics and Interpersonal Comparisons of Utility," *Economic Journal.*
8. Layard, R. G. (ed.) (1972) *Cost Benefit Analysis,* Penguin.
9. Leys, C. (1971) "Politics in Kenya: The Development of Peasant Society," *British Journal of Political Science.*
10. Leys, C. (1974) *Underdevelopment in Africa,* Heinemann.
11. Little, I. M. D. (1957) 2nd ed. *A Critique of Welfare Economics,* O.U.P.
12. Little, I. M. D., and Mirrlees, J. A. (1969) *Manual of Industrial Project Analysis in Developing Countries, Vol. II. Social Cost Benefit Analysis,* O.E.C.D.
13. Milliband, R. (1969) *The State in a Capitalist Society,* Weidenfeld and Nicolson.
14. Plato, *The Republic* (translation B. Jowett, 1908).
15. Samuelson, P. A. (1950) "Evaluation of Real National Income," *Oxford Economic Papers.*
16. Scitovsky, T. (1941) "A Note on Welfare Propositions in Economics," *Review of Economic Studies.*
17. Sen, A. K. (1970) *Collective Choice and Social Welfare,* Oliver & Boyd.
18. Sen, A. K. (1972) "Control Areas and Accounting Prices: An Approach to Economic Evaluation," *Economic Journal.*
19. Sen, A. K. (1973) *Behaviour and the Concept of Preference,* London School of Economics and Political Science.
20. Seton, F. (1972) *Shadow Wages in the Chilean Economy,* O.E.C.D.
21. UNIDO (1972) *Guidelines for Project Evaluation,* United Nations (by P. Dasgupta, S. A. Marglin and A. K. Sen).
22. Weisbrod, B. A. (1968) "Deriving an Implicit Set of Governmental Weights for Income Classes," Reading no. 16, in R. G. Layard (ed.) *Cost Benefit Analysis,* Penguin, 1972.

PART SIX

THE HUMAN COST OF DEVELOPMENT

Economic development is not a smooth, evolutionary process of change. Rather, it is a painful process, which involves breaking up established ways of life and hurting many strongly entrenched vested interests. In the past, development, whether capitalist or socialist, has meant virtually a complete destruction of the old order, with its values and institutions, and their replacement by a new ethic based on a belief in the efficacy of economic progress.

In the first reading, Denis Goulet and Charles Wilber examine the human costs of continued underdevelopment and compare them to the human costs of capitalist and socialist development experience. They also examine the pressure and forces that make the development process a painful one. They conclude that rapid economic growth, while creating and intensifying a whole new set of human costs, may be necessary to overcome the far worse human costs of continued underdevelopment. The article emphasizes E. H. Carr's observation that the cost of conservation falls just as heavily on the underpriviledged as the cost of innovation on those who are deprived of their privileges.

However, whether a growth strategy is followed or one of "redistribution-first," there are always those who gain and those who lose as a result of economic development. This, in turn, generates protest from the losers, which provokes repression from the winners. Richard Falk argues in the second reading that in the context of capitalist development strategies, capital shortage generates a crisis that leads to military takeovers. The crisis is generated by the inability of moderate political elites both to enact redistributive and welfare programs to appease the poor and to make available the investment to sustain economic growth. There is not enough capital to do both. Attempts at compromise satisfy no one. The result is discontent, instability, and economic chaos that invites a takeover by the military and its allies, who are willing and able to impose "discipline" upon society.

Continued underdevelopment is bringing untold suffering to millions of people. Unfortunately, both capitalist and socialist development have generated new suffering in the process of eliminating the old. The human costs of the development process in countries such as Brazil and China have been high indeed. In both the United States and the Soviet Union there has been high human cost accompanying development. The United States has been so interested in money-making and the Soviet Union in catching up that human values often have been sacrificed in the process: genocide of the American Indian, slavery, and sweatshops in the United States; and forced labor, purges, and dictatorship in the Soviet Union attest to this depressing conclusion.

In the final reading of this section, Denis Goulet argues that "liberation" must supplement "development" if the poor countries are to escape the human costs of continued underdevelopment merely to succumb to the human costs of the development process. The hope that Goulet holds out is that the poor countries, while eliminating the sufferings of underdevelopment as rapidly as possible, will draw upon the best from capitalist and socialist experience and combine it with their own uniqueness to produce a new liberated and humanistic civilization.

22

The Human Dilemma of Development

Denis Goulet and Charles K. Wilber

Some argue that, because economic development exacts tremendous social costs, it should be undertaken slowly, only with great deliberation, so as to minimize social disruption. In this light, the orthodox agenda of *rapid* economic growth as the surest route to the elimination of poverty is seriously questioned. The strategy of implementing major economic structural reforms designed to increase output in agriculture and industry is judged against the high price of social change which accompanies rapid development.

Although social change, especially when associated with industrialization, has always entailed a high price, the price of *not* developing is also very high. Historian E. H. Carr notes that "the cost of conservation falls just as heavily on the underprivileged as the cost of innovation on those who are deprived of their privileges."[1] Underdevelopment's high costs include chronic disease, hunger, famine, premature death, and degradation of the human spirit generation after generation. Thus is a painful dilemma posed for development agents conscious of the high social costs of sudden structural changes, yet dedicated to reducing underdevelopment's miseries as rapidly as possible.

THE HIGH SOCIAL COSTS OF DEVELOPMENT

Few writers are more insightful than the sociologist Peter Berger in exposing the high social price of development. The title of Berger's landmark book, *Pyramids of Sacrifice: Political Ethics and Social Change,* is an apt metaphor: The Great Pyramid at Cholula, Mexico, testifies in stone to what Berger calls "the relation among theory, sweat and blood."[2] The pyramid was built as an altar of sacrifice, and the theory legitimizing its construction was brutally simple: "If the gods were not regularly fed with human blood, the universe would

Manuscript prepared for this volume.

fall apart."[3] Although the Aztecs bear the stigma of being history's chief executioners at Cholula, Berger concludes that later generations of leaders everywhere—politicians, military commanders, planners, and revolutionaries, abetted by social theorists—continue to immolate innocent, and usually silent, victims in needless sacrifices to insatiable gods.

Berger views development (in both its capitalist and socialist incarnations) and revolution as contemporary Molochs who devour the living flesh of millions, all in the name of a "better life" for *future* generations. One thinks here of Sartre's play *Dirty Hands* in which Hugo asks: "What is the use of struggling for the liberation of men if we despise them to the point of brainwashing them?" The conversation between Hugo and Hoederer is revealing:

> "If we don't love men, we can't struggle on their behalf."
>
> "I am not interested in what men are but in what they are capable of becoming."
>
> "I, on the contrary, love them for what they are. With all their sloppiness and filth, with all their vices. I love their voices, their warm hands . . . the worried look on their faces and the desperate combat they wage."

Pyramids of Sacrifice needs to be read as a *cri de coeur* against the perpetration of monstrous cruelties—and their legitimization by intellectuals—on living generations of men, women, and children in myriad lands. The criminals are the hosts of planners, social theorists, and change agents who purport to speak *for* the people. Tragedy is compounded by their assumption that their own perception of reality is more correct than that of the masses. Berger denounces that special blend of arrogance and benevolence which too many development enthusiasts and revolutionaries share with missionaries of old, the transformational zeal which denies to poor people that "cognitive respect" of their own perceptions of reality which is theirs as a basic right.

If any aspiration may be said to be universal, across lines of cultural space and individual personality, it is this: Every person and society wants to be treated by others as a being of worth, for its own sake and on its own terms, regardless of its utility or attractiveness to others. Therefore, Berger is right in demanding that planners, revolutionaries, and social scientists show "cognitive respect" for all populations. He himself deserves "cognitive respect" for defending this view against the mainstream of experts who glibly decree the superiority of their own diagnosis of oppression and misery and thereafter proceed to prescribe "appropriate" remedies: economic growth, or revolution and socialist transformation. The stakes are high and in no way can be reduced to the risk of a series of laboratory experiments. Experts who touch people's lives irresponsibly may damage them beyond repair.

Such warnings will remain necessary so long as development keeps confronting societies in distress with a cruel choice between bread and dignity. The facile slogan states that bread can be had with dignity; the harsh reality, however, is that dignity must often be sacrificed to obtain bread, or that the very aspiration after greater dignity becomes distorted as a quest for more bread. *Pyramids* pungently reminds us of two truths: (1) "Not by bread alone does man live," and (2) upon closer examination even the bread may be a stone!

No ethical issue is so resistant to easy answers as that of generations sacrificed now in exchange for the possibility of future development. This agonizing question leads many close to despair. Here one evokes two additional works which closely parallel Berger's own: Barrington Moore's *Reflections on the Causes of Human Misery* and Robert Heilbroner's *An Inquiry into the Human Prospect.* [4] All three authors end their foray into the history of social change on a note of rational pessimism tempered by an appeal to the transrational duty of not despairing. Uniformly they conclude that as much human suffering results from trying to "improve mankind" as from cynically exploiting it; therefore, they tend towards a "hands off history" stance to minimize suffering.

Thus Berger's brief against sacrificing present generations to prepare a better future for their children should be read as one instance of a more generalized disaffection among Western believers in progress. All facile optimism must now be rejected, every easy belief in the necessarily upward movement of history as well as the very imagery of improvement and evolutionary (or revolutionary) emancipation of the human race. Nevertheless, it would be puerile to react by swinging to the other side of the pendulum, since any serious view of history grasps the irreducibly *tragic* nature of social change.

One senses that Berger has grown discouraged over the inability of social science, development theory or revolutionary action to deliver its promised "cargo" at a tolerable human cost. But it is an initial mistake ever to suppose that genuine development can be gained, fully or even in part, at "tolerable" human costs. Therefore, Berger should conclude not by saying "avoid social change (developmental growth and revolution) like the plague." Rather he should say: "Let us engage in an unending struggle against present structural injustices (with their train of alienation, misery, underdevelopment, worship of material well-being, etc.) so as to construct history while we bear witness to transcendence."

Although Berger is right in denying that revolution or development can be ethically pursued at *any* price, he is wrong in omitting the third element in the argument: Doing nothing also makes intolerable exactions in sacrificed generations. Writing before the 1964 military coup, Brazilian economist Celso Furtado described the enormous sacrifices paid by generations of his country

people living in conditions of "underdevelopment": unnecessary deaths, continued abuse of the poor by privileged classes, constant frustration in efforts
to improve their lot. Small wonder, he adds, that

> the masses in the underdeveloped countries have not generally put the
> same high valuation on individual liberty that we do. Since they have not
> had access to the better things of life, they obviously cannot grasp the full
> meaning of the supposed dilemma between liberty and quick develop-
> ment. . . . The liberty enjoyed by the minority in our society is paid for
> by a delay in general economic development; hence [it] is at the expense
> of the welfare of the great majority. . . . Very few of us have sufficient
> awareness of these deeply inhuman characteristics of underdevelopment.
> When we do become fully aware, we understand why the masses are
> prepared for any sacrifice in order to overcome it. If the price of liberty
> for the few had to be poverty of the many, we can be quite certain that
> the probability of preserving freedom would be practically nil.[5]

Furtado's words remind us that most men and women live in conditions
far below those objectively demanded by human dignity. Thus, throughout
history generations have always been "sacrificed." Why, then, should Berger
condemn in absolute terms the prolongation of certain generational sacrifices
a little longer while the progressive emancipation of a populace is being
wrought? The point is this: although Berger correctly laments the high sacrifices demanded in the names of development and revolution, he wrongly
ignores the equally high costs required by the stance of "keeping things as
they are."

THE HUMAN COSTS OF UNDERDEVELOPMENT

Table 1 presents two indicators of the human costs of underdevelopment. To
illustrate, of 12 million children born each year in sub-Saharan Africa, approximately 1.5 million die before they reach their first birthday. If these
countries had the infant mortality rate of the industrialized market economy
countries, the mortality of infants would be approximately 0.1 million. This
means that because of underdevelopment 1.4 million infants die *each year* in
sub-Saharan Africa alone.

The "mathematics of suffering" may be morbid, but it does lend perspective to the human costs of economic *underdevelopment*. Economist Franklyn
Holzman faces the problem of human costs squarely; his consideration of the
problem is worth quoting at length.

> Let us now turn to the case of the nation caught in the "Malthusian trap,"
> nations in which: (1) there has been no increase in the standard of living
> for centuries—perhaps there has even been a decline, (2) increases in

TABLE 1   **The Human Costs of Underdevelopment**

COUNTRIES GROUPED BY NATIONAL INCOME PER CAPITA	INFANT MORTALITY RATE PER THOUSAND LIVE BIRTHS	LIFE EXPECTANCY AT BIRTH IN YEARS
Low income countries		
Less than $400		
Sub-Saharan Africa only	129	48
All except China and India	114	52
China and India only	59	63
Low middle income countries		
$400 to $1700	83	58
Upper middle income countries		
$1700 to $7500	56	65
Industrial market economies	9	76
East European nonmarket economies	19	68

SOURCE: The World Bank, *World Development Report 1986* (New York: Oxford University Press, 1986), pp. 180–181, 232–235.

output lead to a corresponding fall in the death rate so that no change in the standard of living occurs, i.e., those who live remain at subsistence, (3) the death rate is so high relative to the death rate in nations which have experienced secular economic progress that it is fair to say the inability to escape the "Malthusian trap" is responsible for the (premature) death of most of those born, and finally (4) escape from the "trap" requires a rate of investment so high that increases in productivity outrun increases in population. With such nations the case for a high rate of investment for a long period of time (one which enables the nation to escape the "trap") becomes much easier to justify and value judgments easier to make. The essential distinction between this case and that of the progressive economy is that loss of life can no longer be considered an "absolute," i.e., an infinite disutility. It was reasonable to consider it in this way in a progressive economy because loss of life is not comparable by any measure, with other changes in the level of individual welfare. In the case of the "Malthusian trap" nation, however, one is put in the position of having to compare losses of life between periods. That is to say, failure to attempt to escape the "trap" may be considered equivalent to condemning to death, needlessly, members of future generations. Under these circumstances, loss of life would seem to become a legitimate and measurable datum of the system. The question facing the planner is: shall we raise the rate of investment in the present to a point high enough to escape the "trap" even though this will involve a rise in the death rate of the present generation if we know that it will increase the life expectancy and raise the standard of living of countless future generations? No matter what his decision, the planner faced with such a question is responsible for imposing the death sentence on someone. When life and death are compared on this plane, escape from the trap might well seem to be the superior alternative since by simple addition it becomes obvious that more lives would be saved than lost in the process.[6]

Most of the world's populations live in conditions of poverty which are difficult for the affluent West to understand. And the effect of these conditions on the dignity of individuals, the degradation of their very being, cannot be measured.[7] One must, accordingly, contrast this urgent reality of poverty with the allegedly high social costs of development efforts to end poverty. The human cost of economic development has doubtless been very high in the past, but it does not necessarily follow that these costs are an inescapable part of all industrialization or agricultural modernization processes.

There exist several reasons why industrialization is not a painless process. First, there is the need in many countries for radical changes in social structure which often can be brought about only by a social revolution of greater or lesser violence. The old order fights to maintain its dominance while the new order defends itself against counterrevolutionary menaces. And the period of revolution is not restricted to the time of open civil war, but perdures until the inhibiting features of the old social structure are eradicated.

A second reason, closely allied to the first, is the need to develop new social institutions and to socialize people into new habits and values. Peasants must be transformed into factory workers by teaching them new kinds of discipline. People must be convinced that new ways of doing things can be good and beneficial, usually a difficult endeavor. Luddites rose up and smashed the new textile machinery during the British Industrial Revolution, and later Russian peasants tried to sabotage the kolkhoz as an institution. The type of labor discipline required in an industrial society is alien to the habits of a preindustrial society, and it is no easy thing to convince people of the need for new habits and discipline by persuasion alone. Not that the need for discipline and change is not understood, but usually what is understood is not willed ardently enough. Consequently, the passage from one set of habits and values to another is difficult, and often requires some resort to compulsion. This compulsion took the form of the *explicit coercion* of the state police power to expedite the movement from individual to collective farms and to enforce factory discipline in the Soviet Union of the 1930s. In capitalist countries the *implicit coercion* of the market mechanism, under which most must sell their labor where and when they can, transferred labor from rural to urban areas and imposed discipline through the threat of starvation and unemployment.

A third reason why industrialization is painful is the need to increase the rate of capital accumulation, a process which involves widening the margin between consumption and total output. Notwithstanding the prevalence of low consumption levels in underdeveloped countries, these levels cannot be raised substantially in development's early stages. According to Gunnar Myrdal, "Often it is argued that [the] more human approach is what distinguished economic development under democratic conditions from what would take place under a Communist regime—in my opinion a rather dangerous assertion if, realistically, living standards will have to be kept low in order to allow development."[8] The need to limit consumption in favor of capital accumulation can cause a rise in social discontent. The poorer classes will feel that after fighting for the recent revolution, and/or reforms, they are entitled to its fruits. The middle classes and upper classes will resent the curtailment of their former privileges and "luxury" consumption. To keep this unrest from upsetting the development plans or from leading to counterrevolution a powerful government policy of coercion may sometimes be needed. But coercion, as it enables capital to be accumulated, also increases the social cost of doing so. Clearly, development is no smooth evolutionary process of change. On the contrary, says Gerschenkron: ". . . the happy picture of a quiet industrial revolution proceeding without undue stir and thrust has been . . . seldom reproduced in historical reality."[9] The changes needed to initiate economic development are more likely to resemble a gigantic social and political earthquake.

TOWARD A MIDDLE GROUND

On balance, the *human costs* attendant upon capitalist and communist development are probably lower than the *human costs* attaching to continued underdevelopment. And it is particular historical circumstances, rather than the development process itself, which seem to account for the major share of these human costs. The task facing development agents thus becomes one of finding ways to minimize inevitable social costs accompanying economic development efforts and to agree upon standards for evaluating the acceptability of these costs relative to the potential benefits of the process.

Seeking refuge in some predetermined ideological position does not solve the problem, for as Richard Ohmann points out:

> A man who subscribes to a moral or social ideology runs the risk that someone will put it into practice and thereby burden it with a wretched freight of human error and venality. The guillotine becomes an argument against libertarianism, juvenile gang wars an argument against permissive parenthood, the carpetbaggers an argument against emancipation. When this happens, the ideologist may recant; or he may save his ideology by disowning the malpractice as irrelevant perversion. A third response is possible: to accept *la guillotine* along with *la liberté;* but in a man of good will, this requires a strong stomach and a certain obstinacy.[10]

No response seems fully adequate to the problem. Quite possibly no adequate answer exists inasmuch as all relevant normal moral standards in this matter are so ambiguous. Nevertheless, the problem can be understood more clearly by a brief discussion of two factors affecting moral judgments.

The first factor is that "objective conditions control the environment in which behavior takes place."[11] One obvious example of this is a state of war. Restrictions of civil liberties, for example, are usually judged more acceptable in wartime than in time of peace. In Donald Bowles' cryptic phrase, ". . . the death of a political enemy on a battlefield is approved, the domestic execution of a political prisoner is disapproved."[12] A program of economic development is akin to a war on poverty. As such it is likewise an objective condition. Under these conditions, policies to restrict luxury goods consumption, to mobilize underemployed labor for projects such as reforestation, and to control population movements from rural to urban areas could be judged differently than if they were pursued during "peacetime."

Secondly, one must advert to the "ideology affecting the norms by which man evaluates such behavior."[13] In the example just cited, a state of war is an objective condition, while the historical tradition and system of beliefs which shape people's attitudes about civil liberties comprise the ideology or value system. Obviously these two factors interact. The objective conditions can alter the ideological commitments. Even under roughly similar objective conditions, value systems can yield diverse judgments as to the moral status of identical actions. For example, when Nicaragua abrogates democratic procedures it is condemned by some and excused by others. When South Africa, Taiwan, and South Korea do the same the response is reversed by the two groups.

In addition, of course, different value systems will judge the same actions or behavior differently. Raising the price of a good to take advantage of a temporary scarcity in its supply would have been condemned as a sin by Medieval Catholicism; in a capitalist society it would be considered good business practice.

The above discussion highlights the complexity of the problem of evaluating the social costs of economic development. Humanity seems to be faced with a dilemma. On one hand, the failure to overcome underdevelopment *allows* untold human suffering to continue. On the other hand, the process of overcoming these human costs through speeding up development will most likely *generate* some new ones; and the faster the old human costs are overcome the more severe the new. Also, there is the danger that the centralized power needed to generate rapid development will be used, as with Stalin, to consolidate personal power and establish totalitarianism.

Peter Berger issues the challenge that "We must seek solutions to our problems that accept *neither* hunger *nor* terror."[14] But this need not necessarily invalidate the difficult goals of pursuing authentic development and genuine revolution. And by definition neither authentic development nor genuine revolution makes absolutes of success. The qualified pursuit of both is an urgent duty because prevailing structures of underdevelopment perpetuate both hunger and terror.

NOTES

1. E. H. Carr, *What is History?* (New York: Alfred A. Knopf, 1962), p. 102.
2. Peter L. Berger, *Pyramids of Sacrifice: Political Ethics and Social Change* (New York: Basic Books, 1974), p. 5.
3. Ibid.
4. See Barrington Moore, *Reflections on the Causes of Human Misery* (Boston: Beacon Press, 1972) and Robert Heilbroner, *An Inquiry into the Human Prospect* (New York: Norton, 1974).
5. Celso Furtado, "Brazil: What Kind of Revolution?" in Laura Randall, ed., *Economic Development, Evolution or Revolution* (Boston: D.C. Heath & Co., 1964).
6. Franklyn Holzman, "Consumer Sovereignty and the Rate of Economic Development," *Economia Internazionale,* Vol. XI, No. 2 (1956), pp. 15–16.
7. For illuminating views on the effect of poverty on the human spirit see Carolina Maria de Jesus, *Child of the Dark* (New York: E. P. Dutton & Co., 1962), and Oscar Lewis, *The Children of Sanchez* (New York: Random House, 1961).
8. Gunnar Myrdal, *An International Economy* (New York: Harper & Brothers, 1956), p. 164.
9. Alexander Gerschenkron, *Economic Backwardness in Historical Perspective* (New York: Praeger, 1965), p. 213.
10. Richard Ohmann, "GBS on the U.S.S.R." *The Commonweal* (July 24, 1964), p. 519.
11. Karl de Schweinitz, "Economic Growth, Coercion, and Freedom," *World Politics,* Vol. IX, No. 2 (January 1957), p. 168.
12. W. Donald Bowles, "Soviet Russia as a Model for Underdeveloped Areas," *World Politics,* Vol. XIV, No. 3 (April 1962), p. 502.
13. De Schweinitz, op. cit., p. 168.
14. Berger, op. cit., p. xii.

23

Militarisation and Human Rights in the Third World

Richard Falk

1. INTRODUCTION: THE SOCIO-ECONOMIC SETTING

The current global focus on human rights prompts a search for an explanation for the spread of repression in our world. This article considers a part of this overall picture, by focusing on escalating repression in the capitalist portion of the Third World. It examines, in particular the socio-economic setting of capitalist Third World countries in which repressive regimes emerge and stabilise themselves. The perspective taken here is that this setting is being fundamentally shaped by a crisis in capital formation that exists in a variety of forms for all but a few of the resource-rich Third World countries. The crisis is generated by a series of factors. Perhaps the most significant of these is the inability of moderate political elites to maintain stability without redistributive and welfare programmes to pacify the poor, and their consequent inability to sustain growth via re-investment if adequate programmes of this sort are established. There is not enough capital to go around. In these circumstances, attempts at compromise tend to satisfy neither end of the political spectrum. As a result, discontent, instability and economic chaos emerge, creating a context that invites a take-over by those social forces (the military and its allies) willing and able to impose 'discipline' upon the polity. This dynamic is generally played out against an ideological backdrop in which Cold War themes, images and interventionary pressures are manipulated by the participants, as well as by the leadership of multinational corporations.

To provide the grounds for this analysis we first sketch the main dimensions of the setting from which militarised governance arises and the repressive patterns that result; second, we show the extent of the geographical diffusion of repression throughout the Third World during the period 1960–

Reprinted with permission from *Problems of Contemporary Militarism*, Asbjorn Eide and Marek Thee, eds. (New York: St. Martin's Press, 1980), pp. 207–219.

76; and third, we offer some tentative conclusions about the wider impact of this trend for world order values, especially peace and human rights.

2. FORMS OF REPRESSIVE GOVERNANCE: MILITARISATION

The pattern of repressive governance is exhibited in forms corresponding to the exceedingly diverse situations of Third World countries. These variations reflect differences in size, level of economic development, resource endowment, political culture, geopolitical salience and foreign penetration. Nevertheless, despite these diversities—in fact, all the more remarkable because of them—there is an emergent form of militarised repression that shares sufficient features to justify being clustered into a pattern.

2.1 Militarised Governance

The state apparatus is controlled directly or indirectly by the military establishment; military officers are the key leaders and civilian institutions are subordinated, if not altogether eliminated. Typically, control of the state by the military is initially attained by extra-constitutional means, normally by a *coup d'état*. The *coup* is not, however, merely a means of achieving political leadership for military factions of the elite; it represents a long-term commitment, more or less permanent, to restructure state power, even though such restructuring may pass through a number of phases.

2.2 Rightist Ideology

Although some militarised governing systems are leftist in outlook (e.g. Iraq, Libya, Ethiopia) most are anti-leftist which, in contemporary terms, means anti-Marxist in orientation. Therefore, these rightist military regimes identify their countries' social-political futures with the security and prosperity of the urban upper classes working in collaboration with the state bureaucracy. Rightist leaders view the popular sector, or the masses, and sometimes the traditional rural elites, as potential or actual hostile social forces to be demobilised and controlled. Internationally, such regimes are anti-Soviet, anti-Communist in world view, and look to the United States for diplomatic and economic support, as well as for arms.

2.3 Capitalist Development Strategy

The main explanation of rightist militarisation is to overcome obstacles to national economic development through capitalist means. The pretext for military take-over is normally justified by the inability of civilian leadership to maintain order sufficient to check inflation, labour unrest and political turmoil. These social conditions destroy investor confidence and make it difficult to attract capital from abroad in the form of private investment, bank loans or international economic assistance. The military leadership declares its mission as saving the country from radical and destabilising demands for greater 'equity'. Such a role for the new military leadership presupposes the capacity and willingness of government to discipline the poor to accept low wages or acquiesce in unemployment without disrupting productive processes. The economic goal of militarisation in a capitalist context is a high rate of growth in gross national product, regardless of distributive consequences at least for the near term.[1] The poor are 'squeezed', or their expectations 'contained', to assure revenues and stability that benefit the state bureaucracy and most of the privileged classes. Rightist militarisation may produce dramatic results, at least for a time, with respect to economic growth: Brazil, South Korea and Taiwan have all had periods of high annual growth rates. Militarisation along these lines typically occurs because of a crisis in capital formulation.[2] Civilian leaders generally seek to steer a middle course between appeasing the poor and satisfying the rich, generating frustrations on both sides that may erupt into political violence. Civilian governments lack the capability to re-orient the economy to favour the popular sector, as the bourgeois elements in the state will resist such a mandate and are likely to be reinforced in their resistance by outside forces, especially the United States (e.g. Chile under Allende, 1970-3). As a result, constitutionally based civilian leadership lacks the capacity to achieve either *the efficiency* and *external support* of military governance or *the equity* and *participation* of left authoritarian regimes.

In this context, deepening polarisation of the left and right occurs, with important factions of the military being normally and coherently aligned with the right (although not invariably) and capable of tipping the domestic balance by seizing control of the state.

2.4 Militarist 'New Policies'

The leadership of military institutions in Third World countries has also been trained over a long period to regard the principal role of the military as 'internal security', guarding the polity against leftist radical forces eager to subvert the state. Such a role contrasts with the traditional domestic function of the military to act as arbiter among contending civilian forces or as temporary custodian of state power while the civilian sector sorts itself out; this new role involves accepting a more permanent mandate to safeguard the polity and manage the modernisation process. The United States, as part of its response in the early 1960s to the Communist endorsement of 'wars of national liberation', was instrumental, through its aid and training programmes, in orienting key sectors of many Third World military establishments to assume a counter-insurgency outlook towards their own populations. This 'new professionalism' of Third World military elites helps 'legitimise' seizures of power at least within the military establishment itself.[3]

2.5 Coalition with Technocrats

The main pretext of a military take-over is often to 'save' the country from political incompetence and radicalism, as well as to provide the discipline needed to increase economic and political power of the state by means of steady GNP growth, especially in the urban industrial sector. In order to assure realisation of these goals, the state must play a significant role. The military will not simply protect the traditional sectors of economic privilege from interference by the aggrieved sectors of the population; generally, its main objective is to stimulate and sustain economic growth by a sophisticated mixture of fiscal and regulatory policies that make the state an increasingly important participant in the economy. Administered capitalism is the result. Technocrats as expert administrators likewise play key roles. These civil servants share with their military colleagues impatience over the 'inefficiencies' of the conventional politicians who are distracted from true priorities by their search for popularity, their deference to tradition, and their tendency to support sentimental economic goals associated with equity. In the push towards modernity, the military provides a framework, while the technocrats supply planning and overview. Without the technocrats, the generals would be unable to rule for long; at the least, they would be unable to provide society with the kind of disciplined leadership that offers some prospect of restoring confidence in the functioning of a market-oriented economy linked through capital flows and exports to the world economic order.

2.6 Public Enterprise and Investments

As implied, the state enters the economy as principal investor in key industries. The growth-oriented ideology leads in a corporatist direction with the state constantly expanding its economic role.[4] Many basic industries like energy production and distribution, communications and transportation are state-owned in this recent form of militarisation in a Third World capitalist context. The move to the right does not attempt to establish a liberal economic order based on *laissez-faire* market conceptions, nor to supplement market dynamics merely by Keynesian 'fixes' intended to maintain 'full employment' at times when investment levels fall. The new focus is upon efficiency and growth of the economic aggregate, and the leaders accept high levels of unemployment and large-scale poverty for the indefinite future as an unavoidable side-effect of this search for economic viability based on keeping the engine of growth moving regardless of social and political adverse side-effects.

2.7 Ascendant Military Establishment

As might be expected, militarisation along these lines tends to increase defence spending and to diminish budgets for social welfare purposes.[5] By giving the military what it wants for defence expenditure, the governing elite mutes factional disputes within the military and helps to hold succession politics within reasonable bounds.[6] Perhaps most fundamentally, this model of militarised control produces strong states domestically and strengthens their participation in the world system. Statist aspirations for an enhanced status are usually associated with a dynamic military establishment. Hence, the military sector in this kind of polity is often the most dynamic, the most technology-modern, the most rapidly growing, as well as the inspirational source of continuing ideological leadership for the polity.[7]

The priority attached to a military build-up is related to the regional arms races that are aided and abetted by the sales policies of the developed world, especially the United States. These arms sales have been increasing at a dramatic rate during the course of Third World militarisation. Tables 1 and 2 show US military assistance and arms sales to the world and clearly reflect the strategic interests of the US during the relevant period of time. The figures for 1970 and 1975 and the percentage change between those two dates show that Latin America, the Middle East and Africa—all areas in which militarisation and repression are on the rise—have received substantially increased amounts of US military aid while the developed world, excepting Israel, has received no military assistance. A similar pattern is discernible for arms sales. Arms sales from the US to all parts of the world have increased between 1970 and 1975. But the most significant increase occurred in sales to Africa, with sales to South Asia and the Middle East following closely behind.

2.8 Repressive Policies and Apparatus

To assure the success of militarised governance under modern conditions requires the virtual absence of serious manifest political opposition. Given the reality of right/left splits in Third World politics, ascendancy to power by either the right or the left means intense opposition by the other. Harsh means are relied upon to quell opposition. To resist under such conditions requires desperate strategies—kidnappings, terrorism, armed struggle. A vicious circle of repression and resistance ensues. To discipline the polity successfully appears to require reliance on torture and official terror as staple ingredients of rule, at least until the opposition is liquidated or intimidated. An internal security bureaucracy, which includes a network of spies and informers to penetrate all parts of society and often to reach overseas to control exile activity, emerges and grows. As with other aspects of right-wing militarisation, the internal security system is developed in a modern spirit

TABLE 1: US Military Assistance for Years 1966, 1970, 1975 by Regions (Millions of Current Dollars)

REGIONS	1966	1970	PER CENT CHANGE	1975	PER CENT CHANGE
Developing:					
Region 2 (Europe*)	281.3	295.0	+4.8	198.1	−32.8
Region 3 (Latin America)	131.4	26.4	−79.9	156.8	+493.9
Region 4 (Far East)	1,179.3	2,492.8	+111.3	1,243.2	−50.1
Region 5 (South Africa)	9.0	0.5	−94.9	0.6	+20.0
Region 6 (Middle East)	251.1	3.7	−98.5	104.7	+2,729.0
Region 7 (Africa)	36.1	19.4	−46.2	70.5	+263.4
Developed:					
Region 1 (Canada)	49.2	0.0	−100.0	0.0	0
Region 2 (Europe)	1.7	0.0	−100.0	0.0	0
Region 4 (Japan)	90.0	30.0	−66.6	300.0	+900.0
Region 6 (Israel)	5.0	0.0	−100.0	0.0	0
Region 8 (Oceania)					

SOURCE: Computed from figures contained in *US Overseas Loans and Grants and Assistance from International Organisations, Obligations and Loan Authorizations,* 1 July 1945–30 June 1975 (Washington, US AID, 1976).

TABLE 2: US Arms Sales for Years 1966, 1970, 1975 by Regions (Millions of Current Dollars)

REGIONS	1966	1970	PER CENT CHANGE	1975	PER CENT CHANGE
Region 2 (Europe*)	24.277	58.719	+141.8	322.933	+499.9
Region 3 (Latin America)	24.6	25.0	+1.6	154.7	+518.8
Region 4 (Far East)	5.8	61.3	+956.8	439.0	+616.1
Region 5 (South Asia)	10.2	51.4	+403.9	1,419.2	+2,661.0
Region 6 (Middle East)	209.6	143.2	−31.6	2,970.5	+1,974.3
Region 7 (Africa)	7.8	7.8	0	330.0	+4,130.7
Developed:					
Region 1 (Canada)	70.2	53.1	−24.3	102.1	+92.0
Region 2 (Europe)	1,126.423	387.281	−65.5	2,680.767	+592.2
Region 4 (Japan)	16.6	21.2	+27.7	29.6	+39.6
Region 6 (Israel)	72.1	44.9	−37.7	868.7	+1,834.7
Region 8 (Oceania)	52.5	59.4	+13.1	162.7	+173.9

Developed countries: Canada, Japan, Israel, Australia, New Zealand, Belgium, Denmark, France, West Germany, Iceland, Italy, Luxembourg, Netherlands, Norway, United Kingdom, Czechoslovakia, Bulgaria, East Germany, Hungary, Poland, Romania, USSR, Austria, Finland, Ireland, Sweden, Switzerland.
*These European countries are considered 'developing': Greece, Portugal, Turkey, Albania, Malta, Spain, Yugoslavia.
SOURCE: Computed from data in *Foreign Military Sales and Military Assistance Facts* (November 1975).

with outside (usually US) support and guidance.[8] Although militarised regimes vary considerably in their tolerance of political and cultural activity, all of them insist upon 'emergency' prerogatives, as needed, to remove undesirables from the scene and to impose policies designed to intimidate the population from any kind of massive protest.[9]

2.9 Geopolitical Links

Often, but not invariably, militarised regimes of the kind I have been describing come into being with the blessing of the United States government. The precise relationship is difficult to demonstrate in most situations, although recent revelations and investigations often disclose a pattern of CIA support for the transition to militarised rule and its subsequent stabilisation.[10] What seems clear is that a militarised rightist polity tends to attract capital and political support both from the market economies in the industrialised world and from international lending institutions dominated by OECD perspectives. Despite severe abuses of human rights, these regimes are rarely victims of diplomatic pressure from the northern liberal democracies, unless their leaders pursue highly erratic and confrontational policies, such as Amin in Uganda and Qaddafi in Libya. More characteristically, the US-led Western global alliance views the principal examples of such regimes—Brazil, Indonesia and, formerly, Iran—as 'junior partners' in the

TABLE 3: **Dependency of US on Imports of Strategic Raw Materials**

PER CENT IMPORTED	MINERAL	MAJOR FOREIGN SOURCES
100	Manganese	Brazil, Gabon, S. Africa, Zaire
97	Titanium	Australia, India
91	Chromium	USSR, S. Africa, Turkey, Philippines
86	Platinum	USSR, S. Africa, Canada
80	Nickel	Canada, Norway, USSR
88	Aluminium	Jamaica, Surinam, Dominican Republic
88	Tantalum	Australia, Canada, Zaire, Brazil
98	Cobalt	Zaire, Finland, Norway, Canada
86	Tin	Malaysia, Thailand, Bolivia
86	Fluorine	Mexico, Spain, Italy
60	Germanium-Indium	USSR, Canada, Japan
50	Beryllium	Brazil, S. Africa, Uganda
60	Tungsten	Canada, Bolivia, Peru, Mexico
50	Zirconium	Australia, Canada, S. Africa
40	Barite	Ireland, Peru, Mexico
23	Iron ore	Canada, Venezuela, Nigeria, Brazil
21	Lead	Canada, Peru, Australia, Mexico
18	Copper	Canada, Peru, Chile, S. Africa

SOURCE: *United States Military Posture for FY 1977* (Joint Chiefs of Staff, Washington, D.C., 1976).

alliance against radicalism. Iran's intervention in Oman to defeat the Dhofar uprising, Indonesia's invasion of East Timor and Brazil's support for counter-insurgency in southern zone countries illustrate these regional 'peace-keeping' roles. In addition, these regimes have also provided the West, especially the United States, with relatively safe havens for military bases, space stations, geopolitical allies and a comparatively secure and profitable setting for overseas capital and market development, including the operations of multinational corporations.

2.10 Statism

Somewhat contrary to section 2.9, the militarised governance pattern, once relatively secure in power, frequently moves strongly to defend its own statist and nationalist directions. Its logic is to establish control, rather than to defer to its outside patron or 'senior partner'. In this respect, some militarised regimes (or some factions within these regimes), despite their internal reactionary policies, have actually joined in the front ranks of the struggle for a new international economic order. Part of this independent posture in international arenas appears to stem from a quest for international legitimacy on the part of governmental leadership. Experience in Brazil, India, Thailand, South Korea and elsewhere suggests that these militarised regimes cannot count upon achieving legitimacy via the popular endorsement of official policies in elections even if they build up a record of economic successes. Unless rigged, the consistent result of 'opening' the system to electoral politics, even of a restricted kind, has been a repudiation of the economic, political and ideological approach of these militarised regimes. More recently, these regimes have refused to forfeit their nuclear options or to accept US leadership in the area of non-proliferation policy. Brazil, for instance, has been steadily diversifying its trade and investment patterns and has refused to define its diplomatic stance in the United Nations by following the US lead (for example, Brazil voted for the anti-Zionist resolution in the General Assembly in 1975). Even on an economic plane the drive for statist internal control has led these regimes to burden foreign investors with an increasing web of regulatory authority. On another level, the growing burden of foreign indebtedness, built up to $160 billion by the end of 1976, reflects not only the extent to which these militarised polities attracted outside capital, but also their degree of dependence and vulnerability: either they accept external interference in their economy to sustain their credit standing or they lose their credit.

By describing the nature of Third World rightist militarisation in a capitalist context, I am not implying uniformity or conspiracy. I only suggest that some underlying circumstances in the Third World have generated a pattern of response in which some shared characteristics are present and are accentuated by the structure of the world economy.

3. MILITARISM IN THE THIRD WORLD

Depicting trends reinforces the argument that militarism is spreading in the Third World. The spread of rightist forms of militarisation in response to internal crises of capital formation and political order is the central focus of this article. To some extent, however, all forms of militarisation, including leftist forms, reveal the apparent inability of moderate forms of governance to survive into the late 1970s in the Third World.

In collaboration with Charlotte Ebel, Ruthann Johansen and Tom Lindenfeld, I am seeking to develop methods of presenting and interpreting data bearing on these trends. Here we attempt to make the basic case for a spread of militarism, and specifically of right-wing militarism, in a series of *world maps* beginning in 1960. On these maps we indicate those Third World countries subject to militarised rule in each five-year interval since 1960.

We distinguish degrees of militarisation in each of the first four maps. In essence, our view is that militarising pressure is broader than direct control exerted by the military establishment over the governing apparatus or selection of the head of state from the ranks of military officers. Hence, the maps identify those states ruled by military officers, those in which martial law or state of emergency has been declared by the government, and, finally, those in which civilians rule the country but do not allow a political opposition to function normally and depend heavily on the military to keep them in power.

On the fifth map we identify left and right orientations of the militarised governments. We made these judgements on the basis of three criteria: attitudes towards multinationals, pattern of global alignment and socialisation of the economy. Our attempt is to draw these distinctions as reasonably as possible for the most recent year in the eighteen-year period examined.

Even if one objects to a particular decision as to classification, these maps reveal clearly a trend toward rightist forms of militarisation. In Latin America and Africa the shift during the period covered has been specially dramatic. As the preceding discussion of the context of militarisation clarifies, it is the new character of the military outlook that creates occasion for alarm. The ascent to power of the military or of militarised civilians is accompanied by a broadened sense of purpose for the military. The military and their civilian allies now regard their security task as mainly domestic, a matter of protecting the stability of the developmental process against radical social forces. In other words, militarisation is associated, whether wittingly or not, with a new type of politics, that eventuates whatever else in the structures and practices of the rigid state.

In Africa and Asia trends towards militarisation should be associated, in part, with some deferred strains of decolonisation. The post-colonial state has expanded without generally being able to secure a mandate embracing all significant groups encompassed by state boundaries. Hence a crisis of legitimacy has emerged that can be solved in one of two ways: weak governance combined with disorder and economic uncertainty, or strong governance based on imposed authority usually associated with the ascendancy of particular elites. In most third World countries, because the military has been willing to exercise control, the strong governance option has prevailed.

In sum, the maps support the generalisation about the trends towards militarisation, as well as the sub-trends toward rightist variants. Such trends are vectors of change. Some exceptions exist. India's move towards militarised rule with the Emergency Decrees of 1975 has been repudiated at the polls in an election in March of 1977. The elections suggest the mildness of India's move towards militarisation, although reports suggest that Mrs. Gandhi tried unsuccessfully to solicit direct military intervention to offset the adverse election results. It is not clear at all whether the restoration of civilian rule in India will itself enjoy sufficient stability to resist the wider Third World trends; the question is whether the rehabilitation of moderate rule will prove sustainable for long.

4. IMPLICATIONS

There are several significant implications of this trend for the global community. First of all, militarisation encourages the emergence of strong states in many Third world countries. Second, where state power is strong and maintained by military control, a political atmosphere insensitive to international human rights of both an economic and a political character is almost certain to result. Third, a set of militarist Third World governments will be disinclined to push for disarmament initiatives; such an orientation works against a more natural Third World interest in pressing for denuclearisation and disarmament. Fourth, the existence of a large majority of Third World governments that affirm the traditional virtues of sovereignty and statism reinforces the world order *status quo.*

Such a situation creates confusion. On the one hand, militarist governments may push Third World solidarity on a wide variety of issues so as to secure a better relative position for themselves, but, on the other, their framework is traditional statism that includes endorsement of the war system. As such, world order values associated with peace, economic well-being, human rights, ecological balance and positive global identity are not likely to win support from such leadership. Advocacy of a new international economic order is not *necessarily* associated with seeking a just and peaceful world order. And, indeed, an NIEO under militarist auspices is not likely to help the poor strata of national societies satisfy their basic needs in the near future.

In conclusion, alongside the continuing development and spread of the entire spectrum of weaponry is the expansion of militarised governance patterns. The latter augments the former in several damaging respects. While militarism in the Third World is partly a reflection of domestic factors, it is also a consequence of international factors, especially the imperial geopolitics of the United States and the capitalist domination of international economic institutions and procedures.

To reverse the trend of militarised authoritarianism will not be easy. It depends, first of all, on deepening domestic opposition to militarism and authoritarianism, perhaps precipitated by economic failures that extend to deprivations of the poor to the middle classes. Second, prospects for greater global equity, justice and peace will depend on more 'progressive' politics in the leading countries and in the lending practices of the United Nations family of economic assistance agencies like the World Bank and the IMF.

NOTES

1. See, for example, Albert Fishlow, 'Some Reflections on Post–1964 Brazilian Economic Policy' and Philippe C. Schmitter, 'The "Portugalization" of Brazil', in Alfred Stepan (ed.), *Authoritarian Brazil: Origins, Policies, and Future* (Yale University Press, New Haven, Conn., 1973), pp. 69–118, 179–232.
2. See, especially, the penetrating assessment along these lines in Guillermo A. O'Donnell, 'Corporatism and the Question of the State' in James M. Malloy (ed.), *Authoritarianism and Corporatism in Latin America* (University of Pittsburgh Press, Pittsburgh, 1977), pp. 47–88.
3. See Alfred Stepan, *The Military in Politics: Changing Patterns in Brazil* (Princeton University Press, Princeton, 1971); for a more general, carefully nuanced assessment see Abraham F. Lowenthal, 'Armies and Politics in Latin America', *World Politics,* vol. XXVII (1974), pp. 107–30.
4. For elaboration see essays in Malloy, *Authoritarianism and Corporatism in Latin America.*
5. Empirical confirmation in Schmitter, 'The "Portugalization" of Brazil'.
6. See Fernando Pedreira, 'Decompression in Brazil?', *Foreign Affairs,* no. 53 (1975), pp. 498–512.
7. See discussion to this effect in Carlos Estevan Martins, 'Brazil and the United States from the 1960's to the 1970's' in Julio Cotter and Richard F. Fagen (eds.) *Latin America and the United States: The Changing Political Realities* (Stanford University Press, Stanford, California, 1974), pp. 269–301, esp. pp. 298–301.
8. For example, 'United States Policies and Programs in Brazil', *Hearings* of Subcommittee on Western Hemisphere Affairs of Senate Foreign Relations Committee, 92nd Cong., 1st Sess., 4, 5 and 11 May 1971; Michael Klare and Nancy Stein, 'Exporting the Tools of Repression', Reprint no. 104, Center for National Security Studies (Dec. 1976), pp. 1–15; Walden Bellow and Severina Rivera (eds.), *The Logistics of Repression* (Friends of the Filipino Peoples, Washington, D.C., 1977).
9. Norman Gall illustrates this characteristic by reference to the callous disregard of human welfare in relation to train safety and service between outlying workers' communities and Rio de Janeiro. See Gall, 'The Rise of Brazil', *Commentary,* no. 63 (1977), pp. 45–55, at p. 50.
10. For example, Robert L. Borosage and John Marks (eds.), *The CIA File* (Grossman Publishers, New York, 1976); 'Covert Action: Intelligence Activities', *Hearings,* Senate Select Committee to Study Governmental Operations, 94th Cong., 1st Sess., 4–5 Dec. 1975.

24

"Development" . . . or Liberation?

Denis Goulet

Latin Americans in growing numbers now denounce the lexicon of development experts as fraudulent. To illustrate, Gustavo Gutierrez, a Peruvian theologian and social activist, concludes that "the term development conveys a pejorative connotation . . . (and) is gradually being replaced by the term liberation . . . there will be a true development for Latin America only through liberation from the domination by capitalist countries. That implies, of course, a showdown with their natural allies: our natural oligarchies."[1]

Gutierrez is a major spokesman for "theology of liberation." Numerous seminars and conferences have already been held on the theme in Colombia, Mexico, Uruguay, Argentina, and elsewhere. For Gutierrez—as for Gustavo Perez, René Garcia, Rubem Alves, Juan Segundo, Camilo Moncada, Emilio Castro,[2] and others—"liberation" expresses better than "development" the real aspirations of their people for more human living conditions. Gutierrez does not attempt to review all the changes in the definition of development since the Marshall Plan was launched in 1947. This task has already been performed by others.[3] Instead he focuses his critical gaze on three perspectives with one of which most experts in "developed" countries identify.

THREE VIEWS OF DEVELOPMENT

For many economists development is synonymous with economic growth measured in aggregate terms. A country is developed, they hold, when it can sustain, by its own efforts and after having first reached a per capita GNP (Gross National Product) level of $500 (for some observers) or $1000 (for others), an annual rate of growth ranging from 5% to 7%. According to these

Reprinted from the *International Development Review,* Vol. XIII, No. 3 (September 1971), by permission of the publisher. Copyright © 1971 by the Society for International Development.

criteria, certain countries are highly developed, while those on the lowest rungs of the ladder are either underdeveloped or undeveloped. Similar comparisons can also be established between different regions and sectors within a single economy. Although this view is generally repudiated today, it still retains some vestigial influence, thanks to the impact of works like Walt Rostow's *The Stages of Economic Growth* and to the dominant role still played by economists in planning. Even when they give lip-service to other dimensions in development, many economists continue to subordinate all non-economic factors to the practical requirements of their growth models.

The second outlook, far more prevalent today, was summarized at the start of the United Nations' First Development Decade in U Thant's phrase, "development = economic growth + social change." The trouble with this formula is that it either says too much or says too little since not any kind of growth will do, nor any kind of change.

Most social scientists adopt some variant of this conception as their own working definition of development; it is broad enough to embrace a variety of change processes emphasizing either economic, social, cultural or political factors. Nearly always, however, social scientists subordinate value judgments about human goals to the achievement of economic growth, to the creation of new social divisions of labor, to the quest for modern institutions, or to the spread of attitudes deemed compatible with efficient production. The last point is well illustrated by those who affirm that "modernity" is not the presence of factories, but the presence of a certain viewpoint on factories.

Behind an array of theories and special vocabularies, however, lingers the common assumption that "developed" societies ought to serve as models for others. Some observers, eager to minimize culture bias, reject the notion that all societies *ought* to follow patterns set by others. Nevertheless, they assert that modern patterns are inevitable, given the demonstration effects and technological penetration of modern societies throughout the world.

A third stream of development thinkers stresses ethical values. This group has always constituted, in some respects, a heretical minority. Its position centers on qualitative improvement in all societies, and in all groups and individuals within societies. Although all men must surely have enough goods in order to be more human, they say, development itself is simply a means to the human ascent. This perspective, at times called "the French school," is linked to such names as economist François Perroux, social planner Louis Lebret, theorist Jacques Austruy, and practicing politicians like Robert Buron and André Phillip. According to these men and their disciples, social change should be seen in the broadest possible historical context, within which all of humanity is viewed as receiving a summons to assume its own destiny. Their ideas have influenced United Nations agencies in some measure, but they have made their greatest inroads in religious writings on development: papal encyclicals, documents issued by the World Council of Churches and the Pontifical Commission on Justice and Peace, pastoral letters drafted by bishops in several countries. The single geographical area where the French school has achieved considerable penetration is Latin America.

This is why the conclusion reached by Gutierrez is particularly significant. According to Gutierrez, the French school, because of its historicity and its insistence on norms for social goals, is the least objectionable of the three perspectives he criticizes. Nevertheless, he argues, the realities barely hinted at by the French are better expressed by the term "liberation" than by "development." By using the latter term the French school does not dramatize its discontinuities with the other perspectives sharply enough. Worse still, its spokesmen employ such notions as foreign aid, technical cooperation, development planning, and modernization in ways which remain ambiguous at best. Consequently, in the eyes of many Latin Americans "development" has a pejorative connotation: it does not get to the roots of the problem and leads to frustration. Moreover, "development" does not evoke asymmetrical power relations operative in the world or the inability of evolutionary change models to lead, in many countries, to the desired objectives. Therefore, says Gutierrez, it is better to speak of liberation, a term which directly suggests domination, vulnerability in the face of world market forces, weak bargaining positions, the need for basic social changes domestically and for freer foreign policies.

THE LANGUAGE OF LIBERATION

To substitute for "development" the term "liberation" is to engage in what Brazilian educator Paulo Freire calls "cultural action for freedom."[4] Liberation implies the suppression of elitism by a populace which assumes control over its own change processes. Development, on the other hand, although frequently used to describe various change processes, stresses the benefits said to result from them: material prosperity, higher production and expanded consumption, better housing or medical services, wider educational opportunities and employment mobility, and so on. This emphasis, however, errs on two counts. First, it uncritically supports change strategies which value efficiency above all else, even if efficiency must be gained by vesting decisions in the hands of elites—trained managers, skilled technicians, high-level "manpower." A second failing, analyzed by Harvard historian Barrington Moore in *Social Origins of Dictatorship and Democracy,* is the dismissal of violence as unconstructive and the refusal to condemn the violence attendant upon legal change patterns.

Not theologians alone, but social scientists, planners, educators, and some political leaders in Latin America prefer the terminology of liberation to that of development. They unmask the hidden value assumptions of the conventional wisdom and replace them with a deliberate stress on self-development as opposed to aid, foreign investment, and technical assistance. Since

I have written a detailed critique of the Pearson, Peterson, Jackson and other development reports elsewhere,[5] there is no need to repeat here what is there said regarding the value assumptions and critical omissions of these reports. What is germane to the present discussion is the confirmation given these criticisms by Third World spokesmen in UNCTAD (United Nations Conference on Trade and Development) and GATT (General Agreement on Tariffs and Trade) meetings.[6] Not surprisingly, more and more leaders from underdeveloped areas are coming to regard "development" as the lexicon of palliatives. Their recourse to the vocabulary of liberation is a vigorous measure of self-defense, aimed at overcoming the structural vulnerability which denies them control over the economic, political, and cultural forces which impinge upon their societies. Even to speak of liberation, before achieving it, is a first conquest of cultural autonomy. Ultimately what is sought is to alter relationships between director and directed societies, between privileged elites and the populace at large within all societies. Ever more people are coming to understand that "to be underdeveloped" is to be relegated to a subordinate position in history, to be given the role of adjusting to, not of initiating, technological processes.

The language of liberation is being nurtured in societies where a new critical consciousness is being formed. For these societies, the models of genuine development are not those billed by U.S. aid agencies as success stories—South Korea, Greece, Taiwan, and Iran. Industrialization and economic growth have no doubt taken place in these lands, but no basic changes have occurred in class relationships and the distribution of wealth and power; the larger social system remains structurally exploitative. Moreover, economic gains have been won under the tutelage of repressive political regimes. Finally, as one European has observed, "U.S. aid seems to work best in countries which are lackeys of American foreign policy."

Revolutionary Latin Americans reject this kind of development. They look instead to China, Cuba, and Tanzania as examples of success. In China, mass starvation has been abolished and a feudal social system overthrown. Elitism in rulers is systematically uprooted whenever it reappears, and technological gains are subordinated to the cultural creation of a new man capable of autonomy. Cuba, notwithstanding its economic mistakes, freely admitted, has overcome its servile dependence on the United States and asserts itself increasingly in the face of the Soviet Union, upon whom it still relies heavily for financial, technical and military assistance. Moreover, Cuba has abolished illiteracy in sensational fashion, decentralized investment, and reduced the gap in living conditions between the countryside and the cities. And Tanzania is admired because it rejects mass-consumption as a model for society, practices self-reliance in its educational system (choosing to grant prestige to agricultural skills rather than to purely scientific ones geared to large-scale engineering projects), accepts foreign aid only when the overall impact of the projects financed will not create a new elite class within the nation itself, and in general subordinates economic gains to the creation of new African values founded on ancient communitarian practices.

For liberationists, therefore, success is not measured simply by the quantity of benefits gained, but above all by the way in which change processes take place. Visible benefits are no doubt sought, but the decisive test of success is that, in obtaining them, a society will have fostered greater popular autonomy in a non-elitist mode, social creativity instead of imitation, and control over forces of change instead of mere adjustment to them. The crucial question is: Will "underdeveloped" societies become mere consumers of technological civilization or agents of their own transformation? *At stake, therefore, is something more than a war over words; the battle lines are drawn between two conflicting interpretations of historical reality, two competing principles of social organization.* The first values efficiency and social control above all else, the second social justice and the creation of a new man.

Western development scholars are prone to question the validity of the new vocabulary of liberation. As trained social scientists, they doubt its analytical power, explanatory value, and predictive capacities. Yet their scepticism is misplaced inasmuch as empirical social science has itself proved unable to describe reality, let alone to help men change it in acceptable ways. Of late, however, a salutory modesty has begun to take hold of social scientists. Gunnar Myrdal (in *Asian Drama*) confesses the error of his early days as an "expert" on development, and challenges (in *Objectivity in Social Research*) the assumptions behind all value-free theories and research methods. More forcefully still, Alvin Gouldner, in *The Coming Crisis of Western Sociology,* argues the case for a new Utopian, value-centered radical sociology for the future. And economist Egbert de Vries[7] reaches the conclusion that no significant breakthroughs in development theory have been achieved in the last decade. Western development scholars, therefore, themselves lost in deep epistemological quagmire, are ill-advised to scorn the new theories.

One finds in truth great explanatory power, analytical merit, and predictive value in the writings of Latin American social scientists on development, dependence, and domination.[8] The new liberation vocabulary is valid, even empirically, because it lays bare structures of dependence and domination at all levels. Reaching behind the neutral "descriptive" words of developmental wisdom, it unmasks the intolerably high human cost to Latin Americans of economic development, social modernization, political institution-building and cultural westernization. The reality described by these writings is the pervasive impotence of vulnerable societies in the face of the impersonal stimuli which impinge upon them. Furthermore, their vocabulary enjoys high prescriptive value because it shows this powerlessness to be reversible: if domination is a human state of affairs caused and perpetuated by men, it can be overthrown by men. Finally, the highly charged political language of liberation has great predictive value to the extent that it can mobilize collective energies around a value which is the motor of all successful social revolutions—HOPE. Liberated hope is not the cold rational calculus of probability *à la* Herman Kahn or Henry Kissinger, but a daring calculus of *possibility* which reverses the past, shatters the present, and creates a new future.

"DEVELOPMENT" AS A HINGE WORD

In spite of its absolute superiority, however, the language of liberation remains, for many people in the "developed" world, tactically unmanageable. The historical connotations of the word sometimes lead them to resist mobilization around its theme, especially if these people are not themselves oppressors, but inert beneficiaries of impersonal oppressive systems. A second category of people may also find it difficult to respond, namely those insurgent professionals who can subvert "the system" only by mastering its tools and serving as a fifth column in alliance with revolutionary groups on the outside. Understandably, these persons will need to continue using the currently available "professional" terminology. It is considerations such as these which lie behind the question: Can "development" serve a useful hinge role in mobilization? The answer is affirmative if one agrees with political scientist Harvey Wheeler that

> . . . we don't possess a *revolutionary* social science to serve the utopian needs
> of the revolution. And those learned enough to create it are divorced from
> the activists who must prepare the way for the new utopianism. . . .
> Somehow, the radical activists and the radical scientists—the utopians—
> must come together.[9]

Desired changes within "developed" societies can ensue only in the wake of concerted (and much unconcerted) action emanating from a variety of change agents. There can be no objection on principle, therefore, to granting tentative validity to "development" as a hinge word.

For the benefit of those who have not yet been weaned from the sweet milk of palliative incrementalism,[10] "development" needs to be redefined, demystified, and thrust into the arena of moral debate. If critically used as a hinge word, it may open up new perspectives and render the leap into "liberation" possible for many people. Nevertheless, only from the third perspective on development summarized above can one find a suitable platform whence to make this leap of faith. The reason is that, of the three viewpoints, only this ethical, value-laden, humanist approach is rooted in history, and not in abstract theory. Before the language of liberation can sound convincing to the categories of people I have described, it must be shown that "development," as normally understood, alienates even its beneficiaries in compulsive consumption, technological determinisms of various sorts, ecological pathology and warlike policies. Worst of all, it makes those who benefit from development the structural accomplices of the underdevelopment of others. Surely this cannot be what authentic development is. As one reflects on its goals, he discovers that development, viewed as a human project, signifies total liberation. Such liberation aims at freeing men from nature's servitudes, from economic backwardness and oppressive technological institutions, from unjust class structures and political exploiters, from cultural and psychic alienation—in short, from all of life's inhuman agencies.

A new language, able to shatter imprisoning reality, must be born from the clash between vocabularies nurtured in different soils. The first will gestate in a Third World matrix and express the emerging consciousness of those who refuse to be objects, and declare their intent to become subjects, of history. The keys to this vocabulary are the conquest of autonomy and the will to create a new future. At the opposite pole, out of "developed" societies, must arise a subversive redefinition of development itself. Its function will be to destroy the First World's uncritical faith in the universal goodness of its notions of progress, achievement, social harmony, democracy, and modernization. Confrontation between the two is required because neither "development" alone nor "liberation" alone fully transcends both cultural domination and purely negative responses to oppression. Moreover, both terms can be used by symbol manipulators to mystify reality or rationalize palliative change strategies.

Nevertheless, it is clear that competing terminologies of development and liberation are not equally subject to distortion. On the scales of human justice, the interests which they express do not balance each other out. There is indeed, as Camus writes, universal meaning in the rebel's refusal to be treated as something less than a man. And as Marx put it, the oppressed masses are the latent historical carriers of universal human values. The battle to free men is not comparable to the struggle to maintain or expand privilege. Consequently, every trace of elitism and cultural manipulation must be purged from the development vocabulary and replaced with the symbols of liberation. Even then history will not give men any respite; rather, it will propel them into asking: Liberation for what? Ancient teleological questions reappear, concerning the good life, the good society, and men's final purposes. That they should keep arising is no sign of the weakness of men's words, but merely a clue to the grandeur of their historical task. That task is to strive endlessly to outstrip not only alienating material conditions but all particular images of the ideal society as well.

Intellectuals who discuss revolution and violence often utter irresponsible words which place bullets in other people's guns. As they debate development and liberation, the danger they face is less dramatic but no less destructive in the long run. For most of them resort to persuasive political definitions, thereby pre-empting all the intellectual ground upon which descriptive and evocative definitions might find their place. Such habits render genuine liberation impossible since true cultural emancipation admits of no sloganism, no sectarianism, no simplism. Revolutionary consciousness is critical of self no less than of others; and it brooks no verbal cheating even to achieve ideological gains. In final analysis, any liberation vocabulary must do two things. The first is to unmask the alienations disguised by the development lexicon: the alienation of the many in misery, of the few in irresponsible abundance. The second is to transform itself from the rallying cry of victims alone into the victory chant of all men as they empower themselves to enter history with no nostalgia for prehistory.

Success proves difficult because men have never fully learned the lesson implied in a statement by the Indian mystic Rabindranath Tagore that, ultimately, only those values can be truly human which can be truly universal.

NOTES

1. Gustavo Gutierrez Merino, "Notes for a Theology of Liberation," *Theological Studies,* Vol. 31, No. 2 (June 1970), 243–261.
2. The writings of these men are found largely in papers circulated by documentary services such as LADOC (Latin American Bureau, U.S. Catholic Conference), ISAL (Iglesia y Sociedad en América Latina), and the THEOLOGY OF LIBERATION SYMPOSIUM (in Spanish), Bogota.
3. Cf. the excellent work by Jacques Freyssinet, *Le Concept de Sous-Développement,* Mouton, 1966. A brief review of the different meanings attached to the word "development" can be found in Denis Goulet, "That Third World," *The Center Magazine,* Vol. I, No. 6 (September 1968), 47–55.
4. Cf. Paulo Freire, *Cultural Action for Freedom,* Harvard Educational Review and Center for the Study of Development and Social Change, Monograph No. 1, 1970. One may also consult the same author's *Pedagogy of the Oppressed,* Herder and Herder, 1970.
5. Cf. Denis Goulet and Michael Hudson, *The Myth of Aid: the Hidden Agenda of the Development Reports,* IDOC Books, 1970. This work contains two essays, one by Goulet entitled "Domesticating the Third World," and a second by Hudson on "The Political Economy of Foreign Aid."
6. On this cf., e.g., Guy F. Erb, "The Second Session of UNCTAD," *Journal of the World Trade Law,* Vol. 2, No. 3 (May/June 1968), 346–359. For a Latin American view, see the document entitled, "The Latin American Consensus of Viña del Mar," dated May 17, 1969.
7. Egbert de Vries, "A Review of Literature on Development Theory," *International Development Review,* Vol. X, No. 1 (March 1968), 43–49.
8. Cf., e.g., such works as F. Cardoso and E. Falleto, *Dependencia y Desarrollo on América Latina,* Santiago, 1967; Theotonio dos Santos, *El Nuevo caracter de la dependencia,* Santiago, 1968; Celso Furtado, *Dialéctica Do Desenvolvimento,* Rio de Janeiro, 1964; numerous essays by Alberto Guerreiro Ramos (a Brazilian now teaching at UCLA), et al.
9. Harvey Wheeler, "The Limits of Confrontation Politics," *The Center Magazine,* Vol. III, No. 4 (July 1970), 39.
10. The difference between palliative and creative incrementalism is explained in Denis Goulet, *Is Gradualism Dead?,* Council on Religion and International Affairs, 1970.

PART SEVEN

WHAT IS TO BE DONE?

Our values, concept of history, and evaluation of current trends inform our vision of the future. Values shape our sense of what the world ought to be like, highlighting reigning inequities by comparison with some ideal of justice and fairness. History lends a sense of the possible. Its contours mark the actions that humans have taken in changing their world, their repeated successes and failures. A barometer of current trends presents a starting point. Here is our world—where shall we go?

A cogent articulation of a future agenda is thus sensitive to the theoretical foundations coloring our reading of past and present. We must therefore be clear about our theoretical underpinnings and their normative dimensions before constructing an alternative framework.

Orthodox approaches are conservative in nature, actively supporting the status quo. Although the underlying system may need occasional marginal adjustments, orthodox economists usually find it to be satisfactory. Little speculation is necessary since the future is but the natural and proper continuation of the past.

In contrast, radical approaches argue for major structural overhaul. Radical theorists contend that the future cannot and/or should not mirror present trends. That the future cannot assume a similar form is based on their contention that there exist powerful contradictions in the present world; in the dynamics of history these will give birth to a different future. The "should not" is an ethical argument stressing oppressive inequalities in the current world order. Some of those stressing this moral argument focus less on the ineluctable forces of history than on the need for human and humane intervention to bring about a just world order.

Between the conservative and radical extremes lies a continuum of arguments for what is to be done. The first reading in this section, Irma Adelman's "A Poverty-Focused Approach to Development Policy," supports the growth-with-equity school, adhering to the belief that capitalist development is a viable strategy which, with modifications, will generate justice. She begins the essay with the assumption that the accepted priority goal of development is the removal of absolute deprivation. Her approach to poverty alleviation is a productivity-oriented approach that aims to raise the incomes of the poor by increasing both their productivity and their access to productivity-enhancing assets. She concludes that the best overall strategy to help the poor through productivity enhancement is reliance upon agricultural-development-led industrialization.

In addition to internal development policies, adjustments must be made in the hierarchical international order. In focusing on this second dimension we recall the issues of the NIEO, discussed earlier by Lance Taylor. The grievances embodied in the call for a NIEO include such factors as: (1) imbalances in monetary reserves; (2) the way the rich nations benefit disproportionately in the distribution of value added to the products traded between themselves and the poor nations; (3) the First World's wave of protectionism, tariffs, and nontariff barriers, which are in direct contradiction to their rhetoric for free market approaches; (4) the MNCs' application of unfair bargaining advantages; and (5) an overall lack of participation in decision-making. John Griffin and William Rouse argue that "counter-trade" is a development strategy currently being adopted by leading Third World countries that may achieve the long sought restructuring of the world economic order. Counter-trade refers to any contractual arrangement that commits the seller of a good or service to accept in partial or full payment goods or services from the buyer. For Third World countries the widespread adoption of counter-trade represents a new model which potentially can lead to a mutually dependent world community based upon the principles of mutual trust, respect, benefit, and cooperation.

There is another international problem vital to the overcoming of underdevelopment—the arms race. In "The Arms Race and Development," Inga Thorsson, the chairperson of the UN Expert Group on Disarmament and Development, highlights the drains of global military expenditures from productive, developmental uses. This selection ought to be read not only as a theoretical summary of the disarmament-development issue, but also as the concrete, operational product of an international initiative to understand and reverse global militarism. A list of recommendations made by the UN group follows the Thorsson article.

Any developmental agenda for the future must take account of the overwhelming realities of global poverty. A fundamental aim of development policy is purported to be a rise in the general living standards of all peoples—yet by and large, programs have failed miserably.

Paulo Freire, in "Pedagogy of the Oppressed," argues that poverty will only be overcome by the actions of those currently suffering under its chains. Over and against top-down poverty programs, Freire contends that development worthy of humans will come about only when the mass of people recognize their oppression and consciously act to change it. That is, a revolution in ideas and values from within the masses must accompany a transformation of structures. This classic selection from Paulo Freire sets out the ideals of his vision of development. Students interested in the operational mechanisms for putting these ideals into everyday practice are referred to the book of the same name from which this selection is taken.

Richard Falk, also discussing global poverty and human needs, proceeds from the conviction that political factors severely constrain economic policy choices within unacceptably narrow limits and vice versa. For Falk, satisfying human needs—a goal embracing participation, dignity, and creative work as well as basic poverty targets—is unattainable in our world of sovereign states. After cataloging the stalemate in North-South solutions to global poverty, he asserts that no amount of tinkering can fix up the present international system. What is called for (illustrated by an appealing children's story) is "a nonterritorial conception of using the earth, having it all and yet owning no part of it—a reversal of prevalent attitudes and arrangements." The main elements of such a transformation of the future include solidarity, unity, space, time, nature, peace, progress, humility, and spirituality.

Some may doubt the realism of the foregoing chapters. Hard-line realists may charge that these wonderful lofty ideals have little to do with the world we live in. But we must embrace a realism imbued with imagination. If we dare not imagine a future different from the present, change is stillborn. However, with imagination and a clear concept of the world as it should be, we can begin to work on the possibility of a future for humankind.

25

A Poverty-Focused Approach to Development Policy

Irma Adelman

The definition of poverty adopted in this essay is one of abject poverty—a poverty level so severe that it stunts the attainment of human potential. In 1980, 880 million people (22 per cent of the world population) lived below that level. This estimate of the extent of poverty is based on a poverty line specified in terms of the income level required to purchase a nutritional level minimally adequate for calorie replacement at average levels of activity. The World Bank suggests setting the standard at an annual per capita income of U.S. $50 of 1960 purchasing power. There can be little argument that a reduction in the number of people living in such a state of absolute deprivation should be a major objective of economic development and of development assistance. Indeed, many (including myself) would say that this should be the prime objective of economic development.

In this essay, I shall pretend that the removal of absolute deprivation is the accepted priority goal of economic development and shall summarize my understanding of what the pursuit of this goal implies for the design of development policy within developing countries. I shall here leave aside the political problems associated with the adoption of such an approach as well as its foreign assistance implications. With respect to internal politics, I shall assume that a coalition of interests exists that accords high priority to the goal of eradicating absolute deprivation. With respect to foreign assistance, I shall assume the existence of an international consensus that foreign aid ought to aim at supporting policies, financing programs, and establishing an international environment that will enable developing countries to pursue the goal of poverty alleviation effectively. These assumptions will allow me to concentrate upon *what developing countries themselves can and must do to reduce their poverty problems.*

From *Development Strategies Reconsidered,* John P. Lewis and Valeriana Kallab, eds. (New Brunswick, N.J.: Transaction Books, 1986) pp. 49–65. Reprinted by permission.

The approach to poverty alleviation that I shall advocate is a productivity-oriented approach that aims to raise the incomes of the poor by increasing both their productivity and their access to productivity-enhancing assets. I will not advocate an alternative, transfer-oriented approach, whereby the goods and services required for subsistence are delivered to the poor *directly*, for several reasons:

(1) A direct-transfer approach becomes less effective over time, since its benefits, even when the transfer continues unabated, tend to be dissipated into higher prices and into other leakages.[1]

(2) It is beyond the fiscal capacities of virtually all developing countries.

(3) It needs to be maintained forever.

(4) It does not allow for a more differentiated approach to enable the poor to decide on their consumption patterns according to their own priorities as defined by their own circumstances and cultures.

To be appropriate, policy must be rooted in the "stylized facts" of the problem that it seeks to address. Before discussing policy, I shall therefore summarize the stylized facts concerning poverty and income distribution that have been learned from the research of the past decade.

THE THEORY OF POVERTY: LESSONS OF A DECADE

The Structure of Poverty

In developing countries, poverty is overwhelmingly a *rural* phenomenon. In most developing countries, the great majority of the poorest 40 per cent of the population is engaged in agricultural pursuits. The landless and the nearly landless are the poorest of the poor. In urban areas, the majority of the poor are unskilled workers in the service sector; but even they are generally richer than the rural poor. Workers in the manufacturing sector, whether skilled or unskilled, are part of the richest 20–40 per cent of the population. Thus unskilled labor is the major asset owned by the poor, and what determines the course of poverty is the state of demand for and the productivity of their labor.

The Course of Income Distribution During the Development Process

What happens to poverty over time is determined by the rate at which total income grows and by changes in the share of the poor in that income. If the share of income accruing to the poor declines more rapidly than overall income rises, the poor lose from growth; otherwise, they gain. Just *how* the income share of the poor changes with economic development is, therefore, critical to understanding the poverty problem and its alleviation.

The initial phases of the development process, during which a mostly agrarian economy starts industrialization, are almost inevitably marked by substantial increases in the inequality of income distribution. The shares of the poorest fifth, two-fifths, and three-fifths of the population all decrease sharply—thanks to the introduction of a small high-income island in a large low-income sea.

Subsequent phases of the development process are marked by an increase in the share of the population involved in the modern high-income sector of the economy, an increase in the income gap between the high-income and the low-income sectors of the economy, and increases in inequality within both the high-income and the low-income sectors. The shift in population from the low- to the high-income sectors is a force working for reductions in inequality; on the other hand, the increases in mean income differentials among sectors and the widening of income dispersion within sectors are factors making for greater inequality. Overall, the tendency is for inequality to increase, at least for a while. Various simulations have suggested that this increase in inequality will tend to continue until at least half of the population is in the high-income sector.

There is no *automatic* tendency for the distribution of income to improve as countries enter the last phase of their transition to the status of industrial countries. Whether inequality does or does not increase depends upon the policies that countries follow. In particular, it depends upon the extent to which the policies adopted narrow the income gap between the sectors, the extent to which they decrease the dispersion of income within the modern sector, and the relative speed of absorption into the modern sector. Thus, the plot of the income share accruing to the poorest, as a function of development, can be either U-shaped, as hypothesized by Simon Kuznets from a comparison of a sample of developed with mid- to high-income developing countries,[2] or J-shaped, depending on the nature of development strategies chosen.[3]

Trends in the Size Distribution of Income and Poverty

The trends in inequality during the past two decades are consistent with the stylized facts described above. Table 1 presents summary data on the course of the concentration of income and on the poverty ratio from 1960 to 1980 in groups of non-communist less developed countries. The figures in the table were calculated by estimating how the shape of the size distributions in the rural and urban sectors of each country varies with the country's structural characteristics and level of development. These rural and urban distributions were aggregated numerically to produce a single size distribution for each country. The individual country distributions were then again aggregated

TABLE 1   **Trends in Income Distribution and Poverty, 1960–1980**

	OVERALL		ELIMINATING INTER-COUNTRY INEQUALITY[a]		ELIMINATING WITHIN-COUNTRY INEQUALITY[a]	
	1960	1980	1960	1980	1960	1980
Income distribution (*Gini coefficient*[b])						
All non-communist developing countries	.544	.602	.450	.468	.333	.404
Low-income	.407	.450	.383	.427	.113	.118
Middle-income, non-oil	.603	.569	.548	.514	.267	.251
Oil-exporting	.575	.612	.491	.503	.328	.375
Poverty (*poverty ratio*[c]—*percentages*)						
All non-communist developing countries	46.8	30.1	5.2	0.9	8.8	3.5
World	39.8	22.4	9.9	1.6	6.3	2.0

[a]The sum of the only-within and only-between country inequalities does not add up to the overall total because of inter-correlations between the two.

[b]The numbers labeled Gini coefficients are measures of the degree of concentration of the size distribution of income. A higher figure indicates greater inequality.

[c]Percentage of population falling below the poverty level (held fixed in real purchasing power). The definition of absolute poverty adopted for these calculations is that of the World Bank: an annual per capita income of less than U.S. $50 (1960). National currencies were converted into dollars using the Kravis purchasing power parity index for 1975.

SOURCE: Irma Adelman, "The World Distribution of Income," Working Paper, Department of Agricultural Economics (University of California, Berkeley: August 1984).

numerically to produce a single distribution for geopolitical regions. Within a given group of countries, each individual was treated as if he were a citizen of that group.[4] The numbers labeled Gini coefficients are measures of the degree of concentration of the size distribution of income. A higher figure indicates greater inequality.

The figures in the table indicate that, between 1960 and 1980, income inequality in the entire group of non-communist developing countries increased substantially; but separate groups of countries were subject to different trends in income concentration. Income concentration increased quite markedly in the group of low-income non-communist countries and in the group of oil-exporting countries, and it decreased significantly in the middle-income, non-oil-exporting countries. As indicated by the poverty-ratio figures, on the other hand, the amount of absolute poverty (defined as previously indicated) declined. Despite the overall increase in inequality, the percentage of population falling below the poverty level (held fixed in real purchasing power) declined by a third between 1960 and 1980.

To see how much of these trends can be attributed to within-country inequality and how much to inter-country inequality, two experiments were performed. In the third and fourth columns of the table, per capita income in each country was set equal to the average income in the world; the only source of inequality in these columns is, therefore, inequality in the size distribution of income *within* each country. In the fifth and sixth columns, the opposite experiment was performed; each individual in each country was assumed to have a per capita income equal to the country average. Therefore the only source of inequality in the fifth and sixth columns is inequality among countries. The sum of only within-country and only inter-country inequalities exceeds overall inequality because, in all subgroups, countries at the upper and lower extremes of the group had less inequality than countries in the middle (i.e., within-country inequality was negatively correlated with inter-country inequality).

It is clear from these experiments that both within-country inequality and inter-country inequality are important contributors to overall developing-country inequality. Within-country inequality is more important than inter-country inequality in explaining total developing-country inequality; but reductions in *either* source of inequality can make important contributions to poverty reduction. The poverty-ratio lines of Table 1 show that if either of the two forms of inequality could be eliminated (admittedly an extreme assumption), absolute poverty would virtually disappear.

Both within-country inequality and inter-country inequality in the non-communist developing countries increased between 1960 and 1980, but the greater disparities were those generated *within* countries. The dispersion of growth rates among non-communist developing countries also increased, since the middle-income countries grew considerably more rapidly than the low-income countries, and the dispersion in growth rates among the oil-exporting countries went up as well.

Efforts to reduce developing-country poverty therefore must focus both on more participatory growth processes within developing countries and on accelerating the growth rates of the poorer countries.

Policies and Programs Aimed at Reducing Income Inequality Within Developing Countries

How the poor fare during the course of economic development depends on how the distribution of assets, the institutions for asset accumulation, and the institutions for access to markets by the poor all interact with the development strategies chosen.

Chief among assets whose distribution has a significant impact on income distribution and poverty are land and education. The effects of economic change on the poor are critically dependent on land tenure conditions and the size distribution of landholdings. Poverty is greatest where land is divided into many small holdings and where there is a marked concentration of landownership coupled with cultivation by either landless labor or subsistence tenants. In contrast, where commercial farm owners supply most of their own labor, the rural distribution of income is in general more equal, and productivity increases may well improve the distribution of income. Concentration of landownership under circumstances in which small cultivators and landless workers lack alternative employment opportunities permits large landowners to pay low wages and to charge high rents. In addition, these tenurial conditions also increase the probability that innovations that raise average income and productivity in agriculture will have negative consequences for the poor. The opening up of new commercial or technological opportunities to populations with unequal abilities to respond to them widens inequality. Increasing the productivity of land when subsistence farmers and the landless cannot take advantage of that increasing productivity—because of limited access to credit or technologically superior inputs—tends to make for the marginalization of subsistence farmers and small tenants and may even lead to their eviction and dispossession. (An exception to this generalization occurs in the rare circumstances when the increase in the demand for hired labor is sufficiently large to overcome the fall in net income from farming that arises from the price decreases and rent increases that accompany the rise in productivity on larger farms.)

Turning to education's impact on income distribution, a broader incidence of education and literacy is associated with a larger share of income accruing to the middle group of income recipients but, at least initially, may not help the very poor. Increases in education spread the ownership of human capital and reduce inequalities in wage income. They also increase the rate of rural-urban migration—thereby augmenting the share of population that is employed in the higher-income sector and improving the agricultural terms of trade by raising urban demand for food while reducing its supply.

Institutions in factor and product markets are important determinants of how development affects the poor. Structural change associated with development gives rise to processes that simultaneously increase the absorption of some labor and other factors, displace labor and other factors, and generate geographic and sectoral reallocations of employment of labor and other factors. How these processes of absorption, displacement, and labor-force redistribution "net out" in their effect on the poor depends upon the institutional structure of factor and product markets. Segmentation of markets leaves some regions and sectors with labor gluts and others with shortages. Even without market segmentation, socially induced rigidities, the lack of relevant skills, or the absence of capital and information may in the short- or medium-run prevent the poor from escaping the contractionary influences to which they are exposed and finding expansionary ones elsewhere.

If one takes the initial distribution of assets and the structure of institutions as given, the major determinant of the course of income inequality and poverty becomes the overall development strategy chosen. The development strategy defines the basic thrust of economic policy. It combines a definition of policy targets (e.g., export expansion) with an identification of policy instruments (e.g., devaluation or export subsidies). Each strategy is associated with a specific configuration of the structure of production and a particular pattern of factor use. It is the development strategy that determines the pre-tax, pre-transfer (i.e., the primary) distribution of income. It governs the speed of absorption of labor into the modern sector, the extent of the income gap that develops between the modern and the traditional sectors, and the degree of income inequality within sectors.

The primary policy for helping absorption into the modern sectors is to adopt *labor-intensive* modes of expansion in those sectors. The labor intensity of growth can, in principle, be changed either by expanding the share of labor-intensive products and sectors in total employment or by increasing the labor intensity of production of a given mix of outputs (i.e., by appropriate technology). Of the two, the first process appears to be the more effective. Artificial shifts away from best-practice technology for a given factor mix reduce the amount of output obtainable from a given amount of resources. This approach is therefore less effective than shifting the mix of output toward sectors requiring a mix of resources that corresponds more closely to the basic factor endowments of the labor-abundant economies of the developing countries.

Once the choice of development strategy has jelled, policies and programs aimed at changing the primary distribution of income can accomplish very little.[5] This is true of both transfer programs and poverty-oriented projects. The size distribution of income tends to be quite stable around the trend established by the basic choice of development strategy. Following any intervention, even one sustained over time, the size distribution of income tends to return to the pre-intervention distribution. Only large, well-designed, complementary packages of anti-poverty policies and programs can change the primary distribution of income somewhat; but, to be effective, they must essentially amount to a gradual change in the overall development strategy.

TYPES OF ANTI-POVERTY POLICY

If one includes among the "assets" of the poor their personal capacities, trained or otherwise, their incomes consist of the value of the services of the assets owned by them that are sold on the market. In a very basic sense, then, the poverty problem is one of too small a quantity of assets, too low a volume of market sales, and/or too low a market price.

Poverty-focused approaches to policy therefore consist of measures to accomplish one or more of the following policy targets: 1) increase the quantity of assets owned by the poor, 2) increase the volume of their market sales, and 3) increase the prices of the services they sell. The general approaches that have been advocated to achieve a non-immiserating growth process can be grouped under these three headings.

Asset-Oriented Approaches

The quantity of assets owned by the poor can be increased either by redistributing assets to them (e.g., through land reform) or by creating institutions for their preferential access to opportunities for accumulation of further assets (e.g., through subsidized credit or wider access to primary education). Elsewhere I have argued for redistributing land and for tilting new educational opportunities toward the poor.[6] And in the famous World Bank/Sussex study of the middle 1970s, Hollis Chenery and his colleagues emphasized the second strategy, i.e., of concentrating asset *increments* on the poor—primarily on grounds of political feasibility.[7]

My own position is based on the experiences of the non-communist newly industrializing countries, notably Korea and Taiwan, that have successfully combined no deterioration in the relative incomes of the poor with accelerated growth. These examples lead me to advocate 1) tenurial reform in agriculture *before* implementation of policies designed to improve the productivity of agriculture, and 2) massive investments in education *before* rapid industrialization.

My rationale for this sequence, which I have called "redistribution before growth," is twofold: First, a better distribution of the major asset whose productivity is about to be improved, together with more equal access to markets and to opportunities for improving the productivity of that major asset, will obviously diminish the adverse effects of unequal asset distribution on income distribution. Second, the redistributed asset is not as valuable before improvements in productivity as it is after. Redistribution with full compensation would therefore be possible, at least in principle. I have argued, therefore, for the establishment of an internationally financed land-reform fund to: 1) help countries interested in implementing land reform design the reform; and 2) provide international guarantees for the nationally issued industrial and commodity bonds used to compensate the landlords whose land is redistributed.

Chenery's recommendations are more modest. In an approach he calls "redistribution with growth," he advocates differentially allocating a larger share of the proceeds of economic growth to asset accumulation by the poor. If, for example, the growth rate is 6 per cent per year, one-third of the growth (or 2 per cent of GNP) should be devoted to investment in assets owned by the poor or in assets that are complementary to assets owned by the poor. Examples of such investments would be: nutrition, health, and education programs for the poor; investment in irrigation facilities for land owned by the poor; or investment in credit programs or input subsidies aimed at subsistence farmers.

Demand-Generating Strategies

How much of the assets owned by the poor can be monetized on the market depends largely on the development strategy chosen and on the institutions for access to factor markets by the poor. Since the assets owned by the poor consist largely of unskilled labor, development strategies that increase the absolute and relative demand for unskilled labor, coupled with institutions that enhance labor mobility and access to jobs by the poor, are the ones that benefit the poor the most.

Two strategies look promising along these lines: 1) reliance upon export-oriented growth in labor-intensive manufactures and 2) reliance upon agricultural-development-led industrialization. I shall argue that, during the coming decade, the second strategy looks more promising for most developing countries that do not yet have an established position in international markets.

Once institutional conditions that permit reallocations of the labor power of the poor to higher productivity pursuits have been established by education, by removal of barriers to migration, and by dismantling of discrimination in hiring, equitable growth requires that subsequent increases in the rate of economic growth be achieved through measures that stress rapid growth in high-productivity, labor-intensive sectors and activities. An effective anti-poverty strategy must therefore increase the rate of growth of output of high-productivity, labor-intensive sectors and assure that the poor have access to the jobs so created.

The most labor-intensive sectors in any economy are agriculture, light manufacturing, and some types of services, especially construction (many services are skill-intensive rather than labor-intensive); but these are not necessarily the high-productivity, labor-intensive sectors. Generally, labor-intensive manufacturing is a (relatively) high-productivity sector in developing countries. That is, although output per worker is lower than it would be for more capital-intensive modes of producing the same product, it is generally higher than in most of agriculture and labor-intensive services. Policies that focus on labor-intensive growth in different sectors are therefore quite different, depending upon which sectors they stress.

Strategies that emphasize employment growth in manufacturing must focus primarily on *generating* demand for the output of the labor-intensive industries. In smaller nations, this implies that development will have to be oriented toward export markets. The small countries that follow this approach must therefore adopt a strategy of export-led growth and tailor their price and non-price incentives to be compatible with such an approach. In large countries, industrialization can be oriented toward the domestic market, particularly when the distribution of income is not too skewed.[8]

By contrast, a strategy that focuses on agriculture or on services can appeal to *existing* demand but must concentrate on increasing the productivity of labor in these sectors. There are no known technologies for increasing the productivity of purely labor-intensive services. The choice, therefore, is between a labor-intensive manufacturing strategy, on the one hand, and an agricultural strategy on the other. Bhagwati as well as Solis and Montemayor . . . espouse the first of these, while Mellor advocates the second.

The choice between the two strategies depends on two factors: 1) the size of the direct and indirect employment multipliers that result from expanding either labor-intensive manufacturing or agriculture, and 2) comparison of the cost and feasibility of entering export markets with the cost and feasibility of increasing agricultural productivity.

Simulations with the two alternative strategies in a price- and wage-endogenous multi-sectoral model of the Republic of Korea indicate that both strategies can be effective in achieving higher growth and a better distribution of income. However, they also indicate that during periods of low growth in world demand for labor-intensive manufactured exports (which is likely to characterize the rest of the 1980s), the agricultural strategy is more effective. In such conditions, this strategy results in less inequality and poverty, as well as in a higher rate of growth and a better balance of payments.

The basic reasons for the superiority of the agricultural strategy—which Mellor emphasizes in an "agriculture-and employment-led" strategy—are: 1) agriculture is much more labor-intensive than even labor-intensive manufacturing; 2) land-augmenting increases in agricultural productivity generate increases in demand for the labor of the landless—the poorest of the poor; 3) increases in agricultural incomes generate high leakages into demand for labor-intensive manufactures on the consumption side and for manufactured inputs on the production side; 4) expansion in agricultural production is less import-intensive than an equivalent increase in manufacturing production; 5) increases in agricultural output with "good-practice," developing-country technology are less capital-intensive than increases in manufacturing; and 6) the agricultural infrastructure required to increase agricultural productivity (roads, irrigation, and drainage facilities) has a high labor-output ratio.

It should be noted, however, that, to be effective, both strategies have certain institutional and asset-distribution prerequisites.[9] The labor-intensive growth strategy in manufacturing requires a wide distribution of education and low barriers to access to jobs by the poor. The agricultural strategy requires that tenurial conditions in agriculture not be too unfavorable and that small farmers be assured access to the complementary resources (particularly credit and water) that they need to improve agricultural yields.

Both strategies also have implications for price policies. The trade-oriented strategy requires a price policy that does not discriminate against exports by means of an overvalued exchange rate and tariffs. The agricultural strategy requires a price policy that enables farmers to capture some of the benefits from improvements in agricultural productivity. The latter, therefore, implies a terms-of-trade policy that divides the income benefits of increased output more equitably between urban and rural groups.

Price-Increasing Policies

Price-increasing policies can operate through factor or commodity markets, and/or they can increase the productivity of the assets owned by the poor.

Price-increasing policies that operate through *factor markets* must raise the wages of the poor. The labor-intensive growth strategies discussed above can therefore also be wage-increasing policies, since an increase in the demand for labor can either raise the quantity of labor sold or raise the wage rate (or both); but the effects of these policies upon the wages of the poor depend critically on *how the labor market operates.* If the barriers to access to jobs by the poor are low and the amount of unemployment and underemployment is small, an increase in the demand for labor will raise the wage rate of the poor. On the other hand, if there are institutional or economic barriers (for example, obstacles to migration) to an increase in the quantity of labor that can be bought from the poor, an increase in the demand for labor can augment the wage rate of the non-poor while leaving the wage rate of the poor largely unchanged and having only a second-round effect on the employment of the poor. The effects of demand-increasing strategies on the price of labor, therefore, depend critically on the institutional organization of the labor market.

Price-increasing policies that operate through *commodity markets* must raise the prices of the goods produced with the labor of the poor. Since the poor are mostly rural, an increase in the relative price of agricultural output (i.e., an increase in the agricultural terms of trade) will tend to benefit the poor. This is true even though such an increase (if not counteracted by price subsidies for urban consumers) will tend to reduce the real wages of the urban poor—for the urban poor, poor as they are, generally are richer than the rural poor. An increase in the agricultural terms of trade will also tend to benefit landless workers, even though they are net buyers of agricultural produce, by increasing the demand for their labor. This is so because, given the usual employment elasticities in developing-country agriculture, the employment effect raises the entire income of landless labor more or less in proportion to the increase in agricultural prices, whereas the food-price effect reduces only that fraction of their income that the landless spend on purchased food.

Productivity-Increasing Policies

Another way to increase the price of the major asset owned by the poor— their labor—is to increase its productivity. This can be done through 1) upgrading the quality of labor through investment in human capital; 2) increasing the amount of complementary assets employed by the poor (e.g., land or capital); or 3) introducing productivity-enhancing technical change (e.g., land-intensive innovations in agriculture).

Human capital investments. Direct investments in the poor are desirable in and of themselves, as part of providing the poor with the minimal bundle of goods necessary to open up their access to opportunities for a full life. However, the discussion that follows will focus only on how such investments can affect the *productivity* of the poor, thereby enabling them to earn higher incomes, which in turn would permit them at some future date to purchase the minimal bundle of goods on the market with their own earnings.

Investments in the nutrition, education, and health of the poor not only increase their welfare directly, but also enhance their capacities for productive labor. Much of the employment of the poor is physical labor. Not infrequently, the market wage that the poor are paid is not even sufficient to allow them to purchase enough food to replace the calories used in earning that wage.[10] Such wage labor therefore results in exposing the poor to higher morbidity and mortality and to higher health hazards than if they had remained unemployed. Consequently it is not surprising that the productivity of the poor, when employed, remains low. In such circumstances, nutrition supplements or higher wages can raise the productivity of the poor.

Investments in the education of the poor—through adult literacy campaigns and increases in the availability of primary education in rural areas and in other places where the poor reside—spread the ownership of human capital. They qualify the poor for more productive jobs and narrow the distribution of wage income. They also increase the rate of rural-urban migration, thereby providing the poor with access to higher-income employment opportunities and raising the agricultural terms of trade. Primary education of females also tends to reduce population growth.

Although the availability of basic health care for the poor—through mobile clinics, "barefoot doctors," investment in environmental sanitation, potable water, and training in food preparation practices and elementary hygiene—raises the well-being of the poor, there is little evidence of significant direct links with productivity. Better health does, however, increase school attendance and learning while in school. It also raises the efficiency of transforming nutritional intake into caloric output and, therefore, substantially reduces malnutrition. Thus, from a productivity point of view, the contributions of investments in better health are mostly indirect, in that they raise the effectiveness of other productivity-enhancing investments in the poor.

Complementary resources and land-augmenting investments. The primary causes of rural poverty of the rural poor are the meager amount of land that they have to till with their own labor combined with a low demand for hired labor by large cultivators. The most effective productivity improvements for raising the incomes of the rural poor are therefore land-augmenting investments and innovations. Examples of land-augmenting innovations are: irrigation and drainage facilities, which, by allowing water control, may permit multiple cropping; improved seed, which by itself can triple the yield per acre; and fertilizer. These types of investments and innovations stretch the yields from whatever land the poor cultivate, and they significantly raise demand for hired labor by larger farmers.

To be most effective, however, these innovations and investments require making complementary resources available to the poor. For even when the more productive technologies are scale-neutral—as they are in the case of the high-yielding varieties of wheat and rice—the poor are not able to take advantage of these innovations because they do not have access to water, credit, improved seed, the wherewithal with which to buy fertilizer, or the technological know-how disseminated by extension. At least in the early stages of the diffusion of such innovations, productivity-increasing innovations tend to have two opposite effects on the rural poor: They increase the demand for wage labor, since the land-augmenting innovations are all quite labor-intensive; but they also reduce the price of the marketable surplus of small cultivators, since the increase in output from the larger farms generates an increase in overall supply in the face of inelastic demand. Large farmers benefit, since they can increase their sales—but the small ones lose, since they are not able to take advantage of the yield-increasing innovations. Therefore the net impact of agricultural innovations upon the rural poor depends, at least in the early stages, on the share of income that they derive from farming as opposed to wage labor.

The negative effects of the yield-enhancing innovations upon the nearly landless discussed above could be avoided if institutions were developed to provide them with access to the complementary resources with which they, too, could shift to more productive technologies. Small farmers need agricultural extension, improved seed and fertilizer, better irrigation and drainage facilities, and, most of all, credit.

CONCLUSION

Several points emerge from this review of findings derived from the experience with development, poverty, and income distribution over the past decade and a half.

1. Validated strategies, policies, and programs for poverty alleviation do exist. Indeed, there has been substantial progress toward the achievement of this goal between 1960 and 1980 in the non-communist developing countries as a group despite the fact that the distribution of income has become substantially more unequal.

2. Strategies for poverty alleviation are not compatible with just any kind of economic growth. They entail particular kinds of economic growth.

3. Approaches to poverty alleviation require the implementation of mutually consistent and reinforcing multifaceted programs. The most effective approaches entail a combination of several elements: asset-oriented policies that are supported by institutions designed to facilitate the poor's access to jobs; investments that enhance the productivity of assets that the poor possess and can sell; and development strategies that generate a rapid increase in the demand for unskilled labor.

4. More than one method exists to achieve each element of the package described above. The choice among instruments needs to be tailored to each country's particular initial conditions, resource base, size, asset distribution, institutional structure, and sociopolitical configuration—as well as to the external conditions and trends that the country faces at any point in time.

5. Choices among poverty-alleviation packages and programs are inherently *political*. A critical aspect of the political choice among competing goals and instrumentalities is the time dimension.

6. The sequence in which different policy interventions are taken up is important: The most effective approach to poverty alleviation entails implementing asset-oriented policies and institutional changes designed to give the poor access to high-productivity jobs

before, not after, shifting development strategies. If that is done, there is no "trade-off" between growth promotion and poverty alleviation. The same development strategy is then optimal for both goals.

7. Which strategy and which set of policies is most effective for a given country is likely to change over time—as changes take place both in the initial conditions within each country and in the economic and political environment in which the country operates.

8. With all of this in view, two strategies appear to promise the poor the most: 1) reliance upon export-oriented growth in labor-intensive manufactures and 2) reliance upon agricultural-development-led industrialization. During the coming decade—likely to be one of low growth in world demand for labor-intensive manufactured exports—the agriculture-led approach is likely to deliver more in terms of less inequality and poverty, a higher growth rate, and a better balance of payments.

NOTES

1. Irma Adelman and Sherman Robinson, *Income Distribution Policy in Developing Countries: A Case Study of Korea* (Stanford: Stanford University Press and Oxford University Press, 1978), pp. 148–151.
2. Simon Kuznets, "Economic Growth and Income Inequality," *American Economic Review,* Vol. 45, No. 1 (March 1955), pp. 1–28.
3. Irma Adelman and Cynthia Taft Morris, *Economic Growth and Social Equity in Developing Countries* (Stanford: Stanford University Press, 1973); Gary S. Fields, *Poverty, Inequality, and Development* (Cambridge, Cambridge University Press, 1980).
4. For a fuller explanation of this method, see Irma Adelman, *The World Distribution of Income,* Working Paper No. 346, Department of Agricultural and Resource Economics, University of California, Berkeley, August 1984.
5. Adelman and Robinson, *A Case Study of Korea,* op. cit.; Frank J. Lysy and Lance Taylor, *Models of Growth and Distribution for Brazil* (Cambridge: Oxford University Press, 1980).
6. See Irma Adelman, "Beyond Export-Led Growth," *World Development,* Vol. 12, No. 9 (September 1984), pp. 937–49.
7. Hollis Chenery, et al., *Redistribution With Growth* (Cambridge: Oxford University Press, 1974).
8. A. de Janvry and Elizabeth Sadoulet, "Social Articulation as a Condition for Equitable Growth," *Journal of Development Economics,* Vol. 13, No. 3 (December 1983), pp. 275–304.
9. Irma Adelman, *Redistribution Before Growth—A Strategy for Developing Countries* (The Hague: Martinus Nijhof, 1978).
10. Gerry B. Rodgers, "A Conceptualization of Poverty in Rural India," *World Development,* Vol. 4, No. 4 (April 1976), pp. 261–76.

26

Counter-Trade as a Third World Strategy of Development

John C. Griffin, Jr. and William Rouse

Economic relations between Third World and industrialised nations are in the process of fundamental alteration. The structure of trade, the international division of labour, global comparative advantage, access to markets and strategic raw materials, the transfer of technology, and industrial location as well as the 'management' of the global economic system are currently realigning to reflect international economic and political reality. This shift will be profoundly conditioned by the rapidity and pervasiveness of the expansion of counter-trade. The current debt/liquidity crisis has combined with significant global contraction to encourage renewed attention on alternative methods of international exchange. In addition, growing protectionism in the developed nations, falling commodity prices, and developed country intransigence towards Third World demands for new rules to the global economic game, have encouraged the expansion of counter-trade. Simultaneously, the maturation of Third World nationalism has reflected itself in the increased ability of less-developed countries to negotiate 'conditioned' or 'tied' trade arrangements as a means to promote the development process. Thus, from necessity and by design, Third World nations are increasingly adopting counter-trade as a major component of their international economic interaction.

As we shall discuss below, the phenomenon of counter-trade offers incentives to developing and developed nations alike. In an era of illiquidity, uncertainty, and global industrial realignment, counter-trade appears to be an ideal mechanism for maintaining growth, promoting exports and fostering economic diversification. Should both developed and developing nations continue in the longer run to pursue such bilateral reciprocal trade mechanisms, a significant restructuring of the present international arrangement would result. In this critical period of transition, international trade specialists have

From *Third World Quarterly,* Vol. 8, No. 1 (January 1986), pp. 177–204.

been split as to whether the counter-trade phenomenon is merely an *ad hoc,* transitory adjustment to the present economic morass or symptomatic of deeper structural reorientations in the global economy. For policymakers in government, multilateral organisations, and international business, the ephemeral or permanent nature of counter-trading will be crucial to successful future decisionmaking.

Thus, to ascertain the potential for future growth of counter-trading one must understand the origins, mechanisms, and current advantages of counter-trade. After exploring its dynamics, we shall suggest that counter-trade is (1) a development strategy currently being adopted by leading Third World countries that may achieve the long sought restructuring of the global economic order, albeit, in a sporadic, *ad hoc* fashion; and (2) a strategy of economic diversification accepted by some developed nations that reflects increased economic nationalism and autonomy.

HISTORICAL EXAMPLES OF COUNTER-TRADE

The barter of goods and services between societies predates written history. Cashless societies have long designed acceptable rates of exchange that conformed to the cultural reality and needs of both trading groups. Anthropologists have marvelled over the long distance movement of goods by 'primitives' inhabiting the planet tens of thousands of years ago.[1] The key lesson, for our purposes, is that these early trading complexes were reciprocal, bilateral relationships based upon personal ties of mutual trust, benefit, and balance.

Early barter-trade complexes were based upon bilateral clearing arrangements.[2] When the cycle of the trading mechanism was completed, neither participant in the trading relation possessed a chronic 'deficit' or 'surplus' position. While much research has shown that one participant might have an obligation to reciprocate goods to the other trade partner at any given time, the relationship over the long run required a shifting balance between 'deficit' and 'surplus' positions. Chronic surpluses or deficits implied a destabilisation in the trade relationship which early 'primitives' actively sought to avoid.[3] Interestingly, it is the same destabilising adjustment between chronic deficit and surplus nations that international economic systems from the *Pax Britannica* to the Bretton Woods System have failed adequately to address.[4] Chronic imbalances between 'primitive' groups implied a breakdown of mutually shared benefits, respect, and status. In the extreme case, relationships of vertical integration evolved (ie, structured superiority/inferiority) which were and are maintained by physical, psychological, political, and/or economic coercion. It is noteworthy that the beginnings of these relationships of structured inequality in archaic trading complexes coincided with the transaction from redistributive levels of socio-political integration to the formation of the state. The advent of physical coercion and economic coercion within a centralised socio-political framework coincided with relationships based upon structured inequality—within societies as well as between societies.[5]

A second point to be ascertained from the literature on early trading systems is that exchange between 'primitive' groups generally benefitted the entire community. Traded goods were distributed for the mass consumption of the band or tribe, with elaborate ritual and cultural pressures employed to ensure wide participation in the fruits of inter-group exchange.[6] Again, coinciding with the advent of the centralised state, the structure, volume, and division of inter-group exchange began to shift. Increasingly, dominant elites, initially religious and military, later financial, industrial, and technological, usurped control over production and trade arrangements. These structures were shaped to fulfil elite preference patterns and to enhance their superior social position.

Under such circumstances, barter was still the basis of exchange but on terms set by the central elites. An example is in the inter-colonial trade of the Spanish empire in Latin America where barter between the vice-royalties was a common, although illegal practice.[7] Eventually, the logic of these static, over-centralised societies created severe social, political and economic distortions. As such, they were unable to adapt flexibly in the face of revolutionary changes in science, technology, and socio-economic organisation that swept Western Europe during the fifteenth and eighteenth centuries.

By the eighteenth century, the completion of the monetisation of global society and the rise of industrial technologies combined to produce an explosion in inter-societal trade. Globally, a process of vertical integration occurred in which 'advanced' industrial nations were able to subjugate 'developing' regions with new mechanisms of political/military/economic domination.[8] At the same time, the skilled-labour-absorptive nature of the Western industrialisation experience (along with labour unions and state redistributive intervention) allowed the fruits of technological progress and international trade to 'trickle down' and widen the internal market within developed nations.[9] Barter increasingly diminished as a percentage of world trade as gold, pound sterling and, more recently, the US dollar provided a suitable intermediary in the structured inequality of international arrangements. In the dynamic, rapid-change orientation of the expanding capitalist order, monetary means provided rapid information flows, flexibility and convenience as the international exchange of commodities widened.

Periodically, however, barter arrangements were resurrected when global liquidity problems implied limited capacities to maintain vital imports or service existing debt. Argentina, for example, resorted to barter extensively during the 1880s and 1890s due to financial problems surrounding the global depression of that era and the reduction of money flows available for a 'high risk', uncreditworthy nation.[10] In addition, highly nationalistic and protectionistic countries, eg, the US, Germany, Japan, Canada, and Italy used barter during their formative industrialization stages in the latter part of the nine-teenth century to avoid gold losses and to circumvent the use of the key currency at that time—the pound sterling.[11]

In summary, although the world increasingly moved toward monetisa-tion and away from barter during the eighteenth and nineteenth centuries, special circumstances sometimes required the use of non-monetary trade. Specifically, barter proved functional to (1) inter-colonial or inter-common-wealth groups (much like an intra-firm transfer of a modern multinational corporation); (2) the emergent newly industrialising nations of the 1860s and 1890s in order to facilitate nationalistic, protectionistic development; and (3) the dependent less-developed nations crippled by cyclic downturns and financial insolvency.

In the aftermath of World War I, there was an attempt to revive the gold/pound-sterling monetary system of international exchange. Yet, severe socio-economic disintegration and virulent economic nationalism once more reduced participation in such multilateral arrangements. The collapse of the global economic structure and the re-militarisation of society fostered isola-tionistic and predatory policies that deepened the economic contraction and heightened geo-political tensions. Bilateralism, barter, and 'beggar thy neigh-bour' policies dominated in such an environment during the late 1920s, 1930s and early 1940s.

In Germany, where war reparations and debt repayments placed upon the Weimar Republic were severe, hyper-inflationary monetary policies and barter appeared as a short-run expedient to service debt obligations and obtain needed imports. By the 1930s Adolf Hitler's Finance Minister, Hjalmar Schacht, was utilising barter to trade for strategic raw materials (oil, bauxite, copper) with colonies, the Balkans and European trading groups.[12] In addi-tion, the Japanese had implemented barter-type agreements within their co-lonial sphere of influence (Korea, Formosa) and with nations participating in the Greater East Asian Co-Prosperity Sphere (Indonesia and Indochina).[13] Again, access to strategic raw materials was the motivating factor for the use of counter-trade by more developed nations as well as the lack of purchasing power on the part of the weaker developing areas. At the same time, European nations, the US and Japan employed comprehensive inter-governmental agreements of bilateral clearing to continue trade between themselves throughout the 1930s and 1940s.[14]

In the post-World War II era, a new monetary mechanism evolved based upon gold/dollar parity. Still, the functioning of this Bretton Woods accord was not complete or immediate. First, the Soviet Union and her allies were not participants in this system. Barter, thus, became a functional alternative for intra-East Bloc trade as well as for trade between East and West. Second, the post-war reconstruction of Europe and Japan required special pro-grammes and massive assistance. In the shadows of an escalating cold war, US national security objectives mitigated the implementation of punitive, exploitative politico-economic structures in Europe and Japan. Instead, structures based upon mutual benefit arose, with counter-trade at the centre of such an undertaking.

In 1948, the Reciprocal, Standardisation, and Inter-operability (RSI) provisions of NATO utilised counter-trade to transfer technology, share production, and foster indigenous control over strategic military operations. Thus, military sales and the evolution of the military/industrial complexes of Western Europe and the United States have been linked since World War II by counter-trade.[15] These relationships have fostered great homogenisation of NATO (and later Japanese) defence forces as well as insuring that the fruits of technological progress, employment, production, and managerial control over this major contributor to Gross National Product (GNP) have been distributed for the mutual benefit of all parties concerned. For example, in 1975, the Northrop Corporation counter-traded fighter jets to Switzerland in exchange for helping Swiss firms to market $450 million in the Middle East. Northrop employed its extensive contacts in the Middle East to help Swiss elevator producers to win contracts in Egypt and to open several new markets for the Swiss in Saudi Arabia.[16] And currently, the F-18 fighter aircraft is being co-produced by the McDonnell Douglas Corporation and various European countries in Europe as part of a NATO offset arrangement. For example, the Boeing Company is providing the North Atlantic Treaty Organisation (NATO) with 18 AWACS radar planes. To offset the sale to NATO, Boeing is building the planes in Europe with West German and Canadian subcontractors.[17]

On the non-military economic level as well, bilateral clearing arrangements were implemented to allow the re-industrialisation of Europe and Japan. These agreements fostered export growth from these nations and enhanced autonomous, sustainable development. To the present day, conditions are placed upon governments and multinational corporations wishing to invest, produce, and/or trade with these more developed nations. In particular, employment of indigenous managerial capacity, technology and production sharing, and investment restrictions are utilised by European nations, Japan and the US to insure that an equitable sharing of the benefits of international interaction occurs.[18]

Trade within the East European nations (COMECON) and East-West trade, on the other hand, have long been based upon barter. Estimates are that 60 per cent of intra-COMECON trade flows and 50 per cent of East-West trade is counter-trade.[19] From Finnish paper, textile products and ships for Soviet oil; to the German transfer of technology and expertise to build the Trans-Siberian pipeline in exchange for Soviet gas; to Occidental Petroleum's long-term counter-trade deals for the construction of petro-chemical complexes in exchange for access to Soviet markets, oil, and a percentage of the plants' output; East-West trade has been dominated by counter-trade. The Soviet Union, as well, has been a pioneer in bartering arms for strategic resources—oil, copper, tin, etc.—with developing countries. Recent swaps of Soviet arms for Libyan and Iraqi oil exemplify this relationship.

The US government, too, beginning in the early 1950s began encouraging barter under certain conditions. From 1950–73, the US Department of Agriculture used simple barter to obtain strategic materials from abroad and to provide services needed by US government agencies overseas under a barter programme established by the Commodity Credit Corporation Act of 1949 and Section 303 of the Agricultural Trade Development and Assistance Act of 1954 (Public Law 480). Approximately $6.65 billion worth of agricultural commodities were bartered under this programme, which was suspended in 1973 when the Commodity Credit Corporation's stock of commodities was depleted ($1.084 billion of agricultural commodities were exchanged for strategic materials and $4.81 billion for foreign-produced goods and services). However, the Foreign Assistance Act of 1974 re-authorised the US government to barter foreign assistance and services for strategic materials and in 1982 President Reagan temporarily revived the barter programme to complete a dairy products-for-bauxite deal with Jamaica (total $13 million). A second US-Jamaica barter deal was signed in November 1983, exchanging dairy products for one million tons of bauxite. In 1983, an amendment (HR 3544) to the Foreign Assistance Act of 1974 reactivated the barter of US agricultural commodity surpluses for oil and strategic materials for the national defence stockpile.[20]

Another example of modern counter-trading has been the increased use of barter, counter-purchase, and bilateral clearing mechanisms by OPEC nations. Since the 1970s, oil for arms exchanges have been important in Eastern Bloc/OPEC trade as well as advanced developing nations' trade with OPEC (notably Brazil and Israel). In addition, certain OPEC nations (Saudi Arabia, Indonesia and Venezuela) are requiring that more-developed nations import increasing volumes of refined and manufactured goods now produced by these developing nations. Complexes producing petro-chemicals, steel, vegetable oils, phosphates, urea, etc, need markets and the OPEC nations are insisting that developed nations purchase these commodities as a part of linking overall bilateral trade, investment and production arrangements. Most recently, some OPEC nations have resorted to counter-trade as a means to subvert the cartel's own limits on production quotas. Estimates suggest that 1.0–1.5 million barrels of over-quota OPEC oil are being produced daily and counter-traded (much of it to the Soviet Union).[21]

Most recently, less developed nations have begun actively to pursue counter-trade options for international exchange. After witnessing the use of counter-trade among more developed nations, between East and West, between OPEC and the rest of the world, and participating in strategic stockpiling arrangements, most Third World nations are turning to counter-trade as a major trading arrangement. The rapid implementation of 'conditioned' trade and the extensive application of such arrangements in all areas of production, trade, investment, and technology transfer harbour the obvious potential of significantly altering the current global arrangement. After first discussing the specific mechanisms of counter-trade, we shall ignore the incentives for implementing such a trading regime.

DEFINING THE VARIANTS OF COUNTER-TRADE

By definition, the term counter-trade refers to any contractual arrangement that commits the seller of a good or service to accept in partial or full payment goods or services from the buyer. Counter-trade is, thus, a 'tied' or 'conditioned' transaction in which a firm or country is compensated partially or fully by non-monetary means. Within the context of this definition, four principal variants of counter-trade can be usefully delineated.[22]

The four basic variants of counter-trade are simple barter, parallel barter, import compensation barter, and bilateral clearing arrangements.

Simple barter. A simple barter transaction is the direct exchange of goods having offsetting values, without any flow of money taking place. In addition, simple barter is a one-time transaction between two parties only, occuring over a relatively short period of time. Because simple barter is fairly inflexible, it normally is limited to government-to-government agreements. Oil, arms, food, and raw material exchanges tend to dominate these counter-trade transactions.

Examples of simple barter include a $200 million frozen lamb-for-crude oil deal between New Zealand and Iran; a wheat/frozen veal-for-iron pellets deal between Argentina and Peru; and a $585 million steel-making-complex-for-crude oil deal between West Germany and Indonesia.[23] OPEC countries have been leading users of simple barter since 1982 as a means to subvert the mandated oil production quotas set by the cartel. Most recently, a huge $1 billion barter of ten Boeing 747 jetliners for Saudi Arabian oil was consummated in August 1984. (This accord weakened already tenuous spot oil prices and generated intense speculation as to Saudi Arabia's future commitment to OPEC quotas.) The Soviet Union has also bartered arms for oil to OPEC countries, over $2.7 billion in 1983 alone. Much of this oil has then been sold on the open market for hard currency at prices that subvert the OPEC benchmark price. The USSR, via counter-trade, has become an import intermediary for 'over-quota' OPEC oil which is resold for hard currency on world markets.[24] With the exception of the OPEC nations, this form of counter-trade is the least used.

Parallel barter. Also called counter-purchase, parallel barter links the value of exports to the value of imports of unrelated goods, and generally specifies that the value of the second transaction should be a percentage of the first, commonly, but not necessarily 100 per cent. The fact that counter-purchase involves payment in 'non-resultant' products—that is, products not related to any technology or plant developed by the exporting firm—affords participants a greater range of selection and flexibility in their bilateral trade regime. In addition, money is often used in parallel barter transactions because of the lag between the off-setting deliveries of goods. These agreements are generally negotiated between a government trading firm and a private firm, or increasingly, between government-run enterprises of Third World nations (i.e., South-South trading arrangements).

For example, countries such as Romania, East Germany and Iran require that the Japanese import 105 per cent, 110 per cent and 150 per cent, respectively, of the value of the exports Japan sends to their economies over the course of a year. This policy ensures a bilateral balance of trade surplus and enhances hard currency inflows from the more developed nation.

An example of a counter-purchase arrangement between developing nations was the 1983 accord reached by Brazil and Mexico to counter-trade over $2 billion in specific areas of heavy industry. In this arrangement, Brazil will supply oil, sulphur, soybeans and steel technology to Mexico for petrochemicals, oil, oil industry equipment, maize and steel mill equipment.[25] Indonesia, in addition to the above mentioned counter-purchase provisions, requires exporting firms (1) to market targetted products produced in Indonesia; (2) to manufacture some portion of the exported product in Indonesia; and (3) to purchase some inputs from domestic suppliers. These are known as offset barter conditions and are gaining widespread popularity in the Third World—most notable Mexico, Brazil, Nigeria, Saudi Arabia, South Korea and India.[26]

Offset agreements have historically been used in the aerospace and defence-related industries. Recently, General Dynamics and South Korea agreed to a $930 million deal for 36 F-16 fighters whereby the US company contracted certain fuselage sections to Daewoo Heavy Industries, Ltd, a Korean firm.[27] Offsets have also enjoyed popularity in the electronics industry as well as in North-South investment and trading relations.

Import compensation. In contrast to counter-purchase, which is primarily commercial counter-trade, import compensation links the exports and imports of related products and represents a focus on industrial counter-trade. The most common variant of import compensation is the buy-back arrangement, although in recent years more complicated forms such as work contracts and develop-for-import arrangements have also become important.

A buy-back arrangement entails the sale of machinery, equipment, technology, and/or turn-key plants in exchange for repayment with the resultant output. Generally, buy-back deals involve large investments by the exporting firm and long pay back periods, usually between five and twenty years. An example is Occidental Petroleum's (and other international oil companies') multi-billion dollar agreements to develop several oil fields of the People's

Republic of China (PRC). Japan also has entered into long-term contracts with the PRC for technology transfer of oil, coal and steel building projects in exchange for repayment with the resultant product.[28] In another example, Brazil has linked with the USSR, Saudi Arabia, and Iraq to develop a uranium enrichment facility in Somalia. Brazilian construction firms will build the plant, Soviet technology and engineers will provide the enrichment machinery, the Iraqis and Saudis will finance the operation, and the Somalis will provide the uranium deposits. Each participant will be paid in uranium output for use in their respective nuclear development programmes—both commercial and military. The Brazilians have also linked with the USSR to build dams in Mozambique and Angola in exchange for oil.[29]

Develop-for-import arrangements can be viewed as a form of conditioned portfolio or equity loans. An example is the provision of Japanese investment capital to develop the Gunpowder Copper mine in Australia in exchange for 23 per cent of the mine's output. Australian nationals own and operate the facility with the Japanese role being that of financier.[30] Similar agreements have been reached with Exxon Corporation and the Colombian government to develop the $3 billion El Cerrejon Norte coal field, the largest coal field in the world. In this case, aspects of buy-back and develop-for-import arrangements are also being utilised.[31] In an additional example, Japan supplied investment capital to Brazil for the construction of an alumina-aluminium complex on the condition that Brazil repay Japan with 50 per cent of the output.[32] In each of the import compensation variants, it is instructive to note that capital formation, both human and physical, is being exchanged for a commodity output. Thus, an important long-run strategy for the acquisition of particular technologies and skills by developing nations is set in motion. Historically, this has been the key counter-trade technique of East-West trade. Recently, however, many Third World nations have implemented this trading device in order to stimulate capital formation.

Bilateral clearing. This form of counter-trade is based upon government-to-government trade agreements to insure bilateral balance in the international accounts. This balance assures that no net drain of foreign exchange will occur between the signatory parties. In the past, such trade imbalances have seriously weakened attempts by developing nations to promote regional economic integration. The wide gaps between surplus and deficit nations have been at the root of tensions within the Central American Common Market, the Andean Bloc, the Association of Southeast Asian Nations (ASEAN), and the break-up of several African regional groups. ASEAN nations are currently practising bilateral balance within that group and increasingly requiring similar agreements with external trading nations. This form of counter-trade is thought to have the potential of regenerating regional economic cooperation and fostering greater South-South trade.

In the event that trade imbalances result at the end of the bilateral clearing agreement, credits can be used as purchasing power (eg, Brazil and East Germany have established such an arrangement)[33] or surplus commodities can be sold to 'switch' traders at a discount, who then market the goods internationally. One example of switch trading was Malaysia's agreement to take payment in cocoa from Mexico in exchange for Malaysian rubber. The cocoa was then sold, for US dollars, to US confectionery makers.[34]

Also, government-to-government 'swaps' of materials that have high transport costs or are highly perishable are an increasingly important form of bilateral clearing. Australia and Mexico agreed to counter-trade lamb for oil. US companies and China also linked to trade lamb/beef for oil. To cut transport costs, the US firms shipped lamb to Mexico for oil, and Australia shipped lamb to the PRC for oil. A second example is that of the USSR supplying customers for Mexico's oil in the Middle East while Mexico sells oil to Cuba, a Soviet customer. A similar 'swap' has been utilised by Venezuela, West Germany, Cuba and the USSR. In 1983, Soviet oil for Cuba was diverted to West Germany and Venezuelan oil for West Germany was diverted to Cuba.[35]

THE SCOPE OF COUNTER-TRADE

Estimations vary enormously concerning the true magnitude of counter-trade. The reasons for such diverse data projections are numerous. In the first place, counter-trade transactions are not specifically tabulated in standard national accounts data. In the second place, most nations are reluctant to acknowledge counter-trade activity for obvious political reasons, especially as the US, IMF, IBRD, and GATT have openly opposed mandated counter-trade. Third, most multinational corporations are hesitant to divulge counter-trade activity so as to preserve client anonymity. And fourth, most estimates are based on rumours of 'proposed' transactions rather than actual deals. Since many specialists feel that a 10–1 ratio exists between counter-trade proposals and consummated deals, estimates that counter-trade represents 50 percent of world trade are highly exaggerated.

Still there are ranges of plausible estimations. Probably the most conservative plausible estimate has counter-trade (excluding bilateral clearing) at 6 per cent of the total $2.5 trillion world trade—or around $150 billion.[36] Gary Banks, an economist with the Secretariat of GATT, has argued that for counter-trade to be 25 per cent of total world trade, all of world trade outside the OECD would have to be counter-trade (LCDs 16 per cent, Eastern Europe 9 per cent and OPEC 8 per cent).[37] Yet, counter-trade is only 50 per cent of East European trade and much less for other countries. At the upper range of the plausible are Business International and Gary Hufbauer, an economist at the Institute of International Economics, who have suggested that 12–15 per cent of world trade occurs within some form of counter-trade relationship. *The Economist* (London) has recently published a survey on counter-trade which estimates 20 per cent of world trade is now under this trading pattern.[38]

Approximately one hundred nations in the world (both North and South) currently require some form of counter-trade provision, and numerous others are considering its adoption. Roughly half of East-West trade is counter-trade. Over half of the Fortune 500 companies now have separate counter-trade divisions and most of the rest are examining the potential for creating in-house capacity.[39] So, while the exact magnitude of counter-trade may be uncertain, there is no doubt that the growth of counter-trade has been explosive and that the trend toward counter-trade is clearly increasing.

This fact is significant in that during a time period of overall world contraction of trade (1980–83), counter-trade has increased dramatically. Recent interviews with representatives of major MNCs, the American Counter-Trade and Export Association, and the US Departments of Commerce and Treasury, suggest that the rapid growth of counter-trade has not yet abated —in spite of a rebound in world growth and trade during 1984–85.[40]

One explanation for the competitive vigour of counter-trade has been the dramatic fall in the transaction costs of such arrangements. The computer has played a key role in linking buyers and sellers with counter-trade around the world. In Brussels, a counter-trade clearing house was established in 1983 in order to facilitate the global networking of counter-trade activity. Also, informal computerised barter exchanges exist in Paris and Vienna, and the American Counter-Trade and Export Association is in the process of establishing a US exchange in Cleveland, Ohio. Governments are also becoming involved. For example, the Swedish government recently purchased an 8 per cent share in Sukab, a counter-trade organisation formed in 1940 by major Swedish exporters. The French government has sponsored the formation of a counter-trade advisory organisation, ACECO (Association pour la Compensation des Echanges Commerciaux), and in Miami, Florida, the state legislature has authorized the establishment of an 'international barter exchange centre'.[41]

Governments, multinational corporations, and counter-trade specialists now are able to quickly and efficiently market products in a centralised setting. As a result, discounting on counter-trade products has fallen markedly. In the late 1970s and early 1980s, discount rates of 25 per cent—40 per cent were not uncommon in counter-trade agreements. By 1984, discount margins had dropped to 3 per cent—7 per cent with many specialists stating that rates will continue to fall as counter-trade expands and computerisation continues. Discounts, also, will vary according to the ease of disposal of the goods. Generally, raw materials carry the lowest rates of discount (under 5 per cent) while hard-to-market manufactured goods carry the highest discounts.[42]

The formation of the South Bank will also provide developing nations with the opportunity to expand counter-trade. Facilitating counter-trade will be a major goal of this new Third World financial agency.[43] US policy has also facilitated the use of counter-trade in business transactions. In 1982, the US Export Trading Company Act allowed US banks to enter into trading relationships worldwide. This legislation was primarily intended to counter Japanese trading companies and to promote US exports. However, the ETCs will also enable US traders to engage in the growing counter-trade nexus. Similarly, the East European nations have begun to integrate their financing, trading, and production sectors into a single organisation, 'combinats', that will enable more competitive trade and counter-trade relations. Thus, on many levels, counter-trade 'infrastructure' is rapidly evolving to support the expansion of 'conditioned' trade.

The key countries who counter-trade outside the Eastern European nations are Indonesia, Iran, Brazil, Colombia, Mexico, the PRC, Canada, and Australia.

Each of these nations has well-defined programmes for counter-trade as part of their overall development plan and each has openly stated their goals of expanding this method of international interaction. We now explore the reasons for its ascendance and its implications for global relations.

INCENTIVES TO COUNTER-TRADE

> Intensive economic nationalism marked the decade. Exports were curtailed. All the weapons of commercial warfare were brought into play; currencies were devalued, exports were subsidised, tariffs raised, exchanges controlled, quotas imposed and discrimination practiced through preferential systems and *barter deals* [emphasis added]. Each nation sought to sell much and buy little. A vicious spiral of restrictionism produced a further deterioration in world trade.[44]

Written in 1949 to describe the global trading environment of the 1930s, the striking similarities to the 1980s suggest longer term processes in our global economy. These periodic cycles of boom and bust, the so-called Kondratiev-Schumpeterian long waves, have historically been closely associated with intensified utilisation of counter-trade as a mechanism of international exchange. While leaving the important discussion of 'long wave' dynamics aside,[45] it is necessary to stress the increased importance of counter-trade as a method of *circumventing* (at least over the short term) the down cycles of global economic activity. In addition, counter-trade and other protectionist, neo-mercantilist devices were historically important in *exacerbating* (in the long run) the economic stagnation that accompanied periodic depressions in the international system.

The global stagnation of the late 1970s and 1980s provides yet another crucible in which to evaluate the impact of counter-trade as a trading device. Again, as in other cycles of economic contraction, the short-term benefits of administered trade have been significant. While the longer term benefits/costs are yet to be determined, there are some indications that qualitative changes in technology and global geopolitics may render past experiences with counter-trade inappropriate as guides to future impacts.

Short-run Exigencies

The proximate cause of the emergence of counter-trade in the trading regimes of developing nations has been the debt crisis.[46] The resultant lack of liquidity (i.e., US dollars) available to developing nations fostered the need for creative alternatives to maintain required imports and to promote exports.[47] Counter-trade provides such a mechanism for Third World nations to accomplish several short-term objectives: hard currency is conserved; required imports of machinery, food and pharmaceuticals can be maintained; traditional and new exports can be promoted; and growth can be stimulated/maintained in the export sector as well as the import substitution industrial sector.

By counter-trading surplus raw materials for needed imports, nations can benefit in the short run by (1) conserving hard currency that otherwise would have been spent on importables; and (2) indirectly providing a price support for those primary export products. Hard currency can then be used to repay interest on loans, the balance of trade position appears more favourable, and the value of its exports which earn hard currency can be preserved (at least in the short run. In the longer run, however, if many nations engage in such a practice, prices will eventually fall for all).

Generally, Third World nations sell commodities for which they have a comparative advantage and/or established markets for hard currency generation. Counter-trade, as a rule, is utilised to market new products for which (1) no market channels exist; (2) protectionistic barriers exist; and/or (3) inferior quality prohibits sales in more developed nations. Thus, manufactured products produced by an 'infant industry' can enter the world market while enjoying continued tariff protection as well as the marketing skills of multinational corporations.

Increasingly, hard currency products will be counter-traded (1) to other cash-strapped nations (i.e., several deals of Mexican and Venezuelan oil for Central American coffee, bananas, and cattle); (2) in conditions of excess supply (as now confront the markets for oil, copper and tin); or (3) where import compensation schemes allow the transfer of high technology, turnkey plants, and/or managerial concessions for resources (as exemplified by the oil, coal, and copper deals between China and Japan).

In essence, counter-trade allows a country facing severe problems of illiquidity, due to reductions in multilateral and commercial bank lending, falling prices for its export commodities, devaluations, and net capital outflows, to maintain existing economic strategies for growth and to avoid extreme deflationary prescriptions for adjustment in the short run. In the absence of counter-trade, large debtor nations such as Mexico, Brazil, and the Philippines would virtually have to use all of their export earnings to service their debts.[48] Thus, as a short-run expedient, counter-trade has been successfully implemented to avoid the deleterious side-effects of periodic global contraction.

Medium-term Incentives

Since the early 1970s, dramatic changes in the international economic system have required Third World nations to adjust domestic policies to accommodate global market pressures. Over the course of the past fifteen years, unprecedented 'liberalisation', de-regulation, and global integration have simultaneously appeared on the world economic scene. The shift to a floating exchange rate world with the value of currencies determined by global decisionmakers marked the watershed point for this era of change. Financial de-regulation, floating interest rates, and the privatisation of lending followed in short order. As international production expanded, the de-oligopolisation of commodity markets (oil, copper, tin, rubber, etc) and of manufactured production intensified the volatility of international prices for traded goods.

For Third World nations, these changes culminated in growing debt imbalances, declining terms of trade, and stagnating growth. As import substitution industrialisation steadily lost its capacity to generate growth and the international lending community lost its enthusiasm to finance and invest in development projects, Third World nations increasingly were forced to turn to the International Monetary Fund (IMF) for liquidity needs. Yet, the IMF 'conditions' implied internal 'liberalisation', 'de-regulation', and increased integration into the volatile international financial/investment system. And history has shown that for those who attempted to follow this radical neo-conservative stabilisation orthodoxy in the late 1960s and 1970s (i.e., Brazil, Argentina, Chile, Uruguay), the results have been equally disastrous.[49] Countries which re-exposed themselves to monocultural export dependence experienced the stultifying effects of industrial involution.

Thus, counter-trade provides a means to overcome the limitations of economic models of the past. At the same time, counter-trade offers dynamic advantages for the future development of Third World economies. In the medium term, counter-trade promotes several important gains that will enable Third World nations to obtain a larger role in decisionmaking and control over economic processes. Counter-trade fosters stability in industrial planning, terms of trade support, diversified trade relations, a new 'partnership' with multinational corporations, bilateral balance, and disguised austerity programmes.

Because of the volatile nature of demand patterns for Third World exports, many nations view counter-trade as a method of stabilising their export revenue profile. With counter-trade, known exports can be paired to desired imports which facilitates the planning of industrial and agricultural development strategies. In this way, periodic external imbalances and the associated IMF-mandated economic contraction can be avoided. With access to new loans declining, the hard choice for government planners is (1) whether to deflate under an IMF austerity programme and hope for international 'trickle down' to regenerate growth; or (2) implement counter-trade policies immediately in order to return to a growth trajectory. Counter-purchase and compensation arrangements are a primary method of stabilising the fluctuating demand for Third World raw materials so that effective long-term planning can proceed. As a result, most less developed nations now counter-trade on a sectoral basis (i.e., automobiles, oil, railways) to foster overall planning.[50]

In addition, these counter-trade techniques can act as a price support mechanism, thus, maintaining the terms of trade over a longer period of time. In comparison to the volatile nature of international market pricing regimes, counter-trade can reduce the destabilising swings in the relative values of imported to exported goods. Counter-trade is perceived by Third World planners as a key means to stabilise export revenues and import costs where, in the past, attempts to implement such arrangements through cartels have largely been unsuccessful. For example, the ASEAN nations have asked Japan, the EEC, and the US to counter-trade as a means to hold up the real purchasing power of their major exports.

Liquidity and terms of trade are not the only motivating factors that encourage linkage. Many countries (including South Korea, Indonesia, Malaysia, Saudi Arabia, China, Australia and Canada) insist upon counter-trade in spite of solid foreign reserve holdings. For these industrialising nations, linking trade flows is a major tool by which diversification of trading partners and the exertion of national sovereignty over multinational corporations can be achieved. Through diversification, the risks of geo-political chaos can be reduced. Important South-South trading patterns can be cultivated as well. In addition, greater outlets for exportable goods and increased sources for importable goods create a more competitive market, which tends to increase export earnings and to reduce import costs. Counter-trade enables Third World nations to increase the flow of technology, foster new market penetration, new product development, and demand the acquisition of marketing skills by requiring such linkage from multinational corporations. Nationalist governments with a large market potential and/or resource wealth have been able to win such concessions and require that new investments produce larger corresponding export sales. Multinational corporations can also be enlisted to overcome more developed nation protectionism by marketing Third World goods.

Third World planners have sought to eliminate balance-of-payments crises by bilaterally balancing their international accounts. Many industrial and trade activities in Third World nations are nationalised and conducive to counter-trade. Thus, bilateral clearing arrangements between governments and between state trading enterprises have become widespread over the past five years. In addition, *investment performance* conditions placed upon private investors (as in the case of Mexico and Brazil) have insured a favourable balance on these transactions as well. Under investment performance, foreign producers are required to increase their export growth over time to continue to qualify for favourable tax and tariff treatment.

Bilateral balance can also reduce net currency outflows that accompany balance-of-trade deficits. Malaysia recently diversified its imports of rice by increasing imports from Burma (with whom Malaysia runs a balance-of-trade surplus) and reducing rice imports from Thailand (with whom Malaysia runs a balance-of-trade deficit). By means of counter-trade, bilateral balance and diversification of trading relationships were obtained. Colombia also is utilising counter-trade to maintain a positive trade balance. In April 1984 the Colombian Institute of Foreign Trade (INCOMEX) prohibited and/or severely restricted the importation of more than 2,000 products, and set aside thirty-three product categories for counter-trade in order to improve its current account situation. In addition, the counter-traded goods must be above and beyond Colombia's normal export levels.

Interestingly, counter-trade can be utilised as a disguised imposition of an economic austerity programme—without overtly resorting to discriminatory tariff barriers. Third World nations that want to cut imports (and the standard of living) can impose stringent counter-trade regulations and then blame foreign corporations for the lack of imported goods.[51] Protection is, thus, afforded to domestic producers without subverting the present guidelines of the General Agreement on Tariffs and Trade (GATT). Also, counter-trade can be employed as an alternative to an explicit export subsidy, devaluation, or cartel pricing guidelines. By accepting higher prices for imported goods for the same amount of exported commodities, counter-trade becomes a form of discounting that again is not within the coverage of the existing GATT framework.[52]

Finally, counter-trade can actually result in greater control over the international debt imbalance since banks will not provide trade financing for counter-purchase deals unless both contracts are backed by readily available goods. Thus, a balancing check against the borrowing excesses of the past is conveniently performed by the counter-trading mechanism. Also, since many counter-trade deals are long-term in nature, one of the participants is implicitly receiving an advance loan. Counter-trade, thus, can bridge the liquidity problem from the financing side as well (East Germany, for example, owes Brazil [of all countries] over $1 billion in clearing account units that are due in two years, effectively giving the East Germans an interest-free loan.)

Over the medium term, counter-trade is perceived to be highly advantageous by Third World nations. Development planning is enhanced, the distribution of benefits in international interaction is improved, balance of payment distortions are avoided, and goals of economic sovereignty are achieved. In a world of illiquidity, structural transformation, and crisis, counter-trade can provide a stable development option for Third World planners.[53]

Advantages for the North

Although the primary focus of our discussion has centered upon the beneficial incentives that counter-trade offers to Third World nations, it would be incomplete to ignore the important incentives that have induced more developed nations and their multinational corporations to enter the 'linkage' game. While many researchers critical of counter-trade have stressed the long-run 'zero sum' nature of bilateral trade regimes,[54] powerful incentives, both positive and negative, have compelled decisionmakers to enter the 'only game in town'.

More developed countries have not been immune to the growing instability of global market forces that have characterised the past fifteen years. In particular, the Japanese, Canadians, and Europeans began to implement policies in the late 1960s and early 1970s that would reduce their heavy dependence upon strategic raw materials imported from the US. Global diversification of sources for raw materials (oil, coal, copper, soybeans, rubber, tin, etc.), sources to market manufactured goods, sites for offshore production, and sources for international investment have been an important component of these developed nations' economic policies. The Third World has been the central recipient of these diversification strategies. Clearly, economic self-interest as well as national security issues have combined to foster policies that would lead to reduced exposure to the geo-political vagaries of any particular nation. Counter-trade has been received with greater enthusiasm by Japanese, European and Canadian governments and corporations as it is perceived to be a mechanism to improve long-term flexibility and economic sovereignty.

For example, the Japanese have been the most willing nation to accept counter-trade concessions in order to diversify their heavy dependence on imported oil. Nigeria, Indonesia, Peru, Ecuador, Mexico, Iran, Iraq and Saudi Arabia, among others, have established formal counter-trading relationships to exchange oil for manufactured goods. Similarly, the Japanese engage in extensive compensation, buy-back and technology transfer agreements with China (coal, oil, bauxite, copper), Australia (copper, uranium, coal), Chile (copper), Brazil (soybeans, aluminium, bauxite, iron ore), the USSR (timber, oil), Indonesia (oil), etc.

The resource-dependent Europeans, too, have been willing to grant counter-trade concessions in exchange for long-term stability in supply and access to internal markets. The West Germans have linked with the PRC for oil, numerous Middle Eastern nations for oil, and Brazil for copper, bauxite, and uranium. The French have been active counter-traders in Africa and the Middle East, again for long-term supplies of raw materials. The British, while less active, have also engaged in counter-trade in India, China, and Africa.

The specific positive inducements to counter-trade afforded to more developed nations are numerous. They include diversified raw material supplies, diversified market sourcing, access to new markets, expansion of existing markets, a means to unblock frozen profits/dividends, tax and tariff dodges, and 'good faith' gestures by image-conscious multinationals.

Since counter-trade is the 'only game in town', reticent corporate managers risk losing existing markets in the Third World as well as potential markets if they choose not to counter-trade. This negative incentive can be extremely powerful for corporations that must show solid growth performance in a quarter-to-quarter evaluation system. For example, Spain's ENESA was able to win a contract to supply buses for Colombia because they included a counter-trade provision to buy Colombian coffee. ENESA had not been the lowest bidder but had offered the most favourable counter-trade package. Another example involves a US corporation. General Electric lost an important contract for the sale of CAT scanners to Austrian hospitals when Germany's Siemens agreed to increase production of electrical goods at a plant it operates in Austria. Although General Electric had been the lowest bidder, Siemens was able to offset the purchase of its scanners with additional Austrian employment and thus won the contract.[55]

Many multinationals have also viewed counter-trade as a means to free profits and dividends locked inside financially troubled developing nations. By counter-trading for goods at 'artificial' intra-firm prices, commodities can be exported from the troubled nation, sold on the international market, and repatriated to the home country for use. Many multinational banks have utilised this method to obtain delinquent interest and principal payments from cash-poor less-developed nations. An additional advantage that can be used by multinational corporations and private domestic companies is the technique of under-valuing counter-traded commodities to reduce exposure to the tax and tariff laws of Third World nations.[56]

Finally, some Western companies will employ counter-trade as a 'good faith' exercise in order to win long-term sales contracts. By establishing themselves as reliable trading partners, multinationals hope to maintain market links and to create new 'favoured' arrangements in the future.

Recently, more developed nations have themselves begun active counter-trading (as opposed to the reluctant passive counter-trade outlined above). Counter-trade can reduce the costs of expensive capital development incurred by multinational corporations. By moving into the downstream linkages of marketing, information processing, and management, costs and risks can be shifted toward developing nations while more profitable activities can be performed by the multinationals. Other governments have sought to actively pursue 'linked' raw material or manufacturing production. France requires buybacks on metal processing equipment sales financed by government credits. Recently, an aluminum refinery was built in India by France whereby France will be repaid in 50 per cent of the annual output.

For the US, the traditional rhetoric for 'free-trade' has inhibited a strong shift toward counter-trade. Still, in strategic metals, grains, and aerospace, the US has been willing to participate in barter arrangements. While officially opposed to counter-trade, the US Export Trading Company Act of 1982 will facilitate US multinational corporation involvement in 'linked' trade.

As more developed governments and multinational corporations increasingly join the counter-trade system, the long-run dynamics of the mechanism will further integrate the global economy and fundamentally alter the existing status quo between the North and the South.

The Long-term Benefits of Counter-trade: Economic Sovereignty and the NIEO

> Counter-trade represents a substantial and growing departure from the principles of multilateral and largely monetised trade of the post-World War II years. . . . By compelling more developed countries to accept part payment in commodities and to take back additional exports, primary producers are circumventing the international pricing mechanism and achieving what decades of negotiations on international commodity agreements and cartels have failed to achieve.[57]

It is in the longer term that counter-trade offers the most enduring changes for the global system. The maturation of political nationalism and the emergence of struggles for economic self-determination have coincided with the present economic crisis and the transformation of the global economy. For Third World nations, the doctrine of national sovereignty over natural resources along with the emergence of the state as an active participant in economic development have provided the conditions whereby changes in the structures of inter-societal interaction can be made. Having direct experience with the long history of 'managed/administered' trade and having participated in such arrangements, Third World nations are now in a position to utilise this mechanism to alter the terms of trade, distribution of benefits, technology transfers, and flows of resources on a global basis.

Counter-trade, as initially an adaptation to profound economic crisis, has evolved into a strategy by which Third World nations can create a *de facto* NIEO. Many of the stated goals of the NIEO (i.e., increased technology transfer, improved terms of trade, a new 'partnership' with multinational corporations, greater access to more-developed nation markets, more favourable resource flows from North to South, and enhanced self-reliance in food, energy and defence) are accomplished via counter-trade without a formal multilateral declaration of such a radical restructuring. Over the longer term, counter-trade provides the potential whereby global institutional structures can be reshaped to foster a mutual 'dependence' built upon respect, benefit, and cooperation.

For developed nations as well, counter-trade can be a useful long-term mechanism by which greater economic autonomy can be obtained. For the resource-dependent nations of Europe and Japan, diversified input supply and market sourcing enhances their national security and promotes expanded influence within the Third World. By overtly linking their long-run economic destinies with developing nations, cooperative relationships are created that spill over into social, political, and strategic security areas to the benefit of both parties.

It is important to stress that the maturation of Third World nationalism and the enhanced capacity of decisionmakers effectively to debate complex economic issues will intensify the use of counter-trade as a long-term tool for restructuring the global economy. Developing countries have a clear understanding of the inner-working of the global economic system and of the dynamic areas within which they want to participate. As such, the leverage of cheap labour, abundant natural resources, and rapidly growing markets will be linked to the redirection of rewards, information access, and technology flows in international interchange. Having experienced the distorting effects of past development models (i.e., from classical comparative advantage, to import substitution, to state planning, to debt-led growth), nationalist Third World nations are attempting a new strategy. Counter-trade reflects the accumulated wisdom of past experiences as well as a sense of newly obtained economic power that many nationalist developing nations are able to wield in determining the next economic 'order'.[58]

Thus, the long-run incentives to counter-trade are a combination of political and economic factors. For Third World nations and advanced industrial nations, long-run political and economic sovereignty are the motivating bases for the rapid adoption of counter-trade.

CONCLUSIONS: POLICY RESPONSE

Counter-trade is a mechanism that will fundamentally transform international economic relations. For Third World nations, the widespread adoption of 'linked' resource flows represents a new model which potentially can lead to a mutually dependent world community based upon the principles of mutual trust, respect, benefit, and cooperation. Counter-trade as a development model is reshaping inter-societal relations and will widen the range of human resource potential available to the world society.

Yet, nationalist Third World decisionmakers must also recognise that external 'linkage' is a necessary (but not a sufficient) requirement for achieving sustainable, equitable growth. The logic of counter-trade must also begin to be implemented internally within Third World nations if the gains from international restructuring are to be effectively absorbed. Self-reliance, participation, control over resources, and the mutuality of trust, benefits, and respect must simultaneously be cultivated among the population of developing nations. Counter-trade, if it endures, will require a radical transformation of relationships in both the external and internal institutional arrangements of economic, political, and social interaction.

For decisionmakers from more developed nations, counter-trade must be recognised as a culmination of a lengthy historical process whereby the forces of political and economic liberation/sovereignty in the Third World have come of age. Attempts to ignore, subvert, or roll back this inexorable process will only engender hostility and exclusion from the most dynamic growth regions on the planet. Policymakers must take the broader view of planetary realism—that economically, ecologically, and politically our destiny as a human species is tightly interwoven. In so doing, counter-trade can be a mechanism by which advanced industrial nations can begin a shift toward fair trade and, thus, avoid the encroaching reality of predatory competition, protectionism, and global economic stagnation.

Over the coming decade, developing nations will continue to employ counter-trade techniques to develop their export capacities in resources, manufactured goods, and high technology products. Already the US and the EEC have been adversely affected by the influx of foreign cars, steel, electronics goods, etc. But this is merely the tip of the iceberg. Over the rest of this decade a veritable tidal wave of high technology goods, petro-chemical products, agricultural products and raw materials will increase the pressure on US and EEC producers. For these developed nations the difficult choice will be whether to impose greater protectionism as a short-term expedient or to begin playing the 'conditioned' trade game in a concerted, coherent manner. Viewed dynamically, counter-trade offers a transition model toward the return of institutions which promote the positive capacities of a healthy, sustainable society—mutual trust, mutual respect, mutual benefits, mutual cooperation, and mutually reciprocal obligations. After some 5,000 years, the species may have come full circle.

NOTES

1. The literature of economic anthropology is filled with such accounts. See in particular George Dalton, 'Barter', *Journal of Economic Issues* (16) March 1982, p. 182 and Thomas Harding and B. Wallace, *Cultures of the Pacific,* Free Press, 1970.
2. This is true of modern hunter/gatherer, tribal, and chiefdom groups as well. George Dalton, *ibid.* pp. 181–90, and George Dalton (ed), *Primitive, Archaic, and Modern Economies: Essays of Karl Polanyi,* Beacon Press, 1971.

3. David Thomas, 'Exchange systems among the Pemon', *Ethnology,* January 1979, pp 61–2, and lectures on Economic Anthropology, Vanderbilt University, 1979–80.
4. It was J. M. Keynes who predicted that the lack of a suitable adjustment mechanism would become the Achilles heel of the present Bretton Woods system.
5. See Elman Service, *Origins of the State and Civilisation: The Process of Cultural Evolution.* Norton Press, 1975, and Morton Fried, *The Evolution of Political Society,* Random, 1968.
6. See Richard Lee and Irven DeVore, *Kalahari Hunter Gatherers,* Harvard University Press, 1976. Elizabeth Marshall Thomas, *The Harmless People,* Vintage, 1959, and Roger Owen, *et al., North American Indians,* London: Macmillan, 1967.
7. William Glade, *The Latin American Economies,* American Book Press, 1969, pp. 110–49. Thomas Skidmore and Peter Smith, *Modern Latin America,* 1984.
8. L. S. Stavrianos, *Global Rift: The Third World Comes of Age,* William Morrow, 1981, Introduction.
9. Wassily Leontief, 'The distribution of work and income', *Scientific American,* September 1982, pp. 188–90; Joel Novek, 'The mechanisation of work,' *Challenge,* September–October 1984, pp. 43–8.
10. L. S. Stavrianos, *ibid.,* p. 188.
11. *ibid.,* pp. 256–62.
12. Jack Kaikaiti, 'The reincarnation of barter trade as a marketing tool', *Journal of Marketing* (40) April 1976, p. 19. Gary Banks, 'The economics and politics of counter-trade', *The World Economy* (6) June 1983, pp. 181–2.
13. John Dizard, 'The explosion of international barter', *Fortune Magazine,* 7 February 1983, p. 89.
14. Dominic Salvatore, *International Economics,* McGraw Hill, pp. 215–16. Gary Banks, *op cit,* p. 178.
15. Ed Barber, 'The Economic Implications of Military Offsets and Co-Production Arrangements', 18 March 1980, p. 7.
16. James Walsh, 'Counter-trade: not just for East-West anymore', *Journal of World Trade Law* 17(1) January/February, 1983, p. 10.
17. Brad Heller, 'US firms must propose joint ventures to win a slice of huge Saudi contracts', *Wall Street Journal,* 13 April 1984, p. 31.
18. Leo G. B. Welt, *Counter-trade: business practices for today's World market,* American Management Association Publications, 1982. p. 11; Gary Banks, *op. cit.,* p. 160.
19. James Walsh, *op. cit.,* p. 4.
20. For a comprehensive discussion of the US Government barter programme, see Donna V. Vogt, 'US Government International Barter', Congressional Research Report No. 83-211ENR, The Library of Congress, 1983.
21. Dan Morgan, 'Moscow's quest for cash hurts OPEC and East bloc,' *San José Mercury,* 24 August 1984.
22. A counter-trade transaction can either involve government-to-government, company-to-government agency, or company-to-company deals.
23. See the OECD working party of the Trade Committee North-South Trade, 'Developing country attitudes to counter-trade', May, 1984.
24. Dan Morgan, *op. cit.*
25. Leo G. B. Welt, *op. cit.,* p. 61.
26. John Wiecking, 'Counter-trade: its nature and scope', US Department of State, Bureau of Intelligence and Research, report 821-AR, 17 April 1984, pp. 5–7.
27. 'New restrictions on world trade', *Business Week,* 19 July 1982, p. 119. 'Investment performance' is an expanding offset mechanism that Brazil, Mexico, and Canada

are demanding. Under such arrangements, project approval and continuation depends upon the firm's ability to *increase* export levels over time.

28. See Robert Dennis, 'The counter-trade factor in China's modernisation plan', *Columbia Journal of World Business,* Spring 1982, pp. 67–74.

29. *Latin America Reports Brazil,* 4 January 1985, p. 4.

30. Louis Nameth, 'Offsets under fire down under', *Multinational Monitor* 5 (6) June 1984, p. 3.

31. See Harvey Kline, 'Colombia's debate about coal, Exxon, themselves', *Inter-American Economic Affairs* 36(4) Spring 1983, pp. 3–28.

32. James Walsh, *op. cit.,* p. 7.

33. John Dizard, *op. cit.,* p. 95.

34. 'Special report: going under the counter', *Far Eastern Economic Review* 27 January 1983, p. 51.

35. Thomas McVey, 'Countertrade and barter: alternative trade financing by Third World nations', *International Trade Law Journal,* Spring/Summer 1981, p. 7. Also G. B. Souza, 'Counter-trade and barter in Venezuela', *Countertrade and Barter Quarterly* (4) Winter 1984, p. 16.

36. David Yoffie, 'Barter: looking beyond the short-term payoffs and long-term threat', *International Management,* August 1984, p. 36.

37. Gary Banks, *op. cit.,* p. 177.

38. 'Why LDC's want—or think they want—countertrade', *Business International* 31 (35) 31 August 1984, p. 274. Estimations from Gary Hufbauer and *The Economist* were obtained from interviews with William Rouse.

39. 'Counter-trade phenomenon is spreading globally in scope and intensity', *Business International* 30 (51) 23 December 1983, p. 354.

40. Based upon interviews conducted by William Rouse in Cleveland, New York, and Washington in August/September 1984.

41. The Florida centre, authorised by an Act of the Florida legislature in June, would be the first international barter exchange centre. The centre will be governed by a 15-member board of directors, appointed by the State of Governor and legislative leaders. It will have a trading floor similar to that of the New York Stock Exchange or Lloyds of London.

42. Leo G. B. Welt, *op. cit.,* p. 17.

43. 'A helping hand for South-South trade', *South* (London) March 1984, p. 64.

44. William Rouse, 'Counter-trade,' unpublished paper, Spring 1984.

45. Many modern scholars (Jay Forrester and David Gordon among others) have offered various explanations for the empirical fact of forty to fifty year boom/bust cycles.

46. The debt crisis itself is a manifestation of the breakdown of the over-centralised, hierarchical, and elitist growth models pursued by policymakers in past decades. Whether North or South, East or West, strategies of import substitution, capital/petro-chemical intensive industrialisation, state enterprises, export enclaves, and oligopolistic conglomeration have fostered protectionism, gross inefficiencies, heightened inequalities, the demise of participatory democracy, and non-sustainable growth and development. The seeds of a viable society lie germinating at this moment. Whether a new generation of thinkers and policymakers will activate

this potential capacity will be the primary debate for the remainder of this century.

47. The accumulated and growing debt of the Third World, estimated at $850 billion today, and the current strength of the US dollar in which most of these nation's debt is denominated, has encouraged the growth of counter-trade practices. In addition, the reduction of trade finance to less developed nations has forced them to consider counter-trading practices. According to the Bank for International Settlements, bank lending to developing countries increased by only $4.7 billion from the end of 1982 to the end of 1983, compared with a growth of $17 billion for the first half of 1982. Also, banks and Western exporters continue to limit trade finance and export activities in these countries to transactions involving minimum risk. And for specific nations, net capital outflows have been recorded from 1982–4. In addition, the IMF recently (January 1985) announced that lending to developing nations dropped from $13.3 billion in 1983 to $7.5 billion in 1984. The liquidity crunch is very real for developing nations.

48. David Yoffie, *op. cit.,* p. 36.

49. See Alejandro Foxley, *Modern Experiments in Neo-Conservative Economics,* University of California, 1983.

50. John Wicking, *op. cit.,* p. 7.

51. David Yoffie, *op. cit.,* p. 36.

52. For this reason, the Reagan Administration has called for a new 'Round' of GATT talks to focus upon mechanisms to control counter-trade *and* to force Third World nations to liberalise their control of service sector items (i.e., computers, banking, insurance, internal shipping/transport, utilities). Obviously, nationalist less-developed nations have not greeted the prospects of the 'Reagan Round' with enthusiasm.

53. From the authors' viewpoint, only a massive infusion of new liquidity into the international system could slow the rapid spread of counter-trade. Without the rapid availability of credits to revive growth in less developed nations, the political, social, and economic costs of long-term IMF deflation will not be tolerable. The options are for:
    1) US dollar expansion
    2) Japanese Yen expansion
    3) British Pound Sterling expansion
    4) German DeutschMark expansion
    5) SDR expansion
    6) other multilateral agency expansions
    7) private commercial bank expansion
    8) direct foreign investment expansion.

    The governments of the top four alternatives are monetarist in orientation and have historical fears of runaway inflation to temper their enthusiasm for such re-inflation. The major industrial governments recently nixed a proposal to increase by $15 billion the present allocation of SDRs. In addition, the 'Big Four' have proposed and supported real cuts in financing for several multilateral agencies. And finally, the evidence from many sources, including the Bank for International Settlements, has amply documented the major reductions in net lending that is available to Third World nations from the commercial banking sector. Direct foreign investment has been lagging as well.

The prognosis on *all* of the available options for increased liquidity for less developed nations for the rest of the decade is not encouraging. As such, counter-trade truly is the 'only game in town'.

54. See in particular the objections made by Gary Banks (GATT Economist), Ed Barber (Treasury Department Economist), James Walsh (Commerce Department Economist) and Carmen Suro-Bredie (Office of US Trade Representative). These researchers have mainly utilised the neo-classical economic framework to analyse the pros and cons of counter-trade.

55. Stephen Cohen and John Zysman, 'The mercantilist challenge to the liberal international trade order,' Report presented to the 97th Congress, 2nd Session, Joint Economic Committee, 29 December 1982.

56. Leo G.B. Welt, *op. cit.,* p. 11; and *Business International.*

57. 'Special report: going under the counter', *op. cit.,* pp. 49–56.

58. It is important to note that many resource-poor and market-poor developing nations may *not* be able to benefit from the growing counter-trade alternative. Poorer nations with weak negotiating positions could find themselves by-passed by the 'only game in town'.

27

The Arms Race and Development: A Competitive Relationship

Inga Thorsson

THE SECRETARY-GENERAL'S REPORT ON DISARMAMENT AND DEVELOPMENT

In the Final Document of the 1978 Special Session on Disarmament, the General Assembly requested the Secretary-General, with the assistance of a group of experts, to prepare a study on the relationship between disarmament and development. An Expert Group was appointed and, under the able leadership of Inga Thorsson, held ten meetings between 1978 and 1981. The Expert Group was aided in its work by forty research reports which it was able to commission.

The Report of the Secretary-General on the "Study of the Relationship Between Disarmament and Development" was issued on October 5, 1981. The Secretary-General described the study as "an important attempt by the international community to thoroughly investigate the proposition that a balanced and generally acceptable pattern of economic and social development is inextricably related to disarmament". He continued, "The clear and widely shared understanding of this relationship may provide a basis for the formulation of practical measures by Governments that would both promote disarmament and further development". . . . We have presented here excerpts from Inga Thorsson's presentation of the Report in the 2nd Committee of the General Assembly.

Common sense alone tells us that military preparations are an economic burden. The arms race and development are to be viewed in a competitive

Reprinted from *Development* (1982):1, pp. 12–15, 20, the quarterly journal of the Society for International Development.

relationship, particularly in terms of resources. Or to put it another way: the arms race and underdevelopment are not two problems; they are one. They must be solved together, or neither will ever be solved.

It is a historical fact that governments have, over the past 30 years, spent vast resources on armaments, resources which—on grounds of morality, on grounds of equal human justice, on grounds of enlightened self-interest—ought to have been directed to ending world poverty and building for human and material development. In this way world armaments are among the causes of poverty and underdevelopment.

The 1972 U.N. study on this same theme concluded that disarmament and development "stand fundamentally apart". Taking their point of departure, this statement is still true. Ten years ago and, as duties of the industrialized countries went, development was simply equated with development assistance. But since then, the development discussion has been broadened to involve basic structural changes in all societies, within states and among states, including more equitable distribution of income, access to the means of production and greater participation by all groups in decision making, and progress towards the establishment of a New International Economic Order.

In the present study we have introduced a new conceptual framework, defined in a dynamic triangular interrelation between disarmament, development and security. We have taken a broader approach to the problem of security. In our era, national security can no longer be equated with military might. Even less can international security, i.e. security *for all,* do so. Also, we demonstrate that threats to security may be made and aggravated in many ways, including those that go far beyond purely military threats. It was recognized by the first Special Session on Disarmament that the arms race itself has become a threat to the security of nations. Thus, disarmament, particularly nuclear disarmament, would directly enhance security, and, therefore, prospects for development.

National security is not a goal in itself. Its ultimate purpose must be to secure the independence and sovereignty of the national state, the freedom of its citizens—freedom and the means to develop economically, socially and culturally, which defines exactly what we mean by "development". In today's world this can never be achieved by any state at the expense of others. In a world of interdependence, only through global, or international security, will it be possible to reach the objective of national security for the ultimate goal of freedom, well-being and human dignity for people throughout the world.

Today there is an array of intensifying non-military threats which aggravate the security problems of states. Such non-military threats can be described as:

- widespread reductions in prospects for economic growth;
- existing or impending ecological stresses, resource scarcities—notably in the field of energy and certain non-renewable raw materials—and a

growing world population. Today's stresses and constraints may translate into tomorrow's economic stresses and political conflicts;
- the morally unacceptable and politically hazardous polarization of wealth and poverty.

The appalling dimensions of poverty, the destruction of the environment, the accelerating race for arms and the resulting global economic malaise are largely problems of our own making. The Group states that it is well within our collective capabilities and within the earth's carrying capacity to provide for basic needs for the world's entire population, and to make progress towards a more equitable economic order, at a pace politically acceptable to all. The Group reaffirms that the arms race is incompatible with the objectives of a New International Economic Order. Of course, also in the future, economic growth is possible even with a continuing arms race, but it would be relatively slow, and very unevenly distributed both among and within regions of the world. We show, on the other hand, that a co-operative management of interdependence can be in the economic and security interests of all states. But the adoption or rather the evolution of such an outlook is quite improbable if the arms race continues.

It is imperative that non-military challenges to security are treated as non-military. If this is not recognized, if states fail to accept and persevere in tackling these challenges through voluntary measures and co-operation, there is a grave risk that the situation will deteriorate to the point of crisis where, even with a low probability of success, the use of military force could be seen as a way to produce results sufficiently quickly. This is far from being a remote possibility. In recent time there has been a marked and increasing tendency in international relations actually to use or threaten to use military force in response to non-military challenges, not only to "security", but also to the secure supply of goods and the well-being of the nations which face these challenges.

The study has documented that a least 50 million people are directly or indirectly engaged in military activities world-wide. This figure includes, *inter alia,* an estimated 500,000 qualified scientists and engineers engaged in research and development for military purposes.

Military research and development remains by far the largest single objective of scientific enquiry and technological development. Approximately 20 per cent of the world's qualified scientists and engineers were engaged in military work at a cost of around 35,000 million dollars in 1980, or approximately one-quarter of all expenditure on research and development. Virtually all this R and D takes place in the industrialized countries, 85 per cent in the USA and the USSR alone. Adding France and Britain would push this share above 90 per cent.

It stands to reason that even a modest reallocation to development objectives of the current capacity for military R and D could be expected to produce dramatic results in fields like resource conservation and the promotion of new patterns of development, better adapted to meeting the basic needs of ordinary people. This is, *inter alia* evident from the fact, which is also among our findings, that, on an average, a military product requires 20 times as much R and D resources as a civilian product.

The 1972 report on the subject identified more than 70 possible alternative uses. Our present investigations suggest, in more elaborated and detailed ways, for instance, that production workers in the military sector could quite easily transfer their skills to the development, production and installation of solar energy devices. Environment, housing and urban renewal are other areas likely to gain from the possible rechanneling of military R and D. New transport systems, particularly in urban areas, are sorely needed and have long been regarded as a major civilian alternative for the high technology industries in the military sector.

In purely financial terms, world-wide military expenditures by 1981 exceed, as we all know, the astounding level of 520,000 million dollars, representing 6 per cent of world output. Member States certainly realize that this amount is roughly equivalent to the value of all investible capital in all developing countries combined.

The effect on the economic and social spheres in our societies of the arms race extend far beyond the fact that 5 to 6 per cent of the world's resources are not available to help satisfy socially productive needs. The very fact that these resources are spent on armaments accentuates the inefficient allocation of the remaining 94 to 95 per cent, within and between nations. Three fundamental characteristics of the arms race reinforces this disallocation: *first,* the sheer magnitude of the volume of resources; *second,* the composition of expenditure, most particularly the stress on R and D, affecting investment and productivity in the civilian sector; and *third,* the fact that this massive effort has now been sustained for over thirty years.

As an illustration of the contribution which can be made by disarmament measures, even limited, to world development, one study submitted to the Group projects global economic prospects under three types of hypothetical scenarios, *viz.,* a continued arms race, an accelerated arms race, and modest disarmament measures involving the release of some resources for reallocation to the developing countries. Utilizing the United Nations input-output model of world economy it is calculated that an acceleration of the arms race would adversely affect global economic well-being in all but one of the regions of the world. A wealth of numerical data is presented in *chapter III* of the report. I will here highlight some general results. Besides the negative impact on per capita consumption, an accelerated arms race will also result in a decline of the world's stock of capital, reduce the value of non-military exports, and entail reductions in industrial employment in the poorest regions of the world.

In contrast, a scenario of even modest disarmament measures is shown to yield higher per capita consumption for different regions and in addition bring about a higher world GDP, a larger capital stock, a general increase in the agricultural output, to mention only a few of the obvious economic gains. Besides these global economic gains, a scenario of modest disarmament would also yield significant benefits for the poorest regions of the world. This conclusion is by itself of considerable significance when it is remembered that in many cases, increases in military outlays by industrial countries have been accompanied by a decline in their aid transfers, despite the repeated request for the fulfilment of the UN targets for official development assistance and despite the fact that existing volumes of assistance are grossly inadequate to meet the basic aid requirements for the poorer countries. The report shows that even a minor part of savings from modest disarmament has the potential of dramatically enhancing present levels of assistance.

We can make similar calculations for the past. For instance, if half the funds spent on armaments throughout the world from 1970 to 1975 had instead been invested in the civilian sector, it has been calculated[1] that annual output at the end of that period would have been 200,000 million dollars higher than it actually was—a figure in excess of the aggregate GNP of Southern Asia and the mid-African regions. And mark well, this growth would most likely have been achieved without any extra demand for investible resources.

Military outlays fall by definition into the category of consumption and not investment. As a consequence, steadily high or increasing military outlays tend to depress economic growth. This effect may be direct through displacement of investment, and indirect through constraints on productivity.

A study conducted in the late 1960s by Emile Benoit is much cited as showing that military outlays do not have negative effects on economic growth for developing countries. In reality Benoit's own conclusion was more modest.[2] He said:

> Thus we have been unable to establish whether the net growth effects of defence expenditures have been positive or not. On the basis of all the evidence we suspect that it has been positive for the countries in our sample, and at past levels of defence burden, but we have not been able to prove this.

This suspected positive relationship of Benoit's has been contested as spurious, since it was simultaneously correlated with other important socio-economic factors in the economies of those developing countries, particularly a high net inflow of foreign assistance. Based on today's level of research, it can now be confidently refuted. In our study we do recognize that the availability of unutilized and underutilized resources in developing countries may produce short-term results, suggesting a parallelism between high rates of growth and significant military spending, a situation which is, by the way, frequently associated with foreign dependence. In the long run, however, the totality of the socio-economic consequences of sizeable military outlays outweigh any immediate economic spinoffs into the civilian sector.

On the basis of the present report, and the research commissioned for it, we can confidently conclude that military budgets are deadend expenditures in all kinds of economies, be they market, centrally planned, or mixed; be they industrialized or developing. Military expenditures do *not* foster growth. Through their inflationary effects—thoroughly analysed in the study—and the general economic and political malaise to which they contribute, military spending *inhibits* the capital investment required for development. Through the drain on the most valuable research talents and funds, it *restrains* productivity gains and *distorts* growth in science and technology. The military sector is not a great provider of jobs. On the contrary it is shown that military spending is one of the least efficient kinds of public spending. It drains away funds that could relieve poverty and distress. The very nature of military spending heightens tensions, reduces security and underpins the system which makes even more arms necessary.

This study has in my view strengthened the economic and social case for the disarmament-development relationship by identifying military spending as an impediment to economic growth and social development and the arms race as an obstacle to the establishment of a New International Economic Order.

The Group has indicated the political and economic potentials of rationally imperative alternatives in suggesting that policies aimed at implementing the disarmament-development relationship are likely to broaden the base of East-West détente and put the North-South dialogue in a mutually advantageous frame of reference.

Its report should not be considered an individual project. I should like to express a hope for an effective follow-up process, to the benefit, first of all, of the billions of human beings inhabiting this world of ours.

NOTES

1. United Nations Disarmament Fact Sheet, No. 9, "Cost of the Arms Race", 1979.
2. Emile Benoit, *Defence and Economic Growth in Developing Countries,* Lexington Books, 1973, p. 4.

[The following are the recommendations from the report of the group of experts on disarmament and development.]

On the basis of its findings and conclusions, implicit in this entire report and more explicitly summarized above, the Group makes the following recommendations:

1. That all Governments, but particularly those of the major military Powers, should prepare assessments of the nature and magnitude of the short and long-term economic and social costs attributable to their military preparations so that their general public be informed of them.

2. That Governments urgently undertake studies to identify and to publicize the benefits that would be derived from the reallocation of military resources in a balanced and verifiable manner, to address economic and social problems at the national level and to contribute towards reducing the gap in income that currently divides the industrialized nations from the developing world and establishing a new international economic order.

3. A fuller and more systematic compilation and dissemination by Governments of data on the military use of human and material resources and military transfers.

4. That the disarmament-development perspective elaborated in this report be incorporated in a concrete and practical way in the ongoing activities of the United Nations system.

5. That Governments create the necessary prerequisites, including preparations and, where appropriate, planning, to facilitate the conversion of resources freed by disarmament measures to civilian purposes, especially to meet urgent economic and social needs, in particular, in the developing countries.

6. That Governments consider making the results of experiences and preparations in their respective countries available by submitting reports from time to time to the General Assembly on possible solutions to conversion problems.

7. That further consideration be given to establishing an international disarmament fund for development and that the administrative and technical modalities of such a fund be further investigated by the United Nations with due regard to the capabilities of the agencies and institutions currently responsible for the international transfer of resources.

8. That the Secretary-General take appropriate action, through the existing inter-agency consultative mechanism of the Administrative Committee on Coordination, to foster and coordinate the incorporation of the disarmament and development

perspective in the programmes and activities of the United Nations system.

9. That the Department of Public Information and other relevant United Nations organs and agencies, while continuing to emphasize the danger of war—particularly nuclear war—should give increased emphasis in their disarmament-related public information and education activities to the social and economic consequences of the arms race and to the corresponding benefits of disarmament.

28

Pedagogy of the Oppressed

Paulo Freire

While the problem of humanization has always, from an axiological point of view, been man's central problem, it now takes on the character of an inescapable concern.[1] Concern for humanization leads at once to the recognition of dehumanization, not only as an ontological possibility but as an historical reality. And as man perceives the extent of dehumanization, he asks himself if humanization is a viable possibility. Within history, in concrete, objective contexts, both humanization and dehumanization are possibilities for man as an uncompleted being conscious of his incompletion.

But while both humanization and dehumanization are real alternatives, only the first is man's vocation. This vocation is constantly negated, yet it is affirmed by that very negation. It is thwarted by injustice, exploitation, oppression, and the violence of the oppressors; it is affirmed by the yearning of the oppressed for freedom and justice, and by their struggle to recover their lost humanity.

Dehumanization, which marks not only those whose humanity has been stolen, but also (though in a different way) those who have stolen it, is a *distortion* of the vocation of becoming more fully human. This distortion occurs within history but it is not an historical vocation. Indeed, to admit of dehumanization as an historical vocation would lead either to cynicism or to total despair. The struggle for humanization, for the emancipation of labor, for the overcoming of alienation, for the affirmation of men as persons would be meaningless. This struggle is possible only because dehumanization, although a concrete historical fact, is *not* a given destiny but the result of an unjust order that engenders violence in the oppressors, which in turn dehumanizes the oppressed.

Because it is a distortion of being more fully human, sooner or later being less human leads the oppressed to struggle against those who made them so.

Reprinted from the author's *Pedagogy of the Oppressed,* translated by Myra Bergman Ramos (New York: Herder and Herder, 1970), pp. 29–56, by permission of the author and The Seabury Press. Copyright 1970 by Paulo Freire.

In order for this struggle to have meaning, the oppressed must not, in seeking to regain their humanity (which is a way to create it), become in turn oppressors of the oppressors, but rather restorers of the humanity of both.

This, then, is the great humanistic and historical task of the oppressed: to liberate themselves and their oppressors as well. The oppressors, who oppress, exploit, and rape by virtue of their power, cannot find in this power the strength to liberate either the oppressed or themselves. Only power that springs from the weakness of the oppressed will be sufficiently strong to free both. Any attempt to "soften" the power of the oppressor in deference to the weakness of the oppressed almost always manifests itself in the form of false generosity; indeed, the attempt never goes beyond this. In order to have the continued opportunity to express their "generosity," the oppressors must perpetuate injustice as well. An unjust social order is the permanent fount of this "generosity," which is nourished by death, despair, and poverty. This is why the dispensers of false generosity become desperate at the slightest threat to its source.

True generosity consists precisely in fighting to destroy the causes which nourish false charity. False charity constrains the fearful and subdued, the "rejects of life," to extend their trembling hands. True generosity lies in striving so that these hands—whether of individuals or entire peoples—need be extended less and less in supplication, so that more and more they become human hands which work and, working, transform the world.

This lesson and this apprenticeship must come, however, from the oppressed themselves and from those who are truly solidary with them. As individuals or as peoples, by fighting for the restoration of their humanity they will be attempting the restoration of true generosity. Who are better prepared than the oppressed to understand the terrible significance of an oppressive society? Who suffer the effects of oppression more than the oppressed? Who can better understand the necessity of liberation? They will not gain this liberation by chance but through the praxis of their quest for it, through their recognition of the necessity to fight for it. And this fight, because of the purpose given it by the oppressed, will actually constitute an act of love opposing the lovelessness which lies at the heart of the oppressors' violence, lovelessness even when clothed in false generosity.

But almost always, during the initial stage of the struggle, the oppressed, instead of striving for liberation, tend themselves to become oppressors, or "sub-oppressors." The very structure of their thought has been conditioned by the contradictions of the concrete, existential situation by which they were shaped. Their ideal is to be men; but for them, to be men is to be oppressors. This is their model of humanity. This phenomenon derives from the fact that the oppressed, at a certain moment of their existential experience, adopt an attitude of "adhesion" to the oppressor. Under these circumstances they cannot "consider" him sufficiently clearly to objectivize him—to discover him "outside" themselves. This does not necessarily mean that the oppressed are unaware that they are downtrodden. But their perception of themselves as oppressed is impaired by their submersion in the reality of oppression. At this level, their perception of themselves as opposites of the oppressor does not yet signify engagement in a struggle to overcome the contradiction,[2] the one pole aspires not to liberation, but to identification with its opposite pole.

In this situation the oppressed do not see the "new man" as the man to be born from the resolution of this contradiction, as oppression gives way to liberation. For them, the new man is themselves become oppressors. Their vision of the new man is individualistic; because of their identification with the oppressor, they have no consciousness of themselves as persons or as members of an oppressed class. It is not to become free men that they want agrarian reform, but in order to acquire land and thus become landowners— or, more precisely, bosses over other workers. It is a rare peasant who, once "promoted" to overseer, does not become more of a tyrant towards his former comrades than the owner himself. This is because the context of the peasant's situation, that is, oppression, remains unchanged. In this example, the over- seer, in order to make sure of his job, must be as tough as the owner—and more so. Thus is illustrated our previous assertion that during the initial stage of their struggle the oppressed find in the oppressor their model of "man- hood."

Even revolution, which transforms a concrete situation of oppression by establishing the process of liberation, must confront this phenomenon. Many of the oppressed who directly or indirectly participate in revolution intend— conditioned by the myths of the old order—to make it their private revolu- tion. The shadow of their former oppressor is still cast over them.

The "fear of freedom" which afflicts the oppressed,[3] a fear which may equally well lead them to desire the role of oppressor or bind them to the role of oppressed, should be examined. One of the basic elements of the relation- ship between oppressor and oppressed is *prescription*. Every prescription repre- sents the imposition of one man's choice upon another, transforming the consciousness of the man prescribed to into one that conforms with the prescriber's consciousness. Thus, the behavior of the oppressed is a prescribed behavior, following as it does the guidelines of the oppressor.

The oppressed, having internalized the image of the oppressor and adopted his guidelines, are fearful of freedom. Freedom would require them to eject this image and replace it with autonomy and responsibility. Freedom is acquired by conquest, not by gift. It must be pursued constantly and responsibly. Freedom is not an ideal located outside of man; nor is it an idea which becomes myth. It is rather the indispensable condition for the quest for human completion.

To surmount the situation of oppression, men must first critically recog- nize its causes, so that through transforming action they can create a new situation, one which makes possible the pursuit of a fuller humanity. But the struggle to be more fully human has already begun in the authentic struggle to transform the situation. Although the situation of oppression is a dehumanized and dehumanizing totality affecting both the oppressors and those whom they oppress, it is the latter who must, from their stifled humanity, wage for both the struggle for a fuller humanity; the oppressor, who is himself dehumanized because he dehumanizes others, is unable to lead this struggle.

However, the oppressed, who have adapted to the structure of domination in which they are immersed, and have become resigned to it, are inhibited from waging the struggle for freedom so long as they feel incapable of running the risks it requires. Moreover, their struggle for freedom threatens not only the oppressor, but also their own oppressed comrades who are fearful of still greater repression. When they discover within themselves the yearning to be free, they perceive that this yearning can be transformed into reality only when the same yearning is aroused in their comrades. But while dominated by the fear of freedom they refuse to appeal to others, or to listen to the appeals of others, or even to the appeals of their own conscience. They prefer gregariousness to authentic comradeship; they prefer the security of conformity with their state of unfreedom to the creative communion produced by freedom and even the very pursuit of freedom.

The oppressed suffer from the duality which has established itself in their innermost being. They discover that without freedom they cannot exist authentically. Yet, although they desire authentic existence, they fear it. They are at one and the same time themselves and the oppressor whose consciousness they have internalized. The conflict lies in the choice between being wholly themselves or being divided; between ejecting the oppressor within or not ejecting him; between human solidarity or alienation; between following prescriptions or having choices; between being spectators or actors; between acting or having the illusion of acting through the action of the oppressors; between speaking out or being silent, castrated in their power to create and re-create, in their power to transform the world. This is the tragic dilemma of the oppressed which their education must take into account.

[This paper] will present some aspects of what the writer has termed the pedagogy of the oppressed, a pedagogy which must be forged *with*, not *for*, the oppressed (whether individuals or peoples) in the incessant struggle to regain their humanity. This pedagogy makes oppression and its causes objects of reflection by the oppressed, and from that reflection will come their necessary engagement in the struggle for their liberation. And in the struggle this pedagogy will be made and remade.

The central problem is this: How can the oppressed, as divided, unauthentic beings, participate in developing the pedagogy of their liberation? Only as they discover themselves to be "hosts" of the oppressor can they contribute to the midwifery of their liberating pedagogy. As long as they live in the duality in which *to be* is *to be like*, and *to be like* is *to be like the oppressor*, this contribution is impossible. The pedagogy of the oppressed is an instrument for their critical discovery that both they and their oppressors are manifestations of dehumanization.

Liberation is thus a childbirth, and a painful one. The man who emerges is a new man, viable only as the oppressor-oppressed contradiction is superseded by the humanization of all men. Or to put it another way, the solution of this contradiction is born in the labor which brings into the world this new man: no longer oppressor nor longer oppressed, but man in the process of achieving freedom.

This solution cannot be achieved in idealistic terms. In order for the oppressed to be able to wage the struggle for their liberation, they must perceive the reality of oppression not as a closed world from which there is no exit, but as a limiting situation which they can transform. This perception is a necessary but not a sufficient condition for liberation; it must become the motivating force for liberating action. Nor does the discovery by the oppressed that they exist in dialectical relationship to the oppressor, as his antithesis—that without them the oppressor could not exist[4]—in itself constitute liberation. The oppressed can overcome the contradiction in which they are caught only when this perception enlists them in the struggle to free themselves.

The same is true with respect to the individual oppressor as a person. Discovering himself to be an oppressor may cause considerable anguish, but it does not necessarily lead to solidarity with the oppressed. Rationalizing his guilt through paternalistic treatment of the oppressed, all the while holding them fast in a position of dependence, will not do. Solidarity requires that one enter into the situation of those with whom one is solidary; it is a radical posture. If what characterizes the oppressed is their subordination to the consciousness of the master, as Hegel affirms,[5] true solidarity with the oppressed means fighting at their side to transform the objective reality which has made them these "beings for another." The oppressor is solidary with the oppressed only when he stops regarding the oppressed as an abstract category and sees them as persons who have been unjustly dealt with, deprived of their voice, cheated in the sale of their labor—when he stops making pious, sentimental, and individualistic gestures and risks an act of love. True solidarity is found only in the plenitude of this act of love, in its existentiality, in its praxis. To affirm that men are persons and as persons should be free and yet to do nothing tangible to make this affirmation a reality is a farce.

Since it is in a concrete situation that the oppressor-oppressed contradiction is established, the resolution of this contradiction must be *objectively* verifiable. Hence, the radical requirement—both for the man who discovers himself to be an oppressor and for the oppressed—that the concrete situation which begets oppression must be transformed.

To present this radical demand for the objective transformation of reality, to combat subjectivist immobility which would divert the recognition of oppression into patient waiting for oppression to disappear by itself, is not to dismiss the role of subjectivity in the struggle to change structures. On the contrary, one cannot conceive of objectivity without subjectivity. Neither can exist without the other, nor can they be dichotomized. The separation of objectivity from subjectivity, the denial of the latter when analyzing reality or acting upon it, is objectivism. On the other hand, the denial of objectivity in analysis or action, resulting in a subjectivism which leads to solipsistic positions, denies action itself by denying objective reality. Neither objectivism nor subjectivism, nor yet psychologism is propounded here, but rather subjectivity and objectivity in constant dialectical relationship.

To deny the importance of subjectivity in the process of transforming the world and history is naïve and simplistic. It is to admit the impossible: a world without men. This objectivistic position is as ingenuous as that of subjectivism, which postulates men without a world. World and men do not exist apart from each other, they exist in constant interaction. Marx does not espouse such a dichotomy, nor does any other critical, realistic thinker. What Marx criticized and scientifically destroyed was not subjectivity, but subjectivism and psychologism. Just as objective social reality exists not by chance, but as the product of human action, so it is not transformed by chance. If men produce social reality (which in the "inversion of the praxis" turns back upon them and conditions them), then transforming that reality is an historical task, a task for men.

Reality which becomes oppressive results in the contradistinction of men as oppressors and oppressed. The latter, whose task it is to struggle for their liberation together with those who show true solidarity, must acquire a critical awareness of oppression through the praxis of this struggle. One of the gravest obstacles to the achievement of liberation is that oppressive reality absorbs those within it and thereby acts to submerge men's consciousness. Functionally, oppression is domesticating. To no longer be prey to its force, one must emerge from it and turn upon it. This can be done only be means of the praxis: reflection and action upon the world in order to transform it.

Making "real oppression more oppressive still by adding to it the realization of oppression" corresponds to the dialectical relation between the subjective and the objective. Only in this interdependence is an authentic praxis possible, without which it is impossible to resolve the oppressor-oppressed contradiction. To achieve this goal, the oppressed must confront reality critically, simultaneously objectifying and acting upon that reality. A mere perception of reality not followed by this critical intervention will not lead to a transformation of objective reality—precisely because it is not a true perception. This is the case of a purely subjectivist perception by someone who forsakes objective reality and creates a false substitute.

A different type of false perception occurs when a change in objective reality would threaten the individual or class interests of the perceiver. In the first instance, there is no critical intervention in reality because that reality is fictitious; there is none in the second instance because intervention would contradict the class interests of the perceiver. In the latter case the tendency of the perceiver is to behave "neurotically." The fact exists; but both the fact and what may result from it may be prejudicial to him. Thus it becomes necessary, not precisely to deny the fact, but to "see it differently." This rationalization as a defense mechanism coincides in the end with subjectivism. A fact which is not denied but whose truths are rationalized loses its objective base. It ceases to be concrete and becomes a myth created in defense of the class of the perceiver.

Herein lies one of the reasons for the prohibitions and the difficulties . . . designed to dissuade the people from critical intervention in reality. The oppressor knows full well that this intervention would not be to his interest. What *is* to his interest is for the people to continue in a state of submersion, impotent in the face of oppressive reality. . . . "To explain to the masses their own action" is to clarify and illuminate that action, both regarding its relationship of the objective facts by which it was prompted, and regarding its purposes. The more the people unveil this challenging reality which is to be the object of their transforming action, the more critically they enter that reality. In this way they are "consciously activating the subsequent development of their experiences." There would be no human action if there were no objective reality, no world to be the "not I" of man and to challenge him; just as there would be no human action if man were not a "project," if he were not able to transcend himself, to perceive his reality and understand it in order to transform it.

In dialectical thought, word and action are intimately interdependent. But action is human only when it is not merely an occupation but also a preoccupation, that is, when it is not dichotomized from reflection. Reflection, which is essential to action, is implicit in Lukács' requirement of "explaining to the masses their own action," just as it is implicit in the purpose he attributes to this explanation: that of "consciously activating the subsequent development of experience."

For us, however, the requirement is seen not in terms of explaining to, but rather dialoguing with the people about their actions. In any event, no reality transforms itself,[6] and the duty which Lukács ascribes to the revolutionary party of "explaining to the masses their own action" coincides with our affirmation of the need for the critical intervention of the people in reality through the praxis. The pedagogy of the oppressed, which is the pedagogy of men engaged in the fight for their own liberation, has its roots here. And those who recognize, or begin to recognize, themselves as oppressed must be among the developers of this pedagogy. No pedagogy which is truly liberating can remain distant from the oppressed by treating them as unfortunates and by presenting for their emulation models from among the oppressors. The oppressed must be their own example in the struggle for their redemption.

The pedagogy of the oppressed, animated by authentic, humanist (not humanitarian) generosity, presents itself as a pedagogy of man. Pedagogy which begins with the egoistic interests of the oppressors (an egoism cloaked in the false generosity of paternalism) and makes of the oppressed the objects of its humanitarianism, itself maintains and embodies oppression. It is an instrument of dehumanization. This is why, as we affirmed earlier, the pedagogy of the oppressed cannot be developed or practiced by the oppressors. It would be a contradiction in terms if the oppressors not only defended but actually implemented a liberating education.

· · · · · ·

The pedagogy of the oppressed, as a humanist and libertarian pedagogy, has two distinct stages. In the first, the oppressed unveil the world of oppression and through the praxis commit themselves to its transformation. In the second stage, in which the reality of oppression has already been transformed, this pedagogy ceases to belong to the oppressed and becomes a pedagogy of all men in the process of permanent liberation. In both stages, it is always through action in depth that the culture of domination is culturally confronted.[7] In the first stage this confrontation occurs through the change in the way the oppressed perceive the world of oppression; in the second stage, through the expulsion of the myths created and developed in the old order, which like specters haunt the new structure emerging from the revolutionary transformation.

The pedagogy of the first stage must deal with the problem of the oppressed consciousness and the oppressor consciousness, the problem of men who oppress and men who suffer oppression. It must take into account their behavior, their view of the world, and their ethics. A particular problem is the duality of the oppressed: they are contradictory, divided beings, shaped by and existing in a concrete situation of oppression and violence.

Any situation in which "A" objectively exploits "B" or hinders his pursuit of self-affirmation as a responsible person is one of oppression. Such a situation in itself constitutes violence, even when sweetened by false generosity, because it interferes with man's ontological and historical vocation to be more fully human. With the establishment of a relationship of oppression, violence has *already* begun. Never in history has violence been initiated by the oppressed. How could they be the initiators, if they themselves are the result of violence? How could they be the sponsors of something whose objective inauguration called forth their existence as oppressed? There would be no oppressed had there been no prior situation of violence to establish their subjugation.

Violence is initiated by those who oppress, who exploit, who fail to recognize others as persons—not by those who are oppressed, exploited, and unrecognized. It is not the unloved who initiate disaffection, but those who cannot love because they love only themselves. It is not the helpless, subject to terror, who initiate terror, but the violent, who with their power create the concrete situation which begets the "rejects of life." It is not the tyrannized who initiate despotism, but the tyrants. It is not the despised who initiate hatred, but those who despise. It is not those whose humanity is denied them who negate man, but those who denied that humanity (thus negating their own as well). Force is used not by those who have become weak under the preponderance of the strong, but by the strong who have emasculated them.

For the oppressors, however, it is always the oppressed (whom they obviously never call "the oppressed" but—depending on whether they are fellow countrymen or not—"those people" or "the blind and envious masses" or "savages" or "natives" or "subversives") who are disaffected, who are "violent," "barbaric," "wicked," or "ferocious" when they react to the violence of the oppressors.

Yet it is—paradoxical though it may seem—precisely in the response of the oppressed to the violence of their oppressors that a gesture of love may be found. Consciously or unconsciously, the act of rebellion by the oppressed (an act which is always, or nearly always, as violent as the initial violence of the oppressors) can initiate love. Whereas the violence of the oppressors prevents the oppressed from being fully human, the response of the latter to this violence is grounded in the desire to pursue the right to be human. As the oppressors dehumanize others and violate their rights, they themselves also become dehumanized. As the oppressed, fighting to be human, take away the oppressors' power to dominate and suppress, they restore to the oppressors the humanity they had lost in the exercise of oppression.

It is only the oppressed who, by freeing themselves, can free their oppressors. The latter, as an oppressive class, can free neither others nor themselves. It is therefore essential that the oppressed wage the struggle to resolve the contradiction in which they are caught; and the contradiction will be resolved by the appearance of the new man: neither oppressor nor oppressed, but man in the process of liberation. If the goal of the oppressed is to become fully human, they will not achieve their goal by merely reversing the terms of the contradiction, by simply changing poles.

This may seem simplistic; it is not. Resolution of the oppressor-oppressed contradiction indeed implies the disappearance of the oppressors as a dominant class. However, the restraints imposed by the former oppressed on their oppressors, so that the latter cannot reassume their former position, do not constitute *oppression*. An act is oppressive only when it prevents men from being more fully human. Accordingly, these necessary restraints do not *in themselves* signify that yesterday's oppressed have become today's oppressors. Acts which prevent the restoration of the oppressive regime cannot be compared with those which create and maintain it, cannot be compared with those by which a few men deny the majority their right to be human.

However, the moment the new regime hardens into a dominating "bureaucracy"[8] the humanist dimension of the struggle is lost and it is no longer possible to speak of liberation. Hence our insistence that the authentic solution of the oppressor-oppressed contradiction does not lie in a mere reversal of position, in moving from one pole to the other. Nor does it lie in the replacement of the former oppressors with new ones who continue to subjugate the oppressed—all in the name of their liberation.

But even when the contradiction is resolved authentically by a new situation established by the liberated laborers, the former oppressors do not feel liberated. On the contrary, they genuinely consider themselves to be oppressed. Conditioned by the experience of oppressing others, any situation other than their former seems to them like oppression. Formerly, they could eat, dress, wear shoes, be educated, travel, and hear Beethoven; while millions did not eat, had no clothes or shoes, neither studied nor traveled, much less listened to Beethoven. Any restriction on this way of life, in the name of the rights of the community, appears to the former oppressors as a profound violation of their individual rights—although they had no respect for the millions who suffered and died of hunger, pain, sorrow, and despair. For the oppressors, "human beings" refer only to themselves; other people are "things." For the oppressors, there exists only one right: their right to live in peace, over against the right, not always even recognized, but simply conceded, of the oppressed to survival. And they make this concession only because the existence of the oppressed is necessary to their own existence.

This behavior, this way of understanding the world and men (which necessarily makes the oppressors resist the installation of a new regime) is explained by their experience as a dominant class. Once a situation of violence and oppression has been established, it engenders an entire way of life and behavior for those caught up in it—oppressors and oppressed alike. Both are submerged in this situation, and both bear the marks of oppression. Analysis of existential situations of oppression reveals that their inception lay in an act of violence—initiated by those with power. This violence, as a process, is perpetuated from generation to generation of oppressors, who become its heirs and are shaped in its climate. This climate creates in the oppressor a strongly possessive consciousness—possessive of the world and of men. Apart from direct, concrete, material possession of the world and of men, the oppressor consciousness could not understand itself—could not even exist. Fromm said of this consciousness that, without such possession, "it would lose contact with the world." The oppressor consciousness tends to transform everything surrounding it into an object of its domination. The earth, property, production, the creations of men, men themselves, time—everything is reduced to the status of objects at its disposal.

In their unrestrained eagerness to possess, the oppressors develop the conviction that it is possible for them to transform everything into objects of their purchasing power; hence their strictly materialistic concept of existence. Money is the measure of all things, and profit the primary goal. For the oppressors, what is worthwhile is to have more—always more—even at the cost of the oppressed having less or having nothing. For them, *to be* is *to have* and to be the class of the "haves."

As beneficiaries of a situation of oppression, the oppressors cannot perceive that if *having* is a condition of *being*, it is a necessary condition for all men. This is why their generosity is false. Humanity is a "thing," and they possess it as an exclusive right, as inherited property. To the oppressor consciousness, the humanization of the "others," of the people, appears not as the pursuit of full humanity, but as subversion.

The oppressors do not perceive their monopoly on *having more* as a privilege which dehumanizes others and themselves. They cannot see that, in the egoistic pursuit of *having* as a possessing class, they suffocate in their own possessions and no longer *are*; they merely *have*. For them, *having more* is an inalienable right, a right they acquired through their own "effort," with their "courage to take risks." If others do not have more, it is because they are incompetent and lazy, and worst of all is their unjustifiable ingratitude towards the "generous gestures" of the dominant class. Precisely because they are "ungrateful" and "envious," the oppressed are regarded as potential enemies who must be watched.

It could not be otherwise. If the humanization of the oppressed signifies subversion, so also does their freedom; hence the necessity for constant control. And the more the oppressors control the oppressed, the more they change them into apparently inanimate "things." This tendency of the oppressor consciousness to "in-animate" everything and everyone it encounters, in its eagerness to possess, unquestionably corresponds with a tendency to sadism.

> The pleasure in complete domination over another person (or other animate creature) is the very essence of the sadistic drive. Another way of formulating the same thought is to say that the aim of sadism is to transform a man into a thing, something animate into something inanimate, since by complete and absolute control the living loses one essential quality of life—freedom.[9]

Sadistic love is a perverted love—a love of death, not of life. One of the characteristics of the oppressor consciousness and its necrophilic view of the world is thus sadism. As the oppressor consciousness, in order to dominate, tries to deter the drive to search, the restlessness, and the creative power which characterize life, it kills life. More and more, the oppressors are using science and technology as unquestionably powerful instruments for their purpose: the maintenance of the oppressive order through manipulation and repression.[10] The oppressed, as objects, as "things," have no purposes except those their oppressors prescribe for them.

Given the preceding context, another issue of indubitable importance arises: the fact that certain members of the oppressor class join the oppressed in their struggle for liberation, thus moving from one pole of the contradiction to the other. Theirs is a fundamental role, and has been so throughout the history of this struggle. It happens, however, that as they cease to be exploiters or indifferent spectators or simply the heirs of exploitation and move to the side of the exploited, they almost always bring with them the marks of their origin: their prejudices and their deformations, which include a lack of confidence in the people's ability to think, to want, and to know. Accordingly, these adherents to the people's cause constantly run the risk of falling into a type of generosity as malefic as that of the oppressors. The generosity of the oppressors is nourished by an unjust order, which must be maintained in order to justify that generosity. Our converts, on the other hand, truly desire to transform the unjust order; but because of their background they believe that they must be the executors of the transformation. They talk about the people, but they do not trust them; and trusting the people is the indispensable precondition for revolutionary change. A real humanist can be identified more by his trust in the people, which engages him in their struggle, than by a thousand actions in their favor without that trust.

Those who authentically commit themselves to the people must reexamine themselves constantly. This conversion is so radical as not to allow of ambiguous behavior. To affirm this commitment but to consider oneself the proprietor of revolutionary wisdom—which must then be given to (or imposed on) the people—is to retain the old ways. The man who proclaims devotion to the cause of liberation yet is unable to enter into *communion* with the people, whom he continues to regard as totally ignorant, is grievously self-deceived. The convert who approaches the people but feels alarm at each step they take, each doubt they express, and each suggestion they offer, and attempts to impose his "status," remains nostalgic towards his origins.

Conversion to the people requires a profound rebirth. Those who undergo it must take on a new form of existence; they can no longer remain as they were. Only through comradeship with the oppressed can the converts understand their characteristic ways of living and behaving, which in diverse moments reflect the structure of domination. One of these characteristics is the previously mentioned existential duality of the oppressed, who are at the same time themselves and the oppressor whose image they have internalized. Accordingly, until they concretely "discover" their oppressor and in turn their own consciousness, they nearly always express fatalistic attitudes towards their situation.

> The peasant begins to get courage to overcome his dependence when he realizes that he is dependent. Until then, he goes along with the boss and says "What can I do? I'm only a peasant."[11]

When superficially analyzed, this fatalism is sometimes interpreted as a docility that is a trait of national character. Fatalism in the guise of docility is the fruit of an historical and sociological situation, not an essential characteristic of a people's behavior. It almost always is related to the power of destiny or fate or fortune—inevitable forces—or to a distorted view of God. Under the sway of magic and myth, the oppressed (especially the peasants, who are almost submerged in nature)[12] see their suffering, the fruit of exploitation, as the will of God—as if God were the creator of this "organized disorder."

Submerged in reality, the oppressed cannot perceive clearly the "order" which serves the interests of the oppressors whose image they have internalized. Chafing under the restrictions of this order, they often manifest a type of horizontal violence, striking out at their own comrades for the pettiest reasons.

> The colonized man will first manifest this aggressiveness which has been deposited in his bones against his own people. This is the period when the niggers beat each other up, and the police and magistrates do not know which way to turn when faced with the astonishing waves of crime in North Africa. . . . While the settler or the policeman has the right the livelong day to strike the native, to insult him and to make him crawl to them, you will see the native reaching for his knife at the slightest hostile or aggressive glance cast on him by another native; for the last resort of the native is to defend his personality vis-à-vis his brother.[13]

It is possible that in this behavior they are once more manifesting their duality. Because the oppressor exists within their oppressed comrades, when they attack those comrades they are indirectly attacking the oppressor as well.

On the other hand, at a certain point in their existential experience the oppressed feel an irresistible attraction towards the oppressor and his way of life. Sharing this way of life becomes an overpowering aspiration. In their alienation, the oppressed want at any cost to resemble the oppressor, to imitate him, to follow him. This phenomenon is especially prevalent in the middle-class oppressed, who yearn to be equal to the "eminent" men of the upper class. Albert Memmi, in an exceptional analysis of the "colonized mentality," refers to the contempt he felt towards the colonizer, mixed with "passionate" attraction towards him.

> How could the colonizer look after his workers while periodically gunning down a crowd of colonized? How could the colonized deny himself so cruelly yet make such excessive demands? How could he hate the colonizers and yet admire them so passionately? (I too felt this admiration in spite of myself.)[14]

Self-depreciation is another characteristic of the oppressed, which derives from their internalization of the opinion the oppressors hold of them. So often do they hear that they are good for nothing, know nothing and are incapable of learning anything—that they are sick, lazy, and unproductive—that in the end they become convinced of their own unfitness.

> The peasant feels inferior to the boss because the boss seems to be the only one who knows things and is able to run things.[15]

They call themselves ignorant and say the "professor" is the one who has knowledge and to whom they should listen. The criteria of knowledge imposed upon them are the conventional ones. "Why don't you," said a peasant participating in a culture circle, "explain the pictures first? That way it'll take less time and won't give us a headache."

Almost never do they realize that they, too, "know things" they have learned in their relations with the world and with other men. Given the circumstances which have produced their duality, it is only natural that they distrust themselves.

Not infrequently, peasants in educational projects begin to discuss a generative theme in a lively manner, then stop suddenly and say to the educator: "Excuse us, we ought to keep quiet and let you talk. You are the one who knows, we don't know anything." They often insist that there is no difference between them and the animals; when they do admit a difference, it favors the animals. "They are freer than we are."

It is striking, however, to observe how this self-depreciation changes with the first changes in the situation of oppression. I heard a peasant leader say in an *asentamiento*[16] meeting, "They used to say we were unproductive because we were lazy and drunkards. All lies. Now that we are respected as men, we're going to show everyone that we were never drunkards or lazy. We were exploited!"

As long as their ambiguity persists, the oppressed are reluctant to resist, and totally lack confidence in themselves. They have a diffuse, magical belief in the invulnerability and power of the oppressor.[17] The magical force of the landowner's power holds particular sway in the rural areas. A sociologist friend of mine tells of a group of armed peasants in a Latin American country who recently took over a latifundium. For tactical reasons, they planned to hold the landowner as a hostage. But not one peasant had the courage to guard him; his very presence was terrifying. It is also possible that the act of opposing the boss provoked guilt feelings. In truth, the boss was "inside" them.

The oppressed must see examples of the vulnerability of the oppressor so that a contrary conviction can begin to grow within them. Until this occurs, they will continue disheartened, fearful, and beaten.[18] As long as the oppressed remain unaware of the causes of their condition, they fatalistically "accept" their exploitation. Further, they are apt to react in a passive and alienated manner when confronted with the necessity to struggle for their freedom and self-affirmation. Little by little, however, they tend to try out forms of rebellious action. In working towards liberation, one must neither lose sight of this passivity nor overlook the moment of awakening.

Within their unauthentic view of the world and of themselves, the oppressed feel like "things" owned by the oppressor. For the latter, to be is to have, almost always at the expense of those who have nothing. For the oppressed, at a certain point in their existential experience, to be is not to resemble the oppressor, but to be under him, to depend on him. Accordingly, the oppressed are emotionally dependent.

> The peasant is a dependent. He can't say what he wants. Before he discovers his dependence, he suffers. He lets off steam at home, where he shouts at his children, beats them, and despairs. He complains about his wife and thinks everything is dreadful. He doesn't let off steam with the boss because he thinks the boss is a superior being. Lots of times, the peasant gives vent to his sorrows by drinking.[19]

This total emotional dependence can lead the oppressed to what Fromm calls necrophilic behavior: the destruction of life—their own or that of their oppressed fellows.

It is only when the oppressed find the oppressor out and become involved in the organized struggle for their liberation that they begin to believe in themselves. This discovery cannot be purely intellectual but must involve action; nor can it be limited to mere activism, but must include serious reflection: only then will it be a praxis.

Critical and liberating dialogue, which presupposes action, must be carried on with the oppressed at whatever the stage of their struggle for liberation.[20] The content of that dialogue can and should vary in accordance with historical conditions and the level at which the oppressed perceive reality. But to substitute monologue, slogans, and communiqués for dialogue is to attempt to liberate the oppressed with the instruments of domestication. Attempting to liberate the oppressed without their reflective participation in the act of liberation is to treat them as objects which must be saved from a burning building; it is to lead them into the populist pitfall and transform them into masses which can be manipulated.

At all stages of their liberation, the oppressed must see themselves as men engaged in the ontological and historical vocation of becoming more fully human. Reflection and action become imperative when one does not erroneously attempt to dichotomize the content of humanity from its historical forms.

The insistence that the oppressed engage in reflection on their concrete situation is not a call to armchair revolution. On the contrary, reflection—true reflection—leads to action. On the other hand, when the situation calls for action, that action will constitute an authentic praxis only if its consequences become the object of critical reflection. In this sense, the praxis is the new

raison d'être of the oppressed; and the revolution, which inaugurates the historical moment of this *raison d'être,* is not viable apart from their concomitant
conscious involvement. Otherwise, action is pure activism.

To achieve this praxis, however, it is necessary to trust in the oppressed
and in their ability to reason. Whoever lacks this trust will fail to initiate (or
will abandon) dialogue, reflection, and communication, and will fall into
using slogans, communiqués, monologues, and instructions. Superficial con-
versions to the cause of liberation carry this danger.

Political action on the side of the oppressed must be pedagogical action
in the authentic sense of the word, and, therefore, action *with* the oppressed.
Those who work for liberation must not take advantage of the emotional
dependence of the oppressed—dependence that is the fruit of the concrete
situation of domination which surrounds them and which engendered their
unauthentic view of the world. Using their dependence to create still greater
dependence is an oppressor tactic.

Libertarian action must recognize this dependence as a weak point and
must attempt through reflection and action to transform it into independence.
However, not even the best-intentioned leadership can bestow independence
as a gift. The liberation of the oppressed is a liberation of men, not things.
Accordingly, while no one liberates himself by his own efforts alone, neither
is he liberated by others. Liberation, a human phenomenon, cannot be
achieved by semihumans. Any attempt to treat men as semihumans only
dehumanizes them. When men are already dehumanized, due to the oppression they suffer, the process of their liberation must not employ the methods
of dehumanization.

The correct method for a revolutionary leadership to employ in the task
of liberation is, therefore, *not* "libertarian propaganda." Nor can the leadership merely "implant" in the oppressed a belief in freedom, thus thinking to
win their trust. The correct method lies in dialogue. The conviction of the
oppressed that they must fight for their liberation is not a gift bestowed by
the revolutionary leadership, but the result of their own *conscientização.* *

The revolutionary leaders must realize that their own conviction of the
necessity for struggle (an indispensable dimension of revolutionary wisdom)
was not given to them by anyone else—if it is authentic. This conviction
cannot be packaged and sold; it is reached, rather, by means of a totality of
reflection and action. Only the leaders' own involvement in reality, within
an historical situation, led them to criticize this situation and to wish to
change it.

Likewise, the oppressed (who do not commit themselves to the struggle
unless they are convinced, and who, if they do not make such a commitment,

---

*The term *conscientização* refers to learning to perceive social, political, and economic contradictions, and to take action against the oppressive elements of reality.—Ed.

withhold the indispensable conditions for this struggle) must reach this conviction as Subjects, not as Objects. They also must intervene critically in the situation which surrounds them and whose mark they bear; propaganda cannot achieve this. While the conviction of the necessity for struggle (without which the struggle is unfeasible) is indispensable to the revolutionary leadership (indeed, it was this conviction which constituted that leadership), it is also necessary for the oppressed. It is necessary, that is, unless one intends to carry out the transformation *for* the oppressed rather than *with* them. It is my belief that only the latter form of transformation is valid.

The object in presenting these considerations is to defend the eminently pedagogical character of the revolution. The revolutionary leaders of every epoch who have affirmed that the oppressed must accept the struggle for their liberation—an obvious point—have also thereby implicitly recognized the pedagogical aspect of this struggle. Many of these leaders, however (perhaps due to natural and understandable biases against pedagogy), have ended up using the "educational" methods employed by the oppressor. They deny pedagogical action in the liberation process, but they use propaganda to convince.

It is essential for the oppressed to realize that when they accept the struggle for humanization they also accept, from that moment, their total responsibility for the struggle. They must realize that they are fighting not merely for freedom from hunger, but for

> . . . freedom to create and to construct, to wonder and to venture. Such freedom requires that the individual be active and responsible, not a slave or a well-fed cog in the machine. . . . It is not enough that men are not slaves; if social conditions further the existence of automatons, the result will not be love of life, but love of death.[21]

The oppressed, who have been shaped by the death-affirming climate of oppression, must find through their struggle the way to life-affirming humanization, which does not life *simply* in having more to eat (although it does involve having more to eat and cannot fail to include this aspect). The oppressed have been destroyed precisely because their situation has reduced them to things. In order to regain their humanity they must cease to be things and fight as men. This is a radical requirement. They cannot enter the struggle as objects in order *later* to become men.

The struggle begins with men's recognition that they have been destroyed. Propaganda, management, manipulation—all arms of domination—cannot be the instruments of their rehumanization. The only effective instrument is a humanizing pedagogy in which the revolutionary leadership establishes a permanent relationship of dialogue with the oppressed. In a humanizing pedagogy the method ceases to be an instrument by which the teachers (in this instance, the revolutionary leadership) can manipulate the students (in this instance, the oppressed), because it expresses the consciousness of the students themselves.

> The method is, in fact, the external form of consciousness manifest in acts, which takes on the fundamental property of consciousness—its intentionality. The essence of consciousness is being with the world, and this behavior is permanent and unavoidable. Accordingly, consciousness is in essence a "way towards" something apart from itself, outside itself, which surrounds it and which it apprehends by means of its ideational capacity. Consciousness is thus by definition a method, in the most general sense of the word.[22]

A revolutionary leadership must accordingly practice *co-intentional* education. Teachers and students (leadership and people), co-intent on reality, are both Subjects, not only in the task of unveiling that reality, and thereby coming to know it critically, but in the task of re-creating that knowledge. As they attain this knowledge of reality through common reflection and action, they discover themselves as its permanent re-creators. In this way, the presence of the oppressed in the struggle for their liberation will be what it should be: not pseudo-participation, but committed involvement.

NOTES

1. The current movements of rebellion, especially those of youth, while they necessarily reflect the peculiarities of their respective settings, manifest in their essence this preoccupation with man and men as beings in the world and with the world—preoccupation with *what* and *how* they are "being." As they place consumer civilization in judgment, denounce bureaucracies of all types, demand the transformation of the universities (changing the rigid nature of the teacher-student relationship and placing that relationship within the context of reality), propose the transformation of reality itself so that universities can be renewed, attack old orders and established institutions in the attempt to affirm men as the Subjects of decision, all these movements reflect the style of our age, which is more anthropological than anthropocentric.
2. As used throughout this paper, the term "contradiction" denotes the dialectical conflict between opposing social forces.—Translator's note.
3. This fear of freedom is also to be found in the oppressors, though, obviously, in a different form. The oppressed are afraid to embrace freedom; the oppressors are afraid of losing the "freedom" to oppress.
4. See Georg Hegel, *The Phenomenology of Mind* (New York, 1967), pp. 236–237.
5. Analyzing the dialectical relationship between the consciousness of the master and the consciousness of the oppressed, Hegel states: "The one is independent, and its essential nature is to be for itself; the other is dependent, and its essence

is life or existence for another. The former is the Master, or Lord, the latter the Bondsman." Ibid., p. 234.

6. "The materialist doctrine that men are products of circumstances and upbringing, and that, therefore, changed men are products of other circumstances and changed upbringing, forgets that it is men that change circumstances and that the educator himself needs educating." Karl Marx and Friedrich Engels, *Selected Works* (New York, 1968), p. 28.

7. This appears to be the fundamental aspect of Mao's Cultural Revolution.

8. This rigidity should not be identified with restraints that must be imposed on the former oppressors so they cannot restore the oppressive order. Rather, it refers to the revolution which becomes stagnant and turns against the people, using the old repressive, bureaucratic State apparatus (which should have been drastically suppressed, as Marx so often emphasized).

9. Eric Fromm, *The Heart of Man* (New York, 1966), p. 32.

10. Regarding the "dominant forms of social control," see Herbert Marcuse, *One-Dimensional Man* (Boston, 1964) and *Eros and Civilization* (Boston, 1955).

11. Words of a peasant during an interview with the author.

12. See Candido Mendes, *Memento dos vivos—A Esquerda católica no Brasil* (Rio, 1966).

13. Frantz Fanon, *The Wretched of the Earth* (New York, 1968), p. 52.

14. *The Colonizer and the Colonized* (Boston, 1967), p. x.

15. Words of a peasant during an interview with the author.

16. *Asentamiento* refers to a production unit of the Chilean agrarian reform experiment.—Translator's note.

17. "The peasant has an almost instinctive fear of the boss." Interview with a peasant.

18. See Regis Debray, *Revolution in the Revolution?* (New York, 1967).

19. Interview with a peasant.

20. Not in the open, of course; that would only provoke the fury of the oppressor and lead to still greater repression.

21. Fromm, op. cit., pp. 52–53.

22. Alvaro Vieira Pinto, from a work in preparation on the philosophy of science. I consider the quoted portion of great importance for the understanding of a problem-posing pedagogy and wish to thank Professor Vieira Pinto for permission to cite his work prior to publication.

29

Satisfying Human Needs in a World of Sovereign States: Rhetoric, Reality, and Vision

Richard Falk

I. INTRODUCTION

No Quick Solution to World Poverty

The enigma of world poverty continues to baffle people of good will. Why are there so many poor people despite a long period during which the gross planetary product has steadily increased? Some blame capitalism or imperialism; others stress selfish leaders and ruling groups; some talk of the ignorance, corruption, and inefficiency of governments or the backwardness of societies; still others point to nefarious money managers and to obscure machinations by multinational corporations; some suggest that the *real* problem is a result of unchecked population growth; and some contend that poverty remains engrained because the planet is running out of cheap resources.

Of course, there are elements of truth in each line of explanation, and yet we lack the knowledge to assert with any real confidence that a single line of explanation is definitive. We are faced with a reality: grinding poverty for the mass of humanity. And we posit a goal: a world economic and political order that produces enough goods and services and distributes them in such a way as to satisfy the basic material needs of everyone. The gap between reality and goal is what defines the scope of our inquiry.

At the outset, it seems important to assert that there is no technical way to close this gap rapidly. It exists, not out of necessity, but because of the way in which states and the system of states are organized. To change organiza-

Reprinted by permission from *World Faiths and the New World Orders,* Joseph Gremillion and William Ryan, eds. (1978) pp. 109–139.

tional patterns on this scale is a complex, difficult, perhaps impossible under-taking that depends on shifting patterns of perceived interests and on chang-ing value formations. It is a formidable challenge to our institutions and traditions, and calls for a wide range of responses. It calls, especially, on our religious heritages to provide us with clues as to what is wrong and what to do about it, as well as with inspiration to strengthen our resolve.

New Stress on Needs is Ambiguous

The stress on "needs" is, at once, obvious and problematic. It is obvious because the poorest people in the world are numerous and miserable, as well as because the overall arrangement of wealth that allows such disparities to persist is an assault upon our most primitive ethical sensibilities. It is prob-lematic because it encourages a kind of patronizing, philanthropic concern about doing something for "others," conceived as helpless objects, and, there-fore, resists the understanding of poverty as a "structural" consequence of the way in which power and wealth are and have been deployed. Nevertheless, we shall focus on needs because that is the way people are thinking about meeting the challenge of world poverty. This stress on needs proceeds from a non-philanthropic outlook that asks how we must transform domestic and international structures to enable *all* people to enjoy a satisfying life; it does not isolate "the poor" as a distinct category.

The diagnostic question is why it seems so difficult to achieve distribu-tive patterns that satisfy the basic material needs of all people. How should we understand and explain this difficulty? This paper argues that the princi-pal difficulty arises at the interface between politics and economics on both national and international levels. It also argues that mass denial of human needs is not inevitable, but results from the contingent structures of inequal-ity existing between and within states. This can be rectified, although only after an intense and prolonged struggle.

The therapeutic question is what to do to achieve distributional patterns that are designed to satisfy basic material needs. The argument sketched here is that political structures will have to be fundamentally transformed by struggle, facilitated by cultural innovation, and pursued by a variety of non-violent strategies ranging from education to mass civil disobedience, general strikes, and the like. Values constitute the core of what the struggle is about, in reality translating the great religious vision of what has been ethically presupposed for humanity into the actualities of political, economic, and social arrangements. Such an imperative is reinforced by the apocalyptic dangers of persisting with behavioral and organizational patterns premised on the acceptability of *exploitation* (giving rise to personal and collective inequal-ity, including deep poverty for large numbers), of *fragmentation* (associating well-being with a part—whether territory, class, race, religion—rather than the whole of the human species). The possibility of a positive human destiny then, depends upon suffusing activities with a vivid and intensifying sense of human solidarity on all levels of societal interaction.[1]

Obviously, such a vision of the future can only begin to be approximated after a long process. The process can be initiated immediately in appropriate forms within every setting of choice and action. We can begin now, and, given the urgency of the undertaking, there is no time to lose. Yet we cannot expect to achieve rapid results except within domains under our direct control. The length of time needed for a cumulative shift of structures may be as short as several decades or as long as several centuries. We have no way of knowing, or even of assessing the probabilities. The correctness of the stand, and not its rewards, provide us with the basis for action. At the same time, the present rewards are tangible because we are allowed the experience of transformation to the limit of our capacities. We can realize now the emergent future order to some extent by putting into practice the principles and values of humane governance in as many activities as our strength and our circumstances allow.

Overview of the Paper

a. Structural and ideological impasse. In this paper, I shall pursue these themes by considering the current impasse over methods to reduce world poverty and cut the disparities between rich and poor countries. The main conclusion of this first section is that there is no way to circumvent this impasse, given prevailing secular structures and their supportive ideological outlooks. Furthermore, frustration occasioned by this impasse is likely to grow even more acute, resulting in a violent cycle of repression and resistance. In effect, therefore, violence on both sides, repressive violence by those who would manage the status quo, versus revolutionary violence by those who would change it, will increase.

Such a cycle leads to a political dynamic that is mutually futile, as one side fails to achieve "order," and the other side fails to achieve "justice." Without a greater consciousness for what is necessary, the conception of what is possible will remain excessively modest, dooming the revolutionary attempt, even if successful, to shifts in policy and personnel, but failing to break through the cycle of violent and inhumane governance. The effects of the Soviet Revolution are illustrative.

Of course, structural constraints are not everything. The particular orientation of individuals and elites toward global policy issues may be more or less generous, imaginative, and effective. These variations of outlook could make the difference between a relatively steady voyage into the future and disastrous shipwreck. At the same time, the constraints on official leadership arising from the demands of domestic social forces, from the influence of perceived interests, and from traditions of behavior associated with national security and sovereignty, are so great as to make it highly unrealistic to expect much aid and comfort for transformative demands emanating from the centers of established power and authority.[2]

b. Evolution of a consensus. After considering this challenge to the legitimacy and capability of the existing system of world order, I will examine the more encouraging evidence of the evolution of a consensus that is beginning to grasp and depict what is needed to evolve patterns of humane governance for the planet. This consensus is gradually forming despite the practices and tendencies of constituted power. In effect, we cannot, at this stage, expect most official institutions and governing groups, given their sense of priorities, to support a social movement for planetary renewal, although individuals serving in these structures will be influenced by the movement to varying degrees, and may keep the processes of governance from veering to extremes.

c. Uneven process of renewal. This transnational movement of renewal will proceed unevenly. In the advanced industrial countries, the crux of the problem lies in the interplay between runaway technology and the apparatus of state power. The state is too large for humane governance, and yet too small to cope functionally with the planetary agenda. To overcome the predominance of the state presupposes a dialectical unfolding toward values that are simultaneously more communitarian and personally felt, producing decentralization and more universalistic and functionally successful, and as such, requiring greater centralization of organizing structures.[3] Decentralizing potentials are more significant than centralizing ones because it seems so essential to reduce, to the furthest extent possible, the intrusion of bureaucratic ways and means on the life experience of people.

In less industrialized countries the emergence of strong state structures is part of the phenomenon of "catching up," and provides some assurance that political independence can be safeguarded and that global issues will be dealt with in a fairer way. Statism as a short-run response to imperialism enables Third World societies to make effective their quest for national self-assertion, including achieving greater participation in international arenas and more regulation of foreign penetration in their own societies. Such nationalist strategies interfere with interim, stopgap globalist adjustment processes (e.g. inhibits formation of an enlightened law of the oceans), and may have some unfortunate domestic effects, such as a tendency to smother the domestic self-determination dynamic beneath the weight of an effective machinery of repression.

Overall, however, and given sufficient time, it remains a matter of letting history run its course. The dynamic of self-determination at the national level, and of globalization at the international and individual levels, are both reinforced by the weight of social pressures to such an extent that efforts of resistance are led to choose more and more desperate tactics. These pressures may make the interval and process of transition a dangerous and confusing one, as well as making its outcome uncertain. These pressures also establish the specific context in which religious and cultural perspectives possess their greatest relevance: to facilitate transition by reorienting consciousness toward the satisfaction of human needs and the fulfillment of human potential for individual and group development.

II. COMMENTS ON THE MAINSTREAM DEBATE ON THE WORLD ECONOMIC SITUATION

Some widely accepted generalizations can be set forth to provide a normative sense of direction:

- a large and growing number of people live near or below subsistence;

- the overwhelming concentration of these poor people is among non-white populations located in Asia, Africa, and Latin America;

- a much more rapid and relative rate of population increase exists among the non-white poor of the world; —a widening gap exists between the per capita GNP of rich and poor countries currently estimated as 11:1 or 12:1;

- an even more rapidly widening income gap exists within poor countries, resulting in the relative, and in some instances, the absolute decline in the purchasing power of the poorest 40% or so of the population despite overall societal growth;*

- a corresponding absence of influence and power on the part of poor countries in international economic and political arenas;

- a disproportionate use of scarce resources by the rich countries of the North relative to their population, perhaps at a ratio of 15:1 on a per capita basis, affecting price and availability of resources required to meet basic needs;

- a strong correlation since 1945 between the poorest sectors of world society and the location of most instances of large-scale collective violence, including warfare;

- an equally strong correlation between the rich sectors of world society and outlays for defense spending;

---

*The costs to the poorest 40 percent of the population in many countries that followed this 'trickle-down' strategy have now become clear. Not only have their relative incomes and standards of living decreased, sometimes markedly, but there is considerable evidence to suggest that the *absolute incomes of the bottom 10–20 percent may also have fallen."* (emphasis in original). James Grant and Mahbub ul Haq, "Income Redistribution and the International Financing of Development," Annex 2, in Jan Tinbergen, coordinator, *Reshaping the International Order (RIO)*, New York, E. P. Dutton, 1976.

- an intensification of arms race behavior, including nuclear weapons innovations by superpowers, the spread of nuclear capabilities to many additional countries, and the rise of arms spending for sophisticated conventional weaponry; this dynamic increases the likelihood of the outbreak of various forms of warfare, including nuclear war;
- an intensification of authoritarian tendencies, especially throughout the Third World, signifying the decline of moderate politics;
- a mood of growing despair in the rich countries about their economic and political prospects as a consequence of energy costs and options, sustained unemployment and inflation, environmental pressures, terrorist activities, increasing protectionism, and spreading mass disaffection among all societal classes.

These elements of the international situation are not meant to be exhaustive. The purpose of this enumeration is to clarify the grounds of concern about the workings and prospects of the international system. In addition to these various factors, two kinds of linkages, the first between political and economic strategies, and the second, between the domestic political order and the international order, are of fundamental importance.

Idealistic Rhetoric

My analysis proceeds from the conviction that political factors severely constrain available economic policy choices within unacceptably narrow limits and vice versa. These narrow limits reflect a certain stress upon selfish, short-term, domestic concerns that dominate governmental policy-making procedures and make it unrealistic to anticipate any major voluntary adjustments in the international system that could result in substantially greater satisfaction of basic human needs. Put differently, despite idealistic rhetoric, as well as a sense of what needs to be done, altruistic motivation is an exceedingly weak premise for any meaningful program of global reform and perceived selfish motivations are not likely to work for the benefit of the poor.[4]

The only way to avoid this assessment is to envision a reorientation of domestic élites around a more planetary interpretation of national interests coupled with the success of populist politics that successfully revises the domestic allocation of income and wealth. Neither shift is remotely plausible without prior drastic changes in prevailing political consciousness. This will include the emergence of new belief/value orientations that reflect a simultaneous emphasis on the worth of the individual person, on the solidarity of humanity, and on the value of human persistence and evolution.

Such shifts are already underway to some extent, but it will take several decades, at least, until they become dominant; in the interim, stiffening resistance from more traditional and conservative assessments of human nature and political optimality will be encountered. Only by careful examination of prevailing configurations of political power, including their economic dimensions, can we begin to appreciate the magnitude of creating an overall social order of planetary scale that endows all classes and peoples with the opportunity to satisfy basic human needs, a goal more dynamic and ambitious than the elimination of poverty.[5] Poverty could, in theory, be virtually eliminated by welfare payments on an international level without creating a social environment where people have their basic needs, including their sense of dignity, satisfied. Our concern rests with the greater organic attainment of a development process that encompasses everyone, providing work as well as sustenance, dignity as well as material wherewithal, participation as well as benefits.

This insistence on grounding inquiry within the realm of power is especially important where normative concerns are as prominent as they are here. There is often a tendency in international relations to substitute high-minded intentions and words for policy and behavior, or to assume that benevolent adjustments in economic relationships can somehow be achieved by the right technical "fix." The issue of world poverty and the related "development gap" are especially prone to simplistic rhetoric and mechanistic proposals.

Leaders of both rich and poor countries, for a variety of pragmatic reasons, endorse the goals of eliminating poverty as rapidly as possible from the face of the earth. President Jimmy Carter of the United States exhibited a characteristic understanding of this view in a major foreign policy address delivered at Notre Dame University on May 22, 1977: "More than 100 years ago, Abraham Lincoln said that our nation could not exist half slave and half free. We know that a peaceful world cannot long exist one-third rich and two-thirds hungry."[6] To similar effect is a statement by Julius Nyerere, President of Tanzania: "If the rich countries go on getting richer and richer at the expense of the poor, the poor of the world must demand a change, in the same way as the proletariat in the rich countries demanded change in the past. And we do demand change. As far as we are concerned the only question at issue is whether the change comes by dialogue or confrontation."[7]

The formal consensus seems virtually unanimous at such levels of abstraction. Rich and poor leaders alike accept the normative and pragmatic case for a world campaign against both poverty and global disparities. The extent of formal support is also disclosed by the virtually unanimous approval given to the postulates of the new international economic order in key votes at the United Nations; disagreement emerges as soon as action proposals are put forward (e.g. debt cancellation; indexation of commodity prices; national control of foreign investment).

Southern Perspectives

However, even the apparent consensus on goals is deceptive as sharp disagreement becomes quickly evident on the level of explanation and remedy.

Third World representatives, regardless of political orientation, tend to put the blame for Third World poverty on the rich countries and naturally expect these countries to bear the moral and material burdens of rectification. As Adam Nsekela, an African World Bank official, puts it: ". . . why are the poor states poor? The answer is that they are poor because they have been colonized, dominated, drained of their surpluses, locked into bondage in which they are poor and are becoming ever poorer because the rich are rich and are becoming relatively richer."[8] Such a perspective leads, at the very least, to an insistence that a feature of any new international economic order that emerges is that states in the poor sector are helped to become economically more secure. In Mr. Nsekela's words, "The New International Economic Order is about distribution: the distribution of world production, the distribution of the surpluses derived in any country and the distribution of economic power."[9] The standard proposals to achieve these results are outside the scope of this paper, but do include such measures as debt relief, stabilization of commodity prices, increased direct assistance, indexation of prices for primary and finished goods, increased Third World voting power in international economic institutions, and improved terms of trade.*

Whether or not such a Southern perspective also includes a transformation of distributive patterns within the state is, of course, a more sensitive issue. To look outward at other governments or global institutions for capital, technical assistance, or social reform may be to invite intervention that endangers political autonomy. In many instances upholding autonomy is a national goal that is as important, and on occasion, more important, than even economic development. To look inward at inequity is to challenge the legitimacy of the state as currently constituted in a political setting where opposition and dissent are increasingly regarded as criminal activities by the leadership of the society. The more radical positions on social change have certainly concentrated upon the need for drastic restructuring on the domestic level and have regarded international restructuring as desirable, but definitely subsidiary. Whether this domestic restructuring is, in effect and unavoidably a call for some variety of socialism, is an important issue. Can governments that rely on private domestic and foreign capital for development purposes, in other words, achieve distributive justice if they are, indeed, operating from an initial circumstance of mass poverty? How?[10]

Northern Perspectives

The governments of rich countries respond to Third World claims in several ways. The most sophisticated and euphemistic line of resistance is to empha-

---

*The terminology for generalization about rich and poor countries is woefully inadequate. In this paper as generalizations, in some respects deceptive, I refer to poor countries as Third World and Southern, realizing full well that very diverse countries are caught within the net, including rich countries, especially the OPEC members. And for rich countries, with similar caveats, I use the notion Northern, and refer to the market economies of the North as OECD countries.

size the automaticity of mutual benefit created by the positive linkage between "growth" for the North and the South, contending that only adjustments based on the imagery of "mutual gain" are politically feasible,
economically effective, and morally persuasive. Such an outlook argues
against placing additional burdens on the North that will retard its engine of
growth to any extent, on the morally self-serving ground that such an effect
would be especially harmful to the South. As a consequence, large-scale
transfer or redistribution proposals are rejected as "counter-productive" and
"irrational." The most authoritative statement, perhaps, of this convenient
outlook is contained in the Communiqué of the Economic Summit Meeting
held in London during May 1977, and issued on behalf of the seven leading
"industrial democracies":

> The well-being of the developed and developing countries are bound up
> together. The developing countries' growing prosperity benefits industrial
> countries, as the latter's growth benefits developing nations. Both devel-
> oped and developing nations have a mutual interest in maintaining a
> climate conducive to stable growth worldwide.[11]

Even if one grants this dubious premise, what remains to be accounted
for is the assessment of whether or not the character of such growth projected
for the South is likely to benefit the poorer countries and the poorer segments
of these countries. Growth of what? for whom? and over what time period?
These critical normative questions are rarely addressed by liberal internation-
alist advocacy.

The more moderate versions of this mutual gain position argue that the
prosperity of the North is the key to market outlets for the products of the
South, and that the poor countries are poor for reasons disconnected with
their colonial heritage. The essential point in the argument is that these
countries would be no less poor had they not been colonized, and that the
rich countries would be as rich (or richer) even if there had been no colonial
system (e.g. Sweden and Switzerland had no colonies and are rich; Portugal
had colonies and is relatively poor).[12]

Some Northerners go further and provide an even more self-vindicating
account of economic disparities. For example, the British economists Peter
Bauer and John O'Sullivan write that: "Surely the principal reason [for global
disparities] is that nations, peoples, tribes, communities are not equally endowed with those qualities which mainly determine economic achievement."[13] That is, the inequality of result in the world of the late 1970s is an
inevitable reflection of the inequality of endowment and to allege exploitation and injustice is to offer a rationalization for poverty ungrounded in fact
or evidence. Bauer and O'Sullivan go on to attack Northern statesmen for
their fatuous acquiescence to the Southern indictment. They argue that indig-

enous failures of leadership in poor countries are generally responsible for the mass economic plight of their peoples.

This debate as to causation and tactics remains intense and inconclusive. A focus on the level of argumentation tends to overlook more critical issues of political will and capability. The North lacks both the *will* and the *capability* to depart significantly from what it has been doing. Domestic demands for jobs, profits, and inflationary control are predominant, and equalizing concessions to the South are perceived as needless exercises in self-sacrifice for which there is no domestic political constituency of any consequence.

III. SOME PERSPECTIVES ON REFORM

There are a variety of approaches to global economic reform. The strengths and weaknesses of the principal approaches will be examined in this section.

Capital Transfers and Reallocations

a) A painless economic fix? Many Northerners continue to believe it is possible to help the South with massive capital transfers, coupled with domestic reallocations of investment priorities. Barbara Ward, for instance, proposes "a planetary bargain" between the North and South comparable to the Marshall Plan. As of 1947, the United States made large resource transfers (up to 2% of U. S. GNP per year) for a period of years to stimulate European economic expansion. The result, point out its enthusiasts, has been 25 years of mutually beneficial growth. Arguing that a comparable growth potential exists for North-South trade, Barbara Ward calls for a similar resource transfer, but at the level of .7% of GNP (compared with the current .3%) for a sustained period, perhaps for several decades. Her economic case rests on the view that legitimate demand for goods among the Trilateral countries is largely saturated, leading to increasingly destructive competitive interactions, whereas the demand potential in the Third World remains mostly undeveloped ("there is no doubt where marginal productivity is highest— among still undeveloped people, areas, and resources.").[14]

The incentive for Northern [in conjunction with the Organization of Petroleum Exporting Countries (OPEC)] bounty is the lure of mutual benefit associated with the prospect of major increases in the productive capacity and purchasing power of the poor. This kind of economic thinking, the liberal dream of fusing "rationality," "decency," and "self-interest," is expected to come true, and provide the world economy with a painless apolitical "fix." The catch, however, is that there is virtually no chance of winning support for such an approach in most rich countries, and even if such support could be found and the plan put into effect there is no reason to expect poor countries or poor sectors of societies to benefit to any large extent.

The analogy drawn between economic conditions in post-World War II Europe and in the contemporary Third World is unconvincing. First of all, Europe in 1947, had a disabled industrial capability damaged by war that could be rebuilt by an efficient, generally disciplined, work force provided only that the capital became available. In contrast, much of the Third World has an industrial sector that is restricted to a small physical area, that involves only a fraction of the labor force, and that lacks a large reservoir of skilled labor to draw upon for purposes of rapid economic expansion. Third World poverty tends to be concentrated in the rural sector and its alleviation would require dramatic shifts in public investment priorities so as to stimulate overall rural development that would benefit the rural population as a whole.[15]

Secondly, the governmental structures of Europe after World War II were genuinely determined to rebuild their economies in an efficient manner, whereas governments in Third World countries are often unable to organize themselves for large-scale undertakings, being disabled as much by corruption as by capital shortages.

Thirdly, the short-term effects of such a stimulus of Third World productive capacity would be to export Trilateral jobs and markets in a period of rising economic nationalism and protectionist sentiment in the North.

Fourthly, there is no assurance that such a growth spurt, even if it occurred, would bring substantial benefit to the really poor segments of Third World societies—especially the rural poor.

The tensions extend even further. If investment, for instance, was heavy in agricultural development of the sort required for food self-sufficiency then it would deprive North American farmers of part of their market for exportable grains and cereals, depress world prices, and cause severe domestic problems in those countries. In fact the situation of the U.S. farmer is already described as worse than it has been at any time since the depression and steps have been taken by the government to cut back wheat production by as much as 20%. These steps have been taken, incidentally, at a time when famine conditions exist in Laos, Mozambique and elsewhere.

Among others, Arthur Lewis has shown that "mutual gain" based on North-South trade, especially in exports of primary goods, does tie the economic hopes of the South to the prosperity of the North. The tie is not mutual, however, because of the extreme dependence of the South on the stability of commodity markets in the North, and because of the absence of any comparable Northern dependence on Southern prosperity. Lewis favors stimulating the growth of South-South trading relationships, as well as diversifying the productive capacities of Southern countries to reduce their import requirements and overall dependency. These policies, Lewis argues, would be beneficial in promoting viable forms of development in the South. Lewis' analysis is powerful, in part, because it proceeds within the confines of liberal economic analysis to clarify why present structures of North-South relations are exploitative even if growth rates appear to move in tandem.[16]

b) **Naive "econometric" solutions.** Another kind of "fix" is to abstract the quantum of resources needed to overcome world poverty. Roger Hansen, for instance, reports "that two estimates resulting from different approaches and methodologies suggest that absolute poverty could be virtually ended within ten to fifteen years at a cost of $125 billion (in 1973 dollars); and that an asset-transfer policy to assure the 'forgotten 40 percent' of a firm floor above that level in the future might cost approximately $250 billion." As Hansen notes, such a program could be financed for $10–13 billion per year for 15–25 years, "depending on the thoroughness of the job." Since the present flow of aid from OECD countries is at the level of $13.6 billion, with much of it going to middle-level countries or for purposes unrelated to basic needs, it would be possible, Hansen contends, to reallocate this amount around the priorities of the basic human needs approach without even necessitating increases in aid totals.[17] This contention seems so simple that it raises the obvious question: why doesn't it happen?

Hansen also points out that according to a World Bank estimate "a 2 percent annual transfer from the upper classes to the bottom 40 percent of the populations of the developing countries could successfully finance both the short-term and the long-term goals of the strategy over a twenty-five year period."[18] Again, we are intrigued by the apparent triviality of the effort as compared to the grand character of the promised effect; and again, as with an international transfer, the political constraints emerge when we ask "why doesn't this happen?" Here, as well, the technical vision seems flawed: resource transfers by themselves will not induce self-sustaining growth.

How does one get the capital to the countryside intact and then invest it in such a way as to meet the human needs of the poor, including infrastructure deficiencies, in a manner that will generate a dynamic of productive growth? Without convincing scenarios, targets and numbers are misleading, diverting us from an appreciation of the structural difficulties of rural development in a polity where the capital allocation process is generally dominated by growth-oriented technocrats and profit-oriented urban industrial capitalists. Such arithmetic targets are useful to the extent that they underscore the availability of economic capabilities to meet human needs and call attention to the structural distortions of priority and control that make these reallocations highly implausible. However, to the extent that such "econometric" solutions are meant to provide a *real* solution via an appeal to good faith rationality of policy-makers, they are naive about the nature of power, as well as insensitive to the exploitative character of human relationships implicit in capitalism. As Fernando Henrique Cardoso puts it, "Because they fail to recognize the banality—social and economic exploitation of man by man, of one class by another, of some nations by other nations—so-called 'counter-élites' often go round in circles, dreaming of technical solutions."[19]

c) **The Bariloche model.** On a different level of seriousness, large-scale economic models project ways to help the poor and/or eliminate disparities.

Perhaps, the most significant initiative to date is the Bariloche inquiry into the kind of development strategy appropriate for the realization of basic human needs. Unlike "the fix" of resource transfers the Bariloche model examines scenarios that involve indigenous Third World investment reallocations designed to produce a needs-oriented development path.[20] Stress is placed upon the kinds of productive outputs called for to satisfy distributional minima for the poorer sectors of the population, as well as on activating demand from those who are now enduring severe levels of deprivation. The model demonstrates, essentially, that a needs-oriented, demand-pulled "engine of growth" is technically feasible when appropriate resource reallocations are made.

This formal demonstration that needs could be satisfied fulfills an educational function, as well as creates a political instrument of criticism and advocacy. The fact that the Argentinian government has withdrawn support from the Bariloche Foundation, evidently in reaction to the publication and widespread discussion of the model (with its implicit critique of GNP-maximation development strategies that tend to skew investment patterns in directions that perpetuate and even intensify income inequalities), is one indication that rigorous demonstrations of alternate development paths is politically threatening to the extent that makes a needs approach appear feasible.

The technocratic style of reactionary regimes in the South claim that their approach to developmental choices possess 'objectivity' and the toleration of continued poverty is unavoidable for the present. Such approaches dismiss criticism calling for greater equity as sentimental or polemical, or misguided. The Bariloche type of model, with its increasingly rigorous methodology, erodes these official claims to speak objectively, and therefore, helps to expose the ideological and class character of prevailing developmental policy. As such, it is naturally perceived as dangerous by ruling groups, as it weakens the legitimacy of governmental claims to be doing as well as possible on the most explosive of all issues in the South.

Beyond this, such a drastic critique of prevailing policies cannot easily be dismissed as a Marxist effort to overthrow the existing order. Indeed, such model-building is often attacked by those who insist that Marxist categories of perception are the only adequate tools for understanding what is going on at the interface between economics and politics. In these regards, those who favor humane development patterns and yet are disillusioned by hardened ideological claims, can take heart. The Bariloche approach seeks to create a knowledge-base that can give policy-makers a real possibility to shape development patterns in ways that meet the needs of the poor. However, the demonstration of economic feasibility should not be confused with demonstrations of political feasibility. The latter demonstration depends on understanding the basis of the governing coalition in a given country, and the extent of discretion that exists among the leaders to alter the bases of support for that coalition within the bureaucracy and in relation to public opinion.

Coercive Transfers

OPEC, since 1973, has achieved a massive North-South transfer of resources without producing a war, although a rising level of threat occurred during the period of embargo. The bulk of these resources, however, have benefitted only a few countries. Most of the additional oil revenues have been recycled in the North, and have been financing huge arms purchases to build up powerful military establishments in several oil-rich countries, especially Iran and Saudi Arabia. Such a use of the market mechanism to achieve rapid international *redistributive* outcomes is certainly effective, but it does not appear to be generalizable beyond oil, nor does it assure a contribution to international equity, as measured by human effects. Recycling of earnings in safe, productive sectors of the world economy is self-interested behavior by OPEC members. The diversion of resources to poor country economies would almost certainly lead to a global depression, provoking an atmosphere of crisis and danger, as well as depriving the oil producers of their best customers. The OPEC strategy is not, in any event, generalizable because oil has special properties. It is a critical resource for which no available substitute exists in sufficient quantities in the short-run. No other commodity is nearly as vital as oil, although some gains for the South can surely be achieved in other trading contexts by a concerted and intelligent assessment of the market.

It is not realistic to envision the OPEC strategy as capable of solving the challenge of either disparities or poverty. It is true, however, that the radicalization of Iran and Saudi Arabia could make a sizeable difference in the international climate, possibly sufficiently reinforcing the more militant overall demands for a new international economic order to make some genuine restructuring begin to happen.

Nevertheless, there is no reason to suppose that domestic radicalization will produce solid benefits for people other than those living within state boundaries, although the reality of such benefits might stimulate revolutionary activity elsewhere. In essence, the secondary effects of coercive transfers (via resource cartels) are not likely unless, of course, the main militant governments themselves move toward socialism, which in itself is not a likely prospect for the immediate future, or unless, an even less likely prospect, the overall international economy is restructured along non-capitalist lines.

International Institutional Arrangements

There are some possibilities for wealth sharing that exist at the frontiers of technology. The mineral wealth of the ocean sea bed, for example, was for a time conceived to be a part of "the common heritage of mankind" which could be largely administered by international institutions. Most of the income derived could then be distributed according to equity criteria, giving resource-poor Third World countries a source of capital that came without strings or with an interventionary presence, provided only that the recipient governments were pursuing a development strategy of benefit to the society as a whole.

What is now apparent is that ocean idealism has been superseded by selfish pressures to divide up ocean wealth according to criteria of geopolitical clout, technological capability, and availability of venture capital. The expected result is that the richest and most powerful countries will acquire most of the economic benefits, either because a treaty arrangement favorable to their interest is negotiated, or because it isn't, and exploitation then proceeds on the basis of relatively unregulated competition.

Statist imperatives have been in the foreground of the ocean negotiations, exhibiting the extent to which each government seeks the best possible deal for its country regardless of effects on other, less favored, states. This kind of statism implies that there is no real prospect of getting a progressive distributive arrangement based on relative societal need, but that each state will bargain for its "fair share" based on its size, ingenuity, and capability. What becomes more important is that behind these governmental positions have been the special economic interests of the multinational corporations, which have pressured their particular government to create investment incentives that include assuring that the lion's share of economic reward goes to developers.

Here again the main point is that the existing structures of power in global society will be generally reflected in the arrangements that are likely to emerge to govern ocean mineral wealth. Even new sources of wealth are not significantly subject to redistributive pressures. The idealism associated with such global negotiations is subordinated, in practice, to the persisting selfishness of governmental outlooks. This generalization includes the behavior of the Soviet Union (as well as its group of dependent socialist countries) which has taken a position similar to that of the United States on ocean minerals, and seeks an arrangement that will reward its superior developmental technology and its supportive polity. Although the South has so far resisted this solution, it has done so on behalf of Third World governments as a whole, rather than on behalf of equitable arrangements designed to channel profits from ocean mining to the governments of poor societies.

What is evident here is the same pattern that can be discerned everywhere; namely, the predominance of statism. There are small variations among governments as to the degree to which global interests are incorporated, but official behavior seems generally designed to maximize state interests and to conceive of international negotiations as interstate bargaining situations, rather than as a cooperative search for a global solution expressive of human or planetary interests. Given the diffusion of state power associated with the spread of formal independence and with political and military capabilities, there are some international redistributive effects arising from statist logic, but the intranational impacts are barely discernible.

Multinational Corporate Globalism

In a recent full-page advertisement in the *New York Times*, an investment banking firm epitomized the new globalist perspective of big business by a huge picture of electronic equipment dwarfed by four huge globes in the background. The caption read in bold letters: "THE ROOM IS NOW GLOBAL." Underneath was an explanation: "Why? Because the needs of the corporations, governments, and institutions we serve are now global."[21]

Beneath this public display lies the dynamic of corporate growth reinforced by electronic capabilities now available to manage operations spread around the globe almost as efficiently as if their geographical extent was confined to a single city. The particular pattern of interests vary from industrial sector to industrial sector, even from firm to firm. In some areas where the domestic market is being encroached upon by foreign competition there is a growth of economic nationalism in the form of protectionist sentiment. Occasionally, these positions are advocated by a coalition of labor (fearing an export or loss of jobs) and management (fearing losses of domestic markets and profits).

Overall, the Multinational Corporations (MNCs) seek to deal with the world, or with as much of it as possible, as a single market. One tendency, evident in textiles and electronic assembly, is to locate productive facilities where taxes and labor costs are low and environmental regulation minimal. South Korea and Taiwan have been beneficiaries of such policies. It is alleged that the expansion of MNCs weaves a network of trade and investment interests that erode conflicts at the political level and make for a more peaceful world. IBM's motto is expressive of the wider MNC global ethos: "World Peace Through World Trade."

More relevant, however, are MNC claims that jobs, capital, and technology are being beneficially transferred to poor countries. Indeed, spokespeople for the MNC outlook applaud the noninterventionary contributions being made to economic growth throughout the Third World. Such a positive interpretation of MNC roles remains unconvincing. First of all, the beneficiaries of the MNC are a tiny proportion of the work force, who tend to be concentrated among the most skilled, and already well-off workers. Secondly, in countries with mass poverty, MNC operations depend on the creation of stable political conditions, which often require a deliberate effort to eliminate drastic challenges from below. The search for "discipline" to reduce the economic costs of social uncertainty inevitably leads to the denial of human rights, to repression and to subordination of populist claims for redistribution, full employment, and the like.[22] Indochina, Argentina, Indonesia, the

Philippines, and Thailand are among the countries that illustrate political solutions of a highly authoritarian character that can be explained, in part, by the priority their leadership attaches to attracting foreign capital (including loans from international financial institutions). At least for the short-run this insistence upon discipline tends to mean that increased activity by MNCs is not likely to result in greater satisfaction of basic needs of poor peoples. Indeed, the bargaining leverage of the poor may be cut down by government policy to assure an attractive investment climate for MNCs and national capitalists.

Thirdly, economic nationalism in the Third World may be a greater force than the benefits derived from MNC operations. The Brazilian government seems willing, during this present period of its history, to complicate the lives of MNCs so that it can fulfill nationalistic goals, including the reduction of foreign encroachment.

Fourthly, the markets for MNC output have tended to concentrate on the goods that could be purchased by those people with the disposable income, i.e. the middle classes. Necessities associated with nutrition, housing, health, and education are impossible to mass produce for profit when most potential customers lack purchasing power. As a consequence, most MNC production related to the domestic markets of Third World countries is associated with luxury items, thereby widening the consumption gap.

As matters now stand it is difficult to be positive about MNCs as agents of societal change and reform. Their direct impact seems concentrated among favored strata of the population, and their generally unintended, but definite, influence is to encourage repressive tendencies by placing a premium on domestic stability. Such stability in contexts of mass poverty tends to close off avenues of domestic reform for a long time. Often, also, the technological sophistication associated with MNC operations is extended to police administration in these countries, although this "modernization" of law enforcement procedures may occur in the absence of MNCs. In any event, there can be no positive example of a country where high levels of MNC operations have yielded dramatic distribution gains for the poorest sectors or where income disparities have narrowed. Even resource-rich Third World countries have no adopted policies designed to achieve domestic equity.

Domestic Radicalism in the South

a) Economic achievements of socialist regimes. It seems correct to credit socialist governments in the Third World with substantial achievements, at least, with respect to intranational equity. To the extent that resource capabilities exist, the basic needs of the population are met, and internal disparities reduced. External penetration is reduced, as well, either by way of corporate behavior or from foreign governments, and economic structures of self-reliance generated. The trade-offs have involved relinquishing "space" for various kinds of diversity—as the regimen of socialist governance in the Third World has severely inhibited oppositional politics of every variety. A bureaucratic élite has also emerged, threatening to evolve into "a new class," and give rise to domestic disparities. Despite these difficulties, the economic achievements of China, Cuba, and Vietnam suggest that the material needs of Third World populations can be rapidly and substantively satisfied by socialist regimes.

b) Lessons of the Allende experience. These socialist success stories, however, have all involved triumphant revolutionary movements in a position to reshape the apparatus of state power after a prolonged armed struggle. The contrary experience of the Allende period in Chile (1970–73), and possibly of Portugal since 1974, confirms the observation. A mandate for structural reform—in other words, shifting income to the poor and orienting economic planning around needs—engenders resistance from a state bureaucracy dominated by military officers and civil servants wedded to the old order. Such resistance makes it difficult, if not impossible, to carry out a program of domestic reform in an effective manner.

This resistance poses a serious dilemma for a progressive leadership that does not have its own people in dominant positions throughout the state bureaucracy. If the program can be blocked by hostile forces within the official hierarchy then it can be discredited as "incompetent," while if the program is effective despite resistance, then counterrevolutionary forces are mobilized. Allende's experience involved a mixture of these elements: strong bureaucratic resistance, considerable popular success despite obstacles, and a counterrevolutionary takeover justified both by the alleged incompetence of Allende's governance and necessitated by its persisting popularity, which evidently was understood to mean that it was unlikely that Allende could be unseated by constitutional means.

External factors, of course, reinforced this pattern. The United States Government, via the Central Intelligence Agency (CIA) and other intelligence agencies, mounted a campaign of "destabilization" designed to foster an impression of incompetence on the part of the Chilean government. The powerful MNCs, especially International Telephone & Telegraph (ITT), did their best to keep Allende from power and then harassed the government during his tenure. Furthermore, by means of CIA actions and a variety of intergovernmental military relationships, the United States maintained contact with and gave encouragement to the counterrevolutionary leadership in Chile. It remains difficult as yet to assess the cumulative influence of the US role in this period. Pressure was also successfully used at American initiative to deny Allende the benefit of loans and credits from international financial institutions, including the World Bank. These institutions are dominated by OECD capital and voting power, lack any countervailing socialist participation, and therefore, tend to resist any kind of radical redistributive policy by a national government despite the degree to which such a policy does what virtually everyone says is desirable.

A final factor involved the failure of the Soviet Union to take protective action on behalf of Allende to offset the effects of American pressure. Soviet motivation is difficult to fathom, but some speculations are possible. One interpretation suggests that the Soviet expense of offsetting American economic pressure on Cuba may have been as much as the Kremlin was willing to accept for the sake of securing "friendly" governments in Latin America. Another view maintains that Allende was "a Marxist" rather than "a Communist" and, consequently, was not sufficiently deferential to Moscow to engender Soviet support. Finally, detente may have been a factor, especially when considered together with the deference the superpowers have been giving to each other's spheres of influence. Soviet leaders may have regarded Chile as within the American sphere and that serious pro-Allende support would have destroyed detente and its related economic relations.

Whatever the causal sequence accounting for Allende's bloody downfall and the harsh militarist aftermath that has befallen Chilean society since 1973, it has tended to reinforce the Leninist insistence that socialism cannot be introduced except as a sequel to a prior armed struggle. This realization is a grave setback for those social forces in the Third World seeking a non-violent path to a socialist political economy.

Cultural Revolution in the North

Together with the notions of helping the South is a new, and quite autonomous, appreciation that the North itself is suffering from a mixture of pressures that have been provocatively labelled "over-development." Such a term suggests that the alienating and dangerous character of post-industrial civilization is to be partly associated with unchecked technological momentum. In effect, the argument goes, after crossing a certain threshold of affluence, "more means worse."

a) **Disintegrating impact of "over-development."** The idea of "over-development" is vague and needs some elaboration. The real content of the notion derives from the realization that the food we eat, the air we breathe, the water we drink, and the lives we lead are contaminating our bodies and spirits in ways we have yet to understand. A recent scholarly paper concludes that malnutrition from affluent diets is taking almost as great a toll in life expectancy as do protein deficient diets.[23] Along similar lines, a report concludes that at least one of four industrial workers in the United States is exposed, without precaution, to hazardous disease-producing conditions as part of work routine.[24] A great deal more than physical health is at stake, however.

There are numerous signs of the breakdown of values, institutions, morale. These signs include the weakening of family ties, the corruption and incompetence of government, the rise of crime, incredible rates of hard drug use, the loss of neighborliness and community sentiments, and widespread evidence of despair and alienation. It is an extraordinary commentary on the breakdown of civility to note that the richest cities in the richest countries are among the most dangerous for the unwary.

Over-development, of course, is compatible, especially in the United States, with deep pockets of poverty, as well as with high levels of unemployment, specifically among minority youth in the cities. Serious deficiencies associated with race, region and class persist in most so-called rich countries. These rich polities, as an aggregate, nevertheless waste resources in large quantities on fashions, luxury consumption, planned obsolescence, and weapons. This waste by the rich occurs during a period of rising consciousness about satisfying basic needs and, more keenly, at a time of an emerging concern about "limits to growth" not necessarily mechanical limits, but limits connected to the forms of growth and its environmental effects.

b) Ecological ethos—a rising social force. The ecological ethos—a measure of deference to nature—is a rising social force, especially in Western Europe, where green, not red, is becoming the color of radical politics. Its potency is revealed by the expansion of a militant anti-nuclear movement throughout the democratic societies of the industrial world. This movement gains support from many sources, but its principal strength arises from the conviction that official institutions are no longer to be trusted with the protection of human interest, especially where fundamental issues of choice and risk are concerned.

In the nuclear context, many people seem prepared to forego, are perhaps eager to do so, additional energy in exchange for a healthier, more humane surrounding. The prospects of economic growth are no longer as tantalizing as they once were to large numbers of people, especially if the cost is reliance on technologies that are a serious health hazard and that result in further centralization of economic and political activities. On a less spectacular scale than the anti-nuclear movement is the rising resistance throughout the West to dams, highways, and bridges that reflects a growing skepticism about the benefits of progress defined in overly materialist terms.

This skepticism has even penetrated official institutions to varying degrees in different countries, although the dominant consensus in these institutions emphasizes the management of environmental concerns in a fashion that is consistent with rapid domestic growth. A bigger pie—and not a more equitably distributed, stable or smaller pie—remains the major premise of economic policy in every society where the quest for profits and higher aggregate production structures are accepted as goals. This growth bias is especially strong in recent years because profits and net output must be sustained in an atmosphere of sharply escalating costs.

In the background of over-development thinking lie varying degrees of guilt or anxiety about annual allocation of world resources. One assessment suggests that 85% of world resources is being used each year for the benefit of less than 20% of the world's population; the people who comprised this 20% are mainly white Northerners.[25] Over-development prescription adopts the inverse view of "the mutual gain" perspective of liberal internationalists. It suggests that the rich should cut back on their use of scarce resources and allow the poorer countries to have a larger share. This outlook would require drastic changes in domestic economic policies and new trading/monetary relations to become operative without inducing severe disruption. It is not an immediately practical alternative. Nevertheless, the over-development outlook is increasingly endorsed by those who seek an economics with a humane and ecological face.

c) Skepticism towards scientific rationalism. The values challenge directed at the current affluent patterns is also expressed in affirmative ways. There is a remarkable surge of interest in spiritual possibilities of all kinds, bearing witness, I think, to the widespread refusal of people to accept the reign of scientific rationalism. Science and technology are generating the kind of skeptical reaction that had been directed toward religion in earlier generations. The interest in Eastern religions and practices throughout the West expresses, also, a demand for a more drastic religious experience than what is currently available in most of the established religious institutions. This spiritual impulse has been complemented by a variety of questionings directed at the viability of affluent life-styles based upon mainstream careerism. There is an immense growth of various modes of "voluntary simplicity" in these parts of the world, especially in the United States. In these cultural gropings there is much that is faddish, immature, quixotic, but there is also impressive evidence of serious quests for new, more satisfying and suitable cultural forms.[26]

A relevant line of conjecture goes as follows: if voluntary simplicity grows in scope and depth, becomes politically potent via its role in consumerist and anti-nuclear causes, then it may create a new normative climate for political leadership. In this new climate territorial boundaries may come to mean less than what one author has called "earthmanship."[27] Whether such a drastic shift of consciousness can emerge without violent convulsions is, of course, problematic. Recent descriptions of anti-nuclear activity in Europe suggest, for instance, a pattern of intensifying violence. Last summer at a large demonstration one protester was killed and several others maimed in France by highly armed national guard security forces. There appears to be an escalating cycle of militance in the confrontation between the state and its opponents on these issues of technological choice.[28]

d) Shifts in life-styles and religious outlook could make a difference.
In essence, then, shifts in life-style in the North could cut domestic disparities, as well as make a greater proportion of global resources available for the
satisfaction of basic needs of other societies provided, of course, that viable
ways to sustain the world economy are found. For such a movement to
succeed, it would have to draw upon spiritual energies that reformulated the
conditions of happiness and development, including the satisfaction of simplicity.[29] The positive character of this conception would have to prevail
against the whole mobilization and manipulation of highly individualized
tastes based upon accumulation of goods, high style and fashion, and the
identification of success with luxurious living. The rise of such alternative
life-styles would have to displace the widely held presumption that virtually
all sensible people seek to enjoy the energy-intensive middle class life-style
associated with the United States. As one influential commentator puts it,
"Attainment of middle-class style of life is what constitutes development in
countries as widely separated geographically and ideologically as Brazil and
USSR."[30] It would require a reversal of the prevailing policymakers' view that
Brazilians on the whole are better off than say, the Chinese, or more aptly,
to entertain the possibility that the Chinese mode of development, if per-
fected, might do more to satisfy the total needs of people than can the
perfection of the Brazilian mode. The value shift, in effect, would depend
upon "less being better" provided "less" is enough to satisfy basic needs, and
that the non-material benefits of community solidarity, socialist consciousness, and equality were made available and widely dispersed.[31]

It is difficult to determine the strength and durability of these tendencies
toward voluntary simplicity and associated spirituality. To influence the
overall economic setting of the world such tendencies would have to evolve
much further and begin to influence policy-making perspective on global
economic issues. Such an impact cannot be expected for another several
decades, although it is worth noting that the late E. F. Schumacher built an
immense following for ideas associated with decentralization, simplicity, and
appropriate technology. Influential political leaders, at least privately, have
been indicating an appreciation for his kind of approach. It is also relevant
that Schumacher's position and influence was infused by a deeply held religious outlook that seems organically related to the radical view of development that he espouses.

IV. A PERSPECTIVE ON TRANSFORMATION: SOME TENTATIVE COMMENTS

Perhaps more than social science or even fiction, children's literature has the
clearest and most direct insight into the present situation. A familiar theme
in recent children's books is the restoration of the earth after it has been
plundered by human activity.

The Earth Belongs to Everyone

One such story, called *Dinosaurs and all that rubbish,* tells of a man who caused great ruin on earth so that he might have a rocket built to allow a visit to another planet. After he leaves a totally polluted planet behind, some dinosaurs, sleeping for ages underneath the earth, awake and fix things up so that landscapes become green again. The man in his rocket, in the meantime, discovers that the distant star of his dreams is barren and looks elsewhere. He finds, finally, a planet that is green and beautiful, and is excited. The man is astonished to discover that this beautiful habitat is the same earth that he had abandoned in disgust. He pleads, then, with the dinosaurs to be allowed to have some land to live on:

> "Please may I have a small part of it back?" he asked.
> "Please, just a hill, or a tree, or a flower?"

And here is the response of the dinosaur:

> "No," said the dinosaur.
> "Not a part of it,
> but all of it.
> It is all yours
> but it is also mine.
> Remember that.
> This time the earth belongs to everyone,
> not part of it to certain people
> but all of it to everyone,
> to be enjoyed
> and cared for."[32]

It is worth noticing this non-territorial conception of using the earth, having it all and yet of owning no part of it—a reversal of prevalent attitudes and arrangements.

Tinkering Is Not Enough

No amount of tinkering can fix up the present international system. Too many fundamental pressures exist: continuing demographic pressures (increasing population and even more rapidly increasing urbanization), increasing destructiveness and instability of the weapons environment, waste of economic resources to fuel the arms race and to sustain affluent life-styles, sterility of an economistic vision that identifies progress with material growth, and societal fulfillment with entry into the middle classes, moral backwardness of an overall economic and political system that imposes "order" rather than orients investment and production around the satisfaction of basic needs, and short-sightedness of growth patterns that are not ecologically sustainable. These pressures are cumulative, interrelated, and their eventual impact could inflict irreversible damage, foreclosing future options. The logic that controls the state system is no longer tolerable. It is too dangerous, wasteful, and stultifying. It inhibits the sort of economic, political, and cultural development that fulfills individual and collective potentialities at various stages of industrialization.

In these respects even reorientations of national political consciousness can only be understood as transitional, generating dangerous, provocative confrontations between social forces. The efforts of governments to opt for basic needs generally collides with the interests of those who currently manage the international economic and political system. Neither Castro nor Allende, for instance, have had an easy time in the Western Hemisphere, and similarly, those who challenge entrenched interests in the post-industrial states are being met with violence and coercion. There is, for instance, a peaceful movement in the Seattle area of the United States to prevent construction of a large submarine facility for the Trident Submarine, on the basis of substantial evidence that it has been conceived by its designers as a first-strike weapons system.[33] The response of governing bodies has not been to reexamine or even to justify its commitment to weapons that appear to make nuclear war more likely, but to put the protesters in jail for increasingly long terms.

In the OECD world the emergent heroes are those who resist the bland assumptions that we can go on with nuclear power and weapons as if they are benign and inevitable ingredients of human destiny. The refusal to accept such a reality constitutes the center of a movement for transformation in the most affluent countries just as the movement for economic and social equity and against various forms of imperialism constitutes the center of movements for transformation in the Third World.

It is also noteworthy that the convergence of these tendencies is beginning to be evident. Members of the Pacific Life Community, which have led the drive against the Trident, adhere by choice to a life style based on voluntary simplicity, so that their lives will not be in conflict with patterns of living that are, in principle, possible for everyone else on the planet. They also insist upon the wholeness and unity of the species, and self-consciously ignore the boundary between Canada and the United States, soliciting Canadians to take part in activities on American territory as "planetary citizens." Every person has a stake in preventing nuclear war, although Canadians may have a special stake in preventing a Trident base so close to their homes. In striking contrast is the highly territorial response of the governor of the state of Washington, who has publicly warned Canadians to mind their own business, as if the dangers of nuclear war could be cordoned off on the basis of national boundaries.

Main Elements of a Transformative Vision

The main elements of a transformative vision of the future are implicit in what has been written above:

Solidarity—the sense of vital concern about the human species as a focus of emergent loyalty;

Unity—the shared and unified destiny of the planet;

Space—the non-territorial circumference of human concerns;

Time—the extension of human concerns in time to the ancient past and to the most distant future;

Nature—the experience of nature as encompassing, inspiring, and sustaining;

Peace—the renunciation of violence as the collective basis of security and innovation;

Progress—the gradual realization of human potentialities for joy and creativity in all dimensions of individual and collective existence;

Humility—the awareness of limits applicable to human endeavor including an understanding that human society should not proceed with certain lines of scientific investigation and technological innovation; and

Spirituality—the understanding that awe and mystery are as integral to human experience as bread and reason.

In effect, this set of criteria could be espoused on a high enough level of abstraction by virtually anyone, even today. Indeed, even those in positions of significant power in the existing system with its contrary attributes might endorse, quite sincerely, many of these transformative elements. It is the degree of embodiment that makes all the difference! Nominal or ritual embodiment is possible and, possibly, self-deceptive in a damaging way. Power-wielders often seem quiet and serene, even while engaged in destructive activities, because they do not perceive the tension between what they believe and what they do. Part of human adaptability, that has especially high social costs in periods of fundamental challenge, is to disguise contradictions between actions and ideals.

Internalizing a Religious Perspective

The position outlined above is making a radical claim; namely, that the future prospects of the human species depend upon internalizing an essentially religious perspective, sufficient to transform secular outlooks that now dominate the destiny of the planet. Any prudent calculation of probabilities would, of course, heap scorn on this eventuality, and yet, oddly enough it seems more "utopian" to suppose that we can persist on our crowded, depleted, militarized planet inhabited by many who are miserable, some who are desperate, and most who are scared. Any genuine, hard-headed "rationalist," respectful of evidence and trends, would become a "doomsday prophet." Hope, now more than ever, that is not just an unconvincing expectation of a series of technological "miracles," depends on renourishing religious sensibilities.

In the short-term it is difficult to assess whether or not a religious perspective, as integral to the discharge of official functions, allows a power wielder to advance human values more effectively. The resistances seem too formidable. The overriding necessities of wielding power in the current global setting especially in major states, require levels of moral insensitivity that are of a monumental character including a willingness to endorse uses of weapons of mass destruction, to entertain and honor dictators who torture their opponents, to rely on industrial processes that endanger workers and environments, to protect dubious investments and sources of critical raw materials, to orient policy around short-term horizons of expectations. It seems impossible, then, for a religious perspective associated with the values we have set forth to flourish within current realms of secular power.*

In addition to this, religious spokespeople may actually play a regressive role in social issues—for instance on the status of women. A grotesque interaction of secular and religious sensibilities occurred in Somalia two years ago. The government sought to emancipate women from various forms of bondage and was opposed by traditionalist religious leaders citing the Qur'an as their authority. To demonstrate that it meant business, the government rounded up eleven religious leaders actively working against equality for women one morning and executed them later the same day.**

Purely Humanist Positions Cannot Engender Transforming Vision

It is not necessary to be "religious" (in either the formal or existential sense) to have an impulse to do better, to be more ethical, and to be even more empathetic. Such a reformist platform may seem fully consistent with a secular search for stability in the short-run, and hence very practical, or it

---

*A religious perspective can inform almost any political undertaking, often lending it an aura of certitude that vindicates the most extreme, and brutal, behavior. We are using "religious" in a more restricted way associated with shared ideals that are shared by the great religions of the world.

**Bauer and O'Sullivan, note 13, at p. 55, use this incident to support their central conclusion ". . . that the liberal ideas and phraseology of the West, once transported to the Third World, often assume fantastic and distorted forms." I question such an interpretation, and regard it, instead, as a clash between two indigenous approaches to well-being resolved in a manner that discloses the consequences of the failure to curb state power. These failures should not be associated mainly with Third World countries. See, for instance, the Soviet state vis-á-vis its own people; the US vis-á-vis the Vietnamese.

may be appealing mainly for idealistic reasons. And it is obvious that humanism can be accepted by individuals who have no confidence at all in the wider realities of religious affirmation. But such purely humanist positions cannot, in my view, engender the vision or the hope required to build toward transformation; and secularist thinking will never extend social contracts (for the present) to conventional arrangements (for the future).[34]

NOTES

1. A strong argument along these lines is found in the Club of Rome study of Ervin Laszlo and others, *Goals for Mankind,* New York, E. P. Dutton, 1977, esp. pp. 367–424.
2. See Fouad Ajami, "The Global Populists: Third-World Nations and World-Order Crises," Princeton University, Center of International Studies, Research Monograph No. 41, May 1974.
3. I have tried to depict the organizational consequence of this mixture of centralizing functional requirements and decentralizing human requirements in Chapter IV of *A Study of Future Worlds,* New York, Free Press, 1975, pp. 224–276.
4. On what needs to be done see, among others, especially Marc Nerfin's preface and Rodolfo Stavenhagen's chapter in Nerfin, ed., *Another Development,* Uppsala, Sweden, Dag Hammarskjöld Foundation, 1977; also Dieter Senghaas, "If you can't keep up with the rich, keep away," in *Forum of Committee of Correspondence,* 9:1, Sept. 1977, pp. VI-143–VI-145.
5. For clear explanation of the needs focus and distinction between the positive stress of a basic needs approach from the negative stress of a poverty reduction approach see Graciela Chichilnisky, "Development, Basic Needs, and the Future of the International Order," mimeographed, pp. 1–7.
6. For text see *New York Times,* May 23, 1977.
7. Julius Nyerere, "The Economic Challenge: Dialogue or Confrontation," *International Development Review* 1976/1:2–8, at 3.
8. Amon J. Nsekela, "The World Bank and the New International Economic Order," *Development Dialogue* 1977:1, pp. 75–84, at 75–6.
9. *Idem,* at 78.
10. Issue posed in this way by Samir Amin, "Self-Reliance and the New International Economic Order," *Monthly Review,* July/Aug. 1977, pp. 1–21, esp. at 2–3.
11. For text see *New York Times,* May 9, 1977, p. 12.
12. Such a position is comprehensively depicted by Richard Cooper in "A New International Economic Order for Mutual Gain," *Foreign Policy,* Spring 1977, 26:66–122.
13. Peter Bauer and John O'Sullivan, "Ordering the World About: the NIEO," *Policy Review,* Summer 1977, 1:55–69, at 57–8.
14. Barbara Ward, "Seeking a Planetary Bargain," *International Development Review,* 1977/2:34–5, at 34.
15. For data and argument along these lines see Stavenhagen, in Nerfin, note 5, at pp. 40–65, esp. 40–47.
16. As Professor Lewis argues, emphasis on agricultural development is the key to economic autonomy. See, in general W. Arthur Lewis, "The Evolution of the

International Economic Order," Princeton University, Research Program in Development Studies, Discussion Paper No. 74, March 1977, pp. 1–60, esp. 53–60. See also Samir Amin, "Self-Reliance and the New International Economic Order," *Monthly Review,* July/Aug. 1977, 29:1–21.

17. Roger Hansen, "Major U.S. Options on North-South Relations: A Letter to President Carter," in John Sewell and others, *The United States and World Development: Agenda 1977,* Washington, D.C., Overseas Development Council, 1977, pp. 21–142, at 67–9. These figures are specified in greater detail in Mahbub ul Haq, *The Poverty Curtain,* New York, Columbia University Press, 1976, Statistical Annex, Table 5, p. 229.

18. Hansen, p. 68.

19. Fernando Henrique Cardoso, in Nerfin, note 5, pp. 21–39, at 23.

20. For explication of model see Chichilnisky, note 5.

21. *New York Times,* Oct. 3, 1977, p. 48.

22. For lucid argument along these lines Sylvia Ann Hewlett, "Human Rights and Economic Realities: Tradeoffs in Historical Perspective," (mimeographed paper).

23. Erik Ekholm and Frank Record, "The Two Faces of Malnutrition," Washington, D.C., World Watch Paper No. 9, Dec. 1976, pp. 1–63.

24. Report of an official government survey, *New York Times,* Oct. 3, 1977, pp. 1, 22.

25. Chichilnisky, note 5, p. 5.

26. On "voluntary simplicity" see Duane S. Elgin and Arnold Mitchell, "Voluntary Simplicity: Life Style of the Future?" *The Futurist,* Aug. 1977, pp. 200–209, 254–261. In general, see T. Roszak, *The Unfinished Animal,* New York, Harper and Row, 1976.

27. See G. Tyler Miller, Jr., *Living in the Environment: Concepts, Problems, Alternatives,* Belmont, Calif., Wadsworth, 1975, pp. 29–30, 326–330.

28. Anna Gyorgy, "France Kills its First Protester," *The Nation,* Oct. 8, 1977, pp. 330–333; William Sweet, "The Opposition to Nuclear Power in Europe," *Bulletin of Atomic Scientists,* Vol. 33, Dec. 1977, pp. 40–47.

29. Johan Galtung sets forward some suggestive ideas in an essay entitled "Alternative Life Styles in Rich Societies," in Nerfin, note 5, pp. 106–121.

30. Nathan Keyfitz, "World Resources and the World Middle Class," *Scientific American,* July 1976, 235:28–35, at 28. Professor Keyfitz builds his analysis around the presumed superiority of a middle class society, whatever its other features, contending that if resources limit access then "The Chinese rather than the British-Russian pattern of development may be what people will have to settle for." (p. 28).

31. Evidence that value shifts along these lines is taking place is scrupulously and impressively presented in Ronald Inglehart, *The Silent Revolution: Changing Values and Political Styles Among Western Publics,* Princeton, Princeton University Press, 1977.

32. Michael Foreman, *Dinosaurs and all that rubbish,* New York, Thomas Crowell, 1972, pp. 26–7.

33. For an account by a leading participant see Shelley Douglass, "Bangor Summer Reflection," *Year One,* Sept. 1977, III:12–14.

34. Distinction between "contract" and "covenant" attributed to Richard Neuhaus in Samuel Hux, "The Holocaust and the Survival of Tragedy," in *Worldview,* Oct. 1977, pp. 4–10, at 7.

BIBLIOGRAPHY

PART ONE   Theory and Method in Economic Development

BARAN, PAUL. "Economic Progress and Economic Surplus." *Science and Society,* 17, 4 (Fall 1953): 289–317.

CHENERY, HOLLIS, et al. *Redistribution with Growth: An Approach to Policy.* Oxford: Oxford University Press, 1974.

—— and M. SYRAQUIN. *Patterns of Development: 1950–1970.* London: Oxford University Press, 1975.

DONALDSON, LORRAINE. *Economic Development: Analysis and Policy.* Mineola, N.Y.: West Publishing Co., 1984.

FEI, JOHN C. H., and G. RANIS. *Development of the Labor Surplus Economy: Theory and Policy.* Homewood, Ill.: Irwin, 1964.

FRANK, ANDRE GUNDER. "Sociology of Development and Underdevelopment of Sociology." In *Latin America: Underdevelopment or Revolution?* New York: Monthly Review Press, 1969, pp. 21–94.

GOULET, DENIS. *The Cruel Choice.* New York: Atheneum, 1971.

——. "An Ethical Model for the Study of Values." *Harvard Educational Review,* 41, 2 (May 1971).

HIRSCHMAN, ALBERT O. *The Strategy of Economic Development.* New Haven: Yale University Press, 1958.

JAMESON, KENNETH, and CHARLES K. WILBER, eds. *Directions in Economic Development.* Notre Dame, Ind.: University of Notre Dame Press, 1979.

KUZNETS, SIMON S. *Modern Economic Growth.* New Haven: Yale University Press, 1966.

MYRDAL, GUNNAR. *Asian Drama: An Inquiry into the Poverty of Nations.* New York: Pantheon, 1968.

——. *Economic Theory and Underdeveloped Regions.* New York: Harper & Row, 1971.

NURKSE, RAGNAR. *Problems of Capital Formation in Underdeveloped Countries.* Oxford: Basil Blackwell, 1958.

RANIS, GUSTAV, et. al., eds., *Comparative Development Perspectives: Essays in Honor of Lloyd G. Reynolds.* Boulder, Colo.: Westview Press, 1984.

REYNOLDS, LLOYD G. *Image and Reality in Economic Development.* Yale University Economic Growth Center Series. New Haven: Yale University Press, 1977.

STREETEN, PAUL. "Economic Models and Their Usefulness for Planning in South Asia." In *Asian Drama: An Inquiry into the Poverty of Nations* by Gunnar Myrdal. New York: Pantheon, 1968.

TODARO, MICHAEL. *Economic Development in the Third World.* 2nd ed. New York: Longmans, 1981.

UL HAQ, MAHBUB. *The Poverty Curtain: Choice for the Third World.* New York: Columbia University Press, 1976.

WILBER, CHARLES K., ed. "The Methodological Foundations of Development Economics." *World Development,* (Special Issue), 14, 2 (Feb. 1986).

PART TWO   Economic Development and Underdevelopment in Historical Perspective

BAIROCH, PAUL. *The Economic Development of the Third World Since 1900.* Translated from the fourth French edition by Cynthia Postan. Berkeley: University of California Press, 1975.

BARAN, PAUL. "On the Roots of Backwardness." In *The Political Economy of Growth.* New York: Monthly Review Press, 1957: 134–162.

BARRET-BROWN, MICHAEL. *The Economics of Imperialism.* Baltimore: Penguin, 1974.

BHATT, V. V. "Economic Development: An Analytic-Historical Approach." *World Development* 4, no. 7 (July 1976).

FURTADO, CELSO. *Economic Development of Latin America: A Survey from Colonial Times to the Cuban Revolution.* Cambridge, England: Cambridge University Press, 1970.

GERSCHENKRON, ALEXANDER. *Economic Backwardness in Historical Perspective.* New York: Praeger, 1965.

GOULD, JOHN D. *Economic Growth in History: Survey and Analysis.* London: Methuen, 1972.

GRIFFIN, K. B. *The Underdevelopment of Spanish America.* London: G. Allen, 1969.

KITCHING, GAVIN. *Development and Underdevelopment in Historical Perspective: Population, Nationalism and Industrialization.* New York: Methuen, 1982.

MORAWETZ, DAVID. *Twenty-Five Years of Economic Development: 1950 to 1975.* Washington, D.C.: World Bank, 1977.

POLANYI, KARL. *The Great Transformation: The Political and Economic Origins of Our Time.* Boston: Beacon Press, 1957.

REYNOLDS, L. G. *Economic Growth in the Third World, 1850–1980.* Economic Growth Center Series, New Haven: Yale University Press, 1985.

RODNEY, WALTER. *How Europe Underdeveloped Africa.* Dar es Salaam: Tanzania Publishing House, 1972.

ROSTOW, W. W. *Stages of Economic Growth.* 2nd ed. New York: Cambridge University Press, 1971.

THOMAS, C. *Dependence and Transformation.* New York: Monthly Review Press, 1976.

PART THREE   Economic Development in a Revolutionary World: Trade and Dependency

AMIN, SAMIR. *Imperialism and Unequal Development.* New York: Monthly Review Press, 1977.

APTER, DAVID, and LOUIS GOLDMAN, eds. *The Multinational Corporation and Social Change.* New York: Praeger, 1976.

ARRIGHI, G. "Labor Supplies in Historical Perspective: A Study of the Proletarianization of the African Peasantry in Rhodesia." *Journal of Development Studies* 6 (April 1970): 197–234.

BATH, G. RICHARD, and DILMUS JAMES. "Dependency Analysis of Latin America." *Latin American Research Review* 11, No. 2 (1976).

CAPORASO, JAMES A. "Dependence, Dependency, and Power in the Global System: A Structural and Behavioral Analysis." *International Organization* 32, No. 1 (Winter 1978).

CARDOSO, FERNANDO HENRIQUE. "The Consumption of Dependency Theory in the United States." *Latin American Research Review* 12, No. 3 (1977).

———— and ENZO FALETTO. *Dependency and Development in Latin America.* Berkeley: University of California Press, 1978.

DHONTE, PIERRE. *Clockwork Debt: Trade and the External Debt of Developing Countries.* Lexington, Mass.: Heath, 1979.

DOS SANTOS, THEOTONIO. "The Structure of Dependence." *American Economic Review* 60, No. 2 (1970).

EMMANUEL, ARGHIRI. *Unequal Exchange: A Study of the Imperialism of Trade.* New York: Monthly Review Press, 1972.

FRANK, ANDRE GUNDER. *Capitalism and Underdevelopment in Latin America: Historical Studies of Chile and Brazil.* New York: Monthly Review Press, 1967.

GIRLING, ROBERT HENRIQUES. *Multinational Institutions and the Third World: Management, Debt, and Trade Conflicts in the International Economic Order.* New York: Praeger, 1985.

GOTUR, PADMA. "Interest Rates and the Developing World: Interest rates in the developed world have pervasive and important effects on debt, growth and commodity exports in developing countries." *Finance and Development* 20 (Dec. 1983): 33–36.

HELLEINER, G. K., ed. *A World Divided: The Less Developed Countries in the International Economy.* New York: Cambridge University Press, 1976.

HYMER, S. and S. RESNICK. "International Trade and Uneven Development." In Bhagwati, Jones, Mundell, and Vanek, eds., *Trade, Balance of Payments and Growth.* Amsterdam: North Holland, 1971.

KIM, YUNG MYUNG. "Patterns of Dependency and Development: a comparative analysis of radical and conservative state policies in Peru, Egypt, Brazil and South Korea." *Korea and World Affairs,* 8, Winter 1984: 812–44.

MAGDOFF, HARRY. *The Age of Imperialism.* New York: Monthly Review Press, 1969.

MULLER, EDWARD N. "Dependent Economic Development, Aid Dependence on the U.S. and Democratic Breakdown in Third World." *International Studies Quarterly* 29 (December 1985): 445–69.

PREBISCH, RAOUL. "The Role of Commercial Policy in Underdeveloped Countries." *American Economic Review* 49, No. 2 (May 1959).

SINGER, H. W. "The Distribution of Gains Between Investing and Borrowing Countries." *American Economic Review* 40, No. 2 (May 1950).

PART FOUR   Agricultural Institutions and Strategy

ALIER, JUAN MARTINEZ. *Haciendas, Plantations and Collective Farms.* London: Frank Cass, 1977.

BARKIN, DAVID. "Cuban Agriculture: A Strategy of Economic Development." *Studies in Comparative International Development* 7, No. 1 (Spring 1972).

BARRACLOUGH, SOLON, ed. *Agrarian Structure in Latin America.* Lexington, Mass.: Heath, 1973.

BERRY, R. A., and W. CLINE. *Agrarian Structure and Productivity in Developing Countries.* Baltimore: Johns Hopkins University Press, 1979.

CLAY, E. J. and B. B. SCHAFFER, eds. *Room for Manoeuvre: An exploration of public policy planning in agricultural and rural development.* Cranbury, N.J.: Associated Universities Press, Inc., 1984.

FIGUERA, A. "Agrarian Reformisms in Latin America: A Framework and an Instrument of Rural Development." *World Development* 5 (1977).

GANAPATHY, R. S. "The Political Economy of Rural Energy Planning in the Third World." *Review of Radical Political Economics* 15 (Fall 1983): 83–95.

GHAI, D., et al., eds. *Agrarian Systems and Rural Development.* New York: Holmes and Meier, 1979.

GOLDSMITH, ARTHUR. "The Private Sector and Rural Development: Can Agribusiness Help the Small Farmer?" *World Development* 13 (Oct./Nov. 1985): 1125–38.

GRIFFIN, KEITH. *The Political Economy of Agrarian Change.* London: Macmillan, 1974.

———. *Land Concentration and Rural Poverty.* 2nd ed. London: Macmillan, 1980.

GURLEY, JOHN. "Rural Development in China 1949–1972, and the Lessons to Be Learned from It." *World Development* 3, No. 7–8 (July–August 1975).

HEYER, R., P. ROBERTS, and G. WILLIAMS, eds. *Rural Development in Tropical Africa.* London: Macmillan, 1981.

JOHNSTON, BRUCE F. and JOHN W. MELLOR. "The Role of Agriculture in Economic Development." *American Economic Review* 51, No. 4 (September 1961).

——— and P. KILBY. *Agriculture and Structural Transformation: Strategies in Late-Developing Countries.* New York: Oxford University Press, 1975.

——— and W. C. CLARK. *Redesigning Rural Development: A Strategic Perspective.* Baltimore: Johns Hopkins University Press, 1982.

LIPTON, MICHAEL. *Why Poor People Stay Poor: A Study of Urban Bias in World Development.* Cambridge, Mass.: Harvard University Press, 1977.

PEARSE, ANDREW. *Seeds of Plenty, Seeds of Want: Social and Economic Implications of the Green Revolution.* New York: Oxford University Press, 1980.

STAVENHAGEN, RODOLFO, ed. *Agrarian Problems and Peasant Movements in Latin America.* New York: Doubleday, 1970.

PART FIVE   Industrial Institutions and Strategy

CHUDNOVSKY, DANIEL and MASAFUMI NAGAO. *Capital Goods Production in the Third World: An Economic Study of Technological Acquisition.* Dover, N.H.: Frances Pinter (Publishers) Ltd., 1983.

CODY, JOHN, et. al. *Policies for Industrial Progress in Developing Countries.* New York: Oxford University Press, 1980.

CUKOR, GYORGY. *Strategies for Industrialization in Developing Countries.* New York: St. Martin's Press, 1974.

DEYO, F. C. *Dependent Development and Industrial Order: An Asian Case Study.* New York: Praeger, 1981.

GOULET, DENIS. *The Uncertain Promise: Value Conflicts in Technology Transfer.* New York: IDOC North America, 1977.

HIRSCHMAN, ALBERT O. "The Political Economy of Import-Substituting Industrialization in Latin America." *Quarterly Journal of Economics* 82, No. 1 (February 1968).

KIRKPATRICK, C. H. and F. I. NIXSON, ed. *The Industrialisation of Less Developed Countries.* Dover, N.H.: Manchester University Press, 1983.

LEE, E. *Export-Led Industrialization and Development.* International Labour Office, 1981.

ROEMER, M. "Resource-Based Industrialization in the Developing Countries: A Survey." *Journal of Development Economics* 6 (1976).

PART SIX   The Human Cost of Development

ADELMAN, I., and C. T. MORRIS. *Economic Growth and Social Equity in Developing Countries.* Stanford, Calif.: Stanford University Press, 1973.

ALMEIDA-FILHO, NAOMAR DE. "The Psychosocial Costs of Development: Labor, Migration, and Stress in Bahia, Brazil." *Latin American Research Review* 17, No. 3 (1982).

BARRIOS DE CHUNGARA, D. *Let Me Speak!: Testimony of Domitlia, A Woman of the Bolivian Mines.* New York: Monthly Review Press, 1978.

BERGER, PETER. *Pyramids of Sacrifice: Political Ethics and Social Change.* New York: Basic Books, 1974.

BRUNDENIUS, C. and M. LUNDAL. *Development Strategies and Basic Needs in Latin America: Challenges for the 1980's.* Boulder, Colo.: Westview, 1982.

DE JESUS, MARIA CAROLINA. *Child of the Dark.* New York: Dutton, 1962.

ELLIOT, CHARLES. *Patterns of Poverty in the Third World: A Study of Social and Economic Stratification.* New York: Praeger, 1975.

HOLZMAN, FRANKLYN. "Consumer Sovereignty and the Rate of Economic Development." *Economia Internazionale* 11, No. 2 (1958).

LEWIS, W. ARTHUR. "Is Economic Growth Desirable?" In *The Theory of Economic Growth.* Homewood, Ill.: Irwin, 1955.

NAIR, KUSUM. *Blossoms in the Dust.* New York: Praeger, 1962.

O'DONNELL, GUILLERMO. *Modernization and Bureaucratic Authoritarianism: Studies in South American Politics.* Berkeley: Institute for International Studies, University of California, 1973.

SCHWEINTIZ, KARL DE, JR. "Economic Growth, Coercion, and Freedom." *World Politics* 9, No. 2 (January 1957).

PART SEVEN   What Is to Be Done?

AGARWALA, RAMGOPAL. "Planning in Developing Countries: using the lessons of experience to formulate a workable approach." *Finance and Development* 22 (March 1985): 13–16.

AVRAMIC, DRAGOSLAV. "Development Policies for Today." *Journal of World Trade* 17 (May/June 1983): 189–206.

FRANK, ANDRE GUNDER. "Capitalist Underdevelopment or Socialist Revolution?" In *Latin America: Underdevelopment or Revolution?* New York: Monthly Review Press, 1969.

FREIRE, PAULO. *Pedagogy of the Oppressed.* New York: Herder and Herder, 1972.

GRAN, GUY. *Development by People: Citizen Construction of a Just World.* New York: Praeger, 1983.

GUTIERREZ, GUSTAVO. *A Theology of Liberation.* Maryknoll, N.Y.: Orbis Books, 1972.

HIRSCHMAN, ALBERT. *A Bias for Hope.* New Haven: Yale University Press, 1971.

LASZLO, E. *Regional Cooperation Among Developing Countries—The New Imperative of Development in the 1980s.* New York: Pergamon, 1981.

LEONTIEF, W., ANNE CARTER, and PETER PETRI. *The Future of the World Economy.* New York: Oxford University Press, 1977.

MEIER, GERALD M. *Emerging from Poverty: the Economics that Really Matters.* Fair Lawn, N.J.: Oxford University Press, 1984.

MYRDAL, GUNNAR. *The Challenge of World Poverty: A World Anti-Poverty Program in Outline.* New York: Pantheon Books, 1970.

NYERERE, JULIUS K. *Freedom and Development.* Oxford: Oxford University Press, 1974.

SINGH, YYOTI SHANKAR. *A New International Economic Order: Towards a Fair Redistribution of the World's Resources.* New York: Praeger, 1977.

NAME INDEX

Adelman, Irma, 11, 489–490
Ahluwalia, Montek, 339, 343
Alavi, Hamza, 152
Allende, Salvador, 470, 577–578, 583
Althusser, Louis, 144
Alves, Rubem, 480
Amin, Idi, 475
Amin, Samir, 122, 123, 156–164, 165, 305
Apt, Nana, 66
Aquinas, Saint Thomas, 256
Araujo, Arturo, 193, 194, 195, 196
Araujo, Manuel Enrique, 187
Aristotle, 23
Arkwright, Richard, 92
Armah, Ayi Kwei, 322
Arrighi, Giovanni, 150
Arrow, K. J., 394
Auerbach, Paul, 441
Augustine, Saint, 89
Austruy, Jacques, 481

Bahro, Rudolph, 431
Bailey, M., 272
Baily, John, 175, 179
Balassa, Bela, 282
Balibar, Etienne, 144
Balogh, Thomas, 28
Banaji, Jairus, 152
Banerji, Ranadev, 283
Banks, Gary, 517
Baran, Paul, 39, 84, 124, 130, 305
Bardhan, Pranab, 351
Barkin, David, 154–155
Barrios, Gerardo, 180, 181, 182, 186, 197
Bauer, Peter, 6, 38, 568–569, 585n
Benoit, Emile, 537
Berger, Peter, 459–460, 461, 462, 466
Bhaduri, Amit, 351, 397

Bhagwati, Jagdish, 282
Bharadwaj, Krishna, 351
Binswanger, H. P., 400
Blackman, Courtney N., 61
Bosque, Romero, 193
Bowles, Donald, 466
Bradby, Barbara, 148
Brailovsky, Vladimiro, 238
Braverman, A., 397, 402
Brenner, Robert, 123, 134, 137–141
Brewer, Anthony, 163
Bukharin, Nikolay, 438
Burns, E. Bradford, 86
Buron, Robert, 481
Byres, Terry, 437, 439

Cable, Vincent, 293
Camus, Albert, 486
Cardoso, C. F. S., 152
Cardoso, Fernando Henrique, 571
Carr, E. H., 457, 459
Carter, Jimmy, 566
Castro, Emilio, 480
Castro, Fidel, 583
Caves, Richard E., 285
Chayanov, A. V., 365, 368, 369, 370, 371
Chenery, Hollis, 284, 286, 310–311, 500, 501
Cline, William R., 205, 286
Commins, Stephen K., 299, 300
Comte, Auguste, 62
Culbertson, J., 6
Cypher, James M., 156

Dale, William, 223, 234
Debreu, Gerard, 394
De Larosière, Jacques, 227
Dell, Sidney, 204, 232, 237, 241
de Vries, Egbert, 484

SUBJECT INDEX

Accumulation, 160
    autocentric vs. extraverted, 159
    see also Capital accumulation
Action, of oppressed, 547, 555–556
Adjustment capacity, and stabilization,
    237
Administrative capacities, and *dirigisme*,
    34–36
African model, 73, 74–75
Agrarian dualism, 299, 306
Agri-business enterprises, and peasant
    economy, 385–386
Agricultural development
    critical role of, 299
    and environmental constraints,
        313–317, 321–323
    and food aid, 317–321
    and green revolution, 331, 334
    and industrialization, 501, 502–503
    and instability of food supplies,
        328–329
    and poverty, 341, 343–346
    and technical change, 352–355
    see also Cultivation (shifting),
        Deforestation, Rural development,
        Soils
Agricultural policies
    and comparative advantage, 300,
        308–313, 321, 323
    and cooperatives, 358
    and food deficits, 303–324
    and government role in, 359–360
    and industrialization, 418–419
    and redistribution, 356–357
    and rural employment programs,
        357–358
    and underdevelopment, 305–308
Agriculture, 12, 85, 210, 252, 255, 256,
    301, 413

in Africa, 303–308
collectivized, 307–308
commercial vs. peasant economy,
    376–377, 378
and exports, 306, 309–312, 323
vs. industrialization, 436
institutions and strategy, 299–301
and peasant sector, 306
production stagnation of, 331–333
and underdevelopment, 103, 178–179,
    181–184, 190–191, 192–193,
    197–198
see also Latifundia, Rural development
Anti-poverty policy, 500–506
    asset-oriented approaches, 500–501
    demand-generating strategies,
        501–503
    price-increasing policies, 503–504
    productivity-increasing policies,
        504–506
    see also Poverty
Arms race, 474, 490, 533–538
    and military expenditures, 535–538
    and NIEO, 534, 535, 538
    see also Militarization
Articulation, 159
    in peasant economy, 377–382
Articulation of MOP approach, 142,
    144–151
Asset-oriented approaches, 500–501
Autarky, 409, 430
Authenticity, 543–544, 550

Backwardness, *see* Underdevelopment
Balance, *see* External balance, Financial
    balance
Balance-of-payments adjustment, 223,
    225, 226, 235, 242
    and exchange rate policies, 237–239

CONTRIBUTORS

IRMA ADELMAN is professor of economics and agricultural economics, University of California, Berkeley. From 1964 to 1971 she was a chief economic adviser to the Republic of Korea. She is a prolific author in the area of development economics.

PAUL BARAN was professor of economics at Stanford University before his death in 1964. His published works include *The Political Economy of Growth* and, with Paul M. Sweezy, *Monopoly Capital.*

E. BRADFORD BURNS is professor of history, University of California, Los Angeles.

WILLIAM R. CLINE works with the Institute for International Economics in Washington, D.C.

STEPHEN K. COMMINS is coordinator of the Food and Agriculture Project of the African Studies Center, UCLA.

SIDNEY DELL works with the UN Center on Transnational Corporations, New York. He is the author of many articles on economic development issues.

DUDLEY DILLARD is professor of economics at the University of Maryland. He is the author of *The Economics of John Maynard Keynes* and *Economic Development of the North Atlantic Community.*

KLAUS ESSER is head of department, German Development Institute, Federal Republic of Germany.

RICHARD FALK is director of the Center of International Studies at Princeton University. Among his many past posts and honors, Falk has been professor of international law at Princeton; fellow at the Center for Advanced Study in the Behavioral Sciences, Stanford University; a senior fellow at the Institute of World Order, New York; vice-president of the American Society of International Law; and chairman of the Consultative Council, Lawyers' Committee on American Policy Toward Vietnam.

E. V. K. FITZGERALD is professor of development economics at the Institute for Social Studies in the Netherlands. He has served as an economic adviser to the governments of Peru, Mexico, Algeria, Panama, and Nicaragua.

ANDRE GUNDER FRANK has taught economics and social science at the University of Iowa, Michigan State University, Wayne State University, and Sir George Williams University in Montreal. He has also taught at the universities of Brasilia and Chile and at the National University of Mexico. He currently teaches at the

609

University of Amsterdam. He is the author of many pioneer works in dependency theory.

PAULO FREIRE was professor of the history and philosophy of education in the University of Recife, Brazil, until exiled after the military coup in 1964. He then spent five years in Chile, working with UNESCO and the Chilean Institute for Agrarian Reform in programs of adult education. He then served as Educational Consultant to the office of Education of the World Council of Churches in Geneva. He recently returned to Brazil.

AGIT KUMAR GHOSE is a fellow at Queen Elizabeth House, Oxford.

DENIS GOULET is O'Neill Professor of Education for Justice and professor of economics in the Kellogg Institute for International Studies, University of Notre Dame. Trained in philosophy and political science, he has been associated with both aid and research projects in Africa and Latin America and has taught in institutions in Europe and North America. He is the author of *The Cruel Choice, A New Moral Order, The Myth of Aid,* and *Value Conflicts in Technology Transfer.*

JOHN C. GRIFFIN, JR. is with the Monterey Institute.

KEITH GRIFFIN is president of Magdalen College, Oxford University. He is the author of *Underdevelopment in Spanish America, Financing Development in Latin America, Growth and Inequality in Pakistan,* and many other works.

KENNETH P. JAMESON is professor of economics and fellow of the Kellogg Institute at the University of Notre Dame. He has been a Fulbright fellow in Peru and directed the economics division of the Development Studies Program, U.S. Agency for International Development. He has published widely in economics journals and co-authored *Economic Development: Competing Paradigms* and *Religious Values and Economic Development.*

DEEPAK LAL, is professor of political economy, University College (London). He has worked extensively with the World Bank, Washington, D.C.

MICHAEL F. LOFCHIE is professor of political science and director of the African Studies Center, UCLA.

WILLIAM ROUSE is with the Monterey Institute.

DAVID RUCCIO is assistant professor of economics and Director of Latin American Studies, University of Notre Dame.

ALEXANDER SCHEJTMAN is a staff member of the CEPAL Mexico office.

AMARTYA SEN is Drummond Professor of Political Economy, Oxford University, and author of many books and articles on development.

LAWRENCE H. SIMON is assistant professor of philosophy, University of Notre Dame. He has written widely on Marxism.

FRANCES STEWART is fellow of Queen Elizabeth House, Oxford University, and the author of many articles on economic development.

JOSEPH E. STIGLITZ is professor of economics, Princeton University, and a pioneer in the economics of information. He is the author of numerous articles and several books, the most recent being *Economics of the Public Sector.*

R. B. SUTCLIFFE is with the school of economics and politics, Kingston Polytechnic, and the author of the pioneer work, *Industry and Underdevelopment.*

LANCE TAYLOR is professor of economics, Massachusetts Institute of Technology, and the author of many works including *Structural Macroeconomics*.

INGA THORSSON is chairman of the UN Expert Group on Disarmament and Development and under-secretary of state for disarmament in Sweden.

HOWARD J. WIARDA is professor of political science, University of Massachusetts, and Director, Center for Hemispheric Studies, The American Enterprise Institute for Public Policy Research.

CHARLES K. WILBER is professor of economics, the University of Notre Dame. He is the author of *The Soviet Model and Underdeveloped Countries, Directions in Economic Development, Growth with Equity,* and of articles in a variety of economics journals.